श्रीपण्डरीकविट्ठलविरचितो

नर्तननिर्णयः

NARTANANIRṆAYA

OF

PAṆḌARĪKA VIṬṬHALA

कलामूलशास्त्र-ग्रन्थमाला

KALĀMŪLA ŚĀSTRA SERIES

General Editor

KAPILA VATSYAYAN

इ.गा.रा.क.के.क.मू.शा. -२१

I. G. N. C. A. *K. M. S.*- 21

श्रीपण्डरीकविट्ठलविरचितो

नर्तननिर्णयः

NARTANANIRṆAYA

OF

PAṆḌARĪKA VIṬṬHALA

CRITICALLY EDITED AND TRANSLATED WITH COMMENTARY
BY

R. SATHYANARAYANA

VOLUME TWO

INDIRA GANDHI NATIONAL CENTRE FOR THE ARTS
NEW DELHI
AND
MOTILAL BANARSIDASS PUBLISHERS PVT. LTD.
DELHI

First Published 1996

Published by
INDIRA GANDHI NATIONAL CENTRE FOR THE ARTS
Central Vista Mess, Janpath, New Delhi-110001
in association with
MOTILAL BANARSIDASS PUBLISHERS PVT. LTD.
Bungalow Road, Jawahar Nagar, Delhi-110007

ISBN: 81-208-1220-4 (Set)
81-208-1218-2 (Vol. II)
Price: Rs. 650.00 (Vol. II)

Typeset by Neographics
1811, Gyani Bazar, Kotla Mubarkpur
New Delhi-110003
Printed in India
at Shri Jainendra Press
A-45, Naraina Industrial Area, Phase-I
New Dehi-110028

प्रमाणसिद्धान्तविरुद्धमत्र यत्किञ्चिदुक्तं मतिमान्द्यदोषात् ।
उदारभावेन यदार्यचित्ताः प्रसादमाधाय विशोधयन्तु ॥

PREFACE

Nartananirṇaya is an influential, authoritative and original treatise on Indian music and dancing. It was composed by Paṇḍarīka Viṭṭhala of Karnataka in the late sixteenth cent. A.D. under the patronage of the Mughal emperor Akbar. Like many other similar works it is indebted to earlier authorities such as Bharata and Śārṅgadeva (and especially to the latter's commentator, Kallinātha), but is, nevertheless, a valuable primary source for authentic data on the development and trends in these arts of the sixteenth cent. A.D. Paṇḍarīka Vīṭṭhala is the only Indian musicologist who was uniquely authoritative in several cognate art disciplines such as Karnataka music, Hindusthani music, Persian music, classical and folk idioms of dancing, poetics, lexicography, etc. He is much esteemed, respected and borrowed by later authorities on music and dancing in both South India and North India.

Nartananirṇaya comprises four chapters (*prakaraṇas*), viz. Tāladhartṛ (Cymbal Player), Mṛdaṅgi (Mṛdaṅga Player), Gāyaka (Singer) and Nartaka (Dancer). Thus the treatise focusses and climaxes on the final chapter, the previous three chapters are infrastructural, resolved into the auxiliaries of dancing, viz. rhythm content (*naṭṭuvāṅga, tāla* and *mṛdaṅga*), melodic content (*rāga*) and word content (*prabandha*). Such method of exposition is unique to Nartananirṇaya.

The present publication of Nartananirṇaya is issued in three volumes: the first volume contains the first two chapters, viz. Tāladhartṛ prakaraṇam and Mṛdaṅgi prakaraṇam (no. 17 of the KMS series). This second volume comprises the third chapter, viz. Gāyaka Prakaraṇa, subdivided into Rāgādhikaraṇam and Prabandhādhikaraṇam. The third and final volume will comprise the fourth and final chapter, viz. Nartaka prakaraṇam, again subdivided into Nartanādhikaraṇam and Nṛttādhikaraṇam. It will also have a Bibliography and a Text - critique. Each volume is self contained in respect of text, translation, Text-Critical comments, Commentary on the Text as well as numerous indexes relating to the Text and the Commentary.

Nartananirṇaya was composed during the watershed of the history of Indian music and dancing. Each of its chapters reveals flashes of originality, innovation and new trends engendered in the contemporary practice of these arts. Thus, the Rāgādhikaraṇam reflects the dramatic and dynamic changes which were taking place in the melodic content of Indian music at the time. Instances of this include (a) shift in the dynamic equilibrium between *grāma* and *mela* towards the latter, (b) metastability in the concept of *mela* and of *rāga* classification, (c) fluidity in the criteria of rāga-classification, (d) metastability in the *antara, kakalī* and *laghu (or mṛdu) pañcama* notes, (e) Scalar temperament, (f) realignment of *madhyama-grāma rāgas* into *Ṣadje-grāma* (g) transference of the functions of the *grāma* to the *mela* by decentralisation, (h) reorientation in sonance and *daśaprāṇa,* (i) systematic tabulation of *melas* by mathematical and methodological devices, (j) uniformity in *svara vikṛti,* (k) development of *paryāya tattva* and of *pratinidhi tattva* , (l) reorganisation and redistribution of intervals in *rāga* scales (m) individual and collective growth of *rāgas* as a phenomenon in cultural dynamics due to intracultural and inter-cultural forces, (n) mutual interaction between spatio temporal continuity and provincial variance, (o) concretisation or reification (*murtīkaraṃa, dhyeyarupa*) of *rāgas* by intersensory image transference, (p) tonal and visual imagery in relation to mood evocation, (q) recognition and 'classicisation' of melodic material of folk, ethnic, exotic and provincial origin as well as their standardisation within the aesthetic coordinates, (r) development of equations between Hindusthani *rāgas* and Persian *pardahs,* (s) dynamic equilibrium between stabilisation-expansion, stasis-growth, tradition-innovation, etc. in the evolution of *rāgas,* (t) family (or gender) classification of *rāgas* on the criterion of *bhāva-sādṛśya* as an alternative to *svara-sādṛśya.*

Similarly, even though Paṇḍarīka Viṭṭhala is heavily influenced by Kallinātha's commentary on the Prabandhādhyāya of Saṅgītaratnākara of Śārṅgadeva in delineating time-honored musical forms under the suddhasūḍa, ālikrama, viprakīrṇa and sālagasūḍa classification, he offers for the first time eleven new song forms which were renowned in South India. It is noteworthy that unlike the traditionally transmitted *prabandhas* such as the *elā, varṇa, śrīraṇga, dhruva,* etc. candraprakāśa etc. are not described in terms of *aṇgas* and *dhātus.* This is suggestive, as in other areas of Indian music and dance of the time, of a wave of renaissance which had begun to sweep over musical forms also. It is however, equally to be noted, that like many other musicologists of the past, Paṇḍarīka Viṭṭhala so pointedly ignores song forms which were flooding the practice of both Karnataka music (*pada, sulādi, ugābhoga, vṛttanāma, vacana, mantragopya* etc.) and Hindusthani music (e.g. khyāl, Thumri) even in his own homeland and in the very royal courts in which he flourished. Notwithstanding, the original contribution of Nartananirṇaya in its Gāyaka prakaraṇam is substantial and merits serious study. The commentary on both adhikaraṇas endeavours to set the study of *rāgas* and *prabandhas* in a continuous, historical perspective on a pan-Indian canvas.

A new feature is introduced into the second and third volumes of the Nartananirṇaya: The reader's attention is invited to the availability of Text-Critical Comments (TCC) and Commentary on the Text (COT) in terms of the *śloka* number and its *pāda* (quarter e.g. 81d, 128c) on the appropriate recto (translation) pages, where more *pādas* than one are given, the reference may be to each quarter or to their totality. In COT references a hypen indicates range (e.g. 28cd-30abcd, 129-144ab).

I am very thankful to Indira Gandhi National Centre for the Arts and its academic director Dr. Kapila Vatsyayan for asking me to undertake preparing the Nartananirṇaya for inclusion in the KMS Series. I am beholden to Prof. Dr. Satkari Mukhopadhyaya, eminent scholar and teacher as well as coordinator, Kalakosa for his unfailing sympathy, understanding, courtesy and affection. He is indeed a golden bridge between an author and publisher . I have received much help from many individuals and institutions in securing collative material for this edition. I have duly acknowledged such help in the Introduction to the first volume. I acknowledge with much pleasure the help I have received from the learned scholar Vidwan H.V. Nagaraja Rao, M.A. of the Oriental Research Institute, Mysore for his valuable suggestions in respect of Sanskrit grammatical usage. My sincere thanks are due to Vidwan S. Jagannatha, M.A. and my wife Ms. Gowri Sathyanarayana, M.A., RBP for collation and proof-reading and also to my son Sangeetha Vidwan R.S. Nandakumar for preparing the indexes and bibliography.

I thank Sri Ramashis and M/s Neographics for their patient, painstaking, skilful and difficult task of typesetting this work.

Bhāva Navarātrī Prathamā 1994
Trayīlakshmi, Mysore

R. SATHYANARAYANAN

CONTENTS

श्रीपण्डरीकविट्ठलविरचितो

नर्तननिर्णयः

NARTANANIRṆAYA

OF

PAṆḌARĪKA VIṬṬHALA

III. गायकप्रकरणम्

क. रागाधिकरणम्

१. गायनः

शुद्धच्छायालगाभिज्ञो मूर्छनाग्रामतानवित् ।
सतालो रञ्जकं गीतं यो गायति स गायनः ॥ १ ॥
एकेल्लो यमलो वृन्दगायनश्चेति स त्रिधा ।
एक एव तु यो गायेदसावेकेल्लगायनः ॥ २ ॥
सद्वितीयो यमलकः सवृन्दो वृन्दगायनः ।
गातृवादकसङ्घातो वृन्दमित्यभिधीयते ॥ ३ ॥

२. प्रकरणोद्देशः

गायनस्य गुणा दोषाः नादस्थानश्रुतिस्वराः ।
ग्रामश्च मूर्छनास्तानाः प्रस्तारस्तस्य सङ्ख्यकाः ॥ ४ ॥
नष्टोद्दिष्टे ततो वर्णालङ्कारगमकास्ततः ।
स्थायाश्चालप्तिभेदाश्च रागस्य स्थापनं ततः ॥ ५ ॥
रागलक्ष्मस्वरूपाणि प्रबन्धलक्षणानि च ।
प्रबन्धगुणदोषाश्च ततो वाग्गेयकारकः ॥ ६ ॥
इत्युद्दिष्टाः क्रमात्तेषां प्रवक्ष्याम्यथ लक्षणम् ।

३. गायनगुणाः

सुघटश्च सुशारीरो ग्रहमोक्षविचक्षणः ॥ ७ ॥
विविधालप्तिनिपुणः श्रावकः साम्प्रदायिकः ।
आयत्तकण्ठवान् शुद्धच्छायालगविशेषवित् ॥ ८ ॥
जितश्रमः सावधानो गायनानां गुणा दश ।
तत्तत्स्थानं यथायोग्यं घटयन् सुघटः स्मृतः ॥ ९ ॥

III. SINGER

A. RĀGA

1. SINGER

1. He who is proficient in *śuddha* and *chāyālaga* (*rāgas* and *prabandhas*), cognoscente of *mūrchanā, grāma* [and] *tāna,* is possessed of [profound knowledge of] *tāla* and sings songs with aesthetic appeal is (defined as) singer.

2. He is of three kinds *ekella, yamala* and *vṛndagāyana.* He who sings alone (i.e. solo) is [said to be] *ekella-gāyana.*

3. If he sings with another, he is known as *yamala;* if sings with orchestra [he is called] *vṛndagāyana.* An assemblage of singers and instrumentalists is named *vṛnda* (orchestra).

2. CONTENTS OF THE CHAPTER

4. Merits and blemishes of singer, *nāda-sthāna-śruti-svara, grāma mūrchanās* and *tānas, prastāra,* its *saṅkhyās,*

5. *naṣṭa-uddiṣṭa,* then *varṇa-alaṁkāra-gamaka, sthāyas,* varieties of *ālapti, sthāpanā* (establishment) of *rāga,*

6. characteristics and forms of *rāgas,* characteristics of musical compositions, merits and blemishes of musical compositions, next, the music composer,

7ab. these are listed (as contents of this chapter). Now I shall elucidate their characteristics in (the same) order.

3. MERITS OF SINGER

7cd. Sughaṭa, suśārīra, expert in *graha* and *mokṣa,*

8. clever in various kinds of *ālapti,* **śrāvaka, sāmpradāyika** (traditionalist), **āyattakaṇṭhavān** (master of voice), specialist in (the nuances of) *śuddha* and *chāyālaga* (*rāgas* and *prabandhas*),

9. jitaśrama, sāvadhāna—[these] are the ten merits of singer. *Sughaṭa* is [regarded as] one who organizes whatever is (optimally) befitting a given pitch register or position < *sthāna* >

TCC (Text-Critical Comment) 1cd 3ab 6ab 9c
COT (Commentary on Text) 1abcd 2a 7cd-23ab

तारमाधुर्यपुष्टित्वं स्निग्धानुध्वनिकान्तिता ।
तत् सुशारीरमित्युक्तं शरीरेण सहोद्भवात् ॥ १० ॥
गीतारम्भसमास्त्योश्च लयतालग्रहानुगः ।
गीतनिर्वाहकः प्रोक्तो ग्रहमोक्षविचक्षणः ॥ ११ ॥
आलापरूपकालापभञ्जन्यालपनेषु च ।
विविधालप्तिनिपुणस्तत्तदालप्तिकोविदः ॥ १२ ॥
दूरात्तु श्रूयते यस्माद् ध्वनिः श्रावक उच्यते ।
गुरुशिक्षानुसारेण साधकः साम्प्रदायिकः ॥ १३ ॥
स्वाधीनध्वनिप्राचुर्यः स्मृतश्चायत्तकण्ठवान् ।
शुद्धे च्छायालगे चैव हिताहितविचारवान् ॥ १४ ॥
मतिमान् यः स शुद्धादिच्छायालगविशेषवित् ।
अभ्यासतत्परो धीमान् त्रिसन्ध्यं च जितश्रमः ॥ १५ ॥
स्वरेऽधिके विहीने वाऽविरक्तः सावधानकः ।

४. गायनदोषाः

अव्यवस्थितसीत्कारिकपिलाव्यक्तकोद्धडाः ॥ १६ ॥
वितालोद्घुष्टविरसा व्यङ्गाङ्गः सानुनासिकः ।
इत्येते दश दोषाः स्युः प्रसिद्धा गायनादिषु ॥ १७ ॥
स्थानभ्रष्टः स यः प्राप्तुमशक्तस्त्वव्यवस्थितः ।
मुहुः सीत्कारतां कुर्वन् सीत्कारी कथितो बुधैः ॥ १८ ॥
कपिलः स तु यो गायेत् स्वरान्न्यूनाधिकश्रुतीन् ।
गद्गदध्वनिरव्यक्तवर्णस्त्वव्यक्त उच्यते ॥ १९ ॥
छागवच्च ध्वनिं कुर्वन् उद्धडोऽधमगायनः ।
तालज्ञानविहीनो यो वितालस्तालविच्युतः ॥ २० ॥
उद्घुष्टो विरसोद्घोषः काकवत् क्रूरशब्दभाक् ।
विरसो नीरसो वर्ज्यस्वरगानादपस्वरः ॥ २१ ॥
गलगल्लशिरोनेत्रकरादीनां विकारतः ।
गायन् व्यङ्गाङ्गकश्चासावधमाधमगायनः ॥ २२ ॥

10. He is said to be **suśārīra** who[see voice] is replete with sweetness, richness, unctuousness, resonance and lustre in the *tāra* (high register) because [such excellent voice is] born together with (only) the (human) body.

11. He is described as **grahamokṣa-vicakṣaṇa** who follows closely the beginning and end (of song) in *laya* and *tāla* and thus (competently) manages the song.

12. Ālaptīkovida is one who is skilled in various forms of *ālāpa* such as [*rāga-*] *ālāpa, rūpakālāpa* and *bhañjanyālapan.*

13. Śrāvaka is so called because his voice is heard (even) from a distance. He who practices [his art strictly] according to what his teacher has taught is **sāmpradāyika.**

14ab. Āyattakaṇṭhavān is one who has a controlled, abundant voice.

14cd-15ab. He who can discern what is desirable and undesirable in *śuddha* and *chāyālaga* (*rāgas* and *prabandhas*) and is clever (in their special nuances) is **śuddhacchāyālagaviśeṣavit.**

15cd. One who is immersed in repeated study throughout the three divisions of the day and is intelligent is **jitaśrama.**

16ab. He who is not bereft of aesthetic appeal in high (or loud) or low (or soft) tone is **sāvadhānaka.**

4. BLEMISHES OF SINGER

16cd. *Avyavasthita, sītkārī, kapila, avyakta, uddhaḍa,*

17. *vitāla, udghuṣṭa. virasa, vyaṅgāṅga, sānunāsika*—these ten are renowned as the blemishes among the singers etc.

18. One who has strayed from the (desired) pitch and is unable to reach it is **avyavasthita.** One who repeatedly makes a sucking sound (*sīt*) is described by scholars as **sītkārī.**

19. Kapila is one who sings *svaras* with less or more than the (appropriate number of) *śrutis.* **Avyakta** is described as (a singer who is) inarticulate in (the enunciation of) syllables and has a stammering or convulsive voice.

20. Uddhaḍa is a worst singer who repeats sound like a he-goat. **Vitāla** is one who is bereft of *tāla* and has no knowledge of *tāla.*

21. Udghuṣṭa shouts with loud, sapless, harsh sound like a crow. **Virasa** is emotionless (in singing). He is called **apasvara** if he sings the note/s which should be omitted.

22. Vyaṅgāṅga sings by distorting neck, chin, head, eyes and hands. He is the worst of the worst singers.

TCC 10d 12d 16ab 18b 20c
COT -

यदा नासिकया गायन् गीयते सानुनासिकः ।

५. नादस्थानश्रुतिस्वरग्राममूर्छनातानाः

मनो युङ्क्ते विवक्ष्वात्मा हन्ति वह्निं मनोऽनलः ॥ २३ ॥
प्रेरयत्यनिलं प्राणानिलश्चोर्ध्वं क्रमाच्चरन् ।
नाभिहृद्गलशीर्षास्येष्वाविर्भावयति ध्वनिम् ॥ २४ ॥
ध्वनिस्तु नदधातोर्हि सद्भिर्नादो घञि स्मृतः ।
अतिसूक्ष्मः सूक्ष्मपुष्टावतिपुष्टश्च कृत्रिमः ॥ २५ ॥
पञ्चाख्या इति धत्तेऽसौ चतुर्धा व्यवहारतः ।
अनुमन्द्रो नाभिदेशे मन्द्रो हृदि गले पुनः ॥ २६ ॥
मध्यस्तारस्तु मूर्ध्नि स्याद् द्विगुणाश्चोत्तरोत्तराः ।
यन्त्रेऽनुमन्द्रस्थानं स्याद् गायके तदशक्यतः ॥ २७ ॥
मन्द्रादित्रितयं स्थानं व्यवहारेऽभिधीयते ।
हेतवो नादभेदस्य तिर्यक् सच्छिद्रनाडिकाः ॥ २८ ॥
द्वाविंशतिः प्रतिस्थानं सोपानाकारवत् क्रमात् ।
वायुपूरणतस्तासु तावत्यस्तूत्तरोत्तरम् ॥ २९ ॥
भवन्त्युच्चोच्चतरताः श्रुतयः श्राव्यमात्रतः ।
रागादिव्यवहाराय तासु सप्तस्वराः स्थिताः ॥ ३० ॥
षड्जश्च ऋषभश्चैव गान्धारो मध्यमस्तथा ।
पञ्चमो धैवतश्चाथ निषादश्चेत्यनुक्रमात् ॥ ३१ ॥
तेषां संज्ञाः सरिगमपधनीत्यपरा मताः ।
वेदाचलाङ्कश्रुतिषु त्रयोदश्यां श्रुतौ ततः ॥ ३२ ॥
सप्तदश्यां च विंश्यां च द्वाविंश्यां च श्रुतौ क्रमात् ।
षड्जादीनां स्थितिः प्रोक्ता प्रथमा भरतादिभिः ॥ ३३ ॥
असपाः स्वस्वपूर्वातः सञ्चरन्त्युत्तरोत्तरम् ।
त्रिस्त्रिर्गतीस्ते प्रत्येकं यान्ति गश्च चतुर्गतीः ॥ ३४ ॥
यद्यद् रागोपयोगः स्यात् तत्तदिच्छागतिर्भवेत् ।
गन्योर्गती द्वितीये चान्तरकाकलिनौ स्मृतौ ॥ ३५ ॥

23ab. If he sings nasally, he is described as **anunāsika**.

5. NĀḌA-STHĀNA-ŚRUTI-SVARA-GRĀMA-MŪRCHANĀ-TĀNA

23cd. The soul, desirous of self-expression, joins the mind; the mind strikes the fire.

23d-24. The fire (in turn) stimulates the air. The vital air, moving gradually upward manifests the (vocal) sound in [the regions of] navel, heart, throat, head and face.

25ab. The learned opine that [this] sound < *dhvani* > acquires the name *nāda* when (the grammatical suffix called) *'ghañ'* is applied to the stem *'nada'*.

25cd-26a. It take these five names—*atisūkṣma* (very subtle), *sūkṣma* (subtle), *puṣṭa* (strong), *atipuṣṭa* (very strong), and not strong < *apuṣṭa-* weak? > and *kṛtrima* (artificial) respectively.

26b-27ab. It is of four kinds in musical transaction; viz. *anumandra* in the region of the navel, *mandra* in the chest < *hṛdi* >; in the throat again, [it is] *madhya*; *tāra* occurs in the head. They are (each) progressively double (i.e. of the respective predecessor).

27cd-28ab. The *anumandra* register is [obtained] in [musical] instruments, for it is not possible for a singer. [Hence] *mandra* etc. registers (only) are described in [musical] transaction.

28cd-29ab. The generating causes for different musical sounds are horizontal (transverse) hollow tubes [in the body], (numbering) twentytwo in each register [occurring] in order like a staircase.

29cd-30ab. With the [vital] air filling a given number of them one after another in order they [musical sounds—*nādabhedāḥ*] become (progressively) higher and higher; these are called *śrutis* because they are just audible.

30cd-31. For the purpose of [musical] usage such as *rāga*, seven *svaras* abide in them viz. *ṣaḍja, ṛṣabha, gāndhāra, madhyama;* similarly *pañcama, dhaivata* and then *niṣāda*—in this order (of increasing pitch).

32ab. Their other symbols are opined to be *sa, ri, ga, ma, pa, dha* and *ni.*

32cd-33. The initial states of *ṣadja* etc. are declared by Bharata and others to be respectively in the fourth (*veda*), seventh (*acala*), ninth (*aṅka*) *śrutis,* in the thirteenth *śruti,* seventeenth, twentieth and twentysecond *śrutis.*

34. [The *svaras*] other than *sa* and *pa* move from their own respective previous (śrutis) to the [next higher] successive (*śrutis* to attain to their second, third etc. states). Each of them has three such degrees [of movement] but *ga* has four [such] degrees.

35. The degree of movement (of the *svara*) becomes as required according to whatever its use in the [given] *rāga.* The second degrees of movement in *ga* and *ni* are declared to be *antara* and *kākalī* respectively.

TCC 23bcd 24c 25ab 26abcd 27bc 28ab 29bd 30abd 31b 33ac 34ab 35d
COT 23cd 24bcd 25ad 26b 27b 28cd-30abcd 33d 34acd 35cd

पञ्चम्यष्टादशी षष्ठी तथा चैकोनविंशतिः ।
चतस्त्रः श्रुतयश्चैता रागादिष्वप्रयोजकाः ॥ ३६ ॥
शेषा अष्टादशैव स्युः श्रुतयः स्वरबोधकाः ।
न्यूनाधिकैकगतिका मन्द्रतारस्वरा यदि ॥ ३७ ॥
न रागहानिकाः सर्वे स्पष्टता मध्यसप्तके ।
चतुर्विधाः स्वरा वादी संवादी च विवाद्यपि ॥ ३८ ॥
अनुवादीति वादी तु प्रयोगे बहुलः स्वरः ।
अंशः स्थायीति पर्यायो रागोत्पादनहेतुकः ॥ ३९ ॥
श्रुतयो द्वादशाष्टौ वा ययोरन्तरगोचराः ।
मिथः संवादिनौ तौ स्तो गत्यादेश्च विभागतः ॥ ४० ॥
एकश्रुत्यन्तरौ यौ कौ तौ मिथश्च विवादिनौ ।
शेषाणामनुवादित्वं ज्ञेयमन्वर्थतः क्रमात् ॥ ४१ ॥
क्वचिंदशः क्वचिन्न्यासः क्वचित्त्यागस्वरस्तथा ।
तत्तद्रक्त्यनुसारेण रागेषु ग्रहतां नयेत् ॥ ४२ ॥
गीतादिनियतमात्रस्वरो ग्रह इतीरितः ।
प्रयोगे बहुलोंऽशः स्यान्न्यासो गीतसमाप्तिकृत् ॥ ४३ ॥
विदारीवानपन्यासो विदारी छेदकृन्मुहुः ।
सर्वत्र रागतस्त्वेते स्वरभेदा भवन्ति हि ॥ ४४ ॥
षड्जः सर्वत्र रागे च ग्रहो हि, निधपादयः ।
वर्णमात्राः प्रयोज्या ये रक्त्याधिक्यान्न ते स्वराः ॥ ४५ ॥
अशेषा मूर्छनाः प्रोक्ताः षड्जस्थाने मुनीश्वरैः ।
षड्जस्थानस्थितैर्न्याद्यै रजन्याद्या इति स्मृताः ॥ ४६ ॥
मयूरचातकच्छागक्रौञ्चकोकिलदर्दुराः ।
गजश्च सप्त षड्जादीन् क्रमादुच्चारयन्त्यमी ॥ ४७ ॥
हतिः श्रुतिस्ततो लग्नजातोऽनुरणनध्वनिः ।
भावीदीप्तः श्रोतृचित्तं स्वतो रञ्जयति स्वरः ॥ ४८ ॥
स्वराणां निचयो ग्रामो मूर्छनादिसमाश्रितः ।
भरतेनोदितौ शास्त्रे ग्रामौ द्वौ षड्जमध्यमौ ॥ ४९ ॥

36. The fifth and eighteenth, the sixth and nineteenth—these four *śrutis* are useless in *rāgas* etc.

37ab. Only the remaining eighteen *śrutis* awaken (i.e. manifest) the *svaras.*

37cd-38ab. If the *svaras* in the *mandra* and *tāra* (registers) are deficient or excessive by one degree (i.e. *śruti*), each, they do not mar the *rāga* [character]. All [*svaras*] are clear (and exact) in the *madhya* register.

38cd-39a. Svaras are of four kinds, viz. *vādī, saṃvādī, vivādī* and *anuvādī.*

39cd. Vādī is the [most] abundant *svara* in the performance (of a *rāga*) ; *aṁśa* and *sthāyī* are its synonyms; it is the generating cause of producing a *rāga (bhāva).*

40. [A pair of *svaras*] between which an interval of twelve or eight *śrutis* is perceived are *saṁvādīs*; (they are *saṃvādīs* also) by [similar or suitable] apportionment of *gatis*(degrees of movement) etc.

41. Such a pair [of *svaras*] which has an interval of one *śruti* is mutually (defined as) *vivādīs.* The remaining (*svaras*) are to be understood as *anuvādīs.* [These four kinds of *svaras*] are appropriately named.

42. [The selfsame become] sometimes *aṁśa,* sometimes *nyāsa,* similarly the omissible note. (The function of a note as) *graha* (etc.) should be determined according to the aesthetic form of (the given) *rāgas.*

43. The *svara* occurring as a rule, at the beginning of a song [or *rāga*] is called *graha.* The most abundant (*svara* in the rendering of a *rāga*) is *aṁśa*; that which concludes a song is *nyāsa.*

44. That which has *vidārī* is *apanyāsa*; *vidārī* is that which separates (or cuts into segments) repeatedly. Only these *svara* varieties occur everywhere in *rāgas.*

45. Ṣaḍja is of course < *hi* > *graha* in all *rāgas. Ni-dha-pa* etc. (at the beginning of a *rāga*) are (to be regarded as) only syllables (and are used at the beginning only to evoke) copious *raktī*; they are not (*graha*-?) *svaras.*

46. [For,] all *mūrchanās* are described (exclusively) relative to the position of *ṣaḍja* by the sages; *rajanī* etc. (*mūrchanās*) are opined to be [formed] by *ni* etc. established at the position of *ṣaḍja.*

47. Peacock, the *cātaka*-bird (cucculus melanoleucus), he-goat, heron, cuckoo, frog and elephant utter (the notes) *ṣaḍja* etc. respectively.

48. That which 'strikes' is *śruti.* Clinging to it is born the conforming (resonating) sound, imminently bright, and (which) appeals to the listener's heart by itself (and is therefore) called *svara.*

49. Grāma is the assemblage of *svaras* and is the abode of *mūrchanā* etc. Bharata has propounded two *grāmas* viz *ṣaḍja*(*grāma*) and *madhyama*(*grāma*) in the science [of music].

TCC 36d 38b 39a 40bd 41a 42abcd 43bc 46c 47abcd 48ab
COT 36 37abcd 38-41 43abcd-44 45 46b 47a 48a 49-52

षड्जग्रामः पञ्चमे तु सप्तदश्यां श्रुतौ स्थिते ।
स्वरेऽस्मिन् पञ्चमे किन्तु षोडशीं श्रुतिमाश्रिते ॥ ५० ॥
तदैव मध्यमग्रामः सोऽत्र रागे न दृश्यते ।
षड्जग्रामाश्रितान् रागान् सर्वे गायन्ति गायकाः ॥ ५१ ॥
तस्मान्मुख्यतमः षड्जग्राम एव न मध्यमः ।
क्रमात् स्वराणां सप्तानामारोहाच्चावरोहतः ॥ ५२ ॥
मूर्छ्यते यत्र रागो हि श्रोता वा मूर्छना मता ।
ताः सप्त मध्यषड्जेन मूर्छनाऽऽरभ्यतेऽग्रिमा ॥ ५३ ॥
अधस्तनैर्निषादाद्यैः षड्जस्थानस्थितैः क्रमात् ।
षडन्या मूर्छनाः सादींस्तदूर्ध्वं सारयेत् क्रमात् ॥ ५४ ॥
यस्यां यावतिथः षड्जस्तावतिथ्येव मूर्छना ।
आद्या चोत्तरमन्द्रा च रजनी चोत्तरायता ॥ ५५ ॥
शुद्धषड्जा मत्सरीकृताश्वक्रान्ताभिरुद्गता ।
नामान्युक्तानि मुनिभिर्मूर्छनानां यथाक्रमम् ॥ ५६ ॥
गीतोपयोगतस्तासु षाडवौडुवितीकृताः ।
षट्स्वरैः षाडवाः प्रोक्तास्त्वौडुवाः पञ्चभिः स्वरैः ॥ ५७ ॥
शुद्धताना इति ख्याताः पूर्णास्तानक्रियात्मकाः ।
प्रवेशनिग्रहाभ्यां च द्विधा तानक्रिया भवेत् ॥ ५८ ॥
प्रवेशः परसादृश्यमीषत्स्पर्शस्तु निग्रहः ।
व्युत्क्रमात् कूटतानाः स्युः पूर्णापूर्णाः पुरोदिताः ॥ ५९ ॥

६. प्रस्तारः

कश्चित् क्रमं विलिख्यादौ पूर्वपूर्वः परादधः ।
स्वरः स्थाप्यः स चेदग्रे तत्तत्पूर्वस्वरो भवेत् ॥ ६० ॥
प्रस्तारो वामतः कार्यः पुरस्तूपरिवर्तिनः ।
मूलक्रमक्रमात् पृष्ठे शिष्टान् प्रस्तार ईदृशः ॥ ६१ ॥
क्रमात् पूर्वस्वरस्थाङ्कसङ्ख्यान्त्यादिस्वरावलिम् ।
अन्त्यादधोऽधो विलिखेत् कृतं त्यक्त्वा क्रमो भवेत् ॥ ६२ ॥

50-51ab. It is *ṣaḍjagrāma* if *pañcama* (*svara*) resides in the seventeenth *śruti.* But if the *svara pañcama* abides in the sixteenth *śruti,* it is then *madhyama-grāma.* [But] it is not found here (in contemporary musical practice) in (any) *rāga.*

51cd. [All] musicians render all the *rāgas* [as] abiding in *ṣaḍjagrāma* (itself).

52ab. Therefore *ṣaḍjagrāma* alone is the most important, not the *madhyama* (*grāma*).

52cd-53ab. Wherein there is regular ascent and descent of [all] the seven notes and by which the *rāga* and listener are exalted, it is declared to be *mūrchanā.*

53cd. They are seven (in number). The first *mūrchanā* commences with *ṣaḍja* of the middle register.

54. The other six *mūrchanās,* commencing on *ni* etc. lying below and taking the position of *ṣaḍja* should be extended above the one beginning with *sa.*

55ab. Wherein *ṣaḍja* is how-manieth, that *mūrchanā* is as-manieth.

55cd-56. The first [*mūrchanā* being] *uttaramandrā, rajanī, uttarāyatā, śuddhaṣaḍjā, matsarīkṛtā, aśvakrāntā, abhirudgatā*—these names are to be spoken for the *mūrchanās* in (the same) order by the sages.

57. For use in songs, they are rendered *ṣāḍava* and *auḍuva. Ṣāḍavas* are said to be [formed] from six *svaras* and *auḍuvas,* from five *svaras.*

58. Complete (*mūrchanās*) possessed of *tānakriyā* (making of *tānas*) are named *śuddha tānas. Tānakriyā* is of two kinds—*praveśa* and *nigraha.*

59. *Praveśa* is [formed by accomplishing] similarity with the next *svara; nigraha,* by a slight touch [of the note]. Complete and incomplete *tānas* mentioned above become *kūṭa tānas* by irregularity (in the order of *svaras* in ascent and descent).

6. PRASTĀRA

60. First, a [original] *krama* is written; the precedent *svara* should be placed below (its) next (i.e. any given) *svara* [progressively]. If the previous *svara* happens to be the next note, [then the note prior to it and written below it] becomes the previous *svara.*

61. Such tabulation <*prastāra*> should be performed from the left. Further, to the right <*purataḥ*> the remaining *svaras* should be placed below the ones written above in the same order as is found in the original *krama.*

62. The totals of the previous notes etc. of all the *svara* series should be written below the final one progressively (till the end is reached) and it is left there. This gives the original *krama.*

TCC 50d 51c 52acd 53abc 54c 56ac 58d 60ab 61cd 62acd
COT 49-52abcd-56 58-59

यदैकस्वरतश्चान्त्योपान्त्यधारां ततोऽन्यथा ।
मालाप्रस्तारक इति विट्ठलेन प्रकीर्तितः ॥ ६३ ॥

७. सङ्ख्या

अङ्कानेकाङ्कमारभ्य सप्तान्तान् विलिखेत् क्रमात् ।
ऊर्ध्वमूर्ध्वं विहन्यात्तु पूर्वेणाङ्कं परं परम् ॥ ६४ ॥
एकस्वरादितानानां सङ्ख्यैवं जायते स्फुटम् ।

८. नष्टम्

मूर्छनान्त्यस्वरस्थाङ्काः प्रश्नाङ्कैः पातयेत्तु तान् ॥ ६५ ॥
शेषान् प्राक् प्राक् स्वरस्थाङ्कैर्यथा हननसम्भवैः ।
क्रमेण पातयेद् येनाहतिस्तावतिथः स्वरः ॥ ६६ ॥
हतेरभावतः किन्तु कोऽपि पूर्वस्थितः स्वरः ।
स्याद् द्वितीयाच्च गणनं नष्टसिद्धिर्भवेत्तदा ॥ ६७ ॥

९. उद्दिष्टम्

नष्टबोधगता येऽङ्कास्तानन्त्याङ्केषु पातयेत् ।
शिष्ट उद्दिष्टसिद्धिः स्यादित्यभाषत विट्ठलः ॥ ६८ ॥

१०. वर्णाः

गानक्रियोच्यते वर्णः स चतुर्धा निरूपितः ।
स्थाय्यारोह्यवरोही च सञ्चारीत्यथ लक्षणम् ॥ ६९ ॥
स्थित्वा स्थित्वा प्रयोगः स्यादेकस्यैव स्वरस्य यः ।
रागादिव्यवहारेषु स्थायी वर्णः स उच्यते ॥ ७० ॥
आरोहन्ति स्वरा यत्र चारोही स प्रकीर्तितः ।
यत्र चैवावरोहन्ति सोऽवरोहीति गण्यते ॥ ७१ ॥
एतेषां मिश्रणाद् वर्णः सञ्चारी परिकीर्तितः ।

63. If in this the continuous series of the ultimate and penultimate (total, of *svaras*) is witten differently, it is declared by (Paṇḍarīka) Viṭṭhala as *mālāprastāra.*

7. SAṄKHYĀ

64-65ab. The numbers one to seven should be written in order one after the other. If succeeding numbers are progressively multiplied by the previous numbers, then the numbers of *tānas* of one etc. *svaras* arise clearly (from the respective products).

8. NAṢṬA

65cd-66abc. Subtracting the numbers of the end *svaras* of the *mūrchanā* (obtained progressively) from the question number (i.e. number of the required *tāna*), the remainders should be progressively substracted from the *svara* numbers which are obtained by multiplication (of previous *svara*-numbers).

66d. That [number]which remains unmultipliable is the as-manieth *svara* in the *krama.*

67. The reckoning is made to the left second of the unmultipliable number or in its absence, of whatever number precedes it. [Thus] *naṣṭa (pratyaya)* is accomplished.

9. UDDIṢṬA

68. The numbers so obtained from *naṣṭa* [*pratyaya*] should be subtracted from the final number. Viṭṭhala declares that *uddiṣṭa* [*pratyaya*] accrues from the remainder.

10. VARṆAS

69. The act of singing is said to be *varṇa.* It is said to be of four kinds: *sthāyī, ārohī, avarohī* and *sañcārī.* Now [their] definition [will be given].

70. If a single note is executed and sustained repeatedly in [musical] practice such as *rāga,* it is said to be *sthāyī varṇa.*

71. That in which the *svaras* ascend (regularly) is described as *ārohī;* wherein [they] descend (regularly), it is reckoned as *avarohī.*

72ab. *Sañcārī* is said to be (formed) by mixing these.

TCC 63a 64d 66ac 70ad 71d
COT 69a 70d 71bd 72b

११. अलङ्कारा:

i उद्देश:

विशिष्टं वर्णसन्दर्भमलङ्कारं प्रचक्षते ॥ ७२ ॥
तस्य भेदा बहुतरास्तत्र स्थायिगतान् ब्रुवे ।
येषामाद्यन्तयोरेकस्वरास्ते स्थायिनि स्थिता: ॥ ७३ ॥
मन्द्रादिश्चाथ मन्द्रान्तो मन्द्राद्यन्ताह्वयस्तत: ।
मन्द्रमध्याभिध: पश्चात् पञ्चम: क्रमरेचित: ॥ ७४ ॥
स्थायिवर्णगता: पञ्चालङ्कारा: परिकीर्तिता: ।
विस्तीर्ण: सन्निकर्षश्च प्रेङ्खु: प्रच्छादनस्तत: ॥ ७५ ॥
आक्षिप्तबिन्दुहसिता: सप्त चारोहिणि स्थिता: ।
प्रसाद: प्राङ्मुखोत्क्षेपौ परिवर्तोद्वाहितौ तत: ॥ ७६ ॥
निष्कूजितो रेचितश्च स्खलित: क्रमरञ्जितौ ।
ह्लादमानश्च हुङ्कार: श्येन: सञ्चारिवर्णगा: ॥ ७७ ॥
त्रयोदश क्रमादेषामथ लक्षणमुच्यते ।
मन्द्र(:) प्रकरणेऽत्र स्यान्मूर्छनाप्रथमस्वर: ॥ ७८ ॥
स एव द्विगुणस्तार: पञ्चमो मध्य उच्यते ।
लिपौ मन्द्रो बिन्दुशिरास्तारो रेखाशिरा भवेत् ॥ ७९ ॥

ii स्थायिगतालङ्कारा:

मन्द्रमध्यात् परे तारे मन्द्रादि: कथितो यथा ।

सं प सं̍

इति मन्द्रादि: (१)

तद्वैलोम्ये तु मन्द्रान्त:

सं̍ प सं

इति मन्द्रान्त: (२)

मन्द्रयोर्मध्यगे पुन: ॥ ८० ॥

11. ALAMKĀRAS

(i) *List*

72cd. [Any] particular melodic situation is said to be *alaṁkāra.*

73. Its varieties are numerous. Among them, I shall (first) mention [those] occurring in *sthāyī* [*varṇa*]. Those [*alaṁkāras* are said to] abide in *sthāyī* when the selfsame, single *svara* occurs in the beginning, middle and end.

74. *Mandrādi, mandrānta, mandrādyanta, mandramadhya,* further, the fifth [named] *kramarecita,*

75. —[these] five *alaṁkāras* are declared as of *sthāyī-varṇa. Vistīrṇa, sannikarṣa, preṅkha,* then *pracchādana,*

76. *ākṣipta-bindu-hasita*—[these] seven lie in *ārhoī (varṇa). Prasāda, prāṅmukha-utkṣepa, parivarta, udvāhita,*

77-78ab. *niṣkūjita, recita, skhalita, krama, rañjita, hrādamāna, huṁkāra, śyena*—[these] thirteen are of *sañcārī varṇa.* Their characteristics will now be described in [the same] order.

78cd-79. In the context of this topic, *mandra* is [taken to mean] the first note of the *mūrchanā.* When doubled, the selfsame [*svara*] is [denoted as] *tāra.* The fifth (*svara* from *mandra*) is called *madhya.* In notation, the *mandra(svara)* has a dot on its head; the *tāra* [*svara*] has a straight line over its head.

(ii) *Alaṁkāras of Sthāyī-Varṇa*

(1) *Mandrādi*

80ab. If there is *tāra* after *mandra* and *madhya,* it is said to be *madrādi* thus

s̊ p s̍

(2) *Mandrānta*

80c. Mandrānta [is formed] by reversing this.

s̍ p s̊

TCC 74b 75d 76acd 79c 80abc
COT 73c-105 (i) 74c-105

तारे च मन्द्राद्यन्तः स्यात्

सं सं सं

इति मन्द्राद्यन्तः (३)

तारयोर्मध्यगे तथा ।

मन्द्रे च मन्द्रमध्याख्यमलङ्कारविदो विदुः ॥ ८१ ॥

सं सं सं

इति मन्द्रमध्यः (४)

आद्यन्ते मूर्छनादिश्चेत् स्वरो मध्ये द्वितीयकः ।
सैका कलाऽथ चेन्मध्ये सतृतीयचतुर्थके ॥ ८२ ॥
सा द्वितीया पञ्चमाद्यास्त्रयोऽन्तश्चेत् कला परा ।
एवं कलात्रयेणोक्तोऽलङ्कारः क्रमरेचितः ॥ ८३ ॥

संरिसं संगमसं संपधनिसं

इति क्रमरेचितः (५)

iii आरोह्यलङ्काराः

मूर्छनादेः स्वराद्यत्र क्रमेणारोहणं भवेत् ।
स्थित्वा स्थित्वा स्वैर्दीर्घैः स विस्तीर्णोऽभिधीयते ॥ ८४ ॥

सां री गा मा पा धा नी

इति विस्तीर्णः (१)

ह्रस्वैः स्वरैः सन्निकर्षो द्विर्द्विरुक्तैर्निरन्तरैः ।

संसं रिरि गग मम पप धध निनि

इति सन्निकर्षः (२)

स्वरद्वयं समुच्चार्य पूर्वं पूर्वयुतं परम् ॥ ८५ ॥
यदाऽऽन्दोलितमारोहे प्रेङ्खाख्यः कथितो यथा ।

संरि रिग गम मप पध धनि

इति प्रेङ्खः (३)

(3) *Mandrādyanta*

80d-81a. Again, if *tāra* is in between two *mandras*, it is *mandrādyanta.*

s̊ s̍ s̊

(4) *Mandramadhya*

81bcd. Similarly, if there is *mandra* in between two *tāras*, the cognoscente in *alaṁkāras* understand it by the name *mandramadhya.*

s̍ s̊ s̍

(5) *Kramarecita*

82abc. If there is the initial [*svara*] of the *mūrchanā* at the beginning and end, and the second [*svara*] occurs in the middle, it is one phrase.

82d-83. If (instead of the second) there are the third and fourth (*svaras*), it is the second (phrase). If the three (*svaras*) beginning with the fifth (*svara*) are in the middle, it is the next phrase. The *alaṁkāra* [formed] by [these] three phrases in this manner is said to be *kramarecita.*

s̊rs̊ s̊gms̊ s̊pdns̊

(iii) *Ārohī Alaṁkāras*

(1) *Vistīrṇa*

84. Wherein there is, [commencing] from the first *svara* of the *mūrchanā*, regular ascent of long sustained *svaras*, it is said to be *vistīrṇa*

s̊ā rī gā mā pā dhā nī

(2) *Sannikarṣa*

85ab. *Sannikarṣa* is [formed] by short *svaras* each rendered twice continuously (without intervening interval).

s̊s̊ rr gg mm pp dd nn

(3) *Preṅkha*

85cd-86ab. When a pair of *svaras* is such that it contains the just previous [*svara*] progressively, and ascends in a swinging movement, it is called *preṅkha;* thus—

s̊r rg gm mp pd dn

TCC 81d 84a 85ad 86ac

COT 81cd 83d 84abcd 85a 86b 87b

त्रिस्वराद्या कलाऽन्त्ये च पूर्वपूर्वन्तिमाऽऽदिमे ॥ ८६ ॥
कलेस्तस्त्रिस्वरे यत्र तदा प्रच्छादनाभिधः ।

संरिग गमप पधनि

इति प्रच्छादनः (४)

एकान्तरं स्वरयुंगं तादृक् पूर्वयुतं परम् ॥ ८७ ॥
क्रमादारोहति यदा तदाऽऽक्षिप्तं प्रचक्षते ।

संग गप पनि

इति आक्षिप्तः (५)

पूर्वस्वरं त्रिरुच्चार्य सकृत् तत्परकं स्वरम् ॥ ८८ ॥
एवं क्रमं क्रमात् कुर्वन् आरोहे बिन्दुसंज्ञकः ।

संसंसंरि रिरिरिग गगगम मममप पपपध धधधनि

इति बिन्दुः (६)

यत्रैकोत्तरवृद्धाभिरावृत्तिभिरुदीरिताः ॥ ८९ ॥
आरुह्यन्ते स्वराः प्राह हसितं तं मुनीश्वरः ।

स रिरि गगग मममम पपपपप धधधधधध निनिनिनिनिनिनि

इति हसितः (७)

iv. अवरोह्यलङ्कारा:

आरोहेण क्रमादेते सप्त चाप्यवरोहिणि ॥ ९० ॥

v. सञ्चार्यलङ्कारा:

पूर्वः पूर्वः परस्योर्ध्वाधोवर्ती क्रियते स्वरः ।
यदा तदा प्रसादं तमाह श्रीभरतो मुनिः ॥ ९१ ॥

संरिसं रिगरि गमग मपम पधप धनिध

इति प्रसादः (१)

(4) *Pracchādana*

86cd-87ab. Wherein the first phrase has the first three *svaras* (of the *mūrchanā*) and the other phrases of three *svaras* are such that the last *svara* of the previous is the first *svara* of the next, then it is named *pracchādana.*

s̊rg gmp pdn

(5) *Ākṣipta*

87cd-88ab. Similarly, when a pair of *svaras,* omitting an intervening middle *svara* the next [is formed by beginning] with the last note of the previous [phrase] and ascends gradually, then it is decribed as *ākṣipta.*

s̊g gp pn

(6) *Bindu*

88cd-89ab. The precedent (final *svara* of the previous phrase is repeated three times and the next *svara* once; if this progression < *krama* > is executed regularly in ascent, it is named *bindu.*

s̊s̊s̊r rrrg gggm mmmp pppd dddn

(7) *Hasita*

89cd-90ab. Wherein each succeeding *svara* is increased by one than its just predecessor, and gradually ascends, the chief sage declares it to be *hasita.*

s̊ rr ggg mmmm ppppp dddddd nnnnnnn

iv. *Avrohī Alaṁkāras*

90cd. These selfsame seven [*alaṁkāras*] occurring in ascent do so in descent also.

v. *Sañcārī Alaṁkāras*

(1) *Prasāda*

91. Śrī Bharatamuni declared that when a *svara* is preceded and followed by its previous *svara,* it is *prasāda.*

s̊rs̍ rgr gmg mpm pdp dnd

TCC 86cd 89ad 91ab
COT 87b 88b 89b 90ab 91cd-104ab

कला गतागतवती द्विस्वरैकैकहानतः ।
यत्रान्यास्तादृशः स स्यात् प्राङ्मुखः परिकीर्तितः ॥ ९२ ॥

संरिरिसं रिगगरि गममग मपपम पधधप धनिनिध

इति प्राङ्मुखः (२)

त्रिस्वराश्चेत् कला पूर्वा पूर्वत्यागोर्ध्वसङ्क्रमैः ।
यदा तदोत्क्षेपकाख्यः प्रसिद्धो गानवेदिनाम् ॥ ९३ ॥

संरिग रिगम गमप मपध पधनि

इति उत्क्षेपः (३)

स्वरं द्वितीयमुज्झित्वा त्रिस्वराद्या कला यदि ।
त्यक्तादारभ्य तादृश्योऽन्यास्तदा परिवर्तकः ॥ ९४ ॥

संगम रिमप गपध मधनि

इति परिवर्तकः (४)

कलायां त्रीन् स्वरान् गीत्वाऽवरुह्यैकं पराः कलाः ।
यत्रैकैकोज्झिता गीतास्तद्वदुद्वाहितस्तु सः ॥ ९५ ॥

संरिगरि रिगमग गमपम मपधप पधनिध (धनिसंनि)

इति उद्वाहितः (५)

प्रसादस्य कलां गीत्वा तत्कलायास्तृतीयकम् ।
गत्वाऽऽद्यगानाद्भवति निष्कूजितकनामकः ॥ ९६ ॥

संरिसंगसं रिगरिमरि गमगपग मपमधम पधपनिप (धनिधसंनि)

इति निष्कूजितः (६)

आद्यस्वरं द्वितीयं च तृतीयं च द्वितीयकम् ।
पुनः क्रमात् स्वरांस्त्रींश्च गीत्वा चैककला यदि ॥ ९७ ॥
एवं कलाषट्ककं च गीत्वाऽसौ रेचितः स्मृतः ।

संरिगरिसंरिग रिगमगरिगम गमपमगमप मपधपमपध पधनिधपधनि (धनिसंनिधनिसं)

इति रेचितः (७)

(2) *Prāṅmukha*

92. Wherein the phrase has two *svaras* going [up] and [then] coming (down) and [the next phrase begins] by dropping the last *svara*; and the other phrases are formed similarly, it is known as *prāṅmukha*.

s̊rrs̊ rggr gmmg mppm pddn dnnd

(3) *Utkṣepa*

93. If the phrase is formed from three (consecutive) *svaras* and the phrase progresses by dropping the last (*svara*) in the previous phrase (in favour of its next higher) *svara*, it is known as *utkṣepa* among experts in singing.

s̊rg rgm gmp mpd pdn

(4) *Parivartaka*

94. If the first phrase is [composed] of three consecutive *svaras* omitting the second, and the remaining phrases commence from the omitted *svaras* and are similar, then it is *parivartaka*.

s̊gm rmp gpd mdn

(5) *Udvāhita*

95. *Udvāhita* is that in which three (consecutive) *svaras* are sung in the phrase, one (*svara*) is descended and the next phrases are executed, omitting one *svara* after another.

s̊rgr rgmg gmpm mpdp pdnd dns̊n

(6) *Niṣkūjita*

96. The [*alaṁkāra* called] *niṣkūjita* is formed by singing a phrase of *prasāda*, then reaching the third *svara* and then the first.

s̊rs̊gs̊ rgrmr gmgpg mpmdm pdpnp (dnds̊d)

(7) *Recita*

97-98ab. If the first *svara*, second, third, second and then again the first three *svaras* are sung to form the first phrase and thus six phrases are sung, it is recognized as *recita*.

s̊rgrs̊rg rgmgrgm gmpmgmp mpdpmpd pdndpdn (dns̊ndn)

TCC 93b 97d

COT 92d 93d 94d 95d 96d 98b

कलां प्रयुज्य मन्द्रादेर्द्विरुक्तोर्ध्वस्वरान्विताम् ॥ ९८ ॥
अवरुह्येत चेदेष स्खलिताख्यस्तदा भवेत् ।

संगरिममरिगसं रिमगपपगमरि गपमधधमपग मधपनिनिपधम पनिधसंसंधनिप

इति स्खलितः (८)

यत्रासौ क्रम इत्युक्तः कला द्वित्रिचतुःस्वराः ॥ ९९ ॥
आद्यस्वराद्यास्त्रिस्त्रः स्युर्द्वितीयाद्यादयस्तथा ।

संरिसंरिगसंरिगम रिगरिगमरिगमप गमगमपगमपध मपमपधमपधनि पधपधनिपधनिसं

इति क्रमः (९)

द्विरुक्ता यदि मन्द्रान्ता मन्द्रादेः स्युः कलास्तदा ॥ १०० ॥
रञ्जिताख्यो भवेदेष प्रसिद्धो गानवेदिनाम् ।

संगरिसंगरिसं रिमगरिमगरि गपमगपमग मधपमधपम पनिधपनिधप धसंनिधसंनिध

इति रञ्जितः (१०)

ह्रादमाने तु मन्द्रान्ता मन्द्रादेस्तु कला मता ॥ १०१ ॥

संगरिसं रिमगरि गपमग मधपम पनिधप धसंनिध

इति ह्रादमानः (११)

आदिमेन कला यत्र द्विःस्वराद्या गतागतैः ।
स्वरैरेकोत्तरैर्वृद्धैः स हुङ्कारो निगद्यते ॥ १०२ ॥

संरिरिसं संरिगगरिसं संरिगममगरिसं संरिगमपपमगरिसं संरिगमपधधपमगरिसं
संरिगमपधनिनिधपमगरिसं

इति हुङ्कारः (१२)

क्रमात् सरिगमाद्यैः स्याच्छ्येनः संवादियुग्मकैः ।

संप रिध गनि मसं

इति श्येनः (१३)

एते सञ्चार्यलङ्कारा आरोहेण प्रदर्शिताः ॥ १०३ ॥
एतानेवावरोहेण प्राह श्रीभरतो मुनिः ।
इति प्रसिद्धालङ्कारा पञ्चविंशत्युदीरिताः ॥ १०४ ॥

(8) *Skhalita*

98cd-99ab. If the phrase of the [*alaṁkāra*] *mandrādi* is executed such that its higher *svara* is rendered twice and then is descended, then it becomes the one named *skhalita.*

s̊grmmrgs̊ rmgppgmr gpmddmpg mdpnnpdm pnds̍s̍dnp

(9) *Krama*

99cd-100ab. That is said to be *krama* wherein the phrase has clusters of two, three and four *svaras* such that these three begin with the first *svara* and the second [phrase similarly] begins with the second [*svara*].

s̊rs̊rgs̊rgm rgrgmrgmp gmgmpgmpd mpmpdmpdn pdpdnpdns

(10) *Rañjita*

100cd-101ab. If the phrase formed by rendering twice the *mandrādi* [*alaṁkāra* phrase] ends on the *mandra* [*svara*] it is renowned among the experts of singing as the one named *rañjita.*

s̊grs̊grs̊ rmgrmgr gpmgpmg mdpmdpm pndpndp ds̍ndsn̍d

(11) *Hrādamāna*

101cd. It is opined that in *hrādamāna* [*alaṁkāra*] the *mandrādi* phrase ends on the *mandra* [*svara*].

s̊grs̊ rmgr gpmg mdpm pndp ds̍nd

(12) *Huṁkāra*

102. *Huṁkāra* is defined as that [*alaṁkāra*] in which the first phrase is [composed] of the ascent and descent of two (initial) *svaras* and the *svaras* are then progressively increased by one.

s̊rrs̊ s̊rggrs̊ s̊rgmmgrs̊ s̊rgmppmgrs̊ s̊rgmpddpmgrs̊ s̊rgmpdndpmgrs̊

(13) *Śyena*

103ab. *Śyena* is [formed] by the consonant forms of *s r g m* etc. in order.

s̊p rd gn ms̍

103cd-104ab. These *sañcāri-alaṁkāras* are shown (here) in ascent. Śrī Bharatamuni has defined these selfsame [*alaṁkāras*] in descent also.

104cd-105ab. Twentyfive well known *alaṁkāras* are thus described [here]. Because they are endless, they cannot be described in their entirety in *śāstra.*

TCC 101cd

COT 99bc 100cd-101ab 101acd 103b 91cd-104ab 105

अनन्तत्वात्तु ते शास्त्रे न सामस्त्येन कीर्तिताः ।
रक्तिलाभः स्वरज्ञानं वर्णाङ्गानां विचित्रता ।
इति प्रयोजनान्याहुरलङ्कारनिरूपणे ॥ १०५ ॥

१२. गमकाः

गमकः स्वरकम्पः स्यात् श्रोतृहृदयरञ्जकः ।
तस्य भेदास्तु तिरिपः स्फुरितः कम्पितस्ततः ॥ १०६ ॥
लीन आन्दोलितवलित्रिभिन्नकुरुलाहताः ।
उल्लासितः प्लावितश्च मुद्रितो हुंफितस्ततः ॥ १०७ ॥
नामितो मिश्रितः पञ्चदश इत्यथ लक्षणम् ।
लघिष्ठडमरुध्वानकम्पानुकृतिसुन्दरः ॥ १०८ ॥
द्रुततुर्यांशवेगेन **तिरिपः** (१) परिकीर्तितः ।
स्फुरितो द्रुततृतीयांशाद् (२) द्रुतार्धात् **कम्पितं** विदुः (३) ॥ १०९ ॥
द्रुतवेगेन **लीनः** स्याद् (४) **आन्दोलो** लघुवेगतः (५)
वलिर्वेगाधिकत्वेन (६) **त्रिभिन्न**स्तु स उच्यते ॥ ११० ॥
त्रिस्थानेषु सवैचित्र्यमविश्रान्तघनस्वरः (७) ।
कुरुलो वलिरेव स्यात् कण्ठकोमलग्रन्थिलः (८) ॥ १११ ॥
स्वरमग्रिममाहत्य निवृत्तस्**त्वाहतो** भवेत् (९) ।
उल्लासितः क्रमाद् गच्छन् (१०) **प्लावितः** प्लुतमानतः (११) ॥ ११२ ॥
हृदयङ्गमहुङ्कारगम्भीरो **हुंफितो** भवेत् (१२) ।
मुद्रितो मुखमुद्रेण (१३) **नामितो** नमनाद् भवेत् (१४) ॥ ११३ ॥
कतिचिन्मिश्रणान्**मिश्रो** (१५) बहुधाप्यूह्यतां बुधैः ।

१३. स्थायाः

रागस्यावयवः स्थायो वागो गमक उच्यते ॥ ११४ ॥
मयोक्तो गमकः पूर्वं, त्वधुना स्थाय उच्यते ।
भजनः स्थापनगती शब्दढालौ च वाहिनी ॥ ११५ ॥

105cd-ef. The benefits of elucidating *alaṁkāras* are said to be the gain of [aesthetic] appeal, exact knowledge of *svara* [*sthāna,* i.e. pitch], and the splendour of the limbs of melodic movement.

12. GAMAKAS

106. Gamaka is the trembling of a *svara* which is appealing to the listener's heart. Its varieties are: *tiripa, sphurita, kampita,*

107-108ab. *līna, āndolita, vali, tribhinna, kurula, āhata, ullāsita, plāvita, huṁphita, mudrita,* then *nāmita, miśrita*—[these] fifteen. Now their characteristics [will be elucidated].

108cd-109ab. Beautiful simulation of the sound of a light *ḍamaru* (generated) with the speed of a quarter of the *druta* is described as **tiripa**(1).

109c. Sphurita (2) [is the same at the speed] of the a third of the *druta.*

109d. Kampita (3) [is the same at the speed] of half of the *druta.*

110a. Līna(4) occurs at the speed of the *druta.*

110b. Āndola (5) [occurs] at the speed of the *laghu.*

110c. Vali (6) [occurs] at excessive (higher?) speed.

110d-111ab. Tribhinna (7) is said to be a dense, restless *svara* which is beautiful in [all] three registers.

111cd. Kurula (8) is said to be *vali* itself which spirals tenderly (softly) in the throat.

112ab. Āhata (9) is the striking of a *svara* and returning.

112c. Ullāsita (10) is gradual movement [of a *svara*].

112 d. Plāvita (11) is movement of [*svara*] in the measure of (a) *pluta.*

113 ab. Huṁphita (12) is charming, deep *'hum'* sound.

113c. Mudrita (13) is [generated] by closing the mouth (and producing the *svara*).

113d. Nāmita (14) is [formed] by curving [the *svara*].

114ab. Miśra(15) is [formed] by mixing some [of the above *gamakas*]. This should be surmised by scholars to be of many varieties.

13. STHĀYAS

114cd-115ab. Sthāya is an organ of *rāga; vāga* is called *gamaka. Gamaka* has been explained by me above; now *sthāya* will be described:

115cd-116ab. [These are] *bhajana, sthāpana, gati, śabda, ḍhāla, vāhinī* and *chāyā* respectively. Their characteristics will [now] be elucidated in order.

TCC 106c 107a 111ad 112bd 113ab 116a
COT 73-105 (ii) 108-114abcd 115cd 116ab

छाया चेति क्रमात्, तेषां लक्षणं प्रतिपाद्यते ।
रागस्यातिशयाधानाद् भजनः परिकीर्तितः ॥ ११६ ॥
स्थाप्य स्थाप्य पदं रम्यं कृतिः स्थापनिको भवेत् ।
गतिर्गीते विलासः स्यान्मत्तमातङ्गवद् गतिः ॥ ११७ ॥
मुक्तशब्दपरिग्राह्यः शब्दो माधुर्यपुष्टतः ।
चतुर्भेदो भवेच्छब्दः खाङ्गलो नारहाटकः ॥ ११८ ॥
बोम्बको मिश्रकश्चेति, कफजः खाङ्गलो मतः ।
असौ सुस्निग्धमधुरप्रौढतासौकुमार्ययुक् ॥ ११९ ॥
पित्तजो नारहाटः स्याद् रूक्षगम्भीरयुग्ध्वनिः ।
वातजो बोम्बकः स्यात्तु स्थूलनिःसारतायुतः ॥ १२० ॥
एतत्संमिश्रणादुक्तो मिश्रकः सन्निपातजः ।
निःसाररूक्षताहीन उत्तमः परिकीर्तितः ॥ १२१ ॥
खाङ्गलो बोम्बयुक्तश्चेन्मध्यमः कथितो बुधैः ।
बोम्बनाराटसंयुक्तः शब्दानामधमः स्मृतः ॥ १२२ ॥
विलुण्ठनात्मको मुक्ताफलवड् ढाल उच्यते ।
आरोह्यादित्रये निष्ठं कम्पनं वाहिनी भवेत् ॥ १२३ ॥
छायाकाकुः षट्प्रकारा स्वररागान्यरागजा ।
स्याद् देशक्षेत्रयन्त्राणां, तल्लक्षणमथोच्यते ॥ १२४ ॥
श्रुतिन्यूनाधिकत्वेन या स्वराश्रयसंश्रया ।
स्वरान्तरस्य रागे स्यात् स्वरकाकुरसौ मता ॥ १२५ ॥
या रागस्य निजच्छाया रागकाकुं तु तां विदुः ।
सा त्वन्यरागकाकुर्या रागे रागान्तराश्रया ॥ १२६ ॥
सा देशकाकुर्या रागे भवेद् देशस्वभावतः ।
शरीरं क्षेत्रमित्युक्तं प्रतिक्षेत्रनिसर्गतः ॥ १२७ ॥
रागे नानाविधा काकुः क्षेत्रकाकुरिति स्मृता ।
वीणावंशादिकोत्थाऽसौ यन्त्रकाकुः सतां मता ॥ १२८ ॥

116cd. Bhajana (1) is [said to arise] by excessive impregnation with *rāga*(*-bhāva*) [or colour or aesthetic delight].

117ab. Sthāpanikā (2) occurs by the act < *kṛti* > of making a word charming by instituting (it in the *dhātu*) again and again.

117cd. Gati (3) is the sporting pace of a song like the gait of a rutting elephant.

118ab. Taking up of an unattached (free) sound with sweetness and robustness is *śabda* (4).

118cd-119a. *Śabda* is of four kinds, viz. *khāḍgala, nārahāṭa, bombaka* and *miśraka.*

119bcd. Khāḍgala (i) is opined to be phelgm-born. This is unctuous, sweet, mature and tender.

120ab. Nārahāṭa (ii) is bile-born sound [which is] dry and deep.

120cd. Bombaka (iii) is [body-]wind-born and is thick and hollow.

121ab. Miśraka (iv) is said to be their admixture, and is born of *sannipāta.*

121cd. Musical sound is declared to be best if it is without hollowness and dryness.

122. It is said by scholars to be middling if *khāḍgala* is mixed with *bombaka.* The mixture of *bombaka* and *nārahāṭa* is opined to be the worst among voices.

123. Lustrous rolling [of *svaras* in a passage] like a pearl is said to be *ḍhāla* (5). Trembling [of *svaras*] in the three *varṇas* beginning with *ārohi* is *vāhinī* (6).

124. Chāyākāku (7) is of six varieties, viz. *svara-, rāga-, anyarāgaja-, deśa-, kṣetra-* and *yantra-*; their characteristics will be now described:

125. If the *sthāya* belonging to a *svara* abides,— because of the deficiency or excessiveness (in number and magnitude) of *śrutis,*—in another *svara* in a *rāga,* it is opined to be *svarakāku* (i).

126ab. That which elucidates the true shade of a *rāga* is understood to be *rāgakāku* (ii).

126cd. That which (normally) occurs in a (given) *rāga* abides in a different *rāga* is *anyarāgaja kāku* (iii).

127ab. That which occurs in a *rāga* according to the nature of a province is called *deśakāku* (iv).

127cd-128ab. The [human] body is called *kṣetra* (field, soil). Just as it differs from one to another according to its nature, so also there are different *kākus,* according to the nature of the *rāga,* called *kṣetrakāku* (v).

128cd. That which arises from *vīṇā,* flute etc. is opined by experts to be *yantrakāku* (vi) (i.e. instrumental *kāku*)

TCC 116d 118abd 119a 121b 122cd 125b 126bd 128c
COT 116d 117abd 118b 123bd 124a 128bd

१४. आलप्तिभेदाः

वर्णालङ्कारसम्पन्ना गमकस्थायचित्रिता ।
आलप्तिरुच्यते तज्ज्ञैर्बहुवैचित्र्यसंयुता ॥ १२९ ॥
ग्रहांशतारमन्द्राणां न्यासापन्यासयोस्तथा ।
अल्पत्वस्य बहुत्वस्य षाडवौडुवयोरपि ॥ १३० ॥
अभिर्व्यक्तिर्यत्र दृष्टा सा रागालाप उच्यते ।
आलस्यालापयोः सम्यक् प्रकटीकरणं च यत् ॥ १३१ ॥
रागालपनमित्युक्तं लक्ष्यलक्षणकोविदैः ।
आलप्तिर्द्विविधा प्रोक्ता रागवस्तुविशेषणात् ॥ १३२ ॥
स्वस्थानकैश्चतुर्भिर्या क्रियते रूपकं विना ।
रागालप्तिर्यत्र रागः स्वरे संवेश्यते च सः ॥ १३३ ॥
स्थायी, ततश्चतुर्थस्तु द्व्यर्ध इत्यभिधीयते ।
स्थायी स्वरादष्टमस्तु द्विगुणः परिकीर्तितः ॥ १३४ ॥
द्व्यर्धद्विगुणयोर्मध्ये स्थिता अर्धस्वराभिधाः ।
स्थायिनो द्व्यर्धतोऽर्वाक् च स्वरसञ्चालनं तथा ॥ १३५ ॥
स्थायिनोऽधस्तनं चापि वादनात् प्रथमं भवेत् ।
द्व्यर्धस्वरे चालयित्वा न्यसनं तद् द्वितीयकम् ॥ १३६ ॥
अर्धस्वरे चालयित्वा तदेव तु तृतीयकम् ।
द्विगुणं चालयित्वा तु स्थायिन्यासाच्चतुर्थकम् ॥ १३७ ॥
एभिश्चतुर्भिः स्वस्थानै रागालप्तिर्मता सताम् ।
आलाप एव ठायः स्यात् पृथग्भूतविदारिकः ॥ १३८ ॥
रूपकस्थेन रागेण तालेन च विधीयते ।
रूपकालप्तिरेषा तु द्विविधा परिकीर्तिता ॥ १३९ ॥
प्रतिग्रहणिकाद्या च भञ्जनीसंज्ञिका परा ।
विधाय स्थायमालप्ते रूपकावयवो यदि ॥ १४० ॥
प्रतिगृह्येत सा प्रोक्ता प्रतिग्रहणिका बुधैः ।
भञ्जनी द्विविधा ज्ञेया स्थायरूपकभञ्जनात् ॥ १४१ ॥

14. KINDS OF ĀLAPTI

129. Ālapti is described by experts to be that which is replete with *varṇa-alaṁkāra,* lined with *gamaka* and *sthāya* and is possessed of much strange (or characteristic) beauty < *vaicitrya* >.

130-131ab. Wherein there is (clear) articulation of *graha, aṁśa, tāra, mandra,* similarly *nyāsa, apanyāsa, alpatva, bahutva,* also *ṣāḍava* and *auḍuva,* it is said to be *rāgālāpa.*

131cd-132ab. That which manifests well and completely < *samyak* > in [both] *ālaptī* and *ālāpana* is pronounced by experts in [musical] practice and theory as *rāgālapana.*

132cd. Ālapti is said to be of two kinds, being qualified by *rāga* and *vastu.*

133abc. That which is performed in its own four (autonomous, nucleal, melodic) positions without [the song form called] *rūpaka* is *rāgālapti.*

133c-134. The *svara* with which the *rāga* enters is *sthāyī;* the fourth (*svara*) from it is named *dvyardha.* The eighth from *sthāyī-svara* is said to be *dviguṇa.*

135ab. Those [*svaras*] which lie between *dvyardha* and *dviguṇa* are called *ardhasvaras.*

135cd-136ab. Making the *svaras* from the *sthāyī* to the *dvyardha* to move about and the performing in the *svaras* below the *sthāyī* is first *[svasthāna].*

136cd. Making the *svaras* move about in the *dvyardha* and then resting (thereon) is the second *svasthāna.*

137. Making the *ardhasvaras* move about and [doing] the same [resting] is the third *svasthāna.* Making the *dviguṇa* move about and (then) resting on the *sthāyī-svara* is the fourth [*svasthāna*].

138ab. According to the learned, *rāgālapti* is (performed) in these four *svasthānas.*

138cd-139abc. A separated [fragment of] *ālāpa* itself is *ṭhāya.* [*Ālāpa*] executed with a *rāga* abiding in *rūpaka* and having *tāla* is *rūpakālapti.*

139d-104ab. This is averred to be of two kinds: the first is *pratigrahaṇikā;* the other is named *bhañjanī.*

140cd-141ab. If the *sthāya* is established in *ālapti* and (then) the organ of the *rūpaka* (song) is taken up [therefrom], it is declared by scholars to be *pratigrahaṇikā.*

141cd. Bhañjanī is (again) of two kinds by division into *sthāya* and *rūpaka.*

TCC 130d 131a 132cd 133ac 136d
COT 129-144ab

यदा तत्पदमानेन स्थायो रूपकसंस्थितः ।
नानाप्रकारः क्रियते सा ज्ञेया स्थायभञ्जनी ॥ १४२ ॥
तैः पदैस्तेन मानेन समग्रं रूपकं यदि ।
अन्यथा वाऽन्यथा गायेदसौ रूपकभञ्जनी ॥ १४३ ॥
इयमेवोच्यते लोके नेमशब्देन गायकैः ।

१५. स्थापना

स्तोकैः स्तोकैस्तनुस्थायैः प्रसन्नैर्बहुभङ्गिभिः ॥ १४४ ॥
जीवस्वरव्याप्तिमुख्यै रागस्य स्थापना भवेत् ।

१६. रागभेदाः

योऽसौ ध्वनिविशेषस्तु स्वरवर्णविभूषितः ॥ १४५ ॥
रञ्जको जनचित्तानां स रागः कथितो बुधैः ।
स्वराणां क्रमभेदाच्च नानागमकभेदतः ॥ १४६ ॥
षाडवौडुवभेदाच्च सम्पूर्णाद् गतिभेदतः ।
ग्रहांशन्यासभेदाच्च नानादेशजनोद्भवाः ॥ १४७ ॥
अनन्ता रागभेदाः स्यू रूढिदेशस्वराभिधाः ।
शुद्धसालगसङ्कीर्णा इति रागास्त्रिधा पुनः ॥ १४८ ॥
नान्योपजीविनः शुद्धाः केवला रञ्जनात्मकाः ।
छायान्तरेण रक्ता ये रागाः सालगसंज्ञकाः ॥ १४९ ॥
मूलच्छायान्तराद् रक्ता रागा सङ्कीर्णका इति ।
अनन्तत्वात्तु रागाणां प्रत्येकं वक्तुमक्षमः ॥ १५० ॥

१७. रागाणामुद्देशः

केषाञ्चिन्मतमाश्रित्य कतिरागान् वदाम्यहम् ।
शुद्धभैरवहिन्दोलदेशिकारास्ततः परम् ॥ १५१ ॥
श्रीरागः शुद्धनाटश्च नटनारायणश्च षट् ।
रागा देवमयाः ख्यातास्तद्धेतुः कथ्यतेऽधुना ॥ १५२ ॥

142. When a *sthāya* occurring in a *rūpaka* is performed in many different modes (within the limits) measured by the word (or stanza foot?) [to which it is set], it is to be understood as *sthāyabhañjanī.*

143-144ab. If the entire *rūpaka* is sung in [many] alternative ways to the same measure of the same [respective] words, it is *rūpakabhañjanī.* The selfsame is popularly < *loke* > called '*nema*' by singers.

15. STHĀPANĀ

144cd-145ab. [After executing the four *svasthānas,*] the *rāga* (*bhāva*) is fixed with *sthāyas* which are little, clear and bright (intelligible), performed in [their] many postures within the main scope of the *jīvasvara.*

16. KINDS OF RĀGAS

145cd-146ab. That special sound (series), which is ornamented with *svaras* and *varṇas* and is appealing to the minds of people is described by scholars as *rāga.*

146cd-147ab. Because of differences in the order of *svaras,* in the application of numerous *gamaka* varieties, in *ṣāḍava, auḍuva* and *sampūrṇa,* because of differences in [the nature of the] pace, (or in the nature of *svaragati*),

147cd-148ab. because of differences in *graha, aṁśa* and *nyāsa, rāga* varieties produced by people of various regions, *rāga* varieties are endless, and are named after convention, region or *svara.*

148cd. Again, *rāgas* are of three kinds: *śuddha, chāyālaga* and *saṁkīrṇa.*

149ab. The *śuddhas* do not subsist on other [*rāgas*] and [their] appeal is absolute [pure].

149cd. Those [*rāgas*] which become appealing by assuming the shades of other [*rāgas*] are named *sālaga.*

150. *Rāgas* which become appealing because they assume a shade which differs from that of the original *rāga,* are *saṁkīrṇa.* Because of the endlessness of *rāgas* (in number and form), it is not feasible to describe each one of them.

17. LIST OF RĀGAS

151. I shall [now] describe a few *rāgas* based on the opinion of some (authorities): *śuddhabhairava, hindola, deśikāra,* then

152abc. *śrīrāga, śuddhanāṭa, naṭanārāyaṇa*—these six *rāgas* are reputed as divine.

TCC 143c 144c 145a 146d 147ab 148cd 149d 151bc 152b
COT 129-144ab 145cd 146abcd-148abcd-150ab 151-166

सद्योजातोद्भवः शुद्धभैरवो, वामदेवतः ।
हिन्दोलो, देशिकाराख्यस्त्वघोरात्, तत्पुरुषतः ॥ १५३ ॥
श्रीरागः शुद्धनाटाख्योऽपीशानवदनोद्भवः ।
नटनारायणो रागो गिरिजामुखजस्ततः ॥ १५४ ॥
एतेषां वनिताः पुत्राः पञ्च पञ्च क्रमाद् ब्रुवे ।
धन्नासी भैरवी चैव सैन्धवी मारवी तथा ॥ १५५ ॥
आसावरीति पञ्चैताः शुद्धभैरवसुभ्रुवः ।
भैरवः शुद्धललितः पञ्चमः परजस्तथा ॥ १५६ ॥
बङ्गालश्चेति पञ्चैते शुद्धभैरवसूनवः ।
भूपाली च वराली च तोडी प्रथममञ्जरी ॥ १५७ ॥
तुरुष्कतोडिका चेति हिन्दोलस्य च नारिकाः ।
वसन्तः शुद्धबङ्गालः श्यामः सामन्तकस्तथा ॥ १५८ ॥
कामोदश्चेति पञ्चैते हिन्दोलस्य सुता अमी ।
रामक्री बहुली देशी जयतश्रीश्च गुर्जरी ॥ १५९ ॥
देशिकारस्य पञ्चैताः विख्याताश्च वराङ्गनाः ।
ललितश्च विभासश्च सारङ्गस्त्रिवणस्तथा ॥ १६० ॥
कल्याण इति पञ्चैते देशिकारस्य सूनवः ।
गौडी पाडी गुणकरी नादरामक्रिया तथा ॥ १६१ ॥
गुण्डक्रीति च पञ्चैताः श्रीरागस्य हि योषितः ।
टक्कश्च देवगान्धारो मालवः शुद्धगौडकः ॥ १६२ ॥
कर्णाटबङ्गाल इति श्रीरागस्य तनूद्भवाः ।
मालवश्रीश्च देशाक्षी देवक्री मधुमाधवी ॥ १६३ ॥
आहेरी चेति विख्याताः शुद्धनाटवरस्त्रियः ।
जिजावन्तश्च सालङ्गनाटः कर्णाटकस्ततः ॥ १६४ ॥
छायानाटो हम्मीरादिर्नाटो नाटस्य सूनवः ।
वेलावली च काम्बोजी सावेरी सुहवी तथा ॥ १६५ ॥
सौराष्ट्री चेति पञ्चैता नटनारायणस्त्रियः ।

152d-154. Their origin will now be mentioned: *śuddhabhairava* is born of sadyojāta; from Vāmadeva [is born] *hindola; deśikāra* from Aghora; from Tatpuruṣa, *śrīrāga*; the one named *śuddhanāṭa* is born from the face Iśāna [of *Īśvara*]; *naṭanārāyaṇa* [is born] of Girijā's face.

155ab. [Now], I shall mention the five wives and five sons of each of these in order.

155cd-156ab.Dhannāsī, bhairavī, saindhavī, māravī and **āsāvarī**—these five are the wives (lit. women) of *śuddhabhairava.*

156cd-157ab. Bhairava, śuddhalalita, pañcama, paraja, baṅgāla—these five are the sons of *śuddhabhairava.*

157cd-158ab. Bhūpālī, varālī, toḍī, prathamamañjarī, turuṣkatoḍī—these five are the wives of *hindola.*

158cd-159ab. Vasanta, śuddhabaṅgāla, śyāma, sāmanta, kāmoda—these five are the sons of *hindola.*

159cd-160ab. Rāmakrī, bahulī,, deśī, jayataśrī, gurjarī—these five are renowned as the wives of *deśikāra.*

160cd-161ab. Lalita, vibhāsa, sāraṅga, trivaṇa, kalyāṇa—these five are the sons of *deśikāra.*

161cd-162ab. Gauḍī, pāḍī, guṇakarī, nādarāmakriyā, guṇḍakrī—these five are the wives of *śrīrāga.*

162cd-163ab. Ṭakka, devagāndhāra, mālava, śuddhagauḍa, karṇāṭabaṅgāla—these [five] are the sons of *śrīrāga.*

163cd-164ab. Mālavaśrī, deśākṣī, devakrī, madhumādhavī, āherī—these [five] are renowned as the wives of *śuddhanāṭa.*

164cd-165ab. Jijāvanta, sālaṅganāṭa, karnāṭa, chāyānāṭa, hammīranāṭa are the [five] sons of *(śuddha)nāṭa.*

165cd-166ab. Velāvalī, **kāmbojī, sāverī, suhavī, saurāṣṭrī**—these five are the wives of *naṭanārāyaṇa.*

TCC 154b 155a 156b 157cd 159ab 160b 162b 163a 164bd 166b
COT 151-166

मल्हारगौण्डकेदारशङ्कराभरणास्ततः ।
विहगडश्चेति सुता नटनारायणस्य च ॥ १६६ ॥

१८. रागलक्ष्माणि

अथैषां लक्षणं वक्ष्ये मूर्त्याभरणपूर्वकम् ।
चन्द्रनेत्रादिकां संज्ञां ज्ञायतां लोकतः सुधीः ॥ १६७ ॥
सद्योजातोद्भवोऽयं प्रथमगतिगनिः सत्रिकोऽरिः कपर्दी
रक्तश्यामस्त्रिशूली सिततरवसनो भस्मदेहस्त्रिनेत्रः ।
कण्ठे शृङ्गं दधानः श्रवणयुगलतो मुद्रिके चन्द्रजूटो
हैमन्तेऽपि प्रभाते विलसति वृषपो(?गो?) भैरवः शुद्धपूर्वः ॥१६८॥
इति शुद्धभैरवः (१)

सर्वाङ्गे भूषणाढ्या धनिरिगविधुगा सत्रिकाऽस्ता रिधाभ्यां
दूर्वाश्यामा विचित्राम्बररचिततनुर्दाडिमीपुष्पहस्ता ।
नेत्रान्तर्बाष्पयुक्ता धवलसहचरी पूर्वजेराकनाम्रा
पश्यन्ती गीतवर्त्मोषसि बहुधनदा धन्यधन्नासिका सा ॥ १६९ ॥
इति धन्नासी (२)

धन्नासीमेलजाता स्वरसकलयुता चादिमध्यान्तषड्जा
तन्वङ्गी चन्द्रवक्त्रा कनकसमतनुः श्वेतवस्त्रं दधाना ।
भाले सिन्दूरबिन्दुर्विकसितवदना सर्वशृङ्गारकाढ्या
नृत्यन्ती गीयमाना द्रविडजनरता भैरवी सा प्रभाते ॥ १७० ॥
इति भैरवी (३)

भैरव्या मेलजाता स्वरसकलरता सत्रिका चन्द्रवक्त्रा
तन्वङ्गी पद्मनेत्रा विपुलसुजघना मत्तमातङ्गयानी ।
मन्दं मन्दं वदन्ती बहुविधगमकैः सैन्धवी रक्तवस्त्रा
युद्धे योधेश्वराणां विमलतरयशः प्रार्थयन्ती सदा सा ॥ १७१ ॥
इति सैन्धवी (४)

166cd. Ef. **Malhāra, gauṇḍa, kedāra, saṅkarābharana, vihagaḍa**—these [five] are the sons of *naṭanārāyaṇa.*

18. CHARACTERISTICS OF RĀGAS

167. Now, I shall elucidate their characteristics along with their image, ornamentation, etc. Let the intelligent [reader] understand [the meaning of] the symbols *'candra', 'netra',* etc. from [their] popular usage.

Śuddhabhairava and Family

(1) *Śuddhabhairava*

168. This *śuddhabhairava* is born of the Sadyojāta face [of Śiva], has first degree *ga* and *ni*; has threefold *sa*; lacks *ri*; has matted hair; bloodred-mixed dark green complexion; holds the trident; wears bright (white) clothes; body is smeared with ashes; has three eyes; has poison (?gold ornament) in neck; wears ear-seals; wears [crescent] moon in [matted] hair; rides a bull; it is fit to be sung in the cold season, at sunrise.

(2) *Dhannāsī*

169. Dhannāsī (rāgiṇi) wears ornaments all over her body; *dha-ni-ri-ga* are of the first *(vidhu)* degree [of movement]; *sa* is threefold; lacks *ri-dha*; has grass-like intense green complexion; wears charming (strange?) clothes; holds pomegrenate flower in hand; has tear of ecstasy in the corner of eye (has falling tears?); is companion of *dhavala*[*rāga*]; born earlier under the name Irāk; she is singing at dawn; gifts away money in plenty—this fulfilled woman.

(3) *Bhairavī*

170. Bhairavī (rāgiṇi) is born in the *mela* of *dhannāsī;* is complete with all notes; *sa* is at beginning [*graha*], middle [*aṁśa*] and end [*nyāsa*]; is slender; (her) face is [beautiful] like the moon; has golden complexion; wears white clothes; wears a spot of vermilion on forehead; her face blooms [like a flower]; wears all ornaments; dances to the accompaniment of the singing of *draviḍa* people, who are pleased with her, [and is fit to be sung]at dawn.

(4) *Saindhavī*

171. Saindhavī (rāgiṇi) is born of the *mela* of *bhairavī* and is complete with all [seven] *svaras*; *sa* is threefold; she has face like the moon; has a slim body, eyes like the lotus [petal], wide hips, walks [slowly and majestically] like an elephant in rut; sings slowly with many kinds of *gamaka* (or, speaks slowly with coquettry or enthusiasm); wears red clothes, prays for the unblemished success of generals in battle, [and is fit to be sung] always.

TCC 166c 167c 168acd 169acd 170bc 171ab
COT 168-223 168 169 170 171

चन्द्रास्या दीर्घकेशी त्वनलगतिनिगा सत्रिकाऽस्ता रिधाभ्यां
हेमाभा दीर्घरूपा बहुविधकुसुमैर्भूषिता स्निग्धनेत्रा ।
मेवाडस्याग्रजाता मृगशिशुनयनी रक्तवस्त्रं दधाना
चेषद्धास्या स्तुवन्ती युधि नृपतिगणान् मारवी सा सदैव ॥ १७२ ॥

इति मारवी (५)

गान्धारोऽत्राग्निग: स्यात् प्रथमगतिमनिर्मादिमध्यान्तपूर्णा
तन्वङ्गी श्यामवर्णा करधृतमुकुरा सर्वशृङ्गारयुक्ता ।
रम्भाया: काननेषु प्रियविमलयशोऽध्यापयन्ती सुकेशी
गन्धर्वै: स्तूयमाना प्रियरसकरुणा शश्वदासावरी सा ॥ १७३ ॥

इति आसावरी (६)

भस्माङ्ग: कण्ठशृङ्गी श्रवणयुगलत: शङ्खमुद्रे दधान:
पादत्राणे प्रवाले फणिपतिसुजटाबद्धमौलि: प्रमत्त: ।
उज्झालस्यानुयायी पटुनतवचन: किन्नरीवाद्यमान:
पूर्णो धाद्यन्तमध्यस्त्वनलविधुगानिर्भैरव: पूर्वयामे ॥ १७४ ॥

इति भैरव: (७)

सांशाद्यन्त: प्रवीण: शुचितरललितो मारवीमेलजातो
भाले धत्ते सुबिन्दुं कनकसमनिभं शुभ्रवस्त्रं दधान: ।
गौराङ्गश्चम्पमल्लीकुसुमभरशिरा: पङ्कजाक्षो विलासी
कामी ताम्बूलहस्त: प्रतिदिनमुषसि प्रार्थक: खण्डितानाम् ॥ १७५ ॥

इति शुद्धललित: (८)

श्यामं ताम्बूलहस्तं करधृतकुमुदं मारवीमेलजातं
पत्रिं चारिं सुरेशं पिकमृदुवचनं वेणुकं पीतवस्त्रम् ।
लिप्ताङ्गं यक्षपङ्कै: शिरसि सुमुकुटं बालचन्द्रार्कभालं
गायन्तीहात्र नाके सकलसुरवरा: पञ्चमं सुप्रभाते ॥ १७६ ॥

इति पञ्चम: (९)

(5) *Māravī*

172. Māravī (rāgiṇi) has [lovely] face like the moon, long hair; has *ni-ga* of the third *(anala)* degree; has threefold *sa*, lacks *ri* and *dha*; has golden complexion, a tall form, shining eyes; she has bedecked herself with many kinds of flowers; is the first born in Mewad; has [unsteady] eyes like the young deer; wears red apparel; is a little humorous; lauds groups of kings in battle [and is fit to be sung] always.

(6) *Āsāvarī*

173. Āsāvarī (rāgiṇi) has *gāndhāra* of the third (*agni*) degree, *ma-ni* of the first [degree]; *ma* occurs in beginning[*graha*], middle [*aṁśa*] and end [*nyāsa*], she is slim, swarthy; holds a mirror in hand; wears every ornament (or is very amorous in bearing); teaches a lovely parrot her beloved's blameless fame, in a plantain grove; she is lauded by the *gandharvas*; her favourite emotion is mercy [and fit to be sung] always.

(7) *Bhairava*

174. Bhairava (rāgaputra) has ash-smeared body, wears a golden necklace, conch-signet rings in both ears, coral slippers; his matted hair in the head is bound with the king of serpents; he is intoxicated; is a follower of [the Persian mode called] *ujjhāla*; skilled in words; is playing the *kinnarī;* complete [with all *svaras*]; *dha* occurs in the beginning [*graha*], middle [*aṁśa*] and end [*nyāsa*]; *ga-ni* are of the third (*anala*) degree and first (*vidhu*) degree (respectively) (fit to be performed) in the early hours.

(8) *Śuddhalalita*

175. Śuddhalalita (rāgaputra) has *sa* for *aṁśa, graha* and *nyāsa*, skilful (in *vīṇā*?), born in the *māravī-mela*, wears a spot on the forehead, wears bright clothes of the golden hue; has creamy < *gaura* > complexion; wears *campaka* and jasmine flowers on the head, has lotus eyes, is sportive, amorous, holds betel leaf in hand, beseeches his beloved whom he has betrayed, [and is fit to be performed] at dawn.

(9) *Pañcama*

176. Pañcama (rāgaputra) is dark skinned, holds betel leaf in hand, and red lotus in another hand, born in *māravī-mela*, has threefold *pa*, lacks *ri*; he is lord of the gods, speaks softly like a cuckoo, plays on the flute (or holds a goad of bamboo?) and wears yellow clothes; his body is anointed with perfume paste < *yakṣapaṅka* >; he wears a crown on the head; wears the mark of crescent moon and sun on forehead; all gods of the heaven sing [his glories/ fit to be sung] at dawn.

TCC 172bcd 173a 175bcd 176abcd
COT 172 173 174 175 176

सत्रिः सम्पूर्णकोऽसौ द्विविधुगतिगनिस्तालहस्तः सुभार्यः
पृष्ठे पैनाकपाणिर्बहुविधरचितैर्भूषणैः शोभमानः ।
गौरो दीर्घस्वरूपी मृदुवचनपरः सर्वलोकोपकारी
नित्यं याच्यः सदाहर्निशि च सुपरजो भाति चाग्रे नृपाणाम् ॥ १७७ ॥

इति परजः (१०)

अन्त्यो गश्च स्वरौ स्तस्त्रिनयनगतिगौ सत्रिकाढ्यश्च पूर्णो
वामे पाणौ सुमालां शशधरमणिभां शुभ्रवस्त्रं दधानः ।
बङ्गालः पानपात्रं विशदकनकजं सव्यहस्ताग्रभागे
विद्वान् सङ्गीतवेदं पठति च नितरां गद्गदैः कम्पभेदैः ॥ १७८ ॥

इति बङ्गालः (११)

इति शुद्धभैरवपरिवाराः

अस्मिन् रागे भवेतां प्रथमगतिगनी सत्रिकोऽत्रारिपोऽसौ
गौराङ्गः पीतवासा घनकुसुमवने क्रीडको दोलयाने ।
हिन्दोलः स्त्रीसहायः कटकमुकुटमुक्तामहाकुण्डलाढ्यः
प्रातःकाले वसन्ते विचरति चतुरो वामदेवाभिजातः ॥ १७९ ॥

इति हिन्दोलः (१)

जाता मल्हारमेले निगरतिरहिता मादिमध्यान्तरूपा
नासाग्रे स्वर्णपुष्पं कमलनयनयोः कज्जलं कण्ठमालाम् ।
मौक्तेयं भालमध्ये वरतरतिलकं कङ्कणे हस्तमूले
रक्तं वस्त्रं दधाना त्वनवरतमदा याति भूपालिका सा ॥ १८० ॥

इति भूपाली (२)

स्वागारे स्वेच्छया या मृदुतरवचनैः क्रीडिता चालिपुञ्जैः
चित्रं वस्त्रं दधाना कुसुमसुकबरी चामरैर्वीज्यमाना ।
नानाशृङ्गारयुक्ता मदनसहचरी कोमलाङ्गी सुगौरी
सायं पूर्णा त्रिषड्जा त्वनलगतिनिमा राजते सा वराली ॥ १८१ ॥

इति वराली (३)

(10) *Paraja*

177. Paraja (rāgaputra) has threefold *sa*, is complete [in *svaras*], *ga-ni* are of the second and first *(vidhu)* degrees respectively, holds cymbals in hands; his good wife is at his back; holds the *pināka (vīṇā)* in his hands; he is splendid with ornaments made in many ways; he is cream complexioned, tall in form; he tends to speak softly; he is a benefactor of all the world, fit to be wooed always [and fit to be sung] day and night, and is in the presence of kings (is the foremost of kings).

(11) *Baṅgāla*

178. Baṅgāla [rāgaputra] has the final [i.e. *ni*] and *ga svaras* of the third and second (*nayana*) degree respectively; *sa* is threefold; it is complete (with all *svaras*); he holds in his left hand a garland, shining like *candrakānta* gems; he wears white clothes; holds a large wine cup in right hand; a scholar, he always recites music, with low inarticulate (sobbing?) voice < *gadgada* > and different *gamakas.*

Hindola and Family

(1) *Hindola*

179. In this *hindola-rāga, ga-ni* are [each] of the first degree, *sa* is threefold, *ri* is absent; he is cream-complexioned, clad in yellow clothes, sports on a swing in a dense flower garden; he is surrounded with women, wears bracelet, crown, pearls and large earring; he is born of Vāmadeva face [of Śiva], is skilful; he roams about in the morning, [i.e. fit to be sung in the morning] of spring time.

(2) *Bhūpālī*

180. Bhūpālikā (rāgiṇi), born in *malhāra-mela* lacks *ni-ga*, has *ma* as *graha, aṁśa* and *nyāsa*; wears a golden flower at the tip of the nose, collyrium in the eyes, a necklace of pearls, *tilaka* mark on the forehead, bangles at wrists; wears red garments; moves about [and is fit to be sung] always, intoxicated.

(3) *Varālī*

181. Varālī (rāgiṇi) roams at pleasure in her own home, speaking softly and playing with a swarm of bees (with a flock of cuckoos?) wearing beautiful clothes; she has a flowerful fillet of hair; she is fanned with flywhisks, adorned elegantly in many places, is [like a] companion to Cupid; she is tender, cream complexioned, moves about [and is fit to be sung] in the evening; complete with all *svaras*, (the *rāgiṇi)* has threefold *sa, ga-ni* [each of] the third (*agni*) degree; [thus] *varālī* is resplendent.

TCC 177d 179abc 180acd 181ad
COT 177 178 179 180 181

सव्ये हस्ते सुदण्डी त्वपरकरतले तालयुग्मं दधाना
लिप्ताङ्गा चन्दनाद्यैः सुशबरवसना सर्वभूषाभियुक्ता ।
प्रौढा ताम्बूलवक्त्रा विकसितनयना मोहिनी मुक्तचूर्णा
पूर्णा माद्यन्तमध्या प्रथमगतिगनिस्तोडिका प्रातरेव ॥ १८२ ॥

इति तोडी (४)

जाता गौडस्य मेले धरिपरिरहिता चादिमध्यान्तपा या
गौराङ्गी पीतवस्त्रा मृगमदतिलकं भालमध्ये दधाना ।
हस्ते वीणैकवाद्या सरसमधुरवाङ् मुक्तकेशी कुरङ्गी
पीतालङ्कारयुक्ता प्रथमपदपुरा मञ्जरी सा सदैव ॥ १८३ ॥

इति प्रथममञ्जरी (५)

छायानाटस्य मेले प्रकटितसुतनुर्मादिमध्यान्तपूर्णा
गौराङ्गी मूर्ध्नि वेणीं कनकमणिमयं कर्णपुष्पं दधाना ।
प्रौढेषद्रक्तनेत्रा यवनसुवनितावस्त्रवेषादिकाढ्या
द्राक्षां पीत्वा प्रभाते विलसति चतुरा यावनी तोडिका सा ॥ १८४ ॥

इति तुरुष्कतोडी (६)

जातो हिन्दोलमेले स्वरसकलयुतः सत्रिकश्च प्रभाते
त्वारामे क्रीडमानो नवदलकुसुमामोदलुब्धालिवृन्दैः ।
ताम्बूलास्यातिगौरो रतिपतिसदृशो रक्तवस्त्रश्च सार्धं
योषिद्भिः सर्ववाद्यारवरभसमहद्धास्ययुक्तो वसन्तः ॥ १८५ ॥

इति वसन्तः (७)

जातः कर्णाटमेले स्वरसकलरतो म(? स)त्रिकः पूर्णकायः
शुभ्राङ्गः पीतवासा मणिगणरचिते कुण्डले कर्णयोः स्तः ।
आस्ते मौलौ किरीटं करतलकमलः कुङ्कुमालिप्तदेहः
प्रातर्याच्यः प्रमत्तो युवजनसहितः शुद्धबङ्गालकोऽसौ ॥ १८६ ॥

इति शुद्धबङ्गालः (८)

(4) *Toḍī*

182. Toḍī (rāgiṇi) holds in her left hand a *vīṇā* (a staff?) and a pair of cymbals in the other hand; her body is besmeared with sandal paste etc.; she is dressed like a woman of wild mountaineer tribe < *śabara* > wears every ornament; she is mature (or a heroine of the *prauḍhā* class), chews betel; has large, open eyes; is ravishing; has sprinkled sandal powder (on her body; unknotted hair?); (the *rāgiṇi*) is complete (with all *svaras*); has *ma* for *graha, aṁśa* and *nyāsa; ga-ni* are of the first degree [each]. [It is fit to be sung] only in the morning.

(5) *Prathamamañjarī*

183. Prathamamañjarī (rāgiṇi) is born in the *gauḍa-mela;* omits *ri-dha*, has threefold *pa*. She has creamy complexion, wears yellow clothes and yellow ornaments, has the *tilaka* mark of musk on her forehead; she has a *vīṇā* in her hand, speaks gracious and sweet words; wears unknotted hair; [she looks like] a gypsy, always [fit to be sung].

(6) *Turuṣkatoḍī*

184. Yavana[=turuṣka]toḍī (rāgiṇi) is of a (melodic) body born in the *chāyānāṭa-mela,* has *ma* for *graha, aṁśa* and *nyāsa,* complete with all *svaras*; she is of cream complexion; the hair of her head is plaited; she wears a flower of gold and gems in the ears; she is mature (heroine of the *prauḍhā* class), somewhat red-eyed; wears the guise and dress of a *yavana* (Persian) woman and roams about at dawn [at which the *rāgiṇi* is fit to be sung], drinking grape wine—this clever *yavanatoḍī.*

(7) *Vasanta*

185. Vasanta (rāgaputra) is born in *hindola-mela,* has all the *svaras,* and threefold *sa*; he sports at dawn [and is then fit to be sung] in a park, surounded with a swarm of bees, covetous of the fragrance (honey) of the petals of fresh flowers; he chews betel; is very creamy in complexion; he is like Manmatha (Cupid); wears red clothes; he is engaged in great fun (laughter) amidst the blaring sound of all musical instruments, and is in the company of damsels.

(8) *Śuddhabaṅgāla*

186. Śuddhabaṅgāla (rāgaputra) is born in the *karnāṭa-mela,* has all the *svaras*; *ma* (? *sa*) is threefold; has full [perfect], bright (white ?) body, wears yellow clothes; both ears have earrings studded with gems; he has a crown on the head, a lotus in hand; the body is besmeared with vermilion; he is to be wooed [and sung] in the morning; intoxicated, he is in the company of young persons.

TCC 182abc 183ad 185cd 186a
COT 182 183 184 185 186

काकल्या चान्तरेण प्रकटवरतनुः सत्रिकः पूर्णरूपः
श्यामाङ्गः पीतवासा मधुरतररवः कम्पभेदैर्विचित्रैः ।
कण्ठे रत्नैकमालो विरचिततिलकः कुङ्कुमैर्भालमध्ये
रागः श्यामाभिधानस्त्वनवरतमदः कामिनीनां विनोदे ॥ १८७ ॥

इति श्यामः (९)

कर्णाटाख्यस्य मेले प्रकटवरतनुः पूर्णरूपस्त्रिषड्जः
पद्माङ्घ्रिः पद्मनेत्रः श्रवणयुगलतः कुण्डले द्वे दधानः ।
बिभ्रन्मौलौ किरीटं बहुकुसुममयं कण्ठमालां सुवस्त्रं
प्रातःकाले चकास्ति प्रबलगमकवान् प्रौढसामन्तरागः ॥ १८८ ॥

इति सामन्तः (१०)

कामोदः कामरूपी धृतकुमुदकरः श्वेतवस्त्रं दधानः
कस्तूरीबिन्दुभालः कुसुमसुमुकुटः कण्ठमालादिकाढ्यः ।
वक्ता सद्व्यङ्ग्यवाक्यं युवजनसहितो वेत्रहस्तः प्रतापी
सम्पूर्णः सत्रिकोऽसौ विधुगतिगनिकश्चापराह्णे चकास्ति ॥ १८९ ॥

इति कामोदः (११)

इति हिन्दोलपरिवाराः

जातोऽघोराख्यवक्त्रात् त्रिगतिगनिगमाः सत्रिपूर्णोऽत्र रागे
रक्ताङ्गः पद्मनेत्रः सितगजगमनो बाखरेजस्य मित्रम् ।
कण्ठे मुक्तैकमालो धृतमुकुटशिराश्चित्रवासाः सखड्गो
मध्याह्ने योधसङ्घे सुललितशिशिरे देशिकारश्चकास्ति ॥ १९० ॥

इति देशिकारः (१)

पूर्णेन्द्वास्या सुमुक्तामणितरलगला नीलवस्त्रं दधाना
कूर्पासं रक्तवर्णं करचरणयुगे कङ्कणे नूपुरौ च ।
रामक्री चञ्चलाक्षी विमलतरगिरमुद्गारयन्ती विदग्धा
शृङ्गाराढ्या त्रिषड्जा त्वनलगतिगनी राजते सर्वदैव ॥ १९१ ॥

इति रामक्री (२)

(9) *Śyāma*

187. The rāga(putra) called *śyāma* has a (melodic) body manifested with *kākali (niṣāda)* and *antara (gāndhāra)*, full (of *svaras*) in forms, he is swarthy in complexion, clad in yellow garments; *sa* is threefold; his voice is sweet with strange (beautiful) *gamakas*; he has a diamond garland at the throat, and a *tilaka* mark of vermilion in midforehead; he is always [to be sung and] intoxicated in amusement in the company of women.

(10) *Sāmanta*

188. Sāmanta rāga(putra) has a (melodic) body full (of all *svaras*) in form, born in *karnāṭa-mela*; *sa* is threefold; he has lotus(like) feet, lotus(like) eyes and wears two earrings; he has a crown on the head, a garland of many flowers around his neck, and wears excellent clothes; mature (or hero of the *prauḍhā* class), with powerful *gamakas*, this *rāga(putra)* is radiant; [and fit to be sung] in the morning.

(11) *Kāmoda*

189. Kāmoda (rāgaputra) is like Manmatha in appearance (or can assume any form at will), holds a red lotus in hand, wears white clothes, has a spot of musk on forehead, a crown of flowers on head, necklaces etc. (around the neck); he speaks suggestively in the company of young people; he holds a cane in his hand; is valorous; (the *rāgaputra* is) complete with all *svaras*; *sa* is threefold; *ni* is of the first degree; it is radiant [and fit to be sung] in the afternoon.

Deśikāra and Family

(1) *Deśikāra*

190. Deśikāra rāga is born from the Aghora face [of Śiva]; *ni-ga-ma* are [each] of the third degree; *sa* is threefold; it is complete with all *svaras*; he has a red complexion, lotus eyes and the gait of [Indra's] white elephant *(*Airāvata*);* he is the friend of *bākharej*; he has a necklace of pearls and wears a crown on the head; he wears charming (variegated?) clothes, holds a sword; *deśikāra* shines [and should be sung] in the afternoon and in charming winter; he is in the company of soldiers.

(2) *Rāmakrī*

191. Rāmakrī (rāgiṇi) has a [lovely] face like the full moon, wears a necklace of excellent pearls, dark blue clothes, red colured blouse, bangles and anklets; she has unsteady eyes; sings faultless words in high pitch; she is a sophisticated/mature and well decorated (or, is in an erotic mood?); *ṣaḍja* is threefold; *ga-ni* are of the third *(anala)* degree; she is radiant [and fit to be sung] always.

TCC 187bc 188abcd 189a 190bc 191bc
COT 187 188 189 190 191

रामक्रीमेलदृष्टा निगपरिरहिता वापि माद्यन्तमध्या
तन्वङ्गी श्यामवर्णा विलुलितकबरी सव्यहस्ते सुदण्डी ।
ताम्बूलास्या प्रगल्भा मरहठवनितावस्त्रभूषादिकाढ्या
नासायां पीनमुक्ता बहुमतिबहुली शोभते पूर्वयामे ॥ १९२ ॥

इति बहुली (३)

धम्मिल्ले मल्लिमालां श्रवणयुगलतः कुण्डले कण्ठमालां
कूर्पासं शुभ्रवस्त्रं चरणकरयुगे नूपुरौ कङ्कणे च ।
आहङ्गस्य प्रपौत्री मृदुसुकरतले पल्लवं संदधाना
गान्धारान्त्येन्दुगौस्तस्त्रिसमयरिरपा सर्वदा याति देशी ॥ १९३ ॥

इति देशी (४)

नासाग्रे श्रीलवङ्गं जलजकुटिलकेशी कुण्डले श्रोत्रयोर्द्वे
चोलीं कौसुम्भवस्त्रं शिशुविधुतिलकं चाञ्जनं नेत्रयोश्च ।
हस्तद्वन्द्वे सुकाचप्रवलयनिचयं मूर्ध्नि वेणीं दधाना
देशीमेले रुचिज्ञा सकलसुजयतश्रीस्त्रिसा चापराह्ने॥ १९४ ॥

इति जयतश्रीः (५)

सन्धत्ते हस्तमूले करिरदवलयान्यङ्घ्रिमञ्जीरयुग्मं
नासाग्रे हेमपुष्पं कनकसमनिभं कञ्चुकं रक्तवस्त्रम् ।
बिम्बोष्ठी गौरवर्णा द्विवसुसुरचिता मुक्तकच्छाप्यसौ वा
रामक्रीमेलसौख्या त्रिसमयरिरसौ गुर्जरीयं प्रभाते ॥ १९५ ॥

इति गुर्जरी (६)

देशीमेले प्रजातः स्वरसकलयुतो धत्रिकश्चञ्चलाक्षो
हस्ते पद्मं दधानः शुचिवसनरतः श्लिष्टशृङ्गारसर्वः ।
मुग्धस्त्रीसत्समक्षे हसति सकपटं पूर्णताम्बूलवक्त्रः
कामी कामावतारः कुटिलसुललितो भाति धृष्टः प्रभाते ॥ १९६ ॥

इति ललितः (७)

(3) *Bahulī*

192. Bahulī (rāgiṇi) is found in the *rāmakrī-mela;* lacks *ni-ga; ma* is at beginning *(graha), madhya (aṁśa)* and end (*nyāsa*); she is slender, swarthy complexioned; has dangling hair; she holds a good *vīṇā* (staff?) in her right hand; chews betel; she is bold and confident (or heroine of the *pragalbhā* class); she wears the dress and ornaments of a *marāṭhā* woman; she wears a large pearl for nose ring; she is very clever and is splendid [to be sung] in the early hours.

(4) *Deśī*

193. Deśī (rāgiṇi) wears a jasmine garland in her braided hair, earrings in both ears, a garland, blouse, white clothes, bangles and anklets; she is the great-grand-daughter of [the Persian mode] *āhaṅga;* she holds fresh shoots in her soft hands; *gāndhāra* and the final *svara,* (viz. *ni*) are [each] of the first (*indu*) degree; *ri* is threefold; lacks *pa;* she sets out [and is sung] always.

(5) *Jayataśrī*

194. Jayataśrī (rāgiṇi) wears a clove < *śrīlavaṅga* > for nose ring, a lotus in her curly hair, earrings in both ears, a jacket, orange coloured clothes, *tilaka* mark shaped like the crescent moon (on the forehead), collyrium in the eyes and elegant glass bangles; she wears a plait of hair; she is charming in the *deśī-mela,* conquers everyone (with her charm; complete with *svaras?*); *sa* is threefold; [the *rāgiṇi* is to be performed] in the afternoon.

(6) *Gurjarī*

195. Gurjarī (rāgiṇi) wears ivory bangles on wrists and (ivory) anklets, a golden flower in her nose, a blouse of golden hue, and red clothes; she has lips like the [red] *bimba* fruit *(bryonia grandis),* creamy complexion; she is of sixteen years age; she has a freely trailing *kacchā;* she is happy (i.e. born) in the *rāmakrī-mela;* has threefold *ri;* [to be sung] at the dawn.

(7) *Lalita*

196. Lalita (rāgaputra) is born in the *deśī-mela,* has the full complement of *svaras, dha* is threefold; he has unsteady eyes; holds a lotus in the hand; wears white clothes, fully decorated; laughs fraudulently at innocent women; his mouth is full of betel; he is amorous, is a veritable incarnation of Manmatha; he is crooked but charming; is audacious; [is to be sung] at dawn.

TCC 192ab 193abcd 194a 195c 196ac
COT 192 193 194 195 196

गौराङ्गः पङ्कजाक्षः सुशबरवसनो भालकाश्मीरबिन्दु-
मल्लीस्रग्भूष्यकण्ठश्चतुरवरगिरं कीरमध्यापयन् यः।
मेले तातस्य जातस्त्वधिकप्रथममः सत्रिकोऽपः शठोऽसौ
स्वेच्छागामी प्रभाते वदति विनयतां श्रीविभासाख्यरागः॥ १९७॥

इति विभासः (८)

श्यामाङ्गः पीतवासाः प्रबलतरगदाशङ्खचक्राब्जहस्तो
बाणैः शार्ङ्गेण पूर्णः स्फुरदिषुधिकटिस्तार्क्ष्यगो भूषणाढ्यः।
गान्धारो वेदगः स्युर्गुणगतिमनिधाः पक्षगोरिस्त्रिषड्जः
सम्पूर्णश्चापराह्ने प्रचरति चतुरो धीरसारङ्गरागः॥ १९८॥

इति सारङ्गः (९)

देशीसन्मेलजातस्त्रिविधसमयसः पूर्णरूपोऽतिगौरः
कण्ठे मौक्तेयमालो धृतमुकटशिराश्चित्रवासाश्च रम्यः।
पुष्पश्रीकन्दुहस्तो युवजनसहितो मन्मथानन्दकर्ता
शृङ्गारी पण्यवीथ्यां तरुणतिरवणः शोभते सायमेषः॥ १९९॥

इति तिरवणः (१०)

सत्रिः पूर्णो द्विनेत्राग्रियमरिगमनी राजवृन्दैः समेतो
गौरस्ताम्बूलवक्त्रः सिततरवसनः कण्ठरत्नैकमालः।
कञ्जाक्षः छत्रमूर्द्धोभयचमरयुतो रत्नसिंहासनस्थः
कल्याणो यम्मनाद्यः परिजनसहितो राजतेऽसौ दिनान्ते॥ २००॥

इति यम्मनकल्याणः (११)

इति देशिकारपरिवाराः

शृङ्गारी सुन्दरस्तत्पुरुषवदनजः कण्ठनक्षत्रमालः
श्रीरागः श्वेतवासाः प्रथमगतिगता धैवतो रिर्गनी स्युः।
आरोहे धैवतोनस्त्ववगमनयुतः सत्रिपूर्णोऽत्र गौरो
ग्रीष्मे सायं सुनृत्ये विलसति सरसं हस्तलग्नालिपद्मः॥ २०१॥

इति श्रीरागः (१)

(8) *Vibhāsa*

197. Vibhāsa (rāgaputra) is of cream complexion, lotus-eyed, dressed like a man of wild mountaineer tribe < *śabara* >; he wears a vermilion spot on the forehead, a garland of jasmine flowers around the neck; he teaches skilful words to a parrot; he is born in his father's *mela*; employs the first degree *ma* excessively; *sa* is threefold; *pa* is absent; he is [a] fraudulent < *śaṭha* > lover; roams about at will; speaks humbly [to the heroine, and is fit to be sung] at dawn.

(9) *Sāraṅga*

198. Sāraṅga (rāgaputra) is swarthy in complexion; he wears yellow garments, holds a powerful mace, conch, disc and lotus in his (four) hands; a bow called *śāraṅga* and a shining quiver full of arrows is held at his waist; he is well decorated; *ga* is of the fourth (*veda*) degree; *ma-ni-dha* are of the third *(guṇa)* degree; *ri* is of the second *(pakṣa)* degree; *sa* is threefold; it is complete (with *svaras*); this clever, valorous *(sāraṅga)* moves [and is fit to be sung] in the afternoon.

(10) *Tiravaṇa*

199. Tiravaṇa (rāgaputra) is born in the *deśī-mela; sa* is of three conventional usages< *samaya*> [viz. *graha, aṁśa* and *nyāsā*; *sa-ma-pa* are [each] of three degrees; it has a complete form (with all *svaras*); he is very creamy in complexion; wears a pearl necklace, a crown on the head; wears variegated and charming < *citra* > clothes and is charming; he holds a basket full of flowers; he is in the company of young (damsels), generating erotic ecstasy; the youthful *tiravaṇa* is resplendent in the amorous art in the street of the courtesans [and is fit to be sung] in the evening.

(11) *Yammana-kalyāṇa*

200. Yammana-kalyāṇa has threefold *sa*, is complete (with all *svaras); ri, ga, ma, ni* are respectively of the second, second *(netra),* third (*agni*) and second (*yama*) degrees. He is with a train of kings; he is of creamy complexion, chews betel, wears white clothes, a gem-necklace; he is lotus-eyed; has a (royal) umbrella over his head, served with flywhisks on either side; he is seated on a gem throne, surrounded by a train of attendants; he is radiant [and is fit to be sung] at the end of the day.

Śrīrāga and Family

(1) *Śrīrāga*

201. Śrīrāga is well decorated (amorous?), handsome, born of the Tatpuruṣa face [of Śiva]; wears a necklace of star(-shape?- number, i.e. 27?) [gems], white clothes; *dhaivata, ri, ga* and *ni* are of the first degrees; *dhaivata* occurs in ascent but not in descent; *sa* is threefold; it is complete (with all notes); he is of creamy complexion; he is sportive, graceful; he is dancing [and fit to be sung] in the evening in summer; he holds in his hand a lotus swarmed by bees.

TCC 197acd 199d 200cd 201c COT 197 198 199 200 201

रामक्रीमेलजाता धगपरिरहिता सत्रिधा षोडशाढ्या
चित्रं वस्त्रं दधाना करधृतकमलाऽऽकर्णनेत्रा सुकेशी ।
चैत्री मुल्तानिपूर्वी वरयवनपुरीकर्पटीभिश्च सार्धं
सङ्क्रीडन्ती दिनान्ते चतुररतिकला गौरदेहा तु गौडी ॥ २०२ ॥

इति गौडी (२)

गौडीमेले सुलग्ना प्रथमगुणरिनिस्त्यक्तगा पङ्कजाक्षी
भर्तुः सन्तापहन्त्री स्मितविधुवदना गीतनृत्याभियुक्ता ।
गौराङ्गी शुक्लवस्त्रा तरुणतरमदोन्मत्तमातङ्गयानी
शृङ्गाराढ्या हि पाडी युवजनहृदयानन्दिनी वासरान्ते ॥ २०३ ॥

इति पाडी (३)

गूर्जर्या मेलजाता स्फुरिततरसपा न्यादिमध्यान्तपूर्णा
वक्षोहारायताक्षी सितवरवसना रक्तकूर्पासिका या ।
नानाशृङ्गारभूष्या मृदुमधुवचना श्यामलाङ्गी सुतन्वी
भर्तुः सङ्केतकं सद्विमलगुणकरी कामिनी याति सायम् ॥ २०४ ॥

इति गुणकरी (४)

सम्पूर्णा सत्रिका या गुणविधुगनिगा किन्नरीवाद्यहस्ता
श्यामाङ्गी दीर्घनेत्रा गुरुजलजगणैः कण्ठमाल्यादिभूष्या ।
मध्येषद्रक्तवस्त्रा वरगजगमनी स्वर्णकूर्पासयुक्ता
वक्तुं सायं प्रयाति प्रियचरितगुणं नादरामक्रियाऽसौ ॥ २०५ ॥

इति नादरामक्री (५)

गूर्जर्या मेलरक्ता रिधपरिरहिता सत्रिका नीलवस्त्रा
गौरी मुक्तालका या नवनगरचिता कामसङ्केतसंस्था ।
नीपच्छायोपविष्टा विमलकरतले पद्मपत्रं दधाना
गुण्डक्री भामिनी सा प्रियतमपदवीं प्रेक्षतीयं प्रभाते ॥ २०६ ॥

इति गुण्डक्री (६)

(2) *Gauḍī*

202. Gauḍī (rāgiṇi) is born in *rāmakrī-mela;* omits *dha-ga; sa* is threefold; she is sixteen years of age; wears variegated clothes; holds a lotus in hand; eyes (are so long as to) reach the ears; has excellent hair; she belongs to the Persian city of Multān in the East, sporting with a mendicant with matted hair; (playing with dolls made of cotton clothes?); she is skilled in the erotic art; she is creamy complexioned; [fit to be sung] at the end of day in the *caitra* month.

(3) *Pāḍī*

203. Pāḍī (rāgiṇi) is married to the *gauḍī-mela;* [its] *ri* and *ni* are of the first and third *(guṇa)* degree (respectively); *ga* is omitted; she is lotus-eyed; she alleviates the (love-heat) affliction of her husband; she has a smiling, moon-like face; she is engaged in singing and dancing; is cream-complexioned, dressed in white clothes; she moves with the gait of a youthful, lusty elephant in rut; she is erotic (well decorated?) and brings rapture to the hearts of swans [and is fit to be sung] at the end of the day.

(4) *Guṇakarī*

204. Guṇakarī (rāgiṇi) is born in the *gūrjarī-mela*; *sa-pa* sparkle with *sphurita* [*gamaka*]; *ni* occurs at the beginning [*graha*], middle [*aṁśa*] and end [*nyāsa*]; it is complete (with all *svaras*); she wears a garland on her bosom; has large eyes; wears white clothes, a red blouse; is decorated with various ornaments; her speech is soft, and sweet; she is swarthy and slender; this damsel of stainless character sojourns to the rendezvous of her husband [and is fit to be sung] in the evening.

(5) *Nādarāmakrī*

205. Nādarāmakrī (rāgiṇi) is complete (with all *svaras*), has threefold *sa; ni* and *ga* are of third (*guṇa*) and first (*vidhu*) degree (respectively); she holds the musical instrument *kinnarī* in her hands; she is of swarthy complexion; she has long eyes; is decorated with a garland of large lotus (or gems, pearls, coral, conch, etc.); she is [a] *madhyā* [class of heroine], wears reddish clothes, walks like an excellent elephant, wears a golden (hued, laced) blouse; she moves about [and is fit to be sung] in the evening, singing the virtues and deeds of her husband.

(6) *Guṇḍakrī*

206. Guṇḍakrī (rāgiṇi) is affined to the *gūrjarī-mela*; lacks *ri-dha*, has threefold *sa*; she wears dark blue clothes, is creamy complexioned, has loose curls; she is sixteen (*nava*=9, *naga*= mountains=7) years of age and is waiting at the love tryst; sitting in the shade of the *nīpa* tree, holds a lotus leaf in hand; this damsel watches the path of her beloved [for his arrival and is fit to be sung] at the dawn.

TCC 202abc 203bd 204ab 205abcd 206ad
COT 202 203 204 205 206

नृत्यासक्तः सहिष्णुर्नयनगतिगनिः सादिमध्यान्तपूर्णो
वक्षोहारं सरत्नं सुकटकमुकुटं चित्रवस्त्रं दधानः ।
गौरः कामी स टक्को मदनमदभरश्चन्दनालिप्तदेहः
पुष्पाणां कन्दुहस्तो विचरति चतुरः कामदूतः सदाऽसौ ॥ २०७ ॥
इति टक्कः (७)

गान्धारो देवपूर्वस्त्वनलगतिगनिः सत्रिकः पूर्णरूपो
नैरन्तर्यं चकास्ति प्रथमगनिरिधो रत्नसिंहासनस्थः ।
इन्द्राद्यैः स्तूयमानो रसपतिरसिकश्चन्दनालिप्तदेहः
शुभ्रं वस्त्रं दधानः करधृतकुमुदः सर्वभूषाभियुक्तः ॥ २०८ ॥
इति देवगान्धारः (८)

गौडीमेले प्रजातो रिपपरिरहितो वा निमध्यान्तपूर्णो
वीरः शृङ्गारनिष्ठो वरशुकरुचिभा मूसलीकस्य मित्रम् ।
पद्मास्यः पद्मनेत्रः सिततरवसनः कण्ठमाल्यादिभूष्यः
सायंकाले सभायां प्रकटितचतुरो मालवो रागराजः ॥ २०९ ॥
इति मालवः (९)

गुण्डक्रीमेलजातो रसपतिसहितो न्यादिमध्यान्तकोऽपः
कौसुम्भीकेसराणां विमलजलकणैश्चित्रितः श्वेतवासाः ।
काश्मीरस्योर्ध्वपुण्ड्रः सुरभितसुतनुः कण्ठकञ्जाक्षमाल-
स्ताम्बूलास्यो दिनान्ते हरिभजनपरः शोभते शुद्धगौडः ॥ २१० ॥
इति शुद्धगौडः (१०)

बङ्गालान्तश्च कर्णाट इति रिरहितो गादिमध्यान्तकोऽयम्
गौडीसम्मेलभूतः कमलकरतले पुष्पयष्टिं दधानः ।
गौराङ्गः शुक्लवासाः कटकमुकुटकेयूरकाण्ठेयकाढ्यः
कौसुम्भ्युष्णीषधारी परिजनसहितो याति पूर्वाह्णकाले ॥ २११ ॥
इति कर्णाटबङ्गालः (११)
इति श्रीरागपरिवाराः

(7) *Ṭakka*

207. Ṭakka (rāgaputra) is engaged (interested?) in dancing, enduring (patient, agreeable?); *ga-ni* are each of the second (*nayana*) degree; *sa* occurs in the beginning [*graha*], middle [*aṁśa*] and end [*nyāsa*]; complete (with all *svaras*); he wears a diamond garland on bosom, bracelets, crown and variegated clothes; has a creamy complexion; is amorous; he has intense love lust; [so] his body is smeared with sandal paste; he holds a ball of flowers; this clever messenger of love (-god) roams about [and is fit to be sung] always.

(8) *Devagāndhāra*

208. Devagāndhāra (rāgaputra) has *ga-ni* each of the third *(anala)* degree, threefold *sa*; has full [melodic] form (with all *svaras*); is radiant always [to be sung], has *ri-dha* of the first degree. He is seated on a diamond(studded) throne; lauded by Indra and others; he enjoys the erotic (experience), with body besmeared with sandal paste; he wears white clothes, holds a red-lotus in hand and is bedecked with all ornaments.

(9) *Mālava(gauḍa)*

209. Mālava(gauḍa) is born in the *gauḍī-mela;* it may or may not have *ri-pa; ni* is *aṁśa* and *nyāsa*; this (**rāgaputra**) is valorous; he abides in erotic emotion; has the complexion of a parrot; he is a friend of *musalika* (*rāga*); he is lotus-faced, lotus-eyed; wears white clothes, is decorated with garlands etc.; this king of *rāgas* is skilled in (self)expression in the assembly (of connoisseurs) in the evening [which is the appropriate time for its performance].

(10) *Śuddhagauḍa*

210. Śuddhagauḍa (rāgaputra) is born in the *gaṇḍakrī-mela;* he is full of erotic emotion; *ni* is *graha, aṁśa* and *nyāsa*; lacks *pa*; his white clothes are picturesquely stained with the honeydew from the filaments of the safflower; he has a vertical mark of vermilion on the forehead, a fragrant body; wears a garland of lotus (seeds?) around the neck; he chews betel; he is engaged in worshipping Hari; he is radiant [and fit to be sung] in the evening.

(11) *Karnāṭabaṅgāla*

211. Karnāṭabaṅgāla (rāgaputra) is bereft of *ri; ga* is *graha, aṁśa* and *nyāsa*; is born in the *gauḍī-mela;* holds a stalk of flowers in his lotus hand; is creamy complexioned, wears white clothes; also wears wristlets, crown, bracelets and a garland; he wears a head-band of safflowers, roams about with his train of attendants [and is fit to be sung] in the forenoon.

TCC 207bcd 208c 209ad 210ab 211cd
COT 207 208 209 210 211

ईशानास्याभिजातस्त्रिगतिगनिरिधः सत्रिपूर्णः सुधीरो
रक्ताङ्गः कञ्जनेत्रः सिततरवसनः कण्ठमालादिकाढ्यः ।
पाणौ खड्गः प्रतापी स्मितवचनपरः स्निग्धगम्भीरनादः
सन्ध्यायां राजमार्गे शरदि हयगती राजते शुद्धानाटः ॥ २१२ ॥

इति शुद्धनाटः (१)

जाता श्रीरागमेले नवगिरिरचिता सादिमध्यान्तिका या
श्रीखण्डापङ्कचोलीं कुसुमसुवसनं संदधाना मृगाक्षी ।
प्रोढेषद्व्यङ्ग्यवाक्यैः प्रियमुपहसती मालवश्रीः सुतन्वी
चक्रीक्षेपावकर्षैश्चपलकरतलाद् भ्राम्यती सा सदैव ॥ २१३ ॥

इति मालवश्रीः (२)

गान्धाराद्यन्तमध्या गुणगतिरिनिगा धैवतद्विर्गतिर्या
ताम्बूलास्याञ्जनाक्षी कनकमणिमयैर्भूषणैर्भूषिताङ्गी ।
नारायण्यङ्गलग्ना कुसुमसुकबरी कञ्चुकी चित्रवस्त्रा
देशाक्षी राजकन्या प्रतिदिनमुषसि प्रेक्षती मल्लयुद्धम् ॥ २१४ ॥

इति देशाक्षी (३)

गौरी श्रीकोमलाङ्गी कजमुकुलकुचा चित्रकूर्पासवस्त्रा
सर्वाङ्गे भूषणाढ्या मृदुतरवचनोशाकपूर्वा प्रगल्भा ।
वेलावल्येकमेलाधिकविधुगतिमा सत्रिका वा पहीना
देवक्री देवकन्या बहुचतुरतरा राजतेऽह्नोऽन्त्ययामे ॥ २१५ ॥

इति देवक्री (४)

मुग्धा गौरी विचित्राम्बरतनुरचिता सर्वशृङ्गारयुक्ता
माद्यन्तांशाऽरिधा वा द्विगतिगतरिधा वह्निगत्यन्त्यगा च ।
भ्रूरेखाचापधर्त्री मृगशिशुनयना तीव्रनेत्रान्तबाणा
भर्तुर्गेहं सखीभिः सह वरमधुमाधव्युषः सम्प्रयाति ॥ २१६ ॥

इति मधुमाधवी (५)

Śuddhanāṭa and Family

(1) *Śuddhanāṭa*

212. Śuddhanāṭa is born from the Īśāna face [of Śiva]; *ga-ni-ri-dha* are each of the third degree; *sa* is threefold; it is complete (with all *svaras*); he is valiant, red complexioned, lotus-eyed; wears white clothes, garlands etc., he holds a sword in his hand; he is powerful, speaks with a smile; has a smooth, deep voice; he is radiant, riding a horse on a highway [and is fit to be sung] in the evening of autumn.

(2) *Mālavaśrī*

213. Mālavaśrī (rāgiṇi) is born in *śrīrāga-mela,* sixteen years of age (*nava*=9, *giri*=mountain=7), *sa* occurs in the beginning [*graha*], middle [*aṁśa*] and end [*nyāsa*]; she wears a blouse soaked in sandal paste, and clothes (made of) flowers; is fawn-eyed, she is mature (or heroine of the *prauḍhā* class) lover, pokes fun at her beloved with ironical words; she is slender, turns near her nose a nosegay continuously with a restless hand [and is fit to be sung] always.

(3) *Deśākṣī*

214. Deśākṣī (rāgiṇi) has *gāndhāra* at beginning [*graha*], middle *[aṁśa]* and end [*nyāsa*]; *ri-ni-ga* are [each] of the third (*guṇa*) degree; *dhaivata* is of the second degree; she chews betel, has collyrium in eyes, is decorated with gold and diamond jewels; she is married to the *nārāyaṇī-mela,* wears flowers in the braid. She wears a blouse and variegated clothes; this princess watches wrestling matches [and is fit to be sung] at every dawn.

(4) *Devakrī*

215. Devakrī (rāgiṇi) has creamy complexion (or she is a girl of ten), tender-bodied; has breasts like lotus buds, wears variegated blouse and clothes, is decorated all over (the body), is soft spoken, has *uṣṣāk* for her ancestor; is bold and confident (or a heroine of the *pragalbhā* class); belongs to the *velāvali-mela, ma* of the first degree is used excessively; *sa* is threefold; lacks *pa*; she is a celestial nymph, very clever and is resplendent [and fit to be sung] in the last watch of the day.

(5) *Madhumādhavī*

216. Madhumādhavī (rāgiṇi) is innocent, creamy complexioned (or a girl of ten), her body is dressed in strange (? charming) clothes, is decorated in every way; *ma* occurs at beginning [*graha*] and end [*nyāsa*] and is *aṁśa;* lacks *ri-dha* or has *ri-dha* of the second degree; also, the fnal *svara (ni)* and *ga* are of the third *(vahni)* degree; she is possessor of eyebrow-bow, side-glance arrow; she goes to her husband's house along with her friends [and is fit to be sung] at the dawn.

TCC 212ab 213d 214d 215ad 216acd
COT 212 213 214 215 216

चन्द्रद्विस्त्रिर्गताः स्युर्गरिनय इह सुस्निग्धनेत्रा प्रगल्भा
श्यामाऽऽभीरी त्रिषड्जा मृदुवचनपरा मूर्ध्नि वेणीं दधाना ।
मृद्वङ्गी नीलवस्त्रा मृदुगलविलसद्विद्रुमालिश्च कर्णे
ताटङ्काढ्या हि सायं रसपतिनिनदै रासदण्डै रमन्ती ॥ २१७॥

इति आभीरी (६)

श्रीरागस्यैव मेलाद् रिधविधुगतिकः सादिमध्यान्तकोऽसौ
श्यामाङ्गः पीतवासा विरचिततिलकः कुङ्कुमैर्भालमध्ये ।
कण्ठे रत्नैकमालो ललितसुमुरलीवाद्यमानस्त्रिभङ्गी
शृङ्गारी भाति सायं कुसुमशरहितः श्रीजिजावन्तरागः ॥ २१८ ॥

इति जिजावन्तः (७)

गौरस्तारुण्यपूर्णः करधृतकुलिशः सम्भृतानङ्गरूपः
कण्ठे मौक्तेयमालः परिजनसहितः सर्वकिर्मीरवस्त्रः ।
शृङ्गाराढ्यः सुकामी मृदुवचनपरः षड्जमध्यादिकान्तः
प्रीतः केदारमेले दिनपतिविरतौ भाति सालङ्गनाटः ॥ २१९ ॥

इति सालङ्गनाटः (८)

शृङ्गारी पीतवस्त्रः कटकमुकुटसिंहासनच्छत्रयुक्तो
गौराङ्गः श्रीहुसेनीसुहृदभिमदकः पूर्ववागेश्वरीष्टः ।
त्रिस्त्रिर्द्व्येकस्थिताः स्युः स्वररिगधनयः केकिकण्ठाभकोऽसौ
न्याद्यन्तांशोऽरिधो वा विलसति दिवसान्तेऽपि कर्णाटरागः ॥ २२० ॥

इति कर्णाटः (९)

कर्णाटस्य प्रमेले प्रकटितसुतनुस्त्वादिमध्यान्तषड्जः
कण्ठे हारः सरत्नः सितवसनरुचिः पाटलोष्णीशधारी ।
गौराङ्गो रक्तनेत्रः सहचरबहुभिर्वीरशृङ्गारवान् यः
छायानाटो दिनान्ते प्रहसति पथिकान् पुष्पसत्कन्दुहस्तः ॥ २२१ ॥

इति छायानाटः (१०)

(6) *Ābhīrī*

217. Ābhīrī (rāgiṇi) has *ga-ri-ni* of the first, second and third degrees [respectively]; she is affectionate-eyed; bold and confident (or heroine of the *pragalbhā* class), swarthy complexioned; *sa* is threefold; she is soft spoken; she has plaited her hair at the crown of her head; she is soft-bodied, wears dark blue clothes, wears a set of corals around her soft neck, and *tāṭaṅka* earrings in both ears; she rejoices in erotic experience with amorous cries and to the sounds of *rāsadaṇḍa* dance in the evening [which is the appropriate time for singing].

(7) *Jijāvanta*

218. Jijāvanta (rāgaputra) is born in *śrīrāga-mela* itself; (its) *ri-dha* are each of the first degree; *sa* is *graha, aṁśa* and *nyāsa*; he is of swarthy complexion, wears yellow clothes; a *tilaka* of vermilion is composed in the middle of the forehead; he wears a diamond garland; he plays the flute assuming the graceful thrice-bent pose; he is amorous, erotically pleasing and shines [and is fit to be sung] in the evening.

(8) *Sālaṅganāṭa*

219. Sālanganāta (rāgaputra) is creamy complexioned, youthful, holds the weapon thunderbolt <*vajra*> in hand, assumes the form of Manmatha; has a pearl garland around neck; he is surrounded by a train of attendants; all his clothes are multi-coloured; he is well decorated, amorous, soft spoken; *sa* occurs at middle [*aṁśa*], beginning [*graha*] and end [*nyāsa*]; he delights in the *kedāra-mela* and shines [and is fit to be sung] at sunset.

(9) *Karnāṭa*

220. Karnāṭa (rāgaputra) is amorous, yellow-clad, wears wristlets and a crown; he is seated on a throne under royal umbrella; he is creamy complexioned; he is a friend of *śrī husenī* (*rāga*) and delightful; he likes *vāgeśvarī (rāga)* of the east; its *svaras ri-ga-dha-ni* abide respectively in the third, second and first degrees; he is of the hue of the peacock neck (?); *ni* is *graha, nyāsa* and *aṁśa;* or, *ri-dha* are absent; it is splendid [and is fit to be sung] at the end of the day.

(10) *Chāyānāṭa*

221. Chāyānāṭa (rāgaputra) is of a (melodic) form originating in *karnāṭa-mela*; *sa* is its *graha, aṁśa* and *nyāsa*; he wears a diamond necklace, white clothes (he speaks with a smile); '< *smitavadanaruciḥ* >', and a head-band of *pāṭala* flowers (trumpet flower, *bignonia suaveolens*); he is creamy complexioned, red-eyed; is surrounded by many companions; he is involved in the valorous and erotic emotion; he holds a basket (or ball) of flowers; and makes fun of wayfarers [and is fit to be sung] at the end of the day.

TCC 217ad 218ac 220b 221b
COT 217 218 219 220 221

सम्पूर्णो द्विर्गती रिस्त्वनलगतिनिगः सग्रहन्यासकांशः
श्रृङ्गारी यौवनाढ्यः स्मिततरवदनः कन्दुसद्दण्डहस्तः ।
गौरस्ताम्बूलवक्त्रः कुसुमशरसुहृद् रक्तवस्त्रः प्रतापी
चेतः सीमन्तीनीनामनुसरति हमीरादिनाटो हि सायम् ॥ २२२ ॥

इति हमीरनाटः (११)

इति शुद्धनाटपरिवाराः

मुग्धस्त्रीसङ्गतो द्विर्गतिरिगधनयः पूर्णसाद्यन्तमध्यो
रुद्राणीवक्त्रजातः शिखिकुलनटिनी नर्तको भूषणाढ्यः ।
श्यामाङ्गः पीतवस्त्रः करधृतचपलाकान्तिखड्गो दयावान्
प्रावृट्काले नृणां शं प्रकटयति सदा नटनारायणोऽयम् ॥ २२३ ॥

इति नटनारायणः (१)

धित्तां धित्तां धितां तामिति मृदुमुरजं वाद्यमाना सुतन्वी
श्रृङ्गाराढ्या सुगौरी कमलवसनकिर्मीरकूर्पासयुक्ता ।
प्रौढा वेलावली योषसि निजमधुमाधव्यशेषस्वरस्था
धाद्यन्तांशाऽरिधा वा सरपरदसुता सत्कुरायीसहाया ॥ २२४ ॥

इति वेलावली (२)

काम्बोजी मोहिनी या द्विगतिगनिरिधा सत्रिकाढ्याऽनिमा वा
गौरी ताम्बूलवक्त्रा कुसुमजवसनं कञ्चुकं चादधाना ।
कस्तूरीबिन्दुभाला कनकमणिमयैर्भूषणैर्भूषिताङ्गी
कर्णाट्यान्ध्रीसखीभ्यामुषसि विलसती किन्नरीवाद्यहस्ता ॥ २२५ ॥

इति काम्बोजी (३)

धाद्यन्तांशाऽसपा या नयनगुणवती चात्र धान्त्यौ रिगौ स्तः
कस्तूरीबिन्दुभाला मृगशिशुनयना चन्द्रवक्त्रा सुतन्वी ।
सावेरी हारकण्ठा सुशबरवसना पीतकूर्पासयुक्ता
द्व्यष्टाढ्या श्यामवर्णा वरगजगमना सस्मिता सायमेति ॥ २२६ ॥

इति सावेरी (४)

(11) *Hamīranāṭa*

222. Hamīranāṭa (rāgaputra) is complete (with all *svaras*); *ri* is of the second degree, while *ga-ni* are (each) of the third (*anala*) degree; *sa* is *graha, nyāsa* and *aṁśa*; he is amorous and youthful; he has a smiling face; he holds a basket (or ball) of flowers and a staff; he has a creamy complexion; chews betel; is a friend of Manmatha; he wears red clothes; is powerful; his mind (i.e. desire) follows damsels [and is fit to be sung] in the evening.

Naṭanārāyaṇa and Family

(1) *Naṭanārāyaṇa*

223. This *naṭanārāyaṇa-rāga* is in the company of innocent women; its *ri-ga-dha-ni* are [each] of the second degree; it is complete (with all *svaras*); *sa* is at the beginning [*graha*], end [*nyāsa*] and [*aṁśa*]; he is born of the face of Rudrāṇī; dances to the accompaniment of a flock of peacocks; he is decorated; he is swarthy complexioned, wears yellow clothes, holds a sword which flashes like lightning; he is merciful and manifests auspiciousness to human beings [and is fit to be sung] always in the spring season.

(2) *Velāvalī*

224. Velāvalī (rāgiṇi) plays softly on the *muraja* drum: *dhittām dhittām dhitām tām;* she is slender, (well) decorated (amorous?), creamy complexioned (girl of ten years?); she wears clothes of lotus (hue) and multicoloured blouse; she is a mature lover (heroine of the *prauḍhā* class); abides in all notes of the *madhumādhavī (mela); dha* is at the beginning [*graha*], end [*nyāsa*] and [*aṁśa*]*;* or *ri-dha* are (optionally) absent; she is the daughter of *sarpardā* and companion of *kurāyī* (Persian modes).

(3) *Kāmbojī*

225. Kāmbojī (rāgiṇi) is a ravishing woman; its *ni-ri-dha* are of the second degree; *sa* is threefold; *ni-ma* are (optionally? '*vā*') absent; she is creamy complexioned (girl of ten years?), chews betel, wears floral clothes and blouse; she has a spot of musk on forehead, is decorated with ornaments of gold and gems; she shines in the company of maids of Karnāṭa and Āndhra; she holds the *kinnarī* in her hands; she is resplendent [and is to be sung] in predawn hour.

(4) *Sāverī*

226. Sāverī (rāgiṇi) has *dha* at beginning [*graha*], end [*nyāsa*] and *aṁśa;* lacks *sa-pa; dha,* final note (*ni*), *ri* and *ga* are each of the second degree; she has a spot of musk on forehead; she is fawn-eyed, moon-faced, slender; she wears a garland; wears the dress of a woman of wild mountaineer tribe < *śabara* > and yellow blouse; she is of sixteen years of age, swarthy in complexion and walks with [slow majesty of] the gait of an elephant in rut [and is fit to be sung] in the evening with a smile.

TCC 222b 223abd 224acd 225ac 226b COT 222 223 224 225 226

तन्वी श्यामा मृगाक्षी वरकमलमुखी पीतवस्त्रं दधाना
प्रौढा सन्मूर्ध्नि वेणीं द्विजवरगमना कञ्चुकं कर्बुरं च ।
वक्त्रेषद्हास्ययुक्ता दशरसरचिता चामरैर्वीज्यमाना
सावेरीमेलयुक्ता ह्युषसि तु सुहवी सत्रिका पूर्णरूपा ॥ २२७ ॥
इति सुहवी (५)

सावेरीमेलरक्ता स्वरसकलयुता सत्रिका स्वैरिणी या
चित्रं वस्त्रं दधाना कठिनकुचतटे कञ्चुकं मेचकं च ।
गौराङ्गी पङ्कजाक्षी हिमकरवदना दाडिमीबीजदन्ता
सायं शृङ्गारपूर्णा मदनसहचरी याति सौराष्ट्रिका सा ॥ २२८ ॥
इति सौराष्ट्री (६)

सावेरीमेलजातः सपपरिरहितो धग्रहन्यासकांशः
श्यामः पीताम्बरो यो मदनपरिचितः कण्ठमाल्यादिकाढ्यः ।
विद्युन्मेघातिगर्जैरुदितशिखिगणान् नर्तयन् कीर्णपक्षान्
बारामीजन्ममित्रोऽप्युषसि मलहरो भाति मल्हारराग: ॥ २२९ ॥
इति मल्हारः (७)

संस्थो मल्हारमेले स्वरसकलयुतो धैवतांशग्रहान्त्यः
श्यामाङ्गः शङ्खमुक्तावलिरचितगलो भस्मभालः किरातः ।
रम्भापत्रं च मौलौ धरति कटितटे बर्हिणां बर्हजालं
भक्तः शम्भोः प्रभाते सुकरशरधनू राजते गोण्डरागः ॥ २३० ॥
इति गोण्डः (८)

सव्ये दण्डं त्रिशूलं त्वपरकरतले शुभ्रवस्त्रं दधानो
भस्माङ्गो रक्तनेत्रो विमलसुजटिलो द्वीपिचर्मोपविष्टः ।
नासाग्रे दत्तदृष्टिर्गिरिशजपमना वेष्टितः शिष्यवर्गैः
केदारो वाऽरिपोऽस्ति त्रिविधनि सुहवीमेलजातो निशीथे ॥ २३१ ॥
इति केदारः (९)

(5) *Suhavī*

227. Suhavī (rāgiṇi) is slender, swarthy in complexion, fawn-eyed, lotus-faced, wears yellow clothes; she is (a) mature lover (heroine of the *prauḍhā* class); has a plait of hair (on crown of head), moves (gracefully) like a swan; wears a blouse of variegated colours; she has a slightly humorous mouth and is sixteen (*daśa*=ten, *rasa*=six) years of age; she is fanned with flywhisks (on both sides); she is with the *sāverī-mela* and is complete (with all *svaras*); *sa* is threefold; [is fit to be sung] in predawn.

(6) *Saurāṣṭrī*

228. Saurāṣṭrī (rāgiṇi) is complete (with all *svaras*); *sa* is threefold; she is wanton; wears variegated clothes, a dark blue (coloured) blouse on firm breasts; she is creamy complexioned, lotus-eyed and has face like the moon; teeth like pomegrenate seeds; she goes about [and is fit to be sung] in the evening, full of erotic sentiment, (as if) a companion to Manmatha.

(7) *Malhāra*

229. Malhāra rāga-(putra) is born in the *sāverī-mela*, bereft of *sa-pa, dha* is *graha, nyāsa* and *aṁśa*; he is swarthy in complexion, clad in yellow garments, skilled in amours, wears garlands etc.; he dances to the accompaniment of peacocks which spread their feathers and dance in ecstasy at the lightning and thunder-clap; he is a friend of [the Persian mode] *bārāmī* since birth; cleanses (all) sins; is resplendent [and is fit to be sung] at predawn.

(8) *Goṇḍa*

230. Goṇḍa rāga-(putra) abides in the *malhāra-mela*, has all *svaras*; *dhaivata* is *aṁśa, graha, nyāsa;* he is swarthy in complexion; his neck is adorned with strings of conch and pearls; his forehead is besmeared with ashes; he is (dressed as) a mountain tribal hunter <*kirāta*>; he bears a plantain leaf on his head, and peacock feathers around his waist; he is a devotee of Śambhu; holds bow and arrow [and is fit to be sung] at dawn; thus shines the *goṇḍa-rāga*.

(9) *Kedāra*

231. Kedāra (rāgaputra) holds a stick in his left hand and trident in the other; he wears white clothes; his body is besmeared with ashes; his eyes are red; his unblemished hair is matted; he is seated on a tiger-skin; his eyes are focused at the tip of the nose while (mentally) reciting the name of Śiva <*japa*>; he is surrounded by disciples; *ri-pa* are absent; *ni* is threefold; (the *rāgaputra*) is born in the *suhavī-mela;*[should be sung] at night.

TCC 227acd 228abd 229bcd 230acd 231cd
COT 227 228 229 230

गौरो रक्ताम्बरोऽसौ गुरुजलजवरश्रेणिकण्ठः सुरूपी
शृङ्गारी यक्षपङ्कैर्विरचितसुतनुर्भालभस्मैकपुण्ड्रः ।
नृत्यारम्भप्रियो मुद्रितसुगमकवान् शङ्कराभूषणाख्यः
प्रातः साद्यन्तमध्यः प्रचरति मधुमाधव्यशेषस्वरस्थः ॥ २३२ ॥

इति शङ्कराभूषणः (१०)

गौरः सुश्वेतवस्त्रः सुरभितसुतनुर्हस्तताम्बूलधारी
कामी पुष्पेषुधन्वी विरहिजनमनोवेधकः सत्रिकाढ्यः ।
चम्पाजातीसुयूथीविरचितमुकुटः कण्ठमल्लीसुमालः
सायं केदारमेले जनिरुपविलसद् यो विहादिर्गडः स्यात् ॥ २३३ ॥

इति विहागडः (११)

इति नटनारायणपरिवाराः

अनन्तरागाः सन्त्यन्ये नानादेशजनाश्रिताः ।
एतेषामुपरागाः स्युरूह्यन्तां ते च तद्विदैः ॥ २३४ ॥

इति रागलक्ष्माणि

(रागाधिकरणं समाप्तम्)

(10) *Śaṅkarābharaṇa*

232. Śaṅkarābhūṣaṇa *(i.e. śaṅkarābharaṇa-rāgaputra),* is creamy complexioned, dressed in red, wears garlands of large lotuses (diamonds, coral, conchs or pearls); is handsome, amorous, his body is anointed with the paste *yakṣapaṅka* perfume; he wears a mark of ashes on all his forehead; he loves to start dancing; he renders *mudrita-gamaka* excellently (while singing); (the *rāgaputra*) has all the notes of *madhumādhavī;* has *sa* for *graha, nyāsa* and *aṁśa*; he moves about in the morning [when it is fit to be sung].

(11) *Vihāgaḍa*

233. Vihāgaḍa (rāgaputra) is creamy complexioned; wears white clothes; has fragrant body, betel in hand; he is amorous; he holds a bow and flower arrows; he understands the minds of separated lovers; *sa* is threefold; he wears a crown of *campā, jāti* and *mallikā* flowers (in abundance), and a garland of *mallikā* flowers around his neck; it is born in *kedāra-mela;* it shines [and is fit to be sung] in the evening.

234. There are other endless *rāgas,* existing in different regions and [with different] people; let the cognoscente in such matters surmise the auxiliary *rāgas.*

This Ends (Description of) Characteristics of Rāgas.
[END OF RĀGA-ADHIKARAṆA]

TCC 232abcd 233bcd
COT 232 233

III. गायकप्रकरणम्

ख. प्रबन्धाधिकरणम्

१ प्रबन्धावयवाः

धातुमातुविदा येन रचितं लक्षणान्वितम् ।
देशीरागादिषु प्रोक्तं गीतं तद्गानमुच्यते ॥ १ ॥
अनिबद्धं निबद्धं च द्विधा तद्गदितं बुधैः ।
अनिबद्धमबन्धत्वादालप्तिः सा पुरोदिता ॥ २ ॥
अङ्गैश्च धातुभिर्बद्धं निबद्धं त्वधुनोच्यते ।
प्रबन्धो रूपकं वस्तु तस्य संज्ञात्रयं भवेत् ॥ ३ ॥
धातुः प्रबन्धावयवश्चतुर्धा स प्रकीर्तितः ।
गीतमुद्गृह्यते चादौ तेनोद्ग्राहस्तु पूर्वभाक् ॥ ४ ॥
मेलापको द्वितीयः स्यादुद्ग्राहध्रुवमेलनात् ।
ध्रुवत्वाद् ध्रुवसंज्ञस्तु तृतीयो भाग उच्यते ॥ ५ ॥
आभोगः पञ्चमो भागो गीतपूर्णत्वसूचकः ।
ध्रुवाभोगान्तरे कश्चिद् धातुरन्योऽन्तराभिधः ॥ ६ ॥
स तु सालगसूडस्थरूपकेष्वेव दृश्यते ।
चतुर्धातुस्त्रिधातुश्च द्विधातुश्चेति स त्रिधा ॥ ७ ॥
आभोगमेलापकयोः क्वचित् क्वचिदभावतः ।

२ प्रबन्धाङ्गानि

षडङ्गानि प्रबन्धस्य स्वरश्च बिरुदं पदम् ॥ ८ ॥
तेनकः पाटतालौ च पुंसो नेत्रादिकाङ्गवत् ।
तत्र तेनपदे नेत्रे स्तः पाटबिरुदे करौ ॥ ९ ॥

III. SINGER

B. PRABANDHA

1. LIMBS OF PRABANDHA

1. *Gīta* is described as that which is composed by an expert in *dhātu* (music) and *mātu* (words) according to (prescribed) definition in *deśī rāgas,* etc. It is (also) called *gāna.*

2ab. It is said by scholars to be of two kinds: *anibaddha* and *nibaddha.*

2cd-3ab. *Anibaddha* is [so called] because it is not set (to *tāla* etc.); it is *ālapti* (itself, which has been) described before. *Nibaddha* is set (together) to *dhātu* (musical elements) and *aṅgas* (literal components); this (latter) will now be elucidated.

3cd-4ab. It has three names, viz. *prabandha, vastu* [and] *rūpaka. Dhātu* is a limb (organ) of *prabandha*; it is said to be of four kinds.

4cd. [The first is called] *udgrāha* because the song is taken up with it; (it occurs) at the beginning (of the song).

5. *Melāpaka* is the second, [so called] because it joins *udgrāha* and *dhruva. Dhruva* is so named because it is constant; it is declared to be the third part.

6. *Ābhoga* is the fifth part and (its name) indicates the completion of song. There is yet another limb named *antara* in between *dhruva* and ābhoga.

7ab. (But) it is found in the *sālagasūḍa* compositions only.

7cd-8ab. It (*prabandha*) is of three kinds: viz. four-*dhātu*, three-*dhātu* and two-*dhātu;* (the last two are formed) because of the absence here and there of (both or one of) *melāpaka* and *ābhoga.*

2. COMPONENTS OF PRABANDHA

8cd-9ab. The *aṅgas* (components) of *prabandha* are six viz. *svara, biruda, pada, tenaka, pāṭa* and *tāla*; these are like eyes and (other) organs in men.

9cd. Among these, *tena* and *pada* are eyes; *pāṭa* and *biruda,* hands.

TCC 2c 3d 4c 5bc 7ab 8d 9ab

COT 1abcd 2cd 3d 4abcd-6cd 7ab 8b 9-10ab

तालस्वरौ च तत्पादौ प्रबन्धगतिहेतुत: ।
तेनतेनेति तेन: स्यान्मङ्गलस्य प्रकाशक: ॥ १० ॥
पदमर्थद्योतकं च पाटो वाद्याक्षरोद्भव: ।
बिरुदं गुणनामानि तालश्चच्चत्पुटादिक: ॥ ११ ॥
स्वर: सरिगमादि: स्याद्यथायोग्यनिवेशनम् ।
प्रबन्धजातय: पञ्च, षड्भिरङ्गैस्तु मेदिनी ॥ १२ ॥
आनन्दिनी पञ्चभि: स्याच्चतुर्भिर्दीपनी तथा ।
अङ्गैस्त्रिभिर्भावनी स्याद् द्वाभ्यां तारावली स्मृता ॥ १३ ॥
अनिर्युक्तश्च निर्युक्त: प्रबन्धो द्विविधो मत: ।
अनिर्युक्तस्त्वनियमान्निर्युक्तो नियमाद् भवेत् ॥ १४ ॥

३ गणवर्णफलानि

अनुक्तच्छन्दोगीतादौ गणवर्णान् क्रमाद् ब्रुवे ।
मयौ रसौ तजभना अष्टौ वर्णगणास्त्रिका: ॥ १५ ॥
मस्त्रिगो भूमिज: श्रीदो यो लाद्यो वृद्धिकृत् कज: ।
रोऽग्निजो भस्मकृल्लान्त: सो वात्योऽन्त्यगचालिकृत् ॥ १६ ॥
तोऽन्त्यलोऽधनकृच्छून्यो ज: सौर्योऽन्तगरुक्प्रद: ।
भ: सौम्य: कीर्तिकृद् गादिर्न ऐन्द्र: शङ्करस्त्रिल: ॥ १७ ॥
उद्ग्राहादौ ध्रुवादौ चाभोगादौ सुकरं गणम् ।
केऽप्याहु: सतयोरेकस्तत्रास्तु न रजौ तथा ॥ १८ ॥
एवमेकैकगणत: फलमाहुर्विपश्चित: ।
गणयोर्युग्मत: केचिदाहु: फलानि तद्यथा ॥ १९ ॥
मनौ हितौ भयौ भृत्यावुदासीनौ जतौ मतौ ।
रसावराती विज्ञेयौ यद्यद् योगफलं तथा ॥ २० ॥

Tāla and *svara* are its feet because they generate movement in the *prabandha. Tena* is (the sounds) *tena-tena* and is the manifester of auspiciousness.

11. *Pada* is the expressor of meaning; *pāṭa* is born of instrumental sounds; *biruda* is (laudatory) adjectival terms; *tāla* is *caccatpuṭa*, etc.

12ab. *Svara* is *sa-ri-ga-ma* etc. These (components) should be situated (in the *prabandha*) appropriately (as specifically prescribed therefor).

12cd-13. Classes of *prabandha* are five: *medinī* [*jātī-prabandha*] is [formed] from (all) six components; *ānandinī* is [formed] from five; likewise *dīpanī* from four; *bhāvanī* (*jāti prabandha*) is [formed] from three components; *tārāvalī* is said to be [formed] from two [*aṅgas*].

14. *Prabandha* is declared to be (again) of two kinds viz. *aniryukta* and *niryukta*; *aniryukta* (is socalled) because of the lack of (prescriptive) rules; *niryukta* occurs by the presence of (prescriptive) rules.

3. FRUITS ACCRUING FROM THE USE OF SYLLABLE-CLUSTERS

15. I shall [now] elucidate in order the syllables and their clusters (to be employed) at the beginning of songs wherein the metre is not prescribed (with reference to the invisible fruits accruing from their use): *ma-ya, ra-sa, ta-ja, bha-na* are the eight syllabic triad-clusters.

16. (Of these,) *ma* (*gaṇa*) has three *ga-s* (*gurus*), is born of the Earth, gives affluence/auspiciousness; *ya* (*gaṇa*) begins with *la* (*laghu*; followed the two *gurus*), is born of Water and bestows prosperity; *ra* (*gaṇa)* has middle *la* (*laghu*; preceded and followed by a *guru*), is born of Fire and burns (everything, every sin?) to ashes; *sa* (*gaṇa*) is born of Air, has *ga* (*guru*) at end (preceded by two *laghus*) and causes movement.

17. *Ta* (*gaṇa*) has *laghu* at the end (preceded by two *gurus*), causes poverty and is born of Space; *ja* (*gaṇa*) is born of the Sun, has *ga* (*guru*) in middle (enveloped by two *laghus*) and produces disease; *bha (gaṇa)* is born of the Moon, bestows fame and has *ga* (*guru*) at beginning (followed by two *laghus*); *na* (*gaṇa*) is born of Indra, has three *la* (*laghus*) and bestows auspiciousness.

18. Some (authorities) declare that at the beginning of *udgrāha*, of *dhruva* and of *ābhoga*, either *sa* (*gaṇa*) or *ta* (*gaṇa*) may be employed at convenience but never *ra* or *ja* (*gaṇas*).

19. The learned mention the fruits of (employing all) *gaṇas* one by one (at the beginning of *udgrāha, dhruva* or *ābhoga*); others mention the fruits of (employing) pairs of *gaṇas* (in the same positions), thus:

20. *Ma-na* (*gaṇa* pair) are friends (mutually), *bha-ya* are servants, *ja-ta* are indifferent (neither friends nor foes); *ra-sa* should be understood as (mutual) foes; the fruits of (employing) their combinations (in the above positions) are accordingly.

TCC 10a 11abd 12d 13bcd 14d 16abcd 17ab 20c
COT 10abc 11acd 12abcd-13c 14a 15a 16-17 16bc 17bcd 18 19-24ab

मङ्गलं मित्रयोर्योगे भृत्ययोस्तु बलं भवेत् ।
उदासीनद्वये व्याधिः शत्रोर्नायकनाशनम् ॥ २१ ॥
जयो मित्रानुचरयोः संसिद्धिर्भृत्यमित्रयोः ।
मित्रोदासीनयोः कष्टं दुःखं तूदासमित्रयोः ।
मित्रशत्र्वोः पीडनं स्यान्निष्फलं शत्रुमित्रयोः ॥ २२ ॥
भृत्योदासीनयोर्हानिरापत्तूदासभृत्ययोः ।
उदासवैरिणोर्वैरं शत्रूदासीनयोः क्षयः ॥ २३ ॥
हाकम्पं भृत्यशत्र्वोश्च शत्रुभृत्योर्गृहक्षयम् ।
केचिन्मात्रागणान् पञ्च प्राहुस्ते छपचास्तदौ ॥ २४ ॥
स्युः षट् पञ्च चतुस्त्रिद्विसङ्ख्यामात्रायुताः क्रमात् ।
अर्जुनोऽपि गणश्रेष्ठान् त्रीनन्यान् प्राह तद्यथा ॥ २५ ॥
द्विस्त्रिश्चतुर्वर्णगणाश्चत्वारोऽष्टौ च षोडश ।
क्रमाद् रतिगणाः कामगणाः बाणगणाः स्मृताः ॥ २६ ॥
किन्तु तत्र लपूर्वा ये तेष्वादावधिको लघुः ।
वर्णानामष्टवर्गाः स्युरकचाष्टतपा यशौ ॥ २७ ॥
नवपञ्चेषु पञ्चेषु पञ्चवेदाब्धिवर्णगाः ।
सोमो भौमो बुधो जीवः शुक्रः सौरी रविस्तमः ॥ २८ ॥
क्रमादकचटानां तपयशानां च देवताः ।

४. वर्णफलानि

वर्णानां च फलान्याहुरायुस्तेजोऽपकीर्तिता ॥ २९ ॥
सौभाग्यं सुन्दरं व्याधिर्मरणं शून्यता क्रमात् ।
हझघढधरषभाः पञ्च वर्णाऽनुनासिकाः ॥ ३० ॥
कदाचिच्छ्लोकगीतादौ न प्रयोज्या विचक्षणैः ।

21. By combining a pair of friends, auspiciousness accrues; strength, by combining servants (*gaṇa* pair); by (combining) two indifferent illness (results); by foes, destruction of the patron (lauded in the song).

22. By friend-servant, victory; by servant-friend, accomplishment; by friend-indifferent, difficulty, grief from indifferent-friend; by friend-foe, harassment; by foe-friend, futility.

23. Loss (accrues) from (combining) servant-indifferent; misfortune from indifferent-servant; enmity from indifferent-foe; decay from foe-indifferent.

24ab. *Hākampa* (trembling with fear or sorrow with the exclamation '*hā*!') results from servant-enemy; family decay from foe-servant.

24cd-25ab. Some (authorities) describe five *mātrā* (moraic) *gaṇas* (syllabic clusters) viz. *cha, pa, ca, ta* and *da*; the number of *mātrās* these *gaṇas* have are six, five, four, three and two respectively.

25cd-26. Arjuna has mentioned three other excellent *gaṇas;* they are thus: *gaṇas* of two, three or four syllables taking four, eight and sixteen (*mātrās*) respectively are said to be *rati gaṇas, kāma gaṇas* and *bāṇa gaṇas* (in this order).

27ab. But those among them which have *la* (*laghu*) at the beginning (in *prastāra*) have an additional *laghu.*

27cd-28ab. Syllables are of eight classes (commencing respectively with) *a ka ca ṭa ta pa ya* and *śa* possessing nine, five, five (*iṣu*), five, five (*iṣu*), five, four (*veda*) and four (*abdhi*) syllables respectively.

28cd-29ab. The presiding deities of the [syllable] classes *a–ka–ca–ṭa* and of *ta–pa–ya–śa* are Soma (Moon), Mars, Mercury, Jupiter, Venus, Saturn, Sun and Rāhu (*Tamas*) respectively.

4. FRUITS ACCRUING FROM [THE USE OF INDIVIDUAL] SYLLABLES

29cd-30ab. The fruits of these syllables (classes) are longevity (*a*), lustre (*ka*), disrepute (*ca*), prosperity (*ṭa*), beauty (*ta*), disease (*pa*), death (*ya*) and void (*śa*) in order.

30cd-31ab. [The syllables] *ha jha gha ḍha dha ra ṣa bha* and the five nasal consonants should never be employed at the beginning of verse or song by experts.

TCC 21a 22bcdef 23d 24ab 26bcd 27d 28ab 29cd 30cd 31ab
COT 19-24ab 24cd 25c 26cd 27d

क्वचिदन्यैर्विशेषश्च कथितः सोऽभिधीयते ॥ ३१ ॥
नकारो नाशयेल्लक्ष्मीं हकारस्तु हरेद्यशः ।
मकारः सर्वहृत्तस्माद् गीतादौ तत्परित्यजेत् ॥ ३२ ॥
सदाशिवः फलं प्राह प्रतिवर्णं पृथक् पृथक् ।
अकारादिस्वराणां च प्रयोगो धुरि शोभनः ॥ ३३ ॥
कात् सुकीर्तिः खुरी खाच्च गाद्ग्रामोऽरिभयं घतः ।
ङाल्लक्ष्मीश्चात् सदश्वाश्च छाच्छत्रं जात् स्त्रियो मृतिः ॥ ३४ ॥
झात्, तथा स्वमृतिर्ञाच्च टाद् गावष्ठाद् विषं फलम् ।
डाच्छोको ढात् सुवर्णं च णकाराद् रत्नमुत्तमम् ॥ ३५ ॥
तात्तारं थाद् बहुधनं दाच्छ्रेयो धान् महापदः ।
नान्नाशो भारती पाच्च फाद् भोगो बान् महाभयम् ॥ ३६ ॥
भाद् (भाच्च?) भीतिर्मृतिर्माच्च यकाराद् राजतो मृतिः ।
रकाराच्छत्रुतो हानिर्लवौ पुत्रधनप्रदौ ॥ ३७ ॥
सर्वत्र शून्यता शाच्च षात् क्षत्रं तुमुलं तथा ।
सकाराच्छत्रिसाम्यं स्यात् हकारस्तु हरेद्यशः ॥ ३८ ॥
क्षकारात्मा शुभः ख्यातः श्रीर्लक्ष्मीरतिशोभनम् ।
पानेऽभिवादने चैव नकारः शोभनः स्मृतः ॥ ३९ ॥
हरिसंज्ञो हकारश्च जकारो जयवाचकः ।
निषेधवाचकोऽप्यत्र न निन्द्यः काव्यकोविदैः ॥ ४० ॥
उद्ग्राहे नगरांश्चैवमन्तरे सतलांस्तथा ।
आभोगे हटकांश्चैव नववर्णान् परित्यजेत् ॥ ४१ ॥
उद्ग्राहे तु दकारश्च भकारश्चान्तरे तथा ।
आभोगे तु चकारश्च त्रयं लक्ष्मीफलप्रदम् ॥ ४२ ॥
गणवर्णविचारोऽयं नृस्तुतावेव नान्यतः ।

31cd-32. Others have pronounced something special (about the fruits of using certain syllables); this will now be described. The syllable *na* destroys wealth; *ha* pilfers away fame; *ma* purloins everything. Therefore they should be discarded at the beginning of songs.

33. Sadāśiva has declared fruits for [the use of] each syllable separately: The use of *a* etc. vowels (at the beginning of a musical composition of unprescribed metrical structure) results in [endowing] success in battle/fame in high position < *dhuri*>

34. Excellent fame from *ka*, perfumes from *kha*, village from *ga*, fear from foe from *gha*, wealth from *ṅa*, fine horses from *ca*, (royal) umbrella from *cha*, women from *ja*, death (of others),

35. from *jha*, one's own death from *ña*, cattle from *ṭa*, poison from *ṭha*, are the fruits; grief from *ḍa*, gold from *ḍha*, excellent diamond from *ṇa*,

36. pearl from *ta*, large money from *tha*, spiritual accretions from *da*, great status (or calamity) from *dha*, destruction from *na*, experience of Brahman (or Sarasvatī power) from *pa*, sensuous pleasures from *bha*, great fear (or security) from *ba*,

37. fright from *bha*, death from *ma*, death by the king from *ya*, loss from the enemy from *ra; la-va* are endowers of children and money (respectively);

38. all round void from *śa*, battle between kings from *ṣa*, equality (or similarity) in (royal) umbrella from *sa*, while the syllable *ha* purloins fame.

39. The syllable *kṣa* is reputed to bring spiritual auspiciousness, (the syllable) *śri* gives very splendid auspiciousness (wealth). The syllable *na* is splendid while drinking and in greeting.

40. *Ha* symbolises Hari while *ja* bespeaks victory. Experts in poetry should not ignore prescribed syllables.

41. *Na-ga-ra* in *udgrāha*, *sa-ta-la* in *antara* and *ha-ṭa-ka* in *dhruva*—these nine syllables should be avoided.

42. The syllable *da* in *udgrāha*, the syllable *bha* in *antara*, similarly the syllable *ca* in *dhruva*—these three syllables bestow the fruits of wealth (auspiciousness).

43ab. This matter of [using] syllables and [their] clusters pertains only to the laudation of men and not otherwise.

TCC 32c 33d 34ab 35d 36c 37ac 39ac 40c 41c
COT 31cd-32 33d 33-39ab 34a 35d 36abcd 37a 38c 41-42b

५. प्रबन्धानामुद्देशः

एलाकरणढेङ्कीभिर्वर्तन्या झोम्बडेन च ॥ ४३ ॥
लम्भरासैकतालीभिः शुद्धसूडोऽष्टभिः स्मृतः ।
वर्णो वर्णस्वरो गद्यं कैवाडश्चाङ्कचारिणी ॥ ४४ ॥
कन्दस्तुरगलीला च गजलीला द्विपद्यपि ।
चक्रवालः क्रौञ्चपदः स्वरार्थो ध्वनिकुट्टनी ॥ ४५ ॥
आर्या गाथा द्विपथकः कलहंसश्च तोटकः ।
धटो वृत्तं मातृका च तथा रागकदम्बकः ॥ ४६ ॥
पञ्चतालेश्वरस्तालार्णव इत्यालिसंज्ञकाः ।
प्रबन्धाः स्युः क्रमादत्र विंशतिश्चतुरुन्नताः ॥ ४७ ॥
श्रीरङ्गः श्रीविलासः स्यात् पञ्चभङ्गिरतः परम् ।
पञ्चाननोमातिलकौ त्रिपदी च चतुष्पदी ॥ ४८ ॥
षट्पदी वस्तुसंज्ञश्च विजयस्त्रिपथस्तथा ।
चतुर्मुखः सिंहलीलो हंसलीलोऽथ दण्डकः ॥ ४९ ॥
झम्पटः कन्दुकः स्यात् त्रिभङ्गिर्हरविलासकः ।
सुदर्शनः स्वराङ्कः श्रीवर्धनो हर्षवर्धनः ॥ ५० ॥
वदनं चर्चरी चर्या पद्धडी राहडी तथा ।
वीरश्रीर्मङ्गलाचारो धवलो मङ्गलस्तथा ॥ ५१ ॥
ओवी लोली ढोल्लरी च दन्ती षट्त्रिंशदित्यमी ।
प्रबन्धा विप्रकीर्णाख्याः सालगास्तु ध्रुवादयः ॥ ५२ ॥
आद्यो ध्रुवस्ततो मण्ठः प्रतिमण्ठो निःसारुकः ।
अड्डुतालस्ततो रास एकतालीति सप्त ते ॥ ५३ ॥

5. LIST OF PRABANDHAS

43cd-44ab. The *śuddha-sūḍa* [class of *prabandhas*] is [formed] from these eight—*elā, karaṇa, ḍheṅkī, vartanī, jhombaḍa, lambha, rāsa* [and] *ekatālī.*

44cd. *Varṇa, varṇa-svara, gadya, kaivāḍa, aṅkacāriṇī,*

45. *kanda, turagalīlā, gajalīlā, dvipadī, cakravāla, krauñcapada, svarārtha, dhvani-kuṭṭanī,*

46. *āryā, gāthā, dvipatha, kalahaṁsa, toṭaka, dhaṭa, vṛtta, mātṛkā*—likewise *rāgaka-damba,*

47. *pañcatāleśvara, tālārṇava*—these twentyfour *prabandhas* are named *āli* (*krama*) *prabandhas* here in order;

48. *śrīraṅga, śrīvilāsa, pañcabhaṅgi, pañcānana, umātilaka, tripadī, catuṣpadī,*

49. *ṣaṭpadī ,vastu, vijaya, tripatha, caturmukha, siṁhatlīla, haṁsatlīla, daṇḍaka,*

50. *jhampaṭa, kanduka, tribhaṅgi, haravilāsa, sudarśana, svarāṅka, śrīvardhana, harṣavardhana,*

51. *vadana, carcarī, caryā, paddhaḍī, rāhaḍī vīraśrī, maṅgalācāra, dhavala, maṅgala,*

52abc. *ovī, lolī, ḍhollarī, dantī*—these thirtysix *prabandhas* are named *viprakīrṇa.*

52d-53. The *sālaga(sūḍa-prabandha)s* however, are *dhruva,* etc. The first [of these] is *dhruva*; then *maṇṭha, pratimaṇṭha, niḥsāruka, aḍḍatāla, rāsa, ekatālī*—these seven (are the *sālagasūḍa*).

TCC 43cd 44c 46ac47ab 49d 50ad 51ab 52ad
COT 43cd-53cd

६. (I) शुद्धसूडः

i. एला

तत्रैला प्रथमे पादे कार्यं खण्डद्वयं बुधैः ।
वर्णसाम्यं तदैकेन धातुना भिन्नामातुकम् ॥ ५४ ॥
गमकाख्यप्रयोगस्तु कर्तव्यस्तदनन्तरम् ।
पदत्रयं तु कर्तव्यं तच्च पल्लवसंज्ञकम् ॥ ५५ ॥
विलम्बिते तु तत्राद्ये तृतीयं द्रुतमानतः ।
तुल्यधातुकमेवं चेद् गेयं पादत्रयं बुधैः ॥ ५६ ॥
तृतीयाङ्घ्रौ विशेषोऽयं न पल्लवपदस्थितिः ।
प्रयोगोऽन्यस्तु कर्तव्यः सम्बोधकपदान्वितः ॥ ५७ ॥
पादत्रयात्मकश्चैवमुद्ग्राहोऽर्कपदान्वितः ।
मेलापकः प्रयोगश्चेत्तदा रुद्रपदान्वितः ॥ ५८ ॥
प्रभुनामाङ्कितो मध्यविलम्बितपदत्रयम् ।
ध्रुवो भवेत्तत्र पूर्वमेकधातुपदद्वयम् ॥ ५९ ॥
तृतीयं भिन्नधातुः स्यादाभोगस्तदनन्तरम् ।
कार्यो वाग्गेयकारेण स्वाभिधानविभूषितः ॥ ६० ॥
पुनर्गानं विधायास्य न्यासस्तु ध्रुवके भवेत् ।
मण्ठद्वितीयकङ्कालप्रतितालेषु कश्चन ॥ ६१ ॥
तालोऽत्र विनियोक्तव्यो ग्रहस्तु विषमो भवेत् ।
प्रबन्धेऽस्मिन् प्रभोः कार्यं शौर्यधैर्यादिवर्णनम् ॥ ६२ ॥
काममन्मथवत् कान्तजितमित्रविकारिणः ।
मान्धातृसुमती शोभी सुशोभी गीतकोचि(-रु!)रुतः ॥ ६३ ॥
विचित्रो वासव मृदु सुचित्रा इति षोडश ।
नामान्येलापदानां स्युः षोडशानामनुक्रमात् ॥ ६४ ॥

6. (I) ŚUDDHA-SŪḌA-PRABANDHAS

i. *Elā*

54. Among these **elā** (will be described first): it should be composed such that its first foot has two segments, [each] composed with alliteration, with the same *dhātu* (music) but different words.

55. A *prayoga* named *gamaka* is [then] executed; after this, a cluster of three words, named *pallava* is rendered.

56. Of these, the first two [words] are performed in slow tempo; the third, in fast tempo. In this way the learned should sing three feet in the same *dhātu.*

57. There is (however) a difference in the third foot (viz.): non-occurrence of *pallava* words; (instead,) another *prayoga* containing vocative words (addressed to the patron) should be executed.

58. Thus the three feet containing twelve (*arka*) words constitute *udgrāha.* If this (second) *prayoga* is [regarded] as *melāpaka,* then it (=*udgrāha*) has [only] eleven (*rudra*) words.

59. [Following this,] there are three words bearing the name of the king (=patron) in the middle and slow tempi. This is *dhruva.* Of these the first two words are [set] in the same *dhātu.*

60. The third [word] is [set] in different *dhātu.* After this occurs *ābhoga* which is executed by the composer [such that it is] decorated with his own signature.

61ab. Rendering [all this] again, the conclusion is [made on] *dhruva.*

61cd-62. Any one among the *tālas maṇṭha, dvitīya, kaṅkāla* and *pratitāla* should be employed here; *graha* is *viṣama.* Description of the king's valour, courage, etc. should be incorporated in this *prabandha.*

63. *Kāma, manmathavat, kānta, jita, mitra, vikārī, māndhātṛ, sumati, śobhī, suśobhī, gītaka, ucita* (*ruta*!),

64. *vicitra, vāsava, mṛdu, sucitra*—these are the names of the sixteen words constituting the *elā* respectively.

TCC 54ad 55d 56abcd 58b 59cd 61a 63d 64cd
COT 54-76 54d 55ad 56d 57d 58bd 59a 61abcd 62b 63d

समानो मधुरः सान्द्रः कान्तो दीप्तः समाहितः ।
अग्राम्यः सुकुमारश्च प्रसन्नौजस्विनाविति ॥ ६५ ॥
मान्धात्रादि पदेषु स्युः प्राणा दश दशस्विमे ।
निर्वर्णगमकप्रौढः समानप्राण उच्यते॥ ६६ ॥
मधुराख्यस्तु सरलस्तानीकरणसम्भवः ।
धातुतो मातुबाहुल्यः सान्द्रस्तारगतिः स्मृतः ॥ ६७ ॥
मन्मथोद्दीपनध्वानरक्तिता कान्त उच्यते ।
तारस्थानोच्चनादो यः स दीप्त इति कथ्यते ॥ ६८ ॥
सवर्णगमकप्रौढः स्थायिस्थस्तु समाहितः ।
वाक्यावयववर्णा ये पूर्वपूर्वपदान्तिमाः ॥ ६९ ॥
द्वयोर्द्वयोस्त्रयाणां वोत्तरोत्तरपदादिमे ।
तत्तत् स्वरयुता वर्णाऽऽवृत्त्या द्विविधया पुनः ॥ ७० ॥
प्रगीयन्ते चक्रवालरीत्याग्राम्य उदाहृतः ।
सुकुमारो वर्णतानस्वराणां कोमलत्वतः ॥ ७१ ॥
प्रसन्नः स्यात् पदस्थानस्वरादीनां प्रसादतः ।
समासतानबहुल ओजस्वी परिकीर्तितः ॥ ७२ ॥
एभिः सर्वगुणैर्युक्ता विष्णुमाररमात्मिका ।
एला श्रोतुः प्रयोक्तुश्च धर्मकामार्थसिद्धिदा ॥ ७३ ॥
एला सामान्यलक्ष्मैतत् पूर्वाचार्यैरुदीरितम् ।
गणवर्णमात्रादेशसङ्कीर्णात् साऽप्यनेकधा॥ ७४ ॥
ग्रन्थविस्तरभावेन न मयाऽत्र प्रदर्शिता ।
अयं प्रबन्धो निर्युक्तस्तालादिनियमात् पुनः ॥ ७५ ॥
चतुर्धातुस्त्रिधातुर्वा मेलापाभावतो यदा ।
पदतालद्व्यङ्गबद्धाज्जातिस्तारावली भवेत् ॥ ७६ ॥

65-66ab. *Samāna, madhura, sāndra, kānta, dīpta, samāhita, agrāmya, sukumāra, prasanna, ojasvī* are the ten vital elements abiding in the ten words commencing with *māndhātṛ.*

66cd. *Samāna-prāṇa* (1) is defined as (*dhātu*) bereft of syllables (=words) but replete with scholarly *gamakas.*

67. *Madhura* (2) arises from simple melodification. *Sāndra* (3) has words in excess of music and moves in *tāra* (register).

68. Appealing sound illumined with erotic mood is called *kānta* (4). High tone in the *tāra* register is declared to be *dīpta* (5).

69ab. *Samāhita* (6) abides in *sthāyin* (*svara*), has syllabic (i.e. word) content and sophisticated *gamakas.*

69cd-71ab. If, of the syllables constituting the sentence(s) [in the *prabandha*], the ones occurring at the end of the precedent word recur in (clusters of) two or three at the beginning of the next word progressively are set to the selfsame *svaras* and repeated twice and are thus sung as in *cakravāla* style, it is said to be *agrāmya* (7).

71cd. *Sukumāra* (8) arises from the tenderness (softness) in syllable, melody line (*tāna*) and *svaras.*

72. *Prasanna* (9) arises from instantaneous intelligibility of word, register and *svara,* etc. *Ojasvi* (10) is declared to be formed from compound words and (closely interwoven) melody lines in abundance.

73. *Elā,* compounding all these qualities, is of the nature of Viṣṇu, Manmatha and Ramā and bestows the fulfilment of *dharma, artha* and *kāma* to both performer and listener.

74. These general characteristics of the *elā* are (as) described by past preceptors. It (*elā*) is of many kinds according to *gaṇa* (syllabic clustering/moraic affinities), *varṇa* (syllabic structuring), mātrā (moraic quantity), *deśa* (provincial parameters) and *saṅkīrṇa* (admixture/hybrid).

75. Lest this treatise become [too] large, I shall not present them here. This *prabandha* is *niryukta* because it has prescription of *tāla* etc.

76. It is [a] four-*dhātu* (*prabandha*), or, in the absence of *melāpaka,* a three *dhātuka* (*prabandha*). Since it is composed of two *aṅgas* viz. *pada* and *tāla,* it is of *tārāvalī* class.

TCC 65b 66bc 69d 70bc 71ac 72bc 73c 74c 75b
COT 66bc 67ab 68bd 69ab 71acd 72a 74cd

ii. करणः

उद्ग्राहः स्वरबद्धश्च ध्रुवः सर्वाङ्गमिश्रितः ।
यस्याभोगः पदैः कार्यस्तत्र नेतृप्रबन्धयोः ॥ ७७ ॥
गातुर्नामाङ्कितः किन्तूद्ग्राहस्त्विष्टस्वरे भवेत् ।
अंशस्वरे च न्यासः स्यादादितालो द्रुतो लयः ॥ ७८ ॥
सामान्यलक्षणं प्रोक्तं करणस्य मुनीश्वरैः ।
एकैकाङ्गप्रबद्धः स्यात् ध्रुवकः करणे यदि ॥ ७९ ॥
तत्तदङ्गाभिधानं तत्करणं स्यात्तदा पुनः ।
स्वरैश्च पाटैरुद्ग्राहो यदा पाटैः पदैर्ध्रुवः ॥ ८० ॥
तदा तच्चित्रकरणं कोहलादिकसम्मतम् ।
स्यान्मिश्रकरणं यत्र स्वरपाटकतेनकैः ॥ ८१ ॥
बद्धो ध्रुवस्तदा शेषलक्षणं पूर्ववत् स्मृतम् ।
अयं तु तालनियमान्निर्युक्तश्च त्रिधातुकः ॥ ८२ ॥
त्यक्ततारावली जातिर्मेदिन्यादिकजातिमान् ।

iii ढेङ्की

यत्रोद्ग्राहस्य पूर्वार्धं गीयते द्विर्निरन्तरम् ॥ ८३ ॥
उत्तरार्धं सकृत् पश्चात् प्रयोगात्मा भवेन्न वा ।
मेलापकाख्यश्चोद्ग्राहमेलापौ तावतालकौ ॥ ८४ ॥
अथवा ढेङ्किकाताले कङ्काले वा विलम्बिते ।
ध्रुवाभोगौ तु गातव्यावन्यतालाल्लयान्तरे ॥ ८५ ॥
ध्रुवस्त्रिखण्डः खण्डे द्वे गीयेते समधातुनी ।
तृतीयमुच्चमेष द्विः सकृदाभोगकस्ततः ॥ ८६ ॥
पुनर्गीत्वा ध्रुवे न्यासो यस्यां सा ढेङ्किका मता ।
सामान्यलक्षणं चैतत् ढेङ्किकायाः प्रकीर्तितम् ॥ ८७ ॥

ii. *Karaṇa*

77-78ab. *Udgrāha* [of *karaṇa prabandha*] is composed of *svaras*;[its] *dhruva* is a mixture of all (six) *aṅgas*. Its *ābhoga* is composed of words (other than those of *udgrāha* and *dhruva*); in these are incorporated the names of patron, *prabandha* and of the singer (=composer); but the *udgrāha* is [set] in *svaras* of (composer's own) choice.

78cd. The conclusion [of the song] is in the *aṁśa-svara* (of the *rāga*); [its] *tāla* is *ādi*; [its] tempo is fast.

79ab. The general characteristics of *karaṇa* (*prabandha*) are so described by the great sages (of yore).

79cd-80a. If the *dhruva* [*dhātu*] of the *karaṇa* is composed of each *aṅga* (separately), then that *karaṇa* is named after the respective *aṅga*.

80b-81ab. Then again, if its *udgrāha* is composed of *svaras* and *pāṭas* and (its) *dhruva* of *pāṭas* and *padas*, then it is opined by Kohala and others to be *citrakaraṇa*.

81cd-82ab. Where the *dhruva* is composed of *svara, pāṭa* and *tena*, it is *miśrakaraṇa;* other (remaining) characteristics are declared to be as before.

82cd-83ab. This is *niryukta* because of *tāla* prescription; it has three *dhātus*. It is of *medinī* etc. classes, excepting *tārāvalī*.

iii. *Ḍheṅkī*

83cd. Wherein the first half of *udgrāha* is sung twice without pause;

84-85ab. the second half [is rendered] once; and then *melāpaka* [which is] of the nature of *prayoga* (an expedient spanning device, called *gamaka*) may or may not occur; *udgrāha-melāpaka* are [executed] without *tāla* or [executed] in *ḍheṅkī-tāla* or *kaṅkāla* [*tāla*] in slow tempo;

85cd. but *dhruva* and *ābhoga* are sung in a different *tāla* and different tempo;

86abc. *dhruva* is formed of three segments [of which the first] two are sung in the same *dhātu* while the third is (in) higher (pitch);

86cd-87. this (foregoing, viz. *udgrāha, melāpaka* and *dhruva* is executed) twice (followed by) *ābhoga* [rendered] once; then [the whole *prabandha*] is sung again; conclusion is in *dhruva*. Wherein it is so, it is opined to be *ḍheṅkī*. This is declared to be the general definition of *ḍheṅkī*.

TCC 77bcd 80ad 81bc 82a 84a 85c 86c
COT 77ab-83ab 78b 79b 80a 83cd-90ab 84b 85bcd 87b

विशेषा बहुधा नोक्ता मुक्तावल्यादिका भिदाः ।
अयं ढेङ्कीप्रबन्धस्तु मेलापस्य विकल्पतः॥ ८८ ॥
त्रिधातुश्च चतुर्धातुर्यदानियम तालतः ।
अनिर्युक्तश्च निर्युक्तो ढेङ्कीकङ्कालदर्शनात् ॥ ८९ ॥
तारावलीजातिमांश्च पदतालाङ्गबद्धतः ।

iv. वर्तनी, विवर्तनी

यल्लक्षणं स्वराद्यस्य करणे ह्युदितं पुरा ॥ ९० ॥
वर्तन्या अपि तत्सर्वं तालोऽन्यो रासकाद् भवेत् ।
विलम्बितो लयश्चात्र द्विरुद्ग्राहस्तु गीयते ॥ ९१ ॥
ध्रुवाभोगौ सकृद् गायेन्न्यासोऽस्य ध्रुवके भवेत् ।
कङ्काले प्रतिताले च कुडुक्के प्रतिमण्ठके ॥ ९२ ॥
रचिता चेत्तदा ज्ञेया वर्तन्येव विवर्तनी ।
अयं प्रबन्धो निर्युक्तस्तालादि नियमात् पुनः ॥ ९३ ॥
त्रिधातुकोऽपि मेलापनामधातुविहीनतः ।
भावनीजातिमान् तालपदस्वरसुबन्धतः ॥ ९४ ॥

v. झोम्बडः

यस्मिन् उद्ग्राहपूर्वार्धं गीयते द्विः सकृत्ततः ।
उत्तरार्धं प्रयोगाढ्यो भवेन् मेलापको न वा ॥ ९५ ॥
द्विर्गीत्वा ध्रुवमाभोगं सकृन्न्यासो ध्रुवे भवेत् ।
यत्रासौ झोम्बडो नाम ताले निःसारुके तथा ॥ ९६ ॥
कुडुक्के त्रिपुटे वापि प्रतिमण्ठे द्वितीयके ।
यतिलग्ने गारुगौ च रासे च प्रतितालके ॥ ९७ ॥
एकताल्यां भवेदस्य सामान्यलक्षणं स्मृतम् ।
झोम्बडे बहवो भेदा नोक्ता ग्रन्थस्य विस्तरात् ॥ ९८ ॥

88ab. Its numerous specific varieties such as *muktāvalī* will not be expiated here.

88cd-90ab. Because of the ambiguity [in the use] of *melāpaka*, this *ḍheṇkī prabandha* may be of three or four *dhātus*; if [there is] no rule about *tāla*, it is *aniryukta*; alternatively, since *ḍheṅkī* and *kaṅkāla-tālas* are (optionally) seen [in it], it may be *niryukta* (also). Being composed of only two *aṅgas* viz. *pada* and *tāla* it is of *tārāvalī* class.

iv. *Vartanī, Vivartanī*

90cd-91a. Whatever are the characteristics mentioned for *svarakaraṇa* above, they all occur in *vartanī* also;

91bcd. but the *tāla* is other than *rāsa*; here the tempo is slow; *udgrāha* is sung twice;

92ab. *dhruva* and *ābhoga* are [each] sung once; conclusion (of the song) is on *dhruva*.

92cd-93ab. If set to *kaṅkāla, pratitāla, kuḍukkā* or *pratimaṇṭha tāla, vartanī* is to be understood as becoming *vivartanī*.

93cd-94. This *prabandha* is *niryukta* because of the prescription of *tāla* etc.; again, because of the absence of the *dhātu* named *melāpaka*, it is *tridhātuka*; because it is constructed of *tāla, pada* and *svara,* it belongs to *bhāvanī* class.

v. *Jhombaḍa*

95. Wherein the first half of *udgrāha* is sung twice, then the second half, once; *melāpaka*, which is of the nature of *prayoga* (expedient bridging device, called *gamaka*) may or may not occur,

96abc. *dhruva* is sung twice, *ābhoga*, once; conclusion is on *dhruva*; where in it is so, it is named *jhombaḍa.*

96d-98a. [This *prabandha*] occurs in the *tāla niḥsāru, kuḍukka, tripuṭa, pratimaṇṭha, dvitīya, yatilagna, gārugi, rāsa, pratitāla* or *ekatālī.*

98bcd. [This is] opined to be its general definiton. [There are] many varieties in *jhombaḍa*; [but they] are not described [here] lest the treatise become [too] large.

TCC 88b 91b 93a 94a 95c 96a 97b 98bd

COT 88a 89abd 90cd-94 90cd-92abcd 93d 94d 95-99 97-98ac

चतुर्धातुस्त्रिधातुश्च मेलापाभावतो यदि ।
निर्युक्तस्तालनियमाद् द्व्यङ्गात्तारावलेयकः ॥ ९९ ॥

vi. लम्भः

यत्रैकखण्ड उद्ग्राहो द्विखण्डो वा भवेत् पुनः ।
गीयतेऽसौ सकृद् द्विर्वा ध्रुवप्रतिनिधौ ततः ॥ १०० ॥
द्विराभोगो ध्रुवे मुक्तिः स लम्भस्तु त्रिधातुकः ।
तारावलीजातिमांश्च द्व्यङ्गत्वात् पदतालतः ॥ १०१ ॥
तालादीनामनियमादनिर्युक्तो भवेदसौ ।

vii. रासः

यो झोम्बडगतं लक्ष्म गमकस्थानके विना ॥ १०२ ॥
रासको रासतालेन गीयतेऽसौ त्रिधातुकः ।
निर्युक्तस्तालनियमाद् द्व्यङ्गात्तारावलेयकः ॥ १०३ ॥

viii. एकताली

द्विरुद्ग्राहाद् ध्रुवोऽपि द्विः सकृदाभोगकस्ततः ।
न्यासः स्याद् ध्रुवके यत्र सैकताल्येकतालिका ॥ १०४ ॥
अस्यामालापमात्रेण केदिुद्ग्राहमूचिरे ।
आलापो गमकालप्तिरक्षरैर्वर्जिता मता ॥ १०५ ॥
सैव प्रयोगशब्देन मुनिना सम्प्रकीर्तिता ।
तारावलीजातिमांश्च निर्युक्तोऽयं त्रिधातुकः ॥ १०६ ॥

६. (II) आलिक्रमप्रबन्धाः

i. वर्णः

उद्ग्राहध्रुवकौ यत्र बद्धौ कर्णाटभाषया ।
बिरुदैर्वर्णतालेन पदैराभोगकल्पितः ॥ १०७ ॥
स वर्णः स्याच्च निर्युक्तो त्र्यङ्गः किन्तु त्रिधातुकः ।

99. It is four-*dhātu* (*prabandha*), but if *melāpaka* is absent, [it is] three-*dhātu*. It is *niryukta* because of the rule about *tāla*; it is of *tārāvalī* (class) since it has two *aṅgas*.

vi. *Lambha*

100-101ab. Wherein the *udgrāha* is of one or two segments; and again, sung once or, in representation of *dhruva* is sung twice, then *ābhoga* is executed twice and conclusion is on *dhruva*, it is *lambha* [*prabandha*]; it is of three *dhātus*.

101cd-102ab. Because [it has only] two *aṅgas* viz. *pada* and *tāla*, it belongs to *tārāvalī* class. This is *aniryukta* because it has no prescription of *tāla* etc.

vii. *Rāsa*

102cd-103. *Rāsa* [*Prabandha*] is sung to *rāsa-tāla* with the same characteristics as described for *jhombaḍa* except the occurrence of *gamaka* and *sthānaka*. It is of three *dhātus*. It is *niryukta* because of *tāla* restriction; because [it has] two *aṅgas*, it is of *tārāvalī* class.

viii. *Ekatālī*

104. Wherein after *udgrāha* [is executed] twice, *dhruva* [is also rendered] twice, and *ābhoga*, once and conclusion is on *dhruva*, it is *ekatālī* [*prabandha*] which is set in *ekatālī* (*tāla*).

105. Some restrict its *udgrāha* (to be rendered) in *ālāpa* only; *ālāpa* [here] means *gamakālapti* [which is performed] without syllables (=words).

106. Such selfsame [*ālāpa* without syllables] is described by the Muni under the term *prayoga*. This [*prabandha*] is of *tārāvalī* class, *niryukta* and three-*dhātu*.

6. (II) ĀLIKRAMA-PRABANDHAS

i. *Varṇa*

107-108ab. Wherein *udgrāha* and *dhruva* are composed in Karnāṭa (=Kannaḍa) language, with *birudas* in *varṇa-tāla* and *ābhoga* is performed in (other) words, it is *varṇa-prabandha*; it is *niryukta*, three-*dhātu* and has three *aṅgas*.

TCC 99d 102abcd 103ad 104a 106d 107ab 108b
COT 99d 100-102ab 100d 101ab 102cd-103 102d 104-106 104c 105a 106b 107-109ab 107a

अनुक्ताभोगवस्तूनां पदैराभोगकल्पना ॥ १०८ ॥
ओव्यादयस्तु चत्वारो भवन्त्याभोगवर्जिताः ।

ii. वर्णस्वरः

स्वरैः पाटैः पदैस्तेनै रचना वाञ्छितक्रमात् ॥ १०९ ॥
मुक्तिस्तु तेनकैर्वर्णस्वरः स्याद् वर्णतालतः ।
स्वरादेरादिविन्यासाद् वेदाक्षिरचनात्मकः ॥ ११० ॥
अत्र स्वरादिमध्ये तु काभ्यामुद्ग्राहको भवेत् ।
एकेन ध्रुव आभोगः पदैः कार्यस्त्रिधातुकः ॥ १११ ॥
निर्युक्त आनन्दिनीवान् बिरुदस्य विहीनतः ।

iii. गद्यम्

गद्यं पदचयं च्छन्दोबन्धहीनं निगद्यते ॥ ११२ ॥
तत् षोढोत्कलिका चूर्णं ललितं वृत्तगन्धि च ।
खण्डं च चित्रमेतेषां प्रभवः सामवेदतः ॥ ११३ ॥
गातव्योत्कलिका वीरे गौडीमारभटीं श्रिता ।
चूर्णं शान्ते च वैदर्भीं सात्त्वतीं वृत्तिमाश्रितम् ॥ ११४ ॥
पाञ्चालीकैशिकीभ्यां च शृङ्गारे ललितं युतम् ।
शान्ते सपद्यं भारत्यां पाञ्चाल्यां वृत्तगन्धि च ॥ ११५ ॥
वैदर्भीसात्त्वतीभ्यां च खण्डं हास्ये रसे स्मृतम् ।
वैदर्भीकैशिकीचित्रं चित्रं शृङ्गारनिर्भरम् ॥ ११६ ॥
चतूरसेषु नानासु रीतिवृत्तिविचित्रितम् ।
वेणीमिश्रमिति प्राहुरन्ये भेदद्वयं परम् ॥ ११७ ॥
वेणी सर्वैः कृता मिश्रं चूर्णकैर्वृत्तगन्धिभिः ।
द्रुता विलम्बिता मध्या बह्वल्पसमलैः क्रमात् ॥ ११८ ॥

108cd-109ab. In such compositions where *ābhoga* is not specifically mentioned, the *ābhoga* should be composed with words. *Ovī,* etc. four (*prabandhas*) occur without *ābhoga.*

ii. *Varṇa-svara*

109cd-110. *Varṇasvara* is composed with *svaras, pāṭas, padas* and *tenas* in any desired order and its conclusion is with *tenakas*; it is set to *varṇa-tāla.* It has twenty-four (*vedākṣi*) forms by structuring with *svaras* etc. at the beginning.

111-112ab. Among *svaras* etc. any two (occurring in the beginning) become *udgrāha; dhruva* is formed from one (other *aṅga*); *ābhoga* is composed of words; it has three *dhātus.* It is *niryukta*; because of the absence of *biruda,* it is of *ānandinī* (class).

iii. *Gadya*

112cd. *Gadya* is defined as an aggregate of words without a metrical structure.

113. It is sixfold: *utkalikā, cūrṇa, lalita, vṛttagandhi, khaṇḍa* and *citra.* They originate from Sāmaveda.

114. *Utkalikā* (1) is to be sung in heroic sentiment in *gauḍī-rīti* (style) and *ārabhaṭī-vṛtti* (diction); *cūrṇa* (2) [is to be sung] in *śānta* (tranquil) *rasa, vaidarbhī rīti* and *sāttvatī vṛtti.*

115. *Lalita* (3) [is rendered] with *pāñcālī* (style) and *kaiśikī* (diction) and *śṛṅgāra* (erotic) *rasa. Vṛttagandhi* (4) is [to be executed] with verse in *śānta rasa, rīti bhāratī (vṛtti)* and *pāñcālī* style.

116-117ab. *Khaṇḍa* (5) is declared (to be performed) in *vaidarbhī* (sty;e), *sāttvatī* (diction) and in *hāsya* (ludicrous) *rasa. Citra* (6), full of erotic (sentiment, is to be executed)in *vaidrabhī rīti* and *kaiśikī-citra* (diction) in (all the above) four sentiments, various styles and dictions in a beautiful/variegated way.

117cd-118ab. Other [authorities] state two other varieties [of *gadya*] viz. *veṇī* and *miśra. Veṇī* is composed from (a combination of) all (the above varieties); *miśra* is formed from a mixture of *cūrṇaka* and *vṛttagandhi.*

118cd. *Druta* (fast), *vilambita* (slow) and *madhyā* (middle) tempi are generated from densely packed, scant and even (middling) use of *las* (*laghus*) respectively.

TCC 108cd 110ab 111c 112d 114ab 115cd 116d 117b 118bcd
COT 110d 111c 112cd-124 112cd 113d 114bcd 116cd 117abc 118d

पृथग् लगत्वे मिश्रैश्च द्रुतमध्या गतिः परा ।
गतिर्द्रुतविलम्बाख्या त्वन्या मध्यविलम्बिता ॥ ११९ ॥
इति गद्यस्य षट् प्रोक्ताः प्रत्येकं गतयो बुधैः ।
सर्वैश्च गमकैर्वर्णैः प्रणवाद्यमतालकम् ॥ १२० ॥
स्वरैरतालवाक्यानां युतमन्तेऽन्तरान्तरा ।
अवान्तरानेकपदस्यैकतालपदद्वयम् ॥ १२१ ॥
एकत्र वस्तु नामाङ्कं द्विर्द्विर्गीत्वा पृथक् ध्रुवे ।
प्रयोगो द्विविभागाढ्यो गीयते द्विर्विलम्बितम् ॥ १२२ ॥
गातृनामान्यतालेन विलम्बेनान्यतालतः ।
द्रुतं नाम प्रभोर्यत्राभोगे चैतत् समस्तकम् ॥ १२३ ॥
पुनर्गीत्वा गातृपदे न्यासो गद्यं निगद्यते ।
अनिर्युक्तस्त्रिधातुश्च भावनीजातिमानयम् ॥ १२४ ॥

iv. कैवाडः

पाटैर्निरर्थैः सार्थैर्वा स्यातामुद्ग्राहकध्रुवौ ।
पदाभोगश्च कैवाडे न्यसनमुद्ग्राहके भवेत् ॥ १२५ ।
भावनीजातिमांश्चायमनिर्युक्तस्त्रिधातुकः ।

v. अङ्कचारिणी

वीररौद्राढ्यबिरुदैर्बद्धावुद्ग्राहकध्रुवौ ॥ १२६ ॥
पदैस्त्रिवर्ण्यनामाङ्कैराभोगोऽपीष्टतालतः ।
गीयते यत्र सा प्रोक्ता गीतज्ञैरङ्कचारिणी ॥ १२७ ॥
अनिर्युक्तस्त्रिधातुश्च भावनीजातिकोऽप्ययम् ।

vi. कन्दः

आर्यागीतौ वीररसे देशभाषात्मकैः पदैः ॥ १२८ ॥
उद्ग्राहः पाटबिरुदैर्ध्रुवश्चान्यपदान्तरैः ।
आभोगः पाटके न्यासः कन्दः स्यात्तालवर्जितः ॥ १२९ ॥

119. By mixing *la* (*laghus*) and *ga* (*gurus*) differently (in the first half and second half of the word-line, i.e. *mātu*-line) is formed another tempo, viz. *drutamadhyā*; the next tempo is *drutavilambā*; the other is *madhyavilambitā*.

120ab. Thus six tempi are propounded for each *gadya* (variety) by the learned.

120cd. [*Gadya* should be performed as follows:] with all *gamakas* and *varṇas;* commencing with *praṇava* ('*om*') without *tāla*;

121abc. composing *svaras* at the ends of sentences which are not set to *tāla, inter alia* sentences (i.e. in between words) and *inter alia* words (i.e. in between syllables),

121d-122. incorporating the name of the *Vastu* (i.e. *gadya* variety) within the limits of two words in the measure of a single span of any (desired) *tāla* and singing it twice separately in the *dhruva* (*dhātu*); singing the *prayoga* in two segments twice in slow tempo;

123abc. incorporating the singer's (i.e. composer's) name in a different *tāla* in slow tempo, and the king's (patron's) name in yet another *tāla* in fast tempo in the *ābhoga*;

123d-124. singing all this again and concluding (the *gadya-prabandha*) on the name of the singer; wherein it is so it is defined *gadya*. This (*prabandha*) is *aniryukta*; it has three *dhātus* and belongs to the *bhāvanī* class.

iv. *Kaivāḍa*

125-126ab. In *kaivāḍa, udgrāha* and *dhruva* are [composed] of meaningless or meaningful *pāṭas*; *ābhoga* is performed in words; conclusion is on *udgrāha*; it belongs to *bhāvanī* class, is *aniryukta* and of three *dhātus*.

v. *Aṅkacāriṇī*

126cd-127. *Udgrāha* and *dhruva* are [constructed] from *birudas* expressing the heroic and terrible (sentiments); *ābhoga* contains name of the trifold patron (lit. 'described', *varṇya*) sung in words in any desired *tāla*; wherein it is thus sung, it is said to be *aṅkacāriṇī* by experts in song.

128ab. This (*prabandha*) is *aniryukta*, three *dhātu* and is of *bhāvanī* class.

vi. *Kanda*

128cd-129. *Kanda* is [composed] in *āryāgīti* (metre), in heroic sentiment; the *udgrāha* is set in words of the provincial language; *dhruva*, in *pāṭas and birudas; ābhoga* is in other words (than those in *udgrāha* and *dhruva*); conclusion is on *pāṭas*; it has no *tāla*.

TCC 121b 122ac 123bc 125abcd 126c 127cd 128c 129bcd
COT 120ab 124b 125-126ab 126-128ab 127ad 128a 128cd-130ab 128c 128b 129bd

निर्युक्तोऽयं त्रिधातुश्च भावनीजातिमान् भवेत् ।

vii. हयलीला

तुरङ्गलीलातालेन पदैरुद्ग्राहकध्रुवौ ॥ १३० ॥
आभोगोऽन्यपदैर्यत्र हयलीला द्विधा च सा ।
गद्यजा पद्यजा चेति, गद्यबन्धात्तु गद्यजा ॥ १३१ ॥
आर्याया वाश्वललितच्छन्दसः पूर्वपश्चिमौ ।
भागावताललतालौ वा व्यत्ययौ वा सतालकौ ॥ १३२ ॥
यद्वा स्वरैः पदैस्तालाद् बिरुदैरुद्ग्राहबन्धतः ।
पद्यजा इति विख्याता निर्युक्तश्च त्रिधातुकः ॥ १३३ ॥
तारावलीजातिकोऽसौ दीपनीजातिमान् क्वचित् ।

viii. गजलीला

गजलीलेन तालेन गजलीला निगद्यते ॥ १३४ ॥
लक्ष्माश्वललितच्छन्दोहीनान्यद्धयलीलवत् ।

ix. द्विपदी

तालेन करुणानाम्ना द्विपदी परिगीयते ॥ १३५ ॥
छः पञ्च ताः गुरुश्चान्ते चतुर्भिरीदृशैः पदैः ।
कृत्वा पूर्वार्धमुद्ग्राहं परार्धं ध्रुवकं तथा ॥ १३६ ॥
गातृनेतृप्रबन्धाङ्क आभोगोऽपि पदैः स्मृतः ।
यद्वा षष्ठद्वितीयौ जौ षष्ठो वा गुरुमात्रतः ॥ १३७ ॥
अपरे च स्वरान् प्राहुरुद्ग्राहस्यावसानतः ।
यद्वा पादैश्चतुर्भिस्तैरेकैकगुरुसंयुतैः ॥ १३८ ॥
किं वा छात्तगणाभ्यां च पाभ्यां ताल्लगुतोऽथवा ।
छगणेन चतुर्मात्रैस्त्रिभिर्वा छगणाग्रतः ॥ १३९ ॥

130ab. This is *niryukta*, of three *dhātus* and is of *bhāvanī* class.

vii. *Hayalīlā*

130cd-131a. *Hayalīlā* is [composed] in *turaṅgalīlā tāla; udgrāha* and *dhruva* are in words; *ābhoga* [consists] of other words.

131bcd. It is of two kinds: *gadyaja* and *padyaja*; *gadyaja* is [so called] because it is [composed] in prose.

132-133c. When structured in *āryā* or *aśvalalita* metre, its first half and second half are [respectively] with and without *tāla* or *vice versa* or (both are) with *tāla*; [when] *udgrāha* is composed with *svaras, padas, tāla* and *biruda*, it is renowned as *padyaja*.

133d-134ab. It is *niryukta*, three-*dhātu*, is of *tārāvalī* class or sometimes, of *bhāvanī* class.

viii. *Gajalīlā*

134cd-135ab. *Gajalīlā* [*prabandha*] is declared to be set in *gajalīlā-tāla;* its characteristics are the same as of *hayalīlā* excepting [the prescription of] *aśvalalita* metre.

ix. *Dvipadī*

135cd. *Dvipadī* is sung in the *tāla* named *karuṇā*.

136-137ab. The first half is made *udgrāha* from four verse-feet [each] consisting of one *cha* (*gaṇa*), five *ta* (*gaṇas*) with a *guru* at the end; the other half is (made) *dhruva* similarly. *Ābhoga* is declared to be composed of words consisting of names of singer (composer) patron and *prabandha*.

137cd-138. Alternatively, the sixth and second (syllable triads in the verse foot) are *ja* (*gaṇas*) or the sixth is only *guru*; others prescribe *svaras* at the end of *udgrāha*. Alternatively [again,] each of the four verse-feet [of the *dvipadī*] maybe constructed with an additional *guru*.

139. Further [the verse foot may also be composed] with *cha* (*gaṇa*) and two *ta*: *gaṇas* or with two *pa-gaṇas, ta-gaṇas* with a (terminal) *laghu* and *guru*; or [again] with *cha-gaṇa* followed by three *gaṇas* each of four *mātrās*.

TCC 131d 132acd 133b 136a 139abc

COT 130cd-134ab 130c 131a 132a 133c 134d 135b 135cd-140 135c 136-137 138a

चतुर्भिर्यगणैर्युक्ता द्विपदीत्यवदन् परे ।
तारावलीको निर्युक्तस्त्रिधातुर्भावनी क्वचित् ॥ १४० ॥

x. चक्रवालः

प्राक् प्रागक्षर(सं)व्यूहो योऽन्त्यो वर्णचयः स चेत् ।
उत्तरोत्तरवाक्यादौ चक्रवालस्तदोच्यते ॥ १४१ ॥
गद्यपद्यप्रभेदेन द्विविधः कथितो बुधैः ।
उद्ग्राहध्रुवकौ तत्र चाभोगोऽन्यपदैस्ततः ॥ १४२ ॥
तारावलीजातिमांश्च निर्युक्तोऽसौ त्रिधातुकः ।

xi. क्रौञ्चपदः

यत्र स्वरैः पदैः स्यातामुद्ग्राहध्रुवकौ क्रमात् ॥ १४३ ॥
आभोगोऽन्यपदैर्न्यासः उद्ग्राहे प्रतितालतः ।
छन्दोहीनात् क्रौञ्चपदः स्वनामच्छन्दसाऽथवा ॥ १४४ ॥
त्रिधातुस्तालनियमान्निर्युक्तो भाविनेयकः ।

xii. स्वरार्थः

यत्र सप्ताक्षरैरेव षड्जादिस्वरवाचकैः ॥ १४५ ॥
क्रमव्युत्क्रमव्यस्तैश्च समस्तैर्वाञ्छितार्थकैः ।
उद्ग्राहध्रुवकौ स्यातामाभोगोऽन्यपदैः कृतः ॥ १४६ ॥
स्वरार्थः स्यादिष्टतालान् मोक्ष उद्ग्राहके च सः ।
शुद्धमिश्रप्रभेदेन द्विविधः परिकीर्तितः ॥ १४७ ॥
शुद्धः स्वराक्षरैरेव मिश्रस्त्वन्याक्षरैः स्वरैः ।
तारावलीजातिकोऽयमनिर्युक्तस्त्रिधातुकः॥ १४८ ॥

140. [Yet] others state that *dvipadī* [is structured] from four *ya-gaṇas* (in each verse-foot; this *prabandha* is of) *tārāvalī* [class], *niryukta*, of three *dhātus*, and sometimes, of *bhāvanī* class.

x. *Cakravāla*

141. If the letter clusters occurring at the end of preceding (sentences) are (repeated to occur as) the initial letter clusters of the further and further sentences, then it is said to be *cakravāla*.

142. It is described by scholars as being of two kinds, being the prose and verse subvarieties. It has *udgrāha* and *dhruva* (for the first half and second half respectively); then *ābhoga* is performed to different words.

143ab. It is of *tārāvalī* class, *niryukta* and of three *dhātus*.

xi. *Krauñcapada*

143cd-144. Wherein *udgrāha* and *dhruva* are [composed] of *svaras* and words respectively, [and] *ābhoga* is sung in different words and conclusion is in *udgrāha* set to *pratitāla*, it is *krauñcapada* [which may be] without metre or set to (its own) namesake metre.

145ab. It is of three *dhātus*; *niryukta* because of *tāla* restriction and is of *bhāvanī* class.

xii. *Svarārtha*

145cd-147ab. Wherein *udgrāha* and *dhruva* are [composed] of only seven syllables which denote *ṣaḍja* and other *svaras* arranged in regular order, disorder, individually or together yielding the desired [word-]meaning and *ābhoga* is made from other words, it is *svarārtha* (*prabandha*); [it is] set to any desired *tāla* and [its] conclusion is on *udgrāha*.

147cd-148. It is said to be in two subvarieties, viz. *śuddha* and *miśra*; *śuddha* [*svarārtha* is composed] with only *svara* syllables and *miśra*, with other syllables (also). This is of *tārāvalī* class, a *niryukta* and is of three *dhātus*.

TCC 141ac 143a 145b
COT 140bcd 141-143ab 141d 142d 143cd-145ab 144bd 145cd-148 145c 146abcd

xiii. ध्वनिकुट्टनी

मण्ठकङ्कालरहितौ तालौ भिन्नलयात्मकौ ।
सममात्रा यतिच्छेदौ सपदोद्ग्राहकध्रुवौ ॥ १४९ ॥
यत्राभोगः पृथक् तालपदैः स्याद् ध्वनिकुट्टनी ।
तारावलीजातिकोऽसौ निर्युक्तोऽपि त्रिधातुकः ॥ १५० ॥

xiv. आर्या

यत्रार्याच्छन्दसः पूर्वदलोद्ग्राहः स्वरान्तकः ।
द्विः स्याच्चरमभागस्तु सकृद् ध्रुवस्ततः परम् ॥ १५१ ॥
आभोगो न्यास उद्ग्राहे साऽऽर्या तालपदाश्रिता ।
त्रिधातुर्भावनीजातिर्निर्युक्तोऽसौ प्रबन्धकः ॥ १५२ ॥

xv. गाथा

आर्यैव प्राकृते गाथा, षट् पञ्च त्रिपदी च वा ।
निर्युक्तो भावनीजातिस्त्रिधातुश्च भवत्ययम् ॥ १५३ ॥

xvi. द्विपथः

छन्दसा दोधकेन द्विपथ उद्ग्राहमुक्तिकः ।
तालहीनः सतालो वा स च ज्ञेयश्चतुर्विधः ॥ १५४ ॥
स्वरैरेकोऽन्यः प्रयोगैः सोभयानुभयौ परौ ।
उद्ग्राहध्रुवयोर्बद्धः पदैराभोगभूषितः ॥ १५५ ॥
त्रिधातुकश्च निर्युक्तो भावनीजातिमान्क्वाचित् ।
तारावलेयको भूरिभेदाः सन्त्यस्य गानतः ॥ १५६ ॥

xvii. कलहंसः

हंसकच्छन्दसा यत्र झम्पातन्मिततालतः ।
पदैः स्वरैर्निबद्धस्तु कलहंसो द्विधा पुनः ॥ १५७ ॥
गद्यजः पद्यजश्चेति

xiii. *Dhvanikuṭṭanī*

149-150ab. Wherein [the composition] is set to two *tālas* other than *maṇṭha* and *kaṅkāla,* and to different tempi, such that caesurae divide them into even (numbered) *mātrās;* [wherein] the *ābhoga* is (composed) in a separate *tāla* and [to other] words, that is *dhvanikuṭṭanī* (*prabandha*).

150cd. It is of *tārāvalī* class, *niryukta* and is of three *dhātus.*

xiv. *Āryā*

151-152ab. Wherein [the song] is [composed] in *āryā* metre, the first half is *udgrāha* and ends in *svaras,* sung twice and the second half is *dhruva* (sung) once; after this is *ābhoga;* conclusion is on *udgrāha;* it is *āryā* (*prabandha*) which is structured in *pada* and *tāla.*

152cd. This *prabandha* is of three *dhātus,* of *bhāvanī* class and *niryukta.*

xv. *Gāthā*

153. The selfsame *āryā* [composed] in *prākṛta* [language] is *gāthā* and has six, five or three verse feet. It is *niryukta,* of three *dhātus* and of *bhāvanī* class.

xvi. *Dvipatha*

154-155. *Dvipatha* is set in *dodhaka* metre and concludes in *udgrāha;* it has or lacks *tāla;* it is to be understood as of four kinds viz. one with *svaras,* the other with *prayogas,* the next two are with both or without both. It is composed of *udgrāha* and *dhruva;* its *ābhoga* is decorated with words.

156. It is of three *dhātus,* is *niryukta,* and of *bhāvanī* class (but) sometimes of *tārāvalī;* there are numerous varieties in its singing.

xvii. *Kalahaṁsa*

157-158a. Wherein it is structured in *haṁsa* metre, in *jhampā-tāla* or a *tāla* of the same size, in words and *svaras,* it is *kalahaṁsa;* again, it is of two kinds viz. *gadyaja* and *padyaja.*

TCC 150a 151cd 153bd 154a
COT 149-150 149abc 150abd 151-152 151a 152bc 153 153ad 154-156 154a 155b 156bcd 157-159 157ab

स्वरोद्ग्राहस्तु गद्यजः ।
पद्यजस्तु पदोद्ग्राहे ध्रुवस्तच्छेषतो भवेत् ॥ १५८ ॥
आभोगोऽन्यपदैस्त्र्यङ्गो निर्युक्तोऽपि त्रिधातुकः ।

xviii. तोटकः

तोटकच्छन्दसा बद्धः प्रतिपादं पदैः स्वरैः ॥ १५९ ॥
तोटकः पूर्वमुद्ग्राहो ध्रुवश्चरमभागतः ।
आभोगोऽन्यपदैस्त्र्यङ्गो निर्युक्तोऽसौ त्रिधातुकः ॥ १६० ॥

xix. धटः

द्विपद्याद्यार्धवन्मात्रामिततेनाद्यधातुकः ।
पादोत्तरार्धं ध्रुवको धटे मुक्तिस्तु तेनकैः ॥ १६१ ॥
अर्धान्ते च स्वरानन्यैः पदैराभोगमण्डितः ।
द्व्यङ्गस्त्रिधातुर्निर्युक्तो दीपनीजातिमान् क्वचित् ॥ १६२ ॥

xx. वृत्तम्

वृत्तेन छन्दसा तत्तु ग्लिति वृत्तं दशद्वयम् ।
पदैरिष्टेन तालेन बद्धं वृत्तं तदिष्यते ॥ १६३ ॥
पादान्ते वापि वृत्तान्ते स्वराङ्गं तद्विना परे ।
उद्ग्राहध्रुवकौ तत्र पूर्वापरविभागतः ॥ १६४ ॥
आभोगः पदतः कार्यो निर्युक्तश्च त्रिधातुकः ।
क्वचित् तारावलीलग्नो दीपनीजातिमान् क्वचित् ॥ १६५ ॥

xxi. मातृका

एकैकमातृकामन्त्रवर्णपूर्वपदानि चेत् ।
क्रमतः परिगीयन्ते मातृका, सा त्रिधा मता ॥ १६६ ॥
दिव्या च मानुषी दिव्यमानुषी चेति ।

158bcd-159ab. *Gadyaja* has an *udgrāha* of *svaras*; *padyaja* has an *udgrāha* of words; whatever remains [of the *vṛtta*] is *dhruva*; *ābhoga* [is composed with] other words; it has three *aṅgas,* three *dhātus* and is *niryukta.*

xviii. *Toṭaka*

159cd-160. *Toṭaka* [*prabandha*] is [structured] in *toṭaka* metre with words and *svaras* in every verse foot; *udgrāha* is [constituted] by the former part and *dhruva* by the final part. Its *ābhoga* is of other words. It has three *aṅgas,* three *dhātus* and is *niryukta.*

xix. *Dhaṭa*

161. In *dhaṭa* [*prabandha*] *udgrāha*(*ādyadhātu*) consists of [words extending] in *mātrās* [the same quantity as] the first half of *dvipadī*; the second half of the verse foot is *dhruva*; conclusion is on *tenas.*

162. *Svaras* are composed at the end of [the first] half of *dhaṭa*; *ābhoga* is decorated with other words. It has two *aṅgas,* three *dhātus,* is *niryukta* and is sometimes of *dīpanī* class.

xx. *Vṛtta*

163. *Vṛtta* [*prabandha*] is set in *vṛtta* metre; (*vṛtta*) is a metre of twenty syllables consisting of (a series of) *guru* and *laghu*; [the composition is set] in words and any desired *tāla.*

164. At the end of each verse foot or at the end of the *vṛtta,* there is the *svara-aṅga*; according to others, there is not. Here *udgrāha* and *dhruva* occur [by dividing the composition] into the former and latter [halves].

165. *Ābhoga* is made with (other) words; (*vṛtta-prabandha*) is *niryukta,* of three *dhātus,* sometimes belongs to the *tārāvalī* class, sometimes to *dīpanī* class.

xxi. *Mātṛkā*

166-167a. If words beginning with the syllable of *mātṛkā-mantra* (alphabet/ Mother Divinity) are sung one by one in (alphabetical) order, it is *mātṛkā* [*prabandha*]. It is of three kinds viz. *divyā, mānuṣī* and *divyā-mānuṣī.*

TCC 158c 160a 161abc 163a 164abd 165cd 167b-168c
COT 158a 159-160 159cd 161-162 161abc 162c 163-165 163a 164d 165acd 166-171ab 166a

तत्र तु ।
दिव्या संस्कृतया वाचा मार्गतालैश्च गीयते ॥ १६७ ॥
मानुषी प्राकृतगिरा देशीतालैश्च निर्मिता ।
उभयोर्मिश्रणादुक्ता मातृका दिव्यमानुषी ॥ १६८ ॥
गद्यजा पद्यजा चेति मातृका द्विविधा पुनः ।
अत्रोद्ग्राहस्त्वकारादिपदषोडशतो ध्रुवः ॥ १६९ ॥
ककारादि चतुस्त्रिंशत् पदैराभोगकस्ततः ।
दिव्यादिभेदैर्नियतवर्णपूर्वपदैः क्रमात् ॥ १७० ॥
तारावलीजातिमांश्च निर्युक्तोऽसौ त्रिधातुकः ।

xxii. रागकदम्बः

अनेकरागैस्तालैश्च वृत्तैरङ्गैश्च धातुभिः ॥ १७१ ॥
गद्यैः पद्यै रसैर्युक्तो भवेद् रागकदम्बकः ।
चतुर्वृत्तैश्चतुस्तालैः कविराजेप्सिताङ्ककैः ॥ १७२ ॥
रागैश्चतुर्भिः प्राधान्यैर्नन्द्यावर्तो निगद्यते ।
तालेनैकेन गद्येन केचिदेनं जगुर्बुधाः ॥ १७३ ॥
एतस्माद् रागतालाद्यैर्द्विगुणः स्वस्तिको भवेत् ।
अब्जपत्रोऽब्जगर्भश्च भ्रमराम्रेडितौ तथा ॥ १७४ ॥
स्वस्तिकात् पूर्वपूर्वस्माद् द्विगुणः स्यात् परः परः ।
तत्र पूर्वापरौ भागौ स्त उद्ग्राहध्रुवौ क्रमात् ॥ १७५ ॥
खण्डे खण्डेऽन्तिमे रागे पदैराभोगकल्पना ।
द्विधातुकोऽप्यनिर्युक्तो मेदिन्यादिकजातिमान् ॥ १७६ ॥

xxiii. पञ्चतालेश्वरः

वितालः पूर्वमालापः कर्तव्योऽर्थेन संयुतः ।
चच्चत्पुटेन द्विर्गेयं प्रत्येकं पदपञ्चकम् ॥ १७७ ॥
स्वरपाटेप्सितं तं च धातुमातुपृथक्कृतम् ।

167b-168. Among these, *divyā* is sung with Sanskrit words in *mārga-tāla*; *mānuṣī* is composed with prākṛta (vernacular) words in *deśī tālas; divya-mānuṣī* is said to be a mixture of both.

169ab. Again, *mātṛkā* is declared to be of two kinds viz. *gadyaja* (set in prose) and *padyaja* (set in verse).

169cd-170. Here *udgrāha* is formed from sixteeen words commencing [separately] with the vowel '*a*' etc.; *dhruva* is formed from thirtyfour words commencing with the consonant letters beginning with '*ka*' etc.; then *ābhoga* is [composed] with (other) words which begin with fixed letters appropriate to *divyā,* etc. varieties, [rendered] in [regular] order.

171ab. This is of *tārāvalī* class, is *niryukta* and has three *dhātus.*

xxii. *Rāgakadamba*

171cd-172ab. *Rāgakadamba* is formed from many *rāgas, tālas, vṛttas, aṅgas, dhātus* prose passages, verses and sentiments.

172cd-173. *Nandhyāvarta* is defined as formed from four *vṛttas* (metres), four *tālas,aṅgas* of the composer's own choice, and with four *rāgas* chiefly. Other scholars declare it to be [composed] of a single *tāla* and in prose.

174-175ab. *Svastika* [*rāgakadamba*] is [formed] by doubling the *rāgas* and *tālas* relative to this; similarly, among *abjapatra, abjagarbha, bhramara* and *āmreḍita* each is formed by doubling further and further the *rāgas, tālas,* etc. of the just preceding one beginning with *svastika.*

175cd-176. Here (in all *rāgakadamba* varieties) the former and latter parts constitute respectively *udgrāha* and *dhruva* in each segment (of *rāga, tāla* and *vṛtta*). *Ābhoga* is composed with (other) words in the final (segment of each) *rāga.* It is *aniryukta,* of *medinī* etc. class and has two *dhātus.*

xxiii. *Pañcatāleśvara*

177-178ab. [*Pañcatāleśvara prabandha* is performed as follows:] first, *ālāpa* is executed with meaning[ful words]without *tāla*; each word of a cluster of five words is sung twice in *caccatpuṭa tāla.* They may be composed in any desired *svara* and *pāṭas* so as to have separate *dhātu* and *mātu.*

TCC 168c 173a 174a 175acd 176acd 177c 178ac

COT 167d 168bc 169bd 170acd 171b 171cd-176 171c 172acd 173b 174bc 175bd 176bd 177-185 177acd 178ab

द्विचच्चत्पुटमानेन पाटैः पटहसम्भवैः ॥ १७८ ॥
अन्तरश्च ततश्चाचपुटेन पदपञ्चकम् ।
पूर्ववत् त्वन्तरस्तालमानाद् हौडुक्कपाटतः ॥ १७९ ॥
ततस्तु षट्पितापुत्रकेनैव पदपञ्चकम् ।
प्राग्वच्चान्तरः [स्यात्]शङ्खपाटैस्तालद्विमानतः ॥ १८० ॥
सम्पक्केष्टाकतालेन दलषट्कं तु पूर्ववत् ।
तालद्विमानतः कांस्यतालसम्भवपाटकैः ॥ १८१ ॥
अन्तरश्च तथोद्घट्टतालेन पदषट्ककम् ।
पाटैर्मुरजसम्भूतैस्तालद्विमानतोऽन्तरः ॥ १८२ ॥
गातृनेतृप्रबन्धाङ्क आभोगश्चाविलम्बितः ।
उद्घट्टमानात्तेनोऽपि न्यास आलापके भवेत् ॥ १८३ ॥
पञ्चाङ्गकश्च निर्युक्तश्चतुर्धातुस्त्रिधातुकः ।
पञ्चतालेश्वरो यस्मात् तालबन्धविशेषतः ॥ १८४ ॥
वीरावतारः शृङ्गारतिलकश्चेति स द्विधा ।
वीरशृङ्गारयोस्तेन प्रीयन्ते सर्वदेवताः ॥ १८५ ॥

xxiv. तालार्णवः

यथेप्सिताङ्गैर्मार्गाणां तालैर्यद्वाञ्छितक्रमैः ।
आवृत्तिबहुभिर्बद्धस्तालार्णव इतीरितः ॥ १८६ ॥
गद्यजः पद्यजश्चेति स द्विधा परिकीर्तितः ।
तत्र पूर्वार्धमुद्ग्राहश्चरमार्धं ध्रुवस्ततः ॥ १८७ ॥
ध्रुवमध्यपदाभोगे त्वन्यद् रागकदम्बवत् ।

178cd-179a. *Antara* is [then] executed in two measures of *caccatpuṭa* [*tāla*] with *pāṭas* originating in *paṭaha.*

179bcd. Next a cluster of five words is [sung] in *cācapuṭa-tāla; antara* is then performed as before in *pāṭas* originating in *huḍukka* in the measure of (*cācapuṭa*) *tāla.*

180. Then a cluster of five words is [sung] in *ṣaṭpitāputra* [*tāla*] followed by an *antara* consisting of *pāṭas* of *śaṅkha* in two measures of the [*ṣaṭpitāputra*] *tāla.*

181-182a. [Next], a cluster of six petals [of words] is sung in *sampakveṣṭāka-tāla* [followed by] an *antara* consisting of *pāṭas* originating in *kāṁsya-tāla* (bronze cymbals) in two measures of the [same] *tāla.*

182bcd. Similarly, a cluster of six words is [sung] in *udghaṭṭa-tāla* followed by an *antara* consisting of *pāṭas* originating in *muraja* in two measures of the [same] *tāla.*

183. *Ābhoga* contains the names of the performer (composer), patron and *prabandha* in the measure of *udghaṭṭa-tāla* in a tempo other than *vilamba* (i.e. in *madhya* or *druta laya*); the conclusion is on *ālāpa.*

184. [This *prabandha*] has five *aṅgas,* four or three *dhātus,* is *niryukta* and is [aptly named] *pañcatāleśvara* because of the special structuring in [five] *tālas.*

185. It is of two kinds viz. *vīrāvatāra* and *śṛṅgāratilaka* because of application to *vīra* (heroic) and *śṛṅgāra* (erotic) [themes]. All gods are propitiated with this (*prabandha*).

xxiv. *Tālārṇava*

186. *Tālārṇava* is said to be formed by any desired *aṅgas* in any desired way (or *mārga* such as *dakṣiṇa*) in any *tāla* arranged in any desired order, repeated many times.

187-188ab. It is declared to be of two kinds, viz. *gadyaja* (set to prose) and *padyaja* (set to verses). Here (in this *prabandha*) the first half is *udrāha* while the final half is *dhruva. Ābhoga* is [composed] of words occurring in the *dhruva;* the rest is as in *rāgakadamba.*

TCC 178c 179ac 180bc 181b 182ac 183c 184ad 186a 188a
COT 178d 179cd 180d 181bd 182bc 183b 184abc 186-188ab 186ac 188ab

६. (III) **विप्रकीर्णप्रबन्धाः**

i. श्रीरङ्गः

तालै रागैश्चतुर्भिश्च दलैरन्ते पदान्वितः ॥ १८८ ॥
श्रीरङ्गो मेदिनीवांश्च शेषः स्याद् रागपुञ्जवत् ।
न्यासोऽनुक्तस्तु सर्वत्र भवेदुद्ग्राहके स्फुटम् ॥ १८९ ॥

ii. श्रीविलासः

पञ्चभिश्च दलै रागैस्तालैरन्तस्वरात्मकः ।
श्रीविलासोऽपि पृथ्वीवान् शेषः श्रीरङ्गवद्भवेत् ॥ १९० ॥

iii. पञ्चभङ्गिः

रागाभ्यामपि तालाभ्यां दलाभ्यां तेनकान्तकः ।
पञ्चभङ्गिप्रबन्धः स्याच्छेषः श्रीरङ्गवत् स्मृतः ॥ १९१ ॥

iv. पञ्चाननः

पञ्चाननोऽपि पाटान्तो रागाद्यैः पञ्चभङ्गिवत् ।

v. उमातिलकः

त्रिभिस्तालैर्दलै रागैरन्ते बिरुदरञ्जितः ॥ १९२ ॥
स्यादुमातिलकः श्रीदः शेषः श्रीरङ्गवन्मतः ।

vi. त्रिपदी

अङ्घ्रयो यत्र चत्वारो बद्धाः कर्णाटभाषया ॥ १९३ ॥
क्रमाद् द्विनेत्रवेदाग्निसङ्ख्यामात्रागणात्मकाः ।
षष्ठोऽत्र दशमोऽपि स्याद् रतिरन्ये तु मन्मथाः ॥ १९४ ॥
अतालपूर्वपादाभ्यामुद्ग्राहः परतो ध्रुवः ।
किन्तु स्वरप्रयोगोऽत्र सतालः स्यात् पदैः पुनः ॥ १९५ ॥
आभोगस्त्रिपदी ।

6. (III) VIPRAKĪRṆA-PRABANDHAS

i. *Śrīraṅga*

188cd-189. *Śrīraṅga*, composed of four *rāgas*, [four] *tālas* and [four] segments ending < *dala* > (each *dala* consisting of one *rāga* and one *tāla*) with words, is of *medinī* class; the rest is as in *rāgakadamba*; its conclusion is [left] unsaid (in the sources) but is clearly [seen] in *udgrāha* everywhere [in practice].

ii. *Śrīvilāsa*

190. *Śrīvilāsa* is [composed] with five petals [segments]< *dala* >,[five] *rāgas* and [five] *tālas* (i e. one *rāga* and one *tāla* in each *dala*) and concludes on *svaras*; it is also of *medinī* [class]. The rest is as in *śrīraṅga.*

iii. *Pañcabhaṅgi*

191. *Pañcabhaṅgi prabandha* is [formed] from two *rāgas*, two *tālas* and two petals [segments] (with one *rāga* and one *tāla* in each *dala*), ending on *tenakas*; the rest is declared to be as in *śrīraṅga.*

iv. *Pañcānana*

192ab. *Pañcānana* is (also) like *pañcabhaṅgi* in *rāga* etc. but concludes with *pāṭas.*

v. *Umātilaka*

192cd-193ab. *Umātilaka* is [structured] with three *tālas*, segments and *rāgas* [i.e. one *rāga* and one *tāla* in each *dala*] and is embellished with *birudas* at the end; it gives wealth (auspiciousness). The rest is opined to be as in *śrīraṅga.*

vi. *Tripadī*

193cd-194. In *tripadī*, there are four verse feet [composed] in Karnāṭa language containing respectively two (*dvi*), two (*netra*), four (*veda*) and three (*agni*) *mātrā gaṇas* [in which] the sixth and tenth are *rati* [*gaṇas*] and the others are *manmatha* [*gaṇas*].

195-196ab. *Udgrāha* is formed by the former [two] verse feet without *tāla*, and *dhruva* by the latter [two]; but here [in the *dhruva*] occurs the performance of *svaras* set to *tāla*; *ābhoga* is [composed] with [other] words. This is *tripadī.*

TCC 189b 190bc 191d 192d 194d 195ad

COT 188cd-189 188cd 189bc 193a 193cd-196 194d 195-196a 196a

सा स्यान्निर्युक्तश्च त्रिधातुकः ।
तारावलीजातिकोऽसौ पदतालप्रयोगतः ॥ १९६ ॥

vii. चतुष्पदी

कर्णाटभाषया बद्धा वेदपादा अतालकाः ।
नृपमात्रा समे पादे विषमे दशपञ्च च ॥ १९७ ॥
यमकालङ्कृता यस्याः क्रमात् पूर्वपरार्धकौ ।
स्वरतेनावसानौ तावुद्ग्राहध्रुवकौ ततः ॥ १९८ ॥
पदैराभोगको न्यासस्तेनके सा चतुष्पदी ।
त्रिधातुकश्च निर्युक्तो जातिस्तारावलीयकः ॥ १९९ ॥

viii. षट्पदी

यस्याः षडङ्घ्रयोऽतालबद्धाः कर्णाटभाषया ।
द्विर्द्विः कामगणाः प्रोक्ताः प्रतिपादं तथा पुनः ॥ २०० ॥
षष्ठतृतीययोः प्रान्ते विशेषो बाणसंज्ञकः ।
उद्ग्राहस्त्रिपदैः पूर्वैः परैरन्तस्त्रयै(स्वरै?)र्ध्रुवः ॥ २०१ ॥
आभोगोऽपि पदैर्न्यासो जीवनादे तु षट्पदी ।
तारावलीजातिकोऽसौ निर्युक्तश्च त्रिधातुकः ॥ २०२ ॥

ix. वस्तु

यत्र पञ्चाङ्घ्रयस्तत्र स्युः पञ्चदशमात्रकाः ।
चन्द्राग्रीष्वङ्घ्रयस्तुर्यद्वितीयो रविमात्रकौ ॥ २०३ ॥
स्वरपाटौ द्वितीयान्ते शरान्ते स्वरतेनकौ ।
एभिरुद्ग्राहकः पश्चाद् दोधकेन ध्रुवस्ततः ॥ २०४ ॥
आभोगोऽन्यपदैर्न्यासस्तेनके वस्तु तालयुक् ।
आनन्दिनीजातिकोऽसौ निर्युक्तश्च त्रिधातुकः ॥ २०५ ॥

196bcd. It is *niryukta*, has three *dhātus* and because of the application of [the two *aṅgas*] *pada* and *tāla* it is of *tārāvalī* class.

vii. *Catuṣpadī*

197. [*Catuṣpadī prabandha* is that] of which there are four (*veda*) verse feet composed in Karnāṭa language without *tāla* such that the even feet have sixteen (*nṛpa*) *mātrās* and the odd, fifteen (*mātrās*).

198-199ab. It is decorated with *yamaka-alaṁkāra;* the former and latter halves concluding respectively with *svaras* and *tena* are *udgrāha* and *dhruva.* Then *ābhoga* is composed of other words; conclusion is with *tenas.* Such is *catuṣpadī.*

199cd. It is *niryukta,* of three *dhātus;* its class is *tārāvalī.*

viii. *Ṣaṭpadī*

200-201ab. [*Ṣaṭpadī prabandha* is that] wherein occur six verse-feet which are composed in Karnāṭa language, without *tāla* and there are two *kāma gaṇas* in each foot; then again, by special decree, the *gaṇa* named *bāṇa* occurs as the sixth, third and final.

201cd-202. *Udgrāha* is constituted by the former three verse- feet, and *dhruva* by the latter three; *ābhoga* is sung to (other) words; conclusion is with *sthāyi-svara* < *jīvanāda* > of the *rāga;* such is *ṣaṭpadī.* It is of *tārāvalī* class, *niryukta* and has three *dhātus.*

ix. *Vastu*

203. [*Vastu prabandha* is that] wherein [there] are five verse-feet of which the first (*candra*), third (*agni*) and fifth (*iṣu*) are [each] of fifteen *mātrās* while the second and fourth are [each] of twelve (*ravi*) *mātrās.*

204-205ab. *Svara* and *pāṭa* [occur] at the end of the second (verse- foot); *svara* and *tenaka* at the end of the fifth (*sara*). *Udgrāha* is [formed] from [all] these [five]; then *dhruva* is formed by *dodhaka* (*vṛtta*); *ābhoga* [consists] of (other) words; conclusion is on *tenaka.* The *vastu* [*prabandha*] has *tāla.*

205cd. This is of *ānandinī* class, *niryukta* and has three *dhātus.*

TCC 197c 198a 199d 200c 201d 202b 203ac 204ab 205d

COT 197-199 197acd 198a-199 199cd 200-202 200c 201b 201c-202 202b 203-205 204ad-205bcd

x. विजय:

यत्र स्याद् विजयस्ताल उद्ग्राहस्तेनकैः स्वरैः ।
पाटैः पदैर्ध्रुवः पश्चादाभोगोऽन्यपदैः कृतः ॥ २०६ ॥
विजयो नाम पञ्चाङ्गो निर्युक्तश्च त्रिधातुकः ।

xi. त्रिपथ:

त्रिपथः पाटबिरुदैरुद्ग्राहः स्याद् ध्रुवः स्वरैः ॥ २०७ ॥
पदैराभोगः पञ्चाङ्गोऽनिर्युक्तोऽसौ त्रिधातुकः ।

xii. चतुर्मुख:

स्वरैः पाटैः पदैस्तेनैः क्रमात् स्थाय्यादिवर्णगैः ॥ २०८ ॥
उद्ग्राहः पूर्वभागाभ्यां पराभ्यां ध्रुवकस्ततः ।
आभोगोऽन्यपदैः शेषस्त्रिपथवत्तु(-वच्च-)तुर्मुखे ॥ २०९ ॥

xiii. सिंहलील:

यत्रोद्ग्राहः स्वरैः पाटैर्ध्रुवो बिरुदतेनकैः ।
पदाभोगः सिंहलीलस्तालः स्यात् सिंहलीलके ॥ २१० ॥
त्रिधातुकोऽपि निर्युक्तो मेदिनीजातिमानयम् ।

xiv. हंसलील:

यत्र तालो हंसलीलः पदैरुद्ग्राहः कल्पितः ॥ २११ ॥
पाटैर्ध्रुवश्चान्यपदैराभोगो हंसलीलके ।
त्रिधातुकोऽपि निर्युक्तो भावनीजातिमानसौ ॥ २१२ ॥

xv. दण्डक:

दण्डकच्छन्दसः पूर्वद्विदलो पदनिर्मितः ।
उद्ग्राहश्चरमार्धं तु ध्रुवश्च स्वरनिर्मितः ॥ २१३ ॥

x. *Vijaya*

206-207ab. That [*prabandha*] is named *vijaya* wherein the *tāla* is *vijaya*; *udgrāha* is constituted by *tenakas* and *svaras*; *dhruva*, by *pāṭas* and *birudas*; then *ābhoga* is made of different words; it has five *aṅgas,* three *dhātus* and is *niryukta.*

xi. *Tripatha*

207cd-208ab. *Tripatha* has *udgrāha* [composed] of *pāṭas* and *birudas* and *dhruva*, of *svaras*; *ābhoga* is of (other) words; [*tripatha*] has five *aṅgas,* three *dhātus* and is *aniryukta.*

xii. *Caturmukha*

208cd-209. [The *caturmukha prabandha* is constituted] by *svaras, pāṭas,* words and *tenakas*, set to *sthāyi*, etc. *varṇas*; *udgrāha* is formed from the former two parts, and *dhruva* by the latter two. Then *ābhoga* is made with other words; in *caturmukha* (*prabandha*) the rest is as in *tripatha.*

xiii. *Siṁhalīla*

210-211ab. Wherein the *udgrāha* is made of *svaras* and *pāṭas, dhruva* of *birudas* and *tenakas* and *ābhoga* is [made] of (other) words, such is *siṁhalīla* [*prabandha*] in which the *tāla* is *siṁhalīla.* It is *niryukta*, has three-*dhātus* and is of *medinī* class.

xiv. *Haṁsalīla*

211cd-212ab. In *haṁsalīla* [*prabandha*] the *tāla* is *haṁsalīla*; *udgrāha* is composed of words, *dhruva* from *pāṭas* and *ābhoga* from other words. This is *niryukta*, of *bhāvanī* class and has three *dhātus.*

xv. *Daṇḍaka*

213. [In *daṇḍaka prabandha*] the metre is *daṇḍaka*; the first two segments, composed of words form *udgrāha*; the final half is *dhruva*, composed of *svaras*;

TCC 206c 209ab 213c
COT 206-207 206acd 207ab 207-208ab 207c 208a 208cd-209 208d 209d 210-211ab 210cd 212cd-212 211c 212cd 213-214 213a

आभोगोऽन्यपदैर्यत्र निबद्धश्च त्रिधातुकः ।
निर्युक्तो भावनीजातिमानसौ दण्डको भवेत् ॥ २१४ ॥

xvi. झम्पटः

झम्पटस्त्रिपदीगाथाभेदः पूर्वदलद्वयम् ।
यत्रोद्ग्राहस्तृतीयं तु ध्रुव आभोगकः पदैः ॥ २१५ ॥
क्रीडातालस्त्रिधातुर्निर्युक्तस्तारावलीयकः ।

xvii. कन्दुकः

क्रमात् पदैश्च पाटैश्च बिरुदैः कन्दुकः स्मृतः ॥ २१६ ॥
उद्ग्राहः पदपाटाभ्यां ध्रुवो बिरुदबन्धतः ।
आभोगोऽन्यपदैर्दीपिन्यनिर्युक्तस्त्रिधातुकः ॥ २१७ ॥

xviii. त्रिभङ्गिः

स्वरैः पाटैः पदैरुक्तस्त्रिभङ्गिः स च पञ्चधा ।
एकस्त्रिभङ्गिवृत्तेनान्यस्तन्नाम(क)तालतः॥ २१८ ॥
रागैस्तालैस्त्रिभिर्यद्वा भिन्नवृत्तत्रि भिर्युतः ।
ब्रह्मविष्णुशिवस्तुत्या तालद्वैगुण्यमुक्तिकः ॥ २१९ ॥
स्वरपाटकृतोद्ग्राहो ध्रुवः पदविराजितः ।
आभोगोऽन्यपदासक्तश्चतुरङ्गस्त्रिधातुकः ॥ २२० ॥
अनिर्युक्तश्च निर्युक्तो यथासम्भवयोजितः ।

xix. हरविलासः

यत्रैकखण्ड उद्ग्राहो बद्धः सबिरुदैः पदैः ॥ २२१ ॥
पाटैर्बद्धस्ततस्तेनैर्बद्धस्तौ ध्रुवसंज्ञकः ।
रचितान्यपदाभोगः स स्याद् हरविलासकः ॥ २२२ ॥
अनिर्युक्तस्त्रिधातुश्चानन्दिनीजातिमानयम् ।

214. wherein the *ābhoga* is constructed from other words, it is *daṇḍaka,* which is *niryukta,* of *bhāvanī* class and has three *dhātus.*

xvi. *Jhampaṭa*

215-216ab. *Jhampaṭa* is the three verse-feet variety of *gāthā,* wherein the first two feet constitute *udgrāha* and the third, *dhruva; ābhoga* is [composed] of (other) words. (The composition) has *krīḍā tāla,* three *dhātus,* is *niryukta* and is of *tārāvalī* (class).

xvii. *Kanduka*

216cd-217. *Kanduka* [*prabandha*] is said to be formed by words, *pāṭas, birudas*; *udgrāha* is formed by words and *pāṭas; dhruva,* by constructing with *birudas*; *ābhoga* [consists] of other words; it is *aniryukta,* of *dīpanī* class and has three *dhātus.*

xviii. *Tribhaṅgi*

218-219ab. *Tribhaṅgi* is said to be [formed] from *svaras, pāṭas* and *padas*; it is of five kinds; one is [formed] from *tribhaṅgi vṛtta*; another, from the namesake *tāla*; or [the third and fourth are] from three *rāgas* and from [three] *tālas*; [the fifth is] from three different *vṛttas.*

219cd-220a. It is applied in propitiating Brahmā, Viṣṇu and Śiva; its conclusion is in twice the measure of the [respective] *tāla.*

220bc. Its *udgrāha* is made from *svaras* and *pāṭas*; *dhruva* is graced with words; *ābhoga* embraces other words.

220d-221ab. It has four *aṅgas,* three *dhātus* and is *aniryukta* or *niryukta* according to the way it is composed.

xix. *Haravilāsa*

221cd-222. Wherein *udgrāhas* is of one segment, structured with *birudas* and words, [the second segment] is structured with *pāṭas* and [the third] with *tenas* and these (last) two are designated as *dhruva,* and *ābhoga* is constructed with other words, it is *haravilāsa* (*prabandha*).

223ab. This is *aniryukta,* has three *dhātus* and is of *ānandinī* class.

TCC 215a 216ad 217a 218d 219c 220 221d

COT 215-216ab 215acd 216ab 216cd-217 216d 217c 218-221ab 218cd 219bc 220abc 221ab 221cd-233ab 222d 223b

xx. सुदर्शनः

पदैरुद्ग्राहको यत्र बिरुदैस्तेनकैर्ध्रुवः ॥ २२३ ॥
ततः पदान्तराभोगः स सुदर्शननामकः ।
त्रिधातुकश्चानिर्युक्तो दीपनीजातिकस्त्वयम् ॥ २२४ ॥

xxi. स्वराङ्कः

स्वरैः पाटैश्च बिरुदैरुद्ग्राहादित्रयं क्रमात् ।
एकद्वित्राश्च तालाः स्युः स्वराङ्के न्यसनं स्वरैः ॥ २२५ ॥
आभोगोऽन्यपदैः किञ्च गातव्यो मालवश्रिया ।
निर्युक्तकश्चतुर्धातुर्दीपनीजातिमानयम् ॥ २२६ ॥

xxii. श्रीवर्धनः

यत्रोद्ग्राहस्तु बिरुदैः पाटैर्ध्रुवः पदैः स्वरैः ।
तालमानद्वयन्यास आभोगोऽन्यपदात्मकः ॥ २२७ ॥
श्रीवर्धनोऽप्यनिर्युक्तस्त्रिधातुश्चानन्दिनेयकः ।

xxiii. हर्षवर्धनः

पदैश्च बिरुदैर्हर्षवर्धनः स्वरपाटकैः ॥ २२८ ॥
उद्ग्राहे स्यात्तु निर्वाणः शेषः श्रीवर्धनोदितः ।

xxiv. वदनम्

उद्ग्राहे छपदास्तादृक् स्वरपाटयुतध्रुवः ॥ २२९ ॥
आभोगोऽन्यपदैर्यत्र वदनं गदितं बुधैः ।
तथोपवदनं प्रोक्तं छगणच्छदतैर्युतम् ॥ २३० ॥
तथैव वस्तुवदनं छयुगाद्दचछैः कृतम् ।
अनिर्युक्तस्त्रिधातुश्च चतुरङ्गो भवत्यसौ ॥ २३१ ॥

xx. *Sudarśana*

223cd-224. Wherein *udgrāha* is [composed] of words and *dhruva* of *birudas* and *tenakas*; then *ābhoga* is of different words, it is named *sudarśana*; it has three *dhātus*, is *aniryukta* and is of *dīpanī* class.

xxi. *Svarāṅka*

225-226ab. In *svarāṅka* [*prabandha*] *udgrāha* etc. three [*dhātus*] are respectively [made] from *svaras*, *pāṭas* and *birudas* set respectively to one, two and three *tālas* and the conclusion is with *svaras*; *ābhoga* is [constructed] with other words; besides, it should be sung in *mālavaśrī (rāga)*.

226cd. It is *niryukta*, has four *dhātus* and is of *dīpanī* class.

xxii. *Śrīvardhana*

227-228ab. Wherein *udgrāha* is [structured] with *birudas* and *pāṭas* and *dhruva* with words and *svaras*, conclusion is with two measures of the *tāla* [to which the song is set], *ābhoga* contains other words, it is *śrīvardhana* [*prabandha*]; it is *aniryukta*, has three *dhātus* and is of *ānandinī* [class].

xxiii. *Harṣavardhana*

228cd-229ab. *Harṣavardhana* is composed of words and *birudas* [in *udgrāha*] and *svaras* and *pāṭas* [in *dhruva*]; conclusion is on *udgrāha*; the rest is [as] described in *śrīvardhana*.

xxiv. *Vadana*

229cd-230ab. Wherein the *cha, pa, da* (*gaṇas*) are [organised into words] in *udgrāha*, *dhruva* has *svaras* and *pāṭas*, *ābhoga* is [composed] of other words, it is described by scholars as *vadana* [*prabandha*].

230cd-231ab. Similarly *upavadana* is described as consisting of *cha-gaṇa*, *cha-da-ta gaṇas* (in *udgrāha*). Likewise, *vastu-vadana* is made from two *cha-gaṇas*, *da-ca-cha* (*gaṇas* in *udgrāha*). [The *vadana* is] *aniryukta*, has three *dhātus* and has four *aṅgas* [*dīpanī* class].

TCC 223c 224d 225a 226a 228b 229cd 230d 231d

COT 223cd-224 224bd 225-226 225 226bcd 227-228ab 227 228ab 228cd-229ab 228cd 229ab 229cd-231 229cd-230a

xxv. चच्चरी

यत्र हिन्दोलको रागश्छन्दस्तालश्च चच्चरी ।
बहवोऽप्यङ्घ्रयः किन्तु द्वौ द्वौ च प्रासंसंयुतौ ॥ २३२ ॥
सा वसन्तोत्सवे गेया चच्चरी प्राकृतैः पदैः ।
अत्र पूर्वार्धमुद्ग्राह उत्तरार्धं ध्रुवस्ततः ॥ २३३ ॥
आभोगोऽन्यपदैः कार्यः प्रबन्धोऽयं त्रिधातुकः ।
तारावलीजातिमांश्च निर्युक्तः कामदैवतः ॥ २३४ ॥

xxvi. चर्या

आर्यागणैश्चतुर्भिः स्यादङ्घ्रिर्जगणतो विना ।
अध्यात्मगोचरा चर्या पादान्तप्रासशोभिता ॥ २३५ ॥
द्वितीयतालतो यद्वा तन्मात्रामिततालतः ।
अत्र पूर्वापरौ भागावुद्ग्राहध्रुवकौ ततः ॥ २३६ ॥
आभोगोऽन्यपदैर्द्व्यङ्गो निर्युक्तोऽपि त्रिधातुकः ।

xxvii. पद्धडी

नृपमात्रात्मकं छन्दः पदं यत्र विनायकम् ॥ २३७ ॥
युग्मपादान्तरप्रासा बहुभङ्गिविनिर्मिता ।
उद्ग्राहो बिरुदैर्बद्धः स्वरान्तैः पूर्वभागतः ॥ २३८ ॥
ध्रुवोऽपि बिरुदैर्बद्धः पाटान्तैरपरार्धतः ।
पदान्तरैः कृताभोगः पद्धडी सा मता सताम् ॥ २३९ ॥
त्रिधातुकोऽसौ निर्युक्तो जातावानन्दिनेयकः।

xxviii. राहडी

यत्र वीररसेन स्यात् सङ्ग्रामरचितस्तुतिः ॥ २४० ॥
बहुभिश्चरणैर्बद्धा राहडी सा तु कीर्तिता ।

xxv. *Caccarī*

232-233ab. Wherein the *rāga* is *hindola*, metre and *tāla* are *caccarī*, there are many verse-feet but [adjacent] pairs are rhymed, it is *caccarī* [*prabandha*] sung in the spring festival and composed in words of Prākṛta.

233cd-234. Here the former half is *udgrāha*, the latter half is *dhruva*; then *ābhoga* is made with other words. This *prabandha* has three *dhātus*, is *niryukta*, of *tārāvalī* class; its presiding deity is Kāma.

xxvi. *Caryā*

235-236ab. *Caryā* is [composed] with four *gaṇas* of the *āryā* [metre], omitting *jagaṇa*; it abides in spiritual matters and rhymes at the end of the verse-foot. It is set to *dvitīya-tāla* or a *tāla* of same number of *mātrās*.

236cd-237ab. Here the former and latter parts are *udgrāha* and *dhruva* [respectively]. Then *ābhoga* is [executed] with other words. [The composition] has two *aṅgas*, three *dhātus* and is *niryukta*.

xxvii. *Paddhaḍī*

237cd-238ab. [*Paddhaḍī prabandha* has the following characteristics:] the words are set in a metre of sixteen (*nṛpa*) *mātrās* excluding *ya* (? *ja* ? *gaṇa*) such that they rhyme internally in pairs and may be structured in numerous fashions.

238cd-239. *Udgrāha* is composed in the former part in *birudas* ending in *svaras*; *dhruva* also is composed in the latter part in *birudas* but ending in *pāṭas; ābhoga* is made with other words. This is declared by the cognoscente to be *paddhaḍī*.

240ab. This has three *dhātus*, is *niryukta* and *ānandinī* in class.

xxviii. *Rāhaḍī*

240cd-241ab. It is described as *rāhaḍī* [*prabandha*] wherein is a praise of battle composed in the heroic sentiment and set in numerous verse-feet.

TCC 232d 233ab 235b 236b 239c

COT 232-234 232b 235-237ab 235ab 236ad 237a 235 237cd-240 237c 240cd-242ab 240d 241ab

अत्र पूर्वापरौ भागावुद्ग्राहध्रुवकौ पुनः ॥ २४१ ॥
द्व्यङ्गः पदान्तराभोगोऽनिर्युक्तो गुणधातुकः ।

xxix. वीरश्रीः

यत्रोद्ग्राहः पदैर्बद्धो ध्रुवोऽपि बिरुदैस्ततः ॥ २४२ ॥
आभोगोऽन्यपदैर्युक्तो वीरश्रीरिति गीयते ।
अनिर्युक्तस्त्रिधातुश्च भावनीजातिमानयम् ॥ २४३ ॥

xxx. मङ्गलाचारः

यस्तु गद्येन पद्येन गद्यपद्येन वा कृतः ।
निस्सारुताले श्रीरागे त्वर्धान्ते स्वरराजितः ॥ २४४ ॥
मङ्गलाचार उद्ग्राहध्रुवौ द्विदलतः क्रमात् ।
पदाभोगस्त्रिधातुश्च निर्युक्तो भाविनेयकः ॥ २४५ ॥

xxxi. धवलः

त्रिविधो धवलः कीर्तिर्विजयो विक्रमस्तथा ।
चतुर्भिश्चरणैः षड्भिरष्टभिश्च क्रमादसौ ॥ २४६ ॥
विषमस्थं छयुग्मं चेत्तो वा दो वाऽधिकः समे ।
तदा स्यात् कीर्तिधवलो विजये त्वाद्यतुर्ययोः ॥ २४७ ॥
द्वौ दद्वौ षष्ठे द्वितीये छौ शेषौ द्वौ छेन पेन वा ।
प्रथमे च त्रयं दः स्यात् तृतीये दास्त्रयस्तु च ॥ २४८ ॥
तुर्यद्वितीययोश्चैतत् पञ्चमे सप्तमे तथा ।
षष्ठेऽष्टमे दाश्चत्वारो यस्यासौ विक्रमो भवेत् ॥ २४९ ॥
आशीर्भिर्धवलो गेयो विमलादिपदान्वितः ।
यदृच्छया वा धवलो गेयो लोकप्रसिद्धितः ॥ २५० ॥
अत्र सर्वत्र पूर्वार्धमुद्ग्राहः परतो ध्रुवः ।
आभोगोऽन्यपदैर्द्व्यङ्गो निर्युक्तश्च त्रिधातुकः ॥ २५१ ॥

241cd-242ab. Here the former and latter parts are *udgrāha* and *dhruva* respectively; again, *ābhoga* is in other words; it has two *aṅgas*, three *dhātus*, and is *aniryukta.*

xxix. *Vīraśrī*

242cd-243. Where in *udgrāha* is constructed with words and *dhruva* with *birudas*, then *ābhoga* with other words, it is sung as *vīraśrī* [*prabandha*]; it is *aniryukta*, has three *dhātus* and is of *bhāvanī* class.

xxx. *Maṅgalācāra*

244-245a. *Maṅgalācāra* is that which is structured in prose, verse or prose [and] verse, in *niḥsāru-tāla*, *śrīrāga* and is decorated with *svaras* at the end of the [first] half.

245bcd. *Udgrāha* and *dhruva* are [made of] the former and latter segments in order; *ābhoga* is [made] of [other] words; it has three *dhātus*, is *niryukta* and is of *bhāvanī* [class].

xxxi. *Dhavala*

246. *Dhavala* is of three kinds viz. *kīrti*, *vijaya*, similarly *vikrama*, formed with four, six and eight verse-feet respectively.

247abc. If there is a pair of *cha* [*gaṇas*] in the odd [numbered] verse-feet and an additional *ta* or *da* [*gaṇa*] in the even [numbered feet], then it is *kīrti dhavala.*

247d-248ab. In *vijaya* [*dhavala*] there are two *da gaṇas* in the first and fourth (verse-feet), a pair of *cha* [*gaṇas*] in the sixth and second, and the remaining two (verse-feet are constituted) by *cha-* or *sa-* [*gaṇa*].

248cd-249. Wherein there are three *ca* and [one] *da* [*gaṇa*] in the first [verse-foot], the same is true in the fourth and second verse-feet, four *da* [*gaṇas*] in the fifth, seventh, similarly the sixth and eighth (verse-feet), it is *vikrama* [*dhavala*].

250. *Dhavala* is sung in benediction; it contains words such as *vimala*; or it may be sung arbitrarily as established in usage.

251. Here the first half is *udgrāha* and the next [half], *dhruva*; *ābhoga* is in other words everywhere (in all *dhavalas*). It has two *aṅgas*, three *dhātus* and is *niryukta.*

TCC 245c 247ad 248bcd 250b 251a

COT 242ab 243 242cd 243d 244-245 244abcd 246-251 246ab 247cd 250bcd 251 abcd

xxxii. मङ्गलः

यत्रेषुचगणाः पादे पादे चिरलयेन च ।
शङ्खचक्रादिरचितैर्मङ्गलैरुत्तमैः पदैः ॥ २५२ ॥
श्रीरागे मङ्गलो गेयः किञ्च वा मालवश्रिया ।
अत्रापि पूर्वापरयोर्भागयोरुद्ग्राहकध्रुवौ ॥ २५३ ॥
पदाभोगस्त्रिधातुश्च द्व्यङ्गो निर्युक्तकस्तथा ।

xxxiii. ओवी

खण्डत्रयं प्रासयुतं गीयते देशभाषया ॥ २५४ ॥
ओवीपदं तदन्ते चेदोवी तज्ज्ञैस्तदोदिता ।
त्रयाणां चरणानां स्यादेकाद्यावृत्तितो भिदाः ॥ २५५ ॥
आदिमध्यान्तगैः प्रासैरेकाद्यैश्च पदे पदे ।
छन्दोभिर्बहुभिर्गेया ओव्यो जनमनोहराः ॥ २५६ ॥

xxxiv. लोली

सानुप्रासैस्त्रिभिः खण्डैर्मण्डिता प्राकृतैः पदैः ।
प्रान्ते लोलीपदोपेता लोली गेया विचक्षणैः ॥ २५७ ॥

xxxv. ढोल्लरी

दोहडः स्याद्यदा प्रान्ते प्रोल्लसड्ढोल्लरीपदः ।
ढोल्लरी नाम सा प्रोक्ता लाटभाषाविभूषिता ॥ २५८ ॥

xxxvi. दन्ती

अनुप्रासप्रधानं चेत् खण्डत्रयसमन्वितम् ।
दन्ती पदान्वितं प्रान्ते तदा दन्ती निगद्यते ॥ २५९ ॥
ओव्यादीनां चतुर्णां च पूर्वपूर्वद्विखण्डकम् ।
उद्ग्राहः परखण्डं तु ध्रुवः स्याच्च द्विधातवः ॥ २६० ॥

xxxii. *Maṅgala*

252-253ab. *Maṅgala* [*prabandha*] is sung with five (*iṣu*) *ca-gaṇas* in every verse-foot in *vilambita-laya* (slow tempo) containing excellent and auspicious words such as *śaṅkha, cakra,* etc. in *śrīrāga* or sometimes in *mālavaśrī* [*rāga*].

253cd-254ab. Here also the former and latter parts constitute *udgrāha* and *dhruva* [respectively]; *ābhoga* [consists] of (other) words; it has three *dhātus,* two *aṅgas* and is, likewise, *niryukta.*

xxxiii. *Ovī*

254cd-255ab. If three rhyming segments are sung in provincial language containing the word '*ovī*' at the end, then it is declared by experts to be *ovī* [*prabandha*].

255cd-256. By repeating once etc. its vers-feet (*caraṇa*) it forms varieties. The *ovī,* which is attractive to the popular mind may be sung in numerous metres with rhyming at the beginning, middle or end of each verse-foot.

xxxiv. *Lolī*

257. *Lolī* [*prabandha*] is sung by experts in three segments composed in Prākṛta words with alliteration and containing the word '*lolī*' at the end.

xxxv. *Ḍhollarī*

258. If the *dohaḍa* [*prabandha*] is sung with the word '*ḍhollarī*' at the end, graced with words of the *lāṭa* language, it is declared to be named *ḍhollarī.*

xxxvi. *Dantī*

259. *Dantī* is defined as having three segments with preponderant alliteration and having the word '*dantī*' at the end.

260. In the four [*prabandhas*] beginning with *ovī,* the former two segments constitute *udgrāha,* and the latter [one], *dhruva;* they have two *dhātus.*

TCC 252b 253bd 254b 255bcd 256ac 257d 258d
COT 252-254ab 252ac 253abc 254a 254cd-256 255ad 257 258 259

तारावलीजातिमन्तोऽनिर्युक्ताः प्रकीर्तिताः ।
अनुक्ताभोगवस्तूनां पदैराभोगकल्पना ॥ २६१ ॥
ओव्यादयस्तु चत्वारो मेलापाभोगवर्जिताः ।

६. (IV) सालगसूडः

i. षोडशविधो ध्रुवः

उद्ग्राहः क्रियते यस्य द्विखण्डोऽप्येकधातुकः ॥ २६२ ॥
यद्वैकखण्डं द्विर्गायेत् किञ्चिदुच्चस्तृतीयकः ।
भिन्नधातुर्ध्रुवाख्यः स्यात् त्रयमेतत् द्विरभ्यसेत् ॥ २६३ ॥
ततो द्विखण्ड आभोग आदिमः खण्डकः पुनः ।
एकधातुर्द्विखण्डश्च भिन्नधातूच्चकोऽपरः ॥ २६४ ॥
स्तुत्यनामाङ्कितो न्यास उद्ग्राहस्याद्यखण्डतः ।
स ध्रुवः स्यात् षोडशधा पदैरेकार्थवाचकैः ॥ २६५ ॥
एकादशादिकैराद्यखण्डे खण्डे क्रमाद्यथा ।
जयन्तशेखरोत्साहास्ततो मधुरनिर्मलौ ॥ २६६ ॥
कुन्तलः कमलश्चारो नन्दनश्चन्द्रशेखरः ।
कामदो विजयाख्यश्च कन्दर्पजयमङ्गलौ ॥ २६७ ॥
तिलको ललितश्चेति तेषां संज्ञा इमाः क्रमात् ।
शृङ्गारे रासताले च **जयन्तः** (i) स्यात्तु **शेखरः** ॥ २६८ ॥
वीरे निःसारुताले स्याद् (ii) **उत्साहः** प्रतिमण्ठतः (iii) ।
हास्ये च **मधुरो** गेयः करुणे हयलीलया (iv) ॥ २६९ ॥
निर्मलः स्यात्तु शृङ्गारे क्रीडाताले (v) च **कुन्तलः** ।
लघुशेखरतालेन गातव्यश्चाद्भुते रसे (vi) ॥ २७० ॥
विप्रलम्भे तु **कमलो** झम्पातालेन गीयते (vii) ।
चारो वीररसे गेयस्तथा निःसारुतालतः (viii) ॥ २७१ ॥

261-262ab. They are declared to belong to *tārāvalī* class and are *niryukta.* In musical compositions where *ābhoga* is not specified, *ābhoga* is composed with words. The four [*prabandhas*] *ovī* et cetera omit *melāpaka* and *ābhoga.*

6. (IV) SĀLAGASŪḌA-PRABANDHAS

i. *Sixteen Varieties of Dhruva*

262cd-263. [The *dhruva sālaga-sūḍa-prabandha* has the following characteristics:] its *udgrāha* is made in two segments, both composed of the same *dhātu,* or a single segment sung twice; the third [segment] is somewhat higher (in pitch). This segment with different *dhātu* is [the *dhātu* element] named *dhruva.* All these three [segments] should be repeated twice.

264-265ab. Then [follows] *ābhoga* with two segments; the first segment here again, consists of two sections each of which has the same *dhātu,* while the other [segment] in different *dhātu* is higher (in pitch), and bears the name of the patron. Conclusion is with the first segment of *udgrāha.*

265cd-266ab. This is *dhruva* (*gīta*); it is of sixteen varieties, formed by words which possess (or flow towards) a single meaning, located in the first and following segments, beginning with eleven words [and increasing by one regularly].

266cd-268ab. Their names, in order, are *jayanta, śekhara, utsāha, madhura, nirmala, kuntala, kamala, cāra, nandana, candraśekhara, kāmada, vijaya, kandarpa, jayamaṅgala, tilaka* and *lalita.*

268cd-269abc. *Jayanta* (i) is [sung] in *śṛṅgāra* and *rāsa-tāla. Śekhara* (ii) is in *vīra* [*rasa*] and *niḥsāru-tāla. Utsāha* (iii) is in *pratimaṇṭha-tāla* and *hāsya-*[*rasa*].

269d. *Madhura* (iv) is sung in *karuṇa* [*rasa*] and *hayalīla-tāla.*

270. *Nirmala* (v) is in *śṛṅgāra* and *krīḍā tāla. Kuntala* (vi) should be sung in *laghuśekhara-tāla* in *adbhuta-rasa.*

271. *Kamala* (vii) is sung in *vipralambha*[*-śṛṅgāra*] in *jhampā-tāla. Cāra* (viii) is sung in *vīra rasa* and *niḥsāru-tāla.*

TCC 261cd 262a 263a 264b 266a 267c 269cd 271acd
COT 262cd-276ab 265c 268c

वीरशृङ्गारयोरेकताल्या प्रोक्तस्तु **नन्दनः** (ix) ।
प्रतिमण्ठेन शृङ्गारे हास्ये स्या**च्चन्द्रशेखरः** (x) ॥ २७२ ॥
कामदः प्रतिमण्ठेन शृङ्गारे (xi) **विजय**स्ततः ।
हास्ये द्वितीयतालेन (xii) **कन्दर्पो**ऽप्यादितालतः ॥ २७३ ॥
हास्यशृङ्गारकरुणे (xiii) **जयमङ्गल**संज्ञकः ।
क्रीडातालेन शृङ्गारवीरयोः परिगीयते (xiv) ॥ २७४ ॥
एकताल्यां रसे वीरे शृङ्गारे **तिलका**भिधः (xv) ।
विचारप्रतिमण्ठेन शृङ्गारे **ललितः** स्मृतः (xvi) ॥ २७५ ॥
निर्युक्तकस्त्रिधातुश्च द्व्यङ्गस्तारावलेयकः ।

ii. षड्विधो मण्ठः

द्वियत्येकविरामं वा खण्डमुद्ग्राहसंज्ञकम् ॥ २७६ ॥
ततो ध्रुवाख्यं द्विर्गायेद् विकल्पेनान्तरस्ततः ।
तं गीत्वा ध्रुवमागत्य चाभोगो गीयते सकृत् ॥ २७७ ॥
न्यासस्तु ध्रुवके यस्य स मण्ठो मण्ठतालतः ।
षट्प्रकारो भवेदेष तालभेदेन मण्ठकः ॥ २७८ ॥
जयप्रियो मङ्गलश्च सुन्दरो वल्लभस्तथा ।
कलापः कमलश्चेति तेषां तालरसं यथा ॥ २७९ ॥
वीरे **जयप्रियो** जेन (i) शृङ्गारे भेन **मङ्गलः** (ii) ।
सुन्दरस्तेन शृङ्गारे (iii) करुणे रेण **वल्लभः** (iv) ॥ २८० ॥
विरामान्तेन सेन स्यात् **कलापो** हास्यतो रसे (v) ।
झम्पातालेन **कमलो**ऽप्यद्भुतो रसतो भवेत् (vi) ॥ २८१ ॥
रङ्गोद्योतेन तालेन तथा चच्चत्पुटेन च ।
गीतं मण्ठाभिधं प्राहुः केचिल्लक्ष्यविशारदाः ॥ २८२ ॥
इति मण्ठाभिधस्तालो विशेषोऽत्र प्रकीर्तितः ।

272. *Nandana* (ix) is said to be [sung] in *vīra* and *śṛṅgāra* [*rasa*] and in *ekatālī* [*tāla*]. *Candraśekhara* (x) is in *pratimaṇṭha* [*tāla*], *śṛṅgāra* and *hāsya* [*rasas*].

273-274a. *Kāmada* (xi) is in *pratimaṇṭha* [*tāla*] and *śṛṅgāra*; then, *vijaya* (xii) is in *hāsya* and *dvitīya-tāla*. *Kandarpa* (xiii) is in *ādi tāla*, *hāsya*, *śṛṅgāra* and *karuṇa* [*rasas*].

274bcd. The [*dhruva* variety] named *jayamaṅgala* (xiv) is sung in *krīḍā tāla* and in *vīra* and, *śṛṅgāra [rasas].*

275-276ab. *Tilaka* (xv) is in *ekatālī tāla* and *vīra, śṛṅgāra rasas*; *lalita* (xvi) is averred to be (composed with) *vicāra-pratimaṇṭha* [*tāla*] and *śṛṅgāra*. [The *dhruva gīta* is *niryukta*, of three *dhātus*, has two *aṅgas* and [hence] of *tārāvalī* [class].

ii. *Six Varieities of Maṇṭha*

276cd. [In the *maṇṭha-gīta*] the segment named *udgrāha* has two caesuras or one pause (in its words).

277-278ab. Then the [segment] named *dhruva* is rendered twice, then the *antara* is sung optionally; after singing it, *dhruva* is reached and then *ābhoga* is sung once. Conclusion is with *dhruva*; wherein [it is so], it is *maṇṭha gīta* in *maṇṭha-tāla.*

278cd-279c. This *maṇṭha* is of six varieties according to difference in *tāla*, viz. *jayapriya*, *maṅgala*, *sundara*, *vallabha*, *kalāpa* and *kamala*.

279d-280. Their *tāla(s)* and *rasa(s)* are as follows:

Jayapriya (i) is [sung] in *vīra rasa*, and *ja* [*gaṇa*]; *maṅgala* (ii) in *śṛṅgāra* and *bha* [*gaṇa*]; *sundara* (iii) in *ta*[*gaṇa*] and *śṛṅgāra*; *vallabha* (iv) in *karuṇa* and *ra* [*gaṇa*].

281. *Kalāpa* (v) is in *sa* [*gaṇa*] ending in *virāma* and in *hāsya rasa; kamala* (vi) occurs in *jhampā tāla* and *adbhuta rasa.*

282-283ab. Some experts in the practice of music prescribe the *gīta* named *maṇṭha* in *raṅgodyota tāla* and *caccatpuṭa*. Thus the *tāla* named *maṇṭha* is specially prescribed.

TCC 276a 277c 280abd 281acd 281-285 283ab
COT 275c 276cd-283ab 277b 280-281ab

iii. चतुर्धा प्रतिमण्ठः

प्रतिमण्ठादिवस्तूनां लक्षणं मण्ठवन्मतम् ॥ २८३ ॥
उद्ग्राहादिगतं सर्वं भेदस्तालकृतो भवेत् ।
तत्र तु प्रतिमण्ठेन तालेन प्रतिमण्ठकः ॥ २८४ ॥
स चतुर्धाऽमरस्तारो विचारः कुन्द इत्यपि ।
अमरो गुरुणैकेन शृङ्गारे परिगीयते (i) ॥ २८५ ॥
झम्पातालेन वीरे च रौद्रे वा **तार**नामकः (ii) ।
विचारः करुणे गेयो नगणेन विरामतः (iii) ॥ २८६ ॥
कुन्दो विराममध्येन लत्रयेणाद्भुते मतः (iv) ।

iv. षड्विधो निःसारुकः

निःसारुतालतो बद्धो बुधैर्निःसारुको मतः ॥ २८७ ॥
वैकुन्दानन्दकान्ताराः समरो वाञ्छितस्तथा ।
विशालश्चेति स प्रोक्तः षड्विधः पूर्वसूरिभिः ॥ २८८ ॥
कुडुक्काभिधतालेन **वैकुन्दो** मङ्गले भवेत् (i) ।
क्रीडातालेन **चानन्द** आनन्दे गीयते सदा (ii) ॥ २८९ ॥
विप्रलम्भाख्यशृङ्गारे **कान्तारो** रतितालतः (iii) ।
हंसलीलेन तालेन **समरो** वीरगोचरः (iv) ॥ २९० ॥
लत्रयाद् बिन्दुयुग्मेन **वाञ्छितः** सर्वसिद्धिदः (v) ।
लेन द्रुताभ्यां लघुना सम्भोगे स्याद् **विशालकः** (vi) ॥ २९१ ॥

v. षड्विधोऽड्डुतालः

अड्डुतालेन तालेनाड्डुतालः षड्विधो भवेत् ।
निःशङ्कशङ्कशीलाश्च चारोऽथ मकरन्दकः ॥ २९२ ॥
विजयश्चेति, **निःशङ्को** लगदैर्बिन्दुनाद्भुते (i) ।
रसे वीरे च शृङ्गारे **शङ्कः** स्यात् प्रतितालतः (ii) ॥ २९३ ॥

iii. *Four Varieties of Pratimaṇṭha*

283cd-284. All the characteristics of the *vastus pratimaṇṭha* etc. pertaining to *udgrāha* etc. are as in *maṇṭha.* Variety arises [here] because of *tāla* [differences]. Here *pratimaṇṭha* is sung in *pratimaṇṭha-tāla.*

285. It is of four kinds: *amara, tāra, vicāra* and *kunda. Amara* (i) is sung with a single *guru* in *śṛṅgāra.*

286-287ab. [The *pratimaṇṭha* variety] named *tāra* (ii) is in *jhampā-tāla, vīra* or *raudra rasa. Vicāra* (iii) is sung in *karuṇa* and [the *tāla*] *na-gaṇa* with *virāma. Kunda* (iv) is said to be in three *laghus* with *virāma* in the middle, in *adbhuta* [*rasa*].

iv. *Six Varieties of Niḥsāru*

287cd-288. *Niḥsāru-[gīta]* is declared by the learned to be composed in *niḥsāru-tāla.* It is declared by previous authorities to be of six varieties viz. *vaikunda, ānanda, kāntāra, samara, vāñchita* and *viśāla.*

289. *Vaikunda* (i) occurs in the *tāla* named *kaḍukkā* and on auspicious occasions. *Ānanda* (ii) is always sung in *krīḍā tāla* and for blissful occasions.

290. *Kāntāra* (iii) is in *vipralambha-śṛṅgāra* and in *rati tāla. Samara* (iv) is in *haṁsalīla-tāla,* abiding in *vīra*[*rasa*].

291. *Vāñchita* (v) is in a *tāla* of three *laghus* [followed by] two *drutas* and confers every fulfilment. *Viśāla* (vi) is in the *tāla laghu,* two *drutas* and *laghu,* in *sambhoga-śṛṅgāra.*

v. *Six Varieties of Aḍḍatāla*

292-293a. *Aḍḍatāla-gīta* is composed in the *tāla* [named] *aḍḍa tāla.* It is of six varieties, viz. *niḥśaṅka, śaṅka, śīla, cāra, makaranda* and *vijaya.*

293bcd. *Niḥśaṅka* (i) is in [the *tāla*] *laghu, guru, druta* and in *adbhuta* [*rasa*]. *Śaṅka* (ii) is in *vīra* and *śṛṅgāra rasas* and in *prati tāla.*

TCC 283cd 284abd 286a 288-290 291ac 292a 239cd
COT —

झम्पातालेन शान्ते च **शील**: स्यात् (iii) **चार**नामकः ।
द्रुताभ्यां लगुरुभ्यां च रसे वीरेऽद्भुते तथा (iv) ॥ २९४ ॥
मकरन्दोऽपि शृङ्गारे बिन्दुभ्यां गुरुणा भवेत् (v) ।
द्वितीयतालेन रसे वीरे तु **विजय**: स्मृतः (vi) ॥ २९५ ॥

vi. चतुर्विधो रासः

रासको रासतालेन स चालापादिगो मतः ।
चतुर्विधो भवेदेष न लक्ष्ये दृश्यते तथा ॥ २९६ ॥
विनोदो वरदो नन्दः कम्बुजश्च विशेषतः ।
सर्वरासकभेदेषु द्विखण्डोद्ग्राहको भवेत् ॥ २९७ ॥
ध्रुवोऽवसानकालापो **विनोद**: कौतुके भवेत् (i) ।
आलापमध्यध्रुवको **वरदो** देवतास्तुतौ (ii) ॥ २९८ ॥
आलापनिर्मितोद्ग्राहो **नन्द**स्त्वभ्युदये स्मृतः (iii) ।
आलापादिध्रुवो यत्र **कम्बुज**: करुणे भवेत् (iv) ॥ २९९ ॥

vii. त्रिविधैकताली

एकताल्या च तालेनैकताली त्रिविधा मता ।
रामा च चन्द्रिका तद्वद् विपुलेत्यथ लक्षणम् ॥ ३०० ॥
यत्रोद्ग्राहः प्रयोगात्मा पदैरालापतो ध्रुवः ।
पदान्तरकृताऽऽभोगः सा **रामा** (i) **चन्द्रिका** तु सा ॥ ३०१ ॥
उद्ग्राहो द्विदलो यत्र गमकालापको ध्रुवः ।
पदान्तराभोगतः स्याद्यत्यनुप्राससंयुता (ii) ॥ ३०२ ॥
यत्रालापपदोद्ग्राहस्त्वपरालापतो ध्रुवः ।
आभोगोऽन्यपदैः सा तु **विपुला** परिकीर्तिता (iii) ॥ ३०३ ॥
मण्ठादयः प्रबन्धास्तु द्व्यङ्गास्तारावलेयकाः ।
त्रिधातवश्च निर्युक्ताः सान्तराच्चतुर्धातवः ॥ ३०४ ॥

294. Śīla (iii) occurs in *jhampā-tāla* and *śānta*[*rasa*]. [The one] named *cāra* (iv) is, likewise [sung] in the *tāla* two *drutas, laghu, guru* in *vīra* and *adbhutarasa(s).*

295. *Makaranda* (v) occurs in *śṛṅgāra* [*rasa*] and in the *tāla* two *drutas, guru. Vijaya* (vi) is in *dvitīya tāla* and *vīra*[*rasa*].

vi. *Four Varieties of Rāsa*

296-297c. *Rāsaka* is [sung] in *rāsa-tāla;* by having *ālāpa* at the beginning etc. It is of four kinds, but these are not seen in practice viz., *vinoda, varada, nanda* and *kambuja.*

297d. As a special case, a two-segment *udgrāha* occurs in all *rāsaka* varieties.

298. *Vinoda* (i) has *ālāpa* at end of *dhruva dhātu* and is employed in (situations of) eagerness. *Varada* (ii) has *ālāpa* in the middle of *dhruva* [*dhātu*] and employed in praise of gods.

299. *Nanda* (iii) has *ālāpa* composed in *udgrāha* and employed in (situations of) prosperity. *Kambuja* (iv) is [of *rāsaka* variety] wherein *ālāpa* is at the beginning of *dhruva* and occurs in *karuṇa*[*rasa*].

vii. *Three Varieties of Ekatālī*

300. *Ekatālī* [*gīta*] is [sung] in *ekatālī-tāla;* it is opined to be of three kinds, viz. *rāma, candrikā* and likewise *vipulā;* now their definitions [will be given].

301abc. Wherein *udgrāha* is of the nature of (*gamaka*) *prayoga, dhruva* is of words and *ālāpa, ābhoga* is made with other words, it is *rāmā* (i).

301d-302. *Candrikā* (ii) is that wherein *udgrāha* is in two segments, *dhruva* is [made] with *gamakālāpa, ābhoga* is of other words; it has *yati* (caesura) and alliteration.

303. Wherein *udgrāha* is [structured] with *ālāpa* and words, *dhruva* is [made] of another *ālāpa, ābhoga* is of different words; it is averred to be *vipulā* (iii).

304. *Maṇṭha* and other *prabandhas* have two *aṅgas* [and hence] of *tārāvalī* [class]. They have three *dhātus,* but four *dhātus* when the *antara* is present. [They are] *niryukta.*

TCC 294acd 296b 298a 301bcd 304d
COT 296-299 296c 298-299ab 296c 298-299 303-304 304b

(अन्यसूडक्रमः)

सूडक्रमं वदन्त्यन्ये केचिल्लक्ष्यविशारदाः ।
ध्रुवो मण्ठो रूपकश्च झम्पातालस्ततः परम् ॥ ३०५ ॥
त्रिविडश्चाड्डुतालाख्यस्त्वेकतालीति च क्रमात् ।

६. (V) **प्रसिद्धप्रबन्धाः**

प्रसिद्धाः केचिदन्येऽपि कथ्यन्ते लोकवृत्तितः ॥ ३०६ ॥
चन्द्रप्रकाशः सूर्यादिः प्रकाशो नवरत्नकः ।
वीरशृङ्गारको रुद्रप्रकाशो रणरङ्गकः ॥ ३०७ ॥
दशावतारः शरभलीलाख्यश्चतुरङ्गकः ।
ऋतुप्रकाशः शृङ्गारहारश्चेत्यथ लक्षणम् ॥ ३०८ ॥

i. चन्द्रप्रकाशः

खण्डैः षोडशभिश्चन्द्रप्रकाशश्चन्द्रभूपयोः ।
प्रतिखण्डं कलैकैका वर्णनीया मनीषिभिः ॥ ३०९ ॥
स्वरैः पाटैस्तथा तेनैर्बिरुदैः पदसंयुतैः ।
रागैः षोडशभिस्तालैस्तावद्भिः परिगीयते ॥ ३१० ॥
खण्डेऽन्तिमे भवेन्नाम स्वामिनश्च कवेरिह ।

ii. सूर्यप्रकाशः

खण्डैर्द्वादशभिः सूर्यप्रकाशस्तु निगद्यते ॥ ३११ ॥
चन्द्रप्रकाशवच्छेषं चैत्रमासादिवर्णनात् ।
रागैस्तालैश्च तावद्भिः श्लेषः स्याद् रविभूपयोः ॥ ३१२ ॥

iii. नवरत्नम्

अङ्कब्रह्मरसा(?धरा?)खण्डग्रहरत्नरसैस्तथा ।
रागतालदलैश्चैवं नवभिर्नवभिः क्रमात् ॥ ३१३ ॥

[A Different Sūḍakrama]

305-306ab. Some experts in the practice of music propound a different *sūḍakrama* [which consists] of *dhruva, maṇṭha, rūpaka, jhampā-tāla,* then *triviḍa, aḍḍatāla* and *ekatālī* in [this] order.

6. (V) RENOWNED PRABANDHAS

306cd. A few others which are well established in practice will also be [now] described according to their usage in the world:

307-308. *Candraprakāśa, sūryaprakāśa, navaratna, vīraśṛṅgāra, rudraprakāśa, raṇaraṅga, daśāvatāra, śarabhalīla, caturaṅga, ṛtuprakāśa* and *śṛṅgārahāra.* Now [their] characteristics [will be described].

i. *Candraprakāśa*

309. *Candraprakāśa* [is formed] by sixteen segments; in each segment a quality [lit. part, digit] of the moon and the king should be described by the intelligent [composer].

310-311ab. It is sung with *svaras, pāṭas,* similarly *tenas, birudas,* words, sixteen *rāgas* and as many *tālas.* The names of the patron and composer occur in the final segment.

ii. *Sūryaprakāśa*

311cd-312. *Sūryaprakāśa* is defined by twelve segments; the remaining [characteristics are] as in *candraprakāśa;* [it is sung] by describing (the twelve lunar months) *caitra,* etc. in as many *rāgas* and *tālas* with a *śleṣa* (paronomasia, equivoque) between the sun and the king.

iii. *Navaratna*

313-314. Wherein each of nine segments is composed with all *aṅgas,* in nine *rāgas,* nine tālas and nine segments in order in clusters of nine (*aṅka*), nine (*brahma*), nine

---

TCC 305d 306a 307cd 308b 309c 313a

COT 305cd-306bc 308d 309ab-311ab 309b 310 311cd-312 312bd 313-314 313a

सर्वाङ्गबद्धखण्डानि नव यत्र प्रगीयते ।
नवरत्नं तदाख्यातमन्यच्चन्द्रप्रकाशवत् ॥ ३१४ ॥

iv. वीरशृङ्गारः

सकृद् रागेण गातव्यो वीरशृङ्गारसंज्ञकः ।
सप्तभिः सप्तभिस्तालैर्गीतैश्चापि यदृच्छया ॥ ३१५ ॥
आद्यखण्डः पदैरेव गीयतेऽन्येऽपि खण्डकाः ।
पदैः प्रयोगैर्विविधैः पदालापवितालतः ॥ ३१६ ॥
आद्यखण्डपरार्धस्य धातुकश्चान्यमातुकः ।
तं गीत्वोद्ग्राहके न्यासः प्रतिखण्डं भवेदिति ॥ ३१७ ॥
शृङ्गारवर्णनं चात्र श्लेषः स्याद् वीरकामयोः ।
अन्त्यखण्डः पदैः कार्यो नेत्रादिनामभूषितः ॥ ३१८ ॥

v. रुद्रप्रकाशः

एकादशदलै रागैः षडङ्गैस्तेनकान्ततः ।
पुराणोक्तप्रकारेण रुद्राणां वर्णनं क्रमात् ॥ ३१९ ॥
रुद्रप्रकाशनामा स्याच्छेषश्चन्द्रप्रकाशवत् ।

vi. रणरङ्गः

सकृद् रागः सकृत् खण्डः पाटैः सबिरुदैः पदैः ॥ ३२० ॥
वीरे रौद्रे च रङ्गाख्यताले स्याद् रणरङ्गकः ।

vii. दशावतारः

विष्णोर्दशावताराणां प्रत्येकं यत्र वर्ण्यते ॥ ३२१ ॥
सद्गुणं दशभिः खण्डैः षडङ्गैर्वाञ्छितक्रमैः ।
अन्त्यखण्डपदाभोगो अवतारो दशादिमः ॥ ३२२ ॥

(*rasa*), nine (*khaṇḍa*) < *dharākhaṇḍa?* >, nine (*graha*), nine (*ratna*) and nine (*rasa*) respectively, it is *navaratna* [*prabandha*]; the other [characteristics are] as in *candraprakāśa.*

iv. *Vīraśṛṅgāra*

315. [The *prabandha*] named *vīraśṛṅgāra* should be sung in a single *rāga* but in seven *tālas* and seven *gītas* (? segments?) in an arbitrary manner.

316. The first segment is sung only to words; the other segments are [sung] with words, various *gamaka prayogas,* with *ālāpa* of words without *tāla.*

317. The *dhātu* of the latter half of the first segment should be set to different words. After singing it, conclusion is [made] with *udgrāha.* This is true of every segment.

318. [The song] contains description of *śṛṅgāra,* with paronomasia between the hero (*vīra*) and Manmatha. The final segment should be decorated with the name of the patron etc.

v. *Rudraprakāśa*

319-320ab. [The *prabandha*] named *rudraprakāśa* is composed with eleven segments, [eleven] *rāgas* and all [six] *aṅgas* with *tenakas* at the end, containing the description of [the eleven] Rudras as depicted in the *purāṇas;* the rest is as in *candraprakāśa.*

vi. *Raṇaraṅga*

320cd-321ab. *Raṇaraṅga* occurs [composed] in a single *rāga,* single segment set to *pāṭas, birudas* and words, to a *tāla* named *raṅga* in *vīra* and *raudra [rasas].*

vii. *Daśāvatāra*

321cd-322. *Daśāvatāra* is [the *prabandha*] wherein each of the ten incarnations of *Viṣṇu* as well as His excellent qualities are described in ten segments, set to six *aṅgas* in any arbitrary order, and the *ābhoga* is constituted in (other) words by the final segment.

TCC 316b 317ab 320a 322ad

COT 314a 315-318 319-320ab 319cd 320cd-321ab 321cd-322 322abc

viii. शरभलील:

तालै रागैर्दलैरष्टभि: स्याच्छरभलीलक: ।
सर्वाङ्गक: स्वरान्तश्च स्वनामच्छन्दसाऽथवा ॥ ३२३ ॥
मुक्तकेनापि कथित: शेषं पूर्ववदीरितम् ।

ix. चतुरङ्ग:

चतुरङ्गश्चतु:खण्ड: षडङ्गै रागरञ्जितै: ॥ ३२४ ॥
तेनकान्तै: कृतश्चान्त्यपदै: स्त्रैवर्णनं स्मृतम् ।

x. ऋतुप्रकाश:

पुष्पबाणप्रधानेन वसन्तादिकषड्ऋतून् ॥ ३२५ ॥
षड्रागैश्च दलैरङ्गैर्वीरशृङ्गारवर्णनम् ।
वर्ण्यते च क्रमाद्यत्र स स्यादृतुप्रकाशक: ॥ ३२६ ॥

xi. शृङ्गारहार:

स्वैरैरुद्ग्राहको यत्र पदै: शृङ्गारवर्णित: ।
प्रयोगान्ते ध्रुव: पश्चाद् गातृवस्त्वभिधानत: ॥ ३२७ ॥
वितालकपदालापात् पाटैस्तालयुतोऽन्तर: ।
आभोगो नेतृनामाङ्को न्यास उद्ग्राहके भवेत् ॥ ३२८ ॥
शृङ्गारहारनामा स कथितो लक्ष्यवेदिभि: ।

७ गीतगुणा:

व्यक्तं पूर्णं प्रसन्नं च सुकुमारमलङ्कृतम् ॥ ३२९ ॥
समं सुरक्तं श्लक्ष्णं च विकृष्टं मधुरं तथा ।
एते दशगुणा गीते विद्वद्भि: परिकीर्तिता: ॥ ३३० ॥
तत्र **व्यक्तं** स्फुटतराक्षररागपदस्वरै: (i) ।
पूर्णं पूर्णाङ्गगमकं (ii) **प्रसन्नं** प्रकटार्थकम् (iii) ॥ ३३१ ॥

viii. *Śarabhalīla*

323-324ab. *Śarabhalīla* is [composed] in eight *tālas, rāgas* and segments; it has all [six] *aṅgas*, concludes with *svara*; or it is in namesake metre; or it is composed as *muktaka* [verse]; the rest is as [described] before.

ix. *Caturaṅga*

324cd-325ab. *Caturaṅga* is in four segments, in [all] six *aṅgas*, rendered colourful with *rāga*; it concludes with *tenaka*; the final words are said to contain a description of woman.

x. *Ṛtuprakāśa*

325cd-326. Wherein the [*rasas*], *vīra* and *śṛṅgāra* [or the hero's *śṛṅgāra*] and the six seasons such as spring, etc. are described in order with preponderance of the flower-arrowed [Manmatha] in six segments and in six *rāgas* and (six) *tālas*, it is *ṛtuprakāśa*.

xi. *Śṛṅgārahāra*

327-328ab. In [*śṛṅgārahāra prabandha*], *udgrāha* is [constituted] by *svaras*; *śṛṅgāra* is described in words, *dhruva* follows [*gamaka*] *prayoga*; (*dhruva*?) is marked with the names of the singer [composer] and the *vastu* (i.e. *śṛṅgārahāra prabandha*) in *ālāpa* with words but without *tāla*; *antara* is set to *pāṭas* in *tāla*.

328cd-329ab. *Ābhoga* incorporates the patron's name; conclusion is with *udgrāha*. This is named as *śṛṅgārahāra* by exponents of practical music.

7. MERITS OF SONG

329cd-330. *Vyakta, pūrṇa, prasanna, sukumāra, alaṁkṛtam, sama, surakta, ślakṣṇa, vikṛṣṭa, madhura*—these are declared by the learned to be the ten merits of song.

331. Among them *vyakta* (i) accrues from clarity in syllable, *rāga*, words and *svara*. *Pūrṇa* (ii) is perfection in all limbs and *gamaka*. *Prasanna* (iii) is instantaneous intelligibility.

TCC 323abd 325a 327d 328c 330bc 331b

COT 323-324ab 323b 324a 324cd-325ab 325cd-326a 327-329ab 329ab 329cd-334 331acd

सुकुमारं कण्ठभवं (iv) त्रिस्थानोत्थमङ्कृतम् (v) ।
समवर्णलयस्थानं **समं** (vi) वीणादिशब्दतः ॥ ३३२ ॥
कण्ठध्वन्येकतायुक्तं **सुरक्त**मभिधीयते (vii) ।
नीचोच्चद्रुतमध्यादौ श्लक्ष्णत्वे **श्लक्ष्ण** उच्यते (viii) ॥ ३३३ ॥
उच्चैरुच्चारणादुक्तं **विकृष्टं** (ix) **मधुरं** पुनः ।
लावण्यपूर्णं निर्दोषं सारवज्जनरञ्जकम् (x) ॥ ३३४ ॥

८ गीतदोषाः

दुष्टं लोकेन शास्त्रेण श्रुतिकालविरोधि च ।
पुनरुक्तं कलाबाह्यं गतक्रममपार्थकम् ॥ ३३५ ॥
ग्राम्यं सन्दिग्धमित्येवं दशधा गीतदुष्टता ।
पददोषा वाक्यदोषा दोषाश्च रसभावयोः ॥ ३३६ ॥
काव्यालङ्कारदोषाश्च ते सर्वे गीतमाश्रिताः ।

९ वाग्गेयकारः

उच्यते वचनं मातुर्गेयं धातुरिति स्मृतम् ॥ ३३७ ॥
एतद् द्वयं च कुरुते स वै वाग्गेयकारकः ।
शब्दाभिधानालङ्कारच्छन्दोवृत्तिसुरीतिता ॥ ३३८ ॥
रसभावकलाताललयकाकुविवेकता ।
अशेषभाषाप्रतिभा देशीरागप्रवीणता ॥ ३३९ ॥
नानागीतविनिर्माणं प्रबन्धाङ्गप्रगल्भता ।
त्रिस्थानगमकप्रौढिर्विविधालप्तिनैपुणम् ॥ ३४० ॥
अनुच्छिष्टोक्तिता धातुनूतनत्वं सुविज्ञता ॥
रागद्वेषपरित्यागः सुशारीरः सभाजयः ॥ ३४१ ॥

332. *Sukumāra* (iv) is born of a tender (soft) voice. *Alaṁkṛtam* (v) is ranging in [all] three registers. *Sama* (vi) is evenness (in the distribution) of *varṇa(-alaṁkāra)*, tempo and register.

333. Oneness of the voice with the sounds of *vīṇā,* etc. is named *surakta* (vii). Smoothness (in movement) in low and high pitch, fast, middle, etc. (tempi) is said to be *ślakṣṇa* (viii).

334ab. *Vikṛṣṭa* (ix) is utterance in high pitch. Again, *madhura* (x) is full of grace, faultless, pithy and appealing to people.

8. FAULTS OF SONG

335-336ab. Faulty in practical usage and in theory, inconsistency with *śruti* (Vedic authority) and with (one's own) times, reiteration, exceeding the scope of the art (of music and literature), disorder, wrong meaning, vulgarity, ambiguity— these are ten faults of song.

336cd-337ab. Faultiness of word, faultiness of sentence, faultiness in *rasa* and *bhāva*— these [and other defects] in poetry and figures of speech—all these abide in song (also).

9. COMPOSER

337cd-338ab. Word is called *mātu,* and musical element is declared to be *dhātu.* He who creates both is composer.

338cd. [Qualities of an excellent composer are:] Expertise in grammar, lexicon, figures of speech, prosody, diction, style,

339. discernment in sentiment, effective state, time units (phraseology?), *tāla, laya, kāku* (vocal inflexion), intuitive brilliance in the totality of [all] languages, specialisation in *deśī-rāgas,*

340. capacity to compose different kinds of songs (in fast tempo?), learned in the *aṅgas prabandha,* (vocal) maturity in *gamaka,* in (all) the three registers and skill in various forms of *ālapti,*

341. absence of plagiarism, musical innovativeness, adeptness, avoidance of passion and hatred, excellence of voice, stage presence,

---

TCC 335a 336d 338d 340ab 341a
COT 332acd 334b 335-337 336cd-336 337-343

अवधानं गुणैरेभिर्वरो वाग्गेयकारकः ।
न्यूनमात्वधिकंधातु विदधानस्तु मध्यमः ॥ ३४२ ॥
रम्यमातुविनिर्माताऽप्यधमो मन्दधातुकृत् ।
वरो वस्तुकविर्वर्णकविर्मध्यम उच्यते ॥ ३४३ ॥
कुट्टिकारोऽन्यंधातौ तु मातुकारः प्रकीर्तितः ।

१० प्रकरणसमापनम्

विधिप्रबन्धाकलननादवेदाङ्गवेदिनाम् ।
विट्ठलेन स्वरगतिः सुकरं सुगतिः कृता ॥ ३४४ ॥

इति श्रीकर्णाटजातीय पण्डरीकविट्ठलविरचिते
नर्तननिर्णये गायकप्रकरणं तृतीयम् ॥

342. mental focus (attentiveness)– by these qualities is the composer [reckoned as] excellent. The middling [composer] is deficient in words but excessive in musical element.

343. Composer of (only) charming words but of dull music is inferior. Composer of *vastu* [the matic songs] is excellent; composer of descriptive songs [*varṇaka-prabandhas*] is middling.

344ab. [The composer who] sets words for someone else's *dhātu* is [said to be] *kuṭṭikāra.*

10. CONCLUSION OF CHAPTER

344cdef. For those who [seek to] know the limbs of *nādaveda* for composing *prabandhas* according to rules (of the *śāstra*), a facile pathway in melody has been made by (Paṇḍarīka) Viṭṭhala.

END OF THE THIRD CHAPTER ON SINGER
IN NARTANANIRṆAYA COMPOSED BY PAṆḌARĪKA VIṬṬHALA OF KARNĀṬAJĀTI.

TCC 342c 343bc 344c
COT 342-343

PĀṬHA-VIMARŚA

(Text-Critical Comments)

III: SINGER

1. RĀGĀDHIKARAṆA

Primary sources used for collation of this chapterette (*adhikaraṇa*) are as follows: (Portions available are indicated in brackets).

B (3.1.1 to 3.1.160 ab); C (complete); M (complete); RM (NN 3.1.23cd to the end *minus* 25 ab, 47,117); R (complete); T_1 (3.1.16b to the end); T_2 (3.1.213 to the end); T_3 (3.1.23b to 3.1.85 ab).

Secondary sources used are SS (NN.3.1.34,49-52ab); AV (3.1.168 to the end); AS (3.1.168 to the end) and SR (*inter alia*).

1c. *satālo*: B glosses with '*tālena(sa ha) vartamānaḥ*'.

1d. R: dittography: *gītam yati, sa-yo gāyati sa.*

3a. *sadvitīyo*: B contains gloss: *(dvi)tīyena(sa)ha vartamānaḥ.*

3b. *sa-vṛndo*: B has a gloss: *vṛndenasaha vartamānaḥ;* R-*savṛnda;* R-haplographic lacuna upto '*vṛnda*' **3d.**

3b. *gātṛ*: M-*gāna.*

6a. *rāgalakṣma*: M substitutes lectione facilior: *rāmalakṣmaṇa.*

6d. *vāgge*- M.R.: *vāgo.*

9c. B has an apostil: *krameṇa lakṣaṇānyāha.*

10d. R. MS damnum due to poor impression.

12d. -*nyātāpa*: C.R. *dālāpa.*

16ab. All collative sources are unanimous in 'स्वरोधिको विहीनो वा विरक्तः साव-धानकः' which is opaque. It may be translated only with a farfetched construction, by applying the '*ac*' pratyaya: स्वरो यस्यास्तीति etc. and by interpreting विरक्तः as विशेषण रक्तः rather than रक्तिविहीनः. SR includes '*sāvadhāna*' as a *gāyaka-lakṣaṇa* (3.15) which is explicated by Simhabhūpāla (*Saṅgītasudhākara,* comm. on SR loc. cit. p. 155) as '*śrutiniścayajñaḥ*'. This is appropriate. If this meaning is accepted, the text in question should be conjecturally emended as 'स्वरेऽधिके विहीने वाऽविरक्तः सावधानकः'. This editorial liberty is taken here, though with some reluctance, on the strength of NŚ (33.15 ab) स्वरेऽधिके च हीने च ह्यविरक्तोऽवधानकः basing the *avagraha* on the double negative in '*avirakta*' found in this definition by Bharatamuni.

18b. C dittography from '*stv-avyavasthitaḥ*' to '*gāyet*' (**19a**).

20c. *tāla* is preferred to '*kāla*' (R) because of the definition of '*vitāla*' (**20d**).

23b. *gīyate* : B has gloss: *kathyate.*

23c. *yuṅkte* : B glosses with *'prerayati'* and for *'vivakṣuḥ'* it offfers *'vaktum-icchaḥ' vivakṣuḥ sa cāsau ātmā ca saḥ.*

23d. *analaḥ*: B glosses: *agniḥ.*

24c. *anilam*: ibid. *vāyuḥ;* R reveals haplographic loss of *'prāṇānila'*.

25ab. RM: lacuna; R adds: *dhvani(ḥ) dhvanistu nādaḥ*—as gloss?

26b. *vyavahārataḥ*: B explains: *rāgādi vyavahārataḥ* cf. **30c** *infra.*

26cd-27ab. RM: lacuna.

27b. Dittography in C: *dviguṇaścotarottarottaraḥ.*

27c. *nu*: RM substitutes with '*tu*' through graphic similarity.

28a. *sthānam* is accepted in preference to '*sthāne*' (M) because of collative majority.

28b. *vyavahāre*: C.M. *vyavahāro.*

29b. *sopāna*: R replaces '*na*' with *'ṇa'*.

29d. R dittographic repetition: तारस्तत्तारस्तूत्तरोत्तरम् ।

30a. R dittography: *'-ccatarataratarāḥ'*.

30b. *mātrataḥ*: M-*māttarāḥ.*

30d. *tāsu*: gloss in B-*śrutiṣu.*

31b. *stathā*: B.R. *satastataḥ.*

31b. Marginal addition in B:

मयूरचातकच्छागक्रौ(ञ्च)कोकिलदर्दुराः ।

(ग)जश्च सप्त षड्जादी(न्) क्रमादुच्चारयन्त्यमी ॥

The letters in brackets are lost due to damnum and are conjecturally supplied. Compare with SR. 1.3.46cd-47ab.

33a. *viṁśyā ca:* R *vimśatyā.*

33c. *ṣaḍjādīnām*: B has gloss *svarāṇām.*

34a. *asapāḥ svasvapūrvātaḥ*: B offers exegetical note:

न विद्येते सपौ येषु ते असपाः, स्वराः पूर्वातः

RM, R: *svapūrvapūrvātaḥ;* B: *pūrvasmāt.*

34d. *gaśca*: B glosses: *gāndhāraḥ.*

35d. *ganyoḥ*: B has a gloss: *gāndharaniṣādayoḥ.*

36d. *rāgādiṣva-*: T_1, T_2, RM *rāgādyaira-*; R *rāgādyaistva-.*

38b. *saptake*: R dittographs—*saptasaptake.*

39a. *anuvādīti*: T_1, RM-*anuvādī ca;* RM-*anuvādī tu.*

39a. *paryāyo*: B contains gloss *vādinaḥ pa(ryā)yaḥ*

40b. *-rāntaraḥ*: R- *rantara-.*

40d. i. *gatyā*: C *ganyā;* ii. *vibhāgataḥ;* C *tathānimaiḥ*; R *tathā'nimau.*

41a. *-yau*: gloss in B- *svarau.*

42abcd. RM, T_3 -lacuna.

42d. *nayet*: R *gataḥ*

43b. *itīritaḥ*: T_3 corrupts to *-ratīritīḥ*.

43c. *prayoge*: B adds scholiastic note—'*sati*'.

46c. *nyādyaiḥ*: B adds a gloss '*svaraiḥ*'.

47abcd. M, T_1, T_2, RM-lacuna.

48a. *hatiḥ*: M corrupts to '*iti*' through graphical deterioration.

48b. *lagnajāto*: T_3 *lagnajāte*; simple lipography?

50d. *-māśrite*: C *samsthite*, synonymously.

51c. *-māśritān*: R-*mānsthitān*.

52a. *tamaḥ*: R drops'*ma*'.

52cd-53ab. RM, T_1, T_3 substitute सप्तस्वरारोहावरोहा मूर्छना मता ।

53c. *mūrchyate*: R pluralises to '*murchyante*' and probably construes: *mūrchanā(ḥ) mata(ḥ)*.

54c. *sādīn*:, R corrupts to '*nyāsādīn*'.

56a. *matsarīkṛtā*: R has *matsarīkṛd–*

56c. *munibhiḥ*: MS damnum in C; *uktāni* (are declared). RM '*etāni*' (these are).

57a. *gītopayogataḥ*: C, R have a restrictive variant: '*rāgopayogataḥ*'.

58d. *bhavet*: M *(tānakriyā)tmakāḥ;* M repeats **58cd.**

60a. *kañcit*: R *kramavit* (tr. 'a *krama* being written by an expert in *krama*')

60b. *parād*: B glosses with '*svarāt*'.

61cd. B explains: तस्य तस्य अग्रे गतस्य पूर्वस्वरस्य; तस्य पूर्वस्वरो भवतीत्यर्थः । उत्तरस्वरस्य(अ)धः पूर्वस्वरो भवति । पूर्वस्वरस्य अधः उत्तरस्वरो न भवतीत्यर्थः ।

61c. *śiṣṭān*: B explains with '*svarān*'.

62a. - *sthāṅka*: (decomposes to *sthāṅke*).

62c. i. *antyād*: B glosses with '*aṅkād*'; ii. -'*dho'dho*: second syllable added in bottom margin by scribal diaskeusis.

62d. *kṛtam*: B glosses with '*svaram*'.

63a. *yadaika*: R- *tadaika*

64d. *pūrveṇa*: B glosses with '*aṅkena*'.

66a. i. *śeṣān*: B glosses with '*aṅkān*'; ii. *prāk prāk.*: R has lacuna for one syllable.

66c. *yenāhatiḥ*: B has the gloss '*aṅkena hananam*'.

70a. *sthitvā sthitvā*: R *sthitvā so.*

71d. *so'varohītī*: lacuna in R.

74b. '*-ntāhvaya*' to '*madhya-*': R loss due to poor impression in copy.

75d. *stataḥ*: M *smṛtaḥ*

76a. *hasitāḥ*: T_3 has literal inversion '*sahitāḥ*'.

76cd. hypermetry for one syllable.

79c. *binduśiro* is unanimous with all collative sources. Compare with '*mandro* *binduśirā bhavet'* SR. 1.6.8b; R has lacuna for *-stāro rekhāśirāḥ.*

80b. *yathā: tathā* (similarly); RM *punaḥ* (again).

81d. *alaṁkāravido viduḥ.* R *alaṁkāram vidurbudhāḥ.* (Scholars understand it as *alaṁkāra* named *mandramadhya*).

84a. *mūrchanādeḥ:* R *mūrchanādya-*(the beginning *svaras* of the *mūrchanā*).

85a. T_3 breaks off abruptly at the end of this verse-foot.

85d.- *yutam param:* M *pūrvapunam;* R *param param.*

86a. *-mārohe:* RM *mārohet* (let it ascend).

86c. *kala'ntye:* RM *kalānte.*

86d. *-timā" dime.* RM *-yadā"dime*

89a. M has lacuna for '*kramam*'.

90a. *āruhyante:* C, M. *ārohante.*

90d. *cāpya:* M *cātha* !

91a. *pūrvaḥ pūrvaḥ:* R *pūrvapūrvaḥ.*

91b. *adhovartī kriyate:* RM- *adhastācca kriyate* (is rendered below).

93b. *pūrva* omitted in M.

97d. *gītvā:* CR *gatvā* (proceeding)

101cd. C.R reveal lacuna.

101c. *hrāda:* M *krāda,* indicating probable amanuensal origin of this part of the MS.

106c. *tasya* explained in B as '*gamakasya*'.

107a. *āndolitavali:* R lacuna for '*tavali*'

111a. *kaṇṭha* - parablepsia in R

111d. R reads '*komalo granthilo mataḥ*'.

112b. *humphito* : B *gumphito* (strung together)

112d. *plutamānataḥ:* B explains: '*parimāṇataḥ*'.

113a. *huṁkāra:* RM-*huṁkāro;* compare with '*gambhīro*' (deep), SR. 3.95, p.169.

113b. *bhavet:* RM-*tastathā.*

116a. *ceti:* RM-*veti*

116d. Compare with '*prayatnād bhajanam matam*', SR. 3.128, p. 176.

118a. *parigrāhyaḥ:* R-*pratigrāhyaḥ* (should be received, accepted).

118b. *puṣṭataḥ:* M- *ceṣṭitaḥ* (made sweet).

118d. *khāḍgala:* RM- *khāṅgala,* but *khāhula* in parallel texts (e.g. SR. 3.39, p.129).

119a. *bombaka:* M *combaka*!

121b. *sannipātajaḥ:* B, R *sannipātikaḥ.*

122c. *nārāṭa:* R *-nārahāṭa.*

122d. *-madhamaḥ:* M-*nām madhyamaḥ* (middling among sounds!)

125b. *svarāśrayasaṁśrayā:* RM *saṁśrayāt;* cf. *svarāntara* SR. 3.121, p. 175.

126b. *tu:* T_1, R *ca*

126d. *-rāśrayā:* RM-*rāśrayāt*

128c. *-kotthā'sau*: cf. *yantrotthā*, SR. 3.125, p. 176.

130d. Repeated dittographically in R; *-vauḍuva*. The final *'va'* added in top margin during scribal diaskeusis.

131a. Repeated in T_1.

132c. *ālapti*: elision of '*p*' in R.

132d. *rāgavastu*: M- *rāgarūpa*. Cf. SR. 3.190ab, p. 188: सा द्विधा गदिता रागरूपकाभ्यां विशेषणात् ।

Thus *'rāgarūpa'* is a better reading; for, *prabandha, vastu* and *rūpaka* are synonyms of *nibaddha prabandha:* SR. 4.6cd.

संज्ञात्रयं निबद्धस्य प्रबन्धो वस्तु रूपकम् ।

133a. *yā*: R-*yo*! B has a gloss: *ālaptiḥ*.

133c. *rāga(ḥ)svare*: RM *rāgasvaraiḥ*.

136d-137a. T_1 shows lacuna.

143c. *anyathā*: B contains a graphical corruption-] *atyartha'*.

144c. *stokaiḥ stokaiḥ*: B, SR (3.196, p. 194) *-stokastokaiḥ*.

145a. *Jīvasvara* is glossed as *aṁśasvara* in B.

146d. is repeated in R but ends in '*bhedācca'*.

147ab. M shows lacuna; B has *auḍava* for *auḍuva,* always.

148c. *sālaga*: R *sālaṅga*.

148d. *punaḥ*: B *matāḥ* (are opined).

149d. *saṁjñakāḥ*: R *saṁjñikāḥ*.

151b. The two hemistitchs **158cd-159ab** are interpolated here.

151c. *hindola*: C, R *hiṇḍola,* occasionally.

152b. *naṭa-*: T_1 *naṭṭa-*, always.

154b. B explains: ईशानवदनात् पञ्चममुखादुद्भवः ।

154d. *mukhajastataḥ*: R *mukhatastataḥ* (then, from the face of-)

155a. *eteṣām*: B contains a gloss *śuddhabhairavādīnām*.

156b. *subhruvaḥ*: B glosses: *striyaḥ*.

157c. *varālī*: M substitutes *'varāṭī',* always.

157d. *toḍī*: M *toḍikā*.

158cd-159ab are interpolated between **151b** and **151c.**

160b. B breaks off abruptly here and is available again only from NN 3.2.1.

162b. *śrīrāgasya hi yoṣitāḥ*: R, T_1 *rāge hi samāśritāḥ*; C *rāgā samāśritāḥ*.

163a. *Karṇāta* is always *karnāṭa* in T_3.

164a. *Aherī* is unanimously described as *ābhīrī* (*infra, śl.*217)

164b. *śuddhanāṭavara*: M *śuddhanāṭasya ca*

164d. *tataḥ*: R *tathā*.

166b. M-*naṭanārāyaṇasya,* involving hypermetry for 1 syllable.

166c. i. *gauṇḍa*: C, T_1-*goṇḍa;* ii. *kedāra:* T_3- *kedārāḥ; śaṅkarābharaṇa-*

167c. *Jñāyatām* is vulgate reading, but is a solecism: *jānantu?*

168a. i. *ganiḥ*: T_1-*jani ;,* RM, AV-*gani-;* ii. *satri*: M -*śani*!

168c. *śṛṅgam*: M-*śuṅgam*; R-*śṛṅgim.*

168d. i. *prabhāte* (at dawn): R *prabhāve* (at birth); ii. *vṛṣapo:* R *vṛṣabho*!

169a. i. *bhuṣaṇāḍhyā*: R-*ṇādyā;* ii. *ri ga:* R drops *ga.*

169c. *yuktā* (possessed of): C. *muktā (*dropped tear); lacuna in R from -*vala* to *nāmnā* (for thirteen syllables).

169d. Lacuna in R from *paśyantī* to *dhanyadha-* (for seventeen syllables)

170b. *śveta*: C-*ścitra* (wonderful, variegated)

170c. *bhāle*: M *mālā* (garland); T_1-*phāle* (synonym for *bhāle*), always.

171a. *vaktrā*: R *vakrā* (curved)! through lipographical loss.

171b. i. *padma*: R omits '*pa*'; ii. *vipulasu-:;* R omits '*pu*'; AV, AS -*vilasita.*

172b. *bahuvidha*: AV, AS-*vilasita*; -*rbhūṣita snigdhanetrā;* R -*mābhūṣaṇairbhūṣitā sā.*

172c. *nayanā*: R. *nayanī.*

172d. *nṛpatigaṇān*: C *nṛpatim.*

173a. *mani*: R *gani.*

175b. *kanaka*: R omits '*naka*'.

175c. *mallī*: RM *maitrī*

175d. *dina*: R repeats '*di*'. M has lacuna for thirteen syllables from '*prati*' to '*nām*'.

176a. M has lacuna for seven syllables from '*śyamam*' to '*hastam*'.

176b. i. *cārim*: RM-*trārim*; ii. *vastram*: R drops '*va*'.

176c. i. *samukuṭam*: R omits '*su*'; ii. *bhālam*: T_1 *lolam.*

176d. i. -*hātra nāke*: M *pratāke*; ii. *suravarāḥ:* M *sukhakarī;* R has lacuna from '*ke*' to end of **178d.**

177d. Omitted in M.

179a. *gatiganī*: M *matigatī.*

179b. i. *vāsā*: R-*vāsī*!; ii. *dola*: RM *ḍola,* always.

179c. *muktā*: lacuna in AV; *mahā:* AV-*mahān;* AV adds '*manasvī*' at end.

180a. i. *niga*: AV *nima*; ii. *mādi:* AS *gādi.*

180c. *varatara*: AV *taruvara*! (literal inversion).

180d. i. *yāti*: M *pāti* (by graphic similarity); ii. *sa:* M *yāḥ*; RM-'*sa*'.

181a. *cāli*: M *loli.*

181d. i. *tvanala*: RM *hyanala*; R omits '*tva*'; ii. *nimā:* C *ganī;* M *nibha* (by graphic deterioration).

182a. *karatale*: R *kale.*

182b. i. *liptāṅgā*: R *liptāṅgam;* ii. *suśabara:* R *sutaśita*; AS *susita*; M *subhavara.*

182c. *mukta*: M *bhukta* through graphic deterioration.

183a. *rahitā*: R *haritā* (literal inversion)

183d. *purā*: RM *dhurā*!

185c. *ratipati*: AS-*nṛpati*.

185d. *rava*: R *svara*; *vādyarava*: AS *vādasasvara*.

186a. *matrika*: RM *satrika*; *rato:* AV, AS *yutaḥ*.

187b. *Tara* omitted in C, M.

187c. *racitatilakaḥ*: R omits '*-tati*'.

188a. *rūpa*: R adds *pratāpī, triṣaḍjaḥ*.

188b. i. *pamāṅghriḥ*: omitted in R; AV, AS *padmābhaḥ;* ii. *dadhānaḥ:* C *dadhatte*.

188c. *kaṇṭhamālām*: C *komalāṅga*.

188d. *gamaka*: repeated in R.

189a. i. *dhṛta*: M *'dhana'* by graphic deterioration; ii. *kumuda*: RM *mukuṭa*.

190b. *gaja*: omitted in R.

190c. i. *muktaika*: R *ratnaika*; ii. *khaḍgo*: R *khaṅgo*.

191b. *kūrpāsam*: M-*kāryāsam* by graphic deterioration.

191c. *giram udgārayanta vidagdhā*: M *galam nīlam vastram dadhānā*: RM *giram cāraṭantī*; AS *giram cālapantī*.

192a. i. *hṛṣṭā*: C, R *-tṛṣṭā;* AV, AS-*jāta*; ii. *rahitā*: R-*haritā* (by literal in version).

192b. *vilulita*: T_1, C, R *viluṭhita*.

193a. *mālām*: R, RM *mālām*.

193b. *kūrpāsam*: M *kuryāt*.

193c. i. *āhaṅga*: M *prāhaṅga;* ii. *sukara*: C *mukura*; iii. *samdadhānā*: R omits '*sam*'.

193d. *rirapā*: M *raripā* (inversion of vowels); R-lacuna.

194a. i. *śrīlavaṅgam*: R-*strī*-! ii. *kuṇḍali:* R *kumbhika*.

195c. i. *-gauraḥ-:* RM *rakta*; ii. *dvivasu*: RM-omits '*su*'.

196a. *deśīmele prajātaḥ*: C R *jātastātasya mele*.

196c. i. *mugdhastrī*: M *muktaśrī;* ii. *satsamakṣe:* RM *śyamalākṣo*! iii. *hasati*: R omits '*sati*'.

197a. *śabara*. AV-*śabala*!

197c. *prathama-maḥ*: RM-*prathama-dhaḥ;* AS-*prathamataḥ*.

197d. *vinayatām*: T_1-*vinayitām*.

199d. *paṇyavīthyām*: RM-*paṇyavīcyām*!

200c. i. *chatra*: M-*kṣatra;* ii. *camara*: RM-*caraṇa*.

200d. i. *yammanādyaḥ*: R omits '*ya*'. ii. *sahito*: R-*hisato* (literal inversion).

201c. i. *dhaivatonaḥ:* R, AV, AS-*adhaivato'gaḥ* but '*dhaivatonas-tv-avagamanayutaḥ*' is preferred; cf. description of *śrīrāga* by Paṇḍarīka Viṭṭhala in *Sadrāgacandrodaya*, 2.2.25; *avagamana*: AS, AV omit '*va*'. ii. *gauro*: R-*gauri*.

202a. i. *jātā*: RM-*jāyā*; ii. *rahitā:* R-*haritā* (by literal inversion); iii. *satridhā*: RM-*satrika*; iv. *ṣoḍaśāḍhyā*: RM-*ṣoḍaśabdā*.

202b. *sukeśī* (with excellent hair): C *suśīlā* (of good character).

202c. i. *caitrī mutānī*: M-*caitrīsul;* M-*caitrāmul-*; RM-*caitrīmudrā*; ii. *karpaṭibhiśca:* RM-*bhikṣa*.

203b. i. *hantrī*: M *hartrī;* ii. *nṛtyābhiyuktā:* RM, R-*bhisaktā*.

203d. *hṛdayānandinī*: RM *hṛdayanandinī.*

204a. *nyādi*: RM *sādi.*

204b. *sitavara*: AS *varasita* (by inversion).

205a. *guṇavidhu*: M-*vidhuguṇa; ganigā;* R-*nigagā*; the *lakṣaṇa* is either *'guṇavidhu gani'* or *'vidhuguṇa niga'* because it and its neighbours are derivatives of *mālavagauḍa.*

205b. *jalaja*: RM omits final '*ja*'. M repeats **204cd** after **205b.**

205c. i. -*madhyeṣad*: RM-*madhye sad;* ii. *nayanī:* R-*nayanā.*

205d. -*'sau*: RM-*sā.*

206a. *raktā*: RM *yuktā.*

206d. *prayantīyam* (RM) is prefered to the solecistic *prekṣatīyam*?

207b. *sakaṭaka*: (with bangle): RM-*sukaṭaka* (good bangle).

207c. *sa ṭakko*: RM-*suṭaṅko*

207d. *vicarati*: RM-*vicarita*

208c. *rasapatī*: C, M-*rasayati* (flavours, tr. verb).

209a. i. *rahito*: R *harito* (literal inversion); ii. *prajāto* RM-*sujāto*; iii. *madhyānta:* RM-*madhyādi* (actually *ni-trika*, i.e. *ni* is *graha, aṁśa* and *nyāsa*).

209d. *prakaṭita*: (expressed) RM *prakaṭate* (expresses).

210a. i. *sahito*: RM *rahito* (!); ii. *'paḥ:* C, M *yaḥ* by graphic similarity.

210b. *jala*: omitted in R

211c. *keyūra kaṇṭheya*: RM-*ke puṣpa-keyura.*

211d. *kausumbhy-uṣṇīśa*: C, M-*kausumbhoṣṇīśa.*

212a. i. *īśānāsya*: M-*īśānasya*; ii. *ganiridhaḥ:* R omits *gani.*

212b. T_2 commences.

213d. i. *cakrīkṣepāvakarṣaiḥ*: R *cakrīkṣepā ca karṣaiḥ*; *cakrī*- AV, AS *vakra*; ii. *bhrāmyati*: RM-*dhāmyati;* T_1-*śāmyati*; T_2-*vāmyati*!

214d. *prekṣate* MR *prekṣatī;* M-*prakṣati.*

215a. *mukulakucā*: R shows lacuna by haplography.

215d. *devakanyā*: T_1,T_2-*rājakanyā* (princess).

216a. *tanu-racitā*: R *racita tanuḥ* (lexical inversion).

216c. *bhrū*: RM-*bhū*-!

216d. i. *geham*: RM-*gehe*; ii. *vara* omitted in R; AS gives *kila* vice *vara.*

217a. *susnigdha*: RM-*tu snigdha.*

217d. *rasapati*: T_2-*ramayati* (fondles) (by graphic deterioration?)

218a. *vidhugati*: T_2,T_3-*ramayati*!

218c. *samuralī*: RM-*sumuralī.*

220b. *pūrvī*: R-*pūrya*-

221b. i. *saratnaḥ*: T_2-*saralaḥ* (straight, simple); ii. *vasanaḥ*: RM-*vacanaḥ*; this reading would be plausible only with '*smita*' vice '*sita*' and *ruciḥ* meaning taste, instead of hue, lustre.

222b. *yauvanāḍhyāḥ.* T_1,T_2-*nāḍhyā*!

223a. *mugdhaśtrī*: R-*mugdhaḥ;* accepted reading means that *naṭanārāyaṇa* is in the company of innocent women; the reading of R means that he is innocent and is in the company of women.

223b. i. *śikhi*: RM-*śikhina*! ii. *naṭi:* RM-*naṭī*; iii. *nartako*: M-*nartakī* (by graphic similarity).

223d. i. *sadā.* M inverts to '*dasā*'; ii. *'yam:* AV, AS-*'sau.*

224a. Lacuna in C for *-rajam vādyamānā.*

224c. *-yoṣas*: AS-*hyuṣasi*

224d. *kurāyi*: RM-*kurāī;* AS-*kuḍāyī.*

225a. *satrikāḍhyā'nimā*: M-*chā'nivā;* T_2-*satridyutimā vā*! R-*satrikādyā.*

225c. *bhālā*: M-*mālā* (garland); T_2 omits *bhuṣaṇaiḥ* but adds *bhūṣitāṅgī varāṅgī.*

226b. *bhālā:* M-*mālā.*

227a. Lacuna for *mṛgā* in R.

227c. i. *vaktreṣad-vāsa*, M-*ṣaḍ-vāsa;* ii. *daśarasa:* M inverts to *daśasara.*

227d. *tu suhavī*: AV-*susuhavī.*

228a. i. *raktā*: M-*yuktā*; ii. *svara:* R-*svarasva*!

228b. *taṭe*: M-*tale* (synonymous in this context)

228d. *yātī*: AV, AS-*bhāti* (shines, is radiant)

229b. *madana*: C. *vadana* (face)

229c. *śikhigaṇān*: RM-*śikhariṇān*

229d. i. *bārāmī*: M-*vārāmī;* RM-*dhārāmī;* ii. *malaharo:* M-*malaharī.*

230a. *yuto*: M-*pluto*

230c. *barhiṇām*: R-*barhiṇo*

230d. i. *rājate*: R-*rāje*; ii. *goṇḍa:* M-*gauṇḍa.*

231c. *datta*: RM-*tyakta*; *japamanāveṣṭitaḥ* R.-*mano-*

231d. i. *'ripo*: C-*'ridho*; ii. *'sti trividha ni:* RM-*strividha niḥ*

232a. *jalaja*: R omits '*laja*'.

232b. i. *yakṣa*: AV, AS-*padma*; ii. *puṇḍrah:* RM-*mudraḥ*

232c. *nṛtyārambhapriyo mudrita sugamaka*: AV- *nṛtyārambhe priyo'sau muditagamaka* (this beloved moves with delight at the beginning of the dance).

232d. *pracarati*: C *pracarita.*

233b. i. *puṣpeṣu*: C *puṣpeśa;* ii. *virahi*: C-*virati* (pause)! iii. *dhanvī.* RM-*dhanvā.*

233c. *mallī*: RM-*madhye*

233d. *janirupa*: M-*janirati-*; R, RM add '*syāt*' at end; the text of this line is confused in RM.

PĀṬHA-VIMARŚA
(Text-Critical Comments)

III: SINGER

2. PRABANDHĀDHIKARAṆA

Primary sources used for collation of this chapterette (*adhikaraṇa*) are as follows: (Their contributions are indicated in brackets).

B (complete); C (complete); M (complete); R (complete); T_1 (complete); T_2 (up to 3.2.84).

Secondary sources employed are SS (3.2.281-285, 288-290, 292cd, 294ab) and SR (*inter alia*).

2c. *-masambaddha-mabandha-C, L* - hypermetry of 1 syllable

3d. *tasya:* B contains gloss: *prabandhasya*

4c. *gīta*: M, R *gati* (vowel transposition)

5b. *melanāt*: B has gloss: (*sambandha*) *tvāt*·

5c. *dhruva*: M omits '*va*'

7a. *sa*: B glosses: *antarābhidha dhātuḥ*

7d. - *śca dvidhā ta-* T_1 lacuna

8d. *biruda*: T_1 *viruda*, always

9a. *pade*: C *padau*

9d. *birude*: C *birudau*

10a. i. *tat*: B glosses with '*tasya prabandhasya*'; ii. *pādam* ibid. *caraṇau*

11a. *dyotakam*: M lacuna from '*kam*' to '*dhaṭo vṛttam*', **46c**.

11b. *-'rodbhavaḥ*: CR '*rotkaraḥ*'

11d. '*Caccatpuṭa*': is probably a prakṛtised form of '*cañcatpuṭa*', which is etymologically correct. Both forms are used in textual tradition.

12d. *stu*: R-*śca*

13b. *dīpanī*: B, R *dīpinī*, always

13c. *bhāvanī*: B, R *bhavinī*, always

13d. *dvābhyām*: B glosses: *aṅgābhyām*

14d. *niyamād*: R *niyamān-na*!

16a. *mas-trigo*: B glosses: *trayaḥ gāḥ yasmin*

16b. i. *lādyo*: B glosses: *la ādir-yasya;* ii. *kajaḥ* C, M, T_1 T_2, R *rajaḥ:* B glosses: *kāj jalāt-jātaḥ*

16c. *ro*: C, M, T , T_2, R-*ṭho*

16d. *so*: T_1 *mo*

17a. '*dhanakṛc-chūnyo*' C, R *ambarajaḥ;* T_1- *cchaunyo*

17d. *śaṅkaras-trilaḥ*: R *saṅkara;* B explains: *trayaḥ laḥ yasmin*

20c. i. *rāti T_1 T_2-rīti;* ii. *vijñeyau B vijñeyā*

21a. *yoge*: R-*joge*

22b. *bhṛtya-mitrayoḥ T_2 mitra-bhṛtyayoḥ* (transposition of words)

22cd. Lacuna in C, M, T_1, T_2, T_3

22ef. This enumeration is adopted to accommodate 22cd and to correspond to the Kannaḍa edition (*Puṇḍarīkamālā*) of NN.

22d. *syān-niṣphalam T_2 ca niḥphalam*

22f. *śatru*: R *tvari*

23d. *kṣayaḥ* R,T_2 *kṣayam*

24ab. found only in T_2

24b. *bhṛtyaorgṛha* (BR), but C, M, *bhṛtyayorgṛha*!

26b. *'ṣṭau*: R-*chau*

26c. *ratiga*: C *ragati* (transposition of syllables)

26d. *bāṇagaṇāḥ* T_1 T_2 lacuna

27d.B has an explanation:

अ	क	च	ट	त	प	य	श
9	5	5	5	5	5	4	4

28ab. M, T_1, T_2-*nava pañceṣu pañca*; M-*pañcavedāgni*!

29c. *varṇānām*: R-*vargāṇām*; this is a better reading in the context of what precedes and follows immediately; the fruits accruing from using these eight classes are as follows: *a-āyuḥ* (longevity); *ka-tejaḥ* (brightness, brilliance), *ca-apakīrtī* (? *prakīrtita*? illfame ? fame?) *ṭa-saubhāgya* (auspiciousness or wealth), *ta-sundaram* (physical beauty), *pa-vyādhi* (disease), *ya-maraṇa* (death), *śa-śūnyatā* (void); but *varṇānām* is suitable in view of the topic.

29d. *'pa*: R *pra-*

30c. *hajhaghaḍhadharaṣabhāḥ*: C-*hajadyahṛna*? T_1-*ghaḍa-*; B has on right margin (f.18): *ghadhara janaśa javachamabha haṭhama maḍaya* (?) with the legend *'varja(nīyāḥ)'*

30d. *varṇā*: B; *varṇo*

31a. i. *cit*: B-*ca;* ii. *gītā*: B-*rītya*

31b. *na prayojyā*: B dittography

32c. *ma-kāraḥ*: R *bha-ma-kāraḥ*

33d. *dhuri*: T_2 *bhūri* (tr. copious splendour)

34a. *su*(good): B. *tu* (expletive particle)

34b. *grāmo*: C *gāmo*, T_2-*rāmo*

35d. *ṇa-kārād ratnam-uttamam*: M *ca ṇād ratnarucir-ānane*

36c. *bhāratī*: C *tārutī* by graphic loss

37a. *mṛti*: T_1 lacuna

37c. *chatri*: B *kṣatri*

39a. *kṣakarā*: B *kṣapārā-*; R *kṣaya;-* C *kṣapra*; by graphic ambiguity

39c. *pāne*: C *pāte* by graphic ambiguity

40c. *yatra*: C *pyatra*

41c. *haṭa*: C *haṭha*: wrong lectio simplior replacing correct lectio difficilior.

43c. *ḍheṅkī*: C *ṭeṅkī*, always

43d. *jhomba*: T_2- *dgomba* !

44c.- *svaro* : C, R *saro-*; this reading is possibly deliberate and not the product of transmissional elision; in vernacular literature, esp. Kannaḍa, this *prabandha* is consistently mentioned as *varṇasara* by poets over the centuries.

46a. *dvipatha*: R lacuna

46c. *vṛttam*: M lacuna ends.

47a. i. *-śvara*: M-*svara*, by phonetic deterioration; ii. *stālārṇava*: M *tālāvarṇa* (transposition/inversion of words)

47b. i. *ityāli*: lectio difficilior replaced with wrong lectio simplicior '*ityādi*' in T_1; ii. *saṁjñakā*; M-*saṁjñayā*

49d. *haṁsalīlo*: R omits but adds '*parikīrtitaḥ*' at end.

50a. i. *jhampaṭaḥ*: M-*ḍampaṭah*, always (by initial graphic loss), C-*krampaṭah;* ii. *syāt* R *sasyāt*

50d. *śrīvardhano*: R omits '*-rdha*'

51a. *vadanam*: T_1 *candanam*!

51b. *paddhaḍī*: R *ghaddhaḍī*!

52a. *ḍhollarī*: C *ṭhollari* (by phonetic deterioration in amanuensal transmission); T_2- *ḍhodṛtra;* T_1-*ḍhojhallarī* (lectio simplior)

52d. *salagāstu*: T_1 *sālagastu* (collective usage)

54a. *tatrailā*: M *tatraikā* by graphic gain.

54a. *varṇasāmyam*: B glosses: *anuprāsam*

54d. *mātu*: M corrected (wrongly) to *dhātū;* T_1-*mātra*!

55d. *tacca*: M *yacca*

56a. i. *tatra*: B explains '*pallave*'; ii. *ādya*: B explains *dve pade.*

56b. *tṛtīyam*: B has a gloss: *padam*

56c. *tulya*: M *tulyam*

56d. i. *geyam*: T_2 *bhayam*! ii. *dhātu for pāda* in B

58b. B.M, T_2 loss by homoeoteleuta

59cd. R dittography for **58 ab** after **59cd**

61a. *vidhāyāsya*: T_1 lacuna

63d. i. *suśobhī*: R omits; ii-*kocitaḥ* preferred (SR 4.43) to *-korutaḥ* derived by collative consensus.

64cd. -*mā* ... *nā*... ten syllables lost in M

65b. *dīptaḥ*: M *dīptīḥ*

66b. *Daśa* omitted in R, T_1 but R adds '*vacaḥ*' at end. *savarṇa*; M

66c. *nirvarṇa*:

67c. -*stānī*-: R -*tānī*-

69d. *pūrvapūrvapadāntimāḥ-*: T_2 omits first *pūrva;* B glosses *antīmāḥ* as *agrimāḥ*

70b. *-vottaro:* B *cottaro*; R omits *-ttaro*

70c. *tattat*: M *tat*; R *bhavet*

71a. *pragīyante*: B, T, M *pragīyate*; CR *pragīyete*

71c. *tāna*: C *tāla*

72b. *svarādīnām*: C *svarāṇām ca*

72c. *samāsatāna*: B synonymises with *saṅkocatāna*

73c. *prayoktuś-ca*: M-*prayogaś-ca*

74c. *gaṇavarṇamātrā*: transposition of words*: varṇagaṇa*-B*; gaṇamātrāvarṇa* M, T_2.

75b. i. *na* omitted in T_1, T_2; ii. *pradarśita*; B *prakīrtita.*

77b. *-ṅgamiśritaḥ*: C-*ṅgāni śritaḥ*

77c. *yasya*: B has a gloss: *yasya prabandhasya*

77d. *netṛ* : M *netra* always

80a. *tat*: C, T_2, *tattat*

80d. i. *pāṭaih: C-pādaiḥ*; ii. *padaiḥ* T_2-*pādaiḥ*

81bc. T_2 lacuna; i. M-*sammataḥ;* ii. *yatra* C, R *cātra*

82a. *druvastadā*: M *dhruvapado*

84a. *paścāt*: M *yaśca*

85c. *tu*: T_2-*nu* by graphic similarity

86c. *-mucca-*: T_1 omits.

88b. *-valyādikā*: T_1-*valyakābhidāḥ*

91b. *rāsakād*: R has only *'ke'*

93a. *jñeyā*: addition by propria manu at top of folio during diaskeusis

94a. *tridhātu*: C *dvidhātu*

95c. *-gāḍhyo*: T_1 *gādyo*

96a. *dhruvamābho*: T_1 *dhruvābho*

97b. *prati*: lacuna in T_1

98b. *sāmānya*: M, T_2 *sāmānyam*

98d. *granthasya*: omits *'tha'*

99d. *dvyaṅgāt*: R *dvyaṅgās*

102ab. Hypermetry of one syllable is avoided if *'pi'* is omitted, as is done in B; M, T_1, T_2 read *tālādīnām aniyamān-niryukto 'pi'*; this is a contradiction in terms; for, it cannot be a *niryukta* when there is *niyama* relating to *tāla* etc. So *'tālādīnām aniyamād aniryukto bhaved-asau'* is preferred.

102c. *gatam*: M omits *'ga'*

102d. *sthānake*: cf. (SR 4.125d): *sthānkair*

103a. *rāsa*: C *rāma* by graphic loss

103d. *-vale*: T_2 *-valī-*

104a. *dvir-udgrāhād*: B omits final *d*; M-*ho*; T_1 omits first three syllables.

106d. *niryukto*: M omits *r*, B *niryuktā*
107ab. *dhruvakau...baddhau*: M *dhruvako-baddhaḥ*
108b. i. *tryaṅgaḥ*: B *dvyaṅgaḥ*, T_1 *dvyantaḥ*! ii. *dhātu*: R omits
108cd. NN borrows Kallinātha's quotation (p. 269 on SR. 4.181cd-182ab)
108cd-109ab. cf. NN **3.2.261cd-262ab;** SR. 4.310
110a. *varṇa*: M, T_2-*varṇaḥ*
110b. *tālataḥ*: B *lābhataḥ*
111c. *ekena*: B contains gloss: *aṅgena*
112d. *bandha*: T_1 *bandhana*
114ab. *vīre... śrita*: M *vāre gaurī ... śriyā*
115cd. *śānte sapadyam bhāratyām pāñcālyām*: T_2 *sapadṛte sāram pāñ;* T_1 omits first syllable in *pāñcālyām*
116d. *citram*: M lacuna
117b. -*citrayā*: C *citritā*
118b. *vṛttagandhibhiḥ*: B explains: *gadyaiḥ*
118c. *drutā*: B contains a gloss: (-)*yagatā*(-) *druteti*
118d. *bahvalpa*: T_1 *bahulya*
121b. i. -*mante*: M *mete*, ii. *tarā*: R lacuna
122a. i. -*ekatra*: B glosses: *ekasmin khaṇḍe*, ii. *vastu*: B synonymises: *prabandha*
122c. -*gāḍhyo*: T_1-*gādyo*
123b. *vilambena*: B explains: *vilambitalayasahitena*
123c. *drutam*: BR *drutān*
125a. *pāṭaiḥ*: T_2-*pādaiḥ*
125b. -*kadhruvau*: M-*ke bhavet;* M lacuna ending with -*mudgrāha*, **125d.**
125cd. Hypermetry for one syllable; avoidable with '*nyasanam-udgrāhe bhavet*' or '*nyāsam udgrāhake bhavet*'
126c. *vīra*: T_2 omits '*ra*'
127a. *padaiḥ*: T_2 *pādaiḥ*
127cd. T_2 lacuna
128c. *gītau*: M omits '*tau*'
129b. *padāntaraiḥ*: R *padānvitaḥ*
129c. *pāṭake*: B has '*dhruve*' at top of folio margin; R *pāṭakenaiva*
129d. *kandaḥ*: R omits.
131d. *bandhāt tu*: C *bandhā tu.*
132a. *vāśva*: (*aśvalalita chandas*) M *vāśca* (!*lalita candas*?)
132c. *tāla*: M omits.
132d. *satālakau*: M *snātakau*!
133b. Hypermetry for one syllable, avoidable with '-*rudgrāhabandhāt*'; M-*bandhanaḥ*
136a. -*ścānte ca*: R lacuna

139ab. i *gaṇābhyām ca pābhyām*: M-*bhyo ca pādābhyām* (lectio simplicor); ii. *tālla*: R-*bhālla*; B glosses *pābhyām* as *pagaṇābhyām, tāt* as *tagaṇāt* and *laguto* as *laghuguru-bhyām*

139c. *cha*: R *ca*

141a. Hypometry for one syllable: -*prāgakṣarāṇām vyūho*?

141c. -*rottara*: M lacuna

143a. -*vāṁśa*: T_1-*māṁścā*

145b. *bhāvineyakaḥ*: B *'yam bhavedasau;* T_1 *'yam dvidhātukaḥ*

150a. i. -*tāla*: M, T_1 *kāla*; ii. *padaiḥ* C *padau*

151c. *caramabhāgaḥ*: B explains: *dvitīyabhāgaḥ*

151d. *param*: M *pare*

153b. *pañca*: T_1 *padyam*

153d. -*vatyayam* T_1 *vedayam*

154a. *dodhakena*: B glosses: *dodhaka nāmnā* (*vṛttena*)

158c. *padodgrāhe*: M-*dgrāha;* R-*dgrāho*

160a. *pūrvam*: B glosses with *pūrvārdham*

161a.i. -*dyārdha*: M *dyardha*: C *dyartha*! ii. *yanmātrā* C, R *vanmātrā*

161b. -*mitatenādya*: M, B -*mito yatra*

161c. *pādo*: C *pado*

163a. *vṛttena*: B contains a gloss: *vṛttanāmnā*

164a. *vāpi*: C, R *cāpi*

164b. *svarāṅgam*: T_1 *svarāṅge*

164d. *pūrvā*: M *pūrṇā*

165cd. M lacuna between *kvacit* ... *kvacit*

167b-168d. M lacuna

168c. *ubhayoḥ*: B explains: *divyamānuṣyoḥ*

173a. *prādhānyaiḥ*: R *sāmānyaiḥ,* T_2 *prādhānye nan-*

174a. *etasmād*: B has an explanation: *mukhyam nandyāvartāt*

175a. *pūrva*: C, R lacuna

175cd. *bhāgau sta udgrāha*: C *bhāgāvudgrāha*

176a. *khaṇḍe khaṇḍe*: M *khaṇḍaiḥ khaṇḍaiḥ*

176c. *'pya* T_1*'tha*

176d. *nyādi:* T_1 lacuna

177c. *caccatpuṭeṇa*: M *cañcat; vide* **11d** *supra,* always; B glosses with '*tālena*'

178a. *tam*: M, T_2-*te*

178c. *mānena*: B explains: *parimāṇena*

179a. -*ścatata*: T_1 lacuna

179b. -*puṭena*: T_2 lacuna

179c. -*tvantara*: R -*tpañcama*

180b. *pañcakam*: M *paṅkajam*! (transposition)

180c. *-ccāntara*: C, R *-ttv-antara*
181b. *dala*: B contains '*prabhandha-*' in explanation.
182a. *tato* R. *tatho*
182c. *muraja*: C, R *muruja*
183c. i. *udghaṭṭa*: T_2 *udgrāha*! ii. *teno* T_2 *tenā*, T_1 *tene*
184a. - *ścaturdhātustri-*: M *niyukto sutri*
184d. T_1 ends here.
186a. *-tāṅgaiḥ*: CM *to'ṅgaiḥ*
188a. *-ge tva*: CM. *ga a-*
189b. *pañja*: M *puṅga*
190b. i. *rāgai*: C *rālai*! ii. *svarā-* C *carā*; iii. *rāgaistālaiḥ* R-*stālai rāgai* (transposition)
190c. *pṛthvīvān*: B glosses: *medinīvān*
191d. *smṛtaḥ*: R lacuna
192d. *birudu*: T_1 *biruda*
194d. *rati*: M, R *iti*
195a. *bhāgā*: M *pādā*
195d. *punaḥ*: C *smṛtaḥ*
197c. *nṛpa*: B deciphers the numerogram as *ṣoḍaśa.*
198a. *yamakālaṁkṛtā*: B explains: *yamakena alaṁkareṇa alaṁkṛtā*
199d. *tārāvalīyakaḥ*: C *syādatra dīpanī*
200c. *gaṇāḥ*: M *guṇāḥ*
201d. *svarair*: C *strayair*
202b. *jīvanāda*: B offers explanatory note: *yasmin rā* (-) *yaḥ praban*(-)*raḥ gīyate* (-) *rāga*(*sya*) *aṁśasvaraḥ* (*jīvanādā*) *khyaḥ*
203a. *tatra*: B glosses: *sarvaiścaraṇaiḥ*
203c. *candrāgnīṣu aṅghrayaḥ*: B explains: *prathamatṛtīyapañcamāṅghrayaḥ*
204a. *pāṭau*: M *padau*
204ab. B explains: *dvitīyasya caraṇasyānte svarapāṭau syātām; śarasya-pañcama caraṇasthāne svaratenakau syātām ityarthaḥ* ।
205d. *niryuktaśca*: R *niryukto'sau*
206c. *pāṭaiḥ*: R *pādaiḥ*
209a. *pūrvabhāgābhyām*: B explains: (-) *bhyām* ... MS. damnum
209b. *parābhyām*: B explains: *dalena kābhyām*
213c. *-mārdham*: B-*mārdhe*
215a. *tripadī*: B explains: *trayaḥ pādā yasyā 'sau*
216a. *dhātur-niryukta*: M *dhātuśca niryuktakas-tā-*
216d. *kandukaḥ*: T_1 *kaṇḍukaḥ*
217a. *pada*: B *pāda*, M omits.
218c. *ekaḥ*: B explains: *ekaprakāro'yameva; itaraprakārān-āha-eketī* ।
218d. *tannāmatālataḥ*: B explains: *tribhaiginām atālataḥ* । Hypometry for one syllable: *nānyasty tannāmatālataḥ*?
219c. *brahmā* : M *brahma*

220. R lacuna

221d. *sabirudaiḥ*: B explains: *biruda-sahitaḥ*

223c. *padaiḥ*: T_1- *pādaiḥ; padaiḥ* is preferred so as to accord with parallel treatises.

224d. -*stvayam*: M *svayam*, C *stuyam*

225a. *pāṭaisca*: C, M *padaiśca*

226a. *padaiḥ*: R lacuna

228b. Hypermetry for one syllable.

229cd-230ab. M lacuna

230d. i. *chagaṇa*: M, R *chagaṇā;* ii. *chadataiḥ*-M *chadalaiḥ*

231d. *bhavatyasau*: C *bhavedasau*

232d. *dvau dvau*: B explains: *caraṇau*

233a. *geyā*: B *jñeyā*

233b. *padaiḥ*: B adds the note: *kṛteti śeṣaḥ*

235b. *jagaṇato vinā*: B explains: *jagaṇair-vinā ityarthaḥ*

236b. *tanmātrāmitatālataḥ*: *Dvitīyatāla* is ꟾoo (NN. **1.140ab**); *tālas* of the same quantity are ꟾꟾ and oooo. But B assumes the *tāla* to be *SS* and gives its equivalents: SS IIS ISI SII IIII

239c. - *raiḥ kṛtābhogaḥ*: M -*rekatālo gaḥ*

245c. C. lacuna

247a. *chayugmam*: M *cayugmam*

247d. *ādyaturyayoḥ*: B explains: *caraṇayoḥ*

248b. *pena*: C, M *sena*; *pena* is preferred for reasons given in comm. NN **3.2.247d.**

248c. *prathame* : B glosses: *vikramasya prathame caraṇe*

248d. *sena* : B *pena*, M *yena*

250b. i. *vimalādi* : M *vimalāni*; ii. *padānvitaḥ* C *padānvitāḥ*

251a. *sarvatra*: B explains: (-) *raṇāh bhavanti*

252b. *ciralayeṇa*: B offers the note: *vilambitalayena*

253b. *śriyā*: M,T_1 *śriyām*

253d. Hypermetry for one syllable; -*rudgrāhadhruvau*?

254b. *niryuktakastathā*: M, T_1 *niryuktastathā*

255b. -*stadoditā*: B. *rudīritā* variant reading? gloss?):

255c. *ovī*: M *urvī*, always

255d. *vṛtti*: M *vṛta*

256a. *prāsaiḥ*: C *prāntaiḥ*

256c. i. *chandobhiḥ*: C lacuna; ii. *geyā*: M *jñeyā*

257d. *lolī*: T_1 lacuna

258d. *bhāṣā vi*: C, M *bhāṣādi*

261cd-262ab. interpolated in NN **3.2.108 cd-109ab**. Tele-dittograyphy?

262a. *yasya*: M *tasya*

263a. *yadvaika*: M *yadaika*

264b. *ādimaḥ*: B explains: *ābhogasya*

266a. *khaṇḍe*: R lacuna
267c. *kāmado* C, R *kāmodo*
269c. *geyaḥ*: M *jñeyaḥ*
269d. *karuṇe*: B glosses: *rase*; M, T_1 *karuṇo*
271a. *vipralambhe*: B glosses: *rase*
271c. *vīra*: C *vīro*
271d. *tālataḥ*: C *tālakaḥ*
276a. *niryuktastridhātukāśca*: C, M *niryuktakastridhātuśca*
277c. *tam*: B explains: *a(n)taram*
280a. *jena*: M *yena*; B glosses: *jagaṇena*
280b. *bhena*: B glosses: *bhagaṇena;* M *tena*
280d. *reṇa*: M *teṣā-*
281a. *sena*: M *tena*
281cd. *kamalo'pyadbhuto*: T_1 *kamale'pyadbhute*
281-285. quoted in SS (12, pp.147, 148, 152, 153)
283ab. Occurs in SS; it is not clear whether this is of NN or of SS. The text is continuous in SS but this line is not found in any available collative source.
283cd-284ab. Inserted between **285ab-285cd** of NN in SS.
284a. *gatam sarvam*: SS *gataḥ sarva-*
284d. *tālena*: R *tānena*
286a. *ca* : C *'tha*
288-290, 292cd, 294ab quoted in SS (loc. cit.)
291a. *yugmena*: M *yuktena*
291c. *lena*: M *tena*
292a. *aḍḍa*: M *āḍu*
293c. *rase*: C *rāse*
293d. *śaṅkaraḥ syāt pratitālataḥ*: M *śaṅkā syāt pratitālakāḥ*
294a. *śānte*: B explains: *rase*
294cd. B has the note: ooIS (*iti*) *tālena makarando gīyate*; but this is the *tāla* for *cāra-aḍḍatāla;* the *tāla* prescribed for *makaranada* its ooS.
296b. *go mataḥ*: T_1 *gānataḥ*
298a. *'vasāna*: M *'vamāna*!
301b. *padaiḥ*: T_1 *pādaiḥ*
301cd-302ab. M lacuna
304d. *sāntarāccaturdhātavaḥ*: M *-stottarāccādhidhātavaḥ*! C…*rāśca dvi*… T_1…*raccalli*…
305d. *jhampā* T_1 *rūpa*
306a. *triviḍa*: M *tritāla*
307cd. T_1 lacuna; *raṇaraṅgakaḥ*: R + *ṛturaṅgakaḥ*

308b. *līlākhyaśca* C, M *līlāśca*

309c. *pratikhaṇḍam*: M, B *pratikhaṇḍa*. R shows lacuna from **309c** to **320b**, inclusive.

313a. *rasā*: C *dharā*

316b. i. *gīyate*: M; *gīyante;* ii. *khaṇḍakāḥ* M *khaṇḍakaḥ*; B *khaṇḍakam*

317a. *ādya*: M *adya*

317b. -*ścānya*: M lacuna; MS is blank to indicate lacuna.

320a. *rāgaḥ*: M *bhāvā*

322a. *sadguṇam*: M, T_1 *tadguṇam*

322d. *avatāro daśa-* M is preferred to B, C: *vatāro daśamā-* since it is faithful to the name of the *prabandha* in avoiding the ordinal number, at the price of a minor solecism.

323ab. R *tālarāgadalāvaṣṭābhiḥ syāttu śarabhalīlakaḥ*

323d. *svanāma*: M omits *sva*

325a. *tenakāntaiḥ*: M, T_1 *tenakānto*

327d. *gātṛvastva-*: M *gāna yastva-*

328c. *netṛnāmāṅko*: C *netṛṇām* R *netṛṇānām*

330bc. R lacuna

331b. *padasvaraiḥ*: M *padāmbaraiḥ*

335a. *lokena*: R *lokeṇa*

336d. i. *doṣā*: M lacuna; ii. *bhāvayoḥ*: M *bhāṣayoḥ*

338d. i. *vṛtti*: M *ddhṛti;* ii. *rītitā*: M *rīritā*

340a. *nānā*: B, M, T_1 *druta*

340b. *pragalbhatā*: R *prabhasratā*

341a. -*ktitā dhātu*: C,R *nirvandhū*

342c. *nyūna*: R *nūnam*

343b. *dhātukṛt*: M *dhātukam*

343c. *varṇakavi*: M, R lacuna

344c. *prabandhākalana*: M *prabandhalanā*

344d. *vedinām*: R omits *ve* and *nām*

COMMENTARY ON THE TEXT

1. RĀGA-ADHIKARAṆA

1ab. Śuddhacchāyālaga refers to both *rāgas* and *prabandhas*; *rāgas* have another variety viz. *saṁkīrṇa; prabandhas* are also classified into *sūḍa, ālikrama* and *viprakīṇa;* of these *sūḍa* is again divided into *śuddha* (*elā, ḍheṅkī* etc.) and *chāyālaga* (*dhruva, maṇṭha* etc.). So this phrase may be extended, by reading it as *upalakṣaṇa* to cover the totality of *deśī* music. This requirement of the singer, viz. expertise in *deśī* music is mentioned directly or obliquely in parallel definitions in other treatises also. The second phrase, *mūrchanāgrāmatānavit* may be similarly read as *upalakṣaṇa* for *gāndharva* music or *mārga* music. Therefore NN prescribes for the singer thorough familiarity with both *deśī* and *mārga* music. When NN was composed, it was a watershed in the history of Indian music; it witnessed the culmination of the transition of *grāma* into *mela.* Paṇḍarīka Viṭṭhala is himself aware of this important change; thus he says that only *rāgas* of *ṣadjagrāma* were rendered, to the complete exclusion of *madhyamagrāma-rāgas,* by his contemporary colleagues (NN 3.1.51); moreover, he describes *mela* in place of *grāma* in all his works; therefore he requires a musician to equip himself with both ancient music and modern music to cater to both the traditional elite as well as the common man, thus parallelling the *lakṣaṇa* of *gāndharva* (SR 3.12cd-13ab).

1d. Gāyana is synonymous with *gāyaka,* singer, even as *gāyanī* is equivalent with *gāyakī,* i.e. woman singer in NN and elsewhere. This definition of *gāyaka* is the seed from which the contents of the entire chapter III of the NN arise.

The *gāyaka* is described in three grades, *uttama, madhyama* and *adhama* (or *kaniṣṭha*) and their subvarieties *uttamottama, uttma-madhyama... kaniṣṭhādhama* by earlier treatises, a classification ignored by Paṇḍarīka Viṭṭhala. The qualities or requirements of a singer may be compared with those mentioned elsewhere. According to Somesvara (*Mānasollāsa,* 4.16.87) the great qualities required of a singer are an (excellent) voice, nuances *(dhvani),* intelligence, scholarship, skill in employing *gamakas,* expertise in *tāla* and fearlessness. According to him, the most superior singer has the following qualities:

एवं विधैस्तु (=सप्त)गमकैः प्रयोगैर्हृदयोत्थितैः ।
युक्तं गायति यो गीतं स प्रयोगपदान्वितः ॥
ध्वनिं विधार्य यो गीतं श्लक्ष्णं गायति गायकः ।
गायकेषूत्तमो ज्ञेयः प्रवीणो धारणान्वितः ॥
श्वासं निरुध्य सुचिरं नादं गायति विस्तृतम् ।
उत्तमो गायकः ख्यातो गेये निजबलान्वितः ॥

लयतालकलादक्षो वाद्यसन्धिप्रदर्शक : ।
यतिमाने धुतशिरो गायन् सत्कुलगोचरः ॥ (ibid. 4.16, 75-78, p. 8)

Haripāladeva requires the *uttamottama-gāyaka* to be possessed of the following qualities (*Saṅgītasudhākara*, 5.8.15-22); specialisation in *śrutī* and *svara*, scholarship in *rāgas* and *rāgāṅgas*, knowledge of the seven *gītiprabandhas*, versatality in all languages, skills in *tāla* varieties, knowledge of the application of all *pāṭas*, accomplishment in all forms of *nṛtta*, self-experience in *rasas*, expertise in *varṇālaṁkāras*, profound knowledge of the seven *gamakas*, accomplishment in simile, *double entendre*, poetry, etc., capacity to carry on the meaning initiated, awareness of the correct and inappropriate *sthāna*, endurance, conquest of anger, affability, sweetness of voice, scholarship in *mandra, madhyama* and *tāra* registers, facile execution of *gamakas* in all three registers, respectability of family, cleanliness, lustre, gain of popular esteem, ability to champion and defend his own view point and to refute the opponent's view, intrepidity in assemblies, lack of confusion, ability to generate aesthetic delight, pleasant personality and familiarity in the five *vṛttis*.

Somarājadeva (*Saṅgītaratnāvalī*. extr. *Bharatakośa*, p. 827) requires the *gāyaka* to have the ability to perform various modes of *ālapti*, retentivity and attentiveness, knowledge of *rāgāṅga-rāgas* and their respective *graha, aṁśa* and *nyāsa*, skill in performing all song forms, a voice with a range of three registers, knowledge of *tāla*, deep and sweet voice, mastery over voice, firmness, endurance, special expertness in *rāgas*. *Gāndharva-veda* (extr. op. cit. loc. cit.) prescribes expertise in voice, different *ālapti* forms, and in compositional forms as well as scholarship in *rāga, rāgāṅga, bhāsāṅga, kriyāṅga* and *upāṅga-rāgas*.

Pārśvadeva (*Saṅgītasamayasāra*, 8.88-92, p. 86) lists the following as the requirements of a good singer: skill in various modes of *ālapti*, efficiency in commencement and conclusion, use of all three registers, deep, sweet voice, ability to sing all *vastu-prabandhas*, cognoscence in *tāla*, beautiful body outline, excellent organisation of practical details, skill in *rāga* and *rāgāṅga*, endurance, mastery over voice, mental concentration, capacity to insert at appropriate places now and then of scholarly *rāgabhāvas* and training under a great teacher. If two or three of these qualities are missing, the *gāyaka* is *madhyama*; if four or five, he is *kaniṣṭha*. He is said to be *uttamottama* if he can sing *śuddha* and *chāyālaga* songs, preceded by *ālāpa* in all three registers; if he can do so in two registers only, he is *uttama madhyama*; if merely in one register, he is *madhyamādhama* (loc. cit. 8.94-97, p. 86).

Kumbhakarṇa (*Saṅgītarāja*, 2.3.1.16, p. 442) is very elaborate and comprehensive on the subject. Srīkaṇṭha (*Rasakaumudī*, 2.191) compiles the following qualities:

त्रिस्थानालापदक्षो गमकलयकलाकाकुविज्ञोऽतिधीरो
नव्योक्ती रोषरिक्तः सकलजनमनोरञ्जकः सावधानः ।

शुद्धच्छायालगज्ञः श्रमरहिततनुः कोकिलप्रख्यकण्ठ-
स्तालाभिज्ञो ग्रहज्ञः स भुवि निगदितो गायकानां वरेण्यः ॥

Music treatises also describe the requirements of a female singer, which is omitted by Paṇḍarīka Viṭṭhala. Pārśvadeva collects these from 'Ādi'bharata, in a comparative study of the male and female voices (NŚ. 33.5-6, pp. 398-399): women's voices are naturally sweet, while men's voices are strong; the former have the quality of instrumental tone; the latter, vocal sweetness (ibid; MS. in Sri Varalakshmi Academy, Mysore, p. 148). Śārṅgadeva describes her as possessed of beauty, youth and a voice surcharged with sweetness (3.24). Kumbhakarṇa has (*Saṅgītarāja*, 2.3.1.17, p.443):

तारुण्यप्रतिमप्रपञ्चचतुरा माधुर्यधुर्योक्तयो
लावण्यामृतदुग्धसागरकलारूपौधरत्नकराः ।
नानाभावकलाकलापकलिता हृद्या विदग्धप्रिया
गायिन्यो गदिता हि गायनवरैस्तुल्या नृपेणामुना ॥

Srīkaṇṭha (op.cit. 2. 189. 190, p. 37) waxes poetic on the subject of songstresses:

नानारागकलाकलापकुशला बिम्बाधरेणोज्ज्वला
गायिन्योऽखिलगीतवाद्यनिपुणा ताले च दक्षा लये ।
रम्याः कोकिलकण्ठमञ्जुलतरध्वाना प्रगल्भा रसे
साक्षात्कामजयश्रियः सदसि ताः शोभां परं तन्वते ॥

2a. Ekello is uniformly called *ekalo* (=single, unassisted) in other music treatises,: e.g. Someśvara (op.cit 4.16. 54, p.6), Pārśvadeva (op. cit. Ms. loc. cit. p. 146), Śārṅgadeva, (op. cit. 3. 22, 23, p. 154, 155). Kumbhakarṇa (op. cit. 2.3.1.16, p. 443) however, calls the solo vocalist, *ekilla*. In kannaḍa epic poetry *'ekkalagāṇa'* has uniformly meant solo vocalist,: e.g. Nāgacandra (c.1100A.D., *Mallināthāpuāṇam*, 6.98):

नुण्चरदिनाणति माडिदुदुन्मदाळि तावरोयोळगिर्द लक्ष्मिय मनंबेडेवेक्कल गाणनेंबिनं

Aggala (1189A.d. *Candraprabhapurāṇam*, 7. 96):

गीतमनन्दु पाडुविंपाणननुर्वराधिपति लीलेयिनेक्कलगाणनोर्वनुं

Maṅgarasa (1508 A.D. *Jayanṛpakāvya*, 11.65):

अळियेंदेंबेक्कलगाणं स्मरमोहनगीतमनाळापिसुतिरे

and idem. *Śrīpālacaritre* (3.14:) तोडपिनेक्कागाणनिळेगिळिदने

Aṣṭabhāṣākavi Candraśekhara (c. 1430 A.D., *Pampāsthāna-varṇanam*, 74, p.26):

एक्कलयमळवृन्दगायकरेंब मूरुतेरद गायकरोळगे

I am not aware of musicological cognates of this word, if any in telugu and tamil.

7cd-23ab. Gāyana guṇa-gāyana doṣa: The importance of analysing the voice and vocalists into merits and faults as well as characterising these has been recognised from the earliest times in Indian music. Paṇḍarīka Viṭṭhala offers an ecletic mixture of these. Occasionally authorities, e.g. Śārṅgadeva (on *gāyaka-guṇa)* are content with employing selfexplanatory or descriptive terms: the majority however, render the terms more precise with further, detailed characterisation. The following is a compilation of *gāyakaguṇas* (G) and *gāyak-doṣas* (D) from the more important authorities- **Bharatamuni:** G.-1. *śrāvaka* 2. *ghana* 3. *snigdha* 4. *madhura* 5. *avadhānavān, tristhānaśobhī* (NŚ. 33.12-15, p.400).

D. 1. *kapila* 2. *avyavasthita* 3. *saṁdaṣṭa* 4. *kākī* 5. *tumbakī* (ibid. 33.16-20, p. 401).

Someśvara G 1. *śārīra* 2. *dhvani* 3. *medhā* 4. *prauḍhi* 5. *gamakakauśala,* 6. *tālajñatā* 7. *nirbhayatā* (*Mānasollāsa,* 4.16, 87, p. 9)

D. 1. *sthānabhraṣṭa* 2. *apasvara* 3. *bāhya* 4. *kapila* 5. *tumbakī* 6. *kakī* 7. *saṁdaṣṭa* 8. *avyavasthita* 9. *phūtkārī* 10. *jambuka* 11. *vakrī* 12. *karālī* 13. *vinimīlita* 14. *uṣṭragrīva* 15. *prasārī* 16. *uddhaḍa* 17. *kaṁpita* 18. *dhvanihīna* 19. *avyakta* 20. *udghṛṣṭa* (ibid. 4.16. 24-43, pp. 3-5)

Haripāla G. 1. *khāhula* 2. *bombala* 3. *nārāṭa* 4. *miśra (Saṅgītasudhākara,* 5.8.40-44) D.1. *sandaṁśa* 2. *anunāsika* 3. *kākarvara* 4. *karālī* 5. *vakrī* 6. *nimīlaka* 7. *aja* 8. *phullagalla* (ibid. 5.8.45 ff.)

Śārṅgadeva G. 1. *hṛdyaśabda* 2. *suśārīra* 3. *grahamokṣavicakṣaṇa* 4. *rāga-rāgāṅga-bhāṣāṅga-kriyāṅga-upāṅga- kovida* 5. *prabandhagānaniṣṇata* 6. *vividhālaptitattvavit* 7. *sarvasthānottha-gamakeṣu anāyāsa-lasad-gati* 8. *āyattakaṇṭha* 9. *tālajña* 10. *avadhāna* 11. *jitaśrama* 12. *śuddacchāyālagābhijña* 13. *sarvakāku-viśeṣavit* 14. *anekasthāyasañcāra* 15. *sarvadoṣavivarjita* 16. *kriyāpara* 17. *yuktalaya* 18. *sughaṭa* 19. *dhāraṇāvita* 20. *spūrjat-nirjavana* 21. *hāri* 22. *rahaḥ kṛt* 23. *bhajanoddhura* 24. *susampradāya* (SR. 3.13-18ab, pp. 153-154)

D. 1. *saṁdaṣṭa* 2. *udghuṣṭa* 3. *sūtkārī* 4. *bhīta* 5. *śaṅkita* 6. *kampita* 7. *karālī* 8. *vikala* 9. *kākī* 10. *vitāla* 11. *karabha* 12. *udbhaṭa* 13. *jhombaka* 14. *tumbaki* 15. *vakrī* 16. *prasārī* 17. *vinimīlaka* 18. *virasa* 19. *apasvara* 20. *avyakta* 21. *sthānabhraṣṭa* 22. *avyavasthita* 23. *miśraka* 24. *anavadhāna* 25. *sānunāsika* (ibid. 3.25-38, pp. 157-159)

Kumbhakarṇa C. 1. *ālaptikarmaṇi-vijñātaḥ* 2. *ālaptinirmāṇadakṣa* 3. *rājendra-samsadi-akṣobhyaḥ* 4. *vaśyakaṇṭha* 5. *suśārīraśālī* 6. *anekakākupravīṇaḥ* 7. *rāga-upāṅga-kriyaṅgādiṣu-avikala* 8. *bhāṣāṅgavetta* 9. *prāvaṭukānām jetā* 10. *vahanīmārgagāna-āptamārgaḥ* 11. *tāle kāmapravīṇah* 12. *ubhayagaticatura* 13. *sarvakālam-viśramaḥ* 14. *śāstre susampradāyaḥ* 15. *sughaṭa paṭuvara* 16. *vastu-nirmāṇavedī* 17. *sphūrjan-nirjavana paṭuḥ* 18. *paṭudhiyām-agresaraḥ* 19. *gītodgrāhavidhāna-peśalaḥ* 20. *vimukti* *padavī paṇḍaḥ* 21. *amitasiddhimān* 22. *nyunādhikyaga-sāvadhāna dhiṣaṇah* 23. *bahūllāsavān* 24. *aprayatna-gamaka-sthānatrayam-vyāptimān* 25. *śuddhacchāya-lagajñaḥ* 26. *śruti viṣadamatiḥ* 27. *sthānasamsthasvarajñaḥ* (*Saṅgītarāja* 2.3.1.9-12, p. 442) D. 1. *udghuṣṭa* 2. *kapila* (*vikala*) 3. *kāki* 4. *sūtkārī* 5. *sānunāsika* 6. *udghaḍa* 7. *apasvara* 8. *avyakta* 9. *virasa* 10. *vinimīlana* 11. *tumbakī* 12. *bombakī* 13. *vakrī* 14. *sthānabhraṣṭa* 15. *avyavasthita* 16. *prasārī* 17. *karabhȧ* 18. *bhīta* 19 *sandaṣṭa* 20.*anavadhānaka* 21. *kampita* 22. *śaṅkita* 23. *miśra* 24. *karālī* 25. *vitālaka* (ibid. 2.3.1.18-34, pp. 443-445)

Govinda Dīkṣita G. 1. *manojñaśārīra* 2. *hṛdyaśabda* 3. *gītagrahamokṣa-dakṣa* 4. *rāgāṅgādiṣu vicakṣaṇa* 5. *nānāvidhālaptiṣu tattvavedī* 6. *tristhāna gamkeṣu dakṣaḥ* 7. *svādhīna-kaṇṭhaḥ* 8. *sūḍamukhyatālaprabhedākalana-pravīṇaḥ* 9. *svaraśruti parimāṇavedī* 10. *bahuprabandheṣu jitaśramaḥ* 11. *śuddhacchayālaga-prabandheṣu-paṭuḥ* 12. *kākubhede sthāyeṣu nānāvidhatām gateṣu sañcāradakṣaḥ* 13. *mārgadeśī-rāgān śāstrānusāreṇa muhur-gāyati.* D. 1. *sandaṣṭa* 2. *udghuṣṭa* 3. *sītkāra* 4. *śaṅkita* 5. *kampita* 6. *karāli* 7. *kapila* 8. *kākī* 9. *vitāla* 10. *udbhaṭa* 11. *karabha* 12. *sirāla* 13. *jhombaka* 14. *tumbakī* 15. *vakrī* 16. *prasārī* 17. *nimīlaka* 18. *virasa* 19. *apasvara* 20. *avyakta* 21. *avayavastha* 22. *miśraka* 23. *anavadhāna* 24. *sānunāsika* (25. *sthānabhraṣṭa*)

Paṇḍarīka Viṭṭhala gives only ten out of the twenty-five of *gāyanadoṣas* described by Śārṅgadeva. The latter's *udbhaṭa* and *vikala* are transformed into the phonetic variants *uddhaḍa* and *kapila* in the latter. While *kapila* is described by Bharata (NŚ 33.17, p. 401) as a tonal distortion (*vaisvarya*) and displacement (*ghargharāyita*) due to phlegm in the throat (*śleṣmakaṇṭha*). Abhinavagupta (op. cit. on NŚ loc. cit.) derives the word with the gloss कम्पनं कपिस्तं लयतीति । *Udghuṣṭa* of NN includes the *kākī* of SR.

The defects of a singer may be briefly summarised from SR. A vocalist who sings with clenched teeth is *saṁdaṣṭa*. If he sings with divergent shouting voice he is *udghuṣṭa*. If he has a whistling, snorting or sucking breath, he is *sūtkārī*. If afflicted with stagefright, he is *bhīta*. *Saṅkita* is dubious and so sings fast to get it over with. *Kampita* trembles in both body and voice. *Karālī* makes awful faces and opens his mouth wide while singing. *Vikala* sings notes out of pitch; *kākī* crows harshly like a crow; *vitāla* fails in *tāla*. *Karabha* raises his neck like a camel. *Udbhaṭa* the worst vocalist, has voice like a goat. *Jhombaka* has such a strain while singing that veins stand out on his forehead, face and neck. *Tumbakī* puffs up his cheeks like a bitter gourd. *Vakrī* twists his neck while singing. *Prasārī* moves not only in song but also in body on the stage. *Nimīlaka* sings with eyes shut. *Virasa* is a bore. The *apasvara* sings the proscribed note. *Avyakta* sings with convulsive inarticulation. The *sthānabhraṣṭa* fails in reaching the desired (pitch or) register. *Avyavastha* is disorganised in pitch and register. *Miśraka* is mixed up in the various kinds of *rāgas* and mixes up the shades of different *rāgas* in the one he is rendering. *Anavadhānaka* is inattentive in executing characteristic phrases and *gamakas*. *Anunāsika* has a nasal voice.

The singing voice is coeval with the human body capable of musical expression with effortless ease. Its qualities are described as wide scope (in the registers), resonance, appeal, tenderness, sweetness, depth, denseness, smoothness, lustre and expansiveness. Its defects are enumerated as dryness, lack of appeal, weakness of upper partials, saplessness, thinness, harshness, crowing, and inaccuracy in pitch and register. The merits and defects of vocalists are found discussed in the following: Sathyanarayana, R., *Voice Training in Indian Music*, pp. 78-95 in Sangeet Natak, Nos. 53-54, July- Dec. 1979

Idem. *Karnātaka-Saṅgītavāhinī*, pp. 122-128

Idem. *New Creations in Karnatāka Music in 'Smriti'*, C. Narasimha Murthy Memorial Volume, ed. C.N. Mangala, pp. 95, 96

Idem. Foreword, *Viśeṣakṛtimāle*, pp. 1-3

idem. Foreword, *Sirigannaḍadiñcara*, pp. iii, iv

23cd-24. Manoyuṅkte etc. This is an ancient theory of *nāda*-generation in the gross body and is based on *yoga*. It is a polyvalent conceptual model, freely used in diverse disciplines. For example, Caraka (*Caraka-saṁhitā*, 28.6, 7) employs this theory in *Āyurveda* to explain how the soul becomes extrovert and expressive; the same is used in phonetics by Pāṇini in his *Śikṣā* (6, 7):

आत्मा बुद्ध्या समेत्यार्थान् मनो युङ्क्ते विवक्षया ।
मनः कायाग्निमाहन्ति स प्रेरयति मारुतम् ।
मारुतस्तूरसि चरन् मन्द्रं जनयति स्वरम् ॥

This model is adopted, probably for the first time by Mataṅga (*Bṛhaddeśī*, 18-21, p.3), followed by Nānyadeva (*Bharatabhāṣya*, 1.2.9-10, p. 16), Jagadekamalla (*Saṅgītacūḍāmaṇi*, MS in Sri Varalakshmi Academy, Mysore, pp. 4, 5), Śārṅgadeva (SR. 1.3.3, 4) etc. to explain the origin of *nāda* and musical sound in the gross human body. NN however, athetises the role played by *brahmagranthi* at the navel in this.

23c. Vivakṣu, desirous of expression; in explaining *'vivakṣamāṇa'* of SR (1.3.3) in this context both Siṁhabhūpāla and Kallinātha give a linguistic or verbal orientation to the text. Thus Siṁhabhūpāla says *'vaktumicchan' (Saṅgītasudhākara* on SR loc. cit. p. 65) and Kallinātha offers *'bruva icchāyām sani'* (*Saṅgītakalānidhi* on SR loc. cit. p. 64), making out that the desire is for speech expression, thus excluding nondiscursive modes of meaning such as music. This is why *vivakṣā* is translated here in its broadest sense. A further point merits consideration here: the above model explains the origin and manifestation of musical sound in the human body, but not the one generated on musical instruments outside the body. In this case, whatever *nāda* form which the soul intends to generate on an external musical instrument, the soul realises the same within the body in the *upāṁśu* form as an *ābhāsa* (semblance) or virtual image cast upon itself and then externalises the same through expressional endeavour, technique, etc. Adding this semantic dimension, it is proper to interpret *vivakṣā* as desire for expression, intention of manifestation.

24b. Ūrdhvam caran: If the vital air *(prāṇa)* moves upward (and fills the *nāḍis*) *āhata-nāda* is manifested; if it moves downward, *anāhata-nāda* is generated according to Mataṅga (*Bṛhaddeśī*, 23, p. 3).

कन्दस्थानसमुत्थोऽपि समीरः सञ्चरन्नधः ।
ऊर्ध्वं च कुरुते सर्वान्नादान् मूर्धनि तूद्धतान् ॥

Siṁhabhūpāla prefaces the extraction of this passage in explaining *'ūrdhvapathe caran'* (SR 1.3.4) explicitly as follows (p. 65):

स पूर्वं ब्रह्मग्रन्थिस्थितेन वह्निना प्रेरितः सन् ऊर्ध्वमार्गे गच्छन् आघातेन नाभिहृदयकण्ठमूर्धमुखेषु ध्वनिं प्रकटयति । ऊर्ध्वपथ इति प्रकृतगानोपयोगार्थमधोऽप्यनाहतस्य नादस्योत्पत्तेः ।

Paṇḍarīka Viṭṭhala does not speak of *āhata* and *anāhata-nāda* in his works.

24c. Śīrṣa means head; but this has no resonating air cavity to generate the *'apuṣṭa'* or undeveloped sound. So, following Pāṇini (*Pāṇini-śikṣā* 1.9) *mūrdhā/ śīrṣa* is translated into palate which envelops a resonating air cavity.

24d. Āsya: 'Mouth' as translated by Kunhanraja C. (English Translation of *Saṅgītaratnākara* chapter I, p. 46) is not appropriate in this context. When the mouth is closed and sound is generated, both facial muscles, maxillary sinuses and frontal sinuses resonate with it, producing artificial sound. Since it is not produced with open mouth and open throat in the normal way and since it does not have expressive power of natural voice, it is called *kṛtrima,* artificial. This is lucidly brought out by Mataṅga: *sūkṣmanāda* is produced in *guhā* (navel?), *atisūkṣma* in the chest *(hṛdaya), vyakta (=puṣṭa)* in midthroat (*kaṇṭhamadhye*), *avyakta (apuṣṭa)* in the palate *(tāludeśagaḥ)* and *kṛtrima* (=artificial) in the region of the face *(mukhadeśa)* *(Bṛhaddeśī,* 24, 25, p. 3). Jagadekamalla (op. cit. loc. cit. pp. 4-5) endorses this view with acknowledgement to Mataṅga but calls *vyakta* and *avyakta* as *puṣṭa* and *apuṣṭa.*

24d-25a. Dhvani seems to mean specifically voice here, rather than 'sound' generally.

25a. Nadadhātoḥ: This is a grammatical derivation of the word '*nāda*' which is the substrate of all musical sound. *'Nāda'* is obtained by elongating the vowel '*a*' on the first consonant '*n*' in the verbal stem '*nad*'. Such elongation, called '*ghañ*' is applied when the sense of a verb is accomplished (Pāṇini, *Aṣṭādhyāyī* 3.3.13-'*bhāve*'), when applied causatively to a non-subject (ibid. 3.3.19-*'akartari ca kārake saṁjñāyām'*) in both *bhāva* and *karaṇa* (ibid. 6.4.27-*'bhāvakaraṇayoḥ'*) etc. '*Nad*' is an intransitive, seṭ, *parasmaipadi dhātu* of the first (*'bhvādī'*) class (*Dhātūpāṭha* 3.17) which means to sound, to make, resound, vibrate, to make resonant etc. It may also be derived from the verbal root *'ṇad'* (unmanifest sound) by applying *'ghañ'* (Paṇini, 3.3.18). *'Nāda'* is described in the *Prātiśākhya* literature as the fourth of externalised efforts (*saṁghāta=prayatna*) involved in phonation resulting in speech (cf. Anantabhaṭṭa, comm. on Kātyāyana, *Vājsaneyī Prātiśākhyam,* 1.9). Patañjali enumerates eleven of these outward efforts in his *Mahābhāṣya: vivāra, saṁvāra, śvāsa, nāda, ghoṣa, aghoṣa, alpaprāṇa, mahāprāṇa, udātta, anudātta,* and *svarita.*

A definition of *nāda* from the *Yoga* view point would be नाभेरूर्ध्वं हृदि स्थानात् मारुत: प्राणसंज्ञक: । नदति ब्रह्मरन्ध्रान्ते तेन नाद: प्रकीर्तित: ॥ Another approach is from *mantraśāstra* according to which the syllables *'na'* and *'da'* symbolise the creative categories of *prāṇa* air and (*yoga-*)body fire; their combination generates *nāda.* This view is adopted by Mataṅga (*Bṛhaddeśī,* 22, p. 3) and endorsed by Jagadekamalla (op. cit. MS loc. cit.), Śārṅgadeva (op. cit. 1.3.6) etc. Siṁhabhūpāla (op. cit. on SR loc. cit. p. 65) attributes the derivation to lexicographers or grammarians while Kallinātha (op. cit. on SR loc. cit.) ascribes it to *mantraśāstra* experts.

25d. atipuṣṭa. This term is unique to Paṇḍarīka Viṭṭhala who uses it in the same sense in his Sadrāgacandrodaya (1.18) also, but employs '*apuṣṭa*' for the same in Rāgamālā (5) and Rāgamañjarī (1.17) in agreement with his predecessors Mataṅga, Jagadekamalla, Pārśvadeva, Śārṅgadeva etc. In this sense, '*ati*' means 'beyond' and accords well with textual tradition. It may be translated as very strong in the sense of 'head' sound or *tāra* register.

26b. Caturdhā vyavahārataḥ. While *sūkṣma* etc. denote five kinds of sound related to degree of subtlety, grossness and artificiality and to their origin in the human body, *anumandra* etc. refer to the range. These are regarded as of four kinds rather than as different regions of the tone *continuum* probably because of the difference in the quality of sound such as brightness, denseness, shrillness, hollowness etc. While the range of human audibility is some 16-16000 cps, i.e. about 10 registers, only three are admitted into musical transactions in ancient Indian musicology. A recognition is accorded to the difference in range between instrumental and vocal sounds for the first time in theory in the 16th century by Rāmāmātya who mentions *anumandra* in connection with the *vīṇā (Svaramelakalānidhi,* 3.22, p.15; 3.44ab, p. 17), despite his conventional acceptance of only three registers earlier (ibid. 2.4, p. 9). For the first time Paṇḍarīka Viṭṭhala offers a rationale for the recognition of such extention, viz. *anumandra* is inaccessible to the human voice but accessible to musical instruments (NN 3.1.27cd). Just about a generation later (1609 A.D.) Somanātha confirms the use of *anumandra (Rāgavibodha,* 2.19, 22, pp. 62, 63) and also further extension into *atitāra* (ibid. 2.37, 41, pp. 69, 72) in various *vīṇā* keyboards. This came to be well established in the 17th century A.D. (e.g. Veṅkaṭamakhin, *Caturdaṇḍīprakāśikā* 1.76, p. 110).

This range may be compared with that of various musical instruments of the West.

Sl. No.	Instrument	*cps* *from*	*to*	*Octave range approx.*
1.	Threshold: Organ tube 32"	16.4	–	–
2.	Piano	34.7	4186.0	7.0
3.	Bass Viol	41.2	246.9	2.5
4.	Bass Tuba	43.7	349.2	3.0
5.	French Horn	61.7	698.4	3.25
6.	Cello	65.4	880.0	3.75
7.	Bass Clarinet	73.4	698.4	3.25
8.	Tenor Trombone	82.4	493.9	2.5
9.	Kettle Drum	87.3	174.6	1.0
10.	Human Voice			
	(a) Bass	82.4	349.2	2.0
	(b) Baritone	98.0	392.0	2.0
	(c) Tenor	130.8	523.2	2.0
	(d) Alto	174.6	698.4	2.0
	(e) Soprano	246.9	1174.7	2.25
11.	Viola	130.8	1318.5	2.25
12.	Trumpet	164.8	1046.5	2.5
13.	Soprano Clarinet	164.8	1568.0	3.25
14.	Violin	196.0	3125.9	4.0
15.	Flute	261.6	2249.3	3.0
16.	Oboe	261.6	1568.0	2.5
17.	Picolo	532.2	4498.6	3.0
18.	Highest: Organ tube 0.75"	–	8372.0	–
19.	Limit of Overtones useful to music	–	10,000 (approx.)	–
20.	Threshold	–	16,000	–

Thus it is seen that except in the piano and the violin, the range is about three octaves and the total range is about seven octaves. Since pitch is not absolute in Indian music and is relative to a variable reference pitch *(ādhāra śruti)*, and considering that only a small region of the *anumandra* and *atitāra* registers is covered, the range of musical sounds admitted into Indian music from early times and its extension in the 16th century seems well based on convenience and science.

The *Prātiśākhya* literature speaks of seven stages *(sthāna)* for speech. For example, The *Taittirīya Prātiśākhya* has (23.4-9)

सप्त वाचस्थानानि भवन्ति । उपांशुध्वाननिमदउपब्दिमत् मन्द्रमध्यमताराणि । करणवदशब्दममनः प्रयोगमुपांशु । अक्षरव्यञ्जनानामनुपलब्धिर्ध्वानः । उपलब्धिर्निमदः । सशब्दमुपब्दिमत् । उरसि मन्द्रम् । कण्ठे मध्यमम् । शिरसि तारम् ।

The first four stages are subsonic manifestations. Vedic literature is repeatedly explicit on the use of only three octaves. The *Sāmavidhāna-Brāhmaṇa (Sāyaṇabhāṣya)*, *Ṛgveda Prātiśākhyam* (13.41-45 and Uvaṭa's comm. thereon), *Pāṇinī-śikṣā* (7, 8), *Nāradīya-śikṣā* (1.1.7), *Māṇḍūkya-śikṣā* (68); this is true of *Purāṇa* and other literature also: e.g. *Viṣṇudharmottara-purāṇa* (3.18.1), *Vāyu-purāṇa* (25.4), Viṣṇu-śarman, *Pañcatantra* (5.6.53, *Aparīkṣitakārakam, gītarata-gardabha-sṛgāla-kathā*), Amarasiṁha, *Nāmaliṅgānuśāsanam (Amarakośa,* 1.6. *Nāṭyavarga* 2)

27b.Dviguṇaḥ: (i) Physically it means doubled in pitch, i.e. in frequency (i.e. halved in string length etc.) Thus a note in the *madhyasthāna* is double in pitch of its analogue in the *mandra*; note in the *tāra-sthāna* is double in pitch of its analogue in *madhya.*

(ii) It is interpreted in terms of the effort involved in manifesting the note by utterance. Pāṇini (*Aṣṭādhyāyī* 1.1.50) says *'sthāne'ntaratamaḥ'*. Kallinātha interprets Śārṅgadeva's *'dviguṇaścottarottaraḥ'* (SR 1.3.7 p. 66) in this way:

उत्तरोत्तरः मन्द्रादुत्तरो मध्यो, मध्यादुत्तरस्तार इति यावत् । द्विगुणः, गुण उच्चारणप्रयत्नः द्वौ गुणौ यस्येति द्विगुणः । अयमर्थः-मन्द्रस्थानस्थितात् षड्जादिव्यपदेशवतो नादात् मध्यस्थानस्थितः स एव षड्जादिव्यपदेशवांस्ततोऽपि द्विगुणः प्रयत्नसाध्यत्वाद् द्विगुण इति । पूर्वस्थानस्थितात् क्रमेणारोहे सत्यष्टमः स्वर इति यावत् ।

Thus the ancient musicologists in India hold that the force of the air generating the experience of the octave note is double that generating experience of the fundamental. Nānyadeva quotes Nārada (*Nāradīya-śikṣā?*) to purport that such doubling is effected by narrowing the epiglottal orifice in the throat and expelling the breath through it under pressure (*Bharatabhāṣya,* 2.42,43, pp.19, 20)

तीव्रप्रयत्न उच्चैः सर्वशरीराङ्गसन्धिसञ्चारी ।
गात्राणां निग्रहः स्यात् संवृतता कण्ठविवरस्य ॥
वायोः स्वरस्य च तथा गतागते रूक्षता च वर्णस्य ।
मुनयस्तमेवमेनं स्वरमाहुरुदात्तनामानम् ॥

He makes it clear that low *svara* is generated by enlarging the epiglottal orifice (ibid. 2.44, 45, p. 20):

कण्ठविवरस्य पृथुता वायोः स्वरस्य च हीनगामित्वात् ।
स्निग्धमेवमेनं विदुरनुदात्तं तदा मुनयः ॥

It may be noted that the rule *'dviguṇascottarottaraḥ'* is restricted by Paṇḍarīka Viṭṭhala and other earlier authors to only three octaves. This is testimony to their keen power of perception; for, the higher (or lower) one ascends (by octave, fifth) or descends (by the just fourth), the less and less the derived octave coincides with the fundamental, leaving a gap. I have discussed this as 'Assonance Defect Effect' elsewhere (Sathyanarayana, R., *Niḥśaṅkahṛdaya,* pp. 196, 411, 415-418, 485-488 etc.). It is this *(dviguṇa)* acoustical phenomenon that places all the *svarasthānas* of the octave spirally in the tone continuum and makes possible the predictability of their colour. The octave phenomenon inheres three fundamental principles of musical organisation viz.

(a) realisation in practice of the mutual relationship of every note in the octave with its predecessor and successor; the mutual relationships between pairs of successive notes and of the relationship of each note with the fundamental or any other given note.

(b) extrapolation of this to, and application in, various tone regions.

(c) application in temporal rhythm dimension to derive musico-semantic modes such as song or its abstraction, the *rāga.*

26bcd-27a. Anumandro... mūrdhni syāt: Considerable research has gone in recent times into the determination of the relation between a pitch range and the body region believed to generate it. Revesz, for example, admits of a rough ad-hoc relationship between the notes of *mandra, madhya* and *tāra* (low, middle and high registers respectively) to chest, throat and head; but he rejects the existence of a direct spatial association with tone level and its sensation in the body organ: (Revesz, G., *Introduction to the Psychology of Music,* p. 68):

"However, if we compare the tone sensations with the actual spatial impressions (optical and tactual), we soon find that there is not the slightest phenomenological similarity between the spatial and the acoustical concepts of 'height' and 'distance', let alone ideational identity."

Revesz terms this relationship as association by analogy. E. von Hornbostel (*Musicalische Tonsysteme,* cit. Revesz, op. cit. loc. cit.) and W. Koehler (*Akustische Untersuchungen,* cit. idem, op. cit. loc. cit.) do not relate the high-low relationship to height or distance in space but to the intensity of tone-brightness or dullness. But these views are open to question: the spatial association of the high and low tones of the *tāra* and *mandra-svaras* may not be absolutely valid, but it is acoustically established that low notes are generated by slow vibration and high notes, by fast vibration. The frequency of a note is a function of the speed, volume and pressure of the air which is forced through the epiglottis and sets it in vibration. If the air at the bottom of the lungs is expelled without compression, the vibration is low; if it is compressed upto the region of the throat or to a small volume, the force of escape is larger and so the epiglottal fold vibrates faster, and without spreading, directly reaches the head (i.e. the palate). This has been described as '*mūrdhni tāro*' by the authorities. Therefore, the sound levels are related to body space in some sense. The same applies to instrumental sounds by intrapolation into body consciousness. Every vocalist is familiar with the 'feeling' that the *mandra* notes are 'belly' notes and the *tāra* notes are 'head' notes. The view of Hornbostel is based on an intersensory experience (i.e. visual, such as brightness and dullness); in Western music low notes are believed to be dull, and high notes, bright. This does not appear to be true in Indian music, or is, at least, controversial; the brightness of a note depends, among other things on *svarapuṣṭi* (strength or richness of a tone). Also, the brightness of a note is integral to its nature and cannot be isolated as a variable component. Therefore, this, depending on the quality of the voice, tone colour etc. does not seem to be related to regions of sound. On the other hand, ancient Indian music theory recognises that the same note acquires different personalities in different registers: e.g. Mataṅga (op. cit. p. 4)

केचित् स्थानत्रययोगात् त्रिविधां श्रुतिं प्रतिपद्यन्ते

and the sixty-six *śrutis* propounded by Kohala (ibid. p. 7)

28c. Hetu: Mataṅga poses five schools of thought on the relationship between *śruti* and *svara* viz. *tādātmya* (identity), *vivartatva* (inversion), *kāryatva* (causality), *pariṇāmitā* (transformation) and *abhivyañjakatā* (revealing, manifesting) *avayava-avayavī* (part-whole) and himself prefers *pariṇāmavāda.* I have discussed these in detail elsewhere (Sathyanarayana, R., *Niḥśaṅkahṛdaya,* pp. 493-517). On the other hand, Śārṅgadeva prefers causality: This is seen (a) in his expounding an ablative relationship between *śrutī* and *svara: 'śrutibhyaḥ syuḥ svarāḥ'* (SR 1.3.23) (b) his explicit statement to this effect: *'evam svarakāraṇam'* (SR 1.3.25) (c) his use of the term *'hetu'* (generating) cause (SR 1.3.26). Paṇḍarīka Viṭṭhala seems to subscribe to this view in using the word *'hetavaḥ.'*. According to this causal relationship, *śruti* is the material cause for *svara (upādāna kāraṇa)* just as clay is of the pot.

28d-30a. The first available reference to the stair-case analogy for the stepwise progression of *dhvani* is found in Mataṅga (*Bṛhaddeśī,* 27ab. prose) coherently but differently extracted by Siṁhabhūpāla (op.cit. on SR 1.3.22, p. 68) and Kallinātha (op.cit. on ibid. loc. cit. p. 70). According to Mataṅga (*Bṛhaddeśī,* impressi typis), *dhvani* is manifested by the union of body-fire and the body-air *(prāṇa).* It is then swept upward like smoke, by wind and volition. It then fills up body space (chest and above, i.e. components of voice apparatus) step by step. It is thus manifested in these respective places, (by assuming the exact shape of the respective organ of the voice apparatus) differentiated and quantified forms such as *catuḥśruti.*

The extracts of this passage by Siṁhabhūpāla and Kallinātha suggest a different theory: *dhvani* is manifested in space of which it is an attribute. Space is actually one but appears discrete, plural, distinct and finite because it fills different objects (such as a pot). Such occupation is perceived (and evidenced) through the plurality of objects. *Dhvani* possesses the property of filling up and therefore appears in plural manifestations such as *ṣaḍja, ṛṣabha,* etc. and thus produces awareness of exactness, finiteness and distinctness in them even though it is but one. These intervals constitute phenomenal reality (of musical sound) as do the differentiated and proliferated forms of space. Such individuation of a single undifferentiated entity occurs by *puruṣaprayatna,* i.e. volitional or conscious effort. It rises and fills like smoke in various body spaces (of voice apparatus) lying above the navel step by step, and is, in this manner, manifested in plural appearance. This theory has overtones of the grammarian's *(vaiyākaraṇa)* viewpoint as engendered in the *Prātiśākhyās* and *sikṣās* (for detailed discussion see Sathyanarayana, R., *Śruti, Dhvani* and *Sphoṭa* in the Indian Theosophist, 82.10-11, Oct-Nov. 85, pp. 30-47).

According to Mataṅga, it is *dhvani* itself which pervades the supranavel region progressively. It is only later that the concept of *nāḍī*, evidently inspired by *yoga* and *āyurveda* was introduced, and *śruti* was conceived as generated because the vital air flows through the *nāḍīs* and fills them.

Kohala would appear to be the first theorist to relate the upper *nāḍīs* and volitional effort in the generation of *svara* in the human body (extr. Mataṅga, op.cit. p. 12):

ऊर्ध्वनाडीप्रयत्नेन सर्वभित्तिनिघट्टनात् ।
मूर्छितो ध्वनिरामूर्ध्नः स्वरोऽसौ व्यापकः परः ॥

A later work, called *Kohalamatam*, originating in Kerala claims to derive this theory from (an unspecified) *Āgama* work (or *saṅgītaśāstra*) and apportions the *nāḍīs* (said to be) belonging to the various components of the voice apparatus; the origin of the *svaras* is traced to these components in the *Nāradīya-śikṣā*. Kohalamata (Ms. copy in Sri Varalakshmi Acadmy, Mysore) reveals a parallel in the number of *śrutis* and number of *nāḍīs* from which a given *svara* arises (p. 1):

चतस्रो जत्रुबन्धिन्यो नाड्यः कण्ठमुपाश्रिताः ।
तालुमूलस्य बन्धिन्यः तिस्रस्तस्यैव च स्थिताः ।
ओष्ठयोरुभयोर्नाड्यौ बन्धिन्यौ द्वे व्यवस्थिते ।
चतस्रो मूर्ध्निबन्धिन्यो नाड्यो ब्रह्मपथाश्रयाः ।
नाड्यश्चतस्रस्तिष्ठन्ति दन्तानाबद्ध्य सर्वतः ।
कण्ठताल्वोरन्तरा स्युर्नाड्यस्तिस्रस्तु सङ्गताः ।

कण्ठयोर्द्वे बन्धिन्यौ नाड्यौ तत्रैव विष्ठितौ ।
एता (द्वाविं)शतिर्नाड्यो मध्य(?मन्द्रं)नाड्यां हृदि स्थिताः ।
युगपन्मरुताहत्य नादस्तासु प्रवेक्ष्यति ।
त्रुटिकालमिताः स्युस्तु श्रुतयः श्रुतिगोचराः ।
यदूर्ध्वं हृदयग्रन्थेः कपालफलकादधः ।
प्राणश्चरति तत्रैता व्यज्यन्ते श्रुतयः पृथक् ।
व्यक्तिस्थानेषु वर्णानां स्वरसंज्ञां भजन्ति ताः ॥

Śārṅgadeva seems to be the next authority to adopt this theory (SR 1.3. 8, 9), and being a great āyurvedic authority on human anatomy of his times, was probably struck by an anatomical analogue:

'Although no trace of transverse segmentation is visible on the surface of the spinal cord, it is convenient to regard it as being built of a series of superimposed spinal segments or neuromers, to each of which is attached a pair of spinal nerves. Thirty-one pairs of spinal nerves spring from the spinal cord, each nerve having an anterior and posterior root, the latter being characterised by the presence of an oval swelling, termed the spinal ganglion... The pairs of spinal nerves are grouped as follows: cervical—eight, thoracic—twelve, lumbar—five, coccygeal—one and for the sake of convenience the spinal cord is divided into cervical, thoracic, lumbar and sacral regions, corresponding with the attachments of the different groups of nerves' (Gray's Anatomy, pp. 908, 909). This seems to have been extrapolated onto the *yoga* body, and extended into the postulation of three sets of twenty-two pairs of transverse *yoganāḍīs* corresponding to the three registers, *mandra, madhya* and *tāra.* It must be strongly emphasized here that *prāṇa, agni, brahmagranthi, yoganāḍīs* etc. have only a postulatory status and do not warrant exact analogy or correspondence in the physical human body.

30b. Śrāvyamātrataḥ. This offers a definition of *śruti* in terms of aural acuity and suggests the pitch limen criterion as definitive base. The earliest known definition is due to Dattila (*Dattilam*, 9) *"dhvaniviśeṣās-te śravaṇāc-chruti-saṁjñitāḥ"* wherein the *'viśeṣa'* served as a seed for the *'dhvani-vailakṣaṇya'* of Abhinavagupta (*Abhinavabhāratī* on NŚ 28, 26 pr., p. 23) and '*nairantarya*' and '*dhvanyantarāśruti*' of Śārṅgadeva (SR 1.3.12). Therefore '*mātrataḥ*' may be taken in the sense of *'sāmarthya'*. Otherwise, if it is understood as 'merely', everything that is, or may be, heard, including nonmusical sound, becomes *'śruti's;* so, there would be left nothing which is distinctive, differentiating or definitive in the term.

The word *śruti* is derived by applying the *pratyaya 'ktin'* which enjoins action or activity to the verbal stem '*śru*' (class I, transitive, *parasmaipada*, '*aniṭ*'; but class V according to Monier Williams, *A Sanskrit-English Dictionary,* p.1100; *Dhātupāṭha*, 22.44) which means to listen, to hear attentively, to obey. It has been transmitted in two formal streams—the Vedic and Secular. Nānyadeva (*Bharatabhāṣya*, 3.5.82) has:

श्रुतिः श्रूयत इत्येवं ध्वनिरेषोऽभिधीयते ।
शृणोतेः कर्मविहिते प्रत्यये क्तिनि जायते ॥

In Vedic literature *śruti* generally means 'that which is heard'; *'pṛthak śruti'* means 'heard as a distinct or separate entity' e.g. *Ṛkprātiśākhyam* of Śākaṭāyana, 13.40 and Uvaṭa's comm. thereon; *'ekaśruti'* means 'heard at the same pitch' in *Ṛkprātiśākhya, Taittirīya-Prātiśākhya, Vājasaneyī Prātiśākhya* etc.; *'uccaśruti'* in *Ṛktantra* of Śākaṭāyana (3.3.1, p. 15) means 'high tone' (cf. *Ṛktantra-vivṛti,* p. 10 and *Pāribhāṣika-vacana* on the same). *Nārādīya-śikṣā* employs the word *śruti* in technical contexts which seem to be seeds for several conceptual evolutes for *śruti* in secular music (Sathynarayana, R., *Niḥśaṅkahṛdaya,* pp. 200-202).

In secular music, however, *śruti* implies aural threshold, and pitch limen or aural acuity. Kallinātha offers seemingly different explanations. While commenting as *'śravṇāt'* (SR1.3.8) he takes it as 'fit to be heard'—*śravaṇayogyatvāt'*. This seems to be related to the quality of the *svara,* viz. *anuraṇaṇa śakti* (overtone formation), *dīrghatva* (continuity) and *anantaratā* (contiguity) because the *śruti* is *kāraṇa, svara* is *kārya;* the *kāraṇa*-especially the *upādāna kāraṇa* must include the quality of the *kārya* (op.cit., p. 68). However, while commenting on SR 1.3.12cd:

स्यान्निरन्तरता श्रुत्योर्मध्ये ध्वन्यन्तराश्रुतेः ।

he aligns his viewpoint appropriately to '*nirantaratā*' (ibid. pp. 69-70)

मनागुच्चध्वनित्वस्यैव व्यवस्थापकम्—**स्यान्निरन्तरतेति**। श्रुत्योः पूर्वोत्तरतन्त्र्युपपन्नयोर्मध्ये ध्वन्यन्तरा-श्रुतेर्ध्वन्यन्तरस्य पूर्वोत्तरश्रुतिविलक्षणस्य पूर्वश्रुतेः किञ्चिदुच्चस्योत्तरश्रुतेः किञ्चिन्नीचस्य चान्यध्वनेरश्रुतिर-श्रवणम् । अश्रुतेरिति हेतौ पञ्चमी । मध्यगतध्वन्यन्तराश्रवणं निमित्तीकृत्य श्रुत्योर्निरन्तरता यथा स्यात् तथा तन्त्रीः किञ्चिद् दृढीकरणेन मनागुच्चध्वनिः कार्येत्यर्थः ।

He further takes up the untenable position that *dhvani* in its first perception, i.e. at the moment of generation is called '*śruti*' and that *dhvani* in its subsequent perception with continuity and resonance (or overtone formation) is *svara* (ibid. p. 67). I have discussed this temporal view of the *śruti* elsewhere (*Niḥśaṅkahṛdaya,* pp. 356-361, 514-518). Paṇḍarīka Viṭṭhala repeats the *śruti-nāḍī* relationship in *Sadrāgacandrodaya* as also *śruti,* allocations of *svaras* (2.20-22). Besides this, he likens the *śrutis* to mercury resting in *grāhaka-s* (pits) and gives the names of the *śrutis,* viz. *tīvrā, kumudvatī,* etc. in his *Rāgamañjarī* (1.19, 22-24).

By and large, the treatment of *śrutī* in NN is cursory; what is left unsaid is far more than what is said therein. I have discussed the *śruti* in some detail in its manifold facets in *Niḥśaṅkahṛdaya, Śruti: the Scalic Foundation, Śrutijāti: A Four Component Theory* and *Śrutijāti: A Psycho-Acoustical Study,* etc.

30cd. Rāgādi...sthitāḥ: Most authorities, including Paṇḍarīka Viṭṭhala tend to regard the *śruti* as a primary referential matrix from which the *svaras* are derived, while it is more systematic to regard it as a theoretical model. The *antaragata śruti* propounded by Viśvāvasū as well as the four *śrutis* declared by Paṇḍarīka Viṭṭhala (viz. 5,6, 18, 19) as having no musical potential, support this. In any case, the unit of musical transactions is the *svara* and not *śruti. Śruti* is an explanatory and quantifying device of *svaras.*

Rāgādi—*'ādi'* means *gīta,* i.e. the various kinds of *prabandha, vastu* and *rūpaka.*

33d. Prathamā: These positions are defined as *śuddha* in parallel works.

34a. Asapāḥ, i.e. *ri-ga-ma-dha-ni*; this appears to contain a nuance; *ri-ga-ma-dha-ni* move on to the *śrutis* subsequent to the positions of their initial (*śuddha*) state to become modified. Does it mean that *sa* and *pa* themselves move downward for modification? No, they do not move at all; they are invariants. This is a direct consequence of the obsolescence of the *grāma,* in which *sa* occupied the third, viz. *mandā-śruti* and to become *vikṛta,* i.e. *cyuta-ṣaḍja,* causing *ri* to become *vikṛta* at the seventh *śruti* and causing *ni* to became *vikṛti (kaiśikī)* by occupying the first *(tīvrā) śruti;* or *sa* remained at the fourth *śruti (chandovatī)* and yet became *vikṛta (acyuta-ṣaḍja)* because *ni* became *vikṛta (kākali*) at the second *(kumudvatī) śruti;* similarly *pa* was called *vikṛta pañcama* (in *madhyama-grāma*) when it occupied the 16th *(sandīpanī) śruti* instead of the 17th (SR, 1.3.39-45)

34a. Sva-sva-pūrvātaḥ e.g. reckoning from its *śuddha* position viz. seventh *śruti,* if *ri* moves to the eighth, its *gati* is the first; if it moves from the eighth to the ninth, its *gati* is second; if it moves from the ninth to the tenth *śruti* its *gati* is third; similarly, for *ga* the *svapūrva śrutis* are the ninth, tenth, eleventh and twelfth for its first, second, third and fourth *gatis.*

34cd. Tristrī-gatīḥ. *Gati* is translated as degree of movement, abbreviated to 'degree'. Each of *ṛṣabha, madhyama, dhaivata* and *niṣāda* has three *gatis,* while *gāndhāra* has four *gatis.* The seven notes *sa ri ga ma pa dha ni* are defined to be in their initial state *(prathamā-sthiti)* at the 4th, 7th, 9th, 13th, 17th, 20th and 22nd *śrutis* respectively, when their respetive *gati* is zero. The different *gatis* of the *svaras* are compiled in the following table eclectically from Paṇḍarīka Viṭṭhala's NN, *Sadrāga-candrodaya* (1.26-30) and *Rāgamañjarī* (1.27-32).

Svara	*Gati*	*Textual name*	*Śruti number*	*Modern name in*			
				Karnataka music	*Symbol*	*Hindustani music*	*Symbol*
sa	0	ṣaḍja	4	ṣaḍja	sa	kharaj	sa
ri	0	śuddha	7	śuddha ṛṣabha	ra	komal rikhabh	re
	1	catuḥśruti	8	—	ri*	—	
	2	pañcaśruti	9	pañcaśruti ṛṣabha	ri	śuddhari-khabh	
	3	atyucchṛṅkhala	10	ṣaṭśruti ṛṣabha	ru	—	
ga	0	śuddha	9	śuddha gāndhāra	ga	—	
	1	sādhāraṇa	10	sādhāraṇa gāndhāra	gi	komal gāndhār	ga
	2	antara (original)	11	—	gu*	—	
	3	laghu ma	12	(modern) antara gāndhāra	gu	śuddh gāndhār	ga
	4	ūrdhva	13	—	gu+	—	
ma	0	śuddha	13	śuddha madhyama	ma	śuddh madhyam	ma —
	1	prathama	14	—	ma*	—	—
	2	(dvitīya?), pratinidhi	15	—	—	—	—
	3	pratinidhi, laghu pa	16	prati madhyama	mi	tīvra madhyam	ma
pa	0	śuddha	17	pañcama	pa	pañcam	pa
dha	0	śuddha	20	śuddha dhaivata	dha	komal dhaivat	dha
	1	catuḥśruti	21	—	dhi*	—	
	2	pañcaśruti	22	pañcaśruti dhaivata	dhi	śuddh dhaivat	dha
	3	atyucchṛṅkhala	1	ṣaṭśruti dhaivata	dhu	—	—
ni	0	śuddha	22	śuddha niṣāda	na	—	—
	1	kaiśikī	1	kaiśiki niṣāda	ni	komal nikhād	ni
	2	kākalī (original)	2	—	nu*	—	—
	3	laghu sa	3	(modern) kākalī niṣāda	nu nu	śuddh nikhād	ni

The text on *svara-vikṛti* in *Rāgamañjarī* is somewhat confused and opaque; the first *gati ri-dha* are not explicitly stated or named, but used in *śrīrāga* (2.68cd), *mālavakaiśika* (2.64). The third *gati ri-dha* seem to be named *atyucchṛṅkhala* (1.32), but are simply referred to as third *gati ri-dha* (2.36.38). Again, the fourth *gati ga* seems to be named *ūrdhvakhala* (1.31) but mentioned only as fourth *gati ga* in *rāgalakṣaṇa* (2.44a). Mudduveṅkaṭamakhin (*Rāgalakṣaṇa,* 2.141) has called it, appropriately, à *la* Rāmāmātya, (cf. *cyutamadhyamam-gāndhāra, cyutaṣaḍjaniṣāda) śuddhamadhyama gāndhāra,* a name which Tulaja claims to have introduced (*Saṅgītasārāmṛta,* p. 111). Paṇḍarīka Viṭṭhala has designated *ṣaḍja* of the third *śruti* as *laghuṣaḍja, madhyama* at the twelfth *śruti* as *laghu-madhyama* and *pañcama* at the sixteenth *śruti* as *laghu-pañcama* in the *Sadrāgacandrodaya* (1.26, 27). Rāmāmātya has called them *cyutamadhyama-gāndhāra, cyutapañcama-madhyama* and *cyuta-ṣaḍja-niṣāda* respectively (*Svaramelakalānidhi,* 3.29,31-33, 38, 39, 41, 43); Somanātha has named them *mṛdu ma, mṛdu pa* and *mṛdu sa* respectively (1.24 comm.). However, Paṇḍarīka Viṭṭhala, despite the nomenclature in *Sadrāgacandrodaya,* continues to mention them as third *gati ga, ma, ni* in the *Rāgamālā, Rāgamañjarī* and NN. In an opaque passage in *Rāgamañjarī* (1.32ab) he seems to indicate the names *kaiśikī,* (?) and *ūrdhva* for *madhyama* in its three *gatis* viz. at the fourteenth, fifteenth and sixteenth *śrutis;* but he refers to the first *gati ma* as such in the *lakṣaṇa* of *vibhāsa* (NN 3.1.197, *Rāgamālā,* 175).

It is interesting that about a generation later Somanātha has used *gati* for *svaravikṛti* in the same sense (*Rāgavibodha,* 1.29 and comm.).

35cd. Ganyor-gatī-smṛtau. The *ga-ni* of the second *gati* viz. *antara* and *kākalī* at the eleventh and second *śrutis* respectively were acoustically complex and muscially unsatisfactory intervals. This is why their use was prescribed to the minimum in the music of the *grāma* and *jāti;* Mummaḍi Cikkabhūpāla extracts Bharata to say that *antara* and *kākalī* notes were to be used only in such *jātis* in which *ga* and *ni* were little used (*Abhinava Bharatasārasaṅgraha,* p.150);

अस्याल्पनिषादगान्धारासु जातिषु प्रयोगः ।

Śārṅgadeva is even more explicit (SR 1.5.6):

अल्पप्रयोगः सर्वत्र काकली चान्तरः स्वरः ।

In fact, they were not regarded as independent *svaras* at all, and did not have the status or function of *aṁśa-svara.* This is because they had no consonance richness etc. The *ga* and *ni* manifested at the twelfth and third *śrutis* respectively (i.e. the modern '*antara*' and '*kākalī*' notes) were obtained by the *grāma-sādhārṇa* technique, and were employed exclusively in the *madhyamagrāma* and *ṣaḍjagrāma jātis* and *rāgas* respectively. This restriction arose because the maximum intervallic size was restricted to four *śrutis.* However, when the *grāma* gave place to *mela,* the conceptual and empirical parameters had to be realigned to the notion of the *mela*; one such realignment related to the *antara-kākalī* notes. When *madhyama-grāma* merged into the *ṣaḍja-grāma, madhyama-sādhāraṇa* was sought to be accommodated in the *ṣaḍjagrāma* itself. Both the *antara* and *kākalī* were now (in the 16th century A.D.) tempered to their next *śruti* positions; as tribute to tradition and convention, they were still named as *ma* (*laghu ma, mṛdu ma, cyutamadhyama-gāndhāra*) and *sa* (*laghu sa, mṛdu sa, cyutaṣaḍjaniṣāda*). The original *antara* and *kākalī* became diffuse and ambiguous for some time, continued to be used in some *rāgas* in the 16th century, during the transition of the *grāma* to the *mela.* For a while *cyutamadhyamagāndhāra* and *cyutaṣaḍjaniṣāda* were made to represent the *antara* and *kākalī* notes in such *rāgas* as employed the latter, and in course of time displaced them completely. Soon, when *ṣaḍjagrāma* became uniquely established the practice of calling the notes at the twelfth and third *śrutis* as *madhyama* and *ṣaḍja* and of employing the *antra-kākalī* notes was given up; the former were tempered, and out of respect or loyalty to the *grāma* system, the names *antara* and *kākalī* were retained for the new tempered notes. Paṇḍarīka Viṭṭhala is probably indicating this situation when he repeats the second *gati ga-ni* with the names *antara* and *kākalī* in this hemistitch.

36. The four *śrutis* viz. 5th-18th, 6th-19th, though separated by twelfth *śrutis* and therefore could constitute *saṁvādī* pairs are unique in the octave; they are always *antaragata-śrutis* and can never manifest *svaras.* This is a direct consequence of the rule that *sa* and *pa* could never be *vikṛta svaras* and that only *svaras* other than *sa-pa* (hence the use of the phrase *asapāḥ* in NN, 3.1.34a)—but never *sa* and *pa* could move upward into subsequent *śrutis* to attain *vikṛti. Ma* however was divested of its nonomissibility *(avināśitva)* and invariability but was characterised with three *gatis* to align with the transition of *grāma* to *mela.*

37ab. Śeṣa......bodhakāḥ: The disposition of *svaras* in the remaining eighteen *śrutis* is as follows:

1. third *gati dha*/first *gati ni (kaśikī ni)*
2. second *gati ni* (*kākalī ni*)
3. third *gati ni* (*laghu sa*)
4. *ṣaḍja*
5. —
6. —
7. *śuddha ri*
8. first *gatī ri (catuḥśruti ri*)
9. second *gati ri / śuddha ga*
10. third *gati ri*/first *gati ga* (*sādhāraṇa ga*)
11. second *gati ga (gantara ga)*
12. third *gati ga* (*laghu ma*)
13. fourth *gati ga*/ *śuddha ma*

14. first *gati ma*
15. second *gati ma*
16. third *gati ma* (*laghu pa*)
17. *pañcama*
18. —
19. —
20. *śuddha dha*
21. first *gati dha* (*catuḥśruti dha*)
22. second *gati dha/ śuddha ni.*

37cd. Nyūnādhikā... yadi Cf. *Sadrāgacandrodaya,* 2.27, where the principle is extended to *anumandra* (also, Somanātha, op. cit. 2.34, p. 68). This principle is discovered for the first time in the 16th century. This implies that exact intonation was expected only in the middle register, while a certain amount of latitude was allowed in the same notes when executed in the lower or higher registers. This concession was made probably because of the ambiguous status of notes like *catuḥśruti ri-dha, antara gāndhāra, kākalī niṣada,* and *pratimadhyama* (which at this time oscillated between the 15th and 16th *śrutis*). This situation must have then existed in both Karnataka music and Hindustani music because Paṇḍarīka Viṭṭhala and Somanātha enunciate this principle; significantly it is no longer stated in the 18th century and later.

38-41. The fourfold classification of *svaras* into *vādī, saṁvādī, anuvādi* and *vivādi* is an important contribution of Indian music theory to the understanding of the aesthetic experience in music.

Every semantic mode depends for effective expression on an efficient organisation of its symbols. The meaning may emerge from sequential (discursive) or simultaneous (presentational) appearance of the symbols. The clarity and intelligibility of the meaning depends on organising the symbols into groups each of which has a discernible pattern such that there is inter-group and intra-group consistency. The meaning is determined not only by integration of the unitary or group meanings; but syntax, of (i.e. the way in which the symbols are organised or arranged), proximity and distance, relative importance or prominence etc. of the symbols are also relevant to express an intended meaning. Both homophonic music and language have discursive symbols; polyphonic music consists of a progression of simultaneous (or presentational) symbols. The symbols have three functions, viz. signification, connotation and denotation, which are mutually complementary. In language these are more or less fixed and therefore cannot readily be interchanged or displaced, except in special situations involving complex equations. But the symbols in music have only more or less fixed signification while connotation and denotation are impermanent, fluid and limited by personal equations. Therefore, they possess unlimited general, polyvalent application. So possibility for conjugation and reciprocation arises in *svara,* and not word. A more detailed discussion of symbolistic philosophy of meaning may be found in Susanne K. Langer: *Philosophy in a New Key* and *Emotion in Music,* A.N. Whitehead, *Symbolism: Its Meaning and Effect* and Bertrand Russel, *Our Knowledge of the External World* (chapter on Logic as Essence of Philosophy).

In defining *vādi-svara* as most expressive of the personality of a *rāga* through the most prolific recurrence and possessing an interval of twenty two *śrutis,* in defining *saṁvādī* as a conjugate of the *vādī* at the distance of the (just) fourth or (just) fifth and defining it as a *svara* at the distance of nine or thirteen *śrutis* from the *vādī,* ancient Indian musicologists such as Bharata have shown amazing perceptive brilliance. Similarly the *vivādī* is difined as a *svára* of two *śrutis,* reckoned from the *vādī;* all other notes are *anuvādīs.* This means that aesthetic (or sonance) potential of *svara* varies directly with pitch distance. This quality accrues from similarity or identity with itself, which is greatest in the octave note; the next most similarity occurs in the fourth *(madhyama)* and then in the fifth (which is an inverted fourth from the octave), next in the *anuvādīs,* and least in the most proximate, viz. the *vivādī.* These are very appropriately named in Western music theory in terms of sonance (assonance, con-sonance, dis-sonance and in Indian music in terms of expressive potential (*'vad'*): *vādī, saṁ-vādī, anu-vādī* and *vi-vādī. Vivādī* should be interpreted not as a note to be avoided, but as antilogical to the *vādī,* which heightens the effect of the *vādī* by contrast.

The *saṁvādī* etc. are defined in two mutually consistent ways, as explained by Abhinavagupta (op. cit. on Bharata, op. cit. 28.22, 23, pp.16, 17): Bharata and others describe *saṁvāditva* as a phenomenon perceived in single note having a magnitude of nine or thirteen *śrutis,* reckoned from the *vādī;* this is an extension of the concept of *svara -pramāṇa,* e.g. *dviśruti, triśruti, catuḥśruti svara.* So *saṁvāditva* refers to the quality or nature *(svarūpa)* of the note, which accrues to it because of its size, rather than as an interval *(antarāla)*; that is, consonance is a quality of the note, not of an intervening interval. This is the view of Bhaṭṭa Tauta, Abhinavagupta's teacher. In commenting on Bharata's

ययोश्च नवकत्रयोदशकमन्तरं तावन्योन्यं संवादिनौ । (NŚ. 28.22 pr. p.15)

Abhinavagupta says (loc. cit.)

एतच्च स्वराभिधानम् । अन्ये त्वाहुः—अष्टौ नवेति नवका अष्टका उच्यन्ते। स एष त्रयोदश वा द्वादश । एतावत्यः श्रुतयस्तयोरन्तरं ययोस्तौ संवादिनाविति । उपाध्यायास्त्वाहुः—अन्तरमिति स्वरूपं नान्तरालं, तेन नवश्रुतिकं यस्य स्वरूपं स्वरस्य, यस्य च त्रयोदश श्रुतिकत्वं स्वरूपं तौ स्वरूपं परस्परसंवादिनौ ।

The last sentence here would mean *prima facie* that if there are two notes A and B such that they have magnitudes of nine and thirteen *śrutis* respectively when reckoned from a third note C, then A and B are mutually *saṁvādī* notes. This is untenable because it leaves the *vādī* (viz. C) out of consideration; *saṁvādī, anuvādī* and *vivādī* exist only in relation to the *vādī* as indicated in their names. Also, in other contexts such as formation of *auḍuva* etc. Bharata unambiguously means the just fifth (a thirteen *śruti* note from the given *ṣāḍava-* causing note). Therefore the above last sentence should be construed thus: each of A and B is mutually *samvādī* with the *vādī* note. Otherwise, two notes, e.g. *madhyama* and *pañcama* (of *ṣaḍjagrāma*) separated by only four *śrutis* would become mutually *saṁvādis*; thus the *saṁvādī-lakṣaṇa* enunciated by Bharata becomes futile and inconsistent.

The second view of *saṁvāditva* is interval oriented; it considers the phenomenon in terms of a pair of notes, that is, a relational value; two notes are said to be mutually *saṁvādīs* if there is an interval or distance of eight or twelve *śruti*: श्रुतयो द्वादशाष्टौ वा ययोरन्तरगोचरा: मिथ: संवादिनौ तौ स्तो- (SR 1.3.48, 49). Here both the notes are regarded as contributing to the *saṁvādī* character through mutual participation; both notes are *saṁvādins* and the first has (no longer) the character of *vādī*. Further, this relationship is independent of the *vādī* note; i.e. any two notes separated by eight or twelve *śrutis* would be *saṁvādins*, whatever the *vādī* note may be. In the first view, the *saṁvādī* is manifested at the ninth or thirteenth *śruti*; in the second, it is at a distance of eight or twelve *śrutis*. Quantitatively both mean the same; qualitatively however, they seem to be based on different premises.

Abhinavagupta prescribes, besides nine-*śruti* thirteen-*śruti* magnitude, another condition of *saṁvāditva*, viz. sameness of the number of *śrutis* (op. cit. loc. cit. p. 17) elaborating the scope of '*anyo'nya*' in the above passage from Bharata.

अन्योन्यस्येति वचनं तावद् यस्य संवादिनौ मा भूतामिति समानश्रुतिकत्वेन संवदनात् संवादिनौ ।

He owes this idea to Matanga (op. cit. p.14): संवादिनस्तु पुन: समश्रुतिकत्वे त्रयोदशनवान्तर-त्वेनावबोद्धव्या: । This condition is well satisfied in the illustrations offered for *saṁvāditva* by Bharata himself: *sa-pa, ri-dha, ga-ni, sa-ma* in *ṣaḍjagrāma*; *ri-dha, ga-ni, ri-pa, sa-ma* in *madhyama-grāma*. While Bharata seems to have restricted *saṁvāditva* specifically only to these pairs, it was extended by others, (e.g. Matanga through the *maṇḍala prastāra* method, p. 14) to the *vikṛta* notes. Matanga's discussion of consonance is very lucid and very illuminating (op. cit. pp. 14-17; extr. Kallinātha, op. cit. on SR 1.3.47-51, p. 92).

ननु वदनादिकं प्राणिधर्म: कथमचेतनानां स्वराणां सम्भवति ? सत्यम्; वदनं हि नाम रागप्रतिपादकत्वं विवक्षितम्, न वचनमित्यदोष: । संवदनात् संवादी । संवदनं नाम यद्वादिना स्वरेण रागस्य रागत्वं जनितं तन्निर्वाहकत्वम् । विवदनाद् विवादी । विवदनं नाम वाद्यादिभि: स्वरैरुत्पद्यमानाया रक्तेर्विनाशकत्वम् । अनुवदनाद् अनुवादी । अनुवदनं नाम वादिसंवादिसम्पादितरक्त्यनुकूलत्वम् ।

That *saṁvāditva* here refers to a pair of conjugate (or interchangeable) notes is abundantly borne out by the description and illustrations which follow.

Paṇḍarīka Viṭṭhala aligns himself with this latter view (eight or twelve *śrutis*—interval between a pair of notes); in his *Sadrāgacandrodaya* (1.35) he further adds that (not withstanding the fulfilment of this condition) *(śuddha) ma* and *(śuddha) ni* do not bear mutual consonance:

यदन्तरेऽष्टश्रुतयो द्विषड्वा संवादिनौ तौ न निमावथ च ।

He does not explain the reason for this exception. Abhinavagupta notices it; but because he mentions it contiguously with *'samāna-śrutikatva'*, it is to be inferred that the lack of consonance between this pair arises because of the lack of *samāna-śrutikatva* (op. cit. loc. cit. p. 17): यथा मध्यमनिषादयोर्न संवादित्वं सत्यपि ...

Kallinātha is explicit on this point (op. cit. loc. cit. p. 93), and rejects this criterion:

शुद्धयोर्मध्यमनिषादयोः परस्परं संवादित्व(ा)दर्शनादित्यपरितोषेण पक्षान्तरमाह–रिधयोरेव वेति ।
प्रथममन्यविवादिना वित्यविशे(षे)ण कथनं तु समश्रुतिकत्वयोरेव संवाद इति मतानुसारेण ।

He does not subscribe to *samāna-śrutikatva* as a criterion for *saṁvāditva* and holds the twelve- or eight-*śruti* interval alone is both necessary and sufficient for consonance:

अतो द्वादशाष्टश्रुत्यन्तरित्वमात्रमेव संवादिलक्षणामिति सिद्धं भवति ।

It may be noted that Śārṅgadeva and later authorities do not restrict consonance to specifically named pairs; so in the 13th century A.D. the *saṁvāditva* relationship was extended to the *vikṛta svaras* also. This is clear from Kallinātha's commentary. Kallinātha comprehends both viewpoints and conciles them as not really different (op. cit. p. 93):

एवं 'त्रयोदशनवान्तरम्' इति मतङ्गोक्तस्य संवादिलक्षणस्यापि द्वादशाष्टान्तरमेवार्थः ।

Paṇḍarīka Viṭṭhala's definitions of *vādī* etc. are general and uncontroversial. For example, he defines *vivādins* as a pair of notes which are separated by one intervening *śruti* (NN 3.1.41ab). But Śārṅgadeva, probably influenced by Abhinavagupta's words, offers three alternative views on the *vivādī* (SR 1.3.49).

निगावन्यविवादिनौ । रिधयोरेव वा स्यातां तौ तयोर्वा रिधावपि ॥

(1) *Ni-ga* are *vivādins* with respect to all other notes; (2) they are *vivādins* of *ri-dha* (respectively); (3) *ri-dha* are *vivādins* of *ga-ni* respectively. These are widely divergent views. The first means (rather improbably) that each of *ga* and *ni* is a *vivādin* of each of *sa, ri, ma, pa* and *dha*. If so, the condition of one *śruti* intervening interval

is flouted; it means (probably) that they are *vivādins* to the other notes when this condition is fulfilled. For example, *ni* is *vivādī* to *sa* when the former is *kaiśikī* or *kākalī* and the latter is *cyuta* or *acyuta* respectively; to *dha* when both are *śuddha.* Similarly, *ga* is *vivādin* to *ri* when both are *śuddha; ga* is *vivādin* of *ma* when the former is *sādhāraṇa* or *antara* and the latter, *cyuta* or *acyuta* respectively. The second view is valid when the pairs *ri-ga, dha-ni* are both *śuddha,* and is included in the first as a special instance; this view suggests that the *vivāditva* (and *saṁvāditva*) apply only to *śuddha-svaras* (as was prescribed by Bharata-muni). The third view presents an unusual concept of *vivāditva;* when we say that *ga* is *vivādin* of *ri,* this antilogicity accrues not because of its own nature, but because of the nature of *ri;* in other words, *vivāditva* is generated in *ri,* but it culminates, manifests or is reflected in *ga.* The same applies to *ni-dha* also.

Sonance has attracted much discussion in Western music and covers a wide range from the ingenuous theory of pleasing-displeasing to a volumetric theory of sound postulated by Henry Watt (*The Psychology of Sound,* cit. Glen Hayden, *Introduction to Musicology,* p. 91). These theories may be classified into three groups—mathematical, physical and psychophysiological. From Plato and Euclid to Euler and Liebnitz consonance is attributed to simple numerical relationships, e.g. 1:1, 1:2, 2:3, 3:4 between frequencies of notes. It sounds attractive and appeals to one's aesthetic sense of simplicity but presents only a partial view of the phenomenon. More detailed and complex theories of consonance-dissonance have been put forward from the ancient times by Pythagoras, Aristoxenus, Democritus etc. to the later Helmholtz, D' Alembert, Rameau, Tartini, Stumpf, Watt, Seashore, Malmberg, Revesz, Koening etc. The more important among these are due to Helmholtz, Malmberg, Revesz and Stumpf. Helmholtz offers an acoustical theory based on the phenomenon of beats. Beats may be defined as the periodic variations in the intensity of sound at a point because of the coexistence of two wave trains possessing slightly different frequencies. The difference between the frequencies of the two primary sounds give the number of beats. According to Helmholtz, consonance is a continuous sensation of tone while dissonance is a discontinuous, (intermittent) sensation (roughness). That is, consonance is the absence or the minimum occurrence of beats, while dissonance is the opposite. He classified consonance on this basis as absolute (octave, double octave), perfect (fifth and fourth), medial (major third and major sixth), imperfect (minor third and minor sixth) and dissonance (second, seventh, augmented fourth). Beats are most noticeable when they occur at the rate of thirty-three per second, and cease to be sensible at 132 per second. In other words, what is dissonance at low pitch range would cease to be dissonance at higher pitch ranges, and could, at appropriate pitch levels, even be transformed into consonance. The phenomenon is explained with an intersensory (visual) analogy. Just as a flickering light would tire the eye nerves, so also the beats prove tiring to the ear (Helmholtz, *Sensations of Tone,* cit. Charles Culver, *Musical Acoustics,* pp. 82-84; cit. Revesz, *Introduction to the Psychology of Music,* pp. 81-84). This theory has received general acceptance but has certain inconsistencies. For example, there is *sa-pa* consonance at thirtytwo cps—sixtyfour cps but is accompanied with beats while there is dissonance at 2093 cps—3951 cps (*śuddha ṛiṣabha-kākalī-niṣāda*) beats are absent as shown by Stumpf (Carl Stumpf, *Konsonanz und Dissonanz,* cit. Revesz, op. cit. p. 82). In other words, the beat rate depends on the pitch range and not on the nature of the intervals, i.e. not on consonance or dissonance. The main argument against this theory is that consonance is basically a psychoacoustic phenomenon, and the theory leaves out the psychological aspects of the experience altogether and depends only on the physical laws. Basing on the differential tones discovered by Helmholtz, W. Preyer and F. Krueger developed the differential tone theory according to which i. consonance depends on the number of differentials and ii. consonance is inversely proportional to the number of differentials occurring between two tones. This theory has no empirical foundations; there are two-note clangs in which differentials have no effect whatsoever but still the clangs are very dissonant (F. Krueger, *Die Theorie der Konsonanz,* cit. Revesz, op. cit. p. 84). In summary, the physical theories of consonance, including the foregoing, propose that the difference between consonance and dissonance lies in the degree of continuity of the tone sensation.

Carl Stumpf proposes the theory of fusion, in a psychological perspective. The concept of fusion *per se* is not original to Stumpf, but has been mooted from the earliest times by Euclid, and in recent times by Külpe, Meinong, Titchener and Theodor Lipps. Stumpf defines fusion as the approximation of a two-note clang towards unison; consonance is directly proportional to this sensation of unison; dissonance is inversely proportional to it. A statistical analysis of his comprehensive experiments shows that only degree of fusion can be determined but no sharp dividing line may be drawn between consonance and dissonance. Unison, i.e. the sensation of hearing a single tone, resulting from the fusion of two notes, is perceived *in toto,* in a complex way in a single stage and cannot be resolved into simpler elements (Carl Stumpf, op. cit. ibid., pp. 85, 86). Revesz levels many serious objections against this theory such as its validity only in a very limited pitch range, lack of its applicability to two tones not lying within the same octave (fusion diminishes as the octave difference between two consonant notes increases) etc. (Revesz, op. cit. pp. 87, 88). Revesz characterizes the Helmholtz theory as a causative-genetic theory of consonance which endeavours to determine the objective physical basis of the consonance phenomena; on the other hand, Stumpf's theory of fusion represents a descriptive phenomenological concept that strives to trace the consonance phenomena to an ultimate psychological fact, i.e. fusion. The experiments of Seashore and Malmberg also reveal that there are no incontrovertible foundations for the theory of fusion (Carl E. Seashore, *Psychology of Music,* p. 131). Malmberg's experiments show that consonance decreases in the following order: octave, fifth, major sixth, major third, just fourth, etc. The listener was required in this experiment to evaluate consonance on the basis of three criteria viz. smoothness, purity (absence of partials) and unison. These results appear to be acceptable in the context of Western music (C.F. Malmberg, *The Perceptions of Consonance and Dissonance,* Ia. St. Psy. 8.1918, pp. 93-133). Seashore claims that the principle of consonance may be accommodated broadly on two simple criteria viz. smoothness-roughness and purity-resonance.

Investigations in Gestalt psychology and phenomenology on consonance and dissonance have opened up a new dimension towards the understanding of this phenomenon: it has been shown that consonance is compounded of such special features as independence, unitariness, definiteness and balance of proportions. On the other hand, dissonance manifests dependence, need of resolution, instability and dynamic tendency (C.W. Valentiner, *Appreciation of Musical Intervals,* British Journal of Musicology, cit. Revesz, op. cit. p. 90; S.F. Nadel, *"Zur psychologie des Konsonanzerlebens", Zeitschrift für Psychologie,* 101, 1926, cit. ibid., loc. cit.)

The relevance of a discussion of theories of consonance-dissonance in Western music may be questioned at this point by some. This has been answered in the introduction to this discussion. As mentioned therein, the problem is both general and universal to any mode of semantic expression and gains special interest and importance in the context of nondiscursive areas of meaning such as in music. Sonance is a fundamental and universal aspect of every system of music; there are, therefore some similarities in the phenomenon, be it in Indian music or in Western music. The introduction of equal temperament has distanced the problem in Western music from natural consonance-dissonance. Nevertheless, experience shows that tone sensation is not momentary but somewhat spread out in time, and is related to a precedent and successive sensation of tone. In this sense, consonance-dissonance in polyphonic music has semblance with that in homophonic music.

Two other considerations are also relevant here: (i) consonance-dissonance is not absolute; acoustically it varies with pitch range; (ii) it varies with aesthetic taste; it is well known that habituation, i.e. longer and more frequent exposure, dissolves out dissonance rapidly and may even render it pleasant; the dominance of *vivādī* in newly created *rāgas* and in the *rāgas* revived from the past in Karnataka music practice of today is an example of this. Nevertheless, consonance-dissonance has also an objective aspect, and this cannot be negated, neglected or ignored in favour of purely psychological reasons.

Again, the need to resolve tension or stress to rest is a fundamental trait of the human mind. Music may be regarded as involving the process of creating and resolving aesthetic, affective or structural tension in the locus of a moving tone. Such tension is created by interaction of *vivādī* with the *vādī* in the main and to a lesser degree with *saṁvādī* and *anuvādī* in the unfoldment of the melodic form and is medially resolved by the *apanyāsa* and finally by the *nyāsa*. Among the factors which generate such tension are distance from the *graha* (point of origin), *gamaka* and the sizes of the intervals involved. In situations where *ṣaḍja* which is the universal *graha, aṁśa* and *nyāsa* for all *rāgas* in Indian music since the 16th century assumes a secondary role, consonance-dissonance takes the appearance of simulacrum, and the conventional consonance-dissonance becomes displaced. This is comparable with Auffassungs-dissonanz of Louis and Thuille (R. Louis and L. Thuille, *Harmonielehre*, cit. Glen Haydon, *Introduction to Musicology*, p. 92).

A quantitative or statistical approach to *saṁvāda-vivāda* is conspicuously absent in Indian music theory. The characterisation of degrees of sonance in terms of number of *śrutis* is essentially nonempirical, and largely conceptual. It is noteworthy that the attributes of the experience of *saṁvāda* are analysed in Indian music theory into the psychoacoustic attributes of the *svara* (the unit of musical experience) such as *snigdhatā, anuraṇana, śrutyanantara-bhāvitva, svato-rañjana,* etc. The concept of *anuvādī* lying between *saṁvādī* and *vivādī* and *'vādi-saṁvādi-sampādita rakty-anukūla'* attribute is a distinct contribution of Indian music to consonance-dissonance; the concepts of conjugability in the *saṁvādī* and of the accommodation of *vivādin* within the *alpatva-rāgaprāṇa* and in *nigraha-tānakriyā* are equally brilliant.

43ab. Kvacit is related to *svarabhedāḥ* in **44d.**

43cd-44. Rāgaprāṇas mandra, tāra, alpatva, bahutva, ṣāḍava and **auḍuva** are athetised by Paṇḍarīka Viṭṭhala. It is interesting to note that *aṁśa* (*=vādī=sthāyī=jīvasvara,* cf. NN 3.1.39cd, 145), *nyāsa, graha,* etc. are treated as varieties of *svara* rather than as *rāgaprāṇas.*

45. ṣaḍjaḥ ... svarāḥ. This is found in *Sadrāgacandrodaya* (1.51)

सर्वत्र षड्जो ग्रह एव रागे रक्त्यैकहेतोर्निधपादयो ये ।
वर्णाः प्रयोज्या न तु ते स्वराश्च ताः मूर्छनाः षड्जभवा ह्यशेषाः ॥

Whenever phrases like *nidhapamagarisa, dhapamagarisani* are used at the beginning of a song, or occur as the scale of a *rāga, ni, dha,* etc. at the beginning were regarded as *graha* and the scale or phrase classified under *ṣaḍja-grāma* or *madhyama-grāma* depending on the *vikṛta-svaras* they contained. When the *gāndhāra-grāma* and *madhyama-grāma* had disappeared altogether leaving only *ṣaḍja-grāma* behind in musical practice such *ni, dha,* etc. should not be regarded, says Paṇḍarīka Viṭṭhala, as *graha* despite their initial occurrence; for, *sa* is the universal *graha* for all *rāgas* because all extant *rāgas* now belong only to *ṣaḍja-grāma*; such usages do not have the force of *svaras,* but only of ordinary syllables. Also, the scales *nidhapamagarisa, dhapamagarisani*, etc. should be regarded as *mūrchanās* of *ṣaḍja-grāma* only; that is, the initial *ni, dha,* etc. of these are established in the position of *sa* (cf. NN 3.1.46c) to derive these scales by modal shift of tonic; this is why *ni, dha* etc. are in reality *sa* itself, though they are pronounced as *ni, dha, pa,* etc. It is true that notes other than *sa* are prescribed as *graha, aṁśa* and *nyāsa* for some *rāgas* e.g. *karnaṭī, sāverī, deśākṣī.* In such cases, these notes should be understood as specially contributing to the manifestation of the *rāgabhāva,* besides *sa* which also cofunctions as the general *graha,* which when so used does not mar the purport of the *rāga.* To summarise, suppose that phrases such as *nidhapamagarisa, dhapamagarisani, pamagarisanidha* or the *śuddha tānas* or *kūṭa tānas* generated by them have to be employed in *rāgālapti* or song to obtain *rakti.* These should be regarded neither as *mūrchanās* nor *tānas* but are the *varṇālaṁkāras* (q.v.). The scale of any *rāga* in contemporary usage belongs to *ṣaḍja-grāma* and *ṣaḍja-grāma* alone. In this way, Paṇḍarīka Viṭṭhala loses no opportunity, however small, to concile *lakṣaṇa* with *lakṣya,* especially in the context of the revolutionary changes which were occurring in both the theory and practice in music of his times.

46b. Munīśvaraiḥ is an anachronistic and apocryphal reference, made in the hope of gaining the respect and authority of antiquity for changes which were occurring in his own times.

47a. Cātaka: The bird cucculus melanoleucus which is believed to live only on rain drops. *Riṣabha* is likened to the cry of this bird by Kohala and Maheśvara (extr. Mataṅga, op. cit. 63, p. 13) and by SR (1.3.46), *Saṅgītaśiromaṇi* (165), *Saṅgītasārāvalī* (3, p. 7), *Saṅgītamakaranda* (1.13.14), *Catvāriṁśac-chatarāga nirūpaṇam* (1.30-32), etc. It is likened to the cry of the bull elsewhere e.g. *Yājñavalkya-śikṣā* (8.9), *Saṅgītadāmodara* (3.2.3), *Aumāpatam* (20.5, 6), *Bharatabhāṣya* (3.15-18) etc. Similarly, *dhaivata* is likened to the neighing of horse instead of the croaking of the frog. Paṇḍarīka Viṭṭhala omits other attributes of *svara,* first mentioned by Mataṅga (op. cit. pp. 13,16-18) and elaborated by Śārṅgadeva (SR 1.3.52-59) and others.

48a. Hatiḥ: striking (the *nāḍis* by *prāṇavāyu* or striking the medium, e.g. string, skin, etc.) to generate musical sound; this is the cause of all *āhata-nāda.* This sequential theory of *śruti-svara* relationship seems to be quite old and based on the *Naiyāyika* (Logician) philosophy. Paṇḍarīka Viṭṭhala has subscribed to this theory of pitch-perception time in his *Sadrāgacandrodaya* also (1.32cd-33):

यथेश्वरप्रेरितवातचक्रघातात् प्रभूतध्वनिरेव नाड्याम् ।
प्राक् घातमात्रश्रवणात् श्रुतिश्चानुध्वानरूपः स्वरः इत्यकिञ्चित् ॥

Abhinavagupta compiles this theory from contemporary or earlier times and discusses it at some length. Musical sound is distinguished from noise in possessing the attributes of continuity and covibration (in partials: *anu-raṇana*). These attributes are found in a vibrating string or bell, but not in a vibrating rope or stone.

The former have *anuraṇana* while the latter have only *raṇana*. All four have the common property of *raṇana*-sound generation, but only the string, bell, etc. have *anuraṇana* also, which is born the very next moment after *raṇana*. It is this which confers continuity (longevity), naturalness, sweetness and smoothness on the sound and thus makes it *svara*. The sound generated at the very moment of striking or collision (*abhighāta*) is called *'śruti'* and the one which is joined at the next moment by *anuraṇana* (resonance) is called *svara*. Thus the difference between *śruti* and *svara* lies in the sequence of appearance and the *anuraṇana*. Abhinavagupta recognizes this theory, but refutes the argument viz. that the element of time needed for perception of pitch is *śruti*, by saying that such perception time is an integral component of the *śruti* (here, perceived sound) (op. cit. pp. 12, 13, 19).

Kallinātha on the other hand, firmly subscribes to the sequential theory while commenting on the definition *'śravaṇāt śrutayo matāḥ'* (SR 1.3.8), he says that *śrutis* are heard because they are fit to be heard *(śravaṇayogyatva)*. Such fitness accrues from *anuraṇana* which extends *(tāna)* the tone into longer and longer life. Even so, the sound which is just heard at the very first moment of birth is *śruti* (op. cit. on ibid., loc. cit. p. 67).

According to the *Tārkikas* (logicians), *dravya* (matter) and *guṇa* (property) are not born (or perceived) at the same moment; *dravya* is born first and at the moment of its birth it is absolute, i.e. without attributes. At the next moment, owing to union with the sensorium, *guṇa* unites with *dravya*; then the form, nature, etc. of the matter become perceptible. Similarly, *nāda* the *dravya*, generated by collision of objects, is at the moment of generation, absolute, independent. Then it is called *'śruti'*. Then, at the very next moment, the attribute *(guṇa)* called *anuraṇana* joins it; as a consequence, acquiring *snigdhatā, mādhurya, śrutyanantarabhāvitva,* etc. it becomes *svara*. This theory should be considered only in the context of Indian music theory; for, elsewhere, *nāda* or *śabda* is not *dravya* but is itself the *guṇa* of *ākāśa*, space. If this is allowed, the theory becomes invalid.

According to this theory, there is a time lag between the perception of *śruti* and perception of *svara* (so the theory may also be called Time-lag Theory). Kumbhakarṇa asserts that the duration of this time-lag is perceptible to the ear of an acutely intelligent (sensitive) person as the time taken to pierce with sharp needle through thirty-two lotus petals placed one above the other (this is 0.32 *kṣaṇa* which is the fundamental unit on the time scale of the *tālaprāṇa* called *'kāla'*). This is the time measure *(śrutermānam)* of the *śruti*. Just as *dhvani vailakṣaṇya* is pitch limen in the perception of the *śruti*, this measure of duration is the time limen. If it is less than this threshold value, the *śruti* is not perceived (Kumbhakarṇa, *Saṅgītarāja*, 2.1.2.87, 88, p. 79).

The purport of this theory is that there is a time-lag between appearance and sensation. Postulated more than a thousand years ago, it has received abundant experimental support in the area of experimental psychology of music. It is generally found that pitch perception time is inversely proportional to the pitch level.

1. Carl Seashore writes (*Psychology of Music,* pp. 61, 62):

"**Duration**. There are three types of musical situations which may be recognized in the measurement of pitch discrimination: (i) going from one note to another with a complete break between them as in the standard test where we sound two notes, each of which is one second in duration but differing in pitch and separated by a very short interval of time; (ii) legato rise or fall in pitch or pitch vibrato and (iii) sudden shift in a single note without break in tone as an erratic intonation.

"The discrimination is different for each of these, the necessary increment being about twice as large for the first type as the third, and the second falling between these two. These differences are related to the differences in total duration of each tone.

"The minimum duration necessary in order to identify the pitch of a tone clearly varies with the frequency and to some extent with the loudness. It has been found that in order to be heard clearly as a definite pitch, a tone of 128 cps must have a duration of 0.09 second; for 256 cps, about 0.07 second; for 384 cps, about 0.04 second; and for 512 cps, about the same."

2. Charles Culver agrees that a certain minimum time is necessary in order to recognise a definite pitch and pitch difference, but feels that this duration is not related to the pitch level. He opines that not withstanding differences of opinion on the actual time-lag, it may be generally said that there is such a minimum time (Charles A. Culver, *Musical Acoustics,* pp. 47, 48):

"Another aspect of pitch perception which is coming to have increased significance concerns the minimum time required for the ear to recognize a definite pitch. The data bearing on this point are, as yet, not very concordant, but it would appear that the 'pitch-perception time' is more or less independent of the frequency, being of the order of one twentieth of a second.

"Not only can the ear catalogue a note as to pitch in a remarkably short time interval, but it can also a recognize a sound as such when only two vibrations are made. This means that in the region of c_3 we can become conscious of the existence of a sound if it persists for two or three hundredths of a second. However, to recognize the characteristics of a note, anywhere from two to twenty oscillations are necessary."

Modern experimental psychology has collected much data on the time required to perceive the attribute of an object by union with a sense such as sight, hearing or touch.

3. Thus Dashiell (John F. Dashiell, *Fundamentals of General Psychology* , p. 45; ms=millisecond= 1/1000 of a second):

"Simple response to auditory stimuli varies from 120 ms. to 180 ms. to visual stimuli, from 150 ms. to 225 ms. to tactual pressure, from 130 ms to 185 ms.

4. Robert S. Woodworth (*Experimental Psychology*, pp. 298-339) has obtained comparable results.

5. Harvey Fletcher has this to say: the minimum time that a pure tone must excite the ear for definite pitch to be perceived is about one twentieth of a second and this is nearly independent of frequency (*Speech and Hearing*, pp. 152ff).

6. Fritz Winckel states that the time difference between appearance and perception of sound arises because of the indeterminacy of time and frequency. He reports the investigations of M. Joos (*Acoustic Phonetics, inter alia*) who calls this time-lag as 'perception-time smear', which is about 50 ms. This is a remarkably large value; for a phoneme in rapid conversational speech also requires this span of time. Four other factors are relevant in this connection; the onset times (durations required for sounds to become steady or recognizable from the moment of excitation) are different for different musical instruments: trumpet 20 ms, clarinet 50-70 ms, saxophone 36-40 ms, flute 200-300 ms. The average tone colour of a sound series varies with the speed of execution of the series. Secondly the above time constant of 50 ms has a further far reaching significance: it is the time we require to become conscious of one of our sensory impressions. This is called human factor and shown in recent precise measurements, to have a value of 55 ms. This is of great significance in music because this is also the value obtained from damping decrement of the ear resonators. The ability to distinguish pitch has been measured at 50 ms at 100 cps, 20 ms at 1000 cps, and 14 ms at 4000 cps (R. Feldtkeller, *"Hörbarkeit von Instrumentenklängen"*, Acustica, 4:1 1954). However, the time constant varies inversely as power, according to the Bunsen-Roscoe Law, so that stronger stimulations require shorter pitch-perception time smear and *vice versa.* A third factor which is relevant to the time-lag phenomenon is that while a sound event in music cannot occur more rapidly than about twenty in a second, (i.e. 50 ms), it is also found that the boundary necessary for an elementary sound even to become musically effective is from 50 to 100 ms. Fourthly, physiological parameters involved in boundaries of tone spectrum, the speed of succession of tones, evaluation of tone colour, 'space' perception of sounds, ability to determine the direction of a sound source also influence aesthetic perception (Fritz Winckel, *Music, Sound and Sensation*, pp. 42-54).

Abhinavagupta shows amazing awareness of the components involved in the perception of tone at the *śruti* level and of factors involved in the transformation of *śruti* to *svara* such as *dhvani vailakṣaṇya, nairantarya, ūrdhvasparśa, saṁskāra-pradāna, niṣkāsa, kālakalā, nādāṁśa, āyuḥ, sthāna* and *karaṇa.* I have discussed these in (i) *Niḥśaṅkahṛdaya* (ii) *Śruti: the Scalic Foundation* and (iii) *Śruti-jāti: A Psych acoustical Approach* and (iv) *Śruti-jāti: A Four Component Theory.* A fitting conclusion to a discussion of Paṇḍarīka Viṭṭhala's treatment of *śruti-svara* relation (Sequential Theory or Time-lag Theory) would be Abhinavagupta's observation (op. cit. p. 22).

प्रमाणेतिवदन् न कालकला श्रुतिर्नापि नादांशो न चायुर्न स्थानं न करणमिति दर्शयति ।

48. Svara: Paṇḍarīka Viṭṭhala defines *svara* in *Sadrāgacandrodaya* also (1.24):

श्रुतेश्च नैरन्तरभाविको यः स्निग्धोऽनुशब्दात्मक ओजसात्मा ।
श्रोतुर्मनोरञ्जनकारकत्वात् स्वतस्तु तज्ज्ञैरुदितः स्वरोऽसौ ॥

His definition agrees with that of SR (1.3.24cd-25ab) except that Śārṅgadeva, probably following Abhinavagupta, gives *'śrutyanantarabhāvī'* (co-born with *śruti*) and Paṇḍarīka Viṭṭhala changes it to *'bhāvīdīptam'* (illuminated at the future, i.e. next moment) in accordance with their own schools. The attributes are:

śruteśca nairantarabhāvika: contiguous with, inseparable from the *śruti.*

snigdha: smooth, without harshness or roughness.

anuraṇana: heard together with the partials which are self-generated and coeval

ojas: lustre, light, illumination, intensification; body strength, power, vigour; energy, life force; splendour, support; manifestation, appearance; abode.

'Svṛ' and *'svar'* are *parasmaipadī* verbal roots of the first class *('bhvādi')* and mean intensification, lustre, light, illumination. *Chāndogyopaniṣat* which implies these meanings says that *prāṇa* is the *gaṭi* or course for *svara,* i.e. *svara* abides in *prāṇa.* The strength, power, vigour, energy or vitality of the expressive potential and appeal which *nāda* possesses accrue for *svara. Svara* is also the support or abode of *śrutis. Ojas* is a distinct, unique contribution of Paṇḍarīka Viṭṭhala to the definition of *svara.*

svato: independently; without co-operative reasons and without auxiliary causes.

The term *'svara'* may be derived from three verbal etymons: *'rāj'* is a *ubhayapadī-dhātu* of the first class—*'bhvādi'* (*Dhātupāṭha,* 19.74) which means to shine, to appear, to delight, to be illustrious, radiant or resplendent; *rañj* is a *ubhayapadī dhātu* occurring in both *bhvādi* (first) and *divādi* (fourth) classes (*Dhātupāṭha,* 23.30; 26.58) which means to colour, to be affected, delighted, charmed or to illuminate. Kallinātha gives the etymology and grammatical processes involved in deriving this word (op. cit. on ibid., 1.3.24cd-25ab, p. 82).

स्वतः शब्दोपपदात् 'रञ्ज् रागे' इत्यस्माद् धातोः 'अन्येभ्योऽपि दृश्यन्ते (पाणिनिः अष्टाध्यायी 3-2-75) इति डप्रत्यये टिलोपे पूर्वपदस्थतकारादेः पृषोदरादित्वाल्लोपे च स्वर इति रूपसिद्धिः ।

The third is due to Abhinavagupta who derives it (op. cit. on NŚ 28.21, p. 10, 11) from the root '*svṛ*' which is a *parasmaipadi-dhātu* of class I (*bhvādi*) which has two streams of meaning: *śabda* and *upatāpana.* The first includes 'to sound, to resound, to shine' etc.; the second includes 'to warm up; to heat, to hurt, to go' etc.

(*Dhātupaṭha,* 22.34): *svara* is so named because it warms up the heart and causes it to give up its 'middle state' of neutrality or self-abiding and to this end, manifests to be or express itself or coloured, to be aesthetically delightful. Abhinavagupta also gives the conventional derivation: to afford aesthetic delight by itself (i.e. without outside agency):

न ... वोपतापयो: (स्वरा इति–स्वृशब्दोपतापयो:) स्वर आक्षेप इत्यनयो: स्वर शब्द:, तेन शब्दस्वभावां चित्तवृत्तिमध्यस्थतारूपस्वास्थ्यावस्थापरित्याजनेनोपतापयन्तो हृद्यतातिशयत्वात् स्वतामाक्षिपन्त: स्वविषये अभिधानं (अभिरञ्जनं) कुर्वत: स्वरा इत्युक्ता: ।

The variant readings in brackets are from *Bharatakośa* (p. 754).

Mataṅga explains (op. cit. pp. 12,13) that the symbols *s, r, g* etc. are derived from *Āgama,* they are called *svaras* (vowels) for two reasons: they are only incidental carriers of vowels; this is the name taught by credible, respected authorities; he further explains that of all the vowels (*svara)* only two (*a, i*) are used because they have the extraordinary property *(asādhāraṇatva)* of upward movement *(ūrdhva-gāmitva*). This is an extremely perceptive observation and anticipates the recently discovered acoustic phenomenon of formants, which is explained by Charles Culver (*Musical Acoustics,* pp. 157, 158):

"A great amount of research has been carried out in an effort to arrive at an understanding of the acoustical structure of both vowel and consonantal sounds. Such knowledge is highly desirable if one is to make even a beginning in the improvement of the singing or the speaking voice. So far as the vowels are concerned, the following facts have been definitely established:

1. Any given vowel sound is characterised by the presence of one or more definite groups of partials.

2. The partials which go to make up a given characteristic group are more or less symmetrically disposed about some dominant partial.

3. The frequencies appearing in these characteristic groups are much the same, regardless of the fundamental frequency.

4. The various vowel sounds are produced by means of a 'modulating' process which consists of so shaping the mouth and pharyngeal cavities that the proper order and intensity of partials is developed by resonant action."

The formant theory is further useful in explaining colour differences of different musical instruments. Glen Haydon says that the quality of an instrumental sound arises out of the roughness characteristics of the exciting method (op. cit. pp. 78, 79). The investigations of L. Hermann, Helmholtz, F.C. Donders, R. Koenig, W. Koehler, Gutzmann, Carl Stumpf, Leray T. Laase, Seashore, Barret Stout, Horton C. Talley and others into the formant phenomenon (compiled by Revesz, op. cit. pp. 48 et seq.) have established unequivocally that the vowels '*a*' and '*i*' (as well as their combination, '*ai*') have groups of the highest partials and are generated naturally without the need of any voluntary effect in shaping the mouth and other parts of the voice apparatus. Further investigations (which ought to be undertaken by musical acousticians in India) may throw light as to why the consonants *s r g m p d n* were selected to symbolise these sounds.

49-52ab. Grāma: Ādi (49b) includes *varṇālaṁkāra, tāna, jāti, rāga,* etc. *Grāma* has entered into the English language as *'gamut'* through Arabia, Persia, Greece and Spain. Mataṅga emphasizes that it is a theoretical model erected to comprehend and organise the totality of melody, and confers *'vedopavasati'* on it by deriving it from *Sāmaveda* (op. cit. 89ff. pp. 20-21). Pārśvadeva confirms the organisational function of *grāma* (*Saṅgītasamayasāra,* MS No. 67, Oriental Research Institute, Mysore):

स्वराणां मूर्छनाजातिजात्यंशकानां व्यवस्थितश्रुतीनां हि समूहो ग्राम इष्यते ।

Thus the *grāma* quantifies intervals, their modification, sonance etc. relations through the *śruti.* It offers scalic models for *rāgas* through *mūrchanā, śuddha-, kūṭa-, auḍuva* and *ṣāḍavatānas*; it explains melodic structuring by comprehending the *daśa prāṇas* in *rāga* and *jāti*; it comprehends melodic movement and phrasing through *varṇālaṁkāra*; it includes directional tendencies of melodic gravitation such as multiple tonicity in the threefold *grāma,* and tone curvavures *(gamaka)* in terms of *śruti.*

Paṇḍarīka Viṭṭhala borrows the *lakṣaṇas* of *ṣaḍja-grāma (sa-grāma)* and *madhyama-grāma (ma-grāma)* from earlier authorities, e.g. *pañcama* is manifested at the seventeenth, i.e. its own final *śruti* in *sa-grāma* while it does so at the sixteenth, i.e. its penultimate *śruti* in *ma-grāma.* Given a *śruti* allocation of 4,3, 2, 4, 4, 3, 2 for the *śuddha-svaras sa, ri,* etc., Śārṅgadeva offers an alternative definition (SR 1.43cd) viz. *dha* has three *śrutis* in *sa-grāma,* but four in *ma-grāma,* the reverse of which is true with *pañcama*; both refer to the same, identical *śruti* allocations. Bharata is elaborately explicit on such intervallic fixation in the two *grāmas* (NŚ 28.24-26, p. 19; compare with the corresponding text in the NŚ Kāvyamālā edn. 28.26-29, which is even more explicit). Paṇḍarīka Viṭṭhala reiterates uniformly in his works that in his time all *rāgas* were performed only in *sa-grāma* and none in *ma-grāma* (e.g. *Rāgamañjarī,* 1.44, *Sadrāgacandrodaya,* 1.36).

Bharata (NŚ 28. 23 pr. p.15), Dattila (*Dattilam,* 11) and Mataṅga (op. cit. 92, p. 20) describe only *sa-* and *ma-grāmas.* The *Rāmāyaṇa* also mentions only two *grāmas* and seven *(śuddha) jātis* (1.4.4). Among literary sources which mention three *grāmas* may be mentioned *Harivaṁśa,* (*Viṣṇuparvan,* ch. 82), *Pañcatantra* (5.6.3: *gardabhaśṛgāla-kathā*), *Vāyupurāṇam* (II.24.36), *Mārkaṇḍeyapurāṇam* (103.56), *Viṣṇu-dharmottara Purāṇam* (Bombay edn. III.19, p. 315), etc. *Gāndhāra-grāma* is defined by Nārada (*Nāradaśikṣā,* 1.2.4, 5, 6, 9, pp. 10-12; *Saṅgītamakaranda,* 1.50, 62), Nānyadeva (op. cit. 3.2.36, 44; 3.4.76-80), *Yāṣṭika* (cit. Paṇḍarīka Viṭṭhala, *Rāga-*

mañjarī, 1.46), and Ahobala (*Saṅgītapārijāta,* 1.102). Paṇḍarīka Viṭṭhala actually describes this *grāma* in *Rāgamañjarī* (1.46) and implies it in the expression '*mukhyatama*' in NN (3.1.52a). A brief discussion of *ga-grāma* and Viṭṭhala's contribution thereto is therefore relevant here.

Nārada-śikṣā is opaque in the description of *ga-grāma.* The *Saṅgītamakaranda* contains a descriptive passage which finds literal correspondence in SR (1.4.4, 5), for which SR claims the authority of Nārada. But the author of *Saṅgītamakaranda* attributes it to Brahma—'*idam lakṣaṇam brahmaṇoktam*'. According to this, a *śruti* each from *ri* and *ma* accrues to *ga; dha* assumes a *śruti* from *pa; ni* takes on a *śruti* from *dha* and *sa.* This yield the scale *ga*(4) *ma*(3) *pa*(3) *dha*(3) *ni*(4) *sa*(3) *ri*(2). It is to be noted that both *ga-ni* have four *śrutis* each, and the seventh (*ri*) has two *śrutis* as *sa, pa* and *ni* respectively in *sa-grāma* but that the consonance of the fourth (eight-*śruti* interval) which also bestows symmetry and has a size of four *śrutis* as well as a two-*śruti* third (occurring in *sa-grāma*) are absent in *ga-grāma.*

The *gāndhāra-grāma* scale as defined from Yāṣṭika differs from the foregoing. The quotation from Yāṣṭika is invoked by Paṇḍarīka Viṭṭhala as late as in the 16th century but is not sought by Mataṅga and Śārṅgadeva for definition of this *grāma,* while they do so for *rāgalakṣaṇa.* According to this definition, *ri-dha* occupy the positions of *ga-ni, ni-ma* assume the positions of *laghu sa* and *(laghu) pa, ga* takes up the position of *ma* (of *sa-grāma*). Mention of *laghu sa-pa* clearly makes this a contemporised definition; presumably, the positions of the notes referred to are those of *sa-grāma.* This definition leaves out the position of *sa* and *pa.* Consistent with the prescription for other notes, these may be presumed to occupy the positions of *ri* and *dha* respectively. Under these circumstances the scale has the following *śruti* allocation: *ga*(4) *ma*(3) *pa*(4) *dha*(2) *ni*(3) sa(4) *ri*(2). This is unacceptable because it fails to have the thirteen-*śruti* (just fifth) consonance; the *triśruti* of *ni* is reminiscent of the *vikṛta pañcama* of *ma-grāma,* as also the *catuḥśruti* of the sixth note (*sa*). Paṇḍarīka Viṭṭhala borrows another definition of *ga-grāma* from Śārṅgadeva (*Rāgamañjarī,* 1.43, 44) in which the available text of the *Rāgamañjarī* fails to include a significant part of the definition, viz. पश्रुतिं धो, निषादस्तु धश्रुतिं सश्रुतिं श्रितः, so that from the scant definition

स्वस्वपूर्वापरस्वरश्रुतिस्थौ युग्मके गनी ।
गान्धारग्रामकः ख्यातः शार्ङ्गदेवेन सूरिणा ॥

the scale would have the *śruti* allocation *ga*(4) *ma*(3) *pa*(4) *dha*(2) *ni*(4) *sa* (3) *ri*(2). It is inexplicable, unless attributed to a transmissional defect or damnum, how Paṇḍarīka Viṭṭhala would retain such an incomplete definition.

The text in *Bharatabhāṣya* describing *ga-grāma* suffers a lacuna, but the scale may be reconstructed from the *maṇḍala-prastāra.* According to this, six horizontal lines are crossed by five vertical lines. *Ga* is placed at the *īśāna* (northeast) corner, *ma* is placed at the fourth from it in clockwise order, *pa* on the fifth bottom vertical line, *dha* on the second of the same, *ni* at the left extreme of the *ma*-line, *sa* on the extreme left of the *ga*-line and *ri* at the upper extreme of the *dha*-line. This gives a scale for *ga-grāma* having the following *śruti* distribution: *ga*(4) *ma*(3) *pa*(3) *dha*(3) *ni*(4) *sa*(3) *ri*(2) which is exactly the one defined by Śārṅgadeva.

Ahobala offers, as late as the 17th century, the following definition for *ga-grāma*:

श्रुतित्रयसमायुक्तो यदा गो मेरुगो भवेत् ।
गान्धारग्राम आख्यातस्तिस्रभिः श्रुतिभिः परे ।
चतुःश्रुतिः निषादः स्यात् षड्जोऽपि तिसृभिर्युतः ।

According to this, *ga* is at the *meru*, (i.e. the tonic) and has three *śrutis*; all others, including *sa* have three *śrutis* each, except *niṣāda* which has four *śrutis*. Therefore, the *śruti* distribution for this scale is *ga*(3) *ma*(3) *pa*(3) *dha*(3) *ni*(4) *sa*(3) *ri*(3). It is not known on what authority Ahobala gives this definition. This scale possesses the *madhyama*-(eight *śruti*) and *pañcama*-(twelve *śruti*) consonances for *ga*; but neither the tonic nor its fourth have four-*śruti* magnitudes, nor are the consonances abundant. Since *ni* has four *śrutis*, it is sometimes called *ni-grāma*, but with entire lack of theoretical sanction.

The *svara* dispensations in the three *grāmas* may now be tabulated and compared. (Abbreviations: Ṣg-*ṣaḍjagrāma*, Mg-*madhyamagrāma*, Gg-*gāndhāragrāma*, N-Nārada cit Śārṅgadeva, Y-Yāṣṭika cit. Paṇḍarīka Viṭṭhala, Al-Ahobala original, A II-Ahobala realigned).

Śruti No.	*Śruti* Name	Sg	Mg	Gg-N	Gg-Y	Gg-AI	Gg-AII
1	*2*	*3*	*4*	*5*	*6*	*7*	*8*
1.	*tīvrā*			ni			ni
2.	*kumudvatī*						
3.	*mandā*				ni	sa	
4.	*chandovatī*	sa	sa	sa			sa
5.	*dayāvatī*						
6.	*rañjanī*			ri		ri	
7.	*raktikā*	ri	ri		sa		ri
8.	*raudrī*						
9.	*krodhā*	ga	ga		ri	ga	
10.	*vajrikā*			ga			ga
11.	*prasāriṇī*						

1	*2*	*3*	*4*	*5*	*6*	*7*	*8*
12.	*prīti*					ma	
13.	*mārjanī*	ma	ma	ma	ga		ma
14.	*kṣiti*						
15.	*raktā*					pa	
16.	*sandīpanī*		pa	pa	ma		pa
17.	*ālāpinī*	pa					
18.	*madantī*					dha	
19.	*rohiṇī*			dha			dha
20.	*ramyā*	dha	dha		pa		
21.	*ugrā*						
22.	*kṣobhiṇī*	ni	ni		dha	ni	

The following is noteworthy in the above comparative table:

1. *Sa* and *ma* which were the most important notes of the octave have retained their positions and have yet become three-*śruti* intervals in Gg-N.
2. Just as *sa-ma-pa* in Sg and *sa-ma-dha* in Mg, *ga* the most important note in Gg and *ni* its fifth are four-*śruti* intervals in Gg N. In Sg, *ga-ni* are *vivādins* and *ri-dha, anuvādins, sa-ma-pa* are *saṁvādins.* In Mg, *sa-ma,-ri-pa, ri-dha* are *saṁvādins, ga-ni* are *vivādins* and the rest, *anuvādins.* In Gg *ga-dha-ni* are *saṁvādins, ri* is *vivādi, sa-ma-pa* are *anuvādins.*
3. *Vis-a-vis* the notes of Sg and Mg which were in practical use at the times of Bharata, Mataṅga etc. the notes of Gg are too sharp or too flat.
4. Because of textual contiguity, Gg is derived by some (e.g. Fox Strangways, *The Music of Hindostan,* p. 110) with the following *śruti* allocation: 3, 2, 4, 3, 2, 4, 4; but such a derivation is not in accordance with textual tradition on Gg.
5. When the *śruti* allocations of Sg, Mg and Gg are written in order in descent commencing from *sa, ma* and *ga* respectively, it is found that the first telīachord is identical and that the seventh (i.e. the second in ascent) is always a three-*śruti* interval

	1	2	3	4	5	6	7
Sg	4	2	3	4	4	2	3
Mg	4	2	3	4	2	4	3
Gg	4	2	3	4	3	3	3

6. Consonances among *śuddha svaras* are: *sa-ma, ri-dha, ga-ni* in all three *grāmas*; *ma-ni* consonance, not admissible in *śāstra* (vide supra) in Sg, Mg; *sa-pa* only in Sg; *ri-pa* only in Mg; *ga-dha* and *ga-ni* in Gg.

The question is sometimes raised: Gg should be derived from which *grāma*? N. S. Ramachandran (*Rāgas of Karnataka Music,* p. 28, for example), states that there is no clear indication about this. The question does not arise if Śārṅgadeva is attentively studied. He does not derive the Mg or Gg from Sg, but derives all three from the *śruti* allocations of notes which he has independently derived in connection with the *dhruvavīṇā-calavīṇā* experiment on *śrutis.* He obliquely indicates this when he says *'svacaturtha śrutisamsthite'* (SR 1.4.2d) and *'svopāntyaśrutisamsthite* (ibid., 1.4.3a) to locate *pa* in Sg and Mg respectively, and implies the *śruti* allocation scheme of Bharata *et al* when he says *'yad vā dhas-triśrutiḥ ṣadje, madhyame tu catuḥśrutiḥ'.* It is thus clear that he derives the Gg scale from *śruti* allocations empirically and objectively derived for the above mentioned *sāraṇā* experiment. This is supported by another observation: If Gg N had been derived from Mg, *pa,* in donating its final *śruti* (viz. no. 16 *sandīpanī)* to *dha,* would move down to the 15th *śruti, raktā.* Then, because it would be separated by only one *śruti,* viz. *kṣiti* from *ma, ma-pa* would be *vivādins;* this is contrary to established and consistent textual prescriptions or descriptions. Secondly, if Gg is derived from Mg the disposition of the *svaras* would be: *ni* at *tivrā* (1) *sa* at *chandovatī* (4), *ri* at *rañjanī* (6), *ga* at *vajrikā* (10), *ma* at *mārjanī* (13), *pa* at *raktā* (15), *dha* at *rohiṇī* (19), giving a scale *sa* (3) *ri* (2) *ga* (4) *ma* (3) *pa* (2) *dha* (4) *ni* (4); this is but the *dha-mūrchanā (aśvakrāntā)* of Sg and cannot, therefore, be an independent *grāma* (as is claimed in the *Saṅgītaśiromaṇi* of Paṇḍitamaṇḍali, extr. *Bharatakośa,* p. 172).

Gg is generally believed to be posterior to the Sg and Mg. There is no musicological or literary evidence to this effect. Earlier obsolescence cannot be regarded as evidence of earlier genesis. There is no authority which describes Gg alone nor mentioned it as first born. Similarly the equation or ascription of Gg to *sāman* music is fanciful. On the contrary, Veṅkaṭamakhin (*Caturdaṇḍīprakāśikā,* 5.75) mentions, as late as in the 17th century that *sāmavarālī* (which may be shown to be the *kākalī* variety of *uttaramandrā mūrchanā* of Sg) is born of *Sāmaveda*!

Why did Gg become obsolete? It should be remembered that *grāma* was a *theoretical* model created to perform certain functions which were largely organisational. As the materials of music such as intervals, consonance-dissonance etc. changed with change in popular aesthetic taste and because of internal and external stresses, a corresponding change in the conceptual framework became inevitable. Therefore the primary or basic scale which epitomised such framework had also be changed accordingly. Mataṅga is probably the first authority to explicitly state such theoretical function or use of the *grāma* (op. cit. p. 21):

किं वा तस्य प्रयोजनम् ? प्रयोजनं च यथा–स्वरश्रुतिमूर्छनातानजातिरागाणां व्यवस्थापकत्वं नाम प्रयोजनम् ।

Nānyadeva (op. cit. 3.1.54-56) clearly explains why Gg departed to its heavenly abode:

द्वौ ग्रामौ भरतेनोक्तौ, ग्रामो गान्धारपूर्वकः ।
अतितारातिमन्द्रत्वाद् वैस्वर्यं; नोपदर्शितः ॥
स च स्वर्गे नारदाच्चैव गीयते । तथा च दत्तिलः–"स तु नेहोपलभ्यते" इति (दत्तिलम्–11d)
गान्धर्वैर्गीयते स्वर्गे ग्रामो गान्धारपूर्वकः ।
अतितारातिमन्द्रत्वान्नात्र गायन्ति मानवाः ॥

The last verse here has the flavour of a quotation; if so, this explanation dates from a pre-Nānyadeva period. The notes of Gg proved to be too flat or too sharp when compared with the actual notes in use; it was poorer in consonances; catuḥśruti ga (antara) and ni (kākalī) were denied the status of independent notes in Sg and Mg and were prescribed to be used as little as possible; *ga-ni (śuddha)* were according to one school (cf. SR 1.3.49b) *vivādins* of all other notes in the scale. Gg yielded *sa* and *ma* of three *śrutis* each which was inadmissible in *śāstra*; it also yielded a succession of three *śruti* intervals (for *ma-pa-dha*) which again was contrary to musical principles because the three *śruti* interval is weak. (This is why it was relegated to *anuvāditva.*)

It is interesting that nevertheless, Gg continued to enjoy an after-life continuity or description-in-absentia at the hands of later traditionalists; its *mūrchanās* are named in *Nārada-śikṣā* (1.2.9, p. 13), *Saṅgītamakaranda* (1.95), SR (citing Nārada, 1.4.25, 26), *Saṅgītasūryodaya* (3.55, 56, pp. 284, 285) etc. Its *tānas* are named in *Viṣṇudharmottarapurāṇam* (III. ch. 18) and *Vāyupurāṇam* (24.41). Nānyadeva mentions the following *rāgas* of Gg (MS copy in Sri Varalakshmi Academy, Mysore, pp. 279-292); *kosalā, rudrahāsa, gandharvāmoda, vīrahāsa, jīmuta, ṣāḍavaka, piñjarī, raticandra, gāndhāraṣāḍava, tumburupriya, śārada, vegamadhyamā, gāndhāralalita, drāviḍī, śārdūlī, pārvatī, dhanāsikā, kacchellī, pulindī, śakavalīlā, sindhuvalita, cūtamañjarī, himakṛti and svabhāvakṛti* on the authority of Mataṅga, Vṛddha Kaśyapa, Yāṣṭika, Kaśyapa and Vṛddha-Śātātapa. Mataṅga and later authorities do discribe some of these *rāgas* in their works but under Sg or Mg into which *rāgas* were rationalised at their times, even as Rāmāmātya, Paṇḍarīka Viṭṭhala and Somanātha accommodate the *rāgas* of Mg into Sg.

The scales of Sg and Mg were fixed in ancient times through enunciation of the principle of equivalence. Dattila (op. cit. 26-28) gives a formula for their interconversion:

गान्धारं धैवतीकुर्याद द्विश्रुत्युत्कर्षणाद्यदि ।
तद्वशान् मध्यमादींश्च निषादादीन् यथास्थितान् ।
ततोऽभूद् यावतिथ्येषा षड्जग्रामस्य मूर्छना ।
जायते तावतिथ्येव मध्यमग्राममूर्छना ॥
श्रुतिद्वयापकर्षेण गान्धारीकृत्य धैवतम् ।
पूर्वन्मध्यमाद्याश्च भावयेत् षड्जमूर्छनाः ॥

That is, ga of sa-mūrchanā in Sg is raised by two śrutis; it is then regarded as dha; and from this position, a mūrchanā is executed (dha n*i sa ri ga ma pa*) such that they accord with the *śruti* magnitudes of (raised) *ga, ma, pa, dha, ni, sa* and *ri*. The *mūrchanā* so obtained will be identical with the *ma-mūrchanā* of Mg.

Sg 4(*sa*) 3(*ri*) 2(*ga*) 4(*ma*) 4(*pa*) 3(*dha*) 2(*ni*) (i)

If *ga* is raised by two *śrutis, ga* has now four *śrutis*, and *ma*, only two:

Sg 4(*sa*) 3(*ri*) 4(*ga*) 2(*ma*) 4(*pa*) 3(*dha*) 2(*ni*) (ii)

This *'ga'* is regarded as *dha* and a *mūrchanā* is executed with *dha* as base:

Sg 4(*sa*) 3(*ri*) 4(*ga*) 2(*ma*) 4(*pa*) 3(*dha*) 2(*ni*) 4(*sa*) 3(*ri*) (iii)

4(*dha*) 2(*ni*) 4(*sa*) 3(*ri*) 2(*ga*) 4(*ma*) 3(*pa*) (iv)

If (iv) is rewritten to commence on *ma*, it is found to be identical with *mamūrchanā* of Mg:

ma(4) *pa*(3) *dha*(4) *ni*(2) *sa*(2) *sa*(4) *ri*(3) *ga*(2)

Secondly, *dha* of *sa-mūrchanā* in Mg is reduced by two *śrutis* (donating them to *ni*):

Mg 4(*ma*) 3(*pa*) 4(*dha*) 2(*ni*) 4(*sa*) 3(*ri*) 2(*ga*) (v)

4(*ma*) 3(*pa*) 2(*dha*) 4(*ni*) 4(*sa*) 3(*ri*) 2(*ga*) (vi)

This *dha* is regarded as *ga* and made the base of a *mūrchanā*;

2(*ga*) 4(*ma*) 4(*pa*) 3(*dha*) 2(*ni*) 4(*sa*) 3(*ri*) (vii)

If (vii) is rewritten to commence from *sa*, it is found to be identical with *sa-mūrchanā* of Sg:

sa(4) *ri*(3) *ga*(2) *ma*(4) *pa*(4) *dha*(3) *ni*(2)

The following reciprocity between *ga* and *dha* may be noted in the foregoing:

Ga of the first *mūrchanā* of Sg raised by two *śrutis* and transformed into *dha mūrchanā* gives first *mūrchanā* of Mg.

Dha of the first *mūrchanā* of Mg diminished by two *śrutis* and transformed into *ga mūrchanā* gives first *mūrchanā* of Sg.

The reason for such reciprocity becomes clear if the first *mūrchanās* of both *grāmas* are inspected:

Sg	4	3	2	4	4	3	2	(viii)
Mg	4	3	4	2	4	3	2	(ix)

Thus both are identical except that the third and fourth notes in (1), i.e. *ga-ma* are reversed in (ix), i.e. *dha-ni* of Mg. The simplest way of rendering (viii) (ix) identical with (ix) is to raise the third note (*ga*) by two *śrutis*, thus diminishing the fourth note (*ma*) by two *śrutis.* The raised *ga* of (viii) corresponds to *dha* of (ix). Hence the *dha-mūrchanā* is the same as Sg. The same is true, *mutatis mutandis* of lowering of *dha* of (ix) by two *śrutis* and making it *ga-mūrchanā* of (ix) to give Mg.

In this way Dattila muni had provided the musicians of his day a practical and simple method of moving freely by transposition, from Sg to Mg and *vice versa.*

52cd-56. (i) Mūrchanā. The word is derived from *'murch'* or *'mūrch'*, a *parasmaipadi* of class I (*bhvādi*) which means 'to become solid, congeal, become consistent, assume shape or substance, pervade, spread over, have power to take effect on, cause to sound aloud', etc. The *rāga bhāva* becomes crystalised, consistent and congealed because of the *mūrchanā*; the *rāga* assumes shape (contours) and substance (content) in terms of *mūrchanā*; it pervades the tone continuum as well as (performer's and listener's) consciousness through this means; it has the power to affect the listener (*moha*); it elevates the performer and listener (*'mūrchyate yatra rāgo hi śroto vā'*) as well as the *rāga* to the highest pitch *(samucchrāya)*. The *Dhātupāṭha* (7.32) has *'moha samucchrāyayoḥ'*. It confers such elevation at an objective level within the frame of physical or referential parameters and at a subjective level within the frame of psychological parameters of individual performer and listener.

(ii) Sārayet. The word *'sāraṇā'* is derived from the root *'sṛ'* which is a *parasmiapadī*, classified in both the 1st (*'bhvādi'*) and the 3rd (*'juhotyādi'*) classes in *Dhātupāṭha* (22.37.25;17) and means (*'sṛ-gatau'*) to run, to go, to extend; here, to project or extend the *svaras* in a series.

(iii) Mūrchanā is defined slightly differently by different authorities: thus Mataṅga (op. cit. p. 22), Śārṅgadeva (op. cit. 1.4.9) and others define *mūrchanā* as a series of seven notes taken in regular ascent and descent. Kallinātha supports this etymological definition with a grammatical derivation (op. cit. on ibid., loc. cit. p. 104):

यया करणभूतया रागो मूर्छ्यते व्यापत इति, श्रोता मूर्छ्यते मोह्यत इति वा 'मूर्छा मोहसमुच्छ्राययो:' इति धातोर्ण्यन्ताद्युचिप्रत्यये मूर्छनेति रूपम् ।

Haripāla borrows from Tumburu and Kohala and bestows yet another semantic dimension on the word (Saṅgītasudhākara, 5.2.4ab, 5cd, 6)

श्रुतेर्मार्दवमेव स्यान्मूर्छनेत्याह तुम्बुरुः ।
गायतां शृण्वतां चापि भवेद् रागामृते हृदि ।
मनसो मज्जनं याति यत् स्यान्मूर्छनेत्याह कोहलः ॥
तारस्थाने लालनं यत् स्वरस्यासौ तु मूर्छना ॥ (नारदमते) ॥

According to Viśākhila *mūrchanā* and *tāna* are really synonymous (cit. Mataṅga, op. cit. p. 26): but according to the variant reading in *Bharatakośa.* p. 502 the two differ from each other only minutely. Mataṅga rejects this view and defines *mūrchanā* as regular ascent of seven notes while *tāna* is their regular descent (loc. cit.). The variant reading adopted by Siṁhabhūpāla (op. cit. on ibid., loc. cit. p. 114) makes *mūrchanā* the ascent *and* descent of seven notes in order and *tāna*, only the ascent.

(iv) Kramāt has a special significance: it is *mūrchanā* only if the *svaras* ascend and descend in order; if they are disordered, it becomes *kūṭatāna*.

(v) The *mūrchanā* performed two functions: i. to provide and to generate scalic models for comparison, contrast, standardisation and classification of melodic materials such as *rāga*, *jāti* and *gīta* prevailing in actual musical practice: '*jātibhāṣādisiddhyartham*', (Nandikeśvara, cit. Mataṅga, op. cit. p. 32; '*jātirāga-bhāṣādisiddhaye*', Kohala, cit. Mataṅga, loc. cit.) ii. to derive theoretically the registers: two registers with seven-note *mūrchanās* and three registers by twelve note *mūrchanās* as propounded by Nandikeśvara (Mataṅga, loc. cit.). In Karnataka music it continues to serve as a basis of deriving secondary *rāgas* by *grahabheda* during *rāgālapana*.

(vi) Mūrchanā is of four kinds: *pūrṇa* (having all seven notes), *ṣāḍava* (having six notes), *auḍuva* (having five notes) and *sādhāraṇa*; *sādhāraṇa* is again of three kinds, viz. with *antara-gāndhāra*, with *kākalī-niṣāda* and with both. Thus each of the seven *mūrchanās* has four varieties, thus totalling twenty-eight *mūrchanās* in Sg.

(vii) Each *mūrchanā* may be subjected again to the modal shift of tonic, giving rise to seven secondary scales called *kramas*. They have different intervallic permutations and are used in practical music for melodic variety and in theory as secondary melodic models, through permutative techniques known as *prastāra*.

(viii) Yasyām....mūrchanā. This is a simple device to determine the serial number of a *mūrchanā*; this number is the same as the serial number of *sa* in the given *mūrchanā*. Śārṅgadeva extends it to Mg also (SR 1.4.18); it may be applied with equal validity to Gg as shown below:

	No.	*Name (Bharata)*	*Name (Nārada)*	*Saptasvara mūrchanā* *1.*	*2.*	*3.*	*4.*	*5.*	*6.*	*7.*	*Dvādaśasvara mūrchanā*
1	*2*	*3*	*4*	*5*	*6*	*7*	*8*	*9*	*10*	*11*	*12*
Sg	1	*uttara-mandrā*	*uttaravarṇā*	**sa**	ri	ga	ma	pa	dha	ni	dha ni sa ri ga ma pa dha ni sa ri ga
	2	*rajanī*	*abhirudgatā*	ni	**sa**	ri	ga	ma	pa	dha	ni sa ri ga ma pa dha ni sa ri ga ma
	3	*uttarāyatā*	*aśvakrāntā*	dha	ni	**sa**	ri	ga	ma	pa	sa ri ga ma pa dha ni sa ri ga ma pa
	4	*śuddha-ṣaḍjā*	*sauvīrī*	pa	dha	ni	**sa**	ri	ga	ma	ri ga ma pa dha ni sa ri ga ma pa dha

1	*2*	*3*	*4*	*5*	*6*	*7*	*8*	*9*	*10*	*11*	*12*
	5	***matsarīkṛt***	*hṛṣyakā*	ma	pa	dha	ni	**sa**	ri	ga	ga ma pa dha ni sa ri ga ma pa dha ni
	6	***aśvakrāntā***	*uttarāyatā*	ga	ma	pa	dha	ni	**sa**	ri	ma pa dha ni sa ri- ga ma pa dha ni sa
	7	***abhirud-gatā***	*rajanī*	ri	ga	ma	pa	dha	ni	**sa**	pa dha ni sa ri ga ma pa dha ni sa ri
Mg	1	*sauvīrī*	*āpyāyanī*	**ma**	pa	dha	ni	sa	ri	ga	sa ri ga ma pa dha- ni sa ri ga ma pa
	2	*hāriṇāśvā*	*viśvakṛtā*	ga	**ma**	pa	dha	ni	sa	ri	ri ga ma pa dha ni sa ri ga ma pa dha
	3	*kalopa-natā*	*candrā*	ri	ga	**ma**	pa	dha	ni	sa	ga ma pa dha ni sa ri ga ma pa dha ni
	4	*śuddha-madhyā*	*hemā*	sa	ri	ga	**ma**	pa	dha	ni	ma pa dha ni sa ri ga ma pa dha ni sa
	5	*mārgī*	*kapardinī*	ni	sa	ri	ga	**ma**	pa	dha	pa dha ni sa ri ga ma pa dha ni sa ri
	6	*pauravī*	*maitrī*	dha	ni	sa	ri	ga	**ma**	pa	dha ni sa ri ga ma pa dha ni sa ri ga
	7	*hṛṣyakā*	*cāndramasī*	pa	dha	ni	sa	ri	ga	**ma**	ni sa ri ga ma pa dha ni sa ri ga ma
Gg	1		*nandā*	**ga**	ma	pa	dha	ni	sa	ri	
	2		*viśālā*	ri	**ga**	ma	pa	dha	ni	sa	
	3		*sumukhī*	sa	ri	**ga**	ma	pa	dha	ni	
	4		*citrā*	ni	sa	ri	**ga**	ma	pa	dha	
	5		*citravatī*	dha	ni	sa	ri	**ga**	ma	pa	
	6		*sukhā*	pa	dha	ni	sa	ri	**ga**	ma	
	7		*ālāpā*	ma	pa	dha	ni	sa	ri	**ga**	

58-59. Tāna is derived from the verbal stem *'tan'* which is classified as a *ubhayapadī,* transitive and '*seṭ'* in the 8th (*tanoti*) class; it means 'to extend, spread, stretch, propagate, shine, reach to or towards' etc. It belongs also to the fourth (*'divādi'*) class and means 'to sound'. Kallinātha describes (op. cit. on ibid., 1.4.27, p.115) the grammatical devices involved in deriving it:

तन्यते विस्तार्यत इति तनोतेर्धातोः 'अकर्तरि च–' इत्यादिना सूत्रेण कर्मणि घञि तान इति रूपं दायो लाभ इतिवत् ।

Paṇḍarīka Viṭṭhala does not seem to make a clear-cut distinction between *mūrchanā* and *tāna*. As pointed out earlier (comm. on NN 3.1.52 cd- 56, iii, supra) Viśākhila rejects any difference between *mūrchanā* and *tāna*, while Mataṅga offers a weak explanation that in the former the seven notes are in both *āroha* and *avaroha* while in the latter they occur only in *āroha* (Siṁhabhūpāla's reading) or that the former occurs in ascent only while the latter is in descent only (*Bṛhaddeśī*, p. 26). However, he somewhat inconsistently also says (ibid., p. 24) *'idānīṁ pravakṣyāmi ṣāḍavauḍuva-mūrchanāḥ'*. On the other hand, Haripāla (op.cit. 5.2.8) says that *tānas* are rendered only in ascent.

Śuddhatāna: NN describes *ṣāḍava* and *auḍuva* under *mūrchanās*, but defines *śuddhatānas* as *ṣāḍavas, auḍuvas* (so rendered for purposes of *gīta*); the clarity in meaning has here suffered because of brevity. Śārṅgadeva (SR 1.4.27) brings out the difference very clearly.

तानाः स्युर्मूर्छनाः शुद्धाः षाडवौडुवितीकृताः ।

By placing an ingenious construction on *śuddhāḥ* here as applying to both *mūrchanā* and *tāna* to concile with Bharata's position on the subject, Kallināthā says that if related to *mūrchanā* alone, *'tāna'* in this passage would include *kūṭa tāṇas* also in which case the immediately next passage on *tāna* number (fortynine *ṣāḍavas* and thirty-five *auḍuvas*, thus totalling eighty-four in both *grāmas*) would be inconsistent; therefore, *śuddha-mūrchanās* are those which are without *kākalī* and *antara* notes; *śuddha-tānas* are *ṣāḍavas* and *auḍavas* derived from *śuddha-mūrchanās* such that the notes are taken in regular order (*vyutkrama-rahita*), even though similar *tānas* are possible in the other (three ? only *sādhāraṇa* ?) *mūrchanās*. Śārṅgadeva describes only these eightyfour to be consistent with the *Bhāratīya* text (op. cit. p. 116). The omission of derivation from *sādhāraṇa-mūrchanās* is in any case justified: *antara* and *kākalī* notes were ruled to be used very sparingly; if these notes were omitted, they would no longer characterise the *mūrchanā*. If however, these *tānas* are reckoned for all four vareties of *mūrchanā*, they would total up to 84 × 4 = 336 inclusive of both *grāmas*. However, the *tānas* are consistently apportioned as Sg 14, Mg 21, Gg 14 (= 49) uniformly in *Vāyupurāṇam* (24.36), *Viṣṇudharmottarapurāṇam* III.18. p. 315). *Mārkaṇḍeyapurāṇa* (21.54), *Pañcatantra* (5.6.52), *Nāradaśikṣā* (1.2.7, 8) etc. These fortynine *tānas* were named by vārada and prescribed to be sung (i.e. used as scales for different *sāmans* which were rendered) in various *yajñas* in the propitiation of gods according to Nānyadeva (op. cit. 4.137, 138, p.130):

एवं ग्रामत्रयेऽप्यूनपञ्चाशन्नारदोदिताः ।
सामगाने प्रयुज्यन्ते ताना यज्ञोपयोगिनः ॥

On the other hand, the *tānas* applicable in music are eightyfour, as mentioned by Bharata: (ibid., 4.138cd)

गीतोपयोगिनस्ताना भरतेनोपदर्शिताः ।

However, the eightyfour *tānas* are associated with the eightyfour *yajñas* and are named after them by Mataṅga (op. cit. 106-117, pp. 26-28). Such use is noted by Nānyadeva also (op. cit 4.105, 106):

... तेषु यज्ञेषु तानेन स्तोत्रं प्रवर्तते ।
तथा तानस्य प्रशमकर्मनामा च ये क्वचित् ।
स्तोत्रकर्तृप्रियनामा केषाञ्चिदिह दृश्यते ।

Nānyadeva counts altogether 19873 *tānas* from all three *grāmas* (ibid., 4.168). However, Mataṅga and Śārṅgadeva follow Bharata in the enunciation of eightyfour *tānas.*

How are the eightyfour *tānas* obtained? Bharata prescribes these rules: in Sg. each *mūrchanā* may be transformed into a *ṣāḍava* by omitting *sa, ri, pa* or *ni*; in Mg, each *mūrchanā* may be rendered (*ṣāḍavakṛta*) *ṣaḍava* by omitting *sa, ri,* or *ga*; so each *mūrchanā* gives (4+3) seven varieties of *ṣāḍava tānas*; there are, in all (Sg 7 × 4 = 28 and Mg 7 × 3 = 21, i.e. 28 + 21 =) 49 *ṣāḍava tānas* from both *grāmas.* Next, *auḍuva tānas* are formed by omitting also the respective *pañcama-saṁvādins: sa-pa, ri-pa, ni-ga* in Sg, *ga-ni, ri-dha* in Mg. This gives (7 × 3 =) 21 in Sg and (7 × 2 =) 14 in Mg, giving a total of (21 + 14 =) 35 *auḍuva tānas* from both *grāmas.* So the grand total of *tānas* is (49 + 35 =) 84(NŚ 28.33 pr, p. 27). The precise reasons for omitting these particular notes for obtaining *tānas* are not given by any authority. Dattila's dictum (op.cit. 20, p. 4) is helpful in understanding the process of making *tānas*:

पञ्चमं मध्यमग्रामे षड्जग्रामे तु धैवतम् ।
अनाशिनं विजानीयात् सर्वत्रैव तु मध्यमम् ॥

In Sg, *ma* and *dha* cannot be omitted: of the remaining notes, *sa, ri, pa, ni* may be omitted, one by one. How can *pa,* which differentiates Sg from Mg be omitted? Kallinātha poses this question and answers that a *tāna* of a *grāma* is identified by the omitted notes: this itself serves to associate it with the parent *grāma* even in the absence of *pa* (op. cit. on ibid., 1.4.27-31 p. 116):

ननु शुद्धतानेषु केषुचिद्भेदकपञ्चमलोपाद् ग्रामविवेकः कथमिति चेत्; उच्यते–ग्रामविशेषमधिकृत्यैव तत्तत्स्वरविहीनतानाभिधानात् क्वचिद्भेदकपञ्चमाभावेऽपि तानविशेषस्यैव ग्रामभेदकत्वमिति ।

Still, this does not explain why *ga* could not be omitted for *ṣāḍava* formation in Sg, and *dha* or *ni* in Mg. Textual tradition relies heavily on Bharata's injunction as authority on this topic. In *auḍuva* formation, the rule was to omit the *ṣāḍava*-forming note as well as its *pañcama-saṁvādin.* The original purpose was to maintain balance and symmetry in the two tetrachords. But in course of time this proved too restrictive and failed to accommodate many *rāgas* of *deśya* origin. Therefore, it was relaxed with the concession that the *pañcama-saṁvādin or* an *anuvādin* could be omitted to form *auḍuva tānas*: e.g. Mataṅga (op. cit. p. 24):

Mataṅga raises and answers a relevant question: there are certain overlaps or repetitions in reckoning the *tānas*; for example in the *tānas* omitting *sa* in Sg and Mg, the first and seventh *tāna* have both the identical form, viz. *ri ga ma pa dha ni.* Why are such repetitions not excluded? They are included for the sake of completeness: further one stretches into the low (*mandra*) and the other, into the high (*tāra*) register (op.cit. pp. 29-30):

संवादिलोपादौडुवत्वमिति (भरत) वचनात् संवादिस्वराभ्यामौडुवित्वं प्राप्तमिति प्रायिकम्। कदाचिदनु-वादिस्वराभ्यामौडुवित्वं भवत्येव। यथा-पञ्चमऋषभयोः षड्जग्रामे।

As indicated above, *kūṭa tāna* is formed by a group of notes taken in irregular order (SR 1.4.32). It is formed from a *sampūrṇa* or *asampūrṇa-mūrchanā.* The number of *kuṭa tānas* which may be obtained is governed by the simple algebraic principle of the factorial, viz. p = n (n–1) (n–2) (n–3) .... (3) (2) (1), where 'n' is the number of *svaras* and 'p' the number of *tānas* obtained by systematic and complete permutation. Therefore, the number of *kūta tānas* obtained for the *svaras* are:

1 note: 1; 2 notes: 2 × 1 = 2; 3 notes: 3 × 2 × 1 = 6; 4 notes = 4 × 3 × 2 × 1 = 24; 5 notes: 5 × 4 × 3 × 2 × 1 = 120; 6 notes: 6 × 5 × 4 × 3 × 2 × 1 = 720; 7 notes = 7 × 6 × 5 × 4 × 3 × 2 × 1 = 5040.

Tānas containing 1, 2, 3, ..., 7 notes are called *ārcika, gāthika, sāmika, svarāntara, auḍuva, ṣāḍava* and *sampūrṇa* respectively.

Viśākhila is probably the first authority who is aware of this principle and of the scheme of tabulation (*prastāra*). This is indicated by Nānyadeva (op. cit. 4.89, p. 123). They are discussed by Mataṅga *et al.* But it is the matchless Śārṅgadeva who calculates with vast patience, perseverance and precision the total number of possible *kūṭa tānas* (SR 1.4.36-60):

A		B	
sampūrṇa kūṭa tānas	2,82,240	Repetitions in	
ṣāḍava kūṭa tānas	34,560	i. *uttaramandrā-śuddhamadhyā*	63
auḍuva kūṭa tānas	4,800	ii. *rajanī-mārgī*	593
svarāntara kūṭa tānas	768	iii. *uttarāyatā-pauravī*	3425
sāmika kūṭa tānas	156	iv. *purṇa kramas*	392
gāthika kūṭa tānas	44	*ṣāḍava kramas*	48
ārcika kūṭa tānas	14	*auḍuva* ,,	40
Total	3,22,582	*svarāntara* ,,	32
		sāmika ,,	26
		gāthika ,,	22
		ārcika ,,	11
		Total	4652

Thus the actual number of *kūṭa tānas* = 3,22,582–4652 = 3,17,930

Śārṅgadeva seems unaware of twenty-three more repetitions (which I have shown elsewhere): *matsarīkṛt-sauvīrī* = 1; *aśvakrāntā-hāriṇāśva* = 5; *abhirudgatā-kalopanatā* = 17 (total = 23). If these are subtracted further, the actual number of *kūṭa tānas* is 3,17,907.

Finally, we may attempt to answer the question following Mataṅga (op.cit. p. 30): Description of *mūrchanā* may be justified because they are applied in *jāti* and *rāga*: but why are *tānas* described?

As mentioned earlier, the *śuddha-tānas* were used for two purposes: religious and aesthetic; the former is endorsed by Dattila (op. cit. 30, 31), Mataṅga, Śārṅgadeva, Nānyadeva and others; this soon became obsolete because faith in the accrual of their invisible fruits dwindled in course of time, as stated by Haripāladeva (op. cit. 5.2.10):

> यज्ञनामानि तानानां यान्युक्तानीह तानि यत् ।
> नोक्तानि हरिपालेन प्रयोजनमपश्यता ॥

The second purpose has been mentioned by Bharata and his followers viz. *gītopayogitā*. Mataṅga elaborates this further: they are useful in understanding the differences between *rāgas* and (between?) *jātis,* and in understanding *naṣṭa* and *uddiṣṭa* (vide infra) (Mataṅga, op. cit. p. 30):

ननु मूर्छनास्तावत् जातिरागेषूपयोगिन्य इति युक्तं तासां कथनम् : तानास्तु कुत्रोपयुज्यन्ते ? उच्यते; द्वयोर्ग्रामयोर्जातिरागान्यत्वप्रतिपादनार्थं प्रयोगस्तानानाम् । यद्वा नष्टोद्दिष्टसङ्ख्यासिद्ध्यर्थं प्रयोगस्तानानाम् ।

58d-59. Tānakriyā is the musical act of forming a *tāna*, first described by Bharata (NŚ 28.33 pr, p. 27). This is illustrated in strings (of the *vīṇā*) for facile understanding, but can be extended to all musical instruments of the chordophone and aerophone classes. This is indicated by Paṇḍarīka Viṭṭhala when he says that *tānakriyā* may be applied to all *tānas* (by suitable performance techniques). Deflecting a string to make the next higher note enter, i.e. manifest itself at the position of a precedent lower note is *praveśa*; by this technique the precedent *svarasthāna* is made to resemble (*sādṛśyam*) its next higher one; in *nigraha* an unwanted note is slurred over. (Earlier authorities prescribe total omission of the unwanted note. These are thus methods of adding or subtracting a note to form a desired *tāna*.

69a. 'Varṇ' is an *ubhayapadī-dhātu* of the tenth (*curādi*) class and is transitive: it means 'to paint, to colour, dye, depict, picture write, describe, relate; explain, spread, extend; extol, proclaim qualities' (*Dhātupāṭha*, 3.5.83: *varṇakriyā-vistāraguṇa vacaneṣu preraṇe ca*).

Methodology adopted in the treatment of the subject matter of this chapter—as indicated in the sequence—by Śārṅgadeva (whom Paṇḍarīka Viṭṭhala follows) is noteworthy: *śruti,* quantum of musical sound, its accumulation into unit of melodic expression, the *svara*; its modifications, varieties and attributes, its comprehensive theoretical organisation, the *grāma-grāma* apparatus in conceptually genetic sequence, i.e. *mūrchanā* and *tāna*—aids to their precise knowledge, the *prastāra,* etc. *pratyayas*—phraseology and organisation of *tānas* viz. *varṇālaṁkāras.* As indicated above, the *kūṭatānas* number some 3,17,907 and comprehend theoretical possibilities. It is not possible to remember or practise them all in normal practice. Hence Indian music theory has codified the more commonly used melodic phrases under the name of *varṇālaṁkāras.*

Varṇa is *gānakriyā,* i.e. the act of singing (and playing); in other words, melodic kinematics. Just as *varṇa* (syllable) is the fundamental unit for organisation and meaning in language and is a dynamic entity in an articulated flow and phrasing from which meaning emerges, *varṇa,* the articulation and flowing of clusters of *svaras (varṇa)* is the fundamental unit of organisation and meaning in music. This principle was known from the earliest times in Indian music theory and has been explicitly stated by some authorities. Thus Mataṅga, in a beautiful and lucid passage, gives the etymology of *varṇa* (op.cit. p. 33):

ननु कथं वर्णनिष्पत्तिः ? उच्यते—यदा हि स्वरा वर्णकर्षमाकर्षयन्ति गीतवशात्स्थायित्वेन सञ्चारित्वेन आरोहित्वेन अवरोहित्वेन तदा वर्णस्य निष्पत्तिः ।

Siṁhabhūpāla (op.cit. on SR 1.6.1, p. 152):

स्वराणां वक्ष्यमाणप्रकारेण गानक्रिया गानकरणमुच्चारणमिति यावत् ।

Kallinātha (op.cit. on ibid., loc. cit. p. 151)

गानक्रियया वर्णत्वं स्वरपदादेर्वर्णनाद् विस्तारकरणात् ।

Bharatamuni extols the *varṇa* in glowing terms (song without *varṇa* is like night without the moon, river without water, creeper without flowers and woman without ornaments, NŚ 29.45, p. 92) and gives to it the meaning of linear extension (op. cit. 29.18, p. 81)

यदा वर्णोऽनुकर्षति तदा वर्णस्य निष्पत्तिर्ज्ञेया स्वरसमुद्भवा ।

He adds that the theoretical model of the *varṇa* is set up so as to derive the *alaṁkāras* in both the voice and *vīṇā* (as well as other instruments; op.cit. 29.17, p. 80)

शारीरस्वरसम्भूतास्त्रिस्थानगुणगोचराः ।

Abhinavagupta expands this to say that the *varṇas* occur in *vīṇā* etc. also (op.cit. on ibid., loc. cit. p. 81):

शारीरस्वरेषु मुख्येष्वाश्रितेषु लक्षणमिदमुक्तम् । तत्सदृशस्वरोपलम्भ एवान्यत्र वीणादाविति तत्रापि पर्यवस्यतीति न तु वीणादावलङ्काराभावः ।

70d. Sthāyī. Compare with Mataṅga's lucid definition (op.cit. p. 34):

यत्र समाः स्वराः अनुपहतरूपास्तिष्ठन्ति तेभ्यो यद् गीतं वर्णाभिव्यक्तिकृद् यत्र पदे स वर्णः स्थायीत्युच्यते।

71b. Ārohī. cf. Mataṅga (loc. cit.)

यत्र गेयाः स्वरा आरोहन्ति एकैकशः सान्तरा वा स वर्ण आरोहीत्युच्यते ।

71d. Avarohī: Mataṅga (loc. cit.) restricts the descent to one by one:

अवरोहन्ति स्वरा यत्रैकेनैव क्रमेण तु ।
स चावरोही शब्दे तु समनन्तरः स्वरः ॥

72b. Sañcārī: Mataṅga elaborates this further (loc. cit.):

यत्र ताने सञ्चरन्ति स्वरा अन्त्यान्त्यसंहिताः ।
एकैकशो द्विशोवा स सञ्चारी वर्ण उच्यते ॥

73c-105. i. Alaṁkāras: Paṇḍarīka Viṭṭhala describes the selfsame *alaṁkāras* in *Sadrāgacandrodaya* (1.52-80) and *Rāgamālā* (50cd-82) but athetises the topic altogether in *Rāgamañjarī*. Since the initial note of the *mūrchanā* is also called *prasanna* or *mṛdu* in the context of *alaṁkāras* (SR 1.7.7d-8a), he used the synonym *prasanna* as an adjectival prefix in the names of the *sthāyī-alaṁkāras* in *Sadrāgacandrodaya* (in agreement with most authorities) but replaces it with '*mandra*' in NN and *Rāgamālā*. *Prāṅmukha (sañcārī alaṁkāra)* (NN 3.1.92) has been called *prekṣaka* in *Sadrāgacandrodaya* (1.73), where *skhalita* (*sañcārī alaṁkāra* No. 8) has been listed as *lalita* (op. cit. 1.71) obviously due to graphic deterioration during textual transmission.

A brief review of the treatment of *alaṁkāras* by the more important authorities would help in focussing the same in NN in perspective.

Mataṅga explains *alaṁkāra* in analogy with ornaments of men and women (op. cit. p. 34) and draws a parallel between visual and aural delight.

अलङ्कारशब्देन मण्डनमुच्यते; यथा कटककेयूरादिनालङ्कारेण नारी पुरुषो वा मण्डितः शोभामावहेत्, तथा एतैरलङ्कारैः प्रसन्नाद्यादिभिरलङ्कृता वर्णाश्रया गीतिः गातृश्रोतृणां सुखावहा भवतीति । ... व्युत्पत्तिश्च यथा-डुकृञ् करणे धातुरलंशब्दपूर्वः अलङ्कृतमलङ्कारः घञन्तोऽयमलङ्कारशब्दः ।

I. Bharatamuni (NŚ 29.30-44, pp. 87-92; *Kāvyamālā* edn. 29.22ff. differs substantially from what follows in Mataṅga's extraction, pp. 43, 44)

i. **sthāyī** 1. *prasannādi* 2. *prasannānta* 3. *prasannādyanta* 4. *prasannamadhya* 5. *kramarecita* 6. *prastara* 7. *prasāda.*

ii. **ārohī** 1. *niṣkūjita* 2. *cakora*(?) 3. *hasita* 4. *bindu* 5. *preṅkholita* 6. *ākṣipta* 7. *vidhuta* 8. *udvāhita* 9. *hrādamāna* 10. *sampradāna* 11. *sandhipracchādana* 12. *prasannādi* 13. *prasannānta* (i.2 ?)

iii. **avarohī** 1. *vidhṛta* (ii.7 ?) 2. *gātravarṇa* 3. *udgīta* 4. *udvāhita* (ii. 8) 5. *veṇu (veṇi)*

iv. **sañcārī** 1. *mandratāraprasanna* 2. *bindu* (ii.4) 3. *preṅkholita* (ii.5) 4. *kuhara* 5. *veṇu* (iii.5) 6. *rañjita* 7. *upalolaka* 8. *āvartaka* 9. *parāvarta* 10. ? 11. ?

v. **sarva-varṇāśaya** 1. *prasannādi* (i.1) 2. *prasannānta* (i.2) 3. *bindu* (ii.4, iv.2) 4. *kampita* 5. *recita* (i.5) 6. *preṅkholita* (ii.5, iv.3) 7 *tāramandra-mandra (tāramandraprasanna?)* 8. *sama* 9. *saṁnivṛtta* 10. *pravṛtta (saṁnivṛttapravṛtta ?)* 11. *upalolaka* (iv.7) 12. *veṇu* (iii.5)

These are compiled from Mataṅga's extraction (op. cit. pp. 43, 44). When eleven repetitions, two omissions in (iv) one decomposition in (iv) are considered, these *alaṁkāras* are reduced to 33. Mummaḍi Cikkabhūpāla's extraction of Bharata (*AbhinavaBharata sārasaṁgraha,* pp. 162-166) contains thirty three *alaṁkāras,* though with differences in name and description. The inconsistencies in listing and definition may be reconciled thus: the total *alaṁkāras* listed are 39 (*7 sthāyī,* 13 *ārohī,* 5 *avarohī* and 14 *sañcārī*); of these 6 are equivalent and hence repetitious. Among the listed *alaṁkāras* eight, viz. *kramarecita, prasāda, preṅkhita, recita, avalokita, kṣipta, vistīrṇa* and *udvāhita* are left undefined. But six unlisted *alaṁkāras* viz. *ūrmi, apāṅgita, tāra, tāratama, tāramandra-prasanna* and *mandratāra-prasanna* are defined additionally. Among these, the pairs *ūrmi-preṅkhita, apāṅgita-avalokita* are synonymous. The other *alaṁkāras* may be studied similarly.

II. Mataṅga (pp. 35-43) also describes thirty-three *alaṁkāras* without classification, a comparative study of which with NŚ and SR is instructive.

1. *prasannādi* 2. *prasannānta* 3. *prasannādyanta* 4. *prasannamadhya* 5. *sama* 6. *bindu* 7. *nivṛtta-pravṛtta* 8. *veṇu* 9. *kampita* 10. *kuharita* 11. *recita* 12. *preṅkholita* 13. *tāramandra prasanna* 14. *mandratāra-prasanna* 15. *prastāra* 16. *prasāda* 17. *udvāhita* 18. *upalolaka* 19. *krama* 20. *niṣkūjita* 21. *hrādamāna* 22. *rañjita* 23. *āvartaka* 24. *parivartaka* 25. *udghaṭṭita* 26. *ākṣiptikā* 27. *sampradāna* 28. *hasita* 29. *huṁkāra* 30. *sandhipracchādana* 31. *vidhuta* 32. *udgīta* 33. *gātravarṇa*

III Dattila (op. cit. 97b-108)

i. **sthāyī** : 1 *prasannādi* 2. *prasannānta* 3. *prasannamadhya* 4. *prasannādyanta*

ii. **ārohī**: 1 *prasannādi* (i.1)

iii. **avarohi**: 1. *prasannānta* (i.2)

iv. **sañcārī**: 1. *bindu* 2. *nivṛttapravṛtta* 3. *preṅkholita* 4. *tāramandra prasanna* 5. *mandratāraprasanna*

v. miscellaneous: 1. *kampita* 2. *(ku)harita* 3. *recita*

IV. Pārśvadeva (op. cit. 1.42b-46) largely borrows from Dattila but without acknowledgement.

V. Haripāla (op. cit. 5.7.1-20)

i. sthāyī: 1. *prasannādi* 2. *prasannānta* 3. *madhyadīpta* 4. *prasanna- madhya*

ii. ārohī: 1. *sama* 2. *kampita* 3. *kuharita* 4. *recita* (+*prasannādi*, i.1)

iii. avarohī: 1. *prasannānta* (i.2)

iv. sañcārī: 1. *bindu* 2. *sannivṛttapravṛtta* 3. *preṅkholita* 4. *tāramandra-prasanna* 5. *mandratāra-prasanna*

VI. Śārṅgadeva (op. cit. 1.6.1-65)

i. sthāyī: 1. *prasannādi* 2. *prasannānta* 3. *prasannādyanta* 4. *prasannamadhya* 5. *kramarecita* 6. *prastāra* 7. *prasāda*

ii. ārohi: 1. *vistīrṇa* 2. *niṣkarṣa* 2(a) *gātravarṇa* 3. *krama* 3(a) *bindu* 4. *abhyuccaya* 5. *hasita* 6. *preṅkhita* 7. *ākṣipta* 8. *sandhipracchādana* 9. *udgīta* 10. *udvāhita* 11. *trivarṇa* 12. *veṇi*

iii. avarohī: same as ii. 1-12 but in descent

iv. sañcārī: 1. *mandrādi* 2. *mandramadhya* 3. *mandrānta* 4. *prastāra* (i.6) 5. *prasāda* (i.7) 6. *vyāvṛtta* 7. *skhalita* 8. *parivartaka* 9. *ākṣepa* 10. *bindu* (ii.3a) 11. *udvāhita* (ii.6) 12. *ūrmi* 13. *sama* 14. *preṅkha* (ii.13) 15. *niṣkūjita* 16. *śyena* 17. *krama* (ii.3) 18. *udghaṭṭita* 19. *rañjita* 20. *nivṛttapravṛtta* 21. *veṇu* (ii.12) 22. *lalitasvara* 23. *huṁkāra* 24. *hrādamāna* 25. *avalokita*

v. prasiddha: 1. *tāramandra-prasanna* 2. *mandratāra-prasanna* 3. *āvartaka* 4. *sampradāna* 5. *vidhūta* 6. *upalola* 7. *ullāsita*

VII. Kumbhakarṇa (*Saṅgītarāja*, 2.1.3.1-158, pp. 168-182) describes exactly the same sixtythree *alaṁkāras* of Śārṅgadeva, but suggests that the twentyfive *sañcārī alaṅkāras*, like the *ārohī*, could be taken in descent too, thus giving a total of eightyeight *alaṁkāras*.

VIII. Nānyadeva (op. cit. 5.1.1-17):

i. sthāyī: 1. *prasannādi* 2. *prasannānta* 3. *prasannādyanta* 4. *prasannamadhya* 5. *krama-(recita)* 6. *prastāra* 7. *prasāda*

ii. ārohī: 1. *niṣkūjita* 2. *huṁkāra* 3. *hasita* 4. *bindu* 5. *preṅkholita* 6. *kṣipta* 7. *vidhuta* 8. *udvāhita* 9. *hrādamāna* 10. *sampradāna* 11. *sandhipracchādana* 12. *prasannādi* (i.1) 13. *prasannānta* (i.2) 14. *prasannādyanta* (i.3).

iii. avarohī: 1. *vidhuta* 2. *gātravarṇa* 3. *udvāhita* 4. *udgīta* 5. *veṇu*

iv. sañcārī: 1. *mandra* 2. *prasannādi* (i.1) 3. *preṅkhita* 4. *bindu* (ii.5) 5. *sanni vṛtta-pravṛtta* 6. *recita* 7. *kampita* 8. *sama* 9. *kuhara* 10. *veṇu* 11. *rañjita* 12. *upalolaka* 13. *prāvartaka* 14. *parāvṛtta*

If the repetitions are synonymous, the total reduces to thirty-five.

IX. *Saṅgītasaraṇi* (extr. *Bharatakośa*, p. 586): 1. *ekasvara* 2. *dvisvara* 3. *trisvara* 4. *catuḥsvara* 5. *śṛṅkhalī* 6. *nāgapāśa* 7. *maṅgala* 8. *yatimaṅgala* 9. *nandana* 10. *sundara* 11. *kunda* 12. *sarala* 13. *kuṭila* 14. *udbhaṭa*

X. Ahobala (*Saṅgītapārijāta*, 1.221-297, pp.18-33) describes the selfsame *alaṁkāras* as Śārṅgadeva under the same scheme of classification in the same way: however, he gives additional name for the *sthāyī-alaṁkāras: bhadra (prasannādi), nanda (prasannānta), jita (prasannādyanta), soma (prasannamadhya), grīva (krama-recita), bhāla (prastāra), prakāśa (prasāda)*; like Kumbhakarṇa, he counts *sañcārī* in the descent also (1.278d, p. 30). He also describes seven other *alaṁkāras* which are specially interesting to the historian of Karnataka music; for, these are practised even today as beginner's exercises in the name of *tāla-alaṁkāras* (and simply referred to as *alaṁkāras*) set to the seven *sulādi tālas*. These are believed to be composed by the great saint singer Purandaradāsa in the 16th century and are described by Veṅkaṭamakhin (*Caturdaṇḍīprakāśikā*, 3.82-116). Ahobala describes the *svara* patterns for each of these *tālas* and gives their name, for the first time: *indranīla (dhruva), mahāvajra (maṭhya), nirdoṣa (rūpaka), sīra (jhampā), kokila (tripuṭa), āvarta (aḍḍa), sadānanda (laghutāla)*. He has replaced the name *ekatāla* with the more descriptive *laghutāla*; the *svara* patterns given by him are somewhat different from the ones practised today, but the *tāla aṅgas* are the same. His statement that these *tālas* are found applied in songs of his times (exclusively?) is interesting (op. cit. 1.288). He also describes five more *alaṁkāras* which are used in *rāgas*: *cakrākāra, java, śaṅkha, padmanibha and vārida* (op. cit. 1.288cd, 289, p. 31):

गीतोपयोगिनः सप्त तालयुक्ताः प्रदर्शिताः ।
अलङ्काराः पुनः पञ्च रागोपयोगिनः स्मृताः ॥
चक्राकारो जवश्चैव शङ्खः पद्मनिभः स्मृतः ।
वारिदश्चेति तेषां हि लक्षणं चापि कथ्यते ॥

Thus the total numbers of *alaṁkāras* described by Ahobala is 68 (7 + 12 + 12 + 25 + 7 + 5). Sawai Pratāpasiṁha borrows the seven, *indranīla* etc. (*Saṅgītasāra*, 1.205-207) from Ahobala without acknowledgement.

74c-105. (i) Just as the names of the *varṇas* are appropriate, the names of *alaṁkāras* also are both appropriate and meaningful. Thus *mandra* = *mṛdu* = *prasanna* = initial note of *mūrchanā*; *dīpta* = *tāra* = octave note of *mandra*. Paṇḍarīka Viṭṭhala introduces the term *'madhya'* for the fifth note to fulfil a transient need. However in *alaṁkāras* such as *mandra-tāraprasanna, tāramandraprasanna* (not described in NN) the term *prasanna* appears to be used to indicate the initial note obtained after a descent.

The names of the *alaṁkāras* are beautiful and apt. The meanings of some of these are compiled below from Monier Williams, Apte, Macdonell, etc.

83d. kramarecita—bereft of order

84cd. vistīrṇa—enhanced magnitude: in this instance, enhanced duration; drawn out

85a. sannikarṣa—close contact, vicinity, proximation

86b. preṅkha—swing

87b. pracchādana—covering, overlap; *sandhipracchādana*: covering a joint

88b. ākṣipta—drawn together

89b. bindu—dot, point, spot; here, touching the next note in a point, like flash.

90b. hasita—normally, smile or laughter; here, bloom, enlarge (from root *'has'*, cl. 1, p)

91c. prasāda—lucid, luminous, calm, unagitated

92d. prāṅmukha—turned back

93d. utkṣepa—to throw up, raise, to erect

94d. parivartaka—turn round; artificial hiatus to bring out something new

95d. udvāhita—raised (by one *svara*)

96d. niḥ(-ṣ)kūjita—not sounding (the same note)

98b. recita—emptied, drawn out

99b. skhalita—staggered, slipped, fallen, dripping down

99c. krama—ordered, regular

101a. rañjita—coloured, appealing

101c. hrādamāna—making a sound; *hlādamana*—giving delight

103b. śyena—eagle, falcon, a kind of array, a metre.

73c-105. (ii) NN has borrowed the description of *varṇa-alaṁkāras* freely from SR without acknowledgement but with minor changes. So a brief comparison is appropriate here.

Sthāyī alaṁkāras: NN has athetised *prasāda* and *prastāra*, and has substituted *mandra-prasanna* in the first five *alaṁkāras*; this has led to some confusion because SR describes a *sañcārī alaṁkāra* of this name (1.6.30) and Paṇḍarīka Viṭṭhala assumes its definition in the description of *skhalita, rañjita* and *hrādamāna* (NN 3.1.98-101) without describing it, thus rendering his text opaque and ambiguous.

Ārohī: NN has athetised the listing and definition of *gātravarṇa* (ii. 2a), *abhyuccaya* (ii.4), *udgīta* (ii.9), *trivarṇa* (ii.11) and *veṇi* (ii.12) from SR. Again, SR repeats the names (but not definitions) of *prastāra* (i.6, iv.4), *prasāda* (i.7, iv.5), *ākṣepa* (iv.9) *ākṣipta* (ii.7), *bindu* (ii.3, 4, 10), *udvāhita* (ii.10, iv.11), *krama* (ii.6, iv.17), *veṇi* (ii.12), *veṇu* (iv.21).

Sañcārins, NN has omitted *mandrādi, mandra-madhya, mandrānta* (these three should not be confused with *prasannādi, prasanna-madhya* and *prasannānta* described under *sthāyī-alaṁkāras*), *vyāvṛtta, ūrmi, sama, udghaṭṭita, sannivṛtta-pravṛtta, lalitasvara* and *avalokita* (which may be synonymous with *prekṣaka* = *prāṅmukha*). Further, NN has also omitted the seven *prasiddhālaṁkāras* of SR.

The twentyfive *alaṁkāras* of NN have correspondences in SR shown in brackets in the following (i = *sthāyī* ii = *ārohī* iii = *avarohī* iv = *sañcārī*):

i. 1. *mandrādi* (i.1) 2. *mandrānta* (i.2) 3. *mandrādyanta* (i.3) 4. *mandra madhya* (i.4) 5. *kramarecita* (i.5)

ii. 1. *vistīrṇa* (ii.1) 2. *sannikarṣa* (ii.2a *niṣkarṣa*) 3. *preṅkha* (iv.14) 4. *pracchādana* (ii.8 *sandhipracchādana*) 5. *ākṣipta* (ii.7) 6. *bindu* (ii.3; iv.10) 7. *hasita* (ii.5)

iv. 1. *prasāda* (i.7) 2. *prāṅmukha* = *prekṣaka* (iv.25 *avalokita*) 3. *utkṣepa* (iv.9 . *ākṣepa*) 4. *parivarta* (iv.8) 5. *udvāhita* (ii.10; iv.11) iv. 6 *niṣkūjita* (iv.15) 7. *recita(-)* 8. *skhalita* (iv.7) 9. *krama* (ii.6; iv.17) 10. *rañjita* (iv.19) 11. *hrādamāna* (iv.24) 12. *huṁkāra* (iv.23) 13. *śyena* (iv.16)

80abc. Mandrādi and **mandrānta** are different from SR because of the introduction of *madhya* = *pa* in NN; however, *prasannādi* and *prasannānta* of *Sadrāgacandrodaya* (1.58cd, 59ab) are identical with those in SR (1.6.9)

81cd. Mandra-madhya differs from *prasannamadhya* of *Sadrāgacandrodaya* (1.60, *pa sa pa*) but identical in SR (1.6.23)

83ff. Other parallel texts, (e.g. SR 1.6.13) describe two more *sthāyī alaṁkāras*: *prastāra*, -s̊a ri s̍a s̊a ga mas̍a s̊a pa dha ni s̍a) and *prasāda* (s̍a ri s̊a s̍a ga ma s̊a s̍a pa dha ni sa)

84ab. Sannikarṣa is identical with the first *jaṇṭivarise* in *abhyāsagāna* of Karnataka music and illustrates *sphurita gamaka* (q.v. infra)

90ab.ff. Other texts, (e.g. SR 1.6.19, 24, 25) add five *ārohī-alaṁkāras*, viz. *abhyuccaya* (sa ga pa ni), *udgīta* (sa sa sa ri ga ma ma ma pa dha), *udvāhita* (sa ri ri ri ga ma pa pa pa dha), *trivarṇa* (sari gagaga ma pa dhadhadha) and *veṇi* (sasasa ririri gagaga .... ninini).

100cd-101ab. Rañjita: The definition of this *alaṁkāra* is obscure in all the works of Paṇḍarīka Viṭṭhala because he inserts the term *mandrādi-(alaṁkāra)* without first introducing it. This is yet another instance of his borrowal from SR without contextuality. *Mandrādi* is defined thus in SR (1.6.30):

त्रिस्वरा ऽऽद्या कलैकैकमन्द्रत्यागेन चापराः ।
त्रिस्वराश्चेत् कला मन्द्राद्या मन्द्रादिस्तदा भवेत् ॥
यथा—सगरि रिमग गपम मधप पनिध

101cd. Mandrādestu: vide commentary on NN **3.1.100cd-101ab**.

91cd-104ab. Śri Bharato muniḥ is a both anachronistic and apocryphal. These are actually statements of Śārṅgadeva (SR 1.6.33b): *'tamāha śrīkaraṇeśvaraḥ'* and (ibid., 1.6.53 d) *'śrīkaraṇāgraṇīḥ'* (or variant reading in Ānandāśrama edn. *'niḥśaṅkaḥ prāha sanmatiḥ'*)

105. Alaṁkāraprayojanam: Vāyupurāṇam resolves to describe thirty *alaṁkāras* (Calcutta edn. 25.1-21) but in a passage full, of corruption and lacuna (ibid. loc. cit.) gives only seventeen: 1. *sthāpanī* 2. *kramarejina(-ta ?)* 3. *pramāda* (*pra-*

sāda ?) 4. *apramāda* 5. *kumāra* 6. *śyena* 7. *uttara* 8. *bindu* 9. *durghaṭita* (*udghaṭṭita* ?) 10. *ākṣepa* 11. *kāka* 12. *ākṣipta* 13. *prokṣamadhya* 14. *preṅkholita* 15. *prakṣipta* 16. *ghrāsita* and 17. *makṣi-pracchedana (sandhi-pracchādana* ?) (Ānandāśrama edn. 87.1-24, pp. 314-316). The Calcutta edn. of *Vāyupurāṇam* adds eight more: 1. *visvaroṣṭraka*, 2. *āvarta* 3. *kramotpatti* 4. *vistara vamana* 5. *apāṅga* 6. *kutareka* (*kuharita* ?) 7. *ākṣepa skandana (akṣepa + skhalita* ?) 8. *hrāsita* (*hasita* ?). It promises four benefits to the practitioner of *alaṁkāras*: *samsthāna, pramāṇa, vikāra* and *lakṣaṇa* (ibid., 25.22, 23). On the other hand, *Viṣṇudharmottarapurāṇam* mentions only four *alaṁkāras*, viz. *prasannādi, prasannānta, prasannādyanta* and *prasannamadhya* and describes the benefit accruing from their practice as *'surārādhana'* (ibid., III.18, pp. 92, 93)

106. Gamaka is derived from the root *'gamlṛ'* of class I (*'bhvādi'*), *parasmaipadī*, intransitive and without '*iṭ*'; in the causative (*ṇici*) it assumes forms such as *gamayati* and means, among other things 'to cause (the *svara*) to go to or reach toward (another *svara*), cause (the *svara*) to become expressive, to excel, 'to cause (the musically autonomous meaning of the *svara*) to become clear, intelligible, effective, to convey the meaning (of the *svara*). It evolves into the form *'gamaka'* (*ṇic* + *ṇvul*, Pāṇini, *Aṣṭādhyāyi*, 3.1.33) so as to mean, in the context of music, to cause (the *svara*) to be clearly, intelligibly understood. In other words *gamaka* is the immediate agent which actualises the expressive potential of the *svara*; it makes the *svara* specifically meaningful depending on its environment and context. The semantic potential of a *svara* is latent in its *svasthāna*, but becomes expressive when the *svara* moves in regulated directions and speeds. Thus it acquires a volume or envelop in the tone continuum as also continuity or contiguity. In other words, *gamaka* is not any movement of the note, but a definite or special dynamic state in which it acquires a specific aesthetic function. This is what Kallinātha means when he says (op. cit. on SR 3.87ab, p. 168):

श्रोतृचित्तसुखावह इत्यनेन विशिष्टस्यैव कम्पस्य गमकत्वमिष्टम् । अन्यथा विपरीतस्यापि तस्य गमकत्वं स्यात् ।

108-114ab. The manner and extent of displacement of a *svara* for expressive purposes depends on the nature and limitations of the medium (instrument), on the musical and aesthetic exigencies, physical parameters such as the volume, range, accent, etc. and psychoaesthetic parameters such as aesthetic conventions, individual variation and individual preference, cultural parameters such as traditional norms etc. With these variables, *gamakas* may be only broadly classified.

From the historical standpoint, the growth of *gamaka* may be studied quantitatively (in terms of number), conceptually (the mode of defining), classification and its modern form and function. Paṇḍarīka Viṭṭhala appears in the watershed of the evolution of Indian music; his own contribution to *gamaka* and *sthāya* is only in perpetuation of (textual) tradition; nevertheless, because in his age musical and musicological reformation was on the anvil, a brief comparative study would prove instructive.

Bharata does not mention *gamaka* but may have implied it in *kāku*. Mataṅga does not classify or describe *gamakas* but mentions it clearly on four occasions (op. cit. 479, 489, p. 151; *Bhāṣālakṣaṇa,* pp. 110, 129); Nānyadeva (op. cit. 1.5.2.18-23, pp. 139, 140), Someśvara (*Mānasollāsa,* 4.16.65-75, pp. 7, 8), Pārśvadeva (*Saṅgītasamayasāra,* 1.47-55, pp. 4, 5) and Haripāladeva (*Saṅgītasudhākara,* 5.4.1-9) describe only seven *gamakas,* viz. *sphurita, līna, kampita, tiripa, āndolita, āhata,* and *tribhinna*: Nānyadeva seems to describe the application of each to different notes; Someśvara is the first authority to relate the *gamaka* to (i) the sound generated at the navel etc. (ii) the magnitude of movement in terms of the range of *śrutis* involved and (iii) the speed of movement measured in terms of the *tālāṅgas,* viz. *druta* and *laghu*. *Sphurita* moves to the next *śruti* at thrice the speed of *druta* and returns. *Sphurita* at double *druta* speed is *kampita*; *līna* is the same smoothly performed at *druta* speed; in *āndolita,* the *svara* reaches the third *śruti* (from *svasthāna*) at speed of *laghu* and returns again and again; *tiripa* also moves to the third *śruti* and revolves in high speed; in *āhata* the *svara* strikes the immediately next *svara* at speed of the *druta* and returns: ascent and descent in all three registers very quickly is *tribhinna*; *svara* produced with sealed lips is *mudrita*. Later accounts of *gamaka* are content to relate it with only the speed element and not *śruti* range.

Gamakas next proliferated to fifteen at the hands of Śārṅgadeva who adds *vali, kurula, ullāsita, plāvita humphita, nāmita* and *miśrita* (SR 3.87-97ab). Most of later authors borrow from him. Paṇḍarīka Viṭṭhala also has done the same. However, *gamaka* seems to have been described in another sense from about the 13th century While the above seven (and later, fifteen) are *svara-gamakas,* (i.e. *gamaka* involving *svara* displacement), twenty-two *śruti-gamakas* (involving inter- or intra-*śruti* displacements?) have been mentioned by Pālkurike Somanātha (*Paṇḍitārādhya caritramu, Parvata prakaraṇamu,* p. 452) and copied by Nijaguṇa (*Viveka-cintāmaṇi* 4.92, p. 404): *dīrghalālita, dīrghollāsa, dīrghikādīrgha, ullāsita, samollāsita,* etc. If these were not mere fanciful analogies, they must have been very subtle and exacting in their application. It is interesting that Nijaguṇa has designated the seven classical *svara-gamakas* as *'deśī'*.

From about the 18th century the *gamakas* settled down to ten, and tended to *deśī* usage. Parameśvara (*Vīṇālakṣaṇa,* 4.1-15) describes ten: *hommu, pratihata, siṁhāvalokana, jāru, viṭi, nokku, paṭṭu, orika, gamaka, sphurita*. These are elucidated as techniques in *vīṇā* playing, and may be compared with those described by Subbarāma Dīkṣita as recently as in 1905 A.D.: *kampita (kadalimpu), sphurita, pratyāghāta, nokku, āhata (rava* and *khaṇḍimpu), vali, ullāsita (ekkujāru* and *digujāru), kurula, humphita (orika* and *odagimpu), tribhinna, mudrita* and *miśra (Prathamābhyāsa-pustakamu,* Introduction, pp. 17-19). *Saṅgītaratnākara,* a work in Kannaḍa by an anonymous author gives these ten *gamakas* (p.2): *ārohaṇa, avarohaṇa, ḍ(h)ālu, sphurita, kampita, āhata, pratyāhata, tripuccha, āndola* and *mūrchanā*. Tiruveṅkaṭa Kavi describes ten *gamakas*, viz. *kampita, mūrchanā, kāla, sva(! sphu)rita, pratyāhata, ṭhāya, jāru, orika, nokku, ḍālu,* as well as ten vital elements of *vīṇā* playing, viz. *śruti, dhara, lo mel, paṭṭu, viḍupu, taḍe, sama, kattari, laya,* which are modes of plucking the string with the right fingers. According to him, a *svara* plucked on the string with the right finger and trembled with a left finger is *kampita*; taking the notes in ascent and descent are aptly called *ārohaṇa* and *avarohaṇa* respectively; they are together called *mūrchanā*; rendering them in *vilamba, madhya* and *druta tempi* is *kāla*. *Sphurita* consists in pressing the string with (left) thumb (! forefinger?) and midfinger; (i.e. pressing the string with the left forefinger at the fret of the previous note and striking with the left midfinger the plucked string at the fret of the desired note to generate it in an ascending movement); if executed in descent, this is called *pratyāhata*; rendering a note without plucking the string is *ṭhāya*; *jāru* is the mode of obtaining a note without plucking the string but by sliding the left finger. *Orika* (phonetically deteriorated to '*vareku*' in professional parlance) is deflection of the string to generate a note at a fret; in *ḍhālu* notes are obtained in both ascending and descending movement by sliding the left finger (*Saṅgītasāra-sangrahamu,* pp. 23-24).

The modern practice of *gamaka* in Karnataka music, especially in *vīṇā*-playing is by and large reflected in Subbarāma Dīkṣita's treatment of *gamaka* mentioned above. Muddusvāmi Dīkṣita, the great saint composer, singer and *vīṇā* player (and Subbarāma Dīkshita's grand-uncle) has indicated his preference for the ten *gamakas* by saying *'vīṇāgāna-daśa gamaka-kriye'* in the *caraṇa* of his *kṛti 'mīnākṣi me mudam dehi'* in *gamakakriyā rāga.*

Special mention must be made of Somanātha (*Rāgavibodha*, 5.10-167, pp. 123-210) for his brilliant contribution to the study of *gamaka*; he gives an elaborate account of twenty-two techniques of generating notes on the *vīṇā*, viz. *pratihati, āhati, anuhati, ahati, pīḍā, dolana, vikarṣa, gamaka, kampa, gharṣaṇa, mudrā, sparśa, naimnya, pluti, druta, paratā, uccatā, nijatā* (two varieties), *sama, mṛdu, kaṭhina.* He has inaugurated the designation of the *gamakas* with (visual) graphic symbols, and has used them in writing precisely the *ālāpana* of *rāga* segments. Unfortunately, this has been neglected. It is only about a hundred years ago that Chinnaswamy Mudaliyar and Subbarāma Dīkṣita gave to Karnataka music a well developed system of notation including *gamaka* signs.

Ahobala describes some of these and some uniquely, totalling twenty (op. cit. 1.303-313, p. 34): *cyavita, kampita, pratyāhata, dvirāhata, sphurita, anāhata, śānta, tiripa, gharṣaṇa, avagharṣaṇa, vikarṣaṇa, svasthāna, agrāvasthāna, kartarī, punaḥ svasthāna, sphuṭa, naimnya, ḍhālu, gumphita, mudrā.*

Piṅgalanighaṇṭu, Tamil lexicon, is cited by N.S. Ramachandran (*Rāgas* of *Karnataka Music,* 5, p. 157) as giving the following seventeen names which he claims to relate to techniques of *vīṇā* playing and to different tone qualities of the *vīṇā* (but about which nothing more than the names is known): *kalittal, cummai, kambalai, aḷuṅgal, cilaittal, tuvaittal, cilambal, iraṅgal, imizhdāl, vimmal, irattal, eṅgal, kanaittal, taḷaṅgal, karaṅgal, araṟāl* and *iśaittal.*

Gamakas may be broadly classified as relative to vocal music and to instrumental music. Govinda Dīkṣita elucidates on four occasions (*Saṅgītasudhā,* 3.153, 158, 159, 160, pp. 263, 264) the exclusive application of some *gamakas* to the singing voice. Thus the vernacular name *'vāga'* used for *gamaka* since about the 13th century (e.g. SR. 3.97d) is quite appropriate. Most of the ten *gamakas* mentioned in the foregoing account are applicable to instrumental, especially, *vīṇā*-music. Modern Hindustani music characterises styles and schools of *sitār*-playing, as does Karnataka music those of *vīṇā*-playing, on the criterion of *gamaka.* As long ago as 1888 A.D. Allauddin has described *'daśavidh gamak'* (actually only the classical seven!) in his *Sitārśikṣak* (guru) (pp. 13-15): *ḍālu (sūṇṭh), sphurita (jamajamā, murakī, giṭkaḍī), kampita (larajā), āhat (gamak), pratyāhata (ghasīt), tripuccha (masak)* and *āndolita (mīṇḍ).* The *senī gharānā* has developed twenty-two *gamakas* in its *bāj,* viz. *hump(h)it, khādat, gaṇapat, āhat, anāhat, āndolit, prahat, bruvāhat, durāhat, atharat, śānt, tirip, khareśan, okhareśan,, nisuthān,, okharsuthān, kartarī, syunt, nimni, dhāl, suhān* and *madarā.*

Finally, *gamakas* may be broadly classified into the following:

- **i.** those with names possessing general connotation which have acquired a technical parlance, e.g. *līna, āndolita, tribhinna, vali, kampita.*
- **ii.** exclusive to the voice: *humphita, kurula, mudrita.*
- **iii.** exclusive to chordophones: *nokku, hommu, jāru, orika, ḍhālu.*
- **iv.** those that depend on *svara* sequence, e.g. *āhata, tribhinna, ullāsita.*
- **v.** combinations of two or more *gamakas,* e.g. *miśrita* varieties.
- **vi.** those that depend on difference in speeds, e.g. *kampita, līna, plāvita, āndolita,* etc. (in fact, most of the *gamakas* described by Śārṅgadeva and Paṇḍarīka Viṭṭhala belong to this class).

Gamaka names are quite meaningful: *tiripa*-twisted, screw, turn round; *sphurita*—flash suddenly, tremble, throb; *kampita*—quiver, oscillate very fast; *līna,* dissolve or merge into, absorb, become imperceptible, stick to, be immersed, to become integral with; *āndolita*—swing, sway, vacillate; *vali*—fold; *tribhinna*—differing in three ways; *kurula*—curly; *āhata*—struck; *ullāsita*—exuberant, lustrous, projected from sheath; *plāvita*—soaked, immersed, prolated, *humphita*—generating the sound *'hum'* from the navel; *mudrita*—sealed; *miśra*—mixed.

114cd. (i) **Sthāya: 'Sthā'** is an *ubhayapadī-dhātu* of class I (*'bhvādi'*), intransitive, *aniṭ,* which means 'to stand firmly on, to take up a position on' etc. (*Dhātupāṭha,* 22.30). But *'sthāya'* does not appear to be derived from this *dhātu*; it is equated by lexicographers with *'sthāman'* which means station, seat, place, etc.; *sthāya* is given the meaning 'receptacle' according to lexicons by Monier Williams (op. cit. p. 1264).

On the other hand *'sthāya'* seems to be Sanskritisation of the vernacular word, *ṭhāya,* a technical term used in musical parlance. Kallinātha (op. cit. on SR 3.97d p. 171) states that *vāga* is a vernacular expression but is silent on *sthāya;* so also is Siṁhabhūpāla. It is probable that *'ṭhāya'* is transformed into *'sthāya'* for, the word *ṭhāya* is used again and again in Kannaḍa poetry between the 12th and 20th century and used also in Telugu in exactly the same sense in which it is used in *Saṅgītasamayasāra* and SR, but *'sthāya'* is never employed. The following are some sources in Kannaḍa and Telugu which mention *ṭhāya* (*ṭhāyi, ṭhāye*):

Kannaḍa:

Aggaḷa, *Candraprabhapurāṇa,* 7.97
Kamalabhava, *Śāntīśvarapurāṇam,* 7.93 pr.
Janna, *Anantanātha purāṇam,* 6.71; *Yaśodharacarite,* 2.29, 31
Nāgarāja, *Puṇyāsrava,* 7.52 pr.
Devakavi, *Kusumāvalī kāvya,* 1.78
Kumāravyāsa, *Bhārata, Udyogaparva,* 3.96
Maṅgarasa, *Jayanṛpakāvya,* 14.43
Padmakavi, *Vardhamānacaritre,* 12.32
Rāghavāṅka, *Hariścandrakāvya,* 12.30 (*ragaḷe*)
Kanakadāsa, *Mohanataraṅgiṇi,* 22.31
Ratnākaravarṇi, *Bharateśavaibhava,* 5.56
Ṣaḍakṣari, *Rājaśekharavilāsa,* 10.32
Bommarasa, *Saundarapurāṇam,* 17.12
Prasannaveṅkaṭadāsa, Song: '*tande purandaradāsara smarisuve*'
Padmaṇāṅka, *Padmarājapurāṇa,* 3.62, 63
Aṣṭabhāṣākavi Candraśekhara, *Pampāsthāna-varṇanam,* 74, p. 26
Bhīmakavi, *Basavapurāṇam,* 18.10-16
Siṅgirāja, *Siṅgirājapurāṇam,* 36.12
Ambikātanayadatta (20th century), Araḷumaraḷu, p. 416.11

Telugu:

Palkuriki Somanātha, *Basavapurāṇamu, Sakaleśvaru Mādirājayya kathā,* pp. 208, 209.
Puṣpagiri Timmana, *Samīrakumāra vijayamu,* 3.242, 6.200
Bammera Potarāju, *Bhāgavatamu,* 10.1091
Kaṅkaṇṭi Pāparāju, *Uttara-rāmāyaṇamu,* 6.135
Cedalavāḍa Mallayya, *Vipranārāyaṇacaritramu,* 1.6.

Among the Kannaḍa poets mentioned above, several including Pālkuriki Somanātha, Bhīmakavi, Padmaṇāṅka, Aṣṭabhāṣākavi Candraśekhara, Janna and Siṅgirāja mention some *ṭhāyas* by name.

Some authorities on music refer to *sthāya* as *ṭhāya*. Among them may be mentioned Pārśvadeva (op. cit. 2.33 pr., 34, 60, 62, 66, 68, 71, 80, 83, etc.); Paṇḍarīka Viṭṭhala (*Sadrāgacandrodaya,* 3.29; *Rāgamālā,* 116; NN 3.1.138cd); *ṭhāya* was elevated to the status of a *daṇḍī* (supporting pillar) by Tānappa, *guru* of Veṅkaṭamakhin's *guru* who devotes the seventh chapter of *Caturdaṇḍīprakāśikā* to *ṭhāya*.; with Veṅkaṭamakhin the *ṭhāya* acquired a specific and rigid, uniform form.

The primary sources for the study of *ṭhāya* are Pārśvadeva (op. cit. ch. 2), and SR (3.97-189ab); secondary sources are Kumbhakarṇa (op. cit. 3.1.1-132, pp. 555-567), Govinda Dīkṣita (*Saṅgītasudhā,* 3.163-286, pp. 264-273) and Tulaja (*Saṅgītasārāmṛta,* 14, pp. 179-183) all of whom borrow entirely from SR, but Tulaja spuriously claims Bharata as his authority.

ii. Definition: *Sthāya* is defined as the organ or constituent of *rāga* (*rāgasya avayavaḥ*). Kallinātha elaborates this with the comment (op. cit. on SR 3.97cd, p. 171) that it is a melodic situation (a limb of *rāga*) involving *aṁśa* and some other notes but resting on *nyāsa* (final rest), *apanyāsa* (medial rest), *vinyāsa* (intramedial rest other than *vivādī*) or *sanyāsa* (initial pause). Paṇḍarīka Viṭṭhala defines *ṭhāya* as an isolated piece of *ālāpa* itself (loc. cit.). Pārśvadeva offers the best and comprehensive definition (op. cit. 3.33-37, pp. 8.9): *sthāya* is modality of *svara* kinematics *(svarair-vṛttiḥ, svara-vṛttiḥ)*; the specificity in form of a given *sthāya* results from *gati* (kinetic nature), particular *gamakas* employed, nature of the *rāga* of which it is a limb, the other *rāga* whose semblance it seeks to infuse (as in the case of *bhāṣāṅga-rāgas* or *chāyālaga-rāgas*). It is determined by four operational factors (*karaṇa*) viz. *sthāna* or the *svaramaṇḍala* peculiar to the *rāga* which forms the substratum for the four *varṇas* which constitute its melodic body; *tāna* (*śuddha* or *kūṭa tāna*) which forms a *rāga-sañcāra*; *gamakas* with which the *svaras* must be treated to bring out the *rāgabhāva*; *māna* the extent or length of the *sthāya*. *Gamaka,* especially *miśrita-gamaka* plays a significant role in conferring character on a *sthāya,* e.g. *miśra-sthāyas* (SR 3.176-188). *Sthāyas* should not be stereotyped or monotonous but variegated and beautiful as the neck of a peacock.

iii. Classification: SR has described ninetysix *sthāyas* under the following categories: i. *vyakta-asaṁkīrṇa* (clear and distinct, well known) ii. *avyakta saṁkirṇa (aprasīddha)* iii. *miśra* (mixed). These may be classified on following criteria: (a) sequential characteristics e.g. *śabda, vakra, ullāsita* (b) kinetic characteristics e.g. *ḍhāla, ghaṭana, baddha, sthāpanā,* (c) melodic dynamics e.g. *lavanī, bhṛta, komala, sūkṣmānta, ghanatva* (d) oscillatory characteristics e.g. *vahanī, kampita, sthira* (e) *rāga* characteristics e.g. *kākus, jīvasvara, rāgeṣṭa, apasvarābhāsa,* (f) pitch characteristics (registers) e.g. *tīkṣṇa, avaskhalita, kṣipta, prasannamṛdu,* (g) tempo characteristics e.g. *druta, sama, pluta,* (h) taut or loose structuring e.g. *gāḍha, lalitagāḍha, śithila, śithilagāḍha* (i) aesthetic characteristics e.g. *bhajana, chavi, karuṇā, snigdha, sukha,* (j) instrumental characteristics, e.g. *vādyaśabda, yantrakāku,* (k) tone quality characteristics e.g. *kṣetrakāku,* (l) provincial characteristics e.g. *deśakāku,* (m) analogy e.g. *vedadhvani*, (n) miscellaneous e.g. *chāndasa, sukarābhāsa, vicitra, asādhāraṇa* etc.

115cd-116ab. Paṇḍarīka Viṭṭhala treats *sthāyas* only briefly and cursorily. He discusses only these seven, of which *bhajana, sthāpana* and *gati* belong to the category of *sthāyas* differentiated by quality; *śabda, ḍhāla* and *vahanī* belong to the *vyakta (= prasiddha)—asaṁkīrṇa* (distinct) class. *Śabda* belongs to both.

116d. Bhajana. SR adds *'prayatnād'* (3.121) to the definition: since *ādhāna* is a deliberate or conscious act, *'prayatnād'* should be interpreted to mean 'with special effort'. Pārśvadeva (op. cit. 2.88) adds that the expression of *rāgabhāva* arises here out of a good voice.

117ab. Sthāpana: NN alone has described *'pada'* as *'ramya'* (charming). SR (3.129) or its commentators ignore *padam.* This may be interpreted as (i) the *rāgabhāva* should be established with a suitable *sthāya* at each word or verse-foot of the text, or each section of the *rūpakālapti* or *rāgalapti* or (ii) stopped, according to Siṁhabhūpāla, at every step, before proceeding with the next (*'pratipadam'*: SR.3.129b)

117d. Gati: The simile of the gait of an elephant in rut is from SR (3.129, 130) to which Govinda Dīkṣita (*Saṅgītasudhā,* 3.190, p. 266) adds *gabhīra* (serious, majestic). Pārśvadeva (op. cit. 2.39) describes *gati* as a skilful placement of notes to yield sweet delight to the ear; in this case *gati* does not appear to be a very apt name. The swinging, swaying slow movement of notes as described by NN (and SR) seems to do better justice to the name.

118b. Śabda: Muktaśabda here suggests its prosodial analogue, *cakravāla* as pointed out by Kallinātha (op. cit. on SR 3.113, p. 174). Thus the *śabda* consists of a series of phrases each of which begins on the note or notes on which the immediately preceding phrase ends. Siṁhabhūpāla reads it as *'yuktaśabda'* (suitable or appropriate sounds). Besides this traditional meaning, Paṇḍarīka Viṭṭhala interprets *śabda* as voice and comprehends the four kinds of voice viz. *khāḍgala* (which is called *khāhula* elsewhere in both literary and music textual traditions and may possibly be a graphical corruption), *bombaka, nārāṭa* and *miśraka.* This subject is comprehensively treated separately elsewhere, (e.g. SR 3.39-81; Nānyadeva, op. cit. 1.4.91-115) but is rather implausibly linked up with *sthāya* here. After all, there are *sthāyas* which are associated with quality of the voice. *Sadrāgacandrodaya* (3.15) omits *khāhula* etc. in *śabdasthāya.*

123b. Ḍhāla means a shield; but the intended word is *ḍāla* or *ḍālu* which means lustre, radiance, elegance, gracefulness, etc. Pārśvadeva (op. cit. 3.46cd-47ab) likens it to the sounds of round pearls rolling on a glass surface.

123d. Vāhini, more correctly *vāhanī,* adjectival to the term *vahanī.* Much of its *lakṣaṇa* is athetised in NN. In SR (3.115-119ab) *vahanī* is of two kinds depending on its use in song or *ālāpa.* Each of this is again of two subvarieties, viz. *sthira* (static) and *gīta vegāḍhyā* (speedy) as e.g. *gīta sthira vahanī, gīta vegāḍhyā vahanī, ālāpa* *sthiravahanī, alāpa-vegāḍhyā-vahanī.* Each of these four is again of three subvarieties depending on where in the body it is generated (thus relative to the pitch level): *hṛdyā* (chest or *mandra*), *kaṇṭhyā* (throat or *madhya*) and *śīrṣa* (palatal or *tāra*), totalling twelve *vahanī* forms. Amongst these, the *hṛdyā* variety is divided into two classes viz. *utphullā* and *khullā*. In *utphulla* the notes are divergent and open onward; in *khullā* they are centrally convergent and close inward. The *gamaka vali* accommodates these *vahanī* forms; it may be remembered that *gamaka* is an important operational instrument of the *sthāyas.*

124a. Kāku is voice inflexion charged with emotional stress; it is the curvature in tone at the end of sentence to indicate completion of the meaning (*nirākāṅkṣā*) or incompleteness (*sākāṅkṣā*). It pervades all the three registers of the head, throat and head (Bharatamuni, NŚ 17.106-111 pr, pp. 388-396). It suggests speech (vocal) meaning and musical (*vīṇā*) meaning in all three registers (ibid., loc. cit.). Bhoja defines *kāku* (*Sarasvatīkaṇṭhābharaṇa,* extr. *Bharatakośa,* p. 126) as the suggestion of meaning other than the one explicit in the spoken words by modulating the voice differently:

वाक्ये विधीयमानोऽर्थो येनान्यत्वं प्रपद्यते ।
भिन्नकण्ठध्वनिर्धीरैः स काकुरिति कथ्यते ॥

Abhinavagupta speaks of *śārīra-kāku* and *vīṇā-kāku* of Bharata (loc. cit. 106ab) as *artha-kāku* and *svara-kāku*; *artha-kāku* brings out the literal meaning in the sentence in terms of affirmation or negation while *svara-kāku* indicates the mental state (*Abhinavabhāratī* on Bharata, NŚ, 17.106a, p. 388).

अपि च शारीर्यामथ वीणायामित्यादि केचिद् व्याचक्षते–इहार्थकाकुस्तावद् विधिनिषेधाद्यर्थावगमिका, स्वरकाकुस्तु चित्तवृत्तिसूचिका ।

Thus it is clear that the concept of *kāku* is extrapolated from its discursive environment to *sthāya* in a musical setting. It is called *chāyā-kāku* because it aims at bringing out the shade or shadow of meaning accruing elsewhere. Therefore *kāku* serves both an aesthetic and affective function in musical expression. Both functions may be summarised in the expression *'rasa-kāku'* which Abhinavagupta employs (loc.cit. p. 392).

The word *kāku* may be derived in different ways; the root *'ku'* belonging to class II (*'adādi', parasmaipadi*), VI (*'tudādi', ātmanepadi*) and IX (*'kṛyādi'*) *ubhayapadi*) means 'to sound, cry out aloud, mean, hum' etc. (*Dhātupāṭha* 22.54; 28.108 etc.: *ku-śabde, ku-ārtasvare*); in a dimunitive or instantaneous sense, *kā* is prefixed to it by *ādeśa* (substitution, but sometimes addition or subtraction of a letter or a syllable; Patañjali, *Mahābhāṣya* under Pāṇini, *Aṣṭādhyāyī* 1.1.56); or according to Abhinavagupta it is derivable from *'kak'* (class. I, *bhvādi, ātmanepadi, 'kak-laulye'*) which means 'to be unsteady, to wish, to be proud' (*Dhātupāṭha,* 4.16); *kāku* also means tongue; *kāku* is that which is associated with the functions of the tongue in speech (*Abhinavabhāratī,* on NŚ, 17.106d, p. 389):

अत एव काकुस्वरमपि लक्षितम्-कक लौल्ये, लौल्यञ्च साकाङ्क्षते यथा स्वरवैचित्र्यं लक्ष्यते ईषद्यतो वाच्यभूमिः सम्पद्यते सा काकुः ईषदर्थे कुशब्दस्य कादेशः । काकुर्वा जिह्वा तद् व्यापार सम्पाद्यत्वात् काकुः ।

125d. Svara kāku is the familiar phenomenon of one note assuming the shade of the next by encroaching upon the *śrutis* of the latter so that the *sthāya* strengthens the *rāgabhāva.*

126b. Rāga kāku is that *sthāya* which brings out the essence of the personality of the given *rāga* (cf. *jīvasvarasañcāra* in Karnataka music. SR 3.122; Pārśvadeva, op. cit. 2.99).

126c. Ānyarāga kāku is a *sthāya* which inserts the shade of another *rāga* as in *bhāṣāṅga rāgas* and *miśra rāgas* (e.g. *āhari* in Karnataka music) (SR 3.123). *Ānyarāga-kāku* was also called *ṭhāya* popularly, according to Pārśvadeva (op. cit. 2.101), and *'uparāgabhāṣā* (cf. *rāga* or *vesara,* a particular variety of *rāgas* among *grāma-rāgas*).

127a. Deśa kāku is that which brings out the provincial style or idiom of the same *rāga,* (e.g. the characteristic ways of rendering the *rāga nāṭi* in Karnataka, Andhra and Tamilnadu; SR 3.123). This is analogous to dialectical variations of the same language.

128b. Kṣetra kāku. Kṣetra is field; the (human) body is the field of activity of the soul; vide *Bhagavadgītā,* 13.17:

इदं शरीरं कौन्तेय क्षेत्रमित्यभिधीयते ।
एतद्यो वेत्ति तं प्राहुः क्षेत्रज्ञ इति तद्विदः ॥

Every musician is possessed of traits, attitudes, psychological and physiological characteristics which at once set limitations and yet distinguish him or her from all others. This is why there is a personal stamp in his/her music. This is especially true of *rāga* and therefore *sthāya.* Constitution of the voice apparatus or of instrumental touch which is peculiar to each performer, body-postures and similar body parameters influence the style. Thus *kṣetra kāku* is immediately related to personal style of performers in music (SR 3.124).

128d. Yantra-kāku. There are *rāgabhāvas* which are accessible only to certain instruments such as *nāgasvara, vīṇā,* flute, *sitār* etc. and not to the voice. Besides, some *rāgas* sound more effective in one instrumental class than another: e.g. *ṣaṇmukhapriya, siṁhendramadhyama* in *nāgasvara, madhyamāvati* on flute. Again, there are certain musical forms which are evolved for, or more effective in one instrument than another: e.g. *tānam* on *vīṇā, joḍ* and *jhālā on sitār* or *sarod*. Further, tone quality of an instrument (timbre) is an important ingredient of the sensuous pleasure in music; also, the organisation and display of colours and colour mixtures is as important in orchestration as in painting. (SR. 3.125ab; Pārśvadeva, op. cit. 2.102cd-103ab).

129-144ab. Ālaptibhedāḥ. NN has drawn this material from SR (3.189-202, pp. 188-196) but such description is found earlier in Pārśvadeva (op. cit. 2.1-32, pp. 5-7) who claims the authority of Bhoja and Someśvara etc. (loc. cit.). Since the available works of Bhoja and Someśvara do not contain the varieties of *ālapti, svasthāna-catuḥṣṭaya,* etc. it seems that these must have emerged in the 10th-11th century. There is some evidence of *ālapti* from Tamil sources which will be presently mentioned.

Paṇḍarīka Viṭṭhala takes up here the traditional position and does not notice the models of *ālāpa* which must have been evolving at this time in Karnataka (Cf. Taṛnappa's *caturdaṇḍi,* one of which is *ālāpa*). In order to place Viṭṭhala's contribution on the subject in *Sadrāgacandrodaya, Rāgamālā* and NN in proper perspective, it may be studied under the following heads: i. Definitions ii. *Ālapti*: General Description iii. *Rāgālapti* iv. *Rūpakālati* v. Models. A detailed discussion is beyond the scope of this commentary.

i. *Definitions*

The verbal root '*lap*' belonging to the class I ('*bhvādi*'), intransitive, '*seṭ*' and *paramaipadī* and meaning 'toexpress, articulate or speak' ('*vyaktāyām vāci*': *Dhātupāṭha,* 10.8) generates three nominal forms, viz. *ālāpa, ālapti and ālapana* by taking the prefix '*a*' and the *pratyayas ghañ, ktin* and *lyuṭ* in '*bhāve*' respectively, which confer, according to the grammarian Haradatta Miśra *(Padamañjarī,* comm. on Jayāditya and Vāmana, *Kāśikāvṛtti,* 4.1-3ff. on Pāṇini, *Aṣṭādhyāyī*), the masculine, feminine and neuter (hermaphrodite) genders respectively. According to this grammatical theory, '*ghañ*' confers manifestation (*āvirbhāva, upacaya*); '*ktin*' confers concealment (*tirobhāva, apacaya*) and '*lyuṭ*' confers maintenance or subsistence (*sthiti*). Therefore *ālāpa* means manifestation, *ālapti* means concealment; *ālapana* combines these by *paryāyavṛtti* (alternation) in analogy with *kākākṣi-nyāya,* i.e. by aspecting the one at one time and the other at another. In other words, the *rāga* is expressed both by overt (*ālāpa*) and covert (*ālapti*) means. Kallinātha offers four effective analogies to explain how these two opposite processes may be plausibly combined into an integrated expression: (a) when a person X comes towards an assembly his personality is clearly manifest; but when he sits in the assembly his form is cencealed by being mixed up in likenesses of dress, language etc. (b) when a pearl is alone, its perception is clear, uncontaminated: but when strung with varicoloured gems, it assumes the other colours and its manifestation is only partial. (c) When concealed in an assembly, the person 'X' may become somewhat manifest by moving hither and thither in it, and a pearl is manifested to a limited extent among other gems as in the case of *rūpakālapti* (q.v.) when the *rāga* is only partly manifested through *sthāya, pratigraha* and *bhañjanī* (q.v.). (d) *Ālapti* during the execution of four *svasthānas* (q.v.) reveals the *rāga* here and there and at the same time conceals it just as a lady-love adorned by cosmetics and ornaments (Kallinātha uses *varṇa-alaṁkāra* here in *double etendre*) now conceals and now reveals her features, hair, breasts etc. before her beau; the concealed *rāga* is revealed by *pratigraha* and *bhañjanī* even as a male displays his moustache etc. (Kallinātha, op. cit. on SR 3.197-202, pp. 194, 196). Manifestation (*prakaṭīkaraṇa*) of a *rāga* thus proceeds in terms of highlighting the *aṁśa*, its *saṁvādin* etc. (*āvirbhāva*) and underexposing them through the profusion of *anuvādins* and *vivādin*. It should be pointed out that concealment or mystery is as effective in expression as explicit statement. (Grammatical note: '*ghañ*' elongates the vowel '*a*' on the initial consonant of root; cf. Pāṇini, op. cit. 6.4.27; '*ktin*' adds '*ti*' to the root at the end; ibid. 3.3.91; '*lyuṭ*' in '*bhāve*' adds '*ana*' terminally to the root; ibid., 3.3.115.)

The definition of *ālapti* is functional whereas that of *ālāpa* is structural. In *ālapti* the content is stressed: it is a flow consisting of the four *varṇas* (*sthāyī* etc.) and *alaṁkāras* (*bindu, sannikarṣa, hrādamāna* etc.) in which the *svaras* are embellished with appropriate *gamakas* and which are built up into *sthāyas*; thus it is very beautiful or unusual (*vicitra*). On the other hand, *ālāpa* stresses on the physical parameters such as the notes of commencement, final, medial and submedial pauses, range in the *tāra* and *mandra* registers, etc. in terms of which the personality of the *rāga* is built up: these are the psychoacoustic bases for aesthesis. These two are mutually complementary: male and female, content and form, function and structure. Combining them into a single entity is *rāgālapana*.

However, *rūpaka* also means, according to SR (2.25cd) *rāgālāpa* itself which is in the form of a separate segment, i.e. a segment or limb of *rāgālāpa* removed out of its environment and rendered as an independent melodic entity.

रूपकं तद्वदेव (= रागालाप एव) स्यात् पृथग्भूत विदारिकः ।

Therefore, the equation *rāgālāpa* segment = *sthāya* = *ṭhāya* has served Viṭṭhala as a bridge concept to transit from *rāgālapti* to *rūpakālapti*. This has been possible because '*rūpaka*' is amphibious in *rāga* and *prabandha*. Hence the passage

आलाप एव ठायः स्यात् पृथग्भूतविदारिकः ।

is an echo from SR and a suggestive introduction to the topic of *rūpakālapti*. In describing it at a distance from *sthāya*, the author has indicated both its independent status in music and its *deśī* origin. It may be remembered that *ṭhāya* was just about beginning at this time to develop into an important, independent musical form in Karnataka, was codified and proliferated by Tānappācārya and admitted by his illustrious disciple's disciple Veṅkaṭamakhin into the orbit of *śāstra.*

In *rāgālapti* melodic movement is carried out in vowels, nonsensic syllables or syllables of names. The flow is not restricted or measured by *tāla* rhythm. Its appeal lies in its own autonomy and is not augmentative or secondary to discursive meaning. In *rūpakālapti* however, *ālapti* is performed within a song while the latter is in progress and is set to the same *rāga* and *tāla.* This kind of *ālapti* may be done in two ways:

(i) each segment or division of the song is just preceded by a *sthāya* rendered in the same *rāga-tāla* such that the segment is commenced contiguously with the conclusion of the *sthāya.* Since each segment is thus taken up against the close of a *sthāya* it is called *pratigrahaṇikā.* Kallinātha's commentary gives both explanation and derivation of the word:

स्थायं- रागालप्तेरवयवः, विधाय- प्रथमं गीत्वा, रूपकावयवः - प्रकृतस्थायोचितत्वेन स्वाभिमतः प्रबन्धैकदेशो यदि प्रतिगृह्येत- उपदीयते ।

(ii) Such *sthāyas* are composed to accord with the *'pada'* and *'māna'* of the *prabandha* (*rūpaka)* on hand. *Pada* here does not refer to the word text (*mātu*) of the song but to song segments ('foot') as explained by Kallinātha:

पदैः- पदवत् पदानि; यथा वाक्यस्य पदानि अवयवाः, तथा प्रबन्धस्य अवयवा- विदारीभागाः पदानि इत्युच्यन्ते । न तु वाचकानि सुबन्तादीनि वा भाषापदानि । (SR 3.200)

ii. *Ālapti: General Description*

Someśvara describes the general features of *ālapti* in interesting detail (*Manasollāsa,* 4.16.110-113): *ālapti* is characterised by good tessitura (*susthānam*), simplicity (*saralam*), melodiousness (*śrāvyam*), freedom from contamination (with other *rāgas: śuddham*), splendoured with *kāku* (*kākuvirājitam*), well proportioned (*supramāṇam*), well ordered (*kramayuktam*), sung to please both the learned and the laeity (*gītam prauḍha-janapriyam*); it is executed with the carrier vocables *tittaṇam, dandaṇam, tennā, tritti, hū, hā* or name-syllables, (e.g. hari, rāma, etc.) and the vowels ā ī ū ē; it has ornamented notes in *mandra, madhya* and *tāra* registers with the four *varṇas* viz. *sthāyi, ārohī, avarohī* and *sañcārī,* and the various *gamakas: āhata, tiripa,* etc. Such *ālapti* is excellent.

Aḍiyārkunallar, while commenting on Ilaṅgo Aḍigaḷ's words
yāḻaṅguḷaluñ cīru miṭarum
tāḻguraṇṇumai yāṭaloḍivaṟṟin
icainda pāṭalicaiuḍan paduttu
varikku māṭarku muripporuḷiyakki .... acaiyā marapi nicaiyōṉṟārum
(*Cilappadikāram. Araṅgeṟṟukādai,* ll. 26-36, pp. 99-107)

gives many interesting details of *ālapti* based on the authority of the earlier commentary, viz. *Arumpada-vurai*. This is summarised by N.S. Ramacandran *(Rāgas* of *Karnatik Music,* pp. 74, 75. According to Aḍiyārkunallar (c. 15th century A.D.), *ālapti* was commenced on the consonant *'m'* and then developed on the carrier vocables *'ta'* and *'na'* in long and short vowels; *tenna* and *tena* were use in rendering *ālapti* which was classified as *kāṭṭālatti, niravālatti* and *paṇṇālatti* depending on its use with *'accu'* (with *tāla*), with *pāraṇai* (using syllables) and dance; *paṇṇālatti* was used in rendering *paṇs.* The *ālapti* based on *'m'* was called *śuddha,* that on *'na', sālaga* and that on *'ta'*, restricted to Tamil words. *Paṇ(ālatti)* is performed in eight positions of the vocal apparatus, viz. chest, throat, tongue, teeth, uvula, lips, etc. (compare with *Nāradaśikṣā,* 1.5.6-12, and Nānyadeva, op. cit. 3.24-31 on the physiological origin of the seven notes); *ālatti* is rendered by applying the *gamakas* viz. *eḍuttal, paḍuttal, nalidal, kampitam, kuṭilam, oli, uruṭṭu* and *tākku*; it consists of sixteen parts *paṇṇīrmai, muṛaimai, muḍivu, nirai, kurai, kiḻamai, vali, meli, caman, voraiarai, nīrmai,* etc. Aḍiyārkunallar derives some of this information from *Arumpadavurai.*

The *Saṅgītamakaranda* of Nārada also confirms the use of the syllables *'ta'* and *'na'* as carriers (1.2.1 and 1.4.50, 51):

तत्स्वरूपं तन्ननादि चालापं स्वरगर्भजम् ।
आलापो द्विविधो ज्ञेयः स्वरसंयोजने तथा ।
रागालप्ती रूपालप्तिर्द्वयं च परिकीर्तितम् ।
रागालप्तिस्तननादि, रूपको गीतमुच्यते ।

iii. *Rāgālapti*

SR distinguishes *rāgālāpa* and *rāgālapti* thus:

ग्रहांशमन्द्रताराणां न्यासापन्यासयोस्तथा ।
अल्पत्वस्य बहुत्वस्य षाडवौडुवयोरपि ।
अभिर्व्यक्तिर्यत्र दृष्टा स रागालाप उच्यते ॥

(SR 2.2.23, 24ab; cf. NN 3.1.130, 131ab)

रागालप्तिस्तु सा या स्यादनपेक्ष्यैव रूपकम् ।
स्वस्थानैः सा चतुर्भिः स्यादिति गीतविदो विदुः ॥ (ibid. 3.190cd-191ab)

Thus *rāgālapti* reveals the kinetic characteristics of the *rāga* during its elaboration and is executed in four phases each of which is called *svasthāna,* the area of melodic movement. Kallinātha describes *svasthāna* as *rāgālapana-viśrāntipradeśa* (op. cit. on SR 3.191a), i.e. area in which the processes of manifestation and concealment of *rāga* lie progressively. The following account is based eclectically on Pārśvadeva (op. cit. 2.2.-33, pp. 5-8) who describes it for flautists, Śārṅgadeva (op. cit. 3.190-

193), Siṁhabhūpāla (op. cit. on ibid. loc.cit. pp. 192-195) and Kallinātha (op. cit. on ibid., pp. 192-195).

Rāgālapti is performed only in terms of *svaras* but without words; it is executed however, with carrier vocables. It progresses in four areas (*svasthānas*) in which certain notes named *sthāyī, dvyardha, ardhasthita* and *dviguṇa* serve as nuclei around which the melody pervades. *Sthāyī* is the note on which the *rāga* is begun. This is also the *nyāsa* for *ālāpa*. Pārśvadeva enjoins that the flautist should first establish the *nyāsa* and then *sthāyī* relative to it (which is appropriate to the *rāga*). *Dvyardha* is the fourth note from the *sthāyī*, and as noted by Kallinātha, the fourth from *sthāyī*, inclusive of an omissible note, if any. It is called *dvyardha* because it is half (*ardha*) of the *dviguṇa* (eighth from the *sthāyī*) note. The notes lying between the *dvyardha* and *dviguṇa*, i.e. the fifth, sixth and seventh from the *sthāyī* (inclusive of an omissible note, if any), are called *ardhasthita* or *ardhasvara*. The *dvyardha* (fourth from *sthāyī*) is also called *devaṭhāya* according to Pārśvadeva. Melodic movement around these is called *cālaṇa*. Kallinātha adds the important note that in *cālaṇa* the *svaras* should be shaped by *gamakas*, e.g. *sphurita, kampita*, etc. which are natural to the *rāga* and suitable to the *svara*.

The first *svasthāna* is called *mukhacālī*, a term familiar to flautists (cf. Siṁhabhūpāla op. cit. on SR 3.190-196, p. 194) and dancers as an entrée or entrada (*mukha* = entrance, front, forepart, van). Kannaḍa poets such as Kamalabhava and Janna have frequently used this word (sometimes in a *tadbhava* form viz. *mahacāḷeya*). Paṇḍarīka Viṭṭhala (NN 4.2.427-464), Lakṣmīnārāyaṇa (*Saṅgītasūryodaya*, 2.416-436, pp. 175-178), Catura Dāmodara (*Saṅgītadarpaṇam*, 7.40-51, pp. 188, 189), Veda (*Saṅgītamakaranda*, MS. copy in Sri Varalakshmi Academy, Mysore) etc. mention *mukhacālī* as an entrante for dance recitals. The first *svasthāna* is also called *rāgavaktra* by Pārśvadeva, aptly.

The first *svasthāna* consists of *cālana* of *svaras* from *sthāyin* to *dvyardha* and those below *sthāyin* also according to Kallinātha and resting. Śārṅgadeva does not specify the note on which each of the *svasthānas* should conclude. Siṁhabhūpāla interprets Śārṅgadeva on this point as meaning a note limiting the respective *svasthāna*. This is strange, for Pārśvadeva whom he revers as an authority equates *sthāyī* with *nyāsa*. Similarly, Kallinatha construes Śārṅgadeva to mean that all *svasthānas* should rest on the *sthāyī* note itself. For example, Siṁhabhūpāla says:

स्थायिनः स्वराच्चतुर्थे स्वरे चालनं कृत्वा तत्रैव न्यसनम् (p. 195)

but Kallinātha asserts

पूर्वोक्तैः स्वरैः सह द्व्यर्धस्वरमपि चालयित्वा स्थायिन्यासे सति द्वितीयं स्वस्थानम् (p. 193)

While Śārṅgadeva is content to say *'tasmād-adhastane svare cālanam'*, Pārśvadeva prescribes that the melodic movement should proceed to, and include, the third note below the *sthāyin*.

Next, the second *svasthāna* consists of *svaracālana* at the *dvyardha.* Kallinātha adds that this should include, and progress from, the notes below also. The third *svasthāna* consists of melodic movement centred around the fifth, sixth and seventh notes from the *sthāyin* and should rest, according to Siṁhabhūpāla on an *ardhasvara* itself, and according to Kallinātha, on the *sthāyin.* It is clear that in the latter a suitable descending phrase should be composed as a cadence. The third *svasthāna* does not include the *dviguṇa* note. The fourth *svasthāna* has *svaracālana* in the *dviguṇa,* and according to Kallinātha, in the notes beyond also. Pārśvadeva makes an important contribution (which practice seems to have lost favour with succeeding generations): the *dviguṇa* here means the eight notes in all three registers: the *svaracālana* must comprehend the notes spread over in them; a *rūḍhi* should be executed at this stage in the *sthāyas vali* and *vahaṇī.* The melodic movement involved in establishing the *nyāsa-svara* (in each *svasthāna*) is called *utta.*

Mokṣadeva (*Saṅgītarasakalikā,* extr. *Bharatakośa,* p. 800) describes an abridged form of *svasthāna catuṣṭaya* and ascribes the first *svasthāna* (*mukhacālī*) to the sage Nārada. According to him, *mukhacāla* is performed only in two notes (from the *sthāyī*); the second *svasthāna* lies in the four notes in *ardha* (?); the third occurs in four or two notes; the fourth is performed with four notes and the *dviguṇa:*

आद्यस्वरद्वये चालो मुखः स्यादुपजायते ।
स्वस्थानं प्रथमं ख्यातं नारदेन मनीषिणा ।
चतुर्भिस्तु द्वितीयं स्यादर्धस्थं तत् प्रकीर्तितम् ।
स्वरैश्चतुर्भिर्द्वाभ्यां वा यद्भवेत्तत्तृतीयकम् ।
चतुर्भिर्द्विगुणैः प्रोक्तं चतुर्थं स्थानकं बुधैः ।

Pārśvadeva concludes the discussion of *rāgālapti* with *sthāpanā* (recapitulation) which Śārṅgadeva and Paṇḍarīka Viṭṭhala defer to the end of *rūpakālapti.* Pārśvadeva adds a brief but interesting epilogue to *rāgālapti*: *rāgālapti* has two main characterisitics, viz. purity of *kṣetra,* i.e. *rāga,* and absence of *tāla.* Purity of *rāga* is called *kṣetra-śuddhi,* for *rāga* is designated in this context (elsewhere, *kṣetra* is synonymous with the body, which is the abode of the soul) as *kṣetra* in as much as it is the generating cause for the song (op. cit. 2.28, 29ab, p. 7):

रागालप्तिः क्षेत्रशुद्धियुता तालवर्जिता ।
रागस्य शुद्धता क्षेत्रशुद्धिरित्यभिधीयते ।
गीतस्योत्पत्तिहेतुत्वाद् रागः क्षेत्रमिहोच्यते ।

(*Rāga* is also *kṣetra*-field-because it is the field of tone movement, *svaracālana*).

iv. *Rūpakālapti*

Paṇḍarīka Viṭṭhala has treated *vastu* and *rūpaka* as synonyms (NN 3.1.132cd, 139cd): this is in agreement with Śārṅgadeva (op. cit. 4.6cd):

संज्ञात्रयं निबद्धस्य प्रबन्धो वस्तु रूपकम् ।
तच्छब्देनात्र प्रकृतत्वाद् रूपकं परामृश्यते । तस्य पदानि–विदार्यौ अन्तरभागाः ।

Kallinātha has thus resolved a doubt which could arise on the meaning of *'tat'* because of its immediacy or contiguity with *pratigrahaṇikā* to the divisions of which *pada* could refer. If this latter construction is made, i.e. *'tat pada'* and *'tan-māna'* referring to those of *pratigrahaṇikā* it would mean that the *sthāyas* in *sthāya-bhañjanī* are to be composed so as to accord with the divisions and their extents with those of the *pratigrahaṇikā*. This would argue that a model of the latter would have to be first established. In that case, the *rūpakabhañjanī* has no justification in being treated as a separate variety and should have been regarded as a subvariety of *pratigrahaṇikā*. However, it is not clear if Kallinātha's commentary here is born of actual knowledge and experience of the *ālapti* or of exegetical and polemic skill. Siṁhabhūpāla does not comment on *'pada'* or *'māna'*.

In effect, *pratigrahaṇikā* is the kind of *rūpakālapti* in which a suitable *sthāya* is rendered first in the same *rāga* and *tāla* as of the *prabandha* and then immediately is taken up (*'pratigṛhyeta'*) any limb or part of the *prabandha* which is of the choice of the performer and is suitable to the *sthāya*. In *sthāyabhañjanī*, the *sthāya* is inserted as an integral limb of the song (in the same *rāga* and *tāla*). Then the selfsame *sthāya* is rendered to accord with the extent of the song division (or word?) and its *māna* (= *pramāṇena* = *tat- kālaviśrāntiyuktayā kriyayā*, according to Kallinātha) in numerous alternative ways in novel, beautiful ways (*vicitrarītiyuktaḥ*) which is a measure of the creative excellence of the performer (*gātṛ-vādaka-pratibhāviśeṣeṇa udbhāvyate*). These creative variations are in respect of one *sthāya* pertaining to a given *pada*. If the whole *prabandha* is presented in multiple facets in all the divisions in the respective durations, it is called *rūpakabhañjanī*. Kallinātha elaborates the phrase *'anyathā cānyathā gāyet'* (SR 3.201c) thus (p. 196):

अत्रान्यथात्वं नाम प्रबन्धे प्रकृतधातोर्धात्वन्तरपरिग्रहः । तेनात्र वीप्सया समग्रप्रबन्धस्य प्रकृततान-स्थायानुकारिभिस्तानान्तरैस्तत्तद्रागोचितगमकादियुक्तैर्बहुधावयाविन एव पुनः पुनरावृत्तिभिर्गानमभिद्यो-त्यते । तदासौ रूपकभञ्जनी भवति ।

Rāgasthāpana is an epilogue to *rāgālapti* and affords an opportunity, after elaborate delineation, to recapitulate and epitomise the *rāga*. This is done very briefly in short *sthāyas* presented in variegated postures or aspects such that the pervasive *jīvasvara* (= *aṁśa*) is displayed in its multiple facets by repetition so that the essential personality of the *rāga* is apprehended by the listener with effortless ease. This is an important and efficient device which is well worth reviving in modern practice of *rāga* singing in Karnataka music.

v. *Models*

Paṇḍarīka Viṭṭhala, following Śārṅgadeva has offered four models of *ālāpa*: *rāgālapti* (executed in four *svasthānas* and concluding in *sthāpanā*), *sthāya-bhañjanī*, *rūpaka-bhañjanī* and *pratigrahaṇikā*.

Pārśvadeva describes several forms of *ālapti* which are very interesting (op. cit. 1.28-41, pp. 3, 4). Some of these have survived even today directly or indirectly. He prefaces the description with the observation that it is desirable to preface the rendering of a *gīta* or *prabandha* with an *ālāpa* (in the respective *rāga*). He gives the following sixteen varieties of *ālāpa: viṣama* and *prāñjala* each of which has two sub-varieties with word syllables (*sākṣara*) and without them (*anakṣara*), thus totalling four. Each of these has again two forms viz. *sa-tāla* and *vi-tāla* according as whether it is or is not set to *tāla*. Each of these eight varieties may be *śuddha* or *sālaga*. Thus there are sixteen *ālapti* varieties; Pārśvadeva states that they all flourished in practice of his days and that they are described according to usage.

In *śuddha-viṣamālapti*, melodic movement is quite expressive in all four *varṇas* and is articulated over the whole range of the three registers through *alaṁkāras*, *gamakas* and (carrier) syllables; their *graha* and *aṁśa* are not explicit. Its topographical anatomy is uneven.

The *śuddha-prāñjalālapti* is characterised by purity in style (in rendering), i.e. *śuddha-rīti*; it has delightful designs (*prayoga*) in all three registers with suitable rest notes (for its various parts).

No rules of *varṇa*, *sthāyī* (register) or order of presentation are observed in *sālaga-viṣamālapti*. Its movement is ornamented by beautiful *alaṁkāras* and *gamakas*. Its conclusion is marked by effective (*rāga*) *sthāpanā*.

Sālaga-prāñjalālapti presents (an admixture of) different styles, but brings out the essence of the *rāga*. Its tone is *līna* (*līnanādā*); it is exhilarating and has a graceful *nyāsa*.

'Tam', 'ham', 'śa', 'a', 'da', 'na' etc. (carrier) vocables are used, besides the syllables born of *svaras*, (e.g. sa, ri, ga etc.) in rendering *sākṣarālapti*.

Ānkṣarālapti has no syllable content. *Satālālapti* is performed in the three (*sama*, *anāgata*, *atīta*) *grahas*, three (*druta*, *madhya*, *vilambita*) *layas*, *anujāyi* (*sthāya*, op. cit. 2.41, p. 9), *nyāsa*, *apanyāsa* and *vikṛtāṁśalaya* (?). It is set in *vidārī* (i.e. segmented) and in *yatis* (such as *sama*, *viṣama*, *gopuccha*, etc.). *Atālālapti* is *anibaddha* and is executed only in the four *varṇas*.

Śārṅgadeva illustrates *rāgalakṣaṇa* in the *Rāgavivekādhyāya* of SR. with *ākṣiptikā*, *ālāpa*, *karaṇa* and *vartanī*. He describes *ālāpa* of *rāga* as consisting of the ten vital elements *graha*, *aṁśa* etc.; *rūpaka* is described as similar to *ālāpa* but is divided into separate segments (if *rūpaka* is interpreted as *prabandha*; interpreted as *ṭhāya*, only one such segment is considered). *Ākṣiptikā* is a segment of song set to *caccatpuṭa*, etc. *tāla*, *dakṣiṇa*, *vārtika* etc. *mārgas* and to words and to *svaras*. Śārṅgadeva promises to explain *karaṇa* and *vartanī* in the *prabandhādhyāyà* but fails (in the available text) to keep his promise. The *svara- karaṇa* (SR 4.132-135) or *vartanī-prabandha* (ibid., 4.152-154) shows no indication of *rāgālāpa.* Also, the *karaṇa* and *vartanī* illustrations in *rāgalakṣaṇa* have no relation whatsoever with the *prabandhas.*

Nevertheless, an *ālāpa* system based on *karaṇa, vartanī,* etc. was widely prevalent in the 13th century and survived till the 17th century; for, Govinda Dīkṣita (*Saṅgītasudhā,* 2.458-468, pp. 156-158) and Veṅkaṭamakhin (*Caturdaṇḍīprakāśikā,* 6.1-32) describe it. According to both, the *ālāpa* of a *rāga* proceeds in six phases: i. *ākṣiptikā* (vernacular usage: *āyitta*) is aptly named because it projects (reveals) the *rāga*; ii. *rāga-vardhani* (vern. *karaṇa,* cf. Śārṅgadeva's mention of this element of *rāgālāpa,* SR 2.26) is development (lit. increase) of the *rāga*; this is done in three or two *rāga-vardhanis* separated from each other by a short divisive element called iii. *vidārī* which follows each *rāgavardhanī*). Usually two *vidārīs* are employed. The first, lying between the first and second *karaṇa* is called *yaḍupu* in the vernacular while the second, performed between the second and third *karaṇa,* (i.e. *rāgavardhanī*) is called *makariṇī.* iv. *Rāgavardhanī* (and its *vidārī)* is followed by *sthāyī.* This indicates the beginning of the rendering of *tāna*-groups; the first note on which the *tāna* series commences (usually *madhya sa*) is the *sthāyī.* v. *Vartanī* is the collection of *tāna* groups based on different notes, also called *makariṇī* in the vernacular. This stage corresponds to the presentation of *birkās* in *rāgālāpa* in today's Karnataka music. vi. *Yaḍupu(muktāyī)* is the *ālāpa* element which brings it to a close. Govinda Dīkṣita performs the remarkable feat of describing these six phases in the *ālāpa* of each of fifty *rāgas,* incorporating at the same time the more important of structural elements such as *graha, aṁśa,* the *vādī*-foursome, etc. It is interesting that the *ālāpa* of the *rāga nāti* on the *vipañcī* by Raghunāthanāyaka by Govinda Dīkṣita's eldest son Yajñanāryaṇa Dīkṣita in his *Sāhitya-ratnākara* (6.15-17) corresponds to the *ālāpa* description of this *rāga* in the *Saṅgītasudhā.*

Veṅkaṭamakhin, the second son of Govinda Dīkṣita devotes the entire sixth chapter (of 32 verses) of his *Caturdaṇḍīprakāśikā* to *ālāpa.* He asserts that this is based on the *ālāpas* of fifty *rāgas* which his *guru's guru* Tānappa had created. Thus the *ālāpa* commences with *ākṣiptikā* (*āyitta*), proceeds through the first *rāgavardhanī* (=*karaṇa* = *yaḍupu*), its *vidāri* (*muktāyi*)—second *rāgavardhanī* (second *yaḍupu*)—its *vidārī,* third *rāgavardhanī* —its *vidāri* (one or both of which may be present or absent)—*sthāyī -vartanī* (*makariṇī* ,- fourth *rāgavardhani* - fourth *vidāri,* on which the *rāga* concludes. Veṅkaṭamakhin is more detailed in description of the *sthāyī. Sthāyī* is the base note of a *tāna* in *ālāpana.* Including the *tāra-ṣadja,* a *sampūrṇa, ṣāḍava* or *auḍva rāga* has eight, seven or six notes respectively. Two *tānas* in regular ascent are performed on each note of the *rāga* (thus totalling sixteen, fourteen, or twelve *tānas* respectively) such that the respective note is the upper limit, i.e. the *tāna* proceeds from the corresponding note in the lower register, but does not extend beyond the given note in the given register. The same rule applies in descent also. The first *tāna* merely touches this limiting note but does not stay there; but the second stays on it momentarily and concludes on it. This must be repeated for each note of the *rāga*, beginning with the *madhyasthāyī-ṣaḍja*. Each *sthāyī* is named after the respective base note. *Vartanī* (*makariṇī*) consists of melodic movement in the *mandra* register, commencing and concluding on *mandra-ṣaḍja*. Veṅkaṭamakhin probably implies that *vartanī* is a duplication of *sthāyī-vidhi* in the *mandra* register but does not explicitly say so, whereas Govinda Dīkṣita does.

The foregoing models of *rāgālāpa* were widely prevalent in Karnataka, Andhra and Tamilnadu in the 17th century, for this was systematised as a *daṇḍi* by Tānappa in Karnataka, promoted and stabilised in theory in Tanjore by Govinda Dīkṣita and Veṅkaṭamakhin and exclusively practised by musicians as shown by Shahaji, Tulaja and their court musicians (*Saṅgītasārāmṛta,* Ch. 10, pp. 72-111 and numerous *Rāgalakṣaṇa* Mss. in the Sarasvati Mahal Library, Tanjore).

144b. Nema is also the name of a percursive instrumental composition (NN 2.89-92; *nemacālī,* 2.93-96).

145cd-146ab. Definition of rāga. This is due to Mataṅga (op. cit. 281, p. 81) who also offers another. (ibid., 280, p. 81):

स्वरवर्णविशिष्टेन ध्वनिभेदेन वा पुनः ।
रज्यते येन सच्चित्तं स रागः संमतं सताम् ॥

This is the reading adopted by Kallinātha (op. cit. on SR 2.1, p. 2). The first, used in NN is generally more popular. It is in the active voice (*rañjakaḥ*) while the foregoing is in the passive voice. Kallinātha favours both thus (loc. cit.):

रञ्जनं च, रज्यते येन जनचित्तमिति करणव्युत्पत्त्या वा, जनचित्तानि रञ्जयतीति कर्तरि वा "अकर्तरि च कारके संज्ञायां" इति सूत्रेण कर्तर्यप्यभ्यनुज्ञानादुभयथापि घटत इत्यभिसन्धायोक्तं मतङ्गेन ।

Rāga is derived from the root *'rañj'* belonging to class I (*bhvādi*) and IV (*divādi*), *ubhayapadī, 'seṭ'* and means (*Dhātupāṭha,* 23.30, 26.58) 'to be dyed, coloured, affected, moved, excited, glad, charmed, delighted, attracted, enamoured, to rejoice, exult and shine bright'. It has a Greek cognate 'rezo', 'rezeus'.

Rāga evolves from *'rañj'* by the following grammatical process, according to Varadarāja Bhattācārya (*Laghusiddhāntakaumudī,* p. 387):

घञि च भावकरणयोः (पाणिनिः, अष्टाध्यायी, 6.4.27) रञ्जेर्न लोपः स्याद्रागः । अनयोः किम् ? रज्यत्यस्मिन्निति रङ्गः ।

Sadashiva Shastri Joshi gives an excellent explanation of this in his commentary *'Sudhā'* on the same (ibid., loc. cit.)

'रञ्ज् धातोः 'अकर्तरि च कारके संज्ञायाम्' (पाणिनिः, तत्रैव, 3.3.16) इति घञि घकारञकारयोर्लोपे; 'घञि च भावकरणयोः' (तत्रैव, 6.4.27) इति न लोपे 'अत उपाधायाः' (तत्रैव, 7.2.116) इति वृद्धौ,

'चजोः कुघिण्यतोः' (तत्रैव, 7.3.52) इति जस्य कुत्वे विभक्तिकार्ये च 'रागः' इति रूपम् ।

Thus *'rāga'* means the act of colouring; colour, hue, any feeling or passion, interest or joy, delight, beauty (of voice or song).

DHVANI AND RĀGA

145a. Dhvaniviśeṣaḥ. Implicit in the foregoing definition is an overlapping overtone between poetics and music construed around the term *'dhvani'*, a study of which is rewarding. The *rāga* is appealing (*rañjaka*) to *jana* (common man) also, not merely the elite. It is a special kind of sound (*dhvaniviśeṣa*), i.e. sound other than the one used for transactional communication, a sound which is not normally found organised in the referential world; it is abstracted from phenomenal sound, adapted, idealised or refined into a musical symbol. Thus the singing voice is different from speaking voice or voice used for communication or for non-aesthetic expression; sounds of musical instruments are different from sounds of nature, which they often imitate.

Dhvani means suggestiveness in poetry. It is *sui generis.* Its function in language is purely poetic. It illumines latent or implied meaning lying behind or beyond *prima facie* (or literal) meaning. It is the total experience of *kāvya,* not an ingredient or component. It establishes *rasa-saṁvida* (aesthetic rapport) between poet and *sahṛdaya* (aestehtically susceptible and sympathetic) listener.

Similarly, *dhvani* is expressiveness—rather than expression- in *rāga.* It suggests meanings which are autonomous or peculiar to music only and which transcend meanings that accrue from mere sequential or ordered sound patterns. That is, because of *dhvani, rāga* begins where melodic structure and melodic kinesis end. The specific aesthetic experience which characterises a *rāga* is generated by *dhvani* and is *sui generis. Dhvani* is the exclusive poetic function of non-literal sound sequence or pattern such as *rāga.* It is the total experience of *rāga,* not its ingredient or component. The whole is greater than the sum of the parts.

The second definition of *rāga* quoted above from Mataṅga brings out a reaction between musician and listener: *rāga* is that which colours the mind of the *sahṛdaya* in two ways: special (*viśeṣa*) melodic (*svara*) movement (*varṇa*) and different *dhvani.* In this passage *'vā'* should be construed in its *samuccayārtha* (conjunctional or cumulative sense) rather than optional (*vikalpa*) sense. The first of these ways implies that a particular aesthetic experience is uniquely defined for a given *rāga* by melodic movements which are special to it and not by any or every sequence of musical notes. Such speciality— specificity of melodic kinesis is physically analysable into, and defined by the ten vital elements, *graha, aṁśa, nyāsa,* etc. The second way of generating *rāgatva* (quality of being *rāga*) is by *dhvanibheda*—a term which is synonymous with *dhvaniviśeṣa* which is central to the first definition. As suggested above, 'vā' should be construed with an additive force rather than alternative force;

for, *dhvanibheda* and *viśeṣa-svaravarṇa* are mutually complementary rather than mutually exclusive. The former provides the general criterion for *rāgatva* while the latter confers the individuating or differentiating criterion. *Dhvanibheda* may also be interpreted as special inflexion (*kāku*) of the medium of expression. This again parallels the poetic method.

The expression '*svara-varṇa-viśeṣa*' merits further attention: it contains an apparent redundancy because *varṇa,* the act of singing musical phrases includes *svara.* But this expression does not suffer from tautology; for, *svara* here indicates primary aesthetic appeal which it affords in its own autonomy: '*svato rañjayati*'. This quality of experience includes those attributes of *svara* which contribute to its *rañjakatva,* e.g. *snigdhatā, anuraṇana, śrutyanantarabhāvitā, dūraśrāvyatā* and *gamaka,* which constitute its psychoacoustic aspect. I should like to coin here a new word for the psychoacoustic attribute of the *svara,* viz. 'soneme' in analogy with its linguistic cousin, 'phoneme'. Next, *varṇa* signifies melodic kinesis, i.e. the continuous locus of moving sound. It is this single, continuous sound which assumes the character, role and function or the expressional / structural vital elements such as *graha, aṁśa, nyāsa,* etc. which elucidate both the generality and specificity of a *rāga.* This is why Mataṅga includes *svara per se* and its movement, viz. *varṇa* in the definition. Both have the power of beautification—*alaṁkāra.* Beauty is the *sine qua non* of all art. When *svara* is ornamented in a manner which is appropriate to the *rāga* and manifests a particular movement pattern, it becomes *alaṁkāra. Varṇa* is general and *alaṁkāra* is particular.

The term *dhvani* is employed by grammarians and poeticians to connote, among other things, articulate sound, suggestible meaning or suggestible element in meaning. Abhinavagupta illuminates the several semantic dimensions of *dhvani* in his *Dhvanyāloka-locana* (on Ānandavardhana, *Dhvanyāloka,* 1.13, pp. 62-64).

श्रोत्रशष्कुलीं सन्तानेनागता अन्त्याः शब्दाः श्रूयन्त इति प्रक्रियायां शब्दजाः शब्दाः श्रूयमाणा इत्युक्तम्। तेषां घण्टानुरणनरूपत्वं तावदस्ति, ते च ध्वनिशब्देनोक्ताः । यथाह तत्रभवान् भर्तृहरिः—

'यः संयोगविभागाभ्यां करणैरुपजायते ।
स स्फोटः शब्दजाः शब्दा ध्वनयोऽन्यैरुदाहृताः ॥'

एवं घण्टानिर्ह्रादस्थानीयोऽनुरणनात्मोपलक्षितो व्यङ्ग्योऽप्यर्थो ध्वनिरिति व्यवहृतः । तथा श्रूयमाणा ये वर्णा नादशब्दवाच्या अन्त्यबुद्धिनिर्ग्राह्याः स्फोटाभिव्यञ्जकाः ते ध्वनिशब्देनोक्ताः । यथाह स एव तत्रभवान्—

''प्रत्ययैरनुपाख्येयैर्ग्रहणानुग्रहैस्तथा ।
ध्वनिप्रकाशिते शब्दे स्वरूपमवधार्यते ॥''

इति । तेन व्यञ्जकौ शब्दार्थावपीह ध्वनिशब्देनोक्तौ । किञ्च वर्णेषु तावन्मात्रपरिमाणेष्वपि सत्सु; यथोक्तम्—

"अल्पीयसापि यत्नेन शब्दमुच्चारितं मतिः ।
यदि वा नैव गृह्णाति वर्णं वा सकलं स्फुटम् ॥"

इति । तेषु तावत्स्वेव श्रूयमाणेषु वक्तुर्योऽन्यो द्रुतविलम्बितादिवृत्तिभेदात्मा प्रसिद्धादुच्चारण व्यापारादभ्याधिकः स व्यापारो ध्वनिरुक्तः । स एव यदाह—

"शब्दस्योर्ध्वमभिव्यक्तेर्वृत्तिभेदं तु वैकृताः ।
ध्वनयः समुपोहन्ते स्फोटात्मा तैर्न भिद्यते ॥"

इति । अस्माभिरपि प्रसिद्धेभ्यः शब्दव्यापारेभ्योऽभिघातात्पर्यलक्षणारूपेभ्योऽतिरिक्तो व्यापारो ध्वनिरुक्तः । एवं चतुष्कमपि ध्वनिः । तद्योगाच्च समस्तमपि काव्यं ध्वनिः । तेन व्यतिरेकाव्यतिरेकव्यपदेशोऽपि न युक्तः ॥

This passage is translated by K. Krishnamurthy thus (*Dhvanyāloka-locana,* pp. 148-149).

'According to the theory that the last of the sounds coming in a series to the ear are heard, it has been said that the sounds heard are products of (previous) sounds. Indeed, they do possess a quality of resonance as that of a ringing bell; and they have been called here by the term *dhvani.* As observed by the revered Bhartṛhari:

"What is produced by the contact and separation of the organs of speech-production with the relevant places (within the mouth) is *sphoṭa* or (oral) 'sound'. Other sounds produced (echo-like) from these are termed *dhvani* by others (who hold that such sounds too are produced, as against those who hold that such succeeding sounds are suggested by the preceding ones (*Vākyapadīya,* 2.102)" By the same token, even suggested sense which is resonant and comparable to the resonant vibration of a ringing bell comes to be designated by the term *dhvani.* Furthermore, even audible syllables, termed *nāda,* which are fully grasped only after the last of the syllables is heard, and which suggest in their turn the *sphoṭa* (sound-gestalt) as a whole are called *dhvani* (by some grammarians). This again, is supported by the text of the same revered author (i.e. Bhartṛhari):

By means of impressions ineffable, as well as continuity of apprehensions, the sound gestalt is revealed by *dhvani.* It is this sound gestalt in which we grasp a word (as a totality) in its true form (Ibid., 1.83).

Thus it is clear that the term *dhvani* connotes both suggestive expression as well as suggestive sense.

Furthermore even though the duration of uttered syllables is restricted as noted by the authorities in the field:

"However slight be the effort in the utterance of a word, the listener's mind will either not catch any of the syllables thereof, or will catch all the syllables at once."

(Kumārila, *Ślokavārttika,* section on *Sphoṭa,* 10)

Even in the case of the restricted nature of syllables heard, it is seen that on the speaker's part there is some further effort, over and above the effort required for their mere utterance, which results in differences of intensity in the sounds, viz., 'fast', 'slow' and so forth. As Bhartṛhari himself says:

"After the word-sound is revealed, differences in its intensity are brought about by *vaikṛta dhvanis* or transformed evolutes of the initial or primary *dhvani* (i,e. *prākṛta-dhvani*). But the total unit of *sphoṭa* apprehended is never partitioned by them." (*Vākyapadīya,* 1.77)

Taking their (i.e. grammarian's) lead, it is stated by us that the linguistic function over and above those of denotation, intended purport and secondary implication deserves the designation of *dhvani.* Therefore, references to *dhvani* sometimes as distinct from a poem and at other times as identical with a poem are both not without justification.

Thus *dhvani* is articulate sound; it is analogous with the ringing of a bell because while the latter generates sound waves which reach the ear drum sequentially and cause perception, *dhvani* also generates a succession of waves of conventional, contextual and secondary meaning which proceed in an orderly manner and the last wave reaches consciousness to generate suggestible meaning. Secondly, it is *sphoṭa* the universal sound. *Pada-sphoṭa* is an essential part of it and is manifested in consciousness by the last sound in a sound sequence. Each phoneme of a word donates its semantic impress (*saṁskāra*) progressively to the next one so that meaning flashes in consciousness in a burst when the final sound is heard. Poeticians who subscribe to the theory of *sphoṭa* use the term *dhvani* for both the suggestive word and suggestive meaning. *Dhvani* is also used by grammarians to denote the slowness or fastness of enunciation of the phonemes of a word.

A single word, though fixed in its sound content, is individuated when uttered by different persons at different speeds, which is a determinant factor in the comprehension of its meaning. Because some words, besides arousing the conventional, contextual and secondary meaning have also the additional ability of function of manifesting suggested meanings through variable speed in enunciation, the latter is also called *'dhvani'.*

Dhvani may be classified into the embellishable (*vastu*), embellishment (*alaṁkāra*), transient emotion (*bhāva*) and aesthetic configuration (*rasa*).

The foregoing considerations may be extrapolated, *mutatis mutandis* from the spoken articulate sound to the musical articulate sound. The expression of meaning of nonliteral articulate sound through *dhvani* may be regarded as *rāga.* The use of such sounds in varying durations such as *druta* (fast) and *vilambita* (slow) is of fundamental importance in *rāga,* because, other things being equal, it is this structural variability which makes possible a great multiplicity of possible expressions or expressivenesses, each of them conferring specificity or individuality on meaning. The concept of *sphoṭa* may be readily extended to *rāga* because, though temporal sequentiality of the semantic symbols (phonemes in words, words in phrases, phrases in sentences .... in language; *svara in varṇālaṁkāra, varṇālaṁkāra in sthāya, sthāya in akṣiptikā* etc. limbs .... in *rāga*) is inevitable in all discursive semantic modes, the meaning of the whole is perceived in a burst (*sphoṭa*) only at the end of the final symbol, resulting from the progressive accumulation of semantic impresses of individual units or elements of expression. In other words, *dhvani* conveys the whole sense of the *rāga* in a burst and not in stages or phases; these latter are only a methodological necessity; they are only technical parameters.

I have discussed elsewhere the mutual relationships between, *śruti, dhvani* and *sphoṭa,* recapitulation of which here is beyond the scope of the present discussion. (Sathyanarayana R., *Śruti, Dhvani* and *Sphoṭa,* in the *Indian Theosophist,* Thakur (Dr.) Jaideva Singh Felicitation Number, 82.10-11, Oct. Nov. 1985, pp. 30-47.)

146cd-148ab. While discussing the second definition of *rāga* according to Mataṅga it was said that *svara-varṇa-viśeṣa* provided the individuating or distinguishing criterion for *rāgatva; svarāṇām kramabhedāt* means *vakra*; *vakra rāgas* may be further individuated through restricted melodic phrases e.g. *nārāyaṇagaula, ānanda-bhairavī, āhari,* etc. in Karnataka music, *nānāgamakabhedāt*: NN itself provides examples of this by specifying the *gamakas* , e.g. *saindhavī* (171), *baṅgāla* (178), *śyāma* (187),.*sāmanta* (188), *śaṅkarābharaṇa* (232) etc.; examples in *Rāgamañjarī* are *toḍī* (2.11), *guṇakarī* (2.18), *bhairavī* (2.22, 67) *śaṅkarābharaṇa* (2.33), *turuṣkatoḍi* (2.61); *gatibhedhāt*: some *rāgas* are at their best only when rendered at a particular pace: *āharī* is not effective in fast pace, *navarasakannaḍa* is not effective in slow pace etc.; *grahāṁśanyāsabhedāt*: when NN was written, all *rāgas* were rationalised into *ṣaḍja-grāma* and hence possessed *sa* as *graha, aṁśa* and *nyāsa.* However, this was a transition period and other notes than *sa* continued to serve as these *rāga prāṇas*; numerous examples of this are available in *Svaramelakalānidhi,* NN, *Sadrāgacandrodaya, Rāgamañjarī, Rāgavibodha, Saṅgītarāja,* etc.; *nānādeśa-janodbhavāḥ* refers to the varieties of *rāga* found in different places and created by different musicians; it also refers to the variety introduced in *karnāṭa, karnāṭagauḍa, karnātabaṅgāla; toḍī, turuṣkatoḍi* etc., *rūḍhi-deśa-svarābhidhāḥ:* e.g. *guṇakarī, lalita, vihāgaḍa, saṅkarābharaṇa,* etc. *rūḍhi* (i.e. non-*yaugika* names); *toḍī, gaula, kāmboji, mālava, saindhavī, turuṣkatoḍi, yammaṇa-kalyāna, gurjarī, ābhīrī,* etc. (*deśa*); *pañcama, devagāndhāra, madhyamādi (svara)* (cf. *Sadrāgacandrodaya,* 1.79).

148cd-150ab. Rāgabhedas. *Śuddha-rāga* is uncontaminated with shades of other *rāgas* and has excessive appeal; *sālaga* partakes of other *rāgas* for its appeal; *saṅkīrṇa* compounds its own appeal and that of other *rāgas*; these three kinds originate from Śiva himself (*Sadrāgacandrodaya* 2.78). The first available classification of *rāgas* into *mūla* (*śuddha*), *chāyāmātrāśraya* (*sālaga*), *saṅkīrṇa* and *deśaja* is due to Yāṣṭika who explains them to Kāśyapa, according to Mataṅga (op. cit. 365, p. 104).

151-166. For detailed study of *rāga* classification including gender taxonomy, see Sathyanayrayna, R., *Vīṇālakṣaṇa-vimarśe,* pp. 85-91, Commentary on Veṅkaṭamakhin, *Caturdaṇḍīprakāśikā,* Chs. 4, 5; *Iconification in Indian Music* in Vivekananda Patrika, Madras, Aug. 1984, pp. 107-124; *'Hindustāni-Saṅgītadalli-Rāgamūrtīkaraṇa'* in Inchara, Basavarāja Rājaguru Felicitation Volume, Hospet, 1983, pp. 95-131.

167. Numerograms are a time honoured device in Sanskrit. Several works such as the *Saṁkhyāratnakośa* are devoted to its description from time to time; *candra* = 1, *netra, pakṣa, yama(la)* etc. = 2, *agni, vahni, anala,* etc. = 3, *veda* = 4.

RĀGALAKṢAṆA

168-233. Paṇḍarīka Viṭṭhala gives an intervallic description of *rāgas* in *Sadrāgacandrodaya* and *Rāgamañjarī* and combines it with reificatory description in *Rāgamālā* and NN. He also indicates the omissible note, curvature (*vakratā*), time of singing, *gamaka,* affiliation with *mela* and other *rāgas,* the *auḍuva-ṣāḍava-sampūrṇa* variety, etc. He does not use *rāgāṅga-upāṅga-bhāṣāṅga* classification.

In the following, I have endeavoured to develop a contemporary and pan-Indian delineation of each *rāga.* I have traced the evolution of many of these *rāgas* in a historical perspective elsewhere: Sathyanarayana, R., *Vīṇālakṣaṇa-vimarśe,* pp. 94-256; *Karnāṭaka-saṅgīta-vāhinī,* pp. 77-120, 199-219, 233-253, 316; my Commentary on Veṅkaṭamakhin, *Caturdaṇḍīprakāśikā,* Chs. 4, 5. But here I have adopted a different criterion: the *rāgas* of NN are compared with *rāgalakṣaṇa* and *rāgamūrtilakṣaṇa* found in twelve original sources, including two of Paṇḍarīka Viṭṭhala himself, some composed during his own time, some one or two generations earlier and some one or two generations later, so as to give some continuity and some comprehensiveness to the study.

The sources used for comparative study are abbreviated as follows:

SUS *Saṅgītopaniṣat-sāroddhāra* of Sudhākalaśa
SJ *Saṅgītarāja* of Kumbhakarṇa
SMK *Svaramelakalānidhi* of Rāmāmātya
SC *Sadrāgacandrodaya* of Paṇḍarīka Viṭṭhala
RJ *Rāgamañjarī* ofPaṇḍarīka Viṭṭhala
RK *Rasakaumudī* of Śrīkaṇṭha
RV *Rāgavibodha* of Somanātha
SD *Saṅgītadarpaṇa* of Catura Dāmodara
SS *Saṅgītasudhā* of Govinda Dīkṣita (in the name of Raghunātha Nāyaka)
SP *Saṅgītapārijāta* of Ahobala
PS *Pañcamasārasaṁhitā* of Nārada
GP *Gītaprakāśa* of Kṛṣṇadāsa-Baḍajenā-Mahāpātra

SUS and SJ are included here for the reificatory description they offer, though they precede the NN by more than a century. Works later than c. 1650 A.D. such as *Caturdaṇḍīprakāśikā* of Veṅkaṭamakhin, *Hṛdayaprakāśa* and *Hṛdayakautuka* of *Hṛdayanārāyaṇa*, *Rāgataraṅgiṇī* of Locana Jhā, *Rāgaratnākara* of Gandharvarāja, *Catvāriṁśacchata-rāganirūpaṇam* of Nārada etc. are not considered here because the distance in time from NN is somewhat large.

The following abbreviations are used to indicate the intervallic content of the *rāgas*. K=Karnataka music. H=Hindustani music. T= time of singing. X – 3 = svara X is *graha, aṁśa* and *nyāsa*.

Karnāṭaka Music	*Hindustāni Music*
ra *suddha-riṣabha*	*re komal-riṣa(-kha)bh*
ri* *catuḥśruti-riṣabha*	re -*śuddh-riṣa(-kha)bh*
ri *pañcaśruti-riṣabha*	*ga komal gāndhār*
ru *ṣaṭśruti-riṣabha*	ga *śuddh-gāndhār*
ga *śuddha-gāndhāra*	*ma śuddh-madhyam*
gi *sādhārāṇa gāndhāra*	ma *tīvr-madhyam*
gu* *antara-gāndhāra* (original)	*dha komal dhaivat*
gu *antara-gāndhāra* (modern)	dha *śuddh dhaivat*
ma *śuddha-madhyama*	*ni komal niṣā(-khā)d*
mi *pratimadhyama*	ni *śuddh niṣā(-khā)d*
dha *śuddha-dhaivata*	
dhi* *catuḥśruti-dhaivata*	
dhi *pañcaśruti-dhaivata*	
dhu *ṣaṭśruti-dhaivata*	
na *śuddha-nīṣāda*	
ni *kaiśiki-niṣāda*	
nu* *kākali-niṣāda* (original)	
nu *kākali-nīṣāda*	

168. 1. *Śuddhabhairava*

K—sa ra gi ma pa dha ni. H—sa *re ga* ma pa *dha ni.*

SUS—

SJ—

SMK 4.18, p. 22 mentions under *Śrīrāga-mela* but does not describe; *adhama rāga* (5.11, p. 30)

SC 2.2.50cd *bhairava-sampūrṇa*, dha-3, T—morning

RJ 2.11cd omits ri sa-3, T—dawn

RK—

RV 4.11, p.108 *bhairava-sampūrṇa*, dha-*graha aṁśa*, sa-*nyāsa*, T—morning

5.178, p. 213:

डमरुत्रिशूलधारी पन्नगहारी सितो लसद्धसितः ।
धृतशशिगङ्गोऽतिजटोऽजिनविकटो भैरवोऽसमदृक् ॥

SD 2.197, p. 32 *bhairava*—dha-3, omits ri-pa, dha-*mūrchanā*, dha is *vikṛta*.
2.198, p. 32

गङ्गाधरः शशिकलातिलकस्त्रिनेत्रः सर्पैर्विभूषिततनुर्गजकृत्तिवासाः ।
भास्वत् त्रिशूलकर एष नृमुण्डधारी शुभ्राम्बरो जयति भैरव आदिरागः ॥

SS 2.140cd-141cd-141ab, p.115 (from SR) *bhairava*—dha-3, intervals of *nandayanti jāti*; sa-*mandra*, ga-*tāra*

SP 1.379, p. 42 *bhairava*—dha *graha*, ma *nyāsa*, omits ri-pa, *tīvra* ga-ni, *komala* dha, T- morning

PS—

GP 5.2, 16, pp. 34,36 *sampūrṇa*, dha-3, *mandra* ga has *kampita gamaka*. T- afternoon

169. 2. *Dhannāsī*

K— sa ri * gi ma pa dhi* ni. H—sa re* *ga* ma pa dha* *ni*

SUS—

SJ 2.2.2.64, p. 409 sa *graha-nyāsa*, omits ri; ga-pa *alpa*, *sa-grāmarāga*, born of *kaiśikamadhyama jāti*; T- all seasons, morning, heroic sentiment

SMK 4.18, p. 22 *srīrāga-mela*; 5.39, p. 33—*uttama auḍuva*, sa-3, mostly omits ri-dha, T- morning

SC 2.2.26. sa-3, omits ri-dha, T- dawn, *śrīrāga mela*.

RJ 2.66cd, sa-3, omits ri-dha, T- morning, *mālavakaiśika-mela*

RK 2.111, 118, 119, pp. 26, 27: *śrīrāga-mela*, sa-3, omits ri-dha, T- dawn; heroic sentiment.
2.119, p. 27:

नीलोत्पलश्यामलमूर्तिरेषा प्रियं लिखन्ती विरहेण युक्ता ।
श्रीखण्डचर्चा विलसत्कुचास्या धन्नासिका भाति मनोज्ञवेषा ॥

RV 4.31cd, p. 114 sa-3, omits ri-dha, T- morning
5.177, p. 213:

दूर्वाभविभा विरहासहा लिख़न्ती पटे पतिं रुदती ।
स्न्रपितकुचा सितगल्ला स्थिरधम्मिल्ला धनाश्रीः ॥

SD 2.256, p. 44 sa-3, omits ri, *ṣāḍava*, first *mūrchanā* (of *sa-grāma*), heroic sentiment, *desī rāga*: rules of *śruti*, *svara*, *grāma* and *jāti* do not apply (2.289, p. 51)
2.257, p.44:

दूर्वादलश्यामतनुर्मनोज्ञा कान्ते लिखन्ती विरहेण दूना ।
श्वेते कपोले नयनारविन्दनिष्यन्दनिर्धूतकुचा धनाश्रीः ॥

SS 2.936cd-937, p. 207 *śrīrāga-mela,* sa-3, omits ri-dha; *auḍava* according to *vaiṇika* tradition.

SP 1.359, p. 38 *sampūrṇa,* omits ri-dha in ascent, has *śuddha* notes (i.e. of *śrīrāga mela*), ga-*graha,* ma-*nyāsa* (ga-3?)

PS 3.27.p. 13:

नीलोत्पलं कर्णयुगे वहन्ती श्यामा सुकेशी कृशमध्यभागा ।
ईषत्सहासाम्बुजवक्त्ररम्या सा धानुषी पद्मसुचारुनेत्रा ॥

GP 5.41, p. 38 sa-*graha, aṁśa;* ma-*nyāsa,* born of *śuddhakaiśikmadhyama grāma rāga;* omits ri, heroic and erotic sentiment, T- always

170. 3. *Bhairavī*

KH *Svaras* same as in *dhannāsī,* i.e. *srīrāga-mela*

SUS 3.90, 91, p. 65 *bhāṣā* of *bhairava;* नीलांशुका रक्तवर्णा भैरवी शुकवाहना

SJ 2.2.2.148, p. 419 *upāṅga* of *bhairava,* dha-3, ga-*tāra,* ga-*mandra, svaras* of *velāvali* 2.2.3.72

नीलांशुका रक्तवर्णा शुकवाहनमाश्रिता

SMK 4.18, p. 22; 5.25, 26 p. 31 *srīrāgamela, sampūrṇa,* sa-3, T- atter half of day
SC 2.2.26cd. sa-3, *pūrṇa, mudrita-gamaka* in ri-pa; T- always
RJ 2.22 *bhairavī* I: *mālavagauḍa mela;* sa-3; *mudrita gamaka* in ri-pa, *pūrṇa,* T- always
2.67 *bhairavī* II: *mālavakaiśika-mela;* sa-3; *mudrita-gamaka* in ri-pa; *pūrṇa,* T- always
RK 2.111, p. 26, *śrīrāgamela;*
2.117, p. 27:

सुवर्णवर्णा घनवाद्यहस्ता विशालनेत्रा द्विजराजवक्त्रा ।
नित्यं स्थिता स्फाटिकचारुपीठे कैलासशृङ्गे किल भैरवीयम् ॥

RV 4.32, p. 114 *śrīrāgamela,* sa-3, ri-pa have *mudrita gamaka, pūrṇa,* T- always
SD 2.201, p. 33 *sampūrṇa,* ma-3, *sauvīrī mūrchanā, ma-grāma— rāga, svaras* similar to those of *bhairava.*
2.202, p. 33:

स्फटिकरचितपीठे रम्यकैलासशृङ्गे विकचकमलपत्रैरर्चयन्ती महेशम् ।
करधृतघनवाद्या पीतवर्णाऽऽयताक्षी सुकविभिरियमुक्ता भैरवी भैरवस्त्री ॥

SS.2 952-956, p. 209 *bhairavī* is a *mela;* sa ri gi ma pa dha ni/sa re *ga* ma pa *dha ni;* dhi is also occasionally used in musical practice; sa-*nyāsa;* dha-*graha, aṁśa; vādī*- sa, *saṁvādī*-pa; *vivādī*-ni; *anuvādī*-ri-ga-dha

SP 1.375, pp. 41,42 sa-3, komala dha, T- always.

PS 3.115, 116, pp. 11,12, *rāgiṇī,* sung in forenoon:

3.32, p.14:

सरोवरस्था स्फटिकस्य मण्डपे सरोरुहैः शङ्करमर्चयन्ती ।
तालप्रयोगप्रतिबद्धगीतिः गौरीतनु भैरविका सतीयम् ॥

GP—

171. 4. *Saindhavī*

K—sa gu ma pa nu; omits ri-dha; H—sa ga ma pa ni

SUS

SJ 2.2.2.127, 128, p. 417 *Sa-grāma*, sa-*graha*, *nyāsa*; *kampita* in dha, and a little in sa; ma-*mandra*, ga-*bahula*, erotic sentiment, affiliated to *drāviḍī*

रक्तवस्त्रा च हेमाभा मीनवाहनमाश्रिता ।

2.2.3.21, p. 425 *bhāṣā* of *pañcama* according to Yāṣṭika.

2.2.3.70, p. 431 Name given by Yāṣṭika to *Bhūpālī* (2.2.3.68, 69) which is described by *Bhūpāla-pālaka*, as an *aṅga* of *travaṇā*, sa-3, omits ri.

SMK

SC 2.2.27ab *śrirāga-mela*, sa-3, omits ri-pa, excellent *gamakas*, T- always

RJ 2.67cd *mālavaśrī-mela*, sa-3, omits ri-pa, has (excellent) *gamakas*, T- always

RK

RV 4.33, p.114 *srīrāga-mela;* also called *sindhuḍā* in vernacular, sa-3, omits ga-ni, has *gamaka*, T- always

5.215, p. 223:

उच्चतनुस्तनुरतनुर्जघने शोणांशुका त्रिशूलाङ्का ।
गौरी करिगतिरभिमतयुद्धा सैन्धव्यतिक्रुद्धा ॥

SD 2.183, p.30 wife of *bhairava rāga* according to Hanūmān

2.207, p. 35 *sampūrṇa*, sa-3 *utatramandrā mūrchāna*, *ṣāḍava*, omits ri, heroic sentiment, T- always

2.208, p. 35:

त्रिशूलपाणिः शिवभक्तियुक्ता रक्ताम्बरा धारितबन्धुजीवा ।
वीरे रसे गायकगीतवर्णा सा सैन्धवी भैरवरागिणीयम् ॥

The third quarter of this verse is given by Basavappa-Nāyaka II of Keladi *Śivatattvaratnākara*, 6.8.65 thus

प्रचण्डकोपा रसवीरयुक्ता

SS 2.181, 182ab, p. 120 *bhāṣā* of *ṭakka*, sa-3, omits ri-pa, dense with *gamakas*, ga-ma *tāra*; *mandra* sa, all sentiments (from SR)

2.377, p. 148 *upāṅga* of *varāṭī*; *kampita* in dha, sa; ga-*bahula*, *sphurita* in *mandra* ma, erotic sentiment (from SR)

SP
PS 3.30, p.14

सदिन्द्रनीलद्युतिरम्बुजाक्षी प्रवादयन्ती कविलसयन्तम् ।
विचित्ररत्नाभरणा सुकेशी सा सिन्धुडा कान्तसमीपसंस्था ॥

kavilasayantam—delighting the poet? *kapilāsayant(r)am*—playing *kapilāsa vīṇā*?
GP 5.29, p. 37 *pañcamabhāṣā*, pa-3, T- late afternoon, sentiments of love and mercy
5.70, p.41 *āsāvarī* = *mallārī* + *saindhavī* + *toḍī*; *mukhāvarī* = *saindhavī* + *toḍī*

172. 5. *Māravī*

K— sa ra gu ma pa dha nu; H—sa *re* ga ma pa *dha* ni
SUS —
SJ —
SMK —
SC 2.2.22 *mālavagauḍa-mela*, sa-3, omits ri-dha, T- always
RJ 2.17cd *mālavagauḍa-mela*, sa-3, omits ri-dha, T- always
RK —
RV 4.15, p.109 *mālavagauḍa-mela*, popularly called *mārū*; sa-*nyāsa*, ga - *grāhāṁśa*, omits ri-dha, T- always
5.218, p. 224:

इन्दुमुखी कनकाभा दीर्घा लम्बालकातुला चलदृक् ।
अरुणाम्बरा नृपवरांस्त्वरयन्ती मारवी समिते ॥

(*samite*—for battle)
SD 2.289, p. 51 *deśī-rāga*; no rule in *śrutī*, *grāma*, *jāti*, etc.; *deśī-rāga*; rules of *śruti svara*, *grāma*, *jāti* do not apply (2.289, p. 51)
SS —
SP 1.476, 477, p. 64 *śuddhasvaras* (*śrīrāga-mela*!) ga-*graha*, omits dha in ascent, born of *gāndhārocyavatī-jāti*, *āndolita niṣāda*.
PS—
GP—

173. 6. *Āsāvarī*

K— sa ra gu ma* (14th *śruti*), pa dha ni; H—sa *re* ga ma* pa *dha ni*
SUS—
SJ —
SMK —
SC 2.2.18cd *mālavagauḍa-mela*, ma-3, *pūrṇa*, T- always
RJ 2. 16cd *mālavagauḍa-mela*, ma-3 *pūrṇa*, T- always
RK—

RV 4.21, p. 111 *mālavagauḍa-mela*, ma-2, sa-*nyāsa*; *pūrṇa*, T- always 5.216, p. 223:

चलकदलीदलदलमौलिर्मलयाचलगा कलक्वणन्मुरलिः ।
आसावरी सकरुणा बर्हाली शालिनी नीला ॥

(*bharhālī śālinī*—wears peacock feathers around waist)

SD 2.188, p. 30 wife of *śrīrāga*

2.194, p. 31 wife of *mallāri*

2.258, p.45 omits ga-ri, pa (?dha) -3, *auḍuva*, sentiment of mercy; or born of *kakubha*, *dhaivatī jāti*, dha-*aṁśa*, *graha*, omits pa, *ṣāḍava*

2.259, p. 45:

श्रीखण्डशैलशिखरे शिखिपुच्छवस्त्रा मातङ्गमौक्तिककृतोत्तमहारवल्ली ।
आकृष्य चन्दनतरोरुरगं वहन्ती साऽऽसावरीति कथितोज्ज्वलनीलकान्तिः ॥

SS—

SP 1.444, p.58 *gaurī-mela*, omits ga-ni in ascent; ma-*graha*, dha-*aṁśa*, pa-*nyāsa*, T- after second *prahara*

PS 3.31, p.14 *aśvavārī:*

जवाप्रसूनद्युतिरिन्दुवक्त्रा शुकं च पद्मं च करयोर्दधाना ।
क्षौमां शुकाच्छादितगात्रयष्टिर्महाविदग्धा कथिताश्ववारी ॥

GP 5.5, p. 34 *ṣāḍava*

5.44cd-45ab *sāvarī:* dha-*nyāsa*, ga-*tāra*, ma-*mandra*, ma-3, omits pa, sentiment of *karuṇa*.

174. 7. *Bhairava*

K—sa ra gu ma pa dha ni; H—sa *re* ga ma pa *dha ni*

SUS 3.88, 89, p. 64:

भैरवः श्वेतवर्णः स्यादेकवक्त्रोऽष्टहस्तभाक् ।
वृषयानः कृत्तिवासाः कालभैरवरूपभृत् ॥
सर्पत्रिशूलखट्वाङ्गजपमालाभिरन्वितैः ।
वीणापाशफलाब्जैश्च पाणिभिर्भूषितो ह्ययम् ॥

SJ 2.2.2.35, 36, p. 406 dha-3, *bhinnaṣaḍja*-born, *rāgāṅga*, T- autumn, *rasa*: *vipralambha*(+?) *karuṇā*; T- first watch of day, omits pa, sa-ga-*tāra*, ma-*mandra*

2.2.2.37, 38, p. 406:

एकास्याष्टभुज(:) श्वेतवर्णो वृषभवाहनः ।
कृत्तिवासाः सर्पशूलखट्वाङ्गजपमालिका(:) ॥

वीणापाशफलाब्जानि बिभ्राणो भैरवप्रभः ।
कैश्चिद् रागविदां वर्यैः स्मर्यते शूलिरूपभृत् ॥

SC 2.2.50, *hijeja-mela* (sa ra gu ma pa dha ni), dha-3, *pūrṇa*, T-morning
RJ 2.52cd *hijeja-mela*, sa-3, omits ri, T- morning
RK 2.103, p. 25 *mālavagauḍa-mela*, sa-3, omits ri-pa, T- dawn
2.104, p. 25:

गङ्गाधरश्चन्द्रकलोत्तमाङ्गो भुजङ्गमव्यूहविभूषिताङ्गः ।
शुभ्राम्बरः शूलविभूतिधारी स भैरवाख्यो जयति प्रकामम् ॥

RV 4.11, p. 108 *svamela* (*vasantabhairavī*?), dha-*graha, aṁśa*, sa-*nyāsa*, T- morning

5.178, p. 213:

डमरुत्रिशूलधारी पन्नगहारी सितो लसद्भसितः ।
धृतशशिगङ्गोऽतिजटोऽजिनविकटो भैरवोऽसमदृक् ॥

(*asamadṛk–trilocana*)
SD 2.158, p. 26 male *rāga;* born of Aghora face of Śiva (2.161, p. 27); *puruṣa rāga* (12.164, p. 27), T-morning (2.172, p. 28), *grīṣma* season 2.181, p. 29), *puruṣa-rāga* according to Hanūmān (2.183, p. 30)
2.197, 198, p. 32 see under *śuddhabhaīrava*, (NN 3.1.168)
SS 2.140cd-141ab, p. 115 see under *śuddhabhairava* (NN 3.1.168)
SP 1.379, p. 42 dha-3, omits ri-pa, *komala* dha, *tīvra* ga-ni, T- morning
PS—
GP 5.56cd-57ab, p. 40 born of *bhinnaṣadja*, omits ri-pa, dha-*graha, aṁśa*, ma-*nyāsa*, it is sung on auspicious occasions.

175. 8. *Śuddhalalita*

Māravī mela: (SC 2.2.22cd, RJ 2.17cd) = *mālavagauḍa-mela* or *gauḍī-mela*, K—sa ra gu ma pa dha nu; H—sa *re* ga ma pa *dha* ni
SUS 3.113, p. 67 (*lalita*) *bhāṣāṅga rāga*
SJ—
SMK 4.14, p. 22 *mālavagauḍa-mela, uttama rāga* (5.2, p. 29); 5.36, p. 32 sa-3, omits ri, *ṣāḍava*, T- first watch of day, auspicious.
RV 4.22, p.111 *mālavagauḍa-mela,* sa-3, *sampūrṇa* or omits pa, T- dawn
5.172, p. 211:

नीराजयत्युमेशं दीपैरनिशं निशात्यये ललिता ।
विविधालङ्कृतिमिलिता कलितश्वेताम्बरा गौरी ॥

SD 2.166, p. 27 wife of *vasanta-rāga*; T- morning according to Someśvara (2.172, p. 28) to be sung in spring (2.180, p. 29); wife of *hindola* (2.186, p. 30) according to Hanūmān; wife of *pañcama* according to *Rāgārṇava* (2.192, p. 31): *sampūrṇa* or *auḍuva* by omitting ri-pa, sa-3, *śuddhamadhyā mūrchanā*

2.233, p. 40:

> प्रफुल्लसप्तच्छदमाल्ययुक्ता गौरी कृशाङ्गी तरुणी चलाक्षी ।
> विनिश्वसत्सादवशात् प्रभाते विलासवेशा ललितोपदिष्टा ॥ (हिन्दोलभार्या)

RK

SS 2.712-713ab, p. 182 *gurjarī* (=*mālavagauḍa*)-*mela*, sa-3, omits pa, *ṣāḍava* (*lalita*)

SP 1.415, p. 52 *gaurī* (=*mālavagauḍa*)-*mela*, omits pa, sa-*graha aṁśa*, ma-*nyāsa* ? T- always

PS 3.14, p.11. *rāgini.* T- forenoon, wife of *vasanta* (3.23, p.12)

3.50, p.18:

> उषसि केशसंयममात्मनो विदधती शयनोत्थितवत्यसौ ।
> विलुलितालकवल्लिवृतानना सुललिता ललिता कलिता बुधैः ॥

GP 5.8, p. 35 *auḍuva*,

5.59cd-60ab born of *ṭakka*, has facile *svaras* (ni movement), sa-3, omits ri-pa, sa-*mandra*

176. 9. *Pañcama*

Māravī mela (SC 2.2.22cd, RJ 2.17cd)= *mālavagauḍa-mela* or *gauḍī-mela*

K—sa ra gu ma pa dha nu; H—sa *re* ga ma pa *dha* ni

SUS 3.94cd-95, p. 65

> पञ्चमः पञ्चवक्त्रः स्याद्दशहस्तो गजेन्द्रगः ।
> वीणापाशफलाङ्कुशखट्वाङ्गाब्ज(ङ्गवर)भृत्करः ॥
> तालाभयादियुक्पाणिः श्यामलाङ्गश्च कीर्त्यते ।

SJ.2.2.2.110, 111, p. 415 limb (evolute) of *śuddhapañcama*; pa-3; it is *rāgaṅga* according to some and not, according to others.

> पञ्चवक्त्रो दशभुजो श्यामोऽनेकपवाहनः ।
> वीणापाशाब्जमालाहिकलाभयवराङ्कुशान् ।
> खट्वाङ्गमपि बिभ्राणाः पाणिभिः कैश्चिदिष्यते ॥

SC 2.2.19ab *mālavagauḍa-mela*, pa-3, omits ri, T- morning

RJ 2.19cd *mālavagauḍa-mela,* pa-3, omits ri, T- morning

SMK

RK 2.101, 102, p. 25 pa-3, or sa-3, omits ri, or, according to some, *pūrṇa,* erotic sentiment

रक्ताम्बुजाक्षोऽरुणचारुचीरो युवा सुवेषो रतिरङ्गयुक्तः ।
प्रत्यूषकाले विजयी नितान्तं स पञ्चमाख्यः कलकण्ठभाषी ॥

RV 4.21, p. 111 *mālavagauḍa-mela,* pa-3, omits ri, T- dawn

SD 2.161, p. 27 born of Tatpuruṣa face of Śiva, *puruṣa-rāga* (2.164, p. 27), has five wives (2.168, p. 27), T-morning (2.172, p. 28), in autumn (2.181, p. 29), *puruṣa-rāga* according to *Rāgārṇava* (2.190, p. 31), has five wives (2.192, p. 31); *sāḍava,* omits pa (!), sa-3, first *mūrchanā* (of *sa-grāma*), according to some, it is *sampūrṇa,* erotic sentiment (2.282, p. 50)

2.283, p. 50:

रक्ताम्बरो रक्तविशालनेत्रः शृङ्गारयुक्तस्तरुणो मनस्वी ।
प्रभातकाले विजयी च रत्यां सदा प्रियः कोकिलमञ्जुभाषी ॥

SS —

SP 1.370, pp. 40, 41 *gaurī* (=*mālavagauḍa*)-*mela*; omits ri-pa; has *tīvra* ga, sa-*graha,* ma-*aṁśa, nyāsa;* T- always

PS 3.15, p. 11 *pañcamī* T- forenoon; wife of *vasanta* (3.23, p. 12)

3.49, p.18 *pañcamī:*

सङ्गीतगोष्ठीषु गरिष्ठभागं समाश्रिता गायनसम्प्रदायैः ।
खर्वा क्वणन्नूपुरपादयुग्मा सा पञ्चमी पञ्चमवेदविद्या ॥

GP

177. 10. *Paraja*

SUS—

SJ—

SC—

RJ—

SMK—

RK—

RV 4.23, p. 111 *mālavagauḍa-mela,* ga-*graha aṁśa,* sa-*nyāsa, kampita* in dha, ga; T- always

5.219, p. 224:

परज इषुधनुर्धारी हारी गौरस्तनुस्तनुदीर्घः ।
मिथ आहततालवधूशाली स्तवनेन शालिनः ॥

SD—

SS—
SP—
PS—
GP—

178. 11. *Baṅgāla*

K— sa ra gu ma pa dha nu; H—sa *re* ga ma pa *dha* ni

SUS 3.103, p. 66 *megha-bhāṣā;* बङ्गाला पीतवसना गौराङ्गी खड्गगामिनी

SJ 2.2.2.106, 107, p. 414 *Baṅgāla* I: *aṅga* of *ṣāḍava-rāga,* ma-3, *kampita* in sa-pa; T- all seasons; in joy and erotic sentiment: पीतवासा गौरवर्णालङ्कृतः षड्ज-वाहनः ।

Baṅgāla II: ma-*graha nyāsa,* born of *mālavakaśika,* omits ri, *mṛdu* pa (i.e. *mandra*-pa), *tāra*-pa, presiding deity is *kāma.*

SC 2.2.18ab *mālavagauḍa-mela,* sa-3, pūrṇa, T- always

RJ 2.21cd *mālavagauḍa-mela,* sa-3, *pūrṇa,* T- always

SMK

RK 2.105, p. 25 born in *mālavagauḍa-mela,* ga-3, omits ri; but according to Kallinātha, ma-3, *pūrṇa*

2.106, p. 26:

भस्मोज्ज्वलाङ्गस्तरुणार्कवर्णो जटाकलापं शिरसा दधानः ।
कक्षास्थलस्थूलवलत्करण्डो बङ्गालरागः कथितस्तपस्वी ॥

2.129, p. 29 *śuddhabaṅgāla: karnāṭa-mela;* ma-3, *sampūrṇa,* T- morning

2.130, p. 29:

मनोज्ञवेषः कमनीयकेशः प्रफुल्लनेत्रः शरदिन्दुवक्त्रः ।
सदा विलासी नवगेहवासी बङ्गालनामा रविकल्पधामा ॥

RV 4.22ab, p. 111 *mālavagauḍa-mela,* sa-3, *sampūrṇa,* T- always

SD 2.158, p. 26 *puruṣa-rāga; baṅgālī;* wife of *bhairava* (2.167, p. 27). T- morning (2.171, p. 28), *rāgiṇi* of *bhairava* (2.184, p. 30) according toHanūmān, according to *Rāgārṇava* (2.191.31); *pañcama-bhāryā, auḍuva,* sa-3, omits ri-dha, first *mūrchanā* (of *sa-grāma*); according to Kallinātha, ma-3, *sampūrṇa.*

SS 2.322, p. 140 born of *ṣāḍava-rāga,* ma-3, but in practice, pa-*graha*

SP 1.382, p. 43 *sa-mūrchanā;* omits ri-dha, *ni-tivra,* T- morning (*baṅgālī*)

PS

GP 5.5, p. 34 *ṣāḍava*

179. 12. *Hindola*

K—sa gi ma dha ni; H—sa *ga* ma *dha* ni

SUS

SJ 2.2.2.91-94, pp. 412, 413 born of *mārgahindola*, sa-3; *kampita* in ma-pa, *mandra*-ni, ni-ri-sa affiliation, erotic sentiment

SMK 4.25, p. 22 *hindola-mela* (sa ri gi ma pa dha ni); *uttama* (5.3), *auḍuva*, omits ri-dha, sa-3, auspicious, T- always (5.37, p. 33)

SC 2.2.72 *hindola-mela* (sa ra gi ma pa dha ni), (2.2.73) sa-3, omits ri-pa, T-morning

RJ 2.54cd-55, p. 238 *hindola-mela* (sa ri gi ma pa dha ni); omits ri-pa, sa-3, T-morning

RK

RV 4.14ab, p.109 *vasanta-mela*, omits ri-pa, ma-*aṁśa*, sa-*graha nyāsa*, T- dawn

5.174, p. 212:

मालामशोकचम्पककमलानामुद्वहन् महाभूषः ।
ललनान्दोलितदोलालोलो हिन्दोलको गौरः ॥

SD 2.166, p. 27 *rāgiṇi* of *vasanta*; *puruṣa-rāga* with five *rāgiṇis* according to Hanūmān (2.183, 186, p. 30), *rāgiṇi* of *gauḍa* (*mālavagauḍa*) according to *Rāgārṇava* (2.195, p. 31), omits ri-dha, sa-3, *śuddhamadhyā mūrchanā*, has *kākali niṣāda* (nu*) (2.221, p. 38)

2.222, p. 38:

नितम्बिनी मन्दतरङ्गितासु दोलासु खेलासुखमादधानः ।
खर्वः कपोतद्युतिकामयुक्तो हिन्दोलरागः कथितो मुनीन्द्रैः ॥

SS 2.1023, 1024 ab, p. 217 *bhairavi-mela* (sa ri gi ma pa dha ni/sa re *ga* ma pa *dha ni*) sa-3, omits ri-pa, *auḍuva*

SP 1.432, p. 55 omits ri-pa, has *komala dhaivata*; T- after second watch of day; by restoring ri-pa in it, *mārgahindola* is formed.

PS 3.9, 44, pp. 11,19 *puruṣa-rāga:*

लीलाविलासेन पतन् पृथिव्यामुत्थापितस्तत्क्षणमालिवृन्दैः ।
उल्लासयन् गीतरसैर्विदग्धान् हिन्दोलरागः कथितो रसज्ञैः ॥

GP 5.7.56 ab, pp. 35, 40 *auḍuva,* T- spring season (lacuna for *lakṣaṇa*)

180. 13. *Bhūpālī*

Malhāra-mela; *malhāra* is derived from *kedāra-mela* (SC.2.2.37cd-38ab; RJ 2.29 cd, 2.25) i.e. K—sa ri gu ma pa dhi nu; H—sa re ga ma pa dha ni

SUS

SJ 2.2.3.68,70, pp. 430,431 affiliated to *travaṇā,* omits ri, sa-3, described (created?) by *Bhūpālapālaka*(?): in abjectness and shame (modesty); also called *saindhavī*(II)

SMK 4.26, p. 23; 5.35, p. 35 *śrīrāga-mela*; sa-3, omits ma-ni, *auḍuva,* T- morning (*bhūpāla*)

SC 2.2.46, p. 49 *kedāra-mela* (*vide supra*), ga-3,omits ma-ni, T- morning

RJ 2.27, 31cd. *kedāra-mela,* sa-3, omits ma-ni, T- morning

RK 2.141,142, pp. 30, 31 *vasanta mela* (sa ri gi ma pa dha ni/sa re *ga* ma pa *dha ni*) omits ma-ni, but according to some, ri-pa; *śānta rasa.* T- dawn.

उत्तुङ्गवक्षोरुहभारनम्रा गौरी स्फुरत्कुङ्कुमालिप्तदेहा ।
सम्पूर्णशीतांशुमनोज्ञवक्त्रा भूपालिका सैव पतिं स्मरन्ती ॥

RV 4. 36ab, p. 115 *mallāri-mela* (sa ri gu ma pa dhi nu/sa re ga ma pa dha ni) sa-*nyāsa,* ga-*graha aṁśa,* omits ma-ni, T- dawn

5.171, p. 211:

दोलालोला विपिने तरलितवलयं विभूष्य भूपाली ।
कान्ते प्रसितात्यन्तं कुङ्कुमपीता स्मराद्भीता ॥

(*smarād bhītā* = *kāmātura,* lustful)

SD 2.168, p. 27 *rāgiṇi* of *pañcama* according to *Rāgarāgiṇi-matam,* T- morning (2.171, p. 28), T- autumn (2.181, p. 29), *rāgiṇi* of *megha* according to Hanūmān (2.189, p. 30), *rāgiṇi* of *deśākhyā* according to *Rāgārṇava* (2.196, p. 31); sa-3, first *mūrchanā* (of *sa-grāma*), *sampūrṇa* but *auḍuva* by omitting ri-pa according to some; *śānta rasa* (2.266, p. 46)

2.267:

गौरद्युतिः कुङ्कुमलिप्तदेहा तुङ्गस्तनी चन्द्रमुखा मनोज्ञा ।
भर्तुः स्मरन्ती विरहेण दूना भूपालिकेयं रसशान्तियुक्ता ॥

SS 2.1040cd-1041, p. 219 *bhūpāla*; *mela* of *bhairavī* (sa ri gi ma pa dha ni /sa re *ga* ma pa *dha ni*), sa-3, omits ma-ni, *auḍuva*

SP 1.376, p. 42 omits ma-ni, ri-dha *komala,* ga-*graha aṁśa,* ri-*nyāsa,* T- morning

PS 3.19, 63, pp. 12, 21 *rāgiṇi,* T- evening:

स्वनायकं पुष्पलताधिरूढं समुन्मुखी तं समुदीक्षमाणा ।
प्रयाचमाना कुसुमानि शश्वद् भूपालिका सा कथिता सुधीभिः ॥

GP

181. 14. *Varālī*

K—sa ra ga ma pa dha nu; H—sa *re* ga (*atikomal*) ma pa *dha* ni

SUS 3.9, p. 66 *vairāḍī* is *bhāṣā* of *pañcama*; वईराडी भिन्नवर्णा च कृष्णवस्त्रोष्ट्रयायिनी ।

SJ 2.2.2. 104, p. 414 *bhāṣā* of *bhinna pañacama, tāra*-dha,, *mandra*-ma, same *svaras* as of *lāṭī,* sa-*graha nyāsa,* dha-*aṁśa, sampūrṇa,* erotic sentiment.

SMK 4.43, 44, p. 25 *śuddha varālī* is *mela* as shown above; *uttama rāga* (5.2); sa-3, *sampūrṇa,* T- always (5.21cd-22ab)

SC 2.2.59, p. 51 *śuddhavarāṭi-mela* (*vide supra*), sa-3, T- always

RJ 2.23cd, 25cd, *śuddha-varaṭī-mela* (*vide supra*), sa-3, *sampūrṇa,* T- always

RK—

RV 4.27, p.112 *śuddhavarāṭi, svamela, sampūrṇa,* sa- *aṁśa-nyāsa,* ri-*graha,* T- noon

5.187, p. 216:

तरुणी वने सकरुणं गवेषयन्ती पतिं भृशं गौरी ।
नीलाम्बरा वराटी सुरतरुकुसुमोल्लसत्सुषमा ॥

SD 2.166, p. 27 *rāgiṇi* of *vasanta* according to *Rāgarāgiṇī -matam;* T- (*vairaṭī*) after second *prahara* (2.175, p. 29), *rāgiṇi* of *bhairava* according to Hanūmān (2.184, p. 30), of *pañcama* according to *Rāgārṇava* (2.192, p. 31); sa-3, first *mūrchanā* (of *ma-grāma* ?), *sampūrṇa* (2.205, p. 34)

2.206, p. 34:

विनोदयन्ती दयितं सुकेशी सुकङ्कणा चामरचालनेन ।
कर्णे दधाना सुरवृक्षपुष्पं वराङ्गनेयं कथिता वराटी ॥

SS 2.793-795, p.191 *svamela* (*supra*), madhyama is *ṣaṭśruti* (15th *śruti*), sa-3, sa-*vādī,* pa-*saṁvādī,* ma-*vivādī,* ga-dha-ni *anuvādīs.*

SP 1.391, p. 45 *komala* ri, *komala* dha, *tīvra* ni, *dhaivata mūrchanā,* sa-*tīvartra* with *āndolita-gamaka,* T- after second *prahara.*

PS 3.16, 24, pp.12,13 *vārāḍī* is *rāgiṇi* of *hindola,* T- noon.

3.56, p. 20:

कर्णे दधाना सुरपुष्पगुच्छं(युग्मं) सुवृत्तवक्षोजमनोहराङ्गी ।
स्मेरानना भावविलोलनेत्रा गौराङ्गयष्टिः कथिता वराडी ॥

GP 5.3, 24, pp. 34, 37 *sampūrṇa,* born of *bhinnapañcama-rāga,* sa-3, T- after first *prahara.*

182. 15. *Toḍī*

K—sa ra gi ma pa dha ni; H—sa *re ga* ma pa *dha ni*

SUS 3.108, p. 67. *Toṭī, bhāṣā* of *megha,* red complexioned, seated on a mound.

SJ 2.2.2.100, 101, p. 414 evolute of *śuddhaṣāḍava grāma-rāga;* sa-*tāra,* pa has *kampita gamaka;* ma-3, *mandra*-ga, notes are the same as in *śuddhasāḍava,* on joyful occasions, lovers' meeting, erotic sentiment.

2.2.3.53, 55, p. 429 -do-; *śānta* (*śuci*) *rasa,* T- rainy season:

रक्ताङ्गी रक्तवस्त्रा च रक्तांशुवर(रक्ता शम्बर?)वाहना

SMK 5.13, p. 30 *adhama-rāga,* not described

SC 2.2.54, 55 *svamela (supra)*, ma-3, *kampita* in pa, dha; *sampūrṇa,* T-morning

RJ 2.11 *svamela,* ma-3, *kampita* in pa, dha; *sampūrṇa,* T- dawn

RK 3.133, 134, p. 29 *mela* of *karnāṭa,* ma-3, *āhata* and *kampita* in ma-ni, appealing to the singer's own heart; T- daybreak

मृणालकुन्देन्दुसमानगात्री विलिप्तदेहा हरिचन्दनेन ।
विनोदयन्ती विपिने कुरङ्गं तोडी विपञ्चीं दधती कराभ्याम् ॥

RV 4.10, p.108 *svamela,* ga-*graha aṁśa,* sa-*nyāsa, sampūrṇa,* quivering (notes) T- second *prahara*

5.180, p. 214:

कलितविपञ्ची विपिने लालितहरिणारुणाम्बरा हरिणी ।
धवलाङ्गरागरचना मृदुवचना भूषिता तोडी ॥

(*Hariṇī-vāsakasajjā-nāyikā*)

SD 2.166, p. 27 *Toḍī* is *rāgiṇi* of *vasanta* according to *Rāgarāgini-matam,* T- after second *prahara* (2.175, p. 29), *rāgiṇi* of *kauśika* according to Hanūmān (2.185, p. 30), ma-3, *sauvīrī mūrchanā, sampūrṇa, rāgiṇi of kaiśika;* sa-3 according to some (2.211, p. 35, 36)

2.212, p. 36:

तुषारकुन्दोज्ज्वलदेहयष्टिः काश्मीरकर्पूरविलिप्तदेहा ।
विनोदयन्ती हरिणं वनान्ते वीणाधरा राजति टोडिकेयम् ॥

SS—

SP 1.387, p. 44 sa-*mūrchanā;* ri-dha are *komala,* dha-*nyāsa,* ga-*aṁśa,* pa-*nyāsa* in ascent with pa; T- after first *prahara*

PS 3.15, 23, 48, pp. 11, 12, 17 *rāgiṇi* of *vasanta;* T-forenoon

सुनृत्यमानापि सुशीलयुक्ता मुक्तालताकल्पितहारयष्टिः ।
चूताङ्कुरं पाणियुगे वहन्ती जवारुणाङ्गी कथिता सा तु(तो)डी ॥

GP 5.3, 26, pp. 34, 37 *sampūrṇa,* ma-3, born of *śuddha ṣāḍava rāga;* in heroic and erotic sentiments, T- noon

183. 16. *Prathamamañjarī*

(*mālavagauḍa-mela*) K—sa ra ga ma pa dha nu; H- sa *re* ga ma pa *dha* ni

SUS 3.86ab, p. 64 *bhāṣā* of *vasanta.* गौराङ्गी दोलास्था नादपूरिता

SJ 2.2.3, 92, 93, 95, p. 433 *aṅga* of *bhogavardhanī,* born of *kakubha,* pa-3, ga-*mandra,* ri-dha *tāra,* ga-ma *bahula, sampūrṇa,* T- autumn, erotic sentiment; ma-3 found occasionally in usage.

दोलास्था गौरवर्णा च श्रुतिमण्डलवादिनी ।

SMK 4.14, p. 22 *phalamañjarī* born in *mālavagauḍa-mela, adhama-rāga* (5.10) not described

SC 2.2.20 *mālavagauḍa-mela*, pa-3, T- always (in worship)

RJ 2.20 *paṭamañjarī, gaudī-mela*, pa-3, *pūrṇa*, T- always

RK—

RV—

SD 2.168, p.27 *rāgiṇi* of *pañcama* according to *Rāgarāgiṇi-matam* (*paḍhamañjarī*), T- after first *prahara* (2.173, p. 28), *rāgiṇi* of *hindola* according to Hanūmān (2.186, p. 30), of *mallārī* according to *Rāgārṇava* (2.194, p. 31); *paṭamañjarī* has pa-3, *hṛṣyakā mūrchanā; sampūrṇa*, delights the aesthete (2.230, p. 39)

2.231, p. 39:

वियोगिनी कान्तविशी र्णनेत्रा स्त्रजं वहन्ती वपुषा च शुक्लाम् ।
आश्वास्यमाना प्रियया च सख्या सुधूसराङ्गी पटमञ्जरीयम् ॥

SS

SP 1.414, p. 52 *paṭhamañjarī*: pa-3, born of *svaras* of *mālava* (*rāga*); omits ga in ascent.

PS 3.51, p.18 *paṭhamañjarī*; *rāgiṇi* of *vasanta* (3.23, p.12):

सखीकलापैः परिहासलीलया क्वचित् समस्यां परिपूरयन्ती ।
पत्रं मषीं सत्कलमं वहन्ती मञ्जूक्तिशीला पठमञ्जरीयम् ॥

GP 5.4,32, pp. 34,38, *sampūrṇa*, pa-3, dha-ri *tāra*, ga-ma *bahula*, T- morning, in erotic sentiment and on festive occasion.

184. 17. *Turuṣkatoḍī*

Chāyānāṭa-mela (*chāyānāṭa* is *janya* of *karṇaṭagauḍa* sa ru ga ma pa dhi nu, *Sadrāgacandrodaya*, 2.2.36; 2.2.31cd)

SUS —

SJ 2.2.2.134 similar to *toḍī* but ri-ni *bahula*, ga-*alpa*

SMK 4.36, p. 24 *janya* of *kannaḍagauḍa*; *adhama rāga* (5.14, p. 30) but not described

SC 2.2.34 *karnāṭagauḍa mela*, ma-3, *āhata gamaka* in ma-ni, *kampita* in pa, T- sunrise

RJ 2.62 *karnāṭa-mela*, ma-3, *sampūrṇa, kampita* in pa, *āhata* in ma-ni, T- sunrise

RK—

RV 4.8, p.107 *mela* of *mukhāri* or *toḍī*; *sampūrṇa*, ga-3, all notes quiver, T- second *prahara*; popularly called *husenī* (p.120); or ma-3, T- night (4.44, p. 117) called '*irākh*' in the vernacular (4.44 comm. p. 117)

5.181, p. 214:

आयतनीलनिचोला करमालाजप्यमानपतिनामा ।
विरहातुरोच्चागौरी तुरुष्कतोडी महावेणी ॥

SD—
SS—
SP—
PS—
GP—

185. 18. *Vasanta*

Hindola-mela (RJ 2.54) K—sa ri gi ma pa dha ni; H—sa re *ga* ma pa *dha* ni
SUS 3.75, 84-85, pp. 63, 64; main *rāga*:

षड्वदनो दशकरो वसन्तो विद्रुमप्रभः ।
सुतालशङ्खखट्वाङ्गफलचक्राब्जभृत्करः ॥
सवीणौ च करौ यस्य वरदाभयौ तथा ।
वाहनं कोकिला चैत्रे वैशाखे गीयते स च ॥

SJ 2.2.2.77-79, p. 411 affiliated to *hindola, pūrṇa*, sa-3, *mandra*-ni, sa-pa *kampita*, ri-ni-sa *saṅgati*, T- second half of day, spring season, *śānta-rasa:*

विद्रुमाभं दशभुजं षडास्यं कोकिलगतिम् ।
तालखट्वाङ्गचक्राब्जफलशङ्खाश्च षट्करैः ॥
बिभ्राणं वीणया सक्तकरद्वन्द्वं वराभये ।
दधतं पाणियुग्मेन केचित् प्राहुरतद्विदः ॥

SMK 4.23, p. 23 *śuddhavasanta* is born in *sāraṅganāṭa-mela, uttama rāga* (5.3, p. 29) sa-3, omits pa in ascent only, T- fourth watch (5.32, 33ab. p. 32)
SC 2.2.73cd *hindola-mela*, sa-3, *pūrṇa,* T- dawn
RJ 2.56cd *hindola-mela*, sa-3, *pūrṇa*, T- morning, in erotic sentiment
RK 2.137, 139, p. 30 *svamela* (sa ri gi ma pa dha ni), sa-3, *pūrṇa* or omits ri-pa. T- morning, spring season, heroic and terrible sentiments; born of *hindola;* companion of Manmatha.
2.140, p. 30:

शिखण्डिपिच्छोच्चयचारुचूडश्चूताङ्कुरोद्भासुरकर्णपूरः
नव्याम्बुदश्यामतनुर्विलासी वसन्तरागोऽतिमनोहरश्रीः ॥

RV 4.12cd, p. 108 *svamela, pūrṇa,* sa-3, T- dawn

5.173, p. 212:

केशगकिंशुक एष प्रवेशिताम्राङ्कुरः पिकस्य मुखे ।
अरुणवसनो वसन्तो गौरसुवेषो रसालगतः ॥

SD 2.161, p. 26 *puruṣa-rāga* born from Vāmadeva face of Śiva according to *Rāgarāgiṇī-matam; puruṣa-rāga* (2.164, p. 27), its five *bhāṣās* (2.166, p. 27), T- morning (2.172, p. 28) according to Someśvara; T- in spring season (2.181, p. 29); *rāgiṇi* (*vāsantī*) of *srī* according to Hanūmān (2.188, p. 30), of *baṅgālī* according to *Rāgārṇava* (2.191, p. 31); *vasantā; sampūrṇa*, sa-3, *mūrchanā* of *srīrāga* (2.250, p. 43)

2.251, p. 43:

शिखण्डिबर्होच्चबद्धपीडाकर्णावतंसा स्फुरदाम्रपत्रा ।
इन्दीवरश्यामतनुर्मनोज्ञा वसन्तिका स्यादलिमञ्जुलश्रीः ॥

SS 2.615-618, pp. 172, 173 *śuddhavasanta: sālaṅganāṭi-mela* (= *gurjarī* = *mālava gauḍa-mela*), should be sung under this *mela*; ri* dhi* should not be employed in *srīrāga*; should not be rendered *ṣāḍava* by omitting pa in ascent, but it is *sampūrṇa*; sa-3.

SP 1.371, p. 41 sa-*mūrchanā*, ma-*nyāsa*, ga-ni *tīvra*; T- morning

PS 3.23, 47, pp.12, 17 *puruṣa-rāga:*

चूताङ्कुरेणैव कृतावतंसो विघूर्णमानारुणनेत्रपद्मः ।
पीताम्बरः काञ्चनचारुदेहो वसन्तरागो युवतिप्रियश्च ॥

GP 5.2,13, 14, pp. 34-36 *sampūrṇa-rāga*; born of *ṣaḍjamadhyamā*, sa-3, T- spring season; prescribed to be sung from *śrīpañcamī* to the *śayanotsava* of Hari.

186. 19. *Śuddhabaṅgāla*

karnāṭa-mela (RJ 2.57) K—sa ri gu ma pa dhu nu

SUS—

SJ —

SMK 4.35, p. 24 *janya* of *kannaḍagaula*; *adhama-rāga* (5.12, p. 30), not described

SC 4.35 *mela* of *karnāṭagauḍa*; sa-3; has gu* nu*

RJ 2.61 *mela* of *karnāṭa-gauḍa*, ni-3, *sampūrṇa*, T- dawn

RK —

RV 4.43, p.117 *karnāṭa-mela, sampūrṇa*, ma-3, T- dawn

SD —

SS —

SP—

PS —

GP —

187. 20. *Śyāma*

K—sa ra gu* ma pa dha nu*
SUS—
SJ—
SMK 4.55-56, p. 26 sa ra ga ma pa dha nu*; *sampūrṇa,* sa-3, born of *sāmaveda,* T- always
SC 2.2.59cd *śuddha varāṭī-mela;* sa-3, *sampūrṇa,* nu*
RJ 2.24cd *śyāmavarāṭī: varāṭi-mela,* sa-3, *sampūrṇa,* nu*
RK—
RV 4.9, p.107 *svamela,* sa-3, *sampūrṇa,* T- always
SD —
SS —
SP—
PS —
GP —

188. 21. *Sāmanta*

karnāṭa-mela (*vide supra*)
SUS
SJ
SMK 4.60, p. 27 sa ru gu* ma pa dhu* nu*; sa-3, *sampūrṇa,* T- final watch of day
SC 2.2.36, 37 *karnāta-gauḍa-mela, sampūrṇa,* gu*, nu*, T- sunrise
RJ 2.59cd *karnāṭa-mela,* sa-3, gu*, nu*, T- evening
RK 2.131, p. 29 *karnāṭa-mela, sampūrṇa,* sa-3, gu*, nu*, T- dawn
2.132, p. 29:

करधृतकरवालः शत्रुसन्दोहकालः प्रधनविधिकरालः प्रौढकीर्त्या विशालः ।
हृदयनिहितमालः कुङ्कुमव्याप्तभालः स्फुरतिधरणिपालः ख्यातसामन्तरागः ॥

RV 4.41, p. 116, *svamela;* sa-3, T- evening
SD
SS 2.1190-1193ab, p. 235 *svamela*: sa ru gu* ma pa dha nu*; sa-3, sa-*vādī*, pa-*saṁvādī,* ga-ni *vivādī,* (ri-dha *anuvādī*), *sampūrṇa*
SP 1.453, p. 60 *tīvratara* ri, *tīvra* ga, sa-3, T- after third *prahara*
PS
GP

189. 22. *Kāmoda*

SC 2.2.53: K—sa ra gi mi pa dha ni; (RJ 2.49 also)
SUS 3.104ab, p. 66 *bhāṣā* of *megha*: नीलाम्बरा गौरदेहा कामोदा क्रौञ्चयायिनी
SJ 2.2.2.54, p. 408 *kāmoda* I: *grāmarāga,* sa-*grāma,* born of *ṣaḍjamadhyā vesara-rāga,* dha-*aṁśa,* sa-*nyāsa, mandra*-ga, *tāra*-ga

2.2.2.56, p. 408 *kāmoda* II: *grāmarāga*, sa-*grāma*, born of *ṣādjī jāti*, sa-3, ga- *mandra.*
2.2.2.57, p. 408 कामोदाह्वयं(दाख्यं) क्रौञ्चगामिगौरं नीलाम्बरं स्मृतम्
SMK
SC 2.2.53 *svamela* (sa ra gi mi pa dha ni); sa-3, T-end of day
RJ 2.49cd *svamela* (*supra*), sa-3, *sampūrṇa,* T- fourth watch (of day)
RK 2.156, 157, p. 33 *kāmodī*: closely affiliated to *malhāra, svamela, pūrṇa,* dha-3, T- dawn, erotic stimulant
2.158, p. 33:

पीताम्बरा काकलिनादिनीयं सुकेशपाशा विपिने रुदन्ती ।
विलोकयन्ती भयमुद्वहन्ती कामोदिका नाथमनुस्मरन्ती ॥

RV 5.197, p. 218 (*lakṣaṇa* is not given) (*proṣitabhartṛkā nāyikā*)

पीतांशुका सुकेशी शितिः स्मरन्ती पतिं भयाकुलदृक् ।
पिकनादेन विदूना कामोदी कानने रुदती ॥

SD 2.170, p. 28 *kāmodī*: *rāgiṇi* of *naṭanārāyaṇa* according to *Rāgarāgiṇi-matam.* T- after second *prahara* according to Someśvara (2.175, p. 29) *rāgiṇi* of *dīpaka* according to Hanūmān (2.187, p. 30), of *deśākhyā* according to *Rāgārṇava* (2.196, p. 31), *pauravī mūrchanā, pūrṇa,* dha-3, closely affined to *mallāri.*
2.244, p. 42:

पीतं वसाना वसनं सुकेशी वने रुदन्ती पिकनाददूना ।
विलोकयन्ती विदिशोऽतिभीतो कामोदिका कान्तमनुस्मरन्ती ॥

SS
SP
PS 3.14, p. 11 *rāgiṇi,* T- forenoon;
3.66, p. 21:

भर्ता समं पथि सुसम्भाषयन्ती पयोविहारेण सरोरुहाणि ।
विचिन्वती सौरभमोदमाना कामोदरागिण्युदिता मुनीन्द्रैः ॥

GP 5.3, 21, pp. 34,36 *sampūrṇa; sa-grāma,* born of *ṣāḍjī jāti, sa-graha aṁśa,* dha-*nyāsa; mandra*-ga.

190. 23. *Deśikāra*

K—sa ra gu mi pa dha nu; H—sa *re* ga ma pa *dha* ni
SUS
SJ 2.2.2.68, p. 410 *grāma rāga* born in *sa-grāma,* of *revagupta,* according to *Bṛhaddeśī*

SMK *śuddharāmakriya* (*svamela*) 4.27. p 23, *(supra)*; sa-3 *sampūrṇa,* T- afternoon (5.23cd, 24ab)

SC 2.2.64 *deśī: śuddha rāmakrī-mela;* ri-3, omits pa, T- always

RJ 2.39, 41cd *svamela* (*supra*); *deśī*: ri-3, omits pa, T- morning; *deśikāra* (2.40cd): sa-3, *sampūrṇa,* T- forenoon

RK

RV 4.27, p. 112 *deśakāra-śuddharāmakrī; pūrṇa,* sa-3, ma-ni *kampita, svamela,* T- *madhyāhna* (noon)

5.186, p. 215:

मणिमयमकुटो हारी विचित्रवासा लसन् गतावलसः ।
अरुणः कृपाणपाणिर्देशीकारः सरोजाक्षः ॥

SD 2.166, p. 27 *deśī: rāgiṇi* of *vasanta* according to *Rāgarāgiṇi-matam; deśikāra*: T- morning according to Someśvara (2.172, p. 28); *rāgiṇi* of *megha* according to Hanūmān (2.189, p. 30); *deśakārī*: sa-3, *sampūrṇa,* first *mūrchanā* (of *sa-grāma),* mixed with *varāṭī*

2.265, p. 46:

भर्त्रा समं केलिरसं सुकेशी सर्वाङ्गपूर्णा कमलायताक्षी ।
पीनस्तनी रुक्मतनुः सुवेशा सम्पूर्णचन्द्राननदेशकारी ॥

SS 2.1251-3, p. 242 *śuddharāmakrī* (sa ra gu mi pa dha nu); ma has six *śrutis* (15th *śruti*), sa-3, sa-*vādī* , pa-s*aṁvādī,* ga-ni *vivādī,* ri-dha *anuvādī*

SP 1.373, p. 41 lacuna; dha-*mūrchanā,* dha-*aṁśa,* ga-ni *tīvra,* T- morning

PS 3.15, p. 11 T- forenoon, *rāgiṇi* of *hindola* (3.24, p. 13)

3.57, p. 19:

सार्धं सखीभिर्विजने वसन्ती विचित्रवक्षोजनखक्षतानि ।
निरीक्षमाणा मणिदर्पणेषु सा देशकारी कथिता गुणज्ञैः ॥

GP 5.4.40, pp. 34, 38 *deśī: ṣāḍava,* born of *revagupta,* omits pa, ri-3, T—morning, in *karuṇa* and *śānta rasas*

191. 24. *Rāmakrī*

K—sa ra gu ma pa dha nu; H—sa *re* ga ma pa *dha* ni

SUS 3.86, 87, p. 64 *rāmagrī: bhāṣā of vasanta:* गौराङ्गी दोलास्था नादपूरिता

SJ 2.2.3.114, 115, p. 435 *rāmakṛti: aṅga* of *kolāhala* which is born of *ṭakka,* ma-*graha, aṁśa;* sa-*nyāsa;* omits pa-ni (*tāra*-pa *mandra*-pa, T- second half of day, *vipralambha śṛṅgāra,* 2.2.4.4)

दोलारूढा च गौराङ्गी वीणादण्डविभूषिता

SMK —
SC 2.2.16ab *mālavagauḍa-mela,* sa-3, omits ma-ni, T-always
RJ 2.17ab *mālavagauḍa-mela* sa-3, *pūrṇa,* T- always; has form of female ascetic
RK—
RV 4.20, p.110 *mālavagauḍa-mela, sampūrṇa,* sa-3 or ga-3; T- always
5.213, p. 223:

काञ्चनविभातिभासुरभूषा नीलांशुकाधिकं रम्या ।
रामकृतिरणुवदन्ती सुदती दयतेऽन्तिके याते ॥

SD 2.174, p. 28 *rāmakarī,* T- after first *prahara*; *rāgiṇi* of *hindola* according to Hanūmān (2.186, p. 30), of *pañcama* according to *Rāgārṇava* (2.192, p. 31), *pūrṇa,* first *mūrchanā* (of *sa-grāma*), sa-3; sung to *karuṇa rasa*; according to some, omits ri-dha; according to others, omits pa-sa, *sampūrṇa, ṣāḍava* or *auḍuva* accordingly (2.225, 226, p. 38)
2.227, p. 39:

हेमप्रभाभासुरभूषणा च नीलं निचोलं वपुषा वहन्ती ।
कान्ते समीपे कमनीयकण्ठा मानोन्नता रामकरी मतेयम् ॥

SS
SP 1.402, p. 48 *komala* ri, *tīvra* ga, *tīvratara* ma, *komala* dha, *tīvra* ni; omits ga-ni in ascent; pa-*aṃśa,* dha-*mūrchanā,* T- morning
PS 3.14, p.11 *rāgiṇi,* T- forenoon, *rāgiṇi* of *māḷava* (3.20, p. 12)
3.29, p. 13:

प्रतप्तचामीकरचारुवर्णा कर्णावतंसं कमलं वहन्ती ।
पौष्पं धनुः पुष्पशरान् दधाना चन्द्रानना रामकीरी प्रदिष्टा ॥

GP 5.4.31, pp. 34, 37 *sampūrṇa,* sa-3, '*ṣaḍjarṣabhaghanārambhā*' T- '*praharābhyantare*'.

192. 25. *Bahulī*

Rāmakrī-mela (*vide supra*)
SUS
SJ
SMK 4.13, p. 22 *mālavagauḍa-mela; uttama rāga* (5.4, p. 29); ma-3, omits pa, T-first part of day, *ṣāḍava* (5.31, p. 32)
SC 2.2.15 *mālavagauḍa-mela,* ma-3, T- afternoon, omits ga-ni, but sometimes, not.
RJ 2.16 *mālavagauḍa-mela,* ma-3, T- afternoon, omits ga-ni
RK 2.95, 96, p. 24 *mālavagauḍa-mela,* ma-3, omits, or not, ri-dha, T- evening

दूर्वादलश्यामलभव्यगात्रा शय्यातलस्थापितनव्यपात्रा ।
प्रसूनमालापरिबद्धकेशा विलासिनीयं बहुली विभाति ॥

RV 4.20, p. 110 *mālavagauḍa-mela*, sa-3, omits ma-ni, T- afternoon
5.188, p. 216:

श्यामा चलधम्मिल्ला तन्वी ताम्बूलिनी सुकञ्चुकिका ।
बहुलीलेयं बहुली लोलचैलाञ्चला सुगतिः ॥

SD 2.167, p. 27 *rāgiṇi* of *bhairava*, according to *Rāgarāgiṇi-matam.*
SS 2.638, 684, p.179 *gurjarī-mela,* omits ni and becomes *ṣāḍava.*
SP—
PS —
GP —

193. 26. *Deśī*

Affiliated to *āhang;* K-sa ra gi mi pa dha ni; H-sa *re* ga ma pa *dha ni*
SUS—
SJ 2.2.2.67, 68, p. 410 *grāma-rāga, sa-grāma*, born of *revagupta*, ri-3, ga-*mandra*
SMK 5.10, p. 30 *adhama-rāga*
SC 2.2.64 *śuddharāmakrī-mela*; ri-3, omits pa, T- always
RJ 2.41cd *deśikāra-mela,* ri-3, omits pa, T- always
RK —
RV 4. 29cd, p. 113 *deśikāra-mela*, ri-3, ga *alpa*, T- always
SD 2.166, p. 27 *rāgiṇi* of *vasanta* according to *Rāgarāgiṇi-matam*: of ***dīpaka*** according to Hanūmān (2,187, p. 30), of *pañcama* according to *Rāgarṇava* (2.192, p. 31), T- after second *prahara* according to Someśvara
2.241, p. 41 ri-3, omits pa, *vikṛta* ri, *kalopanatā-mūrchanā*
2.242,p. 42:

निद्रालसं सा कपटेन कान्तं विबोधयन्ती सुरतोत्सुकेन ।
गौरी मनोज्ञा शुकपुच्छवस्त्रा ख्याता च देशी रसपूर्णचित्ता ॥

SS —
SP 1.431, p. 55 ri-*aṁśa,* ri-dha *komala*, ga-ni omitted in ascent, sa-*mūrchanā* T- always
PS—
GP 5.5.40, pp. 34,38 *ṣāḍava,* born of *revagupta*, ri-3, ma-ni *saṅgati*, omits pa, T- morning, in *karuṇa* and *śānta-rasas*

194. 27. *Jaitāśrī*

Deśi-mela (*vide supra*)
SUS —

SJ—
SMK—
SC —
RJ —
RK —
RV 4.28cd, p.113 *deśikāra-mela,* sa-*graha nyāsa,* ga-*aṁśa*; ri-dha *alpa* T- morning
5. 176, p. 213:

एषा माथुरवेषा विशेषपटुरकटुदेशभाषाभृत् ।
स्वेशे मदनावेशं करोत्यलेशेन जैताश्री : ॥

SD 2.289, p. 51 *deśī-rāga*; rules of *śruti, svara, grāma, jāti* do not apply.
SS—
SP 1.467, p. 63 *jayaśrī*: ri-dha *komala*, ga-ni *tīvra*, ma-*tīvratara*; omits ri-dha in ascent: ni-*graha*
PS—
GP—

195. 28. *Gurjarī*

Rāmakrī-mela (*vide supra*)

SUS 3.91cd, p. 65 *bhāṣā* of *bhairava:* गौरवर्णा पीतवस्त्रा गुर्जरी मेषगामिनी

SJ 2.2.2.82, 83, pp. 411, 412 *sa-grāma rāga*; born of *pañcama-ṣāḍava*; ri-3, ri -*bahula*, ma-*nyāsa;* ri-*tāra, śānta rasa, sampūrṇa*

मेषगा पीतवस्त्रा च गौराङ्गी कैश्चिदिष्यते

SMK 4.14, p. 22: *mālavagauḍa-mela; uttama-rāga* (5.2, p. 29); *ghūrjarī*; ri-3; omits pa and sometimes includes pa in descent; T- first watch of day.

SC 2.2.13ab *mālavagauḍa-mela,* ni-3, or sa-*nyāsa* (sa has *mudrita-gamaka?*) T- morning

RJ 2.15cd *gauḍī-mela,* ri-3, omits pa. T- morning

RK 2.91,92,pp.23,24 *mālavagauḍa-mela*, ri-3, *sampūrṇa*, T- morning; occasionally it is admixed with *bahulī* and then omits sa.

RV 4.23, p. 111 *mālavagauḍa-mela,* ri-3, omits pa, T- dawn

SD 2. 167, p. 27 *rāgiṇi* of *bhairava* according to *Rāgarāgiṇi-matam*, of *megha* according to Hanūmān (2.189, p. 30), of *pañcama* according to *Rāgārṇava* (2. 192, p. 31), T- morning according to Someśvara (2.171, p. 28); ri-3, *sampūrṇa*, seventh *mūrchanā* (2.268, p. 47)

2.269, p. 47:

श्यामा सुकेशी मलयद्रुमाणां मृदुल्लसत्पल्लवतल्पमध्ये ।
श्रुतिस्वराणां दधतीवभागं तन्त्रीमुखा दक्षिणगुर्जरीयम् ॥

SS 2.496-503, pp. 161, 162 *sampūrṇa* (sa ra gu ma pa dha nu), ri-3, omits pa in descent according to some.

SP 1.417, p. 53 born of *malava(gauḍa),* omits ma-ni in descent; ga-*mūrchanā*; ga-ma and dha-sa are affinities. This is *dākṣiṇātya gurjarī,* T-after first *prahara.*

PS 3.23, p. 12; 3.52, p. 18 *rāgiṇi* of *vasanta*:

कर्णोत्पलालम्बि मधुव्रतानाम् सुश्रृण्वती मञ्जुलकूजितानि ।
कान्तान्तिकं गन्तुमनाः प्रदोषे सा गुर्जरीवेषकलाञ्चिताङ्गी ॥

GP 5.3, 25, pp. 34, 37 *gujjari: sampūrṇa,* ri-3, born of *pañcamaṣāḍava,* sometimes ma is *nyāsa,* T- beginning of day; erotic sentiment

196. 29. *(Kuṭila/Apara) Lalita*

Deśī-mela (*vide supra*)

SUS

SJ 2.2.3.6, pp. 423, 424 *bhāṣāṅga lalita* I: dha-3, sa-*tāra,* ma-*mandra,* pa-*alpa*

2.2.3.7, p. 423 *lalita* II: *ṭakka aṅga,* sa-3, omits ri-pa, *vīra rasa*

2.2.2.12, 13, p. 424 *lalita* III: *bhinnaṣaḍja bhāṣā,* dha-3 *pūrṇa, kampita* in ni-ga-ma, T- in friendship, *hemanta* season, first *prahara* of day

SMK

SC 2.2.64, p. 52 *deśikāra-mela,* sa-3, *pūrṇa,* T- morning

RJ 2.42, p. 235 *deśikāra-mela,* dha-3, *pūrṇa,* T- morning

RK

RV 4.28, p. 113, *deśikāra-mela, sampūrṇa,* sa-*graha nyāsa,* dha-*aṁśa*; or it may omit pa; T- dawn, this is also called *vibhāsa-lalita*

5.172, p. 211:

नीराजयत्युमेशं दीपैरनिशं निशात्यये ललिता ।
विविधालङ्कृतिमिलिता कलितश्वेताम्बरा गौरी ॥

SD 2.166, p. 27 *rāgiṇi* of *vasanta* according to *Rāgarāgiṇi-matam,* of *hindola* according to Hanūmān (2.186, p. 30), of *pañcama* according to *Rāgārṇava* (2.192, p. 31); T-morning according to Someśvara (2.172, p. 28); *śuddhamadhyā mūrchanā,* omits ri-pa, *auḍuva* (*lalitā* I), *sampūrṇa,* dha-3 (*lalitā* II) (2.232, p. 40)

2.233, p. 40:

प्रफुल्लसप्तच्छदमाल्ययुक्ता गौरी कृशाङ्गी तरुणा चलाक्षी ।
विनिश्वसत्सादवशात् प्रभाते विलासवेशा ललितोपदिष्टा ॥

SS 2.712, 713ab, p. 182 *gūrjarī-mela,* sa-3, omits pa, *ṣāḍava*

SP 1.415, p. 52 *gaurī-mela,* omits pa, sa-2, ma-*nyāsa,* T- always

PS 3.14, 23, 50, pp.11, 12,18 *rāgiṇi* of *vasanta,* T- forenoon

उषसि केशसुसंयममात्मनो विदधती शयनोत्थितवत्यसौ ।
विलुलितालकवल्लिवृतानना सुललिता ललिता कलिता बुधैः ॥

GP 5.8, 59, 60, pp. 34, 40 *auḍuva,* born of *ṭakka rāga,* has facile *svaras,* sa-3, omits ri-pa, sa-*mandra*

197. 30. *Vibhāsa*

Deśikāra-mela (RJ 2.43); ma is at 14th *śruti*
SUS —
SJ —
SMK—
SC —
RJ 2.43 *Deśikāra-mela;* sa-3, *sampūrṇa* or *ṣāḍava* by omitting pa; T- always
RK
RV 4.28, p. 113 *lalitā* II is called *vibhāsa lalita; vide supra* on *lalita* (196)
SD 2.168, p. 27 *rāgiṇi* of *pañcama* according to *Rāgarāgiṇi-matam lalitāvat vibhāsastu* (2.2.86, p. 50)
SP 1.384, pp. 43, 44 ma-*tīvratara,* ga-ni *tīvra*; ri-dha *komala,* dha-*graha,* ma-*aṁśa,* ni-*nyāsa*; when ga or pa is *aṁśa,* omits ma-ni in ascent; ga-*mūrchanā,* T- morning
PS—
GP —

198. 31. *Sāraṅga*

K—sa ri gu (*ūrdhva* ga, on 13th *śruti*) mi pa dhu ni
SUS
SJ
SMK
SC 2.2.69 *svamela,* sa-3, *sampūrṇa,* T- afternoon
RJ 2.45, *svamela,* sa-3, *sampūrṇa,* T- afternoon
RK 2.167-169, p. 34 *svamela,* sa-3, *pūrṇa,* T- noon

प्रसूनमालापरिबद्धकेशो वीणां दधानो लसदंसदेशे ।
समं प्रियाभिः सहकारमूले सारङ्गरागो रसिको विभाति ॥

RV 4.46, p. 117 *svamela, sampūrṇa,* sa-3, T- afternoon
5.189, p. 216:

पीताम्बरोऽसिततनुर्ललितालङ्कृतिरुपेतचापेषुः ।
सारङ्गो गरुडाङ्कोऽम्बुजकम्बुगदारिधारिकर : ॥

(*ari* = *cakra,* discus)
SD
SS

SP 1.403, p. 49 dha-*tīvratara*, ni-*tīvra*; *sa-mūrchanā*, ma-*aṁśa*, sa-*nyāsa*, T- after second *prahara*

PS—

GP—

199. 32. *Tiravaṇa (Travaṇī, Trāvaṇā, Travaṇā)*

Deśī-mela (*vide supra*)

SUS 3. 97ab, p. 66 *triguṇa*: *bhāṣā* of *pañcama*;

त्रिगुणा महिषयाना च श्यामला कृष्णचीवरा ।

SJ 2.2.3, 71, p. 31 *trāvaṇī*: *aṅga* of *travaṇā*, born of *bhinnaṣaḍjā*, dha-3, omits ri-pa, T- daybreak

SMK—

SC 2.2.63 *deśikāra-mela*, sa-3, *pūrṇa*, T- end of day

RJ 2.41 *deśikāra-mela*, sa-3, *pūrṇa*, T- evening

RK—

RV 4.29ab, p. 113 *trāvaṇī*: sa-*nyāsa*, ri-*graha aṁśa*, *sampūrṇa*, T- evening

5.196, p. 218:

कदलीमूलासीना पीनकुचाधीननायका तन्वी ।
कनकनिभा शुभहारा त्रावणिका वर्ण्यवेणीका ॥

SD 2.165, p. 27 *trivaṇī* is *rāgiṇi* of *śrī* according to *Rāgarāgiṇi-matam*, of *gauḍa* according to *Rāgārṇava* (2.195, p. 31), T-after third *prahara* according to Someśvara (2.176, p. 29) dha-3, omits pa-ri, *auḍuva* (2.278, p. 49)

2.279, p. 49:

रम्भायाः सुतरोर्मूले निषण्णा पीतवर्णभाक् ।
तन्वङ्गी हारसंयुक्ता प्रियेण त्रिवणा मता ॥

SS 2.171, 172, p. 119 *travaṇā*: sa-3, ga-ma *tāra*, sa-ri *mandra*, ni-sa-dha *saṅgati*, in *vīra rasa*, evening in prayer of Śiva (according to SR).

travaṇodbhavā (2.173, p. 119) ma-*aṁśa*, sa-*nyāsa*, ga-*apanyāsa*, omits pa, *ṣāḍava*; in competitions, T- always

SP 1.461, p. 61 *trivaṇī*: *gaurī-mela*, omits ma, sa-*graha*, ri-*aṁśa*, T- after third *Prahara*

PS—

GP—

200. 33. *Yammana-kalyāṇa*

K—sa ri gu* mi pa dhi nu*

SUS—
SJ—
SMK—
SC 2.2.71 *svamela* (sa ri gi mi pa dhi nu); sa-3, *pūrṇa*, T- evening (*kalyāṇa*)
RJ 2.49 *svamela* (sa ri gu mi pa (dhi) nu), sa-3, *pūrṇa*, T- evening (*kalyāṇa*)
RK 2.162-164, p. 34 *svamela*, sa-3 or ri-3, *sampūrṇa*, T- evening

करे कृपाणं तिलकं ललाटे धत्ते प्रविष्टः समरे प्रचण्डः ।
आरक्तवर्णस्तपनीयभूषः कल्याणरागो मुनिना प्रदिष्टः ॥

RV 4.33cd, p. 114 *svamela*, sa-2, ga-*aṁśa*, T- eventide
5.200, p. 219:

सच्छत्रचामरोऽच्छस्ताम्बूली मौलिरत्नमालावान् ।
कल्याणः सितवासा राजा सिंहासनासीनः ॥

SD 2.170, p. 28 *rāgiṇi* of *naṭanārāyaṇa* (*kalyāṇī*);
SS
SP 1.401, p. 48 ma-*tīvratara*, ga-ni *tīvra*; ga-*graha*, omits ma-ni in ascent. T- after third *prahara*
PS 5.8, 67, pp.12, 21 *kalyāṇi; rāgiṇi* T- evening:

व्याधुतानटनपरिश्रमेण वाला लीलाभिः सदसिकृतादरानटानाम् ।
कल्याणी कलयति हस्तहावहेलं प्रस्थानोन्मुखरितकिङ्किणीकलापम् ॥

GP 5.68, p. 41 *kalyāṇī* is a combination of *nāṭa, karnāṭa, varāṭī*:

कल्याणी नाटकर्णाटवाराटीयोगसम्भवा ।

201. 34. *Śrīrāga*

K—sa ri* gi ma pa dhi* ni
SUS 3.76-78, p. 63 main *rāga*

श्रीरागोऽथ गौरवर्णोऽष्टहस्तश्चतुर्मुखः ।
पाशाब्जपुस्तकाङ्कुशबीजपूरकभृत्करः ॥
वीणा करद्वयेऽस्य स्यादेकश्च वरदः करः ।
विख्यातोऽयं हंसयानो ब्रह्ममूर्तिरिवापरः ॥

SJ 2.2.2.43-45, p. 407 *sa-grāma*, born of *ṣaḍjī jāti*, sa-3 *ma-tāra*, pa-*alpa*, *auḍuva*, *vīra-rasa*, T- spring season, in propitiation of Lord of Lakṣmī; *sampūrṇa* according to some.

केचिदेनं गौरवर्णमष्टबाहुं चतुर्मुखम् ।
पद्मापाशाङ्कुशवरी(करं) बीजपूरकपुस्तकम् ।
बिभ्राणं पाणिषट्केन वीणासक्तकरद्वयम् ।
ब्रह्माणमिव हंसेन गच्छन्तं जगदुर्बुधाः ॥

SMK 4.16, 17, p. 22 sa ri gi ma pa dhi ni, *uttama rāga* (5.3, p. 29); sa-3, omits ga-dha, *auḍuva*; sometimes includes ga-dha (*sampūrṇa*), T- evening, bestows every wealth.

SC 2.2.23, 25 sa ri* gi ma pa dhi* ni, sa-3, omits dha; T- sunset

RJ 2. 68cd-69 sa ri* gu (!) ma pa dhi* ni; sa-3, omits dha-ga; T- evening; gives wealth and auspiciousness

RK 2.109, 112, p. 26 sa ri* gi ma pa dhi* ni; sa-3, omits dha-ga (*auḍuva*) or is *sampūrṇa;* T- end of day; first *mūrchanā.*

2.113, p. 27:

कन्दर्पमूर्तिस्तरुणोऽरुणाम्बरः कर्णावतंसीकृतनव्यपल्लवः ।
षड्जादिसेव्यः क्षितिपालसुन्दरः श्रीरागनामा नितरां विभासते ॥

RV 3.48, p. 97 sa ri* gi ma pa dhi* ni

4.30ab, p. 113 *svamela,* ri-*aṁśa graha,* sa-*nyāsa,* omits dha-ga *(auḍuva)* or includes dha-ga (s*ampūrṇa*), T- eventide.

5.201, p. 219:

कनकातपत्रमूले लोलदुकूले गजाश्रयो राजन् ।
श्रीरागोऽखिलभोगो नीरजराजिं भजन्मौलौ ॥

SD 2.158, p. 26 *puruṣa-rāga;* born from Sadyojāta face of Śiva according to *Rāgarāgiṇi-matam* (2.161, p. 27); one of six *puruṣa rāgas* (2.164, p. 27); a *puruṣa-rāga* according to Hanūmān (2.183, 188, p. 30); T- after third *prahara,* according to Someśvara (2.176, p. 29); sa-3, *pūrṇa,* first *mūrchanā,* has every *guṇa*(?); according to some, ri-3.

2.249, p. 43:

अष्टादशाब्दः स्मरचारुमूर्तिः धीरोल्लसत् पल्लवकर्णपूरः ।
षड्जादिसेव्योऽरुणवस्त्रधारी श्रीरागराजः क्षितिपालमूर्तिः ॥

SS 2.815-817, p. 193 sa ri gi ma pa dhi ni, sa-3, omits ga (*ṣāḍava*) or not (*pūrṇa)*

SP 1.447, p. 58 ri-3, or sa-*graha; tīvra-gāndhāra;* omits ga-dha; T- after third *prahara*

PS 3.22, p. 12, 40, p.16 *puruṣa-rāga:*

लीलाविहारेण वनान्तरेषु चिन्वन् प्रसूनानि वधूसहायः ।
विलासवेशोदित व्यक्तमूर्तिः श्रीराग एष प्रथितः पृथिव्याम् ॥

GP 5.1.10, pp. 34, 35 *sampūrṇa*, sa-3, *svalpa*-pa, *sa-grāma* affiliation; born of *ṣāḍjī jāti;* T- evening, in *vīra and śṛṅgāra rasas.*

202. 35. *Gauḍī*

Rāmakrī-mela (*vide supra*)

SUS 3.80, p. 63 *śrīrāga-bhāṣā:* गौडी भाषा पीतवस्त्रा गौराङ्गी गजवाहना

SJ 2.2.3.46-50,p.428 *bhāṣāṅga of mālavakaiśika* according to Mataṅga; *upāṅga,* sa-3, sa-*mandra* and *tāra,* ni-*bahula;* becomes *upāṅga* of *vasanta* because of affiliation to *hindola;* according to some, pa in *gamaka* is *nyāsa;* performed in *vīraśṛṅgāra,* in speech with the loved ones, etc.

पीतवस्त्रा च गौराङ्गी गजेन्द्रवरवाहना ।

SMK 4.18, p. 22 *gauḍī,* in *śrīrāga-mela; gauḍī, adhama-rāga* (5.10, p. 30); not described

SC 2.2.17cd *mālavagauḍa-mela,* sa-3, omits dha-ga, T- end of day

RJ 2.14cd *mālavagauḍa-mela,* sa-3, omits dha-ga, T- evening

RK 2.99, 100, p. 25 *mālavagauḍa-mela,* sa-3, omits dha-ga, serious mood, T-evening

रसालनव्याङ्कुरकर्णपूरा कादम्बिनीश्यामलमञ्जुदेहा ।
पीयूषनिष्यन्दिमृदुस्वनाढ्या गौडीति युक्ताऽधिककौतुकेन ॥

RV 5.193, p. 217:

क्षीरोदभासिवासा सहजसुहासा प्रलम्बबाहुलता ।
करधृतसाहिच्छत्रा गौडी गौरी सरोजाक्षी ॥

SD 2.165, p. 27 *rāgiṇi* of *śrī* according to *Rāgarāgiṇī-matam;* of *kauśika* according to Hanūmān (2.185, p. 30); of *gauḍa* according to *Rāgārṇava* (2.195, p. 31); T- after third *prahara* according to Someśvara (2.177, p. 29); sa-3, omits ri-pa, first *mūrchanā;* beautiful in every limb is *gaurī* (2.215, p. 36).

2.216, p. 36:

निवेशयन्ती श्रवणे वतंसमाम्राङ्कुरं कोकिलनादरम्या ।
श्यामा मधुस्यन्दितसूक्ष्मनादा गौरीयमुक्ता किल कोहलेन ॥

SS 2.241, p. 129 according to Mataṅga: sa-3, ni-*bahula, mandra*-sa-*alpa.*

SP 1.369, p. 40 *gaurī: komala*-ri, *komal*-dha, ga-ni *tīvra;* omits ga-dha in ascent, T-after third *prahara*

PS 5.18, 22, 43, pp. 12, 16 *gaurī: rāgiṇi* of *śrī*, T- evening:

पुष्पोद्याने सार्धं माली कलापैः क्रीडन्तीयं कोकिलकाकलीभिः ।
वामा श्यामा (?) सद्गुणग्रामसीमा गौरी गौरी गौरवेनोपदिष्टा ॥

GP 5.4.35, pp. 34-38 *sampūrṇa,* born of *mālavakaiśika*, sa-3, *svaras* are graced with *kampita* and *āndolita gamakas*; sung in *vīra* and *śṛṅgāra rasas.*

203. 36. *Pāḍi*

Gauḍī-mela (*vide supra*)

SUS

SJ

SMK 4.29 *śuddharāmakriyā-mela*; *madhyama-rāga* (5.7, p. 29); sa-3, omits ga, *ṣāḍava,* T- fourth watch (5.52, p. 35)

SC 2.2 14ab *mālavagauḍa-mela,* sa-3, omits ga, T- evening

RJ 2.22cd *gauḍī-mela,* sa-3, omits dha-ga or includes them, T- evening, erotic

RK 2.97,98, p. 24 *pālī: mālavagauḍa-mela*; sa-3, omits ga; has many *gamakas*; T- evening

पाली ललाटोदितचन्द्रलेखा प्रफुल्लराजीवसमत्रिनेत्रा ।
भागीरथीपूतजटाकलापा चकास्ति मुक्ताफलचारुहारा ॥

RV 4.17cd, p. 110 *mālavagauḍa-mela*; sa-3, omits ga, T- evening

SD 2.165, p. 27 *pahāḍī: rāgiṇī* of *śrī* according to *Rāgarāgiṇi-matam,* T- after third *prahara* according to Someśvara (2.178, p. 29); is similar to *gaurī,* sa-3, omits ri-pa; *auḍuva*; has a flavour of Āndhra (2.280, p. 49)

2.166, p. 27:

वीणोपगायत्यतिसुन्दराङ्गी रक्ताम्बरा मञ्जुकदम्बमूले ।
श्रीचन्दनाद्रौ स्थितिकारिणी सा श्रीरागकान्ता कथिता पहाडी ॥

SS 2.742-744, p. 186 should be classified under *gurjarī-mela* and not under (*śuddha*)*rāmakriyā* as some moderners do, for it has only *catuḥśruti*-ma, and not *ṣaṭśruti*-ma; sa-3, *ṣāḍava* because it omits ga.

SP 1.448, p. 59 *gaurī-mela*; omits ga, sa-*graha,* ri-*aṁśa nyāsa,* T- after third *prahara*

PS 3.18, 24, 58, pp. 12, 13, 19 *rāgiṇi* of *hindola,* T- evening (*pāhiḍā*)

भर्तुर्दधाना चरणारविन्दं निषेधयन्ती परदेशयानम् ।
प्रकामदाम्पत्यसुखेन मुग्धा सा पाहिडा संकथिता कवीन्द्रैः ॥

GP

204. 37. *Guṇakarī*

Gurjari-mela (*vide supra*)

SUS

SJ

SMK

SC 2.2.12 *gauṇḍakṛti: mālavagauḍa-mela,* sa-3, omits dha, T- dawn
RJ 2.18 *gauḍī-mela, sampūrṇa,* pa has *sphurita gamaka,* T- evening
RK
RV
SD 2.167, p. 27 *rāgiṇi* of *hindola* according to *Rāgarāgiṇi-matam,* of *kauśika* according to Hanūmān (2.185, p. 30), of *baṅgālī* according to *Rāgārṇava* (2.191, p. 31) T- after first *prahara* according to Someśvara (2.174, p. 28); *rajanī mūrchanā;* affiliated to *mālava, auḍuva,* omits ri-dha; ni-3 or sa-3 according to some
2.218, p. 37:

शोकाभिभूतनयनारुणदीनदृष्टिः नम्राननना धरणिधूसरगात्रयष्टिः ।
आमुक्तचारुकबरी प्रियदूरवर्ती संकीर्तिता गुणकरी करुणे कृशाङ्गी ॥

SS
SP 1.405, p. 49 *guṇakriyā*: ri-dha *komala,* omits ga-ni or omits only ga; ga-*graha,* T- after first *prahara*
PS
GP

205. 38. *Nādarāmakriyā*

K—sa ra gi ma pa dha nu; H—sa re *ga* ma pa dha ni
SUS
SJ
SMK 4.41, 42, p. 25 sa ra gi ma pa dha nu (*svamela*)
5.7, 44, pp. 29, 33 *madhyama-rāga,* sa-3, *sampūrṇa,* T- fourth watch
SC 2.2.74, 75 sa ra gi ma pa dha nu (*svamela*); sa-3, *sampūrṇa,* T- evening
RJ 2.53, 54ab sa ra gi ma pa dha ni (*svamela,* but note difference in *niṣāda*), sa-3, *sampūrṇa,* T- evening
RK
RV 4.11, p. 108 *svamela* (sa ra gi ma pa dha nu), sa-3, T- night
SD
SS 2.634-637, p. 175 has *antara-gāndhāra* in actual musical practice and should be therefore classified under *gurjarī mela* and not accorded the status of an independent *mela* by ascribing *sādhāraṇa gāndhāra;* sa-3, *sampūrṇa*
SP 1.455, p. 60 *gaurī-mela,* sa-*graha,* ma-*aṁśa,* ni-*nyāsa*; omits ga in ascent. T- after first *prahara*
PS
GP

206. 39. *Guṇḍakriya*

Gurjarī-mela (*vide supra*)
SUS 3.86, p. 64 *guṇḍagiri: bhāṣā* of *vasanta;* गौराङ्गी दोलास्था नादपूरिता

SJ—

SKM 4.14 p. 22; 5.8, p. 29; 5.24, p. 35 *mālavagauḍa-mela, madhyama-rāga;* sa-3, omits dha, but sometimes includes it; T- forenoon

SC 2.2.12 *gauṇḍakṛti: mālavagauḍa-mela,* sa-3, omits dha; T- dawn

RJ—

RK —

RV 4.18, p. 110 *mālavagauḍa-mela;* sa-3, omits dha, T- morning

SD—

SS 2.576, p. 169 *gurjarī-mela;* sa-3, *sampūrṇa*

SP—

PS —

GP 5.7, 58cd-59ab, pp. 35, 40 *auḍuva;* sa-3, ma-pa *saṅgati,* omits ri-dha, T-beginning of day; any desired *rasa.*

207. 40. *Ṭakka*

K—sa ra gu* ma pa dha nu*

SUS—

SJ—

SMK—

SC 2.2.13 *mālavagauḍa-mela,* sa-3, *sampūrṇa,* has gu*, nu*, T- last watch (of day)

RJ 2.18 *gauḍī-mela,* sa-3, has gu* and nu*; T- evening

RK

RV 4.13, p. 109 *vasanta-mela* (sa ra gu* ma pa dha nu*), *pūrṇa,* sa-3, T- end of day

SD 2.189, p. 30 *rāgiṇi* of *megha* according to Hanūmān; sa-3, *sampūrṇa,* first *mūrchanā* (of sa-*grāma*) (2.270, p. 47)

2.270, p. 47:

शय्यासु सुप्तां नलिनीदलानां वियोगिनीं वीक्ष्य विषण्णचित्ताम् ।
सुवर्णवर्णग्रहमागतः सन् सम्भाषते तां किल टक्कसंज्ञः ॥

SS—

SP 1.434, p. 55 *ābhīrī mūrchanā, komala* ri-dha, omits dha in ascent (*ḍhakka*), T- after third *prahara*

PS—

GP —

208. 41. *Devagāndhāra*

K—sa ra gu ma pa dha nu; H—sa *re* ga ma pa *dha* ni

SUS 3.82, p. 64 *śrīrāgabhāṣā;* रक्ताभा देवगान्धारी पीतचीराश्रयायिनी

SJ—

SMK 4.19, p. 22 *śrīrāga-mela; adhama-rāga* (5.11, p. 20) not described

SC 2.2.22 *mālavagauḍa-mela;* sa-3, *pūrṇa,* T- always

RJ 2.68, *malavakaiśika-mela;* sa-3, *sampūrṇa,* T- always

RK 2.120, 121, p. 28, *śrīrāga-mela;* sa-3, *sampūrṇa,* T- always

गन्धर्वविद्याधरकिन्नराणां नितम्बिनीभिः परिवेष्टितोऽसौ ।
नृत्योत्सवे प्रीतिमुपैति देवगान्धाररागो नितरां प्रसिद्धः ॥

RV 4.18, p. 110 *mālavagauḍa-mela;* ri-*graha,* pa-*aṁśa,* sa-*nyāsa;* omits ga-ni, T- always

5.217, p. 224:

सिंहासनोपवेशी भूषाभिर्भासितः सितः कुमुदी ।
धवलाम्बरः सुरतनुः शृङ्गारी देवगान्धारः ॥

SD—

SS 2.878, 879ab, p. 200 *śrīrāga-mela;* sa-3, *sampūrṇa*

SP 1.460, p. 61 If *bhairavī* becomes *pūrṇa,* it is *devagandhārī;* ga-*mūrchanā,* ga-*graha,* sa-*aṁśa;* if ri is *graha,* ga is omitted in ascent. T- after second *prahara*

PS—

GP—

209. 42. *Mālavagauḍa*

K—sa ra gu ma pa dha nu; H—sa *re* ga ma pa *dha* nu

SUS—

SJ 2.2.2.23, p. 240 *gauḍa upāṅga;* the same as *chāyāgauḍa* (ni = 3, *sphurita ṣaḍja, pūrṇa*) but sans *tiripa gamaka* for ga.

SMK 4.11, 12, p. 22 sa ra gu ma pa dha nu; *svamela, uttama* (5.2, p. 29), ni-3, omits ri-pa (*auḍuva*) but sometimes includes them; T- evening; the very best among *rāgas.*

SC 2.2.8cd-9ab *svaras* as above, ni-3, omits ri-pa, T- evening (*svamela*)

RJ 2.20 *gauḍī-mela,* ni-3, omits ri-pa, T- evening

RK 3.84-88, p. 23 *svaras* as above; ni-3, *rajanī mūrchanā;* occasionally omits ri-pa, T- evening

उत्तुङ्गवक्षोरुहनम्रकान्तकान्तासमालिङ्गितगौरगात्रः ।
हेमस्फुरत् कुण्डलमण्डितास्यो विराजते मालवगौडरागः ॥

RV 4.15, 16, p. 109 *svamela; pūrṇa*-omits or includes ga-dha; ni-3 or sa-3. T- *pradoṣa* (a period of three *muhūrtas* or 48 × 3 minutes, i.e. two hours and twenty four minutes prefacing the night).

5.202, p. 220:

कान्ताचुम्बितलपनश्चलमौलिः किमपि कुण्डली शुकभाः ।
नर्तनशालाशीली मालाभृन्मालवो मत्तः ॥

SD—
SS —
SP 1.430, p. 55 *gaurī-mela,* omits dha, ri-*graha,* omits ga in ascent; if ga occurs in ascent, pa is *graha* and ma is *nyāsa,* T- after third *prahara*
PS 3.20, 26, p. 12, 13 *puruṣa (mālava):*

नितम्बिनीचुम्बितवक्त्रपद्मः शुकद्युतिः कुण्डलवान् प्रमत्तः ।
सङ्गीतशालां प्रविशन् प्रदोषे मालाधरो मालवरागराजः ॥

GP 5.7, 53, 54, pp. 35, 40 *mālava: auḍuva,* born of *ṭakka,* omits ri-pa, ni-3, ga-*bahula* sa-dha *kampita,* T- end of day or night; in *vīra* and *śṛṅgāra rasas.*

210. 43. *Śuddhagauḍa*

Guṇḍakrī-mela (*vide supra*)
SUS—
SJ —
SMK—
SC 2.2.21 *mālavagauḍa mela,* ni-3 omits pa
RJ —
RK —
RV 4.24, p. 112 *mālavagauḍa-mela;* pa-*aṁśa,* sa-*graha nyāsa,* ni-*alpa,* T- *pradoṣa*
5.203, p. 220:

कुङ्कुमकुसुम्भजाम्भः कणकीर्णसिताम्बरः पुरं सुरभिः ।
मृगमदतिलकी ललितो माला ताम्बूलवान् गौडः ॥

(*gauḍa* = *śuddhagauḍa,* comm. on loc. cit).
SD—
SS 2.652-656, p. 176 *gaula*: *svaras* as above; ni-3; ni-*vādī,* ga-*saṁvādī; ṣāḍava* by omitting dha; ri-*aṁśa* according to actual practice; a *saṅkīrṇa rāga* according to some, because of lack of clear cut *vādī,* etc.
SP—
PS —
GP —

211. 44. *Karnāṭabaṅgāla*

Gauḍī-mela (*vide supra*)
SUS—
SJ 2.2.3, 96, p. 433 *aṅga* of *vegarañjī* which is born of *ṭakka* as *bhāṣā*; ga-*graha aṁśa,* sa-*nyāsa,* T- rainy season, in *śṛṅgāra rasa*
SC 2.2.20 *mālavagauḍa-mela,* sa-3, omits ri, T- dawn
RJ 2.15 *mālavagauḍa-mela,* ga-3, omits ri, T- morning

RK—
RV —
SD —
SS 2.697, 698, p. 181 *gurjarī mela*; ga-3, *ṣāḍava* by omitting ni
SP—
PS—
GP 5.5.37, pp. 34, 38 *ṣāḍava*, ga-3, omits sa-pa, born of *ṭakka vaṁśa, śṛṅgāra rasa*

212. 45. *Śuddhanāṭa*

K—sa ru gu ma pa dhu nu
SUS—

SJ 2.3.4.42, p. 459 mentioned in *sadṛśāṁśa sthāya;* but *naṭṭa* (2.2.3.36, p. 427): born of *hindola bhāṣā piñjarī*, sa-3, omits dha-ga, T- second half of day, in *yuddha-vīra* and *adbhuta rasas*; some '*sāhasaniṣṭhura-s*' even omit ma; but this is not found to be true in actual practice: क्रौञ्चासना पीतवस्त्रा मेघश्यामलरूपधृक् ।

SMK 4.37, 38, p. 24 *svaras:* sa ru gu ma pa dhu nu; *uttama* (5.2, p. 29), *sampūrṇa*, sa-3, T- latter half of day (5.20, 21, p. 31)

SC 2.2.29 *svaras* as above; sa-3, *sampūrṇa*, T- fourth watch of day

RJ 2.36, 37 *svaras* as above; sa-3, serious mood, T- evening

RK 2.122-124, p. 28 *svaras* as above; sa-3, replete with *gamakas*, first *mūrchanā*, T- evening

तुरङ्गमारूढविशालबाहुर्विशुद्धचामीकरचारुवर्णः ।
रणे प्रतापी रुधिरार्द्रदेहो विराजते शुद्धनाटाख्यरागः ॥

RV 4.45, p. 117 *svamela*, sa-3, *pūrṇa*, T- *pradoṣa*
5.198, p. 219:

खेटककृपाणपाणिः प्रतर्जयन् वैरिणो रणेऽरुणदृक् ।
हरितालाभो हारी हयचारी धीरधीर्नाटः ॥

SD 2.158, p. 26 *puruṣa rāga; nāṭī, rāgiṇi of naṭanārāyaṇa* according to *Rāgarāgiṇimatam* (2.2.170, p. 28) of *dīpaka* according to Hanūmān (2.187, p. 30), *puruṣa-rāga* according to *Rāgārṇava* (2.190, p. 31); sa-3, *sampūrṇa*, first *mūrchānā;* performed with many kinds of *gamakas* (2.243, p. 42)
2.244, p. 42:

उद्यद्भानुसुहृच्छविर्विकसितं पङ्केरुहं पाणिना स्पृश्यन्ती मधुपानघूर्णनयना तन्वी तमालद्युतिः ।
ताम्बूलाहरणच्छलेन दयितं सङ्केतयन्ती निजं क्रीडाकुञ्जगृहे लवङ्गलतिकामोदानिले कामिनी ॥

SS 2.453-457, p. 156 *svaras* as above, according to vocal tradition: sa-3, sa- *vādin*, pa-*saṁvādin*, ga-ni *vivādins*, ri-dha *anuvādins*

SP 1.435, pp. 55, 56 *svaras* as above, ri-*mūrchanā*, omits dha-ga in descent; T—after third *prahara*

PS 3.62, p. 20:

चिरं नटन्ती शुभरङ्गमध्ये सम्प्रोञ्छयन्ती निखिलं श्रमाम्भः ।
सुगीततालेषु कृतावधाना नाटी सुनाटी परिधानशीला ॥

GP 5.4.11, 33, pp. 34, 35, 38 *sampūrṇa;* similar to *śrīrāga* but with pa not *alpa*; dha-ri *tāra*; ni-*mandra*; powerful *gamakas* (5.11, p. 35); *svaras* have *kampita* and *āndolita gamakas*; T- night; in *hāsya, adbhuta, śṛṅgāra rasas* and on auspicious occasions.

213. 46. *Mālavaśrī*

Śrīrāga-mela (*vide supra*)

SUS—

SJ 2.2.2.40, p. 406 *aṅga* of *mālavakaiśika, pūrṇa*, sa-3, T- fourth *prahara;* in *adbhuta, vīra rasas,* in the *hemanta* season

SMK 4.19, p. 22 *śrīrāga-mela, uttama* (5.4, p. 29), *ṣāḍava*, sa-3, omits ri, auspicious, T- always (5.33cd-34ab, p. 32)

SC 2.2.25cd *śrīrāga-mela,* sa-3, ri-dha *alpa*, T- always

RJ 2.66 *śrīrāga-mela,* sa-3, ri-dha *alpa*, T- always

RK 2.114, 115, p. 27 *śrīrāga-mela,* sa-3, *pūrṇa,* ri-dha alpa, delightful erotic

प्रफुल्लरक्तोत्पलपाणिरेषा मन्दस्मितोद्भासितगल्लयुग्मा ।
स्वैरं निषण्णा सहकारमूले विभाति नित्यं किल मालवश्रीः ॥

RV 4.30, p. 113 *śrīrāga-mela; mālāśrī: pūrṇa* or weak ri-dha; sa-3 or ni-3; sung at the beginning for auspiciousness; T- always

5.210, p. 222 *mālāśrī:*

तन्वी रसालतलगा कलगाना सस्मिता प्रति स्वपतिम् ।
मृगदृक् करगतकमला मालाश्रीर्मालयोल्लसिता ॥

SD 2.168, p. 27 *rāgiṇi* of *pañcama* according to *Rāgarāgiṇi-matam,* of *śrīrāga* according to Hanūmān (2.188, p. 30); T-morning according to Someśvara (2.172, p. 28) *uttaramandrā mūrchanā, sampūrṇa,* sa-3, appealing form; *śṛṅgāra rasa* (2.254, p. 44); *deśī rāga:* rules of *śruti, svara, grāma, jāti* do not apply (2.289, p. 51).

2.254, p. 44:

रक्तोत्पलं हस्ततले नियुक्तं विभावयन्ती तनुदेहवल्ली ।
रसालवृक्षस्य तले निषण्णा स्तोकस्मिता सा किल मालवश्रीः ॥

SS 2.906cd-907ab, p. 204 *śrīrāga-mela,* sa-3, omits ri, *ṣāḍava*

SP 1.365, p. 39 *śuddhasvara-mela* (= *śrīrāga-mela*); ma-*graha,* dha-*aṁśa,* pa-*nyāsa,* T- morning

PS 3.19, 20, 28, pp. 12, 13 *rāgiṇi* of *mālava*, T- evening (*mālasī*)

करे विधूताम्बुजयुग्मरम्या इतस्ततश्चारु विलोकयन्ती ।
कण्ठे स्फुरणमौक्तिकरत्नहारा सा मालसी संकथिता विचित्रा ॥

GP 5.3, 28, pp. 34, 37 *sampūrṇa*, born of *mālavakaiśika*, sa-3, propitiates Śiva; should be performed from the *śayanotsava* of Hari up to *Durgāṣṭamī*.

214. 47. *Deśākṣī*

K—sa ru gu ma pa dhi nu
SUS—
SJ —
SMK— 4.31, 32, p. 23, 24 *svaras* as above; *uttama* (5.4, p. 29); sa-3, *pūrṇa*, omits ma-ni in ascent; T- forenoon (5.30, p. 32)
SC 2.2.30, 31 *svaras* as above (dha?); ga-3, omits ma-ni or is *pūrṇa*; T- morning
RJ 2.38 *svaras* as above (dha?); ga-3, omits ri, T- morning
RK 2.159, 160, p. 33 *svaras* as above; ga-3, *pūrṇa*; T- morning; in *vīra rasa*

सम्पूर्णशीतांशुमनोज्ञवक्त्रा प्रफुल्लराजीवविलोलनेत्रा ।
प्रांशुः प्रसन्ना सविलासबाहुर्देशाक्षिकेयं गदिता मुनीन्द्रैः ॥

RV 4.45ab, p. 117 *svamela*, ga-3; omits ma-ni in ascent; T- dawn
SD—
SS 2.1312-1314, p. 249 *svaras* as above (*svamela*), ga-3, *sampūrṇa*
SP—
PS—
GP—

215. 48. *Devakrī*

Velāvalī-mela (no. 57, sl. no, 224, *vide infra*); affiliated to *usshaq*; ma is at 14th *śruti*.
SUS—
SJ 2.2.4, 9, p. 438 *grāmarāga*, same as *gaudakṛti* in *svaras*, *graha* is dha; *nyāsa*, *aṁśa* is sa, *mandra*-ni, *tāra*-ma, omits ri-pa; in *vīra* and *adbhuta rasas*.

मेघाभा रक्तवसना च गरुडोपरिसंस्थिता ।

SMK 4.36, p. 24; 5.13, p. 30 *kannaḍagaula-mela* (sa ru gu ma pa dhi ni), *adhama rāga*, not described.
SC 2.2.65-67 *svamela* (sa ru? gu ma pa dhi nu); sa-3, omits pa; also called *śuddha-vasanta*, T- always
RJ 2.34cd *kedāra-mela* (sa ri gu ma pa dhi nu); sa-3, omits pa; T- fourth *prahara*.
RK
RV 4.34, p. 114 *kāmbodī-mela*; *pūrṇa* or omits pa, sa-3, T- afternoon

5.191, p. 217:

भासुरतनुरनुगतसुरतरुसूनाऽनूनसौरभा सुमुखी ।
देवकृतिरतुलभूषा मणिमयसिंहासनासीना ॥

SD—
SS —
SP 1.459, p. 61 *devagiri*: ga-ni *tīvra*, ma-*tīvratara*, omits dha-ga in descent; sa-*mūrchanā*,T- after second *prahara*
PS—
GP 5.4, 30, pp. 34, 37 *sampūrṇa*; sa-3, in *vīra rasa*; T- at all times and all seasons; also called *śuddhavasanta*.

The evolution of this *rāga* is of considerable interest and has been studied elsewhere (Sathyanarayana R., (i) *Vīṇālakṣaṇa-vimarśe*, pp. 198-205, 217-219, (ii) *Karnāṭaka-saṅgītavāhinī*, pp. 80, 81, 199, 236, etc., (iii) *Puṇḍarīkamālā*, pp. 53, 234, 235; (iv) *Śrīguruguha: Devakriyā* or *Śuddhasāverī* ? in *Bhāratīya Samskṛti*, vol. 2.12, Bangalore, 1955).

216. 49. *Madhumādhavī*

K—sa ri gu ma pa dhi nu
SUS—
SJ 2.2.2.31, 32, p. 405 *madhyamādi*: born of *ma-grāma*, *sampūrṇa*, ma-3, *śṛṅgāra rasa*, T- first watch of day:

वेणुप्रवीणा अथ वैणिकाश्च पूर्वं प्रयुज्याखिलरागराशेः ।
इमामभीष्टं निजमालपन्ति रागं ततः प्राङ्मुनिभिः प्रदिष्टम् ॥

SMK 4.19, p. 22 *madhyamādi*: *śrīrāga-mela*, *madhyama rāga* (5.7, p. 29), *ṣāḍava*, ma-3, omits ri-dha, T- latter half of day
SC 2.2.44ab *modhyamādi*: *kedāra-mela:* ma-3, omits ri-dha, T- morning
RJ 2.32cd *madhumādhavi: kedāra-mela;* ma-3, omits ri-dha, T- morning
RK—
RV 4.40, p. 116 *madhyamādi: mallāri-mela* (sa ri gu ma pa dhi nu), ma-3, omits ri-dha, T- morning
SD 2.165, p. 27 *rāgiṇi* of *śrī* according to *Rāgarāgiṇi-matam*; *madhyamādi* is *rāgiṇi* of *bhairava* according to Hanūmān (2.184, p. 30), of *bhairava* according to *Rāgārṇava* (2.191, p. 31) T- (*madhumādhavī*) morning according to Someśvara (2.171, p. 28) *madhyamādi*: *rāgāṅga*, ma-3, *sampūrṇa*, *ma-mūrchanā*; sometimes omits ri-dha (2.199, p. 33)
2.200, p. 33:

पत्या सहासं परिरभ्य कामं संचुम्बितास्या कमलायताक्षी ।
स्वर्णच्छविः कुङ्कुमलिप्तदेहा सा मध्यमादिः कथिता मुनीन्द्रैः ॥

SS 2.920, p. 205 *śrīrāga-mela,* ma-3, omits ri-dha
SP 1.381, p. 43 *ma-mūrchanā,* omits ga-dha, ri-ma-ni *aṁśas;* T- morning
PS—
GP —

217. 50. *Ābhīrī*

K—sa ri gi ma pa dha nu

SUS 3.98ab *bhāṣā* of *pañcama;* नीलाम्बरा च गौरा स्यादाभीरी केकिगामिनी

SJ 2.2.3.58-60, p. 429 *bhāṣāṅga* of *pañcama-rāga;* sometimes *aṅga* of *kakubha;* dha-3, *tāra* pa-dha, ni-ri-pa *saṅgati; sampūrṇa,* first *mūrchanā;* sung in battles; नीलवस्त्रा च गौराङ्गी मयूरवरवाहना ।

SMK 4.39, 40, p. 24 *āharī: svamela* (*svaras* as above), *uttama* (5.4, p. 29), sa-3, *pūrṇa,* T- final watch of day
SC 2.2.57 *svamela* (*svaras* as above), sa-3, *pūrṇa,* T- evening
RJ 2.47 *svamela* (*svaras* as above): *āherī:* sa-3, *sampūrṇa, śṛṅgāra,* T- evening
RK—
RV 4.25, p. 112 *ābhīrī: svamela* (*svaras* as above), ga-*aṁśa graha,* sa-*nyāsa, pūrṇa,* T- *pradoṣa*
5.199, p. 219 *abherī:*

गौरश्यामाभेरी विनीलचोला सविद्रुमालिगला ।
ताटङ्काञ्चितकर्णा मृदुतनुवाणिः सुवेणीभृत् ॥

SD 2.170, p. 28 *ābherī: rāgiṇi* of *naṭanārāyaṇa* according to *Rāgarāgiṇī-matam,* T- after third *prahara; ābhīrī:* (2.288, p. 51): similar to *kalyāṇa*
SS 2.1153, 1154, p. 231 *abherī: āharīmela* (*svaras* as above); sa-3, *sampūrṇa.*
SP 1.400, p. 48 *ābhīrī:* (*svaras* as above), *kampita* in dha-ga; sa-pa *aṁśa;* sometimes omits ma in both ascent and descent, T- after third *prahara*
PS—
GP —

218. 51. *Jijāvanta*

Śrīrāga-mela (*vide supra*)
No reference to *jijāvanta* is found in any of the above sources: only RJ equates it with the Persian *parada* viz. *husenī* (2.74)

219. 52. *Sālaṅganāṭi*

Kedāra-mela (sa ri gu ma pa dhi nu)
SUS—
SJ —
SMK 4.20-23, p. 23 *sālaṅganāṭa: svamela* (*svaras* as above) *uttama* (5.5, p. 29) *sampūrṇa,* sa-3, T- latter half of day

SC 2.2.45 *kedāra-mela;* sa-3, *pūrṇa,* T- fourth watch of the day
RJ —
RK —
RV 4.39, p. 116 *sālaṅganāṭa: mallāri-mela; pūrṇa,* sa-3, T- evening
SD 2.170, p. 28 *rāgiṇi* of *naṭanārāyaṇa* according to *Rāgarāgiṇi-matam;* T-after third *prahara* according to Someśvara (2.177, p. 29); *uttaramandrā mūrchanā, sampūrṇa,* sa-3 (2.273, p. 48)
2.273, p. 48:

वीणां दधाना दृढबद्धवेणी सख्यासमं मञ्जुलवृक्षमूले ।
जम्बूनदाभा च निषण्णदेहा सारङ्गनाटा कथिता सुवेषैः ॥
अथवा- करधृतवीणा सख्यासहोपविष्टा च कल्पतरुमूले ।
दृढतरनिबद्धकबरी सारङ्गा सा सुरङ्गिणी प्रोक्ता ॥

SS 2.587-598, pp. 170, 171 *sālaṅganāṭi: gurjarī-mela;* moderners attribute *pañcaśruti* ri-dha notes and hence classify it elsewhere, but it is wrong; sa-3, sa-*vādīn,* pa-*saṁvādī,* ga-ni *vivādins;* ri-dha *anuvādins.*
SP 1.437, p. 56 *sālaṅganāṭa:* born of *śaṅkarābharaṇa,* omits ga, sa-3, T- after third *prahara.*
PS—
GP—

220. 53. *Karnāṭa*

K—sa ru gu* ma pa dhu nu*
SUS 3.93, p. 65 *bhairava-bhāṣā:* कर्णाटी हस्तिगमना नीलाङ्गी रक्तचीवरा ।
SJ 2.2.2.167, 168, p. 421 *karnāṭagauḍa: upāṅga* of *gauḍa, sampūrṇa,* ni-3, ni-dha, ga-sa *saṅgati, karuṇa rasa,* beloved of the people of Karnātaka; all the more enjoyable with *gamakālapti;* T- final watch of the day; Śārṅgadeva has arbitrarily prescribed sa-3, but this is not borne out in actual practice.
SMK 4.33-36, p. 24 *svamela* (sa ru gu ma pa dhi nu); *sampūrṇa* but sometimes omits dha in ascent; ni-3; T- latter half of day; beloved of the people of *Utkala* (Orissa), *uttama-sampūrṇa* (5.3, 29, pp. 29, 32)
SC 2.2.31cd-33 *karnāṭagauḍa: svamela* (*svaras* as above); *karṇata:* ni-3, omits ri-dha or is *sampūrṇa,* T- sunset
RJ 2.57, 59 *karnāṭa: svamela* (*svaras* as above, but ri = *pañcaśruti*!). This should be emended to '*tṛtīya gatiko'pi riḥ*' on the basis of the corresponding texts in SC and NN). *karnāṭa rāga:* ni-3, omits (or not) ri-dha, T- evening
RK 2.125-128, pp. 28, 29 *karnāṭagauḍa: svamela* (sa ri gu ma pa dhi ni; cf. RJ 2.57). It is however, called *karnāṭa-rāga* in reificatory verse:

राजीवनेत्रः पृथुलातपत्रः पद्मं वहन् दक्षिणहस्तकेन ।
स्तुत्यो नृपः किन्नरचारणाद्यैः कर्णाटरागः करवालपाणिः ॥

RV 4.42, p. 116, 117 *karnāṭa: svamela* (sa ru gu ma pa dhi ni); ni-3, *sampūrṇa,* or sometimes omits ri-dha, T- night

5.204, p. 220:

सासिगजदन्तपाणिर्नीलगलो मीनभूषितः कर्णे ।
शृङ्गारवीरपोषी कर्णाटो योषितामिष्टः ॥

SD 2.168, p. 27 *karnāṭī, rāgiṇi* of *pañcama* according to *Rāgarāgiṇī-matam, kānaḍā, rāgiṇi* of *dīpaka* (2.187, p. 30), *karnāṭa, rāgiṇi* of *nāṭa* (2.193, p. 31), T- *karnāṭī* after third *prahara; sampūrṇa,* ni-3, *vikṛta* ni, *mārgī murchanā.* (2.239, p. 41)

2.240, p. 41:

कर्णाटी कमलेक्षणा सुरतरोर्मूले वसन्ती मुहुः श्वासोच्छ्वासविभिन्नमोदममितः सम्पूरयन्ती दिशः ।
कीरं नीलनिचोलजुष्टममितः स्वर्णमया बिभ्रती कान्तारे पिककूजिते स्वदयितं साङ्केतिके पश्यति॥

SS 2.1204, 1205, p. 237 *kannaḍagaula: sāmanta-mela* (sa ru gu ma pa dhu nu), ni-3, *pūrṇa,* but sometimes omits ma.

SP 1.424, 425, p. 54 *karnāṭagaula: svaras* as above; ga-*nyāsa,* ma-*aṁśa, sa-mūrchanā,* sometimes omits dha in ascent, T- after third *prahara.*

PS 3.21, p. 12 *kānaḍā, rāgiṇi* of *mallāra*

3.36, p. 15:

अशोकवृक्षस्य तले निषण्णा वियोगिनी वाष्पकणाञ्चिताक्षी ।
निर्भूषिताङ्गी जटिलैकवेणी सा कानडा हेमलतेव तन्वी ॥

GP 5.1.11, pp. 34, 35 *sampūrṇa;* similar to *naṭṭa* but has ni-3.

221. 54. *Chāyānāṭa*

Karnāta-mela (*vide supra*)

SUS

SJ 2.2.2.150, p. 419 similar to *naṭṭa* but pa-*mandra,* ga-ni *kampita,* ni-*tāra;* sung in *vīra* and *adbhuta rasas*

SMK 4.35, p. 24 *mela* of *kannaḍagaula, adhama* (5.13, p. 30), not described

SC 2.2.36ab *karnāṭagauḍa-mela;* sa-3, has gu*, nu*, T- evening

RJ 2.60cd *karnāṭa-mela;* sa-3; has gu*, nu*, T- evening

RK—

RV —

SD —

SS 2.392cd, 393ab, p. 150 *upāṅga* of *naṭṭa;* if *naṭṭa* has *mṛdu* pa and *kampita gramaka* in ga-ni, it is *chāyānaṭṭa.*

SP 1.438, p. 56 has *svaras* of *śaṅkarābharaṇa;* omits ni in ascent and ga in descent; dha-*graha*, ni-*nyāsa*, ma-*aṁśa*, T- after third *prahara*

PS—

GP—

222. 55. *Hammīranāṭa*

K—sa ri gu ma pa dha nu

SUS—

SJ —

SMK—

SC 2.2.51 *svamela* (*svaras* as above), lacuna for *lakṣaṇa*

RJ 2.63 *svamela* (*svaras* as above), sa-3, *sampūrṇa,* T- third watch of the day

RK—

RV 4.25cd, p. 112 *hamīra: svamela* (*svaras* as above), ga-*graha*, pa-*aṁśa*, sa-*nyāsa*; T- night

SD 2.170, p. 28 *haṁvīrā, rāgiṇi* of *naṭanārāyaṇa* according to *Rāgarāgiṇi- matam*

SS—

SP —

PS —

223. 56. *Naṭ(ṭ)anārāyaṇa*

K—sa ri gu* ma pa dhi nu*

SUS 3.106, p.67 main *rāga*:

नट्टनारायणो रागो नीलवर्णश्चतुर्भुजः ।
शङ्खचक्रगदावीणाकरः स्याद्गरुडवाहनः ॥

SJ 2.2.2.61, 62, p. 409 *aṅga* of *kakubha*; *tāra* ga, *mandra* pa, same *svaras* as *kakubha, sa-grāma*, dha-3

नीलवर्णश्चतुर्बाहुर्नारायण इवापरः ।
शङ्खचक्रगदावीणाकरो गरुडवाहनः
मन्यते कैश्चिदेवायं मतङ्गमतास्थितैः ॥

SMK 4.23, p. 23 *sāraṅganāṭa-mela* (*svaras* as above); *adhama rāga* (5.1, p. 30) not described

SC 2.2.43 *kedāra-mela* (*svaras* as above), sa-3, *pūrṇa,* has gu*, nu*, T- always

RJ 2.30 *kedāra mela* (*svaras* as above), sa-3, *pūrṇa,* has gu*, nu*, T- always; rainy season

RK 2.149, 150, p. 32 *bhāṣā* of *kedāra* (*svaras* as above), sa-3, has gu*, nu*, T- always

नव्याम्बुदश्यामतनुर्मनोज्ञः प्रफुल्लपङ्केरुहलोचनश्रीः ।
चतुर्भुजः शङ्खगदारिपद्मैर्नारायणोऽसौ नितरां विभाति ॥

RV 4.37, p. 115 *mallāri-mela* (*svaras* as above); sa-2, ga-*aṁśa, sampūrṇa,* T-forenoon

इन्दीवरतनुरञ्चलपीतदुकूलो मणिस्फुरन्मकुटः ।
नटनारायण उच्चैः कुण्डलललितो मुदा नृत्येत् ॥

SD 2.159, p. 26; a '*rāga*'; born of the face of Girijā according to *Rāgarāgiṇ-matam* (2.162, 170, pp. 27, 28), *rāgiṇi* of *nāṭa* according to *Rāgārṇava* (2.193, p. 31), T-***hemanta*** season according to Someśvara (2.182, p. 29)

SS—

SP 1.436, p. 56 *velāvalī-mela;* ma- *aṁśa,* ri-*nyāsa*; omits ga in descent, ga-*mūrchanā,* T- after third *prahara*

PS—

GP —

224. 57. *Velāvalī*

Mela of *madhumādhavī*

SUS 3.92, p.65 *bhāṣā* of *bhairava*: वेलाकुली रक्तचीरा गौरा स्याद् वृषभयायिनी ।

SJ 2.2.3.18 *aṅga* of *bhogavardhanī* which is *bhāṣā* of *kakubha*: *sampūrṇa,* ga-*mandra tāra;* dha-3, dha-*kampita gamaka;* in *vipralambha śṛṅgāra;* in propitiation of Hari: वृषगा गौरवर्णा च रक्तवस्त्रेति केचन ।

SMK 4.19, p. 22 *mela* of *śrīrāga; madhyama rāga* (5.7, p. 29), *pūrṇa,* dha-3, but sometimes omits ri-pa in descent; T- dawn (5.50, p. 34)

SC 2.2.41cd *kedāra-mela;* dha-3, omits ri-pa, T- morning

RJ 2.31 *kedāra-mela;* dha-3, omits ri-pa; T- morning

RK 2.147, 148, p. 31 *bhāṣā* of *kedāra*; *pūrṇa,* or omits ri-pa; dha-3; in *vīra rasa.* T- morning

विधाय सङ्केतमियं प्रियेण हेम्नोल्लसद्भूषणमुद्वहन्ती ।
स्मरं स्मरन्ती स्मरकामिनीव वेलावली श्यामतनुर्विभाति ॥

RV 4.39, p. 116 *mallāri-mela;* dha-3, *pūrṇa* or omits ri-pa; T- dawn
5.170, p. 211:

वेलावेली विनीला ताली वनचारिणी तरलहारा ।
तरुणान्वेषणकरुणं करतलतद्दलाभरणा ॥

SD 2.186, p. 30 *rāgiṇi* of *hindola* according to Hanūmān; T- morning according to Someśvara (2.171, p. 27); *pūrṇa, pauravī mūrchanā,* dha-3; in *vīra rasa* (2.221, p. 38)

2.229, p. 38:

सङ्केतदीक्षां दयिते च दत्वा वितन्वती भूषणमङ्गकेषु ।
मुहुः स्मरन्ती स्मरमिष्टदेवं वेलावली नीलसरोजकान्तिः ॥

SS 2.866cd, 867ab, p. 199 *śrīrāga mela:* dha-3, *pūrṇa*

SP 1.409, p. 50 *abhirudgatā mūrchanā; tīvra* ga-ni; when ma-ni are omitted in ascent, sa is *aṁśa;* when ga is omitted in descent it is somewhat *ga-mūrchanā;* T-morning

PS 3.17, p.12, T- noon; *rāgiṇi* of *mallāra* (3.21, p. 12)

3.34, p. 15:

सङ्केतितोत्फुल्ललतानिकुञ्जे कृतस्थितिः कान्तसमागमाय ।
वेलावली चम्कमालमौलिः विचित्रवेषाभरणा निरुक्ता ॥

GP 5.4.34, pp. 34, 38 *sampūrṇa*, dha-3, *mandra*-sa, same notes as of *naṭṭa;* in *śṛṅgāra.*

An affinity between *velāvalī* and *kurāyī* is mentioned for the first time in NN. But similarity of *kuḍāyī* with *deśākh(yā)* has been noted since veËy early times, e.g. Madanapāla (*Ānandasañjīvanī,* extr. *Bharatakośa,* p. 140); SD describes it as '*deśākhya saṁśrayā*' (2.196, p. 31), to be sung similar to *deśākhya* (2.287, p. 51) T- after second *prahara* according to Someśvara (2.175, p. 29); SP describes it (1.456, 457, p. 60) as possessing *tīvra* ga, ga-*graha*, pa-*aṁśa*; omits ga in descent according to some; omits ma-ni in ascent; T- after first *prahara.* Locana (*Rāgataraṅgiṇī,* p. 130, Darabhaṅga edn., śl. 112, 113, Poona edn.) *kalāyī / kulāyī* (*kuḍāyī?*) as an admixture of *aḍānā, kānarā, velāvalī* and *naṭanārāyaṇa,* thus confirming NN.

225. 58. *Kāmbojī*

K—sa ri gu* ma pa dhi nu*

SUS—

SJ 2.3.51, 52, p.429 born as *bhāṣāṅga* of *kakubha* according to Yāṣṭika; *pūrṇa,* dha-3. According to others, sa-3, omits dha-ri, ni-*bahula*, born of *hindola,* has abundant *sañcāri-varṇa*, employed in *śṛṅgāra* and *karuṇa rasas*

SMK 4.61, 62, p. 27 sa ri gu* ma pa dh nu*, *madhyama rāga* (5.6, p. 29), *sampūrṇa,* sa-3, omits ma-ni in ascent; T- evening

SC 4.48 *kedāra-mela;* sa-3, gu*, nu*, omits ma-ni (in *āroha*), T- dawn

RJ 2.32 *kedāra-mela,* sa-3, omits ma-ni, gu*, nu*

RK—

RV 4.34, p. 114 *svamela* (sa ri gu* ma pa dhi nu*); sa-3; *pūrṇa* or omits ni, T-evening

SD 2.159, p. 26, a '*rāga*'

SS 2.1218, 1219, pp. 238, 239 *svamela* (sa ri gu ma pa dhi ni), sa-3

SP 1.411, p. 51 *ga(dha ?)-mūrchanā, tīvra* ga, *uttarāyatā mūrchanā*; omits ma-ni in ascent; ma-dha *aṁśas.*

PS—

GP—

226. 59. *Sāverī*

K—sa ri gu ma pa dhi nu

SUS 3.99, pp. 66 *sāmeri, bhāṣā* of *pañcama*: श्वेतवर्णा नीलावस्त्रा सामेरी स्यान्मृगासना ।

SJ 2.2.3, 85, p. 432 *aṅga* of *rāganti* which is *bhāṣā* of *kakubha*, ni-*graha nyāsa*, dha-*aṁśa*, ga-*tāra*, lacks pa, ri-dha *bahula*, T- autumn; in *hāsya* and *śṛṅgāra*

SMK 4.23, p. 23 *sāraṅganāṭa-mela* (sa ri gu ma pa dhi nu); *adhama-rāga* (5.14, p. 30) dha-3, omits ga-ni, *auḍuva*, T- morning (5.64, p. 36)

SC 2.2.46cd *kedāra-mela,* dha-3, omits sa-pa, T- morning

RJ 2.33 *kedāra-mela,* dha-3, omits sa-pa, T- morning

RK—

RV 4.40, p. 116 *mallāri-mela;* dha-3, omits sa-pa, T- dawn

SD 2.169, p. 28 *rāgiṇi* of *megha* according to *Rāgarāgiṇi-matam;* T- after first *prahara,* (2.173, p. 28)

SS 2.761, p. 188 *gurjarīī-mela;* pa-3, ni-pa omitted; *auḍuva*

SP 1.445, p. 58 *tīvra* ga, ma-*aṁśa*, dha-*graha*, omits ni; omits ga-ni in ascent, T- always

PS—

GP 5.45, p. 39 *śāvarī*? ma-*graha, aṁśa;* dha-*nyāsa*; *mandra*-ma, *tāra* ga, omits pa.

227. 60. *Suhavī*

Sāverī mela (*vide supra*)

SUS—

SJ —

SMK—

SC —

RJ 2.34 *kedāra-mela,* dha-3, *pūrṇa,* T- morning

RK—

SD —

SS —

SP —

PS —

GP—

228. 61. *Saurāṣṭrī*

Sāverī-mela (*vide supra*)

SUS

SJ 2.2.3.109, 110, pp. 434, 435 sa-3, omits ri-pa, *mandra*-dha, ga-ni-dha *bahula;* '*rāṣṭravardhinī*'

नीलाङ्गी कृष्णवसना गजेन्द्रवरवाहना ।

SMK 4.14, p.22 *mālavagaula-mela*; *adhama-rāga* (5.9, p. 30), not described
SC.2.2.47 *kedāra-mela*; sa-3, *pūrṇa*, T- evening
RJ 2.60 *karnāṭa-mela*; sa-3, *pūrṇa*, T- evening, *śṛṅgāra rasa*
RK 2.89.90 p.23 *mālavagauḍa bhāṣā*, *pūrṇa*, sa-3, T- evening

उत्तुङ्गपीनस्तनलोलहारा कर्णोत्पलऽलिध्वनिदत्तचित्ता ।
प्रियान्तिकं याति विलोलबाहुः सौराष्ट्रिका कुङ्कुमलिप्तगल्ला ॥

RV 4.41 p.116 *mallārī-mela*; sa-3, T- evening

चित्राम्बरातिगौरी मेचककञ्चुकिकयातिगूढकुचा ।
शोणरदा विधुवदना मदनार्ता याति सौराष्ट्री ॥

SD 2.169, p. 28 *soraṭi*, *rāgiṇi* of *malhārī* according to *Rāgarāgiṇi-matam*; T- after first *prahara* (2.174, p. 28); *soraṭī* pa-3 but sometimes sa-3, omits ri.
2.277, pp. 48, 49:

पीनोन्नतस्तनतटोत्तमहारवली कर्णोत्पलभ्रमरनादविलग्नचित्ता ।
याति प्रियान्तिकमतिश्लथबाहुवल्ली सौरष्ट्रिका मदनमूर्तिविचारगौरा ॥

SS 2.522cd-523, p.163 *gurjarī*, sa-3, sa-*vādin*, ma-pa *śaṁvādins*, ni-ga *vivādins*
SP 1.474, p. 64 *śrīrāga-mela*; ri-*graha*, ma-*nyāsa; humphita gamaka* on pa and sa; T- after first *prahara*
PS—
GP—

229. 62. *Malhāra*

K— sa ri gu ma pa dhi nu
SUS—
SJ 2.2.2.152, p. 419 *upāṅga* of *andhāli*, dha-3, omits sa-pa, ga-*mandra*, *ṣaḍja-grāma*; T- rainy season
SMK 4.15, p. 24 *malhāri*: *mālavagaula-mela*; *uttama-rāga* (5.41, p. 29); dha-3, *auḍuva;* omits ga-ni, T- dawn (5.38, p. 33)
SC.2.2.4; *kedāra-mela;* dha-3; omits sa-pa, T- dawn
RJ 2.29 *kedāra-mela*; dha-3, omits sa-pa; T- dawn
RK 2.153-155, p. 32 *svamela* (sa ri gu ma pa dhi nu); dha-3, omits sa-pa

वीणातिवादः कलकण्ठनादः सुवर्णवर्णः स्फुरदब्जकर्णः ।
काश्मीरचित्रः शरदिन्दुवक्त्रो मल्हारनामा नितरां विभाति ॥

RV
SD 2.169, p.128 *malhārī*: *rāgiṇi* of *megha* according to *Rāgarāgiṇi-matam*; accord-

ing to Hanūmān also (2.189, p. 30); *malhāra: rāgiṇi* of *bhairava* according to *Rāgārṇava;* (2.193, p. 31); and *mallārī* of *mallārī* (! *mallāra*) (2.194, p. 31); T- (*malhārī*) *forenoon* (2.171, p. 28); *mallārī:* dha-3, omits sa-pa, *auḍuva, pauravī mūrchanā*; T- rainy season; (2.262, p. 45)

2.263, p. 46 (*mallārī*):

गौरी कृशा कोकिलकण्ठनादा गीतछलेनात्मपतिं स्मरन्ती ।
आदाय वीणां मलिना रुदन्ती मल्लारिका यौवनदूनचित्ता ॥

SS 2.728, 729, p.184 *malahārī*: *gurjarī-mela*; omits ni; and is *ṣāḍava* according to some experts omits ga in descent.

SP 1.369, p. 40 *mallārī*; *gaurī-mela*; omits ni; omits ga in descent; sa-*mūrchanā*, T- always.

PS 3.21, p.12, '*rāga*', *mallāra*:

विद्वान् सुशीलोऽतिविहारशील: कान्तप्रियो धार्मिकशीलयुक्त: ।
कामातुर: पिङ्गलनेत्रयुग्म: मल्लारराग: कुसुमप्रियश्च ॥

GP 5.47cd-48ab, p. 39 *mallārī*: *ṣāḍava*; pa-3, omits ga; *mandra-* ma, T- cloudy day; in *śṛṅgāra rasa.*

230. 63. *Goṇḍa*

Malhāra mela (*vide supra*)

SUS—

SJ 2.2.2. 75, p. 411 *gauḍa: aṅga* of *ṭakka*, ni-3, omits pa, T- rainy season, in *karuṇa rasa*

SMK—

SC 2.2.45 *kedāra-mela;* dha-3, *pūrṇa,* T- dawn

RJ 2.29 *kedāra-mela,* dha-3, *purṇa,* T- dawn

RK—

RV 4.36, p.115 *gauḍa*; *mallāri-mela*: dha-3, ni-*alpa*, T- noon

5.184. p. 215:

पलितकचाहितबर्ह: सुकुटजमालो धनु:शरौ कलयन् ।
गौण्ड: किरातवेषो गौ(गै?)रिकरेखोचितोऽलिनिभ: ॥

SD—

SS—

SP 1.458, p. 61 *gauṇḍa*: *tīvra-* ga, omits ga-ni in ascent, sa- *graha, sampūrṇa*, T- always

PS

GP 5.5, 36, pp. 34,38 *ṣāḍava.* ni-3, omits pa, ri-*alpa*, T—end of day, in *vīra* and *śṛṅgāra rasas*

231. 64. *Kedāra*

Suhavī-mela but has 'nu' instead of 'ni'.

SUSv

SJ—

SMK—

SC 2.2.40, *svamela* (sa ri gu ma pa dhi nu), ni-3, omits ri-dha; T- evening.

RJ 2.28 *svamela* (*svaras* as above), ni-3, omits ri-pa, T- night; in *karuṇa rasa*

RK 2.145, 146, p. 31 *svamela* (*svaras* as above), ni-3; (*pūrṇa* or) omits ri-pa; has nu*, T- evening

गङ्गाधरः सुन्दरचन्द्रमौलिर्भुजङ्गमोद्भासुर यज्ञसूत्रः ।
ध्याने निविष्टो धृतयोगपीठः केदाररागो जटिलो विभाति ॥

RV 4.26, p.112 *hammīra-mela* (sa ri gu ma pa dha nu), *alpa* ri-dha; sa-*nyāsa*, ga-*graha aṁśa*, T- night

5.208, p. 221:

जटिलोऽहियोगपट्टः सविधुशकलमौलिरुल्लसद्भसितः ।
गङ्गाधरस्तपस्वी ध्यानरतोऽतीव केदारः ॥

SD 2.165, p. 27 *kedārī, rāgiṇi* of *śrīrāga* according to *Rāgarāgiṇi-matam*, but of *dīpaka* according to Hanūmān (2.187, p. 30); *kedāra, rāgiṇi* of *nāṭa* according to *Rāgārṇava* (2.193, p. 31); *kedārī: mārgī mūrchanā*, has nu, is *auḍuva* by omitting ri-dha, ni-3 (2.236, p. 40)

2.237, p. 4:

जटां दधानः सितचन्द्रमौलिः नागोत्तरीयो धृतयोगपीठः ।
गङ्गाधरो ध्याननिमग्नचित्तः केदाररागः कथितस्तपस्वी ॥

SS—

SP 1.410, p. 51 *kedārī:* ga-ni *tīvra;* omits ri-dha; ga-*graha*, T- after third *prahara*

PS 3.18, p. 11 T- evening; *rāgiṇi* of *mallāra* (3.21, p.12)

3.39, p.16:

स्नात्वा समुत्तीर्णवती सुदेहा केशाग्रनिःस्यन्दितवारिबिन्दुः ।
निष्पीडयन्ती स्तिमितांशुकान्तं केदारिका व्यक्तपयोधरश्रीः ॥

GP 5.52, p. 40 also called *deśapāla*; ni-3; born of *ṭakka*, omits ri-pa, sa has *āndolita gamaka*; T- evening; in *vīra* and *śṛṅgāra rasas*.

232. 65. *Śaṅkarābharaṇa*

Madhumādhavī-mela (*vide supra, śl.* 216)

SUS

SJ 2.2.2.96, p. 413 pa-3, omits ri, ma-*tāra*, ma-dha *bahula*, *madhyamagrāma rāga*; pleases Lord Śiva.

SMK 4.19, p. 22 *śrīrāga-mela*; *adhama rāga* (5.11, p. 30), *sampūrṇa*, sa-3, has the shade of *sāmanta* (5.61, p. 36).

SC 2.2.42 *kedāra-mela*, sa-3, *sampūrṇa*, has *mudrita gamaka*, T- evening

RJ 2.33 *kedāra-mela;* sa-3, *sampūrṇa*, has *mudrita gamaka*, T- evening

RK 2.151, 152, p. 32 *kedāra mela;* sa-3, has *mudrita gamaka*; T- sunrise

RV 4.37, p.115 *mallāri-mela*; *pūrṇa*, sa-3, T- dawn

5.169, p. 211:

गलराजिकमलराजिर्भाले भसिती रतः सदा नृत्ये ।
सुन्दरगौरः शोणाम्बराधरणः शङ्कराभरणः ॥

SD 2.284, p. 50 has the *svaras* of *velāvalī*.

SS 2.1056-1058, p. 221 *svamela* (sa ri gu ma pa dhi nu), sa-3, *sampūrṇa*

SP 1.407, p. 50 sa-*graha*, ga-*nyāsa*, ma-*aṁśa*, ga-ni *tīvra*; has *kampita* and *ḍhālu gamakas;* T- morning

PS—

GP—

233. 66. *Vihāgaḍa*

Kedāra-mela (*vide supra*, śl. 231)

SUS—

SJ—

SMK—

SC—

RJ—

RK—

RV 4.26, p.112 *hammīra-mela* (sa ri gu ma pa dha nu); ni-*graha-aṁśa*; sa-*nyāsa; svaras* have *kampita gamaka*; T- night

5.209, pp. 221, 222:

विधुकरगौरः सुरभिः सुमनःकृतभूषणाम्बरेषुधनुः ।
विरहिजनमनोमोही विहङ्गडः कीरवाही सः ॥

SD—

SS—

SP 1.442, p. 59 ma-*mūrchanā*; omits pa; ga-ni *tīvra*, omits ri in ascent; ga-*graha*, ri-*nyāsa-aṁśa*; T- after third *prahara*

PS—

GP—

CONCLUSION

The foregoing data on the *rāgas* of NN arranged in chronological and regional sequence reveal the following trends:

1. Fluidity in the concept of *mela*
2. Fluidity in the criteria of classification
3. Historical, i.e. spatiotemporal-continuity vs. provincial variation
4. Transition from *grāma* to *mela* in terms of
   (a) scalic temperament; equilibrium between ri*-ri, gu*-gu, dhi**-dhi and nu*-nu; transience of mi in 14th, 15th and 16th *śrutis*; evolution of the *pratinidhi tattva* (principle of representation) and *paryāya tattva* (principle of alternative denomination) in intervals; principle of extension in *svara vikṛti;* e.g. *ūrdhvagāndhāra*
   (b) athetisation in *daśaprāṇa* and sonance
   (c) realignment of intervals and *rāgas* of *madhyama-grāma*
   (d) transfer of the functions of *grāma* to *mela* through the device of decentralisation
   (e) systematisation of the concept and function of *mela* through mathematical and methodological devices
   (f) reorganisation of *rāga* scales in terms of interval redistribution
5. Individual and collective growth of *rāgas* as a phenomenon in cultural dynamics; intracultural and intercultural forces contributing to such growth
6. Pseudosynaesthetic bases in relation to concretisation or reification in music
7. Approximate constancy or coherence in the emergence in *rāgadhyāna* images; tonal and visual imagery in relation to mood evocation; fluidity in *rāgavelā*
8. Provincial origins and characteristics of *rāgas*; their rationalisation/standardisation into art forms
9. Dynamic equilibrium between stabilisation-expansion, stasis-growth, tradition-innovation in the evolution of *rāgas*
10. Persian *pardaḥ*—Indian *rāga* equivalentes.

I have discussed (1-4) in detail in my Commentary on Veṅkaṭamakhin, *Caturdaṇḍīprakāśikā* (chs. 3, 4, 5); (6-7) in my introduction to Gandharvarāja's *Rāgaratnākara* (unpublished) and (10) in the introduction to the present work.

COMMENTARY ON THE TEXT

B. PRABANDHA-ADHIKARAṆA

Paṇḍarīka Viṭṭhala has depended largely on Śārṅgadeva and especially on Kallinātha as sources for material in this chapterette, but for the eleven '*prasiddha prabandhas*' towards the end. So this commentary will devote itself in the main to a comparison of NN with SR and its commentaries, viz. *Saṅgītasudhākara* of Siṁhabhūpāla and *Saṅgītakalānidhi* of Kallinātha. However, an endeavour is also made to present the *prabandhas* in a limited historical perspective with material from sources which are original and authoritative in contribution to the subject.

1a. dhātumātu: All music, *mārga* or *deśi*, arises out of a union of *dhātu* and *mātu*, (terms which the NN does not define: *dhātu* is the musical part of song such as *rāga* and *tāla*; *mātu*—a term in Kannaḍa which means 'word': cf. SR 3.2); the conditions of *gīta*-music are set forth in this verse.

1b. racitam: *Gīta* is composed, i.e. man-made music. It does not proceed from beginningless tradition (*anādisampradāya*) and is not *apauruṣeya* (not man-made) as music of the *Veda* or *gāndharva* music is; *gāndharva* music is *sva-tantra* (independent of human agency) whereas *gīta* or *gāna* is *paratantra* (dependent on a human composer).

1b. lakṣaṇānvitam: Any composed music is not *gīta*; it must be composed, in order to be so described, according to rules (set forth in this chapterette): it must be composed in terms of *dhātu*, *aṅga* and (*gamaka*) *prayoga*.

1c. deśīrāga: *rāgas* other than *grāmarāga*, *jāti* or their evolutes; *rāgas* classified under *śuddha*-, *sālaga* and *saṁkīrṇa* (*Sadrāgacandrodaya* 2.77-78; *Rāgamālā*, 124-128). Elsewhere *deśīrāga* comprehends *rāgāṅga*, *bhāsāṅga*, *upāṅga* and *kriyāṅga*.

1c. Ādi includes *deśī-tāla*, *deśabhāṣā* (vernacular languages), *deśī-chandas*, *rasa*, etc.

1d. gītam: lit. Anything sung; but it has acquired a restricted meaning here as *gāna*, synonymous with *prabandha*. It has also acquired another restricted meaning over the centuries to mean *sālagasūḍa-prabandha*; such use is known in Kannaḍa poetry since at least the twelfth century, e.g. Aggaḷa (*Candraprabhapurāṇam*, 15.52; 15,72), Janna (*Anantanāthapurāṇam*, 10.8 pr). Pālkuriki Somanātha (*Paṇḍitārādhya-caritramu, parvataprakaraṇamu*, pp. 446, 447, 449), Padmaṇāṅka (*Padmarājapurāṇam*, 5.62); Govinda Vaidya (*Kaṇṭhīrava-narasarāja-vijayam*, 8.61). Veṅkaṭamakhin (*Caturdaṇḍīprakāśikā*, 8.2-4) accords theoretical recognition of such usage.

1d. gāna: Paṇḍarīka Viṭṭhala thus synonymises *gīta* with *gāna*. But SR (4.1) takes *gīta* to be of two kinds: *gāndharva* and *gāna*. *Gāndharva* is performed by *gandharvas* (only), has a tradition which has no beginning, confers spiritual merit unfailingly (SR 4.2). He owes this definition to Bharatamuni (NŚ 28.8, 9):

यत्तु तन्त्रीकृतं प्रोक्तं नानातोद्यसमाश्रयम् ।
गान्धर्वमिति तज्ज्ञेयं स्वरतालपदात्मकम् ॥
अत्यर्थमिष्टं देवानां तथा प्रीतिकरं पुनः ।
गन्धर्वाणां यस्माद् हि तस्माद् गान्धर्वमुच्यते ॥

Abhinavagupta elucidates this passage ably (*Abhinavabhāratī*, comm. on NŚ loc. cit p. 6). He first establishes the syntax thus:

अत्यर्थं, देवानामिष्टं, प्रीतिकरं, गन्धर्वाणां (इदं) यस्माद्, हि, तस्माद् गान्धर्वमच्यते

and then proceeds to explain each term:

यस्मात् = यद् रूपाच्च देवानामीश्वराणामिन्द्रियमनःसंवेदनप्रभृतीनाम्, आतोद्यमानत्वेन व्यवहारेण गच्छता अनेनेति देववाद्यानाम्

अत्यर्थम् = अर्थातिक्रमेण बाह्यशब्दादिविषयोल्लङ्घनेन ..... म्

इष्टम् = इच्छायजनं परसंवित् सङ्गतिलाभलक्षणम्; तथा तेन प्रकारेण प्रतीतेः अपवर्गोचितानन्दस्वभाव-विशेषेणावर्जितमित्यपवर्गफलत्वं दर्शितम् । तथा अतिक्रान्तं धनादिनिरपेक्षं चेदं देवानां यजनं यथा पुराणयोगादिभ्योऽधिका प्रीतिः गान्धर्वात् शङ्करस्येति ।

He collates the definitions of *gāndharva* offered by Dattila and Viśākhila, in support of his contention that '*trividham*' in the following passage from Bharata (NŚ 28.11):

गान्धर्वं त्रिविधं विद्यात् स्वरतालपदात्मकम्

should be construed to mean collective rather than individual; he states (loc. cit. on 28.11, p. 7)

.... न त्वत्र विधाशब्दः प्रकारार्थः, एवं हि सति पृथग् पृथग् गान्धर्वव्यवहारो भवेत् । न चैवं, तथा च विशाखिलाचार्यः– 'स्वरपदतालसमवाये तु गान्धर्व'मिति । आत्मग्रहणे नैषां मिश्रीभावः । ... तदुक्तं दत्तिलाचार्येण— 'पदस्थः स्वरसङ्घातस्तालेन सुमितः' – इति। तेन पदताला यादृशा गान्धर्वेण तादृशा गाने स्वरत एव भूयसा ततोपयोगीति तात्पर्यम् ।

Bharatamuni lists the following in '*gāndharvasaṅgraha*' (NŚ 28.20): *svaras,* two *grāmas, mūrchanās, tānas, sthānas. vṛttis, śuṣka* (pure instrumental music), *sādhāraṇa, varṇas, alaṁkāras, dhātus* (instrumental manual techniques), *śrutis, yatis* (*svaragata-gāndharva* in *vīṇā*); *padagata-gāndharva* includes *vyañjana, svaras, varṇas, sandhis, vibhaktis, nāma, ākhyāta, upasarga, nipāta, taddhita, kṛdanta, chandovidhi,* figures of speech such as *upamā* (simile); *padgata-gāndharva* is again divided into *nibaddha* (set to *tāla*) and *anibaddha* (without *tāla*); *tālagata-gāndharva* consists of *dhruva, āvāpa, niṣkrāma, vikṣepa, praveśa, śamyā, tāla, sannipāta, parivarta, vastu, mātrā, prakaraṇa* (*gītis*), *vidārī, yatis, layas, gītas, avayava, mārga, pādabhāga, pāṇi,* etc. (for explanation of these *gāndharva* terms see Sathyanarayana, R., *Niḥśaṅkahṛdaya,* pp. 28-37). By and large, these are ingredients of what came to be known as *mārga* music later; SR and its commentaries are explicit on this point; Kallinātha (op. cit. pp. 203, 204) says: *gāndharva* is *mārga,* and *gāna, deśī*; *gāndharva* is whatever has been described in the *Svaragata* chapter beginning with the *jātis* and ending with *antarabhāṣā-rāgas* in the *Rāgaviveka chapter* of the SR Siṁhabhūpāla says (op. cit. on loc. cit. p. 208) that *gāndharva* is *jāti, grāma-rāga,* etc. He reads SR as '*śrutyādi*' instead of '*jātyādi*' and therefore exends *gāndharva* to include *śruti, svara (vikṛti), grāma, mūrchanā, tāna* and *sādharaṇa* also.

However, Bharatamuni himself does not appear to differentiate between *gāndharva, gīta* and *gāna* and seems to use them synonymously (NŚ 1.51; 6.47; 29.49; 32.27; 37.2; 37.30) besides using it in the sense of the *svaragata,* etc. forms of *gāndharva* (e.g. ibid., 33.23; 34.3: different reading; 37.65; 37.67).

The term *gāndharva* has two streams of meaning: i. etymological and/or grammatical; ii. acronymic. Hemacandra (*Śabdānuśāsanam,* 7.2.165) derives it from '*gandharva*' in *svārtha, 'aṇ' pratyaya, ādivṛddhi* and *alopa (gandharva/gāndharva,* similar to *prajña→prājña*). He pronounces it as synonymous with *gāna, gīti* and *geya.* Bharata's definition of *gāndharva* and Abhinavagupta's commentary thereon seem to imply this approach (*gām dhārayatīti; gandharvāṇāmidam*). The second approach is made by Nārada (*Nāradaśikṣā,* 1.4.12, and Bhaṭṭa Śobhākara, *Vivaraṇa,* comm. on ibid., loc. cit. p.23): *gā* = *gāna*; *dha* = playing on instruments such as *vīṇā; va* = playing on (percussive) instruments, thus suggesting *pada, svara* and *tāla* forms or subdivisions of *gāndharva.* It may be noted in this connection that an ancient authority Nārada has been named as receiving *gāndharva* from Brahmā and propagating it on earth, e.g. Vyāsa, (*Mahābhārata,* 12.210.21 Bombay edn., 12.203. 19 Poona edn.), Bharatamuni (NŚ 1.8 et. seq., 34.3, 33.23; ibid., loc. cit. 'Bha' reading; Chowkhambā edn. 32, 484). Nandikeśvara (*Abhinayadarpaṇam,* 3-10), Dattila (*Dattilam.* 2), Mataṅga (*Bṛhaddeśī,* pp. 17, 20, 21), (Bāṇabhaṭṭa, *Kādambarī,* p. 168); *South Indian Inscriptions,* (p. 126); Abhinavagupta takes Viśākhila as authority for discussion of *gāndharvaśāstra* (op. cit. on loc. cit. 28.11, p. 7). I have discussed in detail the evolution of the concept of *gāndharva* in literary and epigraphic sources elsewhere (*Bharatanāṭya: A Critical Study.* pp. 37-82, *Bhāratīya-saṅgītadalli-paribhāṣā-prayoga,* pp. 25-55).

Śārṅgadeva gives a *sāmānyalakṣaṇa* for *gīta,* be it *gāndharva* or *gāna*: it is a *rañjakasvarasandarbha,* i.e. aesthetically expressive melodic situation. Pārśvadeva has clearly articulated the various ways in which music may be appealing to different sections of listeners (extr. Siṁhabhūpāla, op. cit. on SR 4.1, p. 209): preceptors - even; scholars— explicit (see comm. on NN 3.2.329c: *vyakta*), women—sweet; others-long, protracted; teachers—high and low note, neither fast nor slow, even in words and *tāla*; the learned–grammatical excellence, explicit in words and *svaras;* the belle-melodious, sweet, erotic, readily intelligibile words; common folk–high pitched, abundant *prayoga* (*gamakālapti*? experimental usages?pragmatic or actual performance oriented usages?), heroes—descriptive of heroic deeds, high and low notes, exuberant, *ārabhatī-vṛtti* (see comm. on NN 3.2.114b); separated lovers—erotic sentiment, words exciting amour, word- and *svara* inflexions evoking *karuṇa-rasa;* libertine or paramour *(viṭa)*–antilogical words, magnified by distorted *svara* postures, jesting, full of *hāsya rasa; yogi*–words of mystic, ultimate, spiritual truth, faulting the pleasures of the mundane world; womenfolk-auspicious, benedictory words, performed in marriages, etc.; devotees of god–propitiatory of gods, influences and effects thereof, generating faith, appealing to the heart; contestants—bereft of excellence in *tāla* or *pāṭa,* dry, odd, hard to understand, difficult to traverse, full of experimental usage.

2c. ālapti varieties, viz. *rāgālapti, ṭhāya, pratigrahaṇikā rūpakālapti, bhañjanī-rūpakālapti, sthāya-bhañjanī* and *rūpakabhañjanī* (*nema*).

2d. puroditā*:* see NN 3.1.129-144.

3d. saṁjñātrayam*:* SR (4.6cd) also agrees that *prabandha, vastu* and *rūpaka* are alternative words for *nibaddha.* However, it deals with *rūpakas* separately under the heading '*rūpakaprabandhāḥ*' (4.361ab pr.) as having distinctive character and five varieties viz. *parivṛtta, padāntara, bhañjanī-saṁśrita, khallottara* and *anusāra* under the classification of *uttama, madhyama* and *adhama* (ibid., 4.361cd-373); however, it omits *vastu* altogether except describing *prabandhas* called *vastu* (4.275, 276), *vastv-elā* (4.130, 131) and *vastu-vadana* (4.289). It employs '*vastu*' in the general sense of *nibaddha* only once (4.310ab). Narahari Cakravarti (*Saṅgītasārasaṅgraha,* 1.153-158, p. 19) defines these three somewhat improbably, on the authority of Harināyaka (*Saṅgītasāra*): *prabandha* is *śuddhagīti,* i.e. songs containing *dhātu, aṅga* and *gamakālapti*; *vastu* has three *dhātus* (probably omitting *melāpaka*) and five *aṅgas*; *vastu* has only two *aṅgas* and two *dhātus*; *rūpaka* has two *dhātus* and two *aṅgas.*

4a. Dhātu is used in two senses; melody-rhythm frame of song, as opposed to *mātu*; also, here, as limb or organ thereof. The first is *sāmānya-dharma* of all songs; the second is *ekadeśa-dharma* of a particular song; cf. *rāga* a term applying to the totality of all *rāgas* and as a term applying to a particular *rāga.* It is derived from the root '*ḍudhāñ*' or '*dhā*', an *ubhayapadi-dhātu* of the third ('*juhotyādi*') class which means 'to bear, hold up, nourish' etc. (*dhāraṇapoṣaṇayoḥ*) and assumes the form '*dhātu*' by the addition of the '*tun*' *pratyaya (Uṇādisūtra* 1.69). It means several things: primitive matter or element (= *mahābhūta*), essential ingredient or humour of the body *vāta, pitta* and *kapha*—an analogy offered in SR (4.10): these hold the body and constitute it, as do the *dhātus* the body of the *prabandha*; it also means the seven fluids or secretions of the body chyle, blood, flesh, fat, bone, marrow and semen; chemical element, verbal stem or root, etc.

4b. avayava and **aṅga** (8c):Both mean organ or limb, component part of a body. But here *dhātu* and *aṅga* mean the elements of the musical—and word structures of song respectively.

4cd-6cd. The names of *dhātus* are *yaugika* (derivable meaning), and quite appropriate; *udgrāha* is derived from *ud+ 'gṛh';* take up, grasp; *melāpaka* is derived from '*melana*', to join (*udgrāha* and *dhruva*). *Dhruva* means constant. It means constancy of occurrence or position, indispensability —in the sense of the central part or kernel of song; it also means constancy in recurrence, in the sense of refrain (e.g. the *pallavi* segment of songs, as in *kṛti* of Karnāṭaka music). Someśvara (*Mānasollāsa,* 4.16.97ab, p. 50) defines *dhruva* with both:

पौनःपुन्याद् ध्रुवत्वाच्च ध्रुवकः परिकीर्तितः ।

Antara means medial or intermediate; it mediates *dhruva* and *ābhoga.* It is called '*upāntara*' in popular usage (Kallinātha, op. cit. on SR 4.314-361, p. 342).

The word *ābhoga* means, among other things, curved, winding, serpent, expanded hood of the cobra capella (used by Varuṇa as his umbrella), circumference and fullness; *ābhoga* is used here in the sense of fullness or completeness (*ābhogaḥ paripūrṇatā*) since the *prabandha* attains to completeness with its use. All *Sanskrit* lexicons are agreed on this meaning (e.g. *Amarakośa* 2. *manuṣyavarga* 137; *Vaijayantī,* 7.1.7, p.180; *Medinī, śabdavarga, ga-trika,* śl. 29, p. 23)

Kṛṣṇadāsa Baḍajena Mahāpātra (*Gītaprakāśa,* 1.4, 5, p.4) observes that the *dhātus melāpaka* and *antara* were not used in the musical practice of his times; thus there were only three *dhātus—udgrāha,* occurring at the beginning of the song, *dhruva,* at the middle and *ābhoga,* at the end. *Ābhoga* always carried the names of the composer and the hero (*nāyaka*) of the song. Indeed, during his time these names were incorporated in the *ālāpa* or *ābhoga* cf. CDP. 9. Narahari Cakarvarti (*Saṅgītasārasaṅgraha,* 1.161, p. 20) corroborates these facts on the authority of Harināyaka (*Saṅgītasāra*) and Paṇḍitamaṇḍalī (*Saṅgītaśiromaṇi*).

It may be recalled that the *dhātus udgrāha, melāpaka, dhruva, antara* and *ābhoga* of *geyaprabandha* had different names in *vādyaprabandhas* in the professional parlance of *bhāṇḍikas,* i.e percussionists, viz. *laharī, yeḍupu, anta, upānta* and *muktāyī* respectively. It is interesting to note here that the *antara* was regarded as auxiliary to *dhruva* (or secondary) and was thus regarded as an appendage of the *dhruva* rather than of *ābhoga.*

7a. sālagasūḍa: Musical compositions were classified into *sūḍa, ālikrama* and *viprakīrṇa. Sūḍa* was further divided into two classes, viz. *śuddha* and *chāyālaga* (*sālaga)* (NN 3.2.45-53). Narahari Cakravarti op. cit. 1.156, p.19) quotes Harināyaka *Śaṅgitasāra* to equate *prabandha* with *śuddhagīta* and *viprakīrṇa* with *saṅkīrṇa* = *kṣudra* (cf. *Gītaprakāśa,* p. 3)

7b. eva: *Antara* is also used in *pañcatāleśvara*, a *prabandha* of *ālikrama* class (NN 3.2.178-182) etc. but this is an exception. Veṅkaṭamakhin defends this (*Caturdaṇḍī-prakāśikā*, 8.133, 134) using an argument from *Pūrvamīmāṁsā-śāstra* (in which he was an eminent authority) viz. *'vacanasāmarthya'* (competency of injunction/ ordnance); he is probably indebted to Kallinātha for this (without acknowledgement) who also invokes the same (*Saṅgītakalānidhi* comm. on SR 4.258-264, p. 309). But Veṅkaṭamakhin invokes further the analogy (*nyāya*) or *niṣādasthapati* from *Pūrvamīmāṁsā* in illustration (loc. cit). I have discussed both argument and analogy elsewhere (Sathyanarayana, *Caturdaṇḍīprakāśikā*, Kannaḍa translation, pp. 89, 90). His purport, based on grammatical construction, is that since the use of *antara* is well established in the practice of *pañcatāleśvara*, the relevant prescriptive rule about its use should be relaxed just enough to accommodate this exceptional use. For a discussion of the elasticity of prescription or proscription in Indian music theory see Sathyanarayana, R., *A Study in Tradition, Modernity and Innovation in Indian Music* (in *Sangeet Natak*, 89-90, Dec. 1988, p. 58).

8b. kvacit-kvacit: Some *prabandhas* have no *melāpaka*, some no *ābhoga* and some have neither; some have both. Therefore some *prabandhas* have (all) four *dhātus* (*udgrāha, melāpaka, dhruva* and *abhōga*); some have three (*udgrāha, melāpaka, dhruva* or *udgrāha, dhruva, ābhoga*) and some have only two (*udgrāha* and *dhruva*). A single *dhātu* cannot generate a *prabandha* (because it is relative). The *sālagasūḍa prabandhas* have no *melāpaka*; so they are *tridhātuka*; but in *maṇṭha* and others, the use of *antara* is optional (SR 4.333b: '*tato vaikalpiko'ntaraḥ*') it is not at all used in *dhruva-prabandha.* So *maṇṭha, pratimaṇṭha* etc. are *caturdhātu* if *anatra* is used and *tridhātus,* if not used (Kallinātha, op. cit. on SR 4.314-361, pp. 340, 341). Since *melāpaka* and *antara* were absent according to Mahāpātra, Narahari Cakravarti, etc. the foregoing is modified suitably for the *prabandhas* described by them.

9-10ab. cf. SR 4.14, 15.

10c. Tena is the instrumental case of '*tat*' which denotes Brahman (*Bhagavad-gītā,* 17.23):

ॐ तत्सदिति निर्देशो ब्रह्मणस्त्रिविधः स्मृतः ।

Therefore sound is of the nature of auspiciousness; repetition is indicative of emphasis and abundance. *Tenaka* is a modification of *tena* in the *bhāṇḍīra* language according to Veṅkaṭamakhin (op. cit. 8.14). SR (4.17c) has:

ॐ तत्सदिति निर्देशात् तत्त्वमस्यादिवाक्यतः ।

11a. Pada is word, i.e. a semantic unit in a sentence. This arises out of a relation between *kriyā* (verb) and *kāraka* (case endings of a nominal or pronomial term, both of which confer on the word its different relations of meaning, cf. Veṅkaṭamakhin, op. cit. 8.12). According to some authorities, e.g. Dāmodara, says

Narahari Cakravarti (op. cit.1.169 pr.), *pada* has no separate status of *aṅga* since its functions are carried out by *biruda* and is replaced by *gamaka.* However, both Catura Dāmodara (*Saṅgītadarpaṇam,* 4.363) and of Śubhaṅkara (*Saṅgītadāmodara,* 2, p. 17) do give *pada* as *aṅga* of *prabandha.* Mahāpātra (*Gītaprakāśa,* 1.6 pr. p. 4) mentions only four, viz. *vākya, svara, pāṭa* and *tenaka* as *aṅgas,* among which *vākya* includes *pada* and *biruda.*

11c. biruda, often *viruda.* Pārśvadeva explains it as *viru + da; viru = viruddha,* a meaning well known in Mahārāṣṭra (probably not the modern Mahārāṣṭra, but a region covered by Karnataka and Kuntala); it gives ('*da*') enmity or opposition to others and is therefore so called; it is in the *vīra* (heroic) *rasa* and generates anxiety, worry (and antagonism) in enemies (*Saṅgītasamayasāra,* 4.17cd-19ab, p. 25). Actually, *biruda* is a panegyric adjective expressing *vīra rasa.* It is distinguished from *pada* in that the *pada* is composed in a different *rasa* (Pārśvadeva, op. cit. loc. cit.); or *pada* comprises all words other than *biruda* (SR 4.16d: *tato'nyad vācakaṃ padam*).

11d. Tāla refers to the totality of *mārga, deśī, yugma, ayugma, khaṇḍa, miśra, saṅkīrṇa, parivartana, prakaraṇa, bhaṅga, upabhaṅga, vibhaṅga, mālā, saṅkara, urupu, marma, bandha, līlā, gaṇa, sulādi,* etc. *tālas.*

12a. svara: sa, ri, ga etc. executed by uttering the same symbols at their respective pitch values e.g. *ciṭṭesvara, ettugaḍe-svara, kalpanā-svara* in Karnāṭaka music; *jātisvara, varṇa-tillāna, śabda, daru,* etc. in *bharatanāṭya* when they contain such passages; *sargam* in Hindustani music.

12b. yathāyogya: according to lakṣaṇa of the respective *prabandha.*

12cd-13. SR 4.19-21. Pārśvadeva (op. cit. 4.21 pr. p. 25) offers alternative names for these *jātis* which are also numerograms: *campū* (2: *gadya, padya*) = 2 *aṅgas*; *kavitā* (3: *śakti, vyutpatti, abhyāsa*) = 3 *aṅgas*; *senā* (4: *hasti, aśva, ratha, padāti*) = 4 *aṅgas, nīti* (5: *bheda, parīkṣā, viśvāsa, vacana, mitrakārya*) = 5 *aṅgas*; *śruti* (6: *śikṣā, jyotiṣa, nirukta, nighaṇṭu, chandas, vyākaraṇa*) = 6 *aṅgas* equivalent to *tārāvalī, bhāvanī, dīpanī, ānandinī* and *medinī* respectively. He has borrowed this from Jagadekamalla (*Saṅgītacūḍāmaṇi,* Ms. copy in Sri Varalakshmi Academy, Mysore).

Mahāpātra questions the existence of *tāravalī jāti prabandha*; for according to modern practitioners, he says, *vākya* comprehends *pada* and *biruda* (*pada* is *sup-tiṅ-antam*; *biruda* is *guṇakīrtanam*; only *vākya* comprehending both is acceptable as *aṅga*; *tāla* is not counted as a separate *aṅga* (in *nibaddha-prabandhas*). So a *dīpanī prabandha* of previous authorities is reduced to *tārāvalī* as reckoned by modern practitioners. When such is the case, how can the *sālagasūḍa* (which according to previous authorities e.g. Śārṅgadeva has only two *aṅgas,* viz. *pada* and *tāla,* is now reducible only to *vākya* as a single *aṅga* since *tāla* is not a separate *aṅga* in a *nibaddha prabandha* be regarded as *prabandha* at all? A *prabandha* cannot be formed with only one *aṅga.* For, a *sālagasūḍa-prabandha* is described thus

ताला नवादिका यत्र पाटादि रहिता यदि ।
सूडप्रबन्धः कथितः एकरागनिवेशितः ॥

So, it is barred from the use of *pāṭa*, *tena* and *svara* and is thus reduced to a single *aṅga*, viz. *vākya*. Hence it is called *prabandha* only by *vacanasāmarthya*, even though according to previous authorities it is a *tryaṅga-prabandha* (*pada*, *biruda*, *tāla*). In the opinion of modern practitioners, only a *prabandha* which is composed with *ālāpa* (*gamaka*) also is fit to be called *prabandha*; since all *prabandhas* necessarily contain *pada*, *biruda* and *tāla*, no *tārāvalī-jati-prabandha* is possible.

13c. Bhāvanī is called *pāvanī* or *pāvinī* in Orissan treatises on music such as *Gītaprakāśa*, *Saṅgītasāra* and *Saṅgītasārasaṅgraha*.

14a. niryukta: prescribed to or restricted to the exclusive use of specific *rāga*, *tāla*, *chandas*, *bhāṣā*, *rasa*, etc.

15a. anuktachandaḥ: Some *prabandhas* such as *āryā*, *toṭaka*, *kalahaṁsa*, *krauñcapada*, *dvipatha* are restricted to a namesake metrical structure. These are exempt from the rule prescribing specific *gaṇas* or syllables at the beginning, middle or conclusion of the *udgrāha*, etc. *dhātus*. But in *prabandhas* in which the metre is left to the choice of the composer or there is no metre, rules are framed insisting on the use of certain *varṇas* (syllables) and *gaṇas* (syllable clusters) for the accrual of invisible merits and fruits and on their avoidance to ward off undesirable effects on the patron.

16-17. cf SR 4.58, 59; where only *ga* (*guru*) is mentioned (e.g. *mastrigo*) the other two syllables are *laghus* and *vice versa*. Thus, using S for *guru* and I for *laghu*, the eight *gaṇas* (borrowed from Sanskrit prosody) may be reprsented as follows: ma SSS, ya ISS, ra SIS, sa IIS, ta SSI, ja ISI, bha SII, na III. These may be condensed into the formula: यमाताराजभानसलग

16b. Kam (neuter) means water, e.g. *Amarakośa* (3.3.249b, p. 346), *Vaijayantī* (8.7.3, p. 215), *Medinī* (*Avyavavarga*, *Vyañjana-varga*, 52a, p. 183).

16c. lānta: *laghu* in the middle; *bhasmakṛt*: elsewhere, the fruit is described as death.

17b. Saurya is adjectival to *ja*, means Sun and not Saturn.

17c. Saumya is adjectival to *bha*, means Moon and not Mercury.

17d. śaṅkaraḥ: The fruit is described as longevity elsewhere.

17. Siṁhabhūpāla (op. cit. on SR 4.58-79, p. 227) gives a parallel verse from an unknown source:

मो भूमिः श्रियमातनोति य जलं पृथ्वीं वह्निर्मृतिम्
सो वायुः परदूरदेशगमनं त व्योम शून्यं फलम् ।
जः सूर्यो रुजमादधाति विपुलां भेन्दुर्यशो निर्मलं
नो नाकः सुखमच्युतं तदखिलं ज्ञेयं प्रयत्नाद् बुधैः ॥

18. These rules appear to be unique to NN.

19-24ab. These details are unique to NN. Its source, if any, is not known. The following are the effects on the patron of the song when pairs of *gaṇas* from among the above eight are employed at the beginning of *udgrāha*, etc.

ma.na-na.ma—auspiciousness; bha.ya-ya.bha—power, strength; ja.ta-ta.ja—disease; ra.sa - sa.ra—destruction; ma.bha-ma.ya-na.bha-na.ya— success; bha.ma-ya.ma-bha.na-ya.na—accomplishment; ma-ra ma-sa na-ra na-sa—injury; ra-ma sa-ma ra-na sa-na—futility; bha-ja bha-ta ya-ja ya-ta—destruction/loss; ja-bha ta-bha ja-ya ta-ya—misfortune; ja-ra ja-sa ta-ra ta-sa—enmity; ra-ja sa-ja ra-ta sa-ta—decay; bha-ra bha-sa ya-ra ya-sa— 'hā' kampa (trembling with fear or sorrow with the exclamation '*hā*!'); ra-bha sa-bha ra-ya sa-ya—family decay.

24c. kecit: e.g. Jagadekamalla, *Saṅgītacūḍāmaṇi* (MS. copy, Sri Varalakshmi Academy, Mysore) SR 4.6.33, etc.

24d. mātrāgaṇa: While *mayarasatajabhana gaṇas* are syllabic triads, cha-pa-ca-ta-da are moraic clusters, taking the following forms; *cha* (six *mātrās*) SSS, pa (five *mātrās*), SSI, *ca* (four *mātrās*) SS, *ta* (three *mātrās*) SI, *da* (two *mātrās*) S; a *mātrā* is here a synonym of *laghu*, with the total duration required to utter the five syllables (short) *ka-ca-ṭa-ta pa*. It is not known who defined these first. All early authorities are agreed, while describing the *elā* that they are of ancient origin and are accepted as *matāntara*.

25c. Arjuna: Early authorities, e.g. Jagadekamalla (op. cit. loc. ci.t), SR (4.102, 103) ascribe these *gaṇas* to Arjuna-synonyms such as Dhanañjaya, Savyasāci while describing *mātrailās*. However, Mataṅga (*Bṛhaddeśī*, 460 p. 149) describes *mātrailās* on the authority of Vallabha (about whom little else is known). Therefore Arjuna must be later than Vallabha. There is a treatise entitled *Arjunabharatam* in MS. Its author, Maḍumbi Narasiṁhācārya flourished in the first quarter of the twentieth century A.D.

26cd. The *trikas*, viz. ma-ya-ra-sa-ta-ja-bha-na are fixed in both number of syllables and moraic quantity. The *mātrā gaṇas* viz. *cha-pa-ca-ta-da* are fixed in moraic quantity but not in number of syllables. These *gaṇas* defined by Arjuna, viz. *rati, kāma* and *bāṇa* are fixed in number of syllables but not in moraic quantity and offer much choice to the poet. These are products of *prastāra* of Vedic prosodial prototypes. The names and composition of these *prastāras*, found in some of the better known authorities, are compiled below from Velankar (*Jayadāman*, pp. 117, 118); the sources used are Bh—Bharatamuni, *Nāṭyaśāstram*, Pp—*Prākṛtapaiṅgalam* of Piṅgalanāga; JK—*Jayakīrti, Chando'nuśāsanam*, H—Hemacandra, *Chando'nuśāsanam*, Vjs—*Vṛttajātisamuccaya* of Virahāṅka, Chm—*Chandomañjarī* of Gaṅgādāsa; Vr—*Vṛttaratnākara* of Kedārabhaṭṭa.

Ratigaṇas are derived from the vedic metrical prototype called *atyuktā* which has two syllables per verse foot, and yields the following four permutations:

i. SS: *kāma* (Pp. 2.3), *nau* (Vjs 5.2), *padma* (JK. 2.4), H (2.7), *strī* (Vr. 3.2)

ii. SI : *jatru* (JK. 2.6), *duḥkha* (H. 2.9), *sāra* (Pp. 2.9)

iii. IS: *mahī* (Pp. 2.8); *sukha* (H. 2.10, JK. 2.5)

iv. II : *puṣpa* (H. 2.8), *madhu* (Pp. 2.5), *vali* (JK. 2.7)

Kāmagaṇas are derived by permutation of the vedic prototype, *madhyā*, which has three syllables per foot and yields the following *trikas*:

i. SSS (*ma-gaṇa*): *tālī* (Pp. 2.11), *nārī* (H. 2.11; Vjs. 5.3; Vr. 3.3), *śyāmāṅgī* (JK. 2.8)

ii. ISS (*ya-gaṇa*): *keśā* (H. 2.12; Vr. 3.4.1), *dhūḥ* (H. 2.12), *dhṛti* (Bh. 32.52) *vana* (JK. 2.9), *śaśi* (Pp. 2.15)

iii. SIS (*ra-gaṇa*): *taḍit* (Bh. 32.50), *priyā* (Pp. 2.13); *mṛgī* (H. 2.13, Vr. 3.4); *sudhī* (JK. 2.10)

iv. IIS (*sa-gaṇa*): *pravara* (JK. 2.11); *madana* (H. 2.14), *rajanī* (Bh. 32.54); *ramaṇa* (Pp. 2.17)

v. SSI (*ta-gaṇa*): *pañcāla* (Pp. 2.19); *senā* (JK. 2.12)

vi. ISI (*ja-gaṇa*): *mṛgendra* (Pp. 2.21); *suvastu* (JK. 2.13)

vii. SII (*bha-gaṇa*):*mandara* (Pp. 2.23); *hṛdya* (JK. 2.14)

viii. III (*na-gaṇa*): *kamala* (Pp. 2.25): *dṛk* (JK. 2.15)

Bāṇagaṇas are derived by permuting the vedic prototype *pratiṣṭhā* which has four syllables per foot and yields the following sixteen forms:

i. ISIS (*ja-gaṇa, guru*): *jayā* (Bh. 32.61; JK. 2.21); *nagāṇitā* (*nagāṇikā*, Pp. 2.31), *lāsinī* (Vr. 3.5.1); *vilāsinī* (H. 2.17)

ii. ISII (*ja-gaṇa, laghu*): *japā* (JK. 2.29)

iii. SSIS (*ta-gaṇa, guru*): *tārā* (JK. 2.20); *somapriyā* (H. 2.22)

iv. SSII (*ta-gaṇa, laghu*): *trapu* (JK. 2.28)

v. IIIS (*na-gaṇa, guru*): *madhu* (JK. 2.23): *mṛgavadhū* (H. 2.19; Vjs. 5.4); *satī* (Chm. 2.4.2)

vi. IIII (*na-gaṇa, laghu*): *dayi* (JK. 2.31)

vii. SIIS (*bha-gaṇa, guru*): *lalitā* (H. 2.16): *sumukhī* (H. 2.16; JK. 2.22; Vr. 3.5.2)

viii. SIII (*bha-gaṇa, laghu*): *jatu* (JK. 2.30)

ix. SSSS (*ma-gaṇa, guru*): *kanyā* (H. 2.15; Vr. 3.5); *gīti* (JK. 2.16); *tīrṇā* (Pp. 2.27)

x. SSSI (*ma-gaṇa, laghu*): *vallī* (JK. 2.24)

xi. ISSS (*ya-gaṇa, guru*): *vrīḍā* (H. 2.20; Vr. 3.5.3); *vṛddhi* (JK. 2.17)

xii. SISS (*ra-gaṇa, guru*): *ṛddhi* (JK. 2.18); *puṣpa* (Bh. 32.57); *samṛddhi* (H. 2.18; Vr. 3.5.4)

xiv. SISI (*ra-gaṇa, laghu*): *dhārī* (Pp. 2.29); *vartma* (JK. 2.26)

xv. IISS (*sa-gaṇa, guru*): *bhramarī* (Bh. 32.59), *sumati*(H. 2.21; JK. 2.19; Vr. 3.5.5)

xvi. IISI (*sa-gaṇa, laghu*): *kadalī* (JK. 2.27)

Paṇḍarīka Viṭṭhala's special injunction 'किन्तु तत्र लपूर्वा ये तेष्वादावधिको लघुः' । (NN. 4.2.27ab) without explaining the relationship of these *gaṇas* with *atyuktā,* etc. has rendered the passage somewhat opaque.

27d. a-ka-ca-ṭa-ta-pa-ya-śa: Sanskrit linguistics accept fortytwo basic sounds: nine vowels (*śaktis*) viz. *a i u ṛ lṛ e ai o au* (and their long as well as prolate forms by extension; this is called *a-varga*); the five *sparṣa* (consonants) viz. gutturals (*ka-varga*), palatals (*ca-varga*), linguals (*ṭa-varga*), dentals (*ta-varga*) and labials (*pa-varga*); *antasthas* (semivowels) viz. *y, r, l, v*; *ūṣmans* (sibilants) viz. *ś ṣ s*, *mahāprāṇa* (sonant aspirate) viz. *h*. These are the eight classes mentioned here. Besides these, there are secondary sounds, e.g. nasals *ṅ, ḥ,* (*anusvāra, visarjanīya*), *jihvāmūlīya* and *upadhmānīya*, as well as *ḷ, ḷh.* Their presiding deities and effects are as follows:

a-varga: Moon, longevity
ka-varga: Mars, fame, brightness
ca-varga: Mercury, illfame
ṭa-varga: Jupiter, auspiciousness
ta-varga: Venus, beauty
pa-varga,: Saturn, illness or disease
ya-varga: Sun, death
śa-varga: Rāhu, void

Ahobala (*Saṅgītapārijāta*) gives the fruits of these as वपु (! आयु)ष्पीडा प्रथा विद्या भाग्यं रोगो मृतिर्भयम् (1.520ab, p. 70) and proceeds to give (ibid., 1.521-527, p. 70) a scheme for tabulating the alphabet and corresponding effects):

अकचटतपयशाः स्थाने षष्ठे च सप्तमे ।
भवेदेकादशस्थाने तेषु दुष्टैर्मृतिः फलम् ॥ ५२१ ॥
जीवनं यदि वाच्यस्य ब्रह्मा वा किं शिवोऽथवा ।
पङ्क्तिषूर्ध्वासु तिर्यक्षु कोष्ठाः स्युर्दशपञ्च च ॥ ५२२ ॥
तिर्यक्कोष्ठेष्वकाराद्या वर्णा लेख्याः क्रमेण तु ।
अधोर्ध्वपङ्क्तिगा वर्णा वायुबीजानि सर्वदा ॥ ५२३ ॥
द्वितीयपङ्क्तिगा वर्णा वह्निबीजानि नित्यशः ।

तृतीयायां स्थिता वर्णा भूमिबीजानि केवलम् ॥ ५२४ ॥
चतुर्थपङ्क्तिगा वर्णा वारिबीजानि सन्ततम् ।
अन्त्यपङ्क्तिस्थिता वर्णाः खबीजानीति संमताः ॥ ५२५ ॥
भ्रमो वायुर्मृतिर्वह्नौ भूमौ लक्ष्मीर्जले सुखम् ।
खबीजे धनहानिश्च वाच्यस्येति फलं भवेत् ॥ ५२६ ॥
स्तुत्याद्यश्लोकगीतादौ प्रयोगगणवर्णयोः ।
फलान्येतानि जायन्ते तस्मादेतद् विचारयेत् ॥ ५२७ ॥

The fifty letters of the Ṣanskrit alphabet are classified, ten each, as *vāyubīja*, *agnibīja*, *bhūmibīja*, *jalabīja* and *gaganabīja* in order (Musanūru Veṅkaṭaśāstri, *Vidyārthikalpataruvu*, p. 60)

31cd-32. cf. Ahobala (op. cit. 1.528-529, p.70)

क्वचिदन्यत्र सम्प्रोक्तान् विशेषांस्तान् ब्रवीम्यहम् ।
नकारो नाशयेल्लक्ष्मीं हकारस्तु हरेद्यशः ।
सकारः सर्वहृत्तस्माद् गीतादौ तं परित्यजेत् ॥

33-39ab. Sadāśiva is venerated as an ancient authority on music and dancing occasionally: Śārṅgadeva (SR 1.1.15: first in the list of ancient authorities; 4.328 on *kandarpa dhruva*); Śāradātanaya (*Bhāvaprakāśnam* 1.16: list of authorities), Divākara (list of authorities, quoted by Jammulamaḍaka (Mādhavaśarma comm. ibid., loc. cit. p. 7); Abhinavagupta extracts (*Abhinavabhāratī* on NŚ 29.112, p. 122) a passage from an ancient authority in which different kinds of *vīṇā* are mentioned on the authority of *Sadāśivāgama.* There is also a work on dancing called *Sadāśivabharata* in MS. But NN is the only source to invoke Sadāśiva as on authority on *varṇaphala,* so far as is known.

33d. dhuri: *dhura* means high position, battle, responsibility, etc.

34a. Khurī means perfume, horse, horseshoe, barber's razor, etc.

35d. ratnam: pearl or any other facial jewel.

36a. tāra: high, silver, pearl, pearl necklace, small copper coin, the syllable '*om*', etc.

36b. Mahāpadaḥ may also be decomposed into *mahā* + *āpadaḥ*: great distress or danger.

36c. Bhāratī also means knowledge of Brahman, the power of Sarasvatī etc.

36d. Mahābhayam may also be decomposed into *mahā* + *abhayam*: absolute freedom from fear.

37a. Bhīti and *bhaya* are derived from the same root *'bhī'* and mean the same: fear, anxiety, danger, disease, etc. Fault of repetition may be avoided in this passage by interpreting these terms differently in terms of these meanings, or better, by translating *mahābhaya* as 'absolute freedom from fear' as indicated above.

38c. chatrisāmya: equal rank with a king: in this case it should read '*chatrīsāmya*'.

41-42. Ahobla (op. cit. 1.529cd-531ab, pp.70-71) has a parallel passage:

उद्ग्राहे भगणश्चैवमन्तरे मतलास्तथा ।
आभोगे हटकीश्चैव नववर्णान् परित्यजेत् ॥
उद्ग्राहे तु दकारश्च मकारश्चान्तरे तथा ।
आभोगे तु न(?)कारश्च तत्र लक्ष्मीः फलं भवेत् ॥

43b. nānyataḥ The foregoing fruits apply only in the case of panegyric to the king, patron or donor, but not in prayer or propitiation of gods.

43cd-53cd. Paṇḍarīka Viṭṭhala describes eleven *prabandhas* such as *candra-prakāśa,* not included in the above list, from contemporary musical practice (NN 3.2.306cd-329ab)

DESCRIPTION OF PRABANDHAS: ŚUDDHA-SŪḌAS

NN describes eighty six *prabandhas*: of these, seventy five are borrowed from SR in exactly the same order and in almost complete agreement. In many places, NN has depended more upon Kallinātha's commentary than on the original SR. Of the remaining eleven, which are described from the musical practice of the times, three are of ancient origin. Notwithstanding these eleven, Paṇḍarīka Viṭṭhala assumes a markedly conservative stance, committed to textual, rather than oral tradition. It is true that most of the *prabandhas* described by him did prevail in his times, though often with bewildering complexity and variability; he has athetised much of such variable or controversial detail in his description, often content with only *sāmānyalakṣaṇa* (e.g. *elā, dheṅkī*). But it is equally true that his great contemporaries Vyāsarāya, Purandaradāsa, Vādirāja and Kanakadāsa were ushering in a renaissance in Karnataka music with a horde of new compositional prototypes of which he must have been aware. After all, this change did not originate during his own lifetime (most of which he spent outside Karnātaka), but was inaugurated nearly a century ago by Śrīpādarāya at Muḷabāgalu, barely a hundred miles from Sātanūru where he was born and spent his youth. Yet he acknowledges these haridāsa saints only obliquely (*kecil-lakṣyaviśāradāḥ*' NN, 3.2.305b and in the *daśāvatāra prabandha* NN 3.2.321cd-322). He ignores these compositional varieties as well as the contributions which these haridāsas were making to already existing forms such as *daṇḍaka, gadya* and *harṣavardhana*; he also ignores the profound changes which they brought about in the *ṣālagasūḍa-prabandhas* to transform them into *sulādis.* He also does not take cognizance of yet another great change which had happened in the realm of *tālas*—the *sulādi-tālas,* of which he makes only a passing mention in the *Tāladhāri-prakaraṇa* of the NN.

An attempt is made in the following pages to study his descriptions of *prabandhas* in a historical perspective. Abbreviations used in this study are

BD— *Bṛhaddeśī* of Mataṅgamuni

AC— *Abhilaṣitārtha-cintāmaṇi* (*Mānasollāsa*) of Someśvara III

JS— *Saṅgītacūḍāmaṇi* of Jagadekamalla (MS. Sri Varalakshmi Academy, Mysore)

SS— *Saṅgītasudhākara* of Haripāladeva

PS— *Saṅgītasamayasāra* of Pārśvadeva

SR— *Saṅgītaratnākara* of Śārṅgadeva and commentaries by Siṁhabhūpāla and Kallinātha.

LS— *Saṅgītasūryodaya* of Lakṣmīnārāyaṇa

RK— *Rasakaumudī* of Śrīkaṇṭha

SD— *Śaṅgītadarpaṇam* of Catura Dāmodara

SP— *Saṅgītapārijāta* of Ahobala

Further abbreviations are U—*udgrāha*, M—*melāpaka*, D—*dhruva*, A—*ābhoga* Ar—*antara*, sv—*svara*, pd—*pada*, tl—*tāla*, tn—*tenaka*, pt—*pāṭa*, bd—*biruda*, n—*niryukta*, an—*aniryukta*, n—an—both *niryukta* and *aniryukta*.

The accent however, is on the comparison with SR especially Kallinātha.

54-76. 1. *Elā*

55a. varṇasāmyam: SR (2.33) has mentioned this as *anuprāsa* explicitly. Kallinātha explains (p. 215) '*varṇasāmyamanuprāsaḥ iti tasya lakṣaṇam*'. *Anuprāsa* is alliteration: proximate recurrence of same or similar sounds e.g. '*kim tayā cintayā kānte nitāntā*'. It has two varieties viz. *grāmya* and *lāṭīya* according to Bhāmaha (*Kāvyālaṁkāra*, 2.5-8). Udbhaṭṭa and later rhetoricians have distinguished another variety viz. *upanāgarikā* in which syllables of the same class (*varga*) recurrently combine with the nasal of the same class. Nāgavarma (*Kāvyāvalokanam*, 133) has named it *madhurā*. *Grāmya anuprāṣa* consists of the recurrence of soft or gentle syllables e.g. सलोलमालालीनालिकुलाकुलगलो बलः ।

In *lāṭānuprāsa* a word or a group of syllables repeat at the beginning of the next word. e.g.

दृष्टिं दृष्टिसुखां धेहि चन्द्रश्चन्द्रमुखोदितः ।

The definition '*varṇasamyāmanuprāsaḥ*' is due to Mammaṭa(*Kāvyaprakāśa*, 9.2-5, pp.136-141): *anu*—in accordance with *rasa* etc., *pra*—excellent, *nyāsa*—disposition of syllables. It is of two kinds—*cheka* and *vṛtti*. *Vṛttyanuprāsa* has three further subvarieties viz. *upanāgarikā*, *paruṣā*, *komalā* or *grāmya*. These are described as the three literary styles *vaidarbhī*, *gauḍī* and *pāñcālī* by Vāmana *et al.* A third kind of *anuprāsa* viz. *lāṭānuprāsa* (mentioned above) is again divisible into five subvarieties: recurrence of several words (*anekapadāvṛtti*), recurrence of a single word (*ekapadāvṛtti*), abiding in the same compound (*ekasamāsagata*), abiding in a different compound (*bhinnasamāsagata*), nominal similarity of sounds abiding in a compound and noncompound (*samāsa-asamāsagata nāmasārūpya*).

54d. ekena dhātunā: Kallinātha's interpretation that the same single section should be sung twice does not seem to be plausible (p. 215).

55a. Prayoga is best translated as means, contrivance, expedient device. It is equated here with *gamakālapti* on the authority of SR (4.360, 361):

आलापो गमकालप्तिरक्षरैर्वर्जिता मता ।
सैव प्रयोगशब्देन शार्ङ्गदेवेन शब्दिता ॥

55d. Pallava seems to be unrelated to *pallavi,* opening segment of many song varieties in Karnātaka music and to the namesake special compositional form therein (see Sathyanarayana, R., *Karnāṭaka-saṅgīta-vāhinī,* pp. 390-413).

56d. pādatrayam. The first foot, possessed of two sections, has two words and three *pallava* words; the second foot also has five (2+3) words similarly. The third foot has a total of six words, but no *pallava* words. Each of these sixteen words is separate and distinct. But the music to which the five words of the first foot are set is repeated exactly for the five words of the second foot and six words of the third foot. The first and second word of foot I and foot II are sung as separate sections, but with the same music (thus the two sections have the same music but different words. After the second word (and second section) and before the first *pallava* word, a *gamakālapti* is inserted; *pallava* words (1) and (2) are each rendered in slow tempo while the third *pallava* word is executed in fast tempo. This may be schematically shown thus:

Pāda			*Pada*			
I	1 section 1	2 section 2	*gamaka*	3 P_1 slow	4 P_2 slow	5 P_3 fast
II	6 section 1	7 section 2	*gamaka*	8 P_1 slow	9 P_2 slow	10 P_3 fast
III	11 section 1	12 section 2	13 medium	14 medium	15 slow	16 slow

The words 1-2, 6-7, 11-12 have the same *dhātu.* The words 3-8, 4-9, 5-10 (i.e. P_1, P_2 and P_3 have the same, corresponding *dhātu.* 13,14,15 are rendered as *gamakālapti.*

57d. pada: This is a single word, the twelfth, called *ucita* (*añcita*?).

58b,d. arka-rudra: There are two views on the distribution of words in the different *dhātus.* According to some, *elā* has no *melāpaka* and is hence a *tridhātuka prabandha.* Here, *udgrāha* (U) consists of the words 1 to 12; *dhruva* (D) of 13, 14, 15 and *ābhoga* (A) of 16. According to others, such as Someśvara (AC) and Somarājadeva (*Saṅgītaratnāvalī*), the *elā* has *melāpaka* in the 12th. Hence *elā* is *caturdhātuka prabandha.*

59a. prabhunāma: SR (4.37) etc. have generalised this as the '*stutya*'-*nāma.* Kallinātha has interpreted this (p. 217) as personal god (*iṣṭadevatā*), king etc. Paṇḍarīka Viṭṭhala seems to restrict the use of the *elā* to human subjects only.

61ab. The *elā* is sung in this sequence: U(M)DAU(M)DAD

61cd. These *tālas* may be recollected here for ready reference: *maṇṭha* ISI (NN 1.178), IIS IIS IIS IIS (SR), IIIISI (SD, RK), IoI (CDP 9.342); *kaṅkāla*: *pūrṇa* ooooSI, *khaṇḍa* ooSS, *sama* SSI, *viṣama* ISS (NN 1.192), SSII (CDP 9. 344); *dvitīya* ooI (NN 1.140); *pratitāla* IIoo (NN 1.193) Ioo (SD, CDP 9.345).

62b. viṣama: Kallinātha (on SR 4.39, p. 218) says that *tālagraha-niryukti* is made only in the case of the *elā*, but not other *śuddha-sūḍa-prabandhas.* Veṅkaṭamakhin, who like Paṇḍarīka Viṭṭhala closely follows. Kallinātha endorses this (CDP 9.345-348) and says that the *graha* may be *anāgata* or *atīta.*

63d. rutaḥ: Collative consensus supports this reading but elsewhere it is uniformly '*ucita*'.

66b. daśaprāṇaḥ: How can there be only ten *prāṇas* while the words are sixteen? Kallinātha (on SR 4.40-52, pp. 219-223) and following him, Veṅkaṭamakhin (CDP 9.350-391) answer this clearly: two or more words possessed of the same *dhātu* have the same *prāṇa* even though they may occur in different *pādas*; they assign the following distribution:

The sixteen words (*pada*) of the *elā* are (1) *kāma,* formed as the first word of the first foot in two sections (2) *manmathavat, prayoga* in the first foot (3) *kānta,* first *pallava* word in the first foot, rendered in slow tempo (4) *jita,* second *pallava* word in the first foot, sung in slow tempo (5) *matta* (called *mitra* in NN) third *pallava* word in first foot, in fast tempo.

(6) *vikāri,* first word in two sections in the second foot (7) *māndhātā,* second word in second foot, rendered as *prayoga* (8) *sumatī,* first *pallava* word in the second foot, sung in slow tempo (9) *śobhī,* second *pallava* word in second foot, rendered in slow tempo (10) *suśobhī,* third *pallava* word in second foot, performed in fast tempo.

(11) *gītaka,* first word in third foot, composed in two sections (12) *Ucita,* (*ruta* or *uruta* in NN) consists of vocative words, rendered as *prayoga,* different in *dhātu* than in (2) and (7); last word of U according to some or M according to Someśvara *et al.* (13) *cirtra* first word of *dhruvadhātu,* sung in middle or medium (*madhya*) tempo (14) *vāsava,* second word of *dhruva,* in *madhya-laya* (15) *mṛdu,* third word of *dhruvakhaṇḍa,* (performed in a different *dhātu*) (13) and (14); (14) and (15) contain the name of the hero or patron. (16) *sucitra, ābhoga* word, containing the composer's signature.

Then ten *prāṇas* are distributed among these sixteen words as follows:

(i) *samāna* - *manmathavat* (2), *māndhātā* (7)
(ii) *madhura* - *kānta* (3), *sumati* (8)
(iii) *sāndra* - *jita* (4), *śobhī* (9)
(iv) *kānta* - *matta* (5), *suśobhī* (10)
(v) *dīpta* - *kāma* (1), *vikārī* (6), *gītaka* (11)
(vi) *samāhita* -*ucita* (*ruta* ? *añcita* ? 12)
(vii) *agrāmya* - *vicitra* (13)
(viii) *sukumāra* - *vāsava* (14)
(ix) *prasanna* - *mṛdu* (15)
(x) *ojasvī* - *sucitra* (16)

66c. nirvarṇa: NN has thus modified '*alpākṣara*' of SR (4.48); this is not consistent with the definition of *samāna-prāṇa*: समानोऽल्पाक्षरध्वानो मधुरः स्वल्पनादया i.e. it has few syllables and modicum of melody; it is applied in the first two *prayogas* which consist of *ālapti* without words (SR 4.360, 361). Veṅkaṭamakhin (CDP 9.366) reconciles this contradiction by saying that *prayoga* should be concluded with a modicum of words.

67a. Madhura has a soupcon of melody and of *mūrchanā* (SR 4.48); *alpamūrchāna* means transforming the *mūrchanā* into *tāna,* i.e. into *ṣāḍava* and *auḍava tānas*; *tānīkaraṇa* consists in uttering the first *svara* of the *mūrchanā*, touching lightly one or more intervening *svaras* and proceeding to the next *svaras*; thus it has *alpanāda* also.

67d. Sāndra prāṇa involves denseness of syllables, thinness of *svara* clusters and the entry of *svaras* into the high register. According to Veṅkaṭamakhin (CDP 9. 372, 374), denseness is accomplished by increasing the *mātrās* (syllables); thinness of *svaras* means smallness of *dhātu*. *Sāndra-prāṇa* should be composed in a pitch higher than in the previous word.

68b. Kānta is briefly defined in SR (4.49) as '*kāntaḥ kāntadhvaniḥ*'; *kānta* means, among other things 'desired, loved, dear, pleasing, agreeable, lovely, beautiful'. Paṇḍarīka Viṭṭhala has made explicit this suggestion of the erotic by saying that the voice becomes coloured (colourful?) and illumined or excited while in the erotic mood.

68d. dīpta: SR (4.50a) is succinct: '*dīptastu dīptanādaḥ*'. *Dīpta* means among other things, 'blazing, flaming, hot, shining, bright, brilliant, splendid, excited, agitated and clear'. NN has interpreted it as high tone in *tāra* register.

69a. Gamakaprauḍha: mature and scholarly *gamakas*—is Paṇḍarīka Viṭṭhala's contribution to the definition of *samāhita.*

69b. Sthāyī is interpreted by Kallinātha as *sthāyī-varṇa* but is probably the *sthāyī-svara* of *rāga* in its *svasthāna-catuṣṭaya-ālapti* (NN 3.1.133, 134).

71a. cakravāla: SR (4.50cd) is content with prescribing recurrence only generally and does not specify *cakravāla-bandha*:

अग्राम्योऽक्षरनादानामावृत्त्या समुदाहृतः ।

Paṇḍarīka Viṭṭhala has followed Kallinātha here (p. 222):

तत्राक्षराणामावृत्तिस्तावत् गीते वाक्यावयवेषु पदेषु यान्यक्षराणि तेषां मध्ये पूर्वपूर्वपदान्तिमयोः द्वयोर्द्वयोस्त्रयाणां चक्रवालरीत्या उत्तरपदादिमत्वेनोच्चारणम् एवं तत्तदक्षरगतानामेव स्वराणामुच्चारणं नादानामावृत्तिः ।

Cakravāla is a *śabdālaṁkāra,* i.e. a figure of speech relating to sound structure; it is a variety of *yamakālaṁkāra* called *muktapadagrasta* (lit. taking up again the liberated word). Bhāmaha (*Kāvyālaṁkāra,* 2.9-20: *ādi, madhyānta, pādābhyāsa, yamakāvalī, samastapāda-yamaka*), Daṇḍin (*Kāvyādarśa,* 3.1-77) Vāmana (*Kāvyālaṁkāra-sūtravṛtti,* 4.1-4) and other authorities describe numerous *yamaka* varieties; but its treatment is elaborate with Bharatamuni (NŚ 16.59-86) who describes ten *yamaka* varieties viz. *pādānta, kāncī, samudga, vikrānta, cakravāla, sandaṣṭa, pādādi, āmreḍita, caturvyasita* and *mālā* as *nāṭakāśraya.* He defines *cakravāla* thus (ibid., 16.73):

पूर्वस्यान्तेन पादस्य परस्यादिर्यदा समः ।
चक्रवच्चक्रवालं तद्विज्ञेयं नामतो यथा ॥

and offers a classic illustration (ibid., 16.74):

शैलास्तथा शत्रुभिराहताहता हताश्च भूयस्त्वनुपुङ्खगैः खगैः ।
खगैश्च सर्वैर्युधि सञ्चिताञ्चिताश्चिताधिरूढा निहतास्तलैस्तलैः ॥

71cd. varṇatānasvarāṇām: SR (4.51) describes this as *varṇanādamūrchanā;* Kallinātha says (p. 223) that *mūrchanās* are modified to give *tānas.*

72a. prasanna: instantaneous communication, even as very dry wood or leaves catch fire in a flash. Kallinātha includes *tāna* and *gamaka* by *upalakṣaṇā* (p. 223).

74cd. anekadhā: SR (4.131) mentions 356 varieties of *elā*; Kallinātha details them as follows (p. 251): *nādāvati* etc. four; modified *(vikṛta)* ninetythree; other *vikṛtailās* fifteen; *mātrailās* twenty; *varṇailās* twentyfour; *deśailās: karnāṭī* forty; *lāṭailās* forty; *gauḍī elās* forty; *āndhrī elās* forty; *drāviḍī elās* forty: total 356. Siṁhabhūpāla arrives at the same number from a different route (pp. 251, 252): *śuddhailās* four; *vikṛtailās* 108;, *mātrailās* twenty; *varṇailās* twentyfour; *mātrailās* twelve; *karnāṭailās* six; other *deśailās* four; total 178; add as many *chandasvatī* varieties: total (178 X 2 = 356).

I have discussed the literary, prosodial and musical aspects of the *elā* in the monograph: *Elā: A Literary and Musical Study* (in print).

BD (431-495, pp. 146-152): *Elā* has five feet of which the first two lack alliteration, the third or fourth and fifth feet have alliteration; every foot has four *gītas;* alliteration employed after singing half of the respective foot, the *elā* contains description of sacrifice, auspiciousness, beauty, valour, courage etc. (of the hero). It is set to *maṭṭa, dvitīya, kaṅkāla* or *prati-tāla.* It incorporates the names of the composer and patron, or according to some, of only the latter; it should be composed with attractive song-qualities (*vide* NN 3.2.330-334), prosodial structures, figures of speech and *rasas* . Its *gaṇailās nādāvatī* , *haṁsāvatī* , *nandāvatī, bhadrāvatī* and five (?) *saṅkarailās, ratilekhā, kāmalekhā, bāṇalekhā* and *candralekhā,* its seven *varṇailās* viz. *madanavatī, śaśilekhā, prabhāvatī, mālatī, hemāvatī, kusumavatī,* and *varṇanibandha,* other seven *varṇailās* viz *ramaṇī, candrikā, lakṣmī, padminī, rañjanī, mālatī* and *mohinī;* five *deśailās* viz. *lāṭa, karnāṭa, gauḍa, āndhra* and *drāviḍa* totalling 28 *elās* (493-495, p. 152) are described.

AC (4.16.99-175, pp. 51-59; 4.16.444-524, pp. 69-79): It has two parts of U each consisting of two words in alliteration followed by *gamaka,* then a word containing the patron's name. Then two words are sung in the third foot, followed by M rendered in *gamaka.* Next is D composed with no restrictions of *gaṇa* etc.; then A is sung with the composer's signature. The song rests on D, sung after A. The *elās* described are (illustrated *elās* are marked *): *nādāvatī**, *haṁsavatī**, *bhadrāvatī**, *ratilekhā**, *kāmalekhā**, *bāṇalekhā**, *candralekhā**, *madanavatī**, *śaśilekhā**, *prabhāvalī**, *lalitā**, *bhogavatī**, *kusumāvatī**, eleven varieties of *varṇamālā elās* viz. *madhukarī, susvarī, kariṇī, surasā, prabhañjinī, kubjinī, vipulā, taḍillatā, viśālā, taralā, kāntimatī**, *mālatī, mālinī (viśālā* is read as *viśākhā,* 522a, p. 79).

JS (pp. 25-39) bases treatment of *elās* on the authority of Śailakanyā (Pārvatī), Mataṅga, Pārtha (Dhanañjaya, Arjuna), Bhoja, Paramardī, Someśvara and contemporary musical practice. The *elā* is called *sūḍa* here for the first time and is an indispensable, integral part of *sūḍaprabandha.* It is composed with many *gītaguṇas,* set to *yati, tāla, laya, rasa* and *alaṁkāra* (figures of speech). It has *padas* followed by *a prayoga* and then *pallava* words, which are not restricted by rules of *gaṇas.* This is the first foot; the second is sung exactly similarly. The third foot is followed by M; all these three feet are regarded as a single entity. Then D is sung with rhyming words containing the patron's name; then A is sung with the composer's name. The song rests on D. This work describes the four *śuddha elās nādāvatī* etc., *mātrailās* such as *ratilekhā,* and varieties *rāmā, manoramā, unnata, ramaṇī śānti, lakṣmī, kāmuki, gaurī, saumyā, rativigrahā, jāṅgalā, vijayā, jayamaṅgalā* etc. etc. Hundreds of *elā* subvarieties are described here; the treatment is the most elaborate of all available sources and is the source for later writers such as Śārṅgadeva.

SS (5.7.101-108ab): *Elā* has many varieties and only *nādāvati* is described. It has three feet in U, words set in rhyme, each foot carrying six *gaṇas*; *prayoga* is performed at the end of the foot. This is followed by *pallava* words which are not restricted with rules of *gaṇa*; the second and third feet are similar. M is sung in the fourth foot; all the first three feet of the *elā* are regarded as a single entity. This is followed up by rendering D which contains the patron's name set in rhyme; then A is sung in *tānas*; the song concludes on D.

PS (4.130cd-134, p. 33): It has two feet, with rhyming words, each foot having six *gaṇas*, and a *prayoga* at the end; then follows *pallava-pada* which is not bound by rules of *gaṇa* and *varṇa*; the second foot (of U) is similar; then the third foot containing M is sung; then is rendered D, with *prāsa*, containing the patron's name. Next, A, containing the composer's name is sung. The song concludes on D, 4 d,2 *aṅgas* (pd.bd); an (4.57, p. 28).

LS (5.37-200, pp. 356-381) describes names and *prāṇas* of *elā padas*, with presiding deities: 1. *padmālaya* (*kāma-dīpta*) 2. *patriṇī* (*manmathavat-samāna*: *gamaka*) 3. *rañjanī (kānta-madhura*—P_1) 4 *sumukhī* (*jita-sāndra*—P_2) 5. *śacī* (*matta-kānta*—P_3) 6. *vareṇyakā (vikārī-dīpta)* 7. *vāyuvegā* (*māndhāṭā-samāna-gamaka*) 8 *vedinī (sumati-madhura*—P_1) 9. *mohinī* (*śobhī-sāndra*—P_2) 10. *jayā* (*suśobhī-kānta*—P_3) 11. *gaurī* (*gīta-dīpta*) 12. *brāhmī* (*ucita-samāhita-prayogabahula*, contains vocative words, M optionally) 13. *mātaṅgī* (*vicitra-agrāmya*—D_1) 14. *caṇḍikā* (*vāsava-sukumāra*—D_2) 15. *vijayā* (*mṛdu-prasanna*—D_3) 16. *cāmuṇḍā* (*sucitra-ojasvin*—A).

Next, *varṇa-gaṇas*, their presiding deities and effects, *varṇavargas* and presiding deities, *mātrā gaṇas* are described. *Śuddha gaṇailās*—*nādāvatī* etc. four, the *vikṛtailās rāma, manoramā, unnatā, śānti, nāgarā, vāsavī, ramaṇiyā, viṣamā, samā, lakṣmī, kaumudī, kamotsavā, nandinī, gaurī, ratidehā, maṅgala, ratimaṅgalā* etc. totalling 108 varieties of *vikṛtailā*; *varṇailās* (12) viz. *madhukarī, susvarā, karaṇī, surasā, prabhañjanī, madanavatī, śaśinī, prabhā, mālatī, lalitā, bhogavatī, kusumavatī, kāntimatī, kumudinī, kalikā, kamalā, vimalā, kālindī, vipulā, vidyullatā, viśālā, saralā, taralā, deśailās* and varieties of *karnāṭailā* (20), giving 356 *elā* varieties in all.

RK (3.41-55, pp. 44, 45): *Elā sāmānyalakṣaṇa* concurs with SR, but is ascribed to Bharata etc. (3.46a); distribution of the sixteen *elā* words among the *dhātus*, their names, presiding deities and *prāṇas* are described.

SD (4.380-393, pp. 67-69) borrows *sāmānyalakṣaṇa* from SR.

SP (1.547, p. 72) first half is U, conclusion is with *druta* (! D), second half is in *vilamba laya*.

77ab-83ab 2. *Karaṇa*

78b. iṣṭasvare: If U is construed as *grahasvara*, it becomes consistent with descriptions of *elā* in parallel treatises; otherwise it would mean that the entire U may be composed in *svaras* of the composer's own choice.

79b. munīśvaraiḥ: This is not Bharatamuni but Mataṅga and Kohala.

79b. karaṇasya: This is *svarakaraṇa*; all early authorities are unanimous in regarding this as *prakṛti* (model) and describing other *karaṇa* varieties in terms of deviations from it; description of *miśrakaraṇa* and *citrakaraṇa* here (NN 3.2.80-83) has followed the same method.

80b. tat karaṇam: Hence *karaṇa* is of eight kinds viz. *svara, pāṭa, bandha, pada, tena, biruda, citra* and *miśra*: *pāṭakaraṇa* is again of two kinds—*kramapāṭakaraṇa* and *vyatyāsapāṭakaraṇa* (depending on the use of *pāṭas* in a predetermined order or in disorder respectively). So the *karaṇas* are actually of nine kinds. In each of these U is in *svaras*; D is composed of *svara, pāṭa, pada* etc.; *pāṭa* means *hastapāṭas*, i.e. sounds generated on percussion instruments by manual techniques. In *kramapāṭakaraṇa* the order is *svara-hastapāṭa*; in *vyatyāsapāṭakaraṇa* this is reversed, i.e. *hastapāṭa-svara*; *bandhakaraṇa* has *pāṭas* of *muraja* in its D. In *citrakaraṇa*, U consists of sv and pt while D consists of pd and pt. The mention of Kohala in this connection may be spurious and calculated to confer acceptability at the hands of undiscerning readers. *Miśrakaraṇa* has a mixture of sv, pt, tn in its D.

Each of the above 9 *karaṇas* has three subvarieties viz. *maṅgalārambha, ānada-vardhana* and *kīrtilaharī*. The differences among them lie in the sequence of the *dhātus* in performing the *karaṇas*; if U_1, U_2 are the first half and second half of U and likewise D_1, D_2 are the first half and second half of D respectively, then *maṅgalārambha* has U-D-A-D-U; *ānandavardhana* has U-D-D_2-A-D-U; *kīrtilaharī* has U-D-U_2-A-D-U (cf. SR.4.132-144; CDP 9.85-106)

The prolific variety and subvariety of *prabandhas* in Indian music is amazing; *elā* alone had 356 varieties, and by their systematic admixture, countless. The *jhombaḍa* alone had as many as 3510 subvarieties etc. (vide Sathyanarayana, R., *Karnāṭaka-saṅgīta-vāhinī*, pp. 353-356). Among the seventy-five major *prabandhas* some had namesake *tālas*; rather, they were named after the *tālas* to which they were restricted e.g. *ḍheṅkī, rāsa, ekatālī, varṇa, hayalīla, gajalīla, haṁsalīla, siṁhalīla, tribhaṅgi*, and among *sālagasūḍas* (later, *sulādis*) *maṇṭha, pratimaṇṭha, niḥsāru, aḍḍatālī, rāsa, ekatālī* etc.; some derived their names from the metre in which the song was prescribed to be composed; e.g. *hayalīlā, krauñcapada, āryā, dvipathaka, kalahaṁsa, toṭaka, jhampaṭa, paddhaḍī*; some others derived their names from the words which occurred at the end of the *prabandha* or recurred at the end of each *caraṇa* (stanza) e.g. *maṅgala, dhavala, ovī, ḍhollarī, dantī.*

BD (6.426, 427, p.146; 506, p. 153) describes *karaṇa* in general (506, p. 153) as set to *karaṇayati tāla*; consisting of pt, tn, sv, bd, pd, tl; the initial mention of pt and tn may imply their initial use, i.e. in U and the remaining sv etc. in D; *bandhakaraṇa* (426, p. 146) is composed in *svaras, muraja-pāṭas*; an additional feature is that it is set to the (namesake) *karaṇa tāla*; it is sung by *gandharvas.* (Does this suggest a *mārga* or *gāndharva* origin for *bandhakaraṇa*?) *Paṭakaraṇa* (427, p. 146) is of two kinds: both contain pt and sv; *kevala pāṭakaraṇa* contains *pāṭas* but not words; *akṣarapāṭakaraṇa* has both.

AC describes only three *karaṇa* varieties viz. *bandha-, pāṭa-* and *tena-*; *bandhakaraṇa* (4.16.89, p. 50) is composed with sv, *muraja-pāṭas* and set to *karaṇa tāla. Pāṭa* (*Pada*?)

karaṇa is sung similarly, with *hastapāṭas,* with sv, and words of Prākṛta replacing pt (4.16.90, 91, p. 50). The *svaras* should be composed *vihita,* i.e. appropriate or of one's own choice. *Svarakaraṇa* is sung in two segments, U and D; U is sung with continuous sv in *āditāla;* patron's name is included in A, at the end of which D is repeated and the song concludes on U (4.16, 431, 432, pp. 68, 69). *Pada(Pāda!) karaṇa* is performed without *hastapāṭas,* but with *svaras* (4.16.434, p. 69).

JS (pp. 25, 26) Seven *karaṇas,* sv, pt, *bandha,* pd (sv-pd?), *citra, tenna* and *miśra* are described separately. Sv-*karaṇa* has two *dhātus,* sung to sv without pause (in both U-D) to *drutaśekharatāla* (*karaṇatāla* is not found used in practice); *graha* is in any desired sv, conclusion is on *aṁśa svara;* A contains name of the patron. The sequence is U-D-A-D-U. It has three varieties viz. *maṅgalābharaṇa, kīrtilaharī* and *ānandavardhana* in which the sequences are as described above. *Pāṭakaraṇa:* sv, pt, two *dhātus; bandhakaraṇa:* sv + *murajapāṭas,* two *dhātus; padakaraṇa* two *dhātus,* sv + pd; *citrakaraṇa:* sv, pt, pd (*murajapāṭas*); *tenakaraṇa:* sv, pt, tn; *miśrakaraṇa:* sv, pt, tn; bd at end; three *dhātus.*

SS, (5.7.85-95) *Svarakaraṇa* is model; it has 2-*dhātus,* sv sung (in both U, D) without pause; it is first (U?) performed in *drutaśekhara-tāla* and then (D?) in *karaṇatāla; graha* is in any desired sv; conclusion is on *aṁśa svara.* A has only patron's name; U is sung twice; D, A, once; D is sung again and conclusion is on U: (2U-D-A-D-U). *Pāṭakaraṇa* has (same) two *dhātus;* sv, *hastapāṭas yatis. Bandha karaṇa:* 2 *dhātus,* sv, *muraja-pāṭas;* sv-pd-*karaṇa:* 2 *dhātus,* sweet sv; *citrakaraṇa:* two *dhātus,* pd, sv, *hastapāṭas* of *muraja; tennakaraṇa:* 2 *dhātus,* sv, tn; *miśrakaraṇa:* two *dhātus,* sv, pt, tn; bd at end.

PS (4.135-152cd. pp. 33, 34) *Svara-karaṇa* is described as in JS; but *karaṇatāla* also is offered as alternative to *drutaśekhara* (in theory?) but not carroborated in practice. A contains, besides the patron's name, the composer's name also. *Maṅgalārambha, kīrtilahari,* and *Ānandavardhana* varieties of *svarakaraṇa* are described. The reading '*pādakaraṇa*' replaces *pāṭakaraṇa* in AC and PS and therefore merits the status of a contender for the name. *Pāda, bandha-, svara-, pada-, citra-, tena-* and *miśrakaraṇa* are described as in JS.

Padakaraṇa: 3d, 3 *aṅgas*—sv tl bd, an: *svarakaraṇa:* 3d, 3*aṅgas*— tl bd sv, an or 3d, four *aṅgas*—tl pt bd sv, an; *pāṭakaraṇa:* 3d, 3*aṅgas*—tl bd pt; an: *tena karaṇa:* 3d, four *aṅgas*—sv tn tl bd, an; *citrakaraṇa:* 3d, four *aṅgas*—sv tn tl bd, an: *bandhakaraṇa:* 3d, 4 *aṅgas*— sv bd tl pt, an; *miśrakaraṇa:* 3d 3*aṅgas*—tn pt sv, an (4.45-51, p. 28).

LS (5.207cd-230ab, pp. 381-384) enumerates nine *karaṇas* by considering *pāṭa-* and *vyatyāsa karaṇas* separately. *Svarakaraṇa* is described to accord with the foregoing; A is composed with words which contain the names of patron and composer; the composition is in *druta māna. Birudakaraṇa* has U of sv, D of bd, A of pd; *graha* etc. are as before. The other *karaṇas* are described to accord with JS, PS etc.

RK (3.56.64, pp. 45, 46) describes eight *karaṇas*, holding *krama-* and *vyatyāsa-karaṇas* as subvarieties of *pāṭakaraṇa*. In *svarakaraṇa*, both U and D are composed of dense *svaras*; A has names of both patron and composer; the *tāla* is *rāsaka*. *Bandhakaraṇa* has *pāṭas* of *mṛdaṅga*; it may be recalled that *mṛdaṅga* and *muraja* were regarded as mutually synonymous since Śārṅgadeva's times (SR 6.102, cf. NN 2.47); the *lakṣaṇa* of *bandhakaraṇa* is apocryphally ascribed to Bharata; *maṅgalārambha, ānandavardhana* and *kīrtilaharī* are described as subvarieties of all nine (!) *karaṇas*, giving a total of twentyseven forms of the *prabandha*.

SD (4.394-403, pp.69-70) holds that *karaṇa* has no *sāmānyalakṣaṇa*! *Svarakaraṇa* is set to *rāsaka tāla* and *druta laya*; the details of all nine *karaṇas* agree with the foregoing.

SP has a lacuna for *karaṇa prabandha*.

CDP of Veṅkaṭamakhin (9.85-106) concurs in all details of all nine *karaṇas* and adds that the essential difference between *citrakaraṇa* and *miśrakaraṇa* is that in the former the components are distinguishably mixed up e.g. rice and gingelly, while in the latter they are inseparably mixed up as milk and water. The *karaṇa* has twentyseven varieties because of *kālabheda*, i.e. difference in number and order of performing U-D-A such as in *maṅgalārambha, ānandavardhana* and *kīrtilaharī*.

83cd-90ab. 3. *Ḍheṅkī*

84b. prayogātmā, i.e. of the nature of *gamakālapti*.

85b. Ḍheṅkī-tāla is described as SIS (NN 1.190);

85c. Kaṅkāla tāla has four forms; *pūrṇa* ooooSI, *khaṇḍa* ooSS, *sama* SSI (acc. CDP 9.344, it is SSII, *viṣama* ISS (NN 1.192)

85d. Anya: any *tāla* other than *ḍheṅkī* and *kaṅkāla;* any *laya* other than *vilamba,* i.e. *madhya* or *druta.*

87b. Sā dheṅkikā: Let U_1-U_1-U_2-M-D-A = X and U_1-U_1-U_2-D-A (i.e. sans M) = Y. Then the order of components in singing *ḍheṅkī* is 2X-A-X-D (first word) or 2Y-A-Y-D (first word).

88a. Viśeṣā-dheṅkī is of four appropriately named kinds: *muktāvalī* (nonmetrical), *vṛttabandhinī* (single *vṛtta*), *yugminī* (two *vṛttas*), *vṛttamālā* (numerous *vṛttas*); the last three have each three varieties: *varṇikā* (composed of *varṇa vṛttas*), *gaṇikā* (composed of *gaṇa vṛttas*) and *mātrikā* (composed of *mātrā vṛttas*); together with *muktāvalī,* these total to ten. Each of these has again three subvarieties viz. *samālaṁkaraṇa* (containing even numbered figures of speech), *viṣamālaṁkaraṇa* (having odd numbered figures of speech) and *citrālaṁkaraṇa* (mixture of both). Therefore *ḍheṅkī* has as many as thirty forms (SR 4.145-152; CDP 9.467-481).

89a. cf. **84d** *supra*: *caturdhātuka* if *melāpaka* is present; *tridhātuka,* if not.

89b. Aniyamatālataḥ seems to imply that if U-M have no *tāla,* D-A also have no *tāla.* There is no reference to this in parallel texts.

89d. cf. **85ab** *supra.*

BD (501cd-502ab, p. 153): Melody set to words is of composer's own choice; it has *ḍheṅkī tāla* or has no *tāla*; thus the composition acquired *kaṅkāla-tāla* later.

AC (4.16.547b, p. 81) mentions *ḍheṅkī;* but the text suffers a lacuna for description.

JS (p. 39): It is called *ṭheṅkī* because its U and M are set to *ṭheṅkī tāla*; the sequence of *aṅgas* is as described in SR. Its conclusion is in 2 measures of the *ṭheṅkī tāla. Muktāvalī, vṛttamālā, vṛttabandhinī* and *yugminī* varieties are given, but the subvarieties, *samālaṁkaraṇa* etc. are restricted to *muktāvalī;* the *vṛttas* are classified into *gaṇikā, varṇikā* and *mātrikā.* The *ḍheṅkikā-lakṣaṇa* is ascribed to Mataṅga Muni. *Graha* is *sama* or *viṣama* in *ḍheṅkī tāla.*

SS (5.7.108cd-111ab): U_1-U_1-M-U_2 sung twice in *sama-viṣama-graha* of *dheṅkī tāla;* similarly D_1-D_2-A-D_2 is sung once.

PS (4.95cd-100, p. 30) agrees fully with JS; D has three segments; the first two have words of alliteration, different in *mātu* but same in *dhātu*; the third is different in both *mātu* and *dhātu*; D is executed in a different *tāla* and *laya*; sequence of *aṅgas* is as above; conclusion is in the measure of U. The composition has 4d, two *aṅgas* viz. pd-tl, n-an or 4d, 2 *aṅgas*—pd bd, n-an (4. 57, p. 28).

LS (5.230-241, pp. 384-386): All details of thirty *ḍheṅkī* varieties are same as above; U-M in *ḍheṅkī-tāla* or *kaṅkāla-tāla* or neither; only U-M is in *vilambita-laya*; third D-segment is sung once in high, strong, intense pitch. The four varieties *muktāvalī* etc. and the subvarieties *varṇikā, gaṇikā* and *mātrikā* are as before giving a total of thirty *ḍheṅkī* forms.

RK (3.65cd-69, p.46): Only *ḍheṅkī sāmānyalakṣaṇa* is given, attributed to Bharata etc. apocryphally, but its varieties are not described. Sequence of rendering *aṅgas* is as before.

SD (4.404-408, pp.70-71) describes *sāmānyalakṣaṇa* as before and ascribes thirty forms to '*granthāntara*'.

SP (1.548, p. 72) is brief and incomplete; merely gives sequence U_1-U_1-U_2 and stops.

90cd-94 4. *Vartanī and Vivartinī*

90cd-92ab. Vartanī is sung in this sequence: U-U-D-A-D (first word).

92cd. For *kaṅkāla* and *prati tāla* see commentary on NN 3.2.61cd; *pratimaṇṭha* is III (NN 1.151; but IIS or SII according to SR and SD); *kuḍukkā* is the same as *aḍḍatāla* ooII (NN 1.140). *Vartanī* may be performed in any *deśi tāla* other than *rāsa*; but *vivartinī* is restricted to one of *kaṅkāla, pratitāla, pratimaṇṭha* and *kuḍukka.*

93d. Ādi includes restriction of *laya.*

94d. Both *vartanī* and *vivartinī* are of *bhāvanī jāti, three-dhātu-prabandhas* (cf. SR 4.152-154; CDP 9.60)

BD (429cd-431ab, p. 146) prescribes a *graha* (?); conclusion is on *aṁśa svara* of the *rāga*; contains name of patron and composer (in A?) sung in *svaras* to any *tāla* other than *kaṅkāla, pratitāla, drutamaṇṭha* and *kuḍukka*.

AC has no description.

JS (pp. 25, 26): *Vartanī*, fashioned after *svarakaraṇa* has the sequence 2U-D-A-D and avoids *prati tāla, dhruva, maṭṭa, kaṅkāla* and *kuḍukka*, and *vivartinī* is composed in only one of these *tālas*. In both, there is at first an *ālāpa* without *tāla*.

SS (5.7.95cd-101a): *Vartanī* commences with an *ālāpa* in *svaras* without *tāla*; then follows the sequence 2U-D-A-D and is composed in any *tāla* other than *pratitāla, dhruva, maṇṭha, kaṅkāla* and *kuḍukka*; the main difference from *karaṇa* is that *vartanī* is set in *vilambita laya* while the *karaṇa* is in *druta laya*. *Vivartinī* also avoids the five *tālas pratitāla* etc. (?) and has a *svara-ālāpa* without *tāla* at the beginning.

PS (4.152cd-15ab, p. 35): The sequence of *aṅgas*, avoidance of *tālas* and the difference from *karaṇa prabandha* are as above. *Vivartinī* is sung to one of these five *tālas*. Both begin with a *svarālāpa* sans *tāla*. *Vartanī*: 2d, 3 *aṅgas* viz. sv pt tn, an or 3d, four *aṅgas*— sv bd pd tl, an (4.31, 50, pp. 27, 28) *Vivartinī*: 3d, four *aṅgas*-sv-pd pd tl; an (4.50, p. 28).

LS (5.242-245ab, pp. 386, 387): U-D in sv. A in pd; performed in *kaṅkāla, pratitāla kuḍukka* or *pratimaṇṭha* (?) in *vilambita-laya*; sequence: 2U-D-A-D. *Vivartinī* is not described, but is probably mixed up with *vartanī*. cf. *tāla* prescription.

RK (3.73-76, p. 47): Similar to *svarakaraṇa*, in a *tāla* other than *rāsa*, in *vilambita laya*; sequence is 2U-D-A-D; *vivartinī* is sung in *kaṅkāla, maṇṭha* etc. *tāla*.

SD (4.409-411, p. 71) *vartanī* and *vivartinī* as in SR.

SP (1.549ab, p. 72). *Svaras* are sung in this song.

95-99 5. *Jhombaḍa*

97-98a. Pratitāla, kuḍukka and **pratimaṇṭha** are shown above; *niḥsāru* = *haṁsalīla* ıı́ (NN 1.190), *tripuṭa* oıı (ibid., 1.181), *dvitīya* oıı (ibid., 1.140), *yatilagna* (=*rūpaka*) oı (ibid., 1.152), *gārugi* oooó (ibid., 1.161), *rāsa*= *ādi* ı (ibid., 1.138), *ekatālī* o (ibid 1.150), SR prescribes *maṇṭha tāla* also from an alternative school (4.158) but rejects it because it is not found in the practice of this song.

98c. Bahavo bhedāḥ: SR (4.155-168) counts as many as 3510 forms of *jhombaḍa* thus: *tāraja* with melodic movement in *tāra* register; *atāraja*, without such movement; *tāraja jhombaḍa* has four varieties: U, M, D or A is in *tāra* register. Among these are four of four *dhātus*, three of three *dhātus* (without *melāpaka*); in *atāraja jhombaḍa* there is one of four *dhātus*, one of three *dhātus* thus giving 9 in all. Each of these has two forms: *prabhūtagamaka* (abundant use of *gamaka*, i.e. tonal curvature) and *stoka-gamaka* (modicum of *gamaka*) thus resulting in eighteen *jhombaḍas*; each of these has five forms again: *prāyogika* (?) (is composed in a metre of four *gaṇas* per verse foot), *kramākhya* (in a metre of five *gaṇas* per verse foot), *kramavilāsa* (six *gaṇas* per verse foot), *citra* (seven *gaṇas*) and *vicitralīlā* (eight *gaṇas*); so 90 *jhombaḍas* are got. Each of the 90 *jhombaḍas* forms thirteen varieties according to the figure of speech and *rasa* as follows:

i. Brahmā—*upamā, rūpaka, śleṣā* ii. Viṣṇu—*vīra rasa, vilāsa* iii. Cakreśvara—*vīra* iv. Caṇḍikeśvara—*bībhatsa* v. Narasiṁha—*adbhuta* vi. Bhairava— *bhayānaka* vii. Haṁsa—*hāsya, śṛṅgāra* viii. Siṁha—*vīra, bhayānaka* ix. sāraṅga—*vipralambha* x. Śekhara—*karuṇa* xi. Puṣpasāra—*śṛṅgāra* xii. Pracaṇḍa—*raudra* xiii. Nandīśa—*śānta.* This gives 90 × 13 = 1170 forms of *jhombaḍa.* Each one of them again, is of three kinds—*gadyaja, padyaja* and *gadya-padyaja.* So the total is 3510. An example is *tāraja-caturdhātuka-dhruva-stokagamaka-kramavilāsa-sāraṅga-padyaja jhombaḍa*: its melody lies in the *tāra* register; it has four *dhātus*; of these D ocurs in *tāra* register; a modicum of *gamakas* is employed in it; it is composed in a metre with six *gaṇas* per foot; its theme is *vipralambha-śṛṅgāra.*

99d. dvyaṅga: pd tl.

BD (495-498, pp. 152,153) has an opaque text; there are four feet; first half is sung twice followed by the second half; each half has rhyming (alliterative?) words; this is true of all *pādas*; it is set to any *deśī tāla* other than *kaṅkāla*; it is decorated with *tānas* and figures of speech.

AC (4.16.77-79, p. 49; 535-538, p. 80): the first passage contains only the mention of *jhombaḍa,* set in *dohaka* metre; which is implausible; in the second passage, the sequence of *aṅgas* is (UUDDAD). It may be set to any *tāla* other than *madra* (*maṭṭha*), ***kaṅkāla***, and ***prati tāla***; it is of six varieties because of the use of *gārugi, dvitīya, niḥsāru,* ***ekatālī.***

JS (pp. 40-44) is the source for PS, SR etc. The seeds of evolution—fatal proliferation—are found here. Its *sāmanyalakṣaṇa* prescribes the sequence $U_1 U_1 U_2$ M (±) DDAD where M± indicates *melāpaka* with *gamakas,* optionally employed. According to some, a component called *'bhāga'* (this consists of the *udgrāha* of the original song composed in different or other words so as to complete the intended meaning); *gamaka* occurs in the *jhombaḍa* sometimes in abundance (*prabhūta-gamaka*) and sometimes scarce (*alpagamaka*) even as the shadow of a body sometimes increases and sometimes decreases.

Jhombaḍa is of two classes viz. *tāraja* (in *tāra sthayī*) and *atāraja* (not in *tāra sthāyī*); *tāraja* is again of two kinds, *duṣkara* and *sukara. Duṣkara* has four subvarieties called *pratāpatilaka, pratapasaṅgama, acalapratāpa* and *pratāpavardhana,* depending on the occurrence of U, M, D or A in the *tārasthāna* respectively; these are obviously composed by, or dedicated to Jagadekamalla (whose original name is not known, but who is invariably called Pratāpapṛthvībhuja in his inscriptions).

Next, the *jhombaḍa-prabandha* (*atāraja*) is of three kinds—*prabhūta gamaka, alpagamaka* and *tridhātuka*; the first is called *duṣkara-atāraja.* The first two are appropri-ately named; *tridhātuka* has copious, facile *gamakas* but omits *melāpaka*; the *sukara-atāraja* is of two kinds again—*tridhātuka* and *alpagamaka.* All these seven forms of *jhombaḍa* are required to be composed in *gārugi tāla*; these seven may also be set to *dvitīya tāla*.

There are four other forms of *duṣkara* viz. *udyatpratāpa*, *pratāpayoga*, *sthirapratāpa* and *pratāpaśekhara* (created by or for Jagadekamalla) in which UMD and A are situated in what is called *sthānaka* respectively (this is *tārasthāna*). These are again divided into the three *prabhūta-gamaka* etc. as well as *duṣkara* and *sukara*. Again, the name of the *jhombaḍa* varies with the *tāla* employed; there are three more varieties of *jhombaḍa; gadyaja* is composed in prose words of Sanskrit or regional language, with alliteration; *padyaja* is composed in any metrical form; *gadyapadyaja* contains both prose and verse. The *prabhūta-gamaka-jhombaḍa* varieties are set in *laghuśekhara tāla* while the *alpa- gamaka* varieties are set in *maṭṭa*, *niḥsāru*, *caṇḍaniḥsāru* or *caṇḍatṛtīya*. Those composed in *laghuśekhara* or *kuḍukka tāla* have an A without words (as a special case). Thus there are eighteen *jhombaḍas*.

PS (4.101-130ab, pp. 31-33) copies JS completely: 3d, 2 *aṅgas*—pd tl; n-an, (p. 27).

SS (5.7.114d-116ab, p. 222) describes *jhombaḍa* on the model of *dhvanikuṭṭanī;* a *bhāga* is to be sung as in *dhvanikuṭṭanī;* U has the other words (as befits *bhāga*); it has *gamaka* (*prayoga*) and (*anu-?*) *prāsa* as well as a metrical structure.

LS (5.245cd-268ab, pp. 387-390) follows SR closely.

RK (4.73-76, p. 47) mentions the sequence U_1 U_1 U_2 M (±, *prayoga*) DDAD; ascribed to the *Munis*, the song is set to any one of the ten *tālas* viz. *niḥsāru*, *gārugi*, *rāsa*, *kuḍukka*, *pratimanṭha*, *tripuṭa*, *aḍḍa*, *yatilagna*, *divitīya*, *ekatāli*, as required in the SR (4.156cd-157); its 3510 varieties are mentioned.

SD (4.412-415 ab, pp. 71, 72) mentions the *aṅga* sequence and the ten *tālas* as above; gives the total number as 3510.

SP (1.549cd) U is in *pañcama* and *dhruva* in *ṣaḍja*!

100-102ab 6. *Lambhaka*

100b. vā: So *lambhaka* is of two kinds.

100d. dhruvapratinidhau: If the *lambhaka* has D, U is sung once; if D is absent then U is sung again, in its place.

101a. dvir-ābhogo: SR describes this differently (4.169) यत्र ध्रुवो द्विर्वाभोगो ध्रुवे मुक्तिः । The *vikalpa* (disjunctive) '*vā*' here is interpreted differently: Siṁhabhūpāla. (p. 266) explains this as 'D is to be sung once or twice; so also A'. Kallinātha. (p. 264) places another construction: D is sung twice; A may or may not occur. It is not known whether such differences are due to divergence in practice or merely exercises in literary exegesis. SR has abbreviated the description at the cost of clarity; as usual, Siṁhabhūpāla is content with a syntactical rearrangement; Kallinātha is quite elaborate. So later authorities such as Paṇḍarīka Viṭṭhala and Veṅkaṭamakhin borrow from Kallinātha, rather than from Śārṅgadeva. For example, while describing the *lambhaka* variety called *vilambha*, SR says (4.174): उद्ग्राहा बहवो यस्मिन्। Kallinātha exapands this as follows:

तेन ध्रुवस्थान उद्ग्राह एवं तत् प्रतिनिधित्वेन प्रयुक्त इति नैकधातुत्वम् । (loc. cit.)

Unaware of this, Paṇḍarīka Viṭṭhala amalgamates this as *lambhaka sāmānyalakṣaṇa: 'dhruvapratinidhau tataḥ'*.

101b. sa lambhaḥ: Paṇḍarīka Viṭṭhala has athetised the text considerably here, omitting the alternative descritpion/characterisation of *lambha* as also its varieties. These are furnished here from SR (4.170-174) for the sake of completeness. According to the alternative view (*matāntara*), both U and D_2 have the same *dhātu* in both *jhombaḍa* and *lambhaka*. The sequence of *lambha* are: i. *Alāpalambha*: U has no *tāla*, ii. *Pralambha*: in the absence of D, U is sung again with the same words but different *dhātu*. iii. *Bhāgalambha:* components of different *lambha* varieties are put together. iv. *Lambhapada*—After U of different *dhātus* (and *mātus*?) D (of the same constant *dhātu* and *mātu*) is repeated 3, 4 or 5 times. v. *Anulambha* is the reverse of this; i.e. *dhruva* of variable *dhātu* and *mātu* is executed 3, 4 or 5 times after U of constant *dhātu* and *mātu*. vi. *Upalambha: dhātu* and *mātu* of both U and D are varied (and sung repeatedly). *Lambha, anulambha* and *upalambha* omit A. vii. *Vilambha* has no D or A; U of a constant *dhātu* is sung again and again with different words in place of D.

BD has no description of *lambhaka*.

AC (4.16.539-546, pp. 80, 81): U and D are composed of one verse foot each. Sequence is 2U-2D-A: (contains patron's name)—D (repeated many times); *vilambha*-U (1 foot)—D (1 foot)-A; *pratilambha*-U (different *tāla*, 1 foot)—D (with *tāla*); *bhāgalambha*-U is sung again with different words in *dhātu* of the first half.

In *lambhaka* the U-variety called *bhāga* is invariably the second component; in *jhombaḍa* it is performed optionally to represent *dhruva*.

SS (5.7.116cd-118ab, pp. 222-223): One or two words (feet?) are sung with a little *gamaka*; sequence is U-2D-A-D.

JS (p. 44): U has one or two words (or feet) with a little *gamaka*: U-2D-A-D; it is decorated with two or three *bhāgas*. It has two varieties viz. *vilambha* and *upalambha*; in *vilambha* U is *ālāpa*; D, A are set in *tāla*, conclusion is on D; *upalambha* has U and/or D repeated several times with different words but same *dhātu;* it has no A.

PS. (4.180cd-185ab, p. 37) borrows from JS; 3d, two *aṅgas*—pd tl; an (4.40, p. 27)

LS (5.268cd-276ab, pp. 390, 391) describes sequence as U-2D-A-D, and the varieties *ālāpa, pra-, bhāga-, anu-, upa, vipra-* and *pada lambhas* as in SR (4.170-174).

RK (3.77, p. 47) 2U-2D-2A-D (U: one or two feet)
SD (4.415, p. 72) 2U-2D-2A-D (U: one or two feet)
SP (1.551, p. 72) U-2D-2A-D (U: one or two feet), *vilambita laya*.

102cd-103 7. *Rāsaka*

102d. gamaka-sthānake vinā: NN has athetised *rāsaka-lakṣaṇa* to a great extent. *Rāsaka* is modelled on the *jhombaḍa prabandha* but with an important difference; *jhombaḍa* is characterised with the following: copiousness or modicum of *gamakas*, occurrence or absence of movement in *tārasthāna*, occurrence or absence of M, application of specific *rasa* and figures of speech etc. *Rāsaka* has none of these. Therefore, it is only of three kinds depending on the dispensation of *gaṇa, varṇa* or *mātrā* in each verse foot. (It may be recalled that in *jhombaḍa* there is only *gaṇa*-structuring and that its varieties arising out of *varṇa*- and *mātrā* structuring of the verse foot are ignored because of their obsolescence.) Thus *rāsaka-prabandha* has the following varieties by possessing *mātrā gaṇas* in the verse foot thus: i. *rāsavalaya: cha-gaṇa* ii. *haṁsatilaka: pa-gaṇa* iii. *ratiraṅgaka: ca-gaṇa* iv. *madanāvatāra: ta-gaṇa*. Secondly *varṇarāsaka* has twentyfive subvarieties in respect of the verse foot possessing 6,7, 8, 9......... 29 or 30 syllables. Thirdly, in *mātrā rāsaka*, there are fiftythree subvarieties in respect of the verse foot populated by 8, 9, 10, 11, 12 ... 59, 60 *mātrās*. So the *rāsaka* has altogether eightytwo forms; but *varṇa*-and *mātrā-rāsakas* had lost the sanction of currency, so that only the four varieties *rāsavalaya, haṁsatilaka, ratiraṅgaka* and *madanāvatāra* were known even to the encyclopeadic Śārṅgadeva.

BD has no description.

AC (4.16.547, p. 81) only mentions *rāsaka* among *sūḍa prabandhas* but does not describe it.

SS (5.7.112cd-119, p. 223): *Rāsaka* is composed in *āditāla* (= *rāsatāla*, NN 1.138b) without *gamakas;* the rest is as in *jhompaḍa prabandha*.

JS (p. 44) composed in *ādi (=rāsaka) tāla* without *gamakas*; it follows *jhombaḍa* (*krombaḍa*) in other details; it is of three kinds because of application of *varṇa, gaṇa* and *mātrā* like *lambhaka;* but these are not found in current practice; some prescribe *ālāpa* in its U while others describe the *rāsaka* U with words in one foot.

PS (4.185cd-188ab, p. 37) borrows literally from JS; 3d; two *aṅgas*—pd tl; n-an, p. 27; or 4d; two *aṅgas*—pd bd, n-an (4.57, p. 28)

LS (5.276cd-282, pp. 391, 392) closely follows SR.

RK (3.78, p. 47) *Rāsa* is like *jhombaḍa* without *gamaka* and *sthāna* variation but with *rāsa-tāla*; it has numerous varieties.

SD (4.416, p. 72) same is in RK; there are fiftythree *mātrikā-rāsas* and twentyfive *varṇaja-rāsas.*

SP (1.552ab, p.72): *jhombaḍa* performed in *rasa tāla is rāsa prabandha* (!)

104-106 8. *Ekatālī*

104c. nyāso: cf SR 4.180-181: Siṁhabhūpāla reads '*nyāso yatra*' as '*nyāso' nyatra*' and therefore explains that the conclusion is elsewhere than D or A, i.e. only in U (p. 264).

105a. ālāpamātreṇa: Kallinātha suggests that *ālāpa* should be interpreted as with or without syllabic content (p. 268): मात्रपदेन तस्य वाचकपदरहितत्वमुच्यते, केवलालापेनोद्ग्राहः कर्तव्य इति केषांचिन्मतम्, मतान्तरे तु वाचकपदैरेवोद्ग्राहः कर्तव्य इत्यर्थः ।

It is more consistent to understand absence of *tāla* rather than of words in *ālāpamātreṇa*.

106b. muninā: This is a spurious invocation to the *muni*; this passage is directly borrowed from SR (4.360cd-361ab):

आलापो गमकालप्तिरक्षरैर्वर्जिता मता ।
सैव प्रयोगशब्देन शार्ङ्गदेवेन कीर्तिता ॥

BD (502cd-503ab, p. 153) describes *ekatālī* as having dense alliteration with frequent caesurae: 'यतिर्यत्र द्रुते द्रुते'

AC (4.16.547, p. 81) mentions *ekatālī* as part of *sūḍakrama* but does not describe it.

SS (5.7.120-122b, p. 223) gives sequence 2U-2D-A-D. It has *prāsa, yati* and repeated *dhruva* copiously and is sung in *ekatālī*.

JS (p. 44) gives the sequence of *dhātus* as 2U-2D-AD; it has copious rhyming, caesurae and *druta*; it is composed in *ekatālī*; according to some, its U is made from *ālāpa*.

PS (4.188cd-190, p. 37) copies JS: 3d, two *aṅgas* —pd tl; n (4.40, p. 27)

LS (5.283, 284, p. 392) gives the same sequence for *dhātus*; set in *ekatāla*; according to some it is composed of *ālāpa*; *prāsa, yati* and *druta* are not mentioned.

RK (3.79, 80, p. 48) describes the same as in LS but ascribes the *lakṣaṇa* spuriously to Bharatamuni and others.

SD (4.417, p. 73): same sequence

SP (1.552cd, p. 73): *ekatāla* and *druta laya* are prescribed.

ŚUDDHASŪḌA PRABANDHAS

Classification of *prabandhas* into *sūḍa, ālikrama* and *viprakīrṇa* seems to emerge in the twelfth century A.D. The same is true of division of *sūḍa* into *śuddha* and *chāyālaga* (*sālaga*). *Sūḍa* is not a Sanskrit word; it is explained by Kallinātha as a vernacular word referring to a special group of *gītas* collectively (op. cit. on SR 4.22, pp. 213, 214):

सूड इति गीतविशेषसमूहवाची देशीशब्दः ।

I have shown elsewhere (Sathyanarayana, R., *Sulādis* and *Ugābhogas of Karnātaka Music*, p. 5 and *Śrīpādarāya: A Musical and Literary Study*, under preparation) that it is a Kannaḍa word meaning 'predetermined order', 'by turn' etc. and was applied to a group of songs which were required to be sung in a particular order. This order was called *sūḍakrama*; *sūḷ* also means 'to sound': the *sūḷādi tālas* were so named because (i) they occurred in a predetermined, fixed order (*sūḷakrama*) and (ii) they were performed in a fast tempo with only sounded beats (*chāpu*).

Sūḍa was divided into *śuddha* and *sālaga* (*chāyālaga*). The eight compositional prototypes *elā* etc. described above are *śuddha*; *dhruva, maṇṭha* etc. are *sālagasūḍas* (*Sālaga* is phonetic degeneration of *chāyālaga*); they are so called because they partake of a shade (*chāyā*) of *elā* etc. in architecture. Śārṅgadeva raises an objection to this nomenclature in *pūrvapakṣa*: according to the *ācārya*(*s*), the *elā* etc. are themselves *chāyālaga*; how then, may they be called *śuddha*? For, *śuddha* refers to the time honoured (*mārga*) musical forms *jāti, grāma-rāgas, bhāṣā, vibhāṣā* and *antarabhāṣā rāgas* (described in the first two chapters of SR) as well as the fourteen (*madraka* etc.) *prakaraṇa gītis* (described in the fifth chapter of SR). He reconciles this by saying that it is true, but in the case of *elā* etc. *śuddha* should be interpreted liberally as *śuddhasadṛśa* (similar to *śuddha*) because of the popular application of this term to them (SR 4.312-313b). It is interesting to note that Siṁhabhūpāla once refers to *elā* etc. *śuddhasūḍas* as *'mārga'* (on SR 3.16, p. 135)

The word '*ācārya*' is interpreted by Siṁhabhūpāla as Bharata (p. 335) while Kallinātha is silent. Justification of this equation is not known, though later writers such as Śrīkaṇṭha and Dāmodara ascribe the *śuddha-sūḍas* to Bharata. No such reference is available in the extant sources of the *Nāṭyaśāstram*. Unless these authors are indulging in gaining for their statements the credibility and authority of antiquity, it has to be assumed that such references are found in the work of a later (than UR-NŚ) namesake author; this possibility cannot be entirely ruled out because of the occurrence of the *pañca-bharata* names as well as the reference to Vṛddha-bharata, Ādibharata etc. in later works on music, dance etc.

Kallinātha explains *śuddha* in connection with *elā* etc. (p. 335) as only a proximate expression, a figure of speech: *śuddha* refers to such music as does not exceed or violate established and prescribed rules, whereas *sālaga* refers to music which contravenes them. In other words, *śuddha* and *sālaga* are relative to each other, in terms of the degree of conformity with rules. *Elā* etc. conform more while *dhruva* etc. do (far) less; but, says Siṁhabhūpāla, *śuddha* does not mean complete conformity (p. 335): '*na tu mukhyam śuddhatvam*'. Deviation from rules or tradition in the *sālagasūḍas* has been recorded by Kallinātha and Tulaja and will be discussed in the commentary on *sālagasūḍas*.

Classification presumes the existence of similarities (and dissimilarities) and their recognition. BD does not reveal these in respect of *elā* etc. and does not describe *lambhaka* and *rāsaka*, much less *dhruva, maṇṭha* etc. *Tālaniryukti*, especially nomenclature on the basis of the *tāla*-name must have played an important role in grouping these songs as *śuddha* and *sālaga*. Most of the *śuddhasūḍas* e.g. *karaṇa* (BD 426, 427; AC 4.16.89-91), *ḍheṅkī* (BD 501cd-502ab; JS p. 39; SS 5.7.108-111), *rāsaka* (AC 4.16.547) and *ekatālī* (SS 5.7.120-122; JS p. 44) began their careers with *niryukti* of self-named *tāla* and gradually grew independent of it. It is not clear if both *sūḍa* songs were of *deśī* (non'classical') origin, and were already regarded as groups (cf. Kallinātha '*gītaviśeṣasamūha*' pp. 213, 214) in their *deśī* environment or if only the name *sūḍa* is of *deśī* origin; for, while the *elā* was composed in provincial languages like Kannaḍa also, they were composed in Sanskrit in sophisticated metrical forms and figures of speech etc. The *sālagasūḍas* must have been composed in Sanskrit before *sulādis* were composed in Kannaḍa by the Haridāsas (14th-15th century A.D.), and much later, in Telugu also. Only one *sulādi* of Annamācārya in Sanskrit has survived in both *mātu* and *dhātu* in an inscription in the temple of Śrī Veṅkateśvara in Tirupati.

In its early days, Indian music had developed a conventionally accepted order in the performance of its compositions. There were two such sequences viz. *sūḍakrama* and *ālikrama*. The *viprakīrṇa prabandhas* were associated with activities or special occasions. It is interesting that Someśvara mentions *sūḍakrama* only, but includes other types of composition in the sequence; he includes some e.g. *rāsaka* which he does not describe; he omits *vartanī* and *vivartanī* altogether (AC 4.16.547-554, pp. 81, 82):

करणं च तथैवैला ढेङ्किका झोम्बडस्तथा ।
लम्भको रासकश्चैव तथा स्यादेकतालिका ॥ ५४७ ॥
कन्दवृत्ताधि(?दि)कः कश्चित् प्रबन्धश्चेन् महान् पुनः ।
अल्पः पश्चात् प्रगातव्य एष सूडक्रमः स्मृतः ॥ ५४८ ॥
त्रिपदी षट्पदी चैव धवलो मङ्गलस्तथा ।
उवी च चर्चरी चर्या राहडी दन्तिकस्तथा ॥ ५४९ ॥
एते सूडेष्वतो गेयाः प्रबन्धा लौकिका मताः ।
विप्रकीर्णाः प्रगातव्या व्यापारेषु पृथक् पृथक् ॥ ५५० ॥
त्रिपदी कण्डने चैव ---- प्रबन्धाः परिकीर्तिताः ॥ ५५१-५५४ ॥

Thus Someśvara defines *sūḍakrama* as consisting of larger *prabandhas* such as *elā* followed by smaller ones such as *kanda*; he seems to include *tripadī, ṣaṭpadi… dantī* among the *sūḍas*! Again, early authorities such as BD, JS, PS do not give them in the same order, and even insert other *prabandhas* such as *svarārtha* and *gadya* between, say *vivartinī* and *lambhaka*; only some *karaṇas* such as *svara, pāṭa* and *bandha* are found in the earlier works, that too not together but scattered among others. BD etc. show the earliest phase of these e.g. *elā* (number of feet, *prāsa* instead of *anuprāsa* etc.). It is interesting that SR does not describe *sālagasūḍas* immediately after the *śuddha sūḍas*, but at the very end, after the *viprakīrṇa prabandhas*; the *sālagasūḍas* are implied to be evolutes of the *śuddha sūḍas* and were melting in a crucible of change. The order *śuddha sūḍa-ālikrama-viprakīrṇa-sālagasūḍa* probably reflects the decreasing degree of conformity to rules or norms.

DESCRIPTIONS OF ĀLIKRAMA PRABANDHAS

107-109ab 1. *Varṇa*

107a. udgrāhadhruvakau: SR (4.181cd, 182ab) is not explicit on the *dhātus*. Kallinātha argues (p. 269) that they are indispensable to every *prabandha* and should be composed of *birudas* (unless otherwise stated); he further quotes Śārṅgadeva: '*anuktābhogavastūnām padair ābhogakalpanā*' (SR 4.310ab) to infer that the *varṇa* has an *ābhoga* composed of words. Therefore, it has three *aṅgas*—pd bd tl; so it is of *bhāvanī* class; it has three *dhātus* viz. UDA. Paṇḍarīka Viṭṭhala quotes the above line which is pertinent, but also the next line (SR 4.310cd: '*ovyādayastu catvāro bhavanty-ābhogavarjitāḥ*') but has omitted the line (SR 4.182ab): '*tāla-traividhyatas-tasya traividhyam gaditam budhaiḥ*'; *varṇa tāla* has three forms viz. *tryaśra* (||oo||), *miśra* (oooóooooóoooóSSooS||S) and *caturaśra* (S|ooS) as described in NN (1.172, 173). So *varṇa prabandha* is of three kinds—*tryaśra, miśra* and *caturaśra.*

BD (403, p. 144): bd, tn (?), tl; Kannaḍa language

AC

JS (p. 49): bd; Kannaḍa language; *varṇa tāla;* so three varieties as above.

PS: 2d, two *aṅgas*—bd tl; n-an (4.29, p. 25)

SS

LS (5.285, 286, pp. 392, 393): U-D: bd, A-words, *varṇa tāla*; 3 varieties; Kannaḍa language

RK (3.94, p. 49): bd, *varṇa tāla*; so, three varieties, Kannaḍa language

SD (4.428, p. 74): same as in RK

SP (1.556cd): Kannaḍa language

109cd-112ab 2. *Varṇasvara*

110d. vedākṣi: Of the six *aṅgas, tāla* is fixed to be *varṇa tāla* and bd is absent. Hence only sv pd pt tn remain; with each composed in the beginning, there are four *varṇasvara* varieties viz., *svarādi, padādi, pāṭādi* and *tenādi.* Following SR (4.182, 183), both Siṁhabhūpāla (p. 270) and Kallinātha explain this. In each of these varieties, the remaining three *aṅgas* may be composed in any desired order; in each *varṇa*, then $^4C_3$, i.e. six forms are available. So the total is twentyfour. Paṇḍarīka Viṭṭhala offers this as an additional observation.

111c. ekena dhruva(ḥ): This is not mentioned in SR; Siṁhabhūpāla is also silent. But Kallinātha (p. 270) avers that among *svara* etc. two should constitute U, and two, D; A is composed of words. But '*anuktābhogavastūnām, padair-ābhogakal-panā*' is only a general rule (SR 4.310ab). So, if out of sv pt tn and pd, two occur in U and pd in A, only one *aṅga* remains. So D cannot have two *aṅgas,* as stated by Kallinātha. It would thus appear that Paṇḍarīka Viṭṭhala is more acceptable. If Kallinātha is to be justified, it must be argued that even if there is pd in the two sections of U and D, A should be composed with words again. Veṅkaṭamakhin also takes this view (CDP 9.143). He states additionally that the composition concludes on tn.

BD. (507, p. 153): sv pd pt tn tl; tl is not specified.

AC (4.16.92, p. 50; 4.16.437, p. 69): pt tn pd sv tl; tl is not specified.

JS (p. 40): four kinds: *svarādi, padādi, pāṭādi, tennādi*; tl not mentioned.

PS—3d, 5 *aṅgas* - sv pt pd tn tl, n-an; (4.55, p. 27)

SS (5.7.139cd-140, p. 225): sv tl pd tn; bd not mentioned; A in other words; conclusion on tn

LS (5.287-290ab, p. 393): four forms *svarādi, pāṭādi, padādi, tenādi*; these are of many further varieties.

RK

SD (4.429, p. 75): sv pt pd tn in any desired order; conclusion is on tn.

SP (1.557ab, p. 73): *Varṇa* performed with sv tl is *varṇasvara.*

112cd-124 3. *Gadya*

112cd. chandobandhahīnam: prose, without prosodial or metrical structure.

113d. sāmavedataḥ: *Gadya* is *padya* without prosodial structure; *sāmans* are formed by melodising the *ṛks* which are liberated from metrical or *tāla* restrictions.

114b. Gauḍī is a *rīti*, i.e. style. Vāmana (*Kāvayālaṁkāra-sūtravṛtti*, 1.6-13) holds that style is the soul of poetry; style is characteristic composing of words. Such characteristic is the quality of poetry. It is threefold: *vaidarbhī, gauḍī* and *pāñcālī*, so named probably because of the original, provincial pecularity in literary composition, but in reality, not limited to geographic boundaries. *Rīti* has two aspects: quality of sound and quality of meaning. These have ten qualities (*guṇa*) each:

	Quality	*Śabda-guṇa*	*Artha-guṇa*
1.	*ojas*	taut structure	full development, maturity
2.	*prasāda*	structural laxity	clarity or purity of meaning
3.	*śleṣa*	unity	coordination
4.	*samatā*	sameness of *mārga*	absence of unevenness, or of oddity
5.	*samādhi*	regularity in ascent and descent	vision
6.	*mādhurya*	discreteness of words	speciality or charm in expression
7.	*saukumārya*	softness; absence of harshness	softness; absence of harshness
8.	*udāratā*	'*vikaṭatva*': as if the words are dancing	'*agrāmyatva*': absence of vulgarity
9.	*arthavyakti*	generating of clear meaning	explicitness of context or description
10.	*kānti*	lustre, illumination	emotive intensity

Vaidarbhī rīti has all ten qualities; it is lovely as the tone of the *vīṇā;* it involves, and transcends grammatical perfection, a good poet and a good theme; beyond and above these, it has something without which the words cannot drip sweetness. *Gauḍī rīti* has *ojas* and *kānti*; so it has long, compound word structures and bombast. *Pāñcālī rīti* is a dull style; involving *mādhurya* and *saukumārya*; it lacks bombast; its structure is loose and resembles *purāṇa* style (Vāmana, op. cit. 3.1.1-27; 3.2.1-10).

As Murray says (J. Middleton Murray, *The Problem of Style*, p. 5), 'Whatever goes to make a man's writing recognizable is included in his style'. 'Here then, we have three fairly distinct meanings of the word; style, disengaged; style, as a personal idiosyncracy; style as a technique of expression; style, as the highest achievement of literature.' (ibid., p. 7), The second meaning is relevant to this context.

Other styles such as *lāṭi, āvantikā* and *māgadhī* (note again the provincial association) developed later in Indian Poetics.

114c. Cūrṇa is more familiarly known as *cūrṇikā.*

114d. (ārabhaṭī) vṛtti: mode of diction; *vṛtti* refers to any speciality in costumery and make up (*nepathya*), song, instrumental music, *rasa, bhāva, abhinaya* and *nṛtya*; or, it is the mode of disposition of grace or beauty. Sāgaranandin asseverates (*Nāṭakalakṣaṇaratnakośa*, 1044ff.):

नेपथ्यो गीतवादितरसभावाभिनयनृत्यजातीनां क्वापि विशेषे वर्तनमिति वृत्तिः कथितः । अथवा विलासविन्यासक्रमो वृत्तिरिति ।

Bharatamuni describes, for the first time the origin and characteristics of the different *vṛttis* (NŚ 20). Here *vṛtti* is a my theme. When Lord Nārāyaṇa shrank the earth to a seed and expanded the universe to the ocean (cf. *Vālmīki Rāmāyaṇa*, 7.72; *Kūrmapurāṇa* 13) and lay down to rest on *Ādiśeṣa,* the *Asuras Madhu* and *Kaiṭabha,* intoxicated with their own power and strength, picked a quarrel and provoked him to battle: they hit him with fisticuffs and derisive abuse. A witness to this, Brahmā chided Viṣṇu: 'Why do you tarry with mere words? Is this an occasion of *bhāratī vṛtti*? Destroy them instantly!' Viṣṇu said, 'This *bhāratī vṛtti* itself will turn out to be the cause of my destroying them; the weight (*bhāra*) of (their) words will go on increasing; let this excessiveness of words be known as *bhāratī vṛtti* in the world!' He fought the *asuras* with well formed, neat body movements and *aṅgahāras.* The earth became heavy with the *sthānakas* (stances) he employed; *bhāratī-vṛtti* has originated from this '*bhāra*' (heaviness). It is born of *Ṛgveda,* is speech-predominant, used by men only and contains Sanskrit words. It is called *bhāratī vṛtti* because *bharatas* (actors) employ it.

During this battle the bow of Viṣṇu viz. the *śāraṅga* tripped sharply, intensely and from the power of *sattva* (mental dispositions); *sāttvatī vṛtti* originated from this; it is born of *Yajurveda*; it is called *sāttvatī* because it contains mental dispositions (*sāttvatena*), *nyāyas* (weapon modalities in a battle) and *vṛttas*; it involves intense joy and destruction of grief.

While engaged in executing strange *aṅgahāras,* Viṣṇu tied his hair (*keśa*) into a tuft in a sportive mood. *Kaiśikī vṛtti* originated from such tying of hair. It involves women who wear specially beautiful make-up and costume, numerous songs and dances, enjoyment of, and services to the erotic pleasures.

Ārabhaṭī vṛtti originated from the strange and charming acts of combat and *cāris* in which Viṣṇu engaged with great excitement and enthusiasm. The *ārabhaṭi vṛtti* includes the qualities of a bold person (*ārabhaṭa*) such as speaking many words, deception, bragging and falsehood. It has jumping, leaping, falling down, crossing over, conjuration and magic.

Bharata prescribes *bībhatsa* and *karuṇa-rasas* for *bhāratī vṛtti, vīra, adbhuta* and *śama* (*śānti*) for *sāttvatī, hāsya* and *śṛṅgāra* for *kaiśikī* and *raudra* as well as *bhayānaka* for *ārabhaṭī.* It may be noted that such allocation is at variance with that made for *gadya* varieties with the assignment of *vṛttis* in the NN.

116c. Kaiśikīcitra-vṛtti is, according to Kallinātha, *kaiśikī-vṛtti* admixed under the influence of *bhāratī* etc. (on SR 4.190, p. 271):

कैशिकवृत्तेश्चित्रत्वं भारत्यादिभिर्वृत्त्यन्तरैः सह साङ्कर्येणेति वेदितव्यम् ।

116d. citram: citra-gadya; cf SR (4.190, 191)

शृङ्गारे वैष्णवं चित्रं चित्रकैशिकवृत्तिजम् ।
वैदर्भ्या रचितं रीत्या नानारीतिविचित्रया ॥

117ab. Parallel texts such as SR give the complexion and presiding deities for the six *gadya* varieties as follows: *utkalikā—red,* Rudra; *cūrṇa—yellow,* Brahma; *lalita—white,* Madana; *vṛttagandhi*—yellow, Muni; *khaṇḍa—white,* Gaṇeśa; *citra—variegated* colour, Viṣṇu.

117c. Veṇī, miśra: Veṅkaṭamakhin (CDP 9.216) seems to imply the *veṇī* and *miśra* varieties for each of the six *gadyas.* This does not seem plausible since the *veṇī* is described as a mixture of all six, and *miśra* a mixture of *cūrṇa* and *vṛttagandhi*; the eight varieties of *gadya* described in SR accord with those found in parallel texts; the *veṇī* and *miśra* may be regarded as compiled in SR from a different school.

118d. bahvalpa samalaiḥ: Herein is implied a natural and logical relationship between *gati* (= *laya*) and syllabic density; in *drutagati*(fast)-*gadya,* only short syllables (*laghu*) are closely packed; in *vilambagati-gadya, laghus* are few and *gurus* are abundant; in *madhyagati-gadya* both *laghus* and *gurus* are equitably distributed.

120ab. ṣaṭ-gatayaḥ: drutavilambitā profuse *laghus* in first half, profuse *gurus* in second half; the name *druta-vilambitā* is thus apposite; this avoids *guru* in first half and *laghu* in the second half of the verse foot. If the *laghus* and *gurus* are equally distributed it is *druta-madhyā; madhyavilambitā* consists of *laghus* and *gurus* in equal (or equitable) proportions in the first half and only *gurus* in the second half.

Thus each of the six *gadya* varieties has six *gati* subvarieties, giving altogether thirtysix *gadya* forms. Śārṅgadeva or his commentators do not extend these subvarieties to the *veṇī* and *miśra*; it is not clear why. Siṁhabhūpāla derives these thirtysix *gadya* forms somewhat differently (p. 274):

उत्कलिकायाः द्रुता गतिः, चूर्णे विलम्बिता गतिः, ललिते मध्या गतिः, वृत्तगंधिनि द्रुतमध्यागतिः, खण्डे द्रुतविलम्बिता गतिरिति ... बहुभिर्लघुभिरुत्कलिका कर्तव्या। अल्पैर्लघुभिश्चूर्णकम्। समैर्लघुभिर्ललितम्। पृथक् स्थितैर्लघुभिर्वृत्तगन्धि। पृथक्स्थितैर्गुरुभिः खण्डम्। मिश्रितैर्मिश्रमिति। एतेषामुक्तषड्विधगतियुक्तत्वेन षड्विधत्वे षट्त्रिंशद् (३६) भेदाः।

124b. gadyam nigadyate: The *sāmānyalakṣaṇa* and mode of singing *gadya* described in the above nine hemistitches may be summarised here: First, the syllable '*aum*' is sung without *tāla*; the words of the *gadya* should be recited without *tāla* (as in *kāvyavācana,* poetry recitation) set to the fifteen *gamakas* and the four *varṇas* (*alaṁkāras*). Solfeggio passages should be sung in between sentences, in between words, in between syllables of words (passages such as *ciṭṭa-svara, ettugaḍe-svara, kalpanā-svara* in Karnātaka music and *sargam* in Hindustanī music). Then, two words containing the name of the *gadya* variety should be sung with *tāla*, and repeated again, once. After this, *gamakālapti* is performed twice; next, a word containing the composer's signature, set to *tāla*, followed by a word incorporating the patron's name also set to *tāla* in *vilamba laya* (i.e. with modicum of *laghus*), is performed. These two *tālas* must be different or in different *layas.* The same is repeated in *druta* (*madhya*? cf. Kallinātha p. 273) *laya.* Then the whole *prabandha* is sung again as described above, and commencing with the two words set to *tāla*, the rest should be completed in *vilamba laya* in a different (third) *tāla.* Thus concludes the *gadya.* Here U is the first portion without *tāla*; the two words, set to *tāla* and repeated twice, constitute D; the last portion commencing with *gamakālapti* (*prayoga*) is A. It is *aniryukta* since there is no restriction of *tāla, rāga, chandas* etc., it is of *bhāvanī jāti* and is *tridhātuka* (UDA). Compare with SR (4.184-198).

BD (400, p. 144): opaque text with lacuna

---- क्षोन्ति तदपि सम्मतः।
व्रातो यस्य भवेत् तालो वर्णनीयस्य संज्ञया।
गीयते यत् तदत्राहुर्गद्यं गीतविशारदाः॥

AC (4.16.247-249, p. 27): *Gadya* has no restriction of verse feet (or words) and of prosody; it is densely populated with compound words; it has sv but no tl. The patron's name is sung at the end with *tāla.* Someśvara offers the following illustration (he does not describe the varieties of *gadya*):

अतसीपुष्पप्रकरसमानकायकान्ति उ(-न्त्यु)त्सङ्गविष्टरोपविष्टलक्ष्मीलोललोचनचारुचषकपेपीयमाना गण्यलावण्य पीयूषरसविरसामृतकरबिम्बविडम्बिना कम्बुना विलूनबाणबाहुचक्रेण चक्रेण प्रतिहतत्रि-दिवपतिपरिपन्थिभुजोद्धटमदोत्कट गदया जनितनिखिलनाकनायकनिकायकामिनीनयनारविन्देन विराजमानकरचतुष्टयमयस्तम्भबिभ्रमभुजदण्डमण्डलमाखण्डलपुरःसरसुरसहस्रसमभ्यर्चितपादपद्म-युगलम् अनिशं अशेषत्रिभुवनत्राणपरायणनारायणं अहरहरर्चयतां जपतां ध्यायतां ध्यायिनां च भूयो भूयो भवभीषणभूमिविभ्रान्तयो न भवन्ति भवन्ति च विलासविभवविजितजम्भारातिविभूतयो भूतयः ।

JS (pp. 14,15) is probably the source for SR to describe *gadya*; its 6 varieties are characterised thus: *vṛttagandhi*—portions of *padya* (*vṛtta*), *cūrṇa*—two, three or four feet (words?) compounded or discrete; *utkalikā*—*gauḍī-rīti*; *lalita*—in five feet (words?) compounded together; *khaṇḍa*—large and small feet in '*prakrānta*' (aforesaid) *rītibhaṅgīs; citra*—various *rītis;* the *rīti, rasa, vṛtti* and *veda* affiliation for these are: *vṛttagandhi-pāñcālī, śānta bhāratī, sāma*; *cūrṇa-vaidarbhī, śānta, sāttvatī*; *utkalikā-gauḍī, vīra, ārabhaṭī*; *lalita-pāñcālī, śṛṅgāra, kaiśikī*; *khaṇḍa–vaidarbhī, hāsya, sāttvatī*; *citra-vaidarbhī, śṛṅgāra, kaiśikī*. Procedure of singing: '*aum*' sans *tāla*; its feet (words?) with six or eight *yamakas*; rendered with all *gamakas* and *varṇa* (*alaṁkāras*) in *vilambita, madhya* and *druta svaras* at the ends of words without *tāla* in between; then two words containing name of *prabandha*, with *tāla*; the six *gatis* viz. *vilamba, madhya, druta, drutamadhyā, madhyavilambā* and *drutavilambitā* are next described with reference to distribution of *laghu* and *guru* syllables as above; therefore, there are thirtysix forms of *gadya*; *daivī-gadya* is in Samskṛta.

PS (4.162cd-180ab, pp. 35-37) as in JS; lacuna for four *gatis* in impressi typis; but text is complete in MS (Sri Varalakshmi Academy, Mysore); 3d–three *aṅgas*—pd tl sv; n-an; (4.31, p. 27)

SS (5.7.50cd-57ab, pp. 214, 215): *vṛttagandhi–padyagadyānusāri; cūrṇa*—compounded or discrete words: *utkalikā*—'*utkalikā'śabdāḍambarayuktam*'; *khaṇḍa*—'*rītībhaṅgasaṁyuktam*'; *lalita*—five compounded words (or feet); *citra*—variegated; any suitable *tāla*; has expertise in *svaras* and variegated charm in rendering: A contains name of composer and patron; *gadya* is pleasing to the gods.

LS (5.290cd-309, pp. 393-396): same as in SR

RK

SD (4.430, p.75) describes *gadya* merely as array of words without metre; many varieties are described in other treatises.

SP (1.557cd, p. 73): merely '*chandohīnam padakadambakam*'.

125-126ab 4. *Kaivāḍa*

125a. nirarthaiḥ-sārthair vā: NN seems to be content with only these two varieties by athetisation of '*sa śuddhair-miśritaiḥ pāṭaiḥ śuddho miśra iti dvidhā*' (SR 4.200). If there is a lacuna in NN for this passage, then *kaivāḍa* is of four kinds: *śuddha-sārthaka, śuddha-nirarthaka, miśra-sārthaka, miśra-nirarthaka.*

125bc. pada: A is composed of the names of the patron and composer.

syātām... nyasanam. Paṇḍarīka Viṭṭhala has improved the description in SR(4.199) by resolving the ambiguity and potential misimplication in पाटै: स्यातां ध्रुवोद्ग्राहौ

Kaivāḍa is a Kannaḍa word which means intervention or interference; lit. 'putting one's hand to'. Kallinātha derives it from Samskṛta (p. 275): *hasta-kai; pāṭa> vāḍa* by phonetic degeneration; it is so called because of the preponderance of *kara(=hasta) pāṭas*:

कैवाड इति करपाटप्रधानत्वात् तद्भवापभ्रंशपदेनेयं संज्ञा ।

As mentioned above *kaivāḍa* means intervention, *hastakṣepa*; it seems more likely that *karapāṭa* is a Sanskritisation of *kaivāḍa* rather than *kaivāḍa* being an *apabhraṁśa* or *tadbhava*; for, this *prabandha* has been consistently called *kaivāṭa/kaivāḍa* from the time of Mataṅga (BD 427, 428, p. 146).

BD (427cd-428ab, p. 146): sung only with pt and/or pd (*akṣara*); tl; sung by *gandharvas*(=expert musician? 'classical' musician? association with *gāndharva* music ?)

AC (4.16.86, p. 50; 4.16.430, p. 68): pt of many kinds (*pādaiḥ, padaiḥ* are mislections); tl; contains name of patron/hero; '*bhavyaiḥ*' and '*navyaiḥ*' are variaelectionness describing *pāṭas.*

JS (p. 49). Four kinds viz. *śuddha-sārthaka, śuddha-nirarthaka, miśra-sārthaka, miśra-nirarthaka* are described: A in bd; conclusion is on U; contains name of *prabandha.*

PS 3d; three *aṅgas*—pd bd tl; an (4.45, p. 28)

SS (5.167-169, p. 229). *kaivāra; hastapāṭas,* tl; four varieties mentioned above; A in other words (containing names of *prabandha*, composer and hero).

LS (5.310-312, p. 396). U-D in *hastapāṭas;* name of *prabandha* in A; conclusion is on U; four varieties as mentioned above; *karapāṭa* has undergone *apabhraṁśa* into *kaivāḍa.* According to some, there is *ālāpa* of words at the beginning of A.

RK

SD (4.431, 432ab, p. 75): U-D in pt only; four varieties; conclusion is on D (!)

SP (1.558, p. 73): UD in pt only; A and antara (!) in pd.

126-128ab 5. *Aṅkacāriṇī*

127a. trivarṇya: NN is influenced by Kallinātha:

अत्र वीरशब्देन दानवीरो दयावीरो युद्धवीर इति त्रिविधोऽपि वीरो गृह्यते । तेन त्रिविधवीराश्रितानि बिरुदानि ग्राह्याणि ।

127d. aṅkacāriṇi: Parallel treatises (e.g. SR 4.201-204) describe six subvarieties: i. *vāsavī*—eight *birudas* in one *tāla* ii. *kalikā*—sixteen *birudas* in two *tālas* iii. *vṛttā*—thirtytwo *birudas* in three *tālas* iv. *vīravatī*—fiftytwo *biruḍas* in four *tālas* v. *vedottara*—

one hundred four *birudas* in five *tālas* vi. *jātimatī*—no rule for number of *tālas* and *birudas.*

128a. aniryukta: Restriction refers only to number of *tālas* and not to specific *tālas.*

BD mentions (386b, p. 242) but has lacuna for description.

AC (4.16.8-10, p. 42): bd; tl of choice, contains name of patron/hero; an illustration is given:

असुरकुलान्तक-दैत्यवंशदावानल।बाणबाहुवनकुठार-रावणान्तःपुररावण-संसारसागरतरण-यमलार्जुन-प्रभञ्जन-मधुकैटभसूदन-गोपीजननयनेन्दीवरचन्द्र-धर्मलताप्रसवकन्द-बलिकुञ्जर-बन्धनस्तम्भ-त्रिदशगण-कृतारम्भ-त्रिजगत्त्राण! रक्ष मां देव नारायण ॥

The above example contains twelve *birudas,* presumably rendered in a single *tāla.*

AC does not classify *aṅkacāriṇī* into six kinds.

JS (pp. 44-45) describes above six varieties; A in other words (presumably incorporating name of patron/hero and composer) performed with two spans of the *tāla.*

PS 3d, two *aṅgas*—bd tl; an (4.41, p. 27)

SS

LS (5.313cd- 321ab, pp. 396, 397): U-D in bd; A has name of *prabandha;* six varieties as above.

RK

SD (4.418b, p. 73) mentions, but does not describe, *aṅkacārinī.*

SP (1.559ab, p. 73): सर्वार्थस्य च गीतस्य गानं चेदङ्गचारिणी !

128cd-130ab 6. *Kanda*

128c. Aryāgīti is also called *skandha*(*ka*) whence the name of the *prabandha: kanda* is derived by phonetic degeneration; when the *āryā* verse contains 8 *caturmātrās* in each half, it is called *āryāgīti;* according to some, it is *āryā* itself, extended by two *mātrās* in each half, i.e. 32 and 29 *mātrās* respectively. (Bharatamuni, NŚ 16.167; Hemacandra, *Chando'nuśāsanam,* 4.13; Jayadeva, *Jayadevacchandas,* 4.14; Jayakīrti, *Chando'nuśāsanam,* 5.13-18; Piṅgalanāga; *Chandaḥśāstram,* 4.31; Virahāṅka, *Vṛttajātisamuccaya,* 4.9; Kedārabhaṭṭa, *Vṛttaratnākara,* 2.11.)

NN describes the *āryā-prabandha* (3.2.151, 152), but not the *āryā* or *āryāgīti* metre. The description is thus not self contained, a fallacy from which even great authorities such as Śārṅgadeva are not exempted. Many early authorities have classified the *prabandhas* on the basis of the names of *tāla, chandas, jāti* etc. So the serial order of presentation is occasionally affected.

Piṅgalanāga has defined *āryāgīti* (as a form of *āryā* metre): '*ardhe vasugaṇa āryāgītiḥ*' (loc. cit.). Kedārabhaṭṭa (loc. cit.) coins a verse which is both its *lakṣya* and *lakṣaṇa*:

आर्यापूर्वार्धं यदि गुरुणैकेनाधिकेन निधने युक्तम् ।
इतरत्तद्वन्निखिलं दलं यदीयमुदितैवमार्यागीतिः ।

Āryāgīti also has the six varieties similar to those of *āryā*.

Āryā is a metre in Sanskrit; it is called *skandhaka* or *saṅkīrṇa* in Prākṛta, and is described by Svayambhū (*Svayambūcchandas*, 1.3), Hemacandra (loc.cit.) and others; there are eight *caturmātrā-gaṇas* in its half; among these, the sixth is a *madhya-guru* (or *ja-gaṇa*) or *sarva laghu* (*na-gaṇa*); *ja-gaṇa* should not occur in the odd positions; Halāyudhabhaṭṭa (*Mṛtasañjīvanī*, comm. on Piṅgala, op. cit. 4.31) offers the following illustration:

अजमजरममरमेकं प्रत्यक्चैतन्यमीश्वरं ब्रह्मपरम् ।
आत्मानं भावयतो भवमुक्तिः स्यादितीयमार्यागीतिः ॥

128b. deśabhāṣā: Elsewhere (BD, AC, SR, vide infra), this is prescribed to be Kannaḍa.

129b. padāntaraiḥ: consisting of the names of composer and hero/patron.

129d. Kandaḥ has twentynine forms arising out of systematic decomposition of each *guru* into *laghus* progressively. Their names—and the *nth guru*, which is decomposed (cumulatively from the right towards the left) which gives the *kanda* its particular form are given below; e.g. 30 means that the 30th (last) *guru* is decomposed; twentyseven means that the 30th, 29th, 28th and 27th *gurus* are decomposed (SR 4.205 cd-209ab):

Pavana thirty, *ravi* twentynine, *chanda* twentyeight, *havyavāhana* twentyseven, *suranātha* twentysix, *samudra* twentyfive, *varuṇa* twentyfour, *śaśi* twenty-three, *śaila* twentytwo, *madhu* twentyone, *mādhava* twenty, *makaradhvaja* nineteen, *jayanta* eighteen, *madhupa* seventeen, *śuka* sixteen, *sārasa* fifteen, *kekinī* fourteen, *hari* thirteen, *hariṇi* twelve, *hasti* eleven, *kādamba* ten, *kārmuka* nine, *naya* eight, *vinaya* seven, *vikrama* six, *utsāha* five, *dharma* four, *artha* three, *kāma* two.

BD (396, 317, p. 143): *Kanda* is a mixutre of Kannaḍa etc. words; pt. bd; no tl; it is very well known in practice.

AC (4.16.292, p. 32): Only in Kannaḍa words; pd, bd, no tl.

JS (p. 21): *Kandaka* metre; no tl; has words of Kannaḍa etc., and pt. A in other words, conclusion is on charming pt. The twentynine forms of *kanda* mentioned above are named and characterised.

PS 3d, two *aṅgas*—pt bd, n (4.42, p. 27)

SS

LS (5.321cd-330, pp. 398, 399): Words of Kannaḍa, Lāṭa etc. *vīra rasa,* conclusion on pt; no *tāla*; twentynine varieties as above.

RK

SD

SP (1.559cd, p. 73): It is sung in one *khaṇḍa* in *vilamba gati.*

130cd-134ab 7. *Hayalīlā*

130c. turaṅgalīla tāla: '*virāmāntadrutadvayāt drutau turaṅgalīlaḥ syāt*' (NN 1.176): oooo

131a. anyapadaiḥ: words not occurring in U or D

132. āryā: see commentary on NN 3.2.151a.

132a. Aśvalalita is synonymous with *hayalīlā*, and *haya=turaṅga*; so this is a *niryukta prabandha* by *svanāmaka chandas* (namesake metre). *Aśvalalita* metre occurs in two forms, with twentytwo and twentythree syllables per verse foot; the first is described by Bharata (NŚ 16.100, 101) as having the *gaṇa* disposition: *na ja bha ja bha ja bha ga*; this is compiled by H.D. Velankar (*Jayadāman,* 1.22.2, p. 143) from the Chowkhamba (Kashi) edition of the NŚ (16.100, 101). However, this prosodial form is not supported in the Kāvyamālā edition of NŚ (15.98-100) or the Baroda (G.O.S.) edition (15.137-139) wherein *aśvalalita* is a metre with twentythree syllables to the foot with the following *gaṇa* disposition: *na ja bha ja bha ja bha la ga* with caesura at 11th and 23rd (i.e. 11, 12) syllables. This agrees with the definitions given by Jayadeva (*Jayadevacchandas* 7.26), Jayakīrti (*Chando'nuśāsanam,* 2.248), Piṅgalanāga (*Chandaḥśāstram,* 7.27); Kedārabhaṭṭa (*Vṛttaratnākara,* 3.101) and is called *lalitā* by Hemacandra (*Chando'nuśāsanam,* 2.358); it is also called *adritanayā* by Gaṅgādāsa (*Chandomañjarī,* 2.231) and others. It is described in an alternative form by Hemacandra (op. cit. 2.358, commentary) and Virahāṅka (*Vṛttajātisamuccaya,* 5.47) as *hayalīlagati,* in which the final *bha gaṇa* is replaced by *ja-gaṇa,* i.e. *na ja bha ja bha ja ja la ga.*

As already mentioned, Bharata inclines to the former version and offers an illustration (G.O.S. edn. 15.139):

विविधतुरङ्गनागरथयौधसङ्कुलमलं बलं समुदितं
शरशक्तिकुन्तपरिघासियष्टिविततं बहुप्रहरणम् ।
रिपुशतमुक्तशस्त्ररवभीतशङ्कितभटं भयाकुलदिशं
कुतमभिवीक्ष्य संयुगमुखे समर्पितगुणं त्वयाश्वललितम् ॥

AC gives (14.16.332, p. 37) the definition of *aśvalalita* as follows:

नजौ भजौ भजौ भो ल्गौ शङ्करार्कविरामकम् ।
तदश्वललितं नाम विकृतौ वृत्तमुच्यते ॥

and contributes the following example:

जयति जिताखिलासुरपुरः पुरन्दरपुरन्ध्रिगीतचरितः
सुखशयितः फणीन्द्रशयने तुषारकिरणावदातरुचिनि ।
निखिलजगज्जनार्थितशुभैः फणाभिमुखतां गतैः कृतपदः
स्फटिकधराधरस्य शिखरे जलौघभरितो घन इव भवन् ॥

Kallinātha (pp. 281, 282) quotes Piṅgalanāga (*Chandaḥśāstram*, 7. 26) for *lakṣaṇa*

अश्वललितं न्जो भ्जौ भ्जौ भ्लौ ग्रुद्रादित्यः ।

and Halāyudhabhaṭṭa (*Mṛtasañjīvanī,* comm. ibid. loc. cit.) for *lakṣya* of this metre:

पवनविधूतवीचीचपलं विलोकयति जीवितं तनुभृतां
वपुरपि हीयमानमनिशं जरावनितया वशीकृतमिदम् ।
सपदि निपीडनव्यतिकरं यमादिव नराधिपान्नरपशुः
परवनितामवेक्ष्य कुरुते तथापि हतबुद्धिरश्वललितम् ॥

133c. vikhyātā: Gadyaja-hayalīlā has no subvarieties; but the *padyaja-hayalīlā* has the following eight: i. tl in first half (U) but not in the second half (D) ii. tl in latter half but not in former half iii. tl in both halves iv. U has sv, pd, bd. Siṁhabhūpāla (p. 282) differs: U in sv, D in bd; U and D in *tāla.* The varieties i, ii and iii have U composed in pd. If these four are composed in *āryā* metre instead of *aśvalalita,* there are four more; together with *gadyaja-hayalīlā,* the total is nine.

134d. dīpanījātimān kvacit: i, ii and iii above have only two *aṅgas,* pd tl; in iv, there are sv pd bd tl; so the first three are of *tārāvalī,* and the fourth, of *dīpanī* class.

BD (412, p. 145): (one) half (i.e.) U in sv and *turagalīlā-yati* (? *tāla*); the other half in bd. Since BD does not specify which half, one more variety is possible by exchanging sv and bd in the two *dhātus.* This seems to be the earliest form of this composition.

AC (4.16.332, p. 37): First half is sv; second half is bd; *gaṇas* composed in *hayalīlā* (metre).

JS (p. 21) describes four varieties as above; *hayalīla-tāla;* only two *dhātus*; A in other words.

PS 3rd, four *aṅgas*—sv bd pd t1; n (4.54, p. 27)

SS

LS (5.331-338, pp. 399, 400): *gadyaja* and eight *padyaja* forms as above; *hayalīla-tāla; āryā* or *hayalīlā* metre (*na ja bha ja bha ja bha la ga*)

RK (3. 116, 117, p. 52) *Aśvalīla* is *gadyaja* and *padyaja*; the latter is in *hayalīla tāla* and is of four kinds; *āryā* metre; first half has tl; second half has (! no) tl.

SD

SP (1.560ab, p. 73) *Turagalīla* is in *śampā-tāla*; gives pleasure.

134-135ab 8. *Gajalīla*

134c. gajalīla tāla: (NN 1.162)

गजलीले विरामान्तमुक्तं लघुचतुष्टयम् (।।।।́)

135b. anyat : *gadyaja* and four *padyaja* varieties and *āryā* metre, thus resulting in five varieties

BD (413, p. 145) *gajalīla-tāla*; (rest is like *hayalīla*?)

AC (4.16.333-335, pp. 37-38): composed in *gajalīla tāla*, but rest is like *hayalīla;* illustration:

भवनाशकरं सकलार्तिहरं प्रणमामि हरं भवदोषहरम्

JS (p. 21): like *hayalīla* without *chandas*, but in *gajalīla tāla.*

PS 3d, four *aṅgas*—sv pd bd tl; an (?n) (4.56, p. 28)

SS–

LS (5.339-341ab, p. 400): one *gadyaja* and four *padyaja* varieties like *hayalīla* without namesake metre.

RK (3.115, p. 51): similar to *hayalīla* except *chandas*; composed in *gajalīla-tāla*

SD–

SP (1.560cd, p. 73): composed in *dhruva tāla* (!)

135cd-140 9. *Dvipadī*

135c. karuṇā tāla (NN 1.176): गुरुणैकेन करुणाताल: सद्भि: प्रकीर्तित: (ऽ). AC lifts *tāla niryukti.*

136-137. This is *dvipadī sāmānyalakṣaṇa*, not so explicitly stated in parallel texts in terms of *dhātu-aṅga* allocation.

138a. apare: This is AC (vide infra).

140b. Dvipadī is a *mātrā-vṛtta* (moraic metre) with two equal feet. Each line has six *mātrās* followed by five *caturmātrās* and a final *guru*. The first and fifth *caturmātrās* should have *ja-gaṇa* or *sarvalaghu*; but the *ja-gaṇa* cannot be used elsewhere; if *sarvalaghu* is used in the above positions, *yati* occurs after the first *laghu*, i.e. a new word must commence with the second *laghu*. According to Jayakīrti (*Chando'nuśāsanam*, 6.28) *dvipadī* is a Sanskrit metre; but Hemacandra classifies it among Prākṛta metres (*Chado'nuśāsanam*, 4.64-67).

Thus the *dvipadī-prakṛti* (model) is a *cha-gaṇa*, five *ta-gaṇas* (according to NN; elsewhere, it is five *bha-gaṇas*) and a final *guru*. This has eight modifications mentioned below (mentioned without names in NN but with names in SR 4.215-219):

i *śuddhā*: *cha bha bha bha bha bha ga* (NN *cha ta ta ta ta ta ga*); alternatively, *cha ja bha bha bha ja ga*; according to Siṁhabhūpāla, *cha ja bha bha bha bha bha ja ga*; sv between U and D (i.e. first half and second half); tl of one's own choice.

ii *khaṇḍā* has only first two feet of *śuddhā*, but not the 3rd and 4th feet.
iii *mātrā* has *guru* in place of *ja-gaṇa* (in sixth position).
iv *sampūrṇā* contains a *guru* in excess at the end of each foot of *śuddhā*.
v *mānavī*: Each quarter has *cha-gaṇa* followed by two *ta-gaṇas*.
vi *candrikā*: Each quater is structured thus: *pa pa ta la ga*.
vii *dhṛti:* Each quarter has *cha* followed by three *caturmātrā-gaṇas*.
viii *tārā*: Each quarter has *cha ya ya ya ya ga*.

140c. tārāvalī: two *aṅgas* viz. pd tl.

140c. niryukta because of prescription of *karuṇā-tāla* and *dvipadī* metre.

140d. bhāvanī: pd, tl, sv according to others.

BD (428cd-429ab, p. 426): *(kara-ru?)ṇā tāla, dvipadī-vṛtta.*

AC (4.16.273-275, p. 30) structure: *cha ta ta ta ta ga*; *ja* in second and sixth *gaṇas*, illustration:

भवजलनिधिदूषितमकरौघनिरन्तरदन्तुरान्तरं
विषयविशेषभोगविरहानलहेतिनितान्तभीषणम् ।
निरवधिबोधसेतुपरिकल्पनकोविदखिन्नमानसो
मुहुरहमुक्तितीर्षुरनाशं भगवत्पदयो: स्मरामि ॥

sv must be composed at the end of two quarters; tl of one's own choice.

JS. (p. 23) *karaṇa (karuṇā?) tāla; gamakālapti* at end of (first) half; A in other words; in two spans o*f tāla*; six varieties described as above.

PS—

SS (5.76b-78c, pp. 217, 218): *karaṇa tāla, gamaka* in middle; A in other words; in two spans of *tāla*

LS (5.341cd-351, pp. 400, 401): Eight varieties aforesaid. First half is U; second half is D, A in other words, containing three names (of *prabandha*, patron/hero, composer)

RK—

SD—

SP (1.561ab, p. 73): three *aśvagatis* (?), two segments.

141-143ab. 10. *Cakravāla*

141d. cakravāla: see commentary on NN 3.2.71a.

Also found in Kannaḍa and Telugu, it is called *samdaṣṭa yamaka.* Numerous instances of this may be found in a range of prosodial structures such as *vṛtta, kanda, ragaḷe, gadya* etc. (e.g. Candrarāja, *Madanatilakam,* 1.5; Śāntinātha, *Sukumāracaritam,* 8.66; Guṇavarma II, *Puṣpadanta purāṇam,* 10.45; Ranna, *Ajitatīrthakara purā-*

ṇatilakam, 4.79 pr; Nemicandra, *Līlāvati*, 4.145 pr; Rudrabhaṭṭa, *Jagannāthavijayam*, 12.57ff., E.C. 6.161). A tenth century example of (*muktapada grahaṇa*) *cakravāla* may be given here from Janna (*Ajitatīrthakara purāṇatilakam*, 4.7 pr.):

जयजय-जगत्त्रयपतिकिरीटकूटकोटिकिरीटमणिमसृण-चारुचञ्चन्नखमयूखोदन्तमयूखमण्डल मण्डलीभूतसकलदिक्पाल-मालामौळिमणिकिरणजाल-बालातपच्छायारुणित-तरुणपारिजातपल्लवाय-मानपादपल्लव-पल्लवितकुसुमितानल्पकल्पलतायमान ----द्वात्रिंशदिन्द्रमणिमयकिरीटकोटिघटित-घट्टितपादपीठ-पीठीकृतमन्दराचलशिखरशिखरीभूत-तिलकायमानमहनीयमहिमोदय-महिमोदयोद्धासि-भगवज्जिनेन्द्रवृन्दवृन्दारक-श्रीमदजितभट्टारक जिन ----

142d. ābhoga: The aforesaid syllabic recurrence is imperative in U and D, but not in A; for otherwise the names of *prabandha*, patron/hero and composer would become distorted.

BD (424, p. 146): recurrence of end syllables of words in *yamakālaṁkāra*.

AC (4.16.304-307, pp. 33, 34): recurrence of end syllables of words in *yamakālaṁkāra*; it occurs in two forms viz. *gadya* and *padya*; contains name of hero/patron at the end(A). Example of *gadyacakravāla*:

कमलाकुचकलशकेलिकल्पितकस्तूरिकापत्रभङ्ग-पत्रभङ्गविषादनवपूतनाप्रलयकर-करकलितसुदर्शनानुगृहीतपुरन्दर-दरचकित-भक्तजनवत्सल-कौस्तुभप्रभाजालसहस्ररचनाविदग्ध-दग्धनिखिलदुरित-भगवन्नारायण-नमस्ते ।

example of *padyacakravāla*:

शशाङ्कलकलङ्किकुमुदम् ।
नवहतेतिहिमकर ॥
करे तदसमं विलसितम् ।
विजयते जयते तव यशः ॥

JS (p. 22): recurrence of end syllables of words; desired *tāla;* two kinds—*gadya* and *padya*: A in other words; conclusion in two spans of *tāla*.

PS 3d, two *aṅgas*—pd tl; n-an (4.43, p. 26)

SS

LS (5.341cd-351, pp. 400-401): aforesaid recurrence in U-D, not A; auspicious RK.

SD (4.431, pp. 75, 76): aforesaid recurrence; *gadya-padya* varieties.

SP (1.561cd-562ab, p. 73): recurrence as above.

143cd-145ab 11. *Krauñcapada*

144ab. nyāsa udgrāhe: SR (4.221) agrees: *svara-nyāsaḥ*

144b. pratitāla (NN1.193): लौ द्रुतौ प्रतितालः स्यात् (॥००)

144d. svanāmacchandasā: *Krauñcapadā (-pāda)* is *samamātrāvṛtta* with twentyfive syllables in every quarter having caesurae (*yati*) after 5, 5, 8 syllables: its *gaṇa* structure is भमसभननननग (Bharata, NŚ 15.144-148, pp. 278, 279); Hemacandra, *Chando'nuśāsanam*, 2.372; Jayakīrti, *Chando'nuśāsanam*, 2.258; Jayadeva, *Jayadevacchandas*, 7.29; Piṅgalanāga, *Chandaḥśāstram*, 7.30; Kedārabhaṭṭa, *Vṛttaratnākara*, 3.104; Virahāṅka, *Vṛttajātisamuccaya*, 5.49). Two illustrations are available for the *vṛtta* and one for the *prabandha*. Thus Bharata (op. cit. 15.147, p. 279):

यः किल दाक्षं विद्रुतसोमं क्रतुवरमचमसमपगतकलशं
पातितयूपं क्षिप्तचषालं विचयनमसमिधमपशुकचरुकम् ।
कार्मुकमुक्तेनाशु चकार व्यपगतसुरगणपितृगणमिषुणा
नित्यमसौ ते दैत्यगणारिः प्रदहतु मखमिव रिपुगणमखिलम् ॥

The second is from Halāyudhabhaṭṭa (on Piṅgalanāga, loc. cit.) quoted by Kallinātha (p. 287)and Veṅkaṭamakhin (CDP 9.275) and interpolated in NŚ (16.148, p. 279):

या कपिलाक्षी पिङ्गलकेशी कलिरुचिरनुदिनमनुनयकठिना
दीर्घतराभिः स्थूलसिराभिः परिवृतवपुरतिशयकुटिलगतिः ।
आयतजङ्घा निम्नकपोला लघुतरकुचयुगपरिगतहृदया
सा परिहार्या क्रौञ्चपदा स्त्री ध्रुवमिह निरवधि सुखमभिलषिता ॥

Someśvara offers another example, his own composition (AC 4.16.238, p. 25):

श्रोत्रपुटान्तः प्राप्तनिवेशः कुलिशशिखर (इव रिपु)हृदयभिदां
यस्य निनादो दैत्यपतीनां समरशिरसि भयभरकृतिं कुरुते ।
निर्जननारी(लोचन)नीलोत्पलवनविकसनसकलहिमकरः
श्रीपतिशङ्खः पातु स युष्मान्दरविकसितदलनवकुमुदनिभः ॥

BD (408, p. 144): *pratitāla;* pd sv; this is the view of the cognoscente in *gāndharva.*

AC (4.16.237-239, pp, 25, 26): structure of *krauñcapada-vṛtta*: भमसभननननग with *yatis* after 5, 5, 8 and 7 syllables. For illustrations of *krauñcapada* see above.

JS (p. 21): *krauñcapada* metre: *pratitāla*, sv, A in other words and other sv.

PS 3d, three *aṅgas*—pd pt tl; n-an, (4.48, p. 27)

SS

LS (5.354-357, p. 402): pd, then sv; conclusion on sv; *prati tāla*; in *gadya* or namesake metre; U and D at different pitch levels; U in sv, D in pd, A in three names.

Metrical structure: भमसमननननग

RK (3.95, p. 49): pd (U), sv (D); *prati tāla*; namesake metre.

SD (4.433cd-434, p. 76): as in RK; in namesake metre of *muktaka.*

SP (1.563cd-564, pp. 73, 74): pd sv pd pt pd (tn?), pd bd pd (?)

145cd-148 12. *Svarārtha*

145c. sapta: *sa ri ga ma pa dha ni*

146a. krama e.g. *sariga māpani*; *vyutkrama* e.g. *nī pada, nīsari*

146b. samasta e.g. *sari, sama, dāsa, pada, samapāda, nī-mari, maga gari, niga*; *vyasta* e.g. *nī, mā, mām, sā, pā.*

146d. anya: other than such above combinations (e.g. *sariga*) like *akṣaravyūha*, Someśvara etc.

148a. eva: The *varṇa* commencing with words *'sarigāni dāni*, in *toḍi rāga* by Rāmasvāmi Dīkṣita is an example of *śuddha-svarārtha-prabandha.*

148d. ayam: SR (4.22, 223) *et al* distinguish seven forms of *śuddhasvarārtha* obtained by combining one, two, three...seven notes, and many other varieties by their combination; they are countless in *miśrasvarārtha.* Siṁhabhūpāla says (p. 289) that they were obsolete in his time.

BD (504cd-505ab, p. 153): a *vastu* in which the desired meaning is brought out only with sv.

AC (4.16.11-12, p.42): sv syllables taken in regular or irregular order are arranged to yield desired meaning. An example is given:

समागमागमा पापमादम (पाप) धानि (नी समागम) । धा (दा) समानीमानि धा (मा)नि पापसन्निगमागमा

JS (p. 26): Meaning is expounded through *svara* syllables; two kinds—*śuddha, miśra*; two kinds again by regular and irregular order of sv; *śuddha-svarārtha*—only seven sv; appropriate to the *rāga, śruti* and *sthāna* are employed; if mixed with other letters of the alphabet, it is *miśra-svarārtha*; by using one (*śaśi*), two (*stana*), three (*agni*), four (*veda*), five (*iṣu*), six (*sva*) and seven (*svara*) *svara*-syllables to generate single or synonymous meaning, *svarārtha* is of seven kinds. It has A in other words; conclusion is on U.

P. (4.157cd-162ab, p. 35): borrows from JS as above; 3d, three *aṅgas*—sv bd tl; an (4.44, p. 27)

SS

LS (5.358-363, p. 403): composer's intended meaning brought out in *sariga* etc. syllables or a ā i ī etc. vowels ingeniously; conclusion on U; two kinds—*śuddha,* and *miśra; śuddha*—only with *svaras*; *miśra:* sv + vowels or sv + other consonants; U-D composed only with these; A in other words; seven forms by using one, two, three...... *svaras.*

RK.

SD (4.435, 436, p. 76): as above (JS)

SP (1.562cd-563ab, p. 73): aptly named; intended meaning obtained only with *svara* syllables

149-150 13. *Dhvanikuṭṭanī*

149ab. NN thus summarises SR (4.225): '*ḍheṅkīvad tāladvayena*' and Kallinātha (p. 289 on ibid. loc. cit.):

यथा ढेङ्कीमिथो लयान्तरयुक्तेन तालद्वयेन गीयते, तथेयमपि मिथो भिन्नलयेन भिन्नतालेन गातव्येत्यतिदेशार्थः ।

Since it prescribes different tempi—'*bhinnalayātmakau*'—comparison with *dheṅkī prabandha* and proscription of M—'*melāpako na ca*' (SR loc. cit.)—have been rendered unnecessary. *Atideśa* means extended application, a rule providing for more than the usual rule, extending the *dharma* of something to something else; here, extending the *lakṣaṇa* of *ḍheṅkī* to *dhvanikuṭṭanī*. It is defined as 'उक्तेन साधनम्', 'अन्यत्रैव प्रणीतायाः कृत्स्नाया धर्मसंहतेः' *Pūrvamīmāṁsā* distinguishes five forms of *atideśa* viz. *śāstra-*, *kārya-*, *nimitta-*, *vyapadeśa-*, *rūpa-*; grammarians have adopted a sixth also viz. *tādātmya*.

149c. Yati is natural pause (usually in the middle of a verse foot) after a cluster of syllables.

150a. pṛthak-tāla: This rule implies, or includes: 'लयान्तरेऽन्यतालेन ध्रुवाभोगौ' stated by SR (4.143) in the context of *ḍheṅkī prabandha*.

150b. (pṛthak) padaiḥ: words other than those in U or D, and containing the names of composer and patron/hero.

150d. Niryukta: because *maṇṭha* and *kaṅkāla-tālas* are ruled out.

BD. (501, p. 153): *Mātrā* and *dhvani* are even (equal?), followed by pause; other *tāla* (than in *jhombaḍa*, viz. *kaṅkāla)*.

AC (4.16.60-62, pp. 47-48): Composed in pd containing intended meaning, in two tl, in only *samā yati* but not *viṣamā;* an example is given:

संसारतारणं जगत्कारणं त्रिदशपतिपालनं नौमि तं हरिम्
दितिकुलसूदनं दनुजघातनं जलधिजलशायिनं नौमि हरिम् ।
कंसवंशनाशकरण मनुजदेह वासुदेव मत्स्यकूर्मकालरुद्र
वदन नरसिंहवामनाङ्गरामरामकृष्णबुद्धकल्किरूप देव नमोस्तु ते ॥

JS (p. 40): *Dhvanikuṭṭanī* is like *ḍheṅkī* but without *maṇṭha or kaṅkāla tālas*; it has mediate caesurae; D is in a *tāla* other than in U.

PS 3d, two *aṅgas*—pd tl, an (4.41, p. 26)

SS (5.7.111cd-114c): *Maṇṭha* and *kaṅkāla-tālas* should not be used; first part of U is sung twice; the second part is sung once in *gamakālapti*; M is sung twice in high pitch. A is rendered once; conclusion is on D.

LS (5. 364, 365, p. 403): U and D in different *tālas* and *layas*, *tālas* other than *maṇṭha* and *kaṅkāla*, *yati* at equal (even?) *mātrās*; A in (other) words.

RK–

SD–

SP (1.566cd, p. 74): '*arthāntaram bhāti*'!

151-152 14. *Āryā*

151a. Āryā chandas is a very famous, ancient, Sanskrit *mātrāvṛtta* of two feet. The first foot, i.e. first half has seven *caturmātrās* with final *guru*; the second has five *caturmātrās*, *laghu*, *caturmātrā* and *guru*. Thus the moraic quantity is thirty *mātrās* in the first and twentyseven in the second. Throughout the metre, *ja-gaṇa* must be avoided in odd (*caturmātrā*) positions. However, the sixth *caturmātrā gaṇa* in the first half must be a *ja-gaṇa* (ISI) or a *na-gaṇa* with a *laghu*, i.e. *sarvalaghu* (IIII). If it is *sarvalaghu*, there is *yati* after the first *laghu*, i.e. a new word must begin with the second *laghu*. But if the *sarvalaghu* occurs at the seventh *gaṇa* in the first half or the fifth *gaṇa* in the second, a new word should begin with the first *laghu* therein (Bharata, NŚ 15.195-227, pp. 287-293; Hemacandra, *Chando'nuśāsanam*, 4.1-2; Jayakīrti, *Chando'nuśāsanam*, 5.1-3; Jayadeva, *Jayadevacchandas*, 4.6-7; Piṅgalanāga, *Chandaḥśāstram*, 4.14-21; Kedārabhaṭṭa, *Vṛttaratnākara*, 2.1-2; Virahāṅka, *Vṛttajāti-samuccaya*, 1.23-25).

Thus Piṅgalanāga defines *āryā* with the aphorism (op. cit. loc. cit.)

रारा अर्धं चार्यार्धम् अत्रायुङ्नज् षष्ठो ज् न्लौ वा, न्लौ चेत् पदं द्वितीयादि, सप्तमः प्रथमादि, अन्त्ये पञ्चमः षष्ठश्च ल् ।

Kedārabhaṭṭa gives a *śloka* which is at once its definition and example (op. cit. loc. cit.)

लक्ष्मैतत् सप्तगणा गोपेता भवति नेह विषमे जः ।
षष्ठोऽयं न लघू वा प्रथमेऽर्धे नियतमार्यायाः ॥
षष्ठो द्वितीयलान् न्ले परके मुखलाच्च सयतिपदनियमः ।
चरमेऽर्धे पञ्चमके तस्मादिह भवति षष्ठो लः ॥

(For a detailed study of this definition see Sathyanarayana, R., *Caturdaṇḍīprakāśikā*, Kan. tr., pp. 103, 104.)

Some examples of the *āryā* are given below:

1. Harṣavardhana, *Ratnāvalī-nāṭakam* (1.6)

द्वीपादन्यस्मादपि मध्यादपि जलनिधेर्दिश्योऽप्यन्तात् ।
आनीय झटिति घटयति विधिरभिमतमभिमुखीभूताः ॥

2. Nāgavarma, *Kannaḍakādambarī* (5.78)

दूरं मुक्तालतया बिससितया विप्रलोभ्यमानो मे ।
हंस इव दर्शिताशो मानसजन्मा त्वया नीतः ॥

3. Someśvara, AC (4.16.255, p. 28)

दलयतु दुरितमशेषं युष्माकं कंसवैरिणश्चक्रम् ।
यद् दैत्यकण्ठविपिनं छिन्द(न्न?)दपि न जायते कुण्ठम् ॥

Āryā has the following ten varieties (Piṅgalanāga, op.cit. 4.22-27)

i. *pathyā*: *Yati* completes the word at the end of third *caturmātrā gaṇa* in each half of *āryā*: e.g. Bharata (NŚ 15.293, p. 219):

मुक्तमृदुपद्मनेत्रा सितदीर्घबहुलमृदुकेशी ।
कस्य तु पृथुमृदुजघना तनुबाह्वंसोदरी पथ्या ॥

ii. *vipulā*: The verse-foot proceeds without such *yati*: e.g. Bharata (NŚ 15.214, p. 290):

विपुलजघनवदनस्तननयनैस्ताम्राधरोष्ठकरचरणैः ।
आयतनासागण्डैर्ललाटकर्णैः शुभा कन्या ॥

iii. *capalā*: The second and fourth are *ja-gaṇas*, preceded and followed by a *guru*.

iv. *mukhacapalā*: Aforesaid definition of *capalā* occurs in the *mukha* (first half) of *āryā*: e.g. Bharata (NŚ 15.218, p. 290):

आर्यामुखे तु चपला तथापि चार्या न मे यतः सा तु ।
दक्षा गृहकृत्येषु तथा दुःखे भवति दुःखार्ता ॥

v. *jaghana-capalā*: Aforesaid definition of *capalā* occurs in the *jaghana* (second half) of *āryā*:

वरमृगनयने चपलासि वरोरु शशाङ्कदर्पणनिभास्ये ।
कामस्य सारभूते न पूर्वमदचारुजघनेन ॥

vi. *mahācapalā*: Aforesaid definition of *capalā* occurs in both halves.

vii. (*āryā*) *gīti*: Both halves of *āryā*, especially the third and fourth quarters, are similar.

viii. *udgīti*: The two halves of *āryā* are interchanged.

ix. *āryāgīti*: This has been explained above (comm. on NN 3.2.128c).

x. *upagīti*: Aforesaid definition of *pathyā* occurs in both halves of *āryā*.

The *āryā* has a total of fourteen *caturmātrā-gaṇas* (seven per foot); among these, the sixth (in each foot) is ruled to be *ja-gaṇa* or *sarvalaghu,* leaving twelve *caturmātrā-gaṇas.* If each of these is composed of only *gurus,* then there are 24 *gurus* in all; a *guru* is prescribed to occur at the end of each half; so the total number of *gurus* is twentysix. This is regarded as *prakṛti.* If each of these is decomposed into two *laghus,* the *āryā* becomes modified. Therefore, there are twentysix varieties of *āryā* (the number after the hyphen indicates the number of *gurus* decomposed):

lakṣmī-0 *vṛddhi*-1 *buddhi*-2 *līlā*-3 *lajjā*-4 *kṣamā*-5 *dīrghā*-6 *gaurī*-7 *rājī*-8 *jyotsnā*-9 *chāyā*-10 *kānti*-11 *mahī*-12 *matī*-13 *kīrti*-14 *manoramā*-15 *rohiṇī*-16 *viśālā*-17 *vasudhā*-18 *śivā*-19 *hariṇī*-20 *cakrā*-21 *sārasī*-22 *kurarī*-23 *haṁsī*-24 *vadhū*-25

Abhinavagupta (*Abhinavabhārati,* comm. on NŚ 15.222-227, p. 291) gives a beautiful example in which the *āryā* is *sarvalaghu:*

शिशिरतरकिरणपरिकरसकलकलविरचित कपिशकचनिचय ।
समहृदय(तनुविनिहितधरणिधरवरसुत जयजय शिवा)

He quotes from an anonymous authority on the staggering number of *āryās* derivable by permutation (loc. cit. p. 292):

आर्याः शतसहस्राणि ज्ञेया ह्येकान्नविंशतिः ।
अष्टौ कोट्यः सहस्राणि विंशतिश्च प्रमाणतः ॥

152b. sā"ryā: This is the manner of singing the *āryā*: this *vṛtta* has two segments (*dala*). The first consists of the whole of the first foot and first half of the second foot. The second segment consists of the second half of the second foot. First segment is U; this is sung twice; sv are composed at the end (of the second rendering). According to SR (4.225) sv may be composed at the end of the (first) foot; second segment is D. A is composed of words not contained in U or D and includes the names of the *prabandha,* patron/hero and composer. Conclusion is on U. So the sequence is 2U-sv-D-A-U.

152c. Bhāvanī jāti, because *āryā* has sv pd tl. SR does not mention tl but Kallinātha does (p. 292). AC is more explicit (4.16.253, p. 28): *'tālenaikena kenacit.'* Thus Paṇḍarīka Viṭṭhala seems to imply the inclusion of tl in this *prabandha* by classifying it as *bhāvanī.*

152d. Niryukta, because *āryā* metre is prescribed.

BD mentions *āryā* (379b, p. 142; 398a, p. 143) but suffers lacuna for its description.

AC (4.16, 254, 255, p. 28): *Mātrā* disposition in *āryā* is 12.10.8/2.10.15. For an example, see above.

JS (p. 20) gives *sāmānyalakṣaṇa* in agreement with above, mentions and describes five *āryā* forms viz. *vipulā, capalā, jaghanā, mukhacapalā* and *pathyā.* The manner of singing is as outlined in commentary on NN 3.2.152b.

PS 3d, three *aṅgas*—sv pd tl, n. (4.46, p. 27).

SS–

LS (5.366-376, pp. 404, 405): *sāmānyalakṣaṇa*: U-first half, D-second half; A-names of *prabandha*, patron/hero, composer; sequence: 2U-sv-D-A-U. Sv may be sung at the end of the quarters or at the end of the first half; twenty-six varieties beginning with *lakṣmī* and ending with *vadhū* are described.

RK

SD

SP (1.566cd: p. 74): set in *āryā* metre.

153 15. *Gāthā*

153a. āryaiva: The difference between *āryā* and *gāthā* is one of language; the former is composed in Sanskrit and the latter, in Prākṛta. There are two forms of *gāthā* in Indian Prosody: The first has four equal feet and nine syllables per foot, such that they are structured as a *ma-gaṇa* followed by two *sa-gaṇas*: SSS IIS IIS. This is called *gāthā* by Jayakīrti (*Chando'nuśāsanam*, 2.83) and *kanaka* by Hemacandra (*Chando'nuśāsanam*, 2.97). This is relatively rare. The second form is the one described for *āryā* above and adopted by Hemacandra (ibid., 7.73), Jayadeva (*Jayadevacchandas*, 7.36), Piṅgalanāga (*Chandaḥśāstram*, 8.1), Kedārabhaṭṭa, (*Vṛttaratnākara*, 5.12).

But Śārṅgadeva compiles a second view of the *gāthā*, according to which it may have three, five or six feet instead of four (SR 4.231, 232):

आर्यैव प्राकृते गेया स्यात् पञ्चचरणाथ वा ।
त्रिपदी षट्पदी गाथेत्यपरे सूरयो जगुः ॥

Siṁhabhūpāla reads *'caraṇa'* in the above as *ca-gaṇa* (p. 293). This ascribes to SR the view that *gāthā* is derived by composing five *ca-gaṇas* in each of the four quarters of *āryā*. In this case, *gāthā* is not specifically restricted to the *gāthā* metre, because the disjunctive '*vā*' would mean that *gāthā* is composed in Prākṛta or in five *ca-gaṇas* in each of its feet. In this case, *gāthā* does not have four feet, but three or six.

153d. Niryukta, because Prākṛta language is prescribed.

BD mentions *gāthā* (379c, p. 142; 398d, p. 143) but suffers a lacuna for its description.

AC (4.16.256-257, p. 28): Same as *āryā* but in Prākṛta language. An example is given:

यो सूसोरारुद्धज अलं लच्छीणाहस्सणमहभन्नीये ।
जं सुमरिउँण यापद्रुभोन्स्वशिरैः संनिमत्स्वोविरयो ॥

JS (p. 22): Composed in Prākṛta with 3, 5 or 6 feet; so it is of three kinds; it has varieties such as *lakṣmī*.

SS (5.7 72cd-74ab, p. 217): *gāthā* is like *āryā* (which is not described by it), but in 3, 5 or 6 feet; its structure is of *āryā*, composed in Prākṛta words, in any *rāga* and *tāla*; it narrates a story from *purāṇa* etc. or poetry.

PS 3d, three *aṅgas*-sv pd tl; n (4.46, p. 27)

LS (5.377, p. 405): set in 3, 5 or 6 feet in words of Prākṛta

RK–

SD–

SP–

154-156 16. *Dvipatha*

154a. dodhakena: Kallinātha (on SR 4.232c, p. 294) establishes the useful equations *dvipathaka=dodhaka=dohā* (in Prākṛta) so that *dvipathaka* has a *niryukti* of namesake metre. *Dohā* is of course a well known metre in both ancient *Prākṛta* and many North Indian languages such as Hindī.

Dodhaka is *sama catuṣpadī-varṇa-vṛtta* with eleven syllables to the quarter, structured as भभभगग (Bharata, NŚ 15.37-39, p. 257; Hemacandra ,*Chando'nu'śāsanam*, 2.130; Jayadeva, *Jayadevacchandas*, 6.19; Jayakīrti, *Chando'nuśāsanam*, 2.97; Piṅgalanāga, *Chandaḥśāstram*, 6.18; *Prākṛtapaiṅgalam*, 2.104; Virahāṅka, *Vṛttajāti-samuccaya*, 5.24; Kedārabhaṭṭa, *Vṛttaratnākara*, 3.33; Virahāṅka also calls it *bhittaka*, op. cit. 4.55 and *taraṅgaka*, op. cit. 4.22). *Prākṛtapaiṅgala* also calls it *bandhu*; 2.100.

Some examples of this *vṛtta* are:

Bharata, NŚ (15.39):

प्रस्खलिताग्रपदप्रविचारं मत्तविघूर्णितगात्रविलासम् ।
पश्य विलासिनि कुञ्जरमेतं दोधकवृत्तमयं प्रकरोति ॥

AC (4.16, 263, p. 29): (*dodhaka*)

नौमि पदाम्बरुहद्वितयं ते माधव बाधितदैत्यकुटुम्ब ।
येन सरामि भवाम्बुधिपारं दुस्तरमस्तसमस्तविकल्पम् ॥

AC (4.16.260, p. 29) (*dvipatha*):

कुवलयकिसलयकान्तिर्वः सौख्यं वितरतु विष्णुः ।
त्रिभुवनसम्भवपरिरक्षासंहरणप्रभ विष्णुः ॥

155b. ubhayānubhayau parau: *Dvipathaka* is of four kinds: i. U-D both composed in sv with or without tl ii. both composed in (*gamakālapti*) *prayoga* in tl iii. both composed in both sv and *prayoga* iv. both bereft of both, composed only in pd.

156b. bhāvanī, when composed in sv pd tl

156c. tārāvalī, when composed in pd tl only.

156d. bhūribhedāḥ: *Dohā* is an ancient time-honoured Prākṛta metre; among the earliest examples are those composed by Buddhist Tāntrikas. It is a very popular metre in many North Indian languages used extensively by poets and saint singers. *Prākṛta-dohā* has 9 varieties: *sārasa, bhramara, hamsa, kurara, candralekhā, kuñjara, tilaka, haṁsakrīḍā, mayūra,* which accrue from differences in *mātrā* quantities in the odd and even feet, and more varieties by interchange and extrapolation. The last variety viz. *mayūra* is formed by retaining the original foot structure and suffixing a *śikhāpada,* i.e. an appendix of five, six or seven *laghus.* (For details, see SR 4.232-241); *śikhāpada* seems to have been a popular compositional device in early Indian music e.g. *śikhāpda* in *elās,* which I have discussed in detail elsewhere (Sathynarayana, R., *Elā; A Literary and Musical Study,* under print).

BD mentions *dvipathaka* (379d, p. 142) but has lacuna for description.

AC (4.16.158-161, pp. 28, 29): *dvipathaka* and *dodhaka* (4.16.262-264, p. 29, vide supra) are separate *prabandhas. Dvipathaka* (not restricted to *dodhaka vṛtta*) has three *gaṇas* and a final *guru* in odd feet, and two *gaṇas* with a pair of final *gurus* in the even feet; *ja-gaṇa* should be avoided; it has sv, but not set to tl. An illustration is given (4.16.260, p. 29; vide supra).

JS (p. 23) is the source for SR. Four *dvipathaka* varieties and its nine kinds as discussed above (comm. on NN 3.2.155b, 156d) are described in detail.

SS (5.7.74cd-76ab, p. 217): *dohā* metre in Prākṛta, desired tl, A in other words; conclusion on sv in two spans of *tāla.*

PS 3d, three *aṅgas*-sv pd tl; n (4.46, p. 27)

LS (5.378-396, pp. 406-408): mentions *niryukti* of *dvipathaka* metre—*bha-bha-bha-ga-ga*; four varieties, nine kinds and *śikhāpada* (which has five *laghus* here and the *dvipatha* possessing the *śikhāpada* suffix is named *śikhādvipatha* here; such a *prabandha* avoids equal moraic quantity in its feet). *Dvipathaka* has many varieties, but these are obsolete.

RK–

SD–

SP (1.565cd. p. 74): *Dvipathaka* has two forms: *nibaddha* and *anibaddha* .

157-159ab 17. *Kalahaṁsa*

157a. haṁsakacchandasā: This shows that the influence of Kallinātha is greater on NN than of Śārṅgadeva himself. Śārṅgadeva has, in fact prescribed the *kalahaṁsa* metre (4.242a). There is actually a metre called *kalahaṁsa* as will be seen presently. Both Kallinātha and Paṇḍarīka Viṭṭhala ignore this (obvious *chandoniryukti* of a namesake metre).The latter abbreviates (?) the name to *haṁsaka.* All collative sources of the text are unanimous on this reading. But it is not unlikely that it may have been *haṁsākhya á la* Kallinātha.

The *haṁsa* mentioned by Paṇḍarīka Viṭṭhala is a *sama-catuṣpadī* metre structured with *bha-ga-ga* in every foot and is so described in *Prākṛtapaiṅgala* (2.37). It is variously called *bhūtalatanvī* (Bharata, NŚ 32.65, 66, p. 309), *kuntalatanvī* (Hemacandra, *Chando'nuśāsanam*, 2.33; also, *akṣaropapada*, 2.25), *kāñcanamālā* (Jayakīrti, *Chando'nuśāsanam*, 2.23), *akṣarapaṅkti* (Virahāṅka, *Vṛttajātisamuccaya*, 5.5), *paṅkti* (Kedārabhaṭṭa, *Vṛttaratnākara*, 3.6) etc. It is very unlikely that this is the metre in which *kalahaṁsa-prabandha* was composed, in view of the examples available.

Kallinātha's commentary on the prescription of *kalahaṁsa-chandas* (SR 4.242a) is confusing. He equates this metre with *haṁsākhya* (*haṁsa*-named?) on the authority of a verse ascribed to Bharatamuni, which describes the metre (p. 297):

कलहंसस्य छन्दसो लक्षणं भारतीये जगत्यां नर्कुटभेदेषु मुनिनोक्तम्; यथा–
"द्वितीयसप्तमान्त्यं चतुर्थं यदा गुरुर्यदा च षष्ठो दशमोऽपि वा ।
अथोदिता हि पादे त्वथ जागते भवेदिदं तु हंसाख्यमिति स्मृतम् ॥"
इति । इदमेवोदाहरणं च । --- हंसाख्यमेव कलहंसम् ।

Veṅkaṭamakhin, who like Paṇḍarīka Viṭṭhala depends more on Kallinātha than on Śārṅgadeva borrows the same passage, claiming it to be written by the Mahātmā Bharata in the *Ādibharata* (CDP 9. 278, 279). However, the available versions of NŚ do not contain this verse, which gives a verse foot ISISISSIISIS, i.e. जरभर in *gaṇa* disposition.

Further, *haṁsākhya* is claimed to be a variety of *narkuṭa* belonging to the prosodial prototype called *jagatī* by Kallinātha. This is not true. NŚ describes eight varieties of *narkuṭa* under *jagatī* metre (32.273-292, pp. 351-355) viz. *rathottara* (*rathoddhati*, र न र ल ग), *budbuda* (स न स त ग), *varṁśapatra* (भ र न भ न ल ग),*udgatā* (स ज स स ज ग), *śivākṣarā (pramitākṣarā*, स ज स स), *haṁsavatī (dhvajiṇī*, स ज स ग भ र न ग ग) , *haṁsāsya* (स र भ र) and *toṭaka* (स स स स). *Haṁsāsya* is described in NŚ (32.290, 291, p. 355) thus:

दशमं सप्तमं यत्र चतुर्थकमथ षष्ठम् ।
तृतीयं निधनं गुरु कथितं (हंसास्यं) नर्कुटं जगतीगतम् ॥

and an example in Prākṛta follows:

दिअहंसा वसन्ते सळिळासए कुसुमासादळुद्धा कमण्णअरे ।
णळिणीपत्तमज्झे परिहिण्डिदा गमणाआसखिण्णा भमरावली ॥
(दिव्यहंसा वसन्ते सलिलाशये कुसुमास्वादलुब्धा कमलाकरे ।
नलिनीपत्रमध्ये परिहिण्डिता गमनायासखिन्ना भ्रमरावली ॥)

The illustration conforms to the *lakṣaṇa* viz. स र भ र. Even if it is assumed that *haṁsāsya* has generated *haṁsākhya* by graphic deterioration, this *lakṣaṇa* does not agree with the one quoted by Kallinātha (and Veṅkaṭamakhin) which yields a *gaṇa* disposition ज र भ र.

On the other hand, *kalahaṁsa* is a very well known metre in Sanskrit. Its *gaṇa* sequence is न भ ज य; it is so described by Hemacandra (*Chando'nuśāsanam*, 2.160), Jayakīrti (*Chando'nuśāsanam*, 2.132) and under the name *drutapadā* by Kedārabhaṭṭa (*Vṛttaratnākara*, 3.64.11) *et al.* Jayakīrti (op. cit. 2.142) also calls it *drutapadā* and divides the foot with *yatis* at 4, 8. Someśvara agrees with this description of *kalahaṁsa* (AC 4.16.324, 325, p. 26) and gives an example which accords with it:

पादो नभजयैर्युक्तः कर्तव्यः स्वमनीषया ।
पश्चात् स्वराः प्रयोक्तव्याः प्रबन्धे कलहंसके ॥
भुवनधारण-महाबल-विष्णो ।

Candrarāja (*Madanatilakam*, 10.83) corroborates this with an example of *kalahaṁsa* (also called *drutapada* in the work) in Kannaḍa:

पाडियनैदे तेरि धर्ममिदेम्मं
नडगिगुत्तमडसित्तेनसेंदुं
मिडुकदंते मरलुंदिद पांगिं
मडदिरोडिसुगुमेग्गननेंदुं

Only the 4th, 8th, 11th and 12th syllables in each foot are *gurus*, thus yielding the *gaṇa* disposition नभजय.

It is thus clear that Śārṅgadeva meant this *kalahaṁsa*. It is strange that this *vṛtta*, so well known to the Prosodists of Karnataka and Maharashtra escaped the meticulous scholarship of Kallinātha. Paṇḍarīka Viṭṭhala has added to the confusion by being content with the ambiguous '*haṁsaka*' which could be an abbreviation for *kalahaṁsa* or for *haṁsākhya*; this confusion could have been avoided if he had followed Śārṅgadeva instead of Kallinātha.

157b. jhampā-tanmita tālataḥ: (NN.1.153) झम्पाताले विरामान्तं द्रुतद्वन्द्वं लघुस्तथा। (००ı); '*tanmita-tālaḥ*' means any *deśī-tāla* whose *āvarta* (cycle) has the same time quantity as *jhampā tāla*. Kallinātha elaborates '*jhampāditālataḥ*' of SR (4.242) with '*ādi-śabdena tanmātrasammita-deśītālāntaram gṛhyate*' (p. 298). NN is more explicit here.

158a. gadyajaḥ padyajaḥ: SR (4.243) has called these, *varṇaja* and *mātrika* more appropriately. Paṇḍarīka Viṭṭhala has so modified the statement of SR that if the *kalahaṁsa* is composed in prose, sv should be first sung and then the words. The basis of such modification is Kallinātha (p. 298):

वर्णजः पद्यरूपः मात्रिको गद्यरूपः, वर्णजस्योक्तलक्षणानुसारेण नियतगणबद्धत्वात् पद्यरूपत्वम्; मात्रिकस्यानियतगणबद्धत्वात् गद्यरूपत्वम् ।

BD (423, p.146): Each verse foot is first rendered, followed by sv; composed in *jhampā* etc. tl.

AC (4.16.324, 325, p. 36): see above.

JS (p. 27): describes only *mātrā-kalahaṁsa* which has 14 *laghus* in odd numbered feet and *graha* (?9) in even numbered feet (in a *viṣama-catuṣpadī*).

PS 3d, 3 *aṅgas*—pd pt tl, n-an (4.48, p. 27)

SS (5.7.66b-68a, p. 216): *kalahaṁsī prabandha*, in *kalahaṁsa* metre in *śampā tāla* (2.68ab: ० ० 'ı); sv sung after first foot. A in other words; conclusion is on sv.

LS (5.397-401ab, pp. 408, 409): *haṁsākhya* metre; sv first, then pd of first foot; *jhampā* or equivalent tl; sv preponderates at end of (each) foot; *padyaja, gadyaja* varieties; U—first half; D—second half; A in other words, including (the three) names.

ṚK (3.129, p. 53) describes only *gadya* variety; sv first, then pd; *chandas* has *bhajaya* (!) *gaṇas.*

SD—

SP. (1.565ab, p. 74) composed in the tl *haṁsanāda*!

159cd-160. 18. *Toṭaka*

159c. Toṭakacchandas is a *sama catuṣpadī* with twelve syllables per quarter, a *prastāra* of the metric prototype *jagatī*, structured as ससस स (Piṅgala, *Chandaḥśāstram* 6.31, *Prākṛtapaiṅgalam* 2.129; Bharata, NŚ 32.288, 289, p. 354; Hemacandra, *Chando'nuśāsanam,* 2.162; Jayakīrtī, *Chando'nuśāsanam,* 2.121; Jayadeva, *Jayadevacchandas,* 6.33; Kedārabhaṭṭa, *Vṛttaratnākra,* 3.47; Virahāṅka, *Vṛttajātisamuccaya,* 5.27; also *chittaka,* ibid., 4.54; also *nandinī,* ibid., 3.20; also *bhramarāvali,* ibid., 4.61)

Three example are available; thus Bharata (NŚ 32.289, p. 354):

रमणीसहिदो रअणीविरमे गगणङ्गणए खगकोसिअओ ।
अ(नुवाया)सए हि विघाट्टदओ परिमण्टदि कोटरअं सुहिदम् ॥
(रमणीसहितो रजनीविरमे गगनाङ्गणे खगकौशिकः ।
अनुवायसैर्हि विघट्टितः परिमण्ठति कोटरं सुहितम् ॥)

Halāyudhabhaṭṭa (*Mṛtasañjīvanī,* comm. on Piṅgala, loc. cit.):

त्यज तोटकमर्थवियोगकरं प्रमदाधिकृतं व्यसनोपहतम् ।
उपधाभिरशुद्धमतिं सचिवं नरनायक! भीरुकमायुधिकम् ॥

Someśvara (AC 4.16.266, p. 29):

अतिवामनरूपधरस्य हरेः सदृशौ न धराधरवारिनिधी ।
पदमात्रममुष्य गुणान् कथयेयुरमी मनुजाः कथमल्पधियः ॥

159d. pratipādam padaiḥ svaraiḥ: SR (4.244-245) does not declare this *lakṣaṇa* for the *toṭaka* foot; NN has athetised the *lakṣaṇa* therein that sv should occur at the end of each foot.

BD–

AC (4.16.267, p. 29): in *toṭaka* metre (ससससस); four feet; Sanskrit or Prākṛta; in any desired *rāga* and *tāla*. For an example, see above.

JS–

PS lacuna

SS–

LS–

RK–

SD–

SP (1.569ab, p. 74): composed in *toṭaka-vṛtta.*

161-162 19. *Dhaṭa*

This *prabandha* is called '*ghaṭa*' by some (e.g. SR 4.244, 245; CDP 9.68); in *dhaṭa-ghaṭa,* one is probably derived by graphic deterioration of the other.

161a. dvipadī (see NN 3.2.136 and comm. on same): *cha*–5 *ta* (or 5 *bha*)-*ga.* The first half of *dhaṭa* should be composed with such structure.

161b. Adya is the collative consensus; if conjecturally emended to *'ardha'*, it confers textual consistency as well as concurrence with parallel treatises such as SR (4.246), Somarāja (*Saṅgītaratnāvalī*? extr. *Bharatakośa*, p. 292), JS, AC (see below) etc. Siṁhabhūpāla also explains the text similarly (p. 301); but Kallinātha (p. 301) says:

द्विपद्यां ... यावन्मात्रमर्धमुक्तं तावन्मात्रमेव पूर्वार्धमुद्ग्राहसंज्ञकं घटे तेनैर्बद्धं कर्तव्यमित्यर्थः ।

His attempt to justify this interpretation on the ground that the expression *ardha* is relative and the sense would remain uncompleted if not explained this way is weak.

161c. padottarārdham: If the text is emended to mean half of the *vṛtta,* it would gain the support of parallel works.

162c. dvyaṅgaḥ: '*Tryaṅgaḥ*' accords well with the stated *lakṣaṇa.* It is of *dīpanī-jāti* because of pd, tn and (accruing from *dvipadī*) tl, if it also has sv according to a different school; if only pd, tn and tl are present, its class is *bhāvanī.* Kallinātha is silent, but Veṅkaṭamakhin (CDP 9.68) classifies *ghaṭa* as a *dvijāti prabandha* under *dīpanī* and *bhāvanī.*

BD–

AC–

JS (p. 24): First half in *dvipadī,* second in tn, or *vice versa;* A in other words; conclusion is on tn; any desired tl.

SS (5.7.77d-79ab, p. 218) as in JS.

PS 3d; three *aṅgas*—pd tn tl, n (4.47, p. 27)

LS (5.401cd-402ab, p. 409): First half in *dvipadī* metre, U; second in pd. *Prabandha* is called *ghaṭa.*

RK–

SD–

SP (1.567ab, p. 74) *dhaṭṭa, sādabāhulya* (*śabda-? pāda-?*)

163-165 20. *Vṛtta*

163a. vṛttena chandasā: '*Vṛtta*' has a general meaning: any verse form of four feet with a definite prosodial structure; it also means a specific metre of this name and a specific namesake *prabandha.* Śārṅgadeva mentions both views while describing *toṭaka prabandha* (SR 4.244cd-245), is personally inclined to the first and compiles the second from others. *Kanda, turaga* (=*haya*) *līlā, krauñcapada, āryā, gāthā, dvipatha, kalahaṁsa, dvipadī, toṭaka, tripadī, ṣaṭpadī* etc. are restricted (*niryukta*) to namesake metres and therefore may be called *vṛttaprabandhas.* Śārṅgadeva accords only half consent to this view; for non-consent, he argues that according to other (ancient) teachers *vṛtta* is (also) a specific metre with a definite prosodial structure; this *prabandha* employs it by prescription and is so named *vṛtta.* However, he does not characterise the *vṛtta.*

The *vṛtta* metre appears in two forms—as *varṇa vṛtta samacatuṣpadī*—in Indian metrics. First, it has ten syllables per quarter, structured as भभभग (Bharata, NŚ, Chowkhamba edn. 32.217; it is also called *dodhaka* by Bharata, NŚ 15.37.39, p. 257, *sāravatī* by *Prākṛtapaiṅgala,* 2.94 and *citragati* by Hemacandra, *Chando'nuśāsanam* , 2.113 and by Jayakīrti, *Chando'nuśāsanam,* 2.89). Second, it takes twenty syllables per quarter, structured as रजरजरजलग, or more simply, ten units of *laghu-guru.* The former is defined by most of the prosodists e.g. Hemacandra (*Chando'nuśanam,* 2.335), Jayadeva (*Jayadevacchandas,* 7.23), Jayakīrti (*Chando'nuśāsanam,* 2.232) and Kedārabhaṭṭa (*Vṛttaratnākara,* 3.98) and the latter by Piṅgalanāga (*Chandaḥśāstram,* 7.24: '*gliti vṛttam*'.

Besides the above, a third form of *vṛtta* is also defined by Kedārabhaṭṭa (*Vṛttaratnākara,* 3.40; it is called *vṛntā* by Hemacandra, Jayakīrti, Jayadeva, Piṅgalanāga *et al.*). This has the *gaṇa* disposition ननसगग and thus has eleven syllables per quarter.

As mentioned above, SR does not define the specific form of *vṛtta,* but leaves the question open; but Kallinātha shows here his personal preferene to Piṅgala's definition (and this lead is taken up by Paṇḍarīka Viṭṭhala and Veṅkaṭamakhin) and extracts an illustration from the latter's commentator, Halāyudhabhaṭṭa (*Mṛtasañjīvanī*, on op. cit. 7.23):

गात्रदु:खकारि कर्मनिर्मितं भवत्यनर्थहेतुरत्र
तेन सर्वमात्मतुल्यमीक्षमाण उत्तमं सुखं भजस्व ।
विद्धि बुद्धिपूर्वकं ममोपदेशवाक्यमेतदादरेण
साधुवृत्तमुत्तमं महाकुलप्रसूतमेति नो हि जन्म ॥

AC (4.16.244, 245, p. 26) offers an illustration for the same form:

(वेध)सा मनोहरस्वरस्तवायगीयमान वृत्तसाम
राजते जगत्त्रयेऽपि यस्य दुष्टदैत्यवंशदाहि धाम ।
सर्वपापहारि पावनं हरे: सदा स्मरामि तस्य नाम
कीर्तयामि वाऽद्भुतं चरित्रमस्य विष्टपत्रयीललाम ॥

Two illustrations may be given for the third form viz.ननसगग; the first is by Nārāyaṇa Purohita in his commentary *Maṇinidhi* on *Vṛttaratnākara* (3.12):

अलमलमतिनिपुणैर्वाक्यैर्यदुवर विसृज सृतिं रुद्धाम् ।
अनुनयतमथजनं स्निग्धं तवमयरसलहरी वृत्त ।

The second is offered by Kalidāsa in his commentary *Śrutabodha* on V*ṛttaratnākara* (loc. cit.):

श्रीनिधाङ्गगुणिनीन्दुकराणां सत्यलोकमुनिबृन्दमिदं तत् ।
धन्यमेव तव दर्शनकाले स्वागतादि वचनं लभते यत् ॥

As pointed out already, NN favours the form '*gliti daśadvayam*', i.e. रजरजरजलग.

164d. pūrvāparavibhāgataḥ: U-*pāda* 1-2, D-*pāda* 3-4.

165a. padataḥ: other than those in U and D (and containing names of *prabandha*, patron/hero, composer).

165cd. Tārāvalī because *vṛtta* has pd and tl if it omits sv (according to some; if it has sv also according to others it should be *bhāvanī;* it is described in this latter manner by PS (see below). However, it is not clear how it could be *dīpanī*; probably, it takes bd also optionally. Veṅkaṭamakhin also describes it (CDP 9.67, 68) as *bhāvanī*, but Kallinātha is silent.

While concluding his description of *vṛtta prabandha*, Śārṅgadeva refers the reader for the numerous varieties of *vṛtta* metre to a work called *Chandoviciti* (SR 4.248ab):

छन्दश्चित्यां विचेतव्याश्छन्दसां बहवो भिदा: ।

Kallinātha merely says (p. 301): '*chandovicitisaṁjñakena granthena ityarthaḥ*'. But Siṁhabhūpāla makes Śārṅgadeva its author (p. 302): '*chandovicitināmni* ***madīye*** *granthe vilokanīyāḥ*' (emphasis is mine). There are several works of this name: a text on *Vedāṅga-chandas*, alternative name of *Yādavaprakāśa's* commentary on Piṅgala, of Piṅgala's *Chandaḥśāstra* (*Chandaḥsūtra*), of *Jānāśrayīchandas*, of *Ratnamañjuṣā*, of a work by Gargya, of *Daṇḍin*, of a work in Buddhist Pāli, etc. But no work of this name written by or ascribed to Śārṅgadeva is known.

BD (400, p. 144) mentions *vṛtta* (378b, p. 142) but the description is opaque due to corruption.

AC (4.16.244-246, pp. 26, 27). *Vṛtta* varieties are endless; according to Mataṅga, *vṛtta prabandha* should be composed in *vṛtta* metre which has for its structure three *ra-ja*(*gaṇa*) units followed by *guru* and *laghu*. For an illustration, see above.

JS (pp.16-17): The *vṛttas, sama, viṣama, ardhasama* etc. varieties are discussed in general; *laksaṇa* of *guru, laghu, gaṇas* etc. is given. *Vṛtta prabandha* is sung in any *vṛtta*, in any *tāla* suitable to the metre, with or without sv; when sv is present, it is sung at the end of the *pāda* or at the end of he *vṛtta* itself. A is composed in words other than those in the *vṛtta*.

SS (5.7.57cd-64ab): the eight *gaṇas ma, ya* etc. are described; the *vṛtta prabandha* has pt tn tl and bd suitable to the theme in all (any) *rāgas*.

PS 3d, three *aṅgas*—pd tl sv, n (4.46, p. 27)

LS (5.7.402cd-403, pp. 409, 410): sung in *vṛtta* metre; according to some, it has (sv, and according to others) no sv; the U,D and A(?) are composed in the metre.

RK—

SD—

SP (1.567cd, p. 74): composed in all metres.

166-171ab 21. *Mātṛkā*

166a. Mātṛkā means alphabet or mother goddess. For Sanskrit alphabet (see comm. on NN 3.2.27d). Mother goddesses are variously described, *Pūrṇodarī, Virajā* etc. 50 (Nijaguṇa Śivayogi, *Vivekacitāmaṇi,* 8.506), *Brāhmī* etc. 7or 8, *Śrī, Lakṣmī* etc. 7 or 8, *Kālī, Kauśika* etc. 7 (Musunūri Veṅkaṭaśāstri, *Vidyārtikalpataruvu,* 80), *Vyāpinī, Tāpinī* etc. 8 (*Śāradatilaka*), *Gaurī, Padmā* etc. 17(*Bahvṛcapariśiṣṭa, Nṛsiṁhapārijāta*). The *bīja-mantras* of these deities are the *mātṛkā mantra varṇa,* or the *kalāmātṛkās* (*Nāradīyapurāna*) etc.

The *bījakṣaras* of *mantras* are *acyuta, ānandabhairava, iṣṭadaiva, īśvara* etc., words.

167d. mārga tālas: *caccatpuṭa* etc. five *tālas* (NN 1.110-114)

168b. deśi tālas: *ādi* etc. *tālas* (NN 1.138-195)

168c. miśraṇād: Sanskrit—*deśī tāla,* Prākṛta—*mārgatāla*

169b. mātṛkā: cf SR (4.251):

उभयोर्मिश्रणादुक्ता मातृका दिव्यमानुषी ।
अनिबद्धा निबद्धा च द्विधा सा गद्यपद्यजा ॥

Does '*sā*' here refer to the *mātṛkā-prabandha* as such or (because of proximity) to its variety *divyamānuṣī* alone? Paṇḍarīka Viṭṭhala has avoided this ambiguity and explicitly states that each of *divyā*, *mānuṣī* and *divyamānuṣī* has two varieties, viz. *nibaddha* and *anibaddha*.

169d. padaṣoḍaśato AC (4.16.310-314, pp. 32, 33) gives the following illustration for the *mātṛkā* U, a creation of his own:

असौ शरण्यः शरणागतानाम् । आकारमाहात्म्यपरास्तकामः ।
इष्टार्थदायी सततं प्रजानाम् । ईशानकल्पः कलिकालतेजाः ।
उदारनेपथ्यधरः परेषाम् । ऊष्माणमन्तं शमयन् रणेषु ।
ऋत्विक्द्विजैराहिततिग्मतेजा । एकातपत्रं कलयन् प्रभुत्वम् ।
ऐश्वर्यवीरो हरिणेक्षणानाम् । ओष्ठप्रकम्पात् परमात्तझम्पः ॥
औदार्यवान् बिभ्रदवोढरागाम् । अङ्के विपञ्चीमिव पक्षलक्ष्मीम् ।
अः केनचिन्नूनमसौ पृथिव्याम् ।
(कृतावतारः किल कारणेन ।) सोमेश्वरक्ष्मापतिरभ्रगङ्गा । तरङ्गसंस्पर्धियशाश्चकास्ति ।

170a. kakārādi catustriṁśat: In the *mahāṣoḍhā nyāsa* of *Śrīvidyātantra*, the following *mantra* names commencing from *ka* to *kṣa* have been prescribed for *yoginī nyāsa*:

कालरात्री खण्डिता गायत्री घण्टाकर्षिणी ङार्णा चण्डा छाया जया झङ्कारिणी ज्ञानरूपा टङ्कहस्ता ठङ्कारिणी डामरी ढङ्कारिणी णार्णा तामसी स्थाणु दाक्षायणी धात्री नारी पार्वती फट्कारिणी बन्धिनी भद्रकाली महामाया यशस्विनी रमा लम्बोष्ठी वरदा श्री षण्डा सरस्वती हंसवती क्षमावती ।

The D and A of *mātṛkā prabandha* may be composed from these. While Kallinātha requires the D to be composed of twentyfive words commencing with *ka* through *ma* (p. 303), Paṇḍarīka Viṭṭhala mentions only thirtyfour; the syllable to be omitted is not known.

170c. niyata: the unclassified consonants from *ya* to *kṣa*.

170d. varṇapūrvapadaiḥ: *divyā*—Sanskrit words; *mānuṣī*—Prākṛta words; *divyamānuṣī*—mixture of both. Paṇḍarīka Viṭṭhala has thus erroneously interpreted Kallinātha's words (p. 303):

दिव्यादिभेदानुसारेणानियतवर्णपूर्वकैः संस्कृतादिपदैर्गातृनेत्रप्रबन्धनामाङ्कितो गातव्यः ।

According to other ancient authorities A of *mātṛkā* varieties should be composed thus: *divyā*—Sanskrit words commencing from the letters *ya* to *kṣa*, *mārga tālas*; *mānuṣī*—words of Prākṛta, *deśī tālas*; *divyamānuṣī*—Sanskrit words, *deśī tālas*, Prākṛta words, *mārga tālas*; Siṁhabhūpāla asseverates that the *mātṛkā prabandha* is of the nature of the entirety of *mantras* and of the pantheon; so it bestows all fruits and fulfilments; he therefore exhorts that it should be performed when one is pure, full of faith and attentiveness. Sung otherwise, demerit (sin?) accrues.

171b. niryukta in *tāla*; has two *aṅgas*—pd, tl and so belongs to *tārāvalī* class.

BD (503, 504, p.153): Intended meaning is sung in words, each commencing with a *mātṛkā* letter.

AC (4.16.310-315, pp. 34-35): as in BD; no rule on *rāga* or tl.

JS (p. 13) as in BD; three kinds: *divyā*—Sanskrit, *divya tāla; manuṣī*-Prākṛta, *deśī tāla; divyamānuṣī-bhāṣā-vaicitrya, mārga* and *deśī tālas;* again of two kinds: *nibaddha, anibaddha; mātṛkā* delights king, gods, sages, *gandharvas* etc. and extols *upaniṣadic* doctrines. JS describes it as the first *prabandha*; composed of bd pt pd tl.

SS (5.7.35cd-39ab): first to be described; as in BD; composed in Sanskrit or Prākṛta, or their mixture, with pd pt bd tl.

PS 3d, three *aṅgas*—pd bd tl; n (4.47, p. 27)

LS (5.404-411ab, pp. 410-411): composed in words commencing with each of the fifty alphabets; *divyā, mānuṣī* as above; *divyamanusī* in *maṇipravāla* language (a mixture of South Indian languages and Sanskrit); *nibaddha-anibaddha mātṛkās.* U in sixteen words each beginning on a different vowel; D in thirtyfive words commencing from *ka* to *kṣa.* A in Sanskrit, *deśī tāla.*

RK

SD (4.437-440, pp, 76, 77): as in BD; a few sentences are sung prior to *mātṛkā-mantra varṇas; divyā* etc. three varieties as above; *anibaddha* and *nībaddha* varieties as above; *mātṛkā* is *sarvamantramayī, sarvasiddhipradāyinī.*

SP (1.538, p. 78): as in BD; *sarvamantramayī, sarvasiddhipradāyinī.*

171cd-176 22. *Rāgakadamba*

171c. rāgaiḥ: Among *rāga, tāla, vṛtta, rasa* etc. which may be applied to a *prabandha, rāga* is the most prominent; hence it is mentioned first; also, this is why the *prabandha* is named *rāgakadamba*; every *vṛtta,* its half or quarter in the *prabandha* may have a different *rāga*; hence, *aneka rāgaiḥ, rāgakadamba.*

171c. tālaiḥ: each *vṛtta* is set in a different *tāla.*

172a. gadyaih: AC (4.16.51, p. 46) declares that this song may be composed in prose without tl; the plural implies different forms or segments of *gadya* to suit the various *rāgas, rasas* etc.

172a. Padyaiḥ is redundant to *vṛttaiḥ.*

172a. rasaiḥ: Each *vṛtta,* or each of its parts, or each of the *gadya* segments should express a *rasa* such as *śānta, vīra* etc.

172c. tālaiḥ: Each of four *vṛttas* is set to a different *tāla.*

172d. Aṅgakaiḥ implies the *prabandha jāti.* Among the six *aṅgas,* pd and tl are already indicated. If only these occur, *nandyāvarta rāgakaḍamba* is a *tārāvalī.* If the composer employs one, two, three or all four of sv, pt, bd and tn, the composition is of *bhāvanī, dīpanī, ānandinī* or *medinī jāti* respectively.

173b. nandyāvarta: NN has omitted a line from SR (4.254) in the definition of *nandyāvarta*:

नन्द्यावर्तो भवेत्तस्य तालमानद्वयेन वा ।

The meaning of the disjunctive '*vā*' here is: if the *tāla* of the *prabandha* has a long span e.g. *simhanandana*, U and D may both be encompassed within a single *āvarta* of the *tāla;* if the *tāla* has a short span e.g. *ādi, jhampā* etc. these may be accommodated in its two *āvartas.*

174b. dviguṇaḥ: *Svastika rāgakadamba* is composed in eight *rāgas*, eight *tālas* and eight *vṛttas* (or two of each).

174c. Abjagarbha is included in *abjapatra* according to Simhabhūpāla (p. 306). Kallinātha adds (p. 304) that according to some, *svastika* defined as above, itself is *abjagarbha.*

175b. paraḥ-paraḥ-svastika or *abjagarbha*—eight (or two each) *rāgas, tālas* and *vṛttas*; *abjapatra*—sixteen (or four of each); *bhramara*—thirtytwo (or eight of each); *āmreḍita*—sixtyfour (or sixteen of each). JS, AC and SS do not describe these *rāgakadamba* kinds.

175d. udgrāhadhruvau: Whatever the variety, the first half constitutes U and the second D.

176b. ābhoga: Śārngadeva and others do not mention A separately for *rāgakadamba*; but as required in the general rule अनुक्ताभोगवस्तूनां पदैराभोगकल्पना (SR 4.310), A must be composed for *rāgakadamba* with words other than those in the *vṛttas*; in the concluding section of the final *rāga* the names of *prabandha*, patron and composer should be incorporated.

176d. ādi: This composition has no rule for the number or order of the *angas*; so it can have two, three, four, five or all six *angas* (in whatever order) and hence may be of any of the five *jātis.*

Rāgakadamba was a scholarly but popular *prabandha.* Gopālanāyaka of Karnataka had composed, in the late 13th or early 14th century *bhramarasvastika* and *amreḍitasvastika* varieties which were quite well known in the middle of the 15th century and are mentioned by Kallinātha (p. 305) in illustration. It may be remarked that these are the only songs he offers as illustrations from contemporary musical practice in the entire *prabandhādhyāya* of the SR. It is strange that he refers to them as *svastikas* rather than as *rāgakadambas.* Thus Gopālanāyaka's *bhramarasvastika* was composed in thirtytwo *rāgas* and thirtytwo *tālas*, its U being in the *rāga mālavaśrī* and the *tāla simhanandana*; it was a *tārāvalī*, consisting of only pd, tl; he had composed another *bhramara* with pd pt sv tn tl (i.e. without bd) in the *rāga velāvalī* and the *tāla darpaṇa*, an *ānandinī*; he had also composed *medinī rāgakadamba.*

The *rāgakadamba* corresponds somewhat to the *rāgatālamālikā-prabandha* of Karnataka music.

BD—

AC (4.16.50-51, p. 46): *Nandyāvarta* and *svastika* are composed respectively in four and eight *vṛttas, rāgas* and *tālas*; they are composed with *tāla* if in verse and without *tāla* if in prose.

JS (p. 46): *Nandyāvarta* and *svastika* as in AC; A in other words; conclusion on U in two *tāla* spans; *svastika* in many *rāgas*.

SS (5.35cd-39ab): *Nandyāvarta* and *svastika* as in AC; A in other words; conclusion on U in two *tāla* spans.

PS 3d, two *aṅgas*—pd tl; n-an (4.43, p. 26).

LS (5.411cd-418, pp. 411-412): all four varieties as in NN; conclusion on *gadya* according to some.

RK (3.98-100, p. 50): only *nandyāvarta* and *svatika* as in AC; the former is in *gadya* according to some.

SD (4.441-446ab, p. 77): all four varieties as in NN; varieties formed by progressively doubling *rāgas* etc. beyond *abjapatra* not found in usage.

SP (1.569cd, p. 74): called *rāgamiśra*: '*rāgāṇām miśraṇādeva sammato rāgamiśrakaḥ*'.

177-185 23. *Pañcatāleśvara*

177a. Rāgaiḥ is *sākṣarālapti* but is *rāgālapti* in parallel texts. This is clearly stated by Siṁhabhūpāla (p. 310):

'यद्यप्यालापशब्देनाप्यतालत्वं लभ्यते, तथाप्यत्र विहिततालप्राप्तिः स्यादिति तन्निरासार्थमुक्तमताल इति'

(Absence of *tāla* is implied in the word '*ālāpa*'; even then, absence of *tāla* is explicitly stated in '*atāla*' in order to obviate a possible doubt that an appropriate *tāla* may be applicable.)
and by Kallinātha (p. 306):

अत्रालापशब्देन रागालाप उच्यते, न तु गमकालप्तिः ।

177c. caccatpuṭena: *Pañcatāleśvara* is so named because it is required to be composed in the five *mārga tālas, caccatpuṭa, cācatpuṭa, ṣaṭpitāputraka, sampakveṣṭāka* and *udghaṭṭa* for details of which see NN1.110-114.

177d. padapañcakam: If these five words are denoted by p_1 p_2 p_3 p_4 p_5, then they are sung in this order- p_1 p_1-p_2 p_2-p_3 p_3-p_4 p_4-p_5 p_5.

178a. īpsitam: without restriction that the *pāṭas* of only such instruments, that only such and such *svaras*, that only such and such *aṅgas*, in only such and such order shoud be composed.

178b. pṛthak: After *ālāpa*, the first word is sung; then *svaras* (or *pāṭas*) in a different *dhātu;* the word is sung again; next *pāṭas* (or *svaras*) are rendered in different melody. Now the second word is sung; this is followed by *svaras/pāṭa* in different *dhātu*. The second word is sung (in the same) *dhātu*; then the *pāṭa/svara* follows in different *dhātu*. Care should be exercised that the order *svara-svara* or *pāṭa-pāṭa* is avoided between the words. The remaining three words are performed in the same manner. This is the manner of singing the *pañcatāleśvara* and is true of all the five segments.

178d. paṭahasambhavaiḥ: For such *pāṭas*, NN 1.12-16. SR (6.822) mentions sixteen *pāṭākṣaras* for *paṭaha*: *ka kha ga gha ṭa ṭha ḍa ḍha ṇa ta tha da dha na ra ha.*

179a. antara: Expedient bridge between D and A prescribed for only *sālagasūḍa-prabandhas.* (For its use in *pañcatāleśvara* see comm. on NN 3.2.7b.)

179c. pūrvavat: With this *atideśa* (extended application), it should be understood that an *antara* should be composed in *huḍukkā pāṭas* in two *tāla* spans.

179d. Hauḍukka *pāṭas* are obtained by omitting '*dem*' from *paṭaha pāṭas* and adding '*majhem*' (SR 6.1076, 1077):

कुर्वीत पाटहान् वर्णानिह देङ्कारवर्जितान् ।
अत्रान्यैरधिकावुक्तौ मझेङ्कारौ मनीषिभिः ॥

180d. śaṅkhapāṭaiḥ: sounds such as *ghum ghum tho digi* etc. (Kallinātha, p. 308).

181b. Dala is understood as pd here. The use of sv and pt which were prescribed in the singing of five or six words in *caccatpuṭa* etc. *tālas* is not specifically mentioned here. But they must be taken as implied here by *pūrvavat.*

181d. kāṁsyatālasambhavapāṭakaiḥ: *pāṭas* preponderant with *tatakaṭa.*

182b. padaṣaṭkakam: thus totalling twentyseven words in the *pañcatāleśvara.*

182c. murajapāṭaiḥ: *paṭaha-pāṭas* in which *takiṭatom* are prominent.

183b. Ābhoga should be composed in *udghaṭṭa tāla* itself, after the *antara* of *muraja pāṭas* in two spans of the same *tāla*, in *druta* or *madhya-laya.* After A, tn is composed in the same *tāla.* Because *tena* signifies auspiciousness, this is called *maṅgalavākya* elsewhere (SR 4.263, JS p.14, RK 3.112 etc.).

184a. pañca: Bd is omitted; hence *ānandinī* in *jāti.*

184a. niryukta JS (p.14) and RK (3.114) further require that *pañcatāleśvara* should be sung in one of the *rāgas*, viz. *śrī, mālavaśrī, velāvalī, toḍī, naṭṭā* and *śuddhavarāṭī.*

184b. dhātukam: UDA-*antara*; if A is omitted, only three *dhātus* in each of the sub-compositions (in *caccatpuṭa* etc.). cf. Kallinātha (p. 309):

त्रिधातवोऽवान्तरप्रबन्धाः पञ्च । महाप्रबन्धस्त्वाभोगेन सह चतुर्धातुरित्यवगन्तव्यः ।

184c. īśvara: It is like the master or king in respect of all other *prabandhas*; cf. also commentary on NN 3.2.177c.

BD—

AC—

JS (pp. 13, 14). as in NN; the number of words is explicitly mentioned as twentyseven; *rāganiryukti* is given as aforesaid (comm. on NN 3.2.184a); *vīrāvatāra* and *śṛṅgāratilaka* are described.

SS (5.7.39cd): as in NN; *Mṛdaṅga* is mentioned *vice muraja*; A is called *maṅgalavākya;* the composition is dear to the gods; it should be sung in *śuddha-* or *rāgāṅga rāgas.*

PS 3d, 4 *aṅgas*—sv bd tn tl; an (4.51, p. 27)

LS (5.418cd-434, pp. 413-415): as in NN. A also contains words of benediction; U and D are each set to three *tālas*. According to Kohala and others, the first two words in each segment constitute U while the remaining three form D. All gods are propitiated by the *prabandha* which yields the fruits of the *agniṣṭoma* etc. *yajñas* and of bathing in the celestial river to the performer, patron and listeners.

RK (3.103-114, pp. 50-51): as in NN; *rāgas* prescribed as above (comm. NN 3.2.184a).

SD (4.446-455ab, pp. 78-79): as in NN.

SP (1.570cd, p.74): *pañcatāla* is composed in five *tālas.*

186-188ab 24. *Tālārṇava*

186a. īpsitāṅgaiḥ: The *prabandha* may have two, three, four, five or six *aṅgas* and therefore may belong to any of the five classes.

186c. āvṛttibahubhiḥ: Paṇḍarīka Viṭṭhala has thus modified '*bhūritālaḥ*' of SR (4.265a). He seems to mean that the same number of *tālas* are repeated over and over again. But SR means that the number of *tālas* is very large. This is why it is *tālārṇava*, ocean of *tālas.*

188a. dhruvamadhyapada: The general rule is that A is composed of words other than those in U, M or D. *Tālārṇava* is an exception; its A is constituted by words which occur in D; so the names of the *prabandha*, patron and composer have to be incorporated in D itself; there is no A other than this. This exception is made only by Paṇḍarīka Viṭṭhala.

188b. anyat: There are some differences: *Tālārṇava* has only one *rāga,* not many as in *rāgakadamba*; progressive doubling of the number of components applies to *tāla* and *vṛtta* alone but not to *rāga.*

BD—

AC (4.16.52, p.46): composed in many *tālas,* one *rāga,* prose or verse.

JS—

SS (5.7.133cd-134): as in AC.

PS 2d, 2 *aṅgas*—pd tl; an (4.26, p. 25); 3d, two *angas*—pd tl, n-an, (4.43, p. 26)

LS (5.434cd-435, p. 415): composed in many *tālas*; two kinds: prose or verse.

RK (3.118cd, p. 52): as in LS

SD (4.455, p. 79): as in LS; name is apt.

SP (1.570ab, p. 74): composed in many *tālas.*

DESCRITPIONS OF VIPRAKĪRṆA PRABANDHAS

Among the thirtsix *viprakīrṇa-prabandhas*, BD describes only eight. AC, twenty-seven; JS, 35; SS, 22; PS describes none, but summarises all information (*dhātus, aṅgas, niryukta* etc.) but directly borrows it form JS; LS and SD are content mostly in following SR (as NN, CDP etc. do). SP is frivolous, uninformed. Therefore, the following commentary will draw upon only BD, AC, JS, SS and PS where pertinent.

188cd-189 1. *Śrīraṅga*

188c. caturbhiḥ: This is only a restriction of number and not of specific *rāgas* or *tālas*. So the *prabandha* is *aniryukta*.

188d. padānvitaḥ: Since this is a *medinī prabandha*, sv pd pt bd tn and tl must be accommodated in four sections; pd is the final *aṅga*. Kallinātha adds that each *rāga* must include all *aṅgas*, of which pd is the last (p. 311).

189b. rāgapuñjavat: SR and other authorities do not refer to *rāgakadamba*; NN (and CDP) picks this up from Kallinātha, thus making the *prabandha* a *medinī*. Veṅkaṭamakhin expands '*rāgakadambavat*' (CDP 9.71-75) and declares that each of the four sections is composed in a different *rāga* and *tāla*; words must necessarily occur at the end; the remaining sv etc. five *aṅgas* may be composed in any desired order; in each section, U is the first half and D, the second half. The composition has no M or A, but the names of *prabandha*, patron and composer are incorporated into the fourth section.

189c. nyāso'nuktastu: This is an independent remark of Paṇḍarīka Viṭṭhala.

190-192 ab. 2. *Śrīvilāsa*
3. *Pañcabhaṅgi*
4. *Pañcānana*
5. *Umātilaka*

śrīraṅgavat: See comm. on NN. 3.2.189b.

The five *prabandhas śrīraṅga, śrīvilāsa, pañcabhaṅgi, pañcānana* and *umātilaka* are considered as an interrelated set by AC, JS, SR and most post-SR treatises, including NN and CDP, because of some common features viz. division into two, three, four, five segments, employment of six *aṅgas*, *rāgamālikā-tālamālikā* form, and compulsory use of a specific *aṅga* in the beginning and end. It would seem, therefore, that they were looked upon as a group. But these five are seperate *prabandhas*; there is no rule that they should be performed in any particular order, nor that all of them should be necessarily performed in the same recital. They differ from *ālikrama prabandhas* such as *rāgakadamba* and *tālārṇava* which take the *rāgamālikā* or *tālamālikā* form on individual merit, not as a group; a common criterion for classifying is found only among these five in *viprakīrṇa prabandhas*.

AC (4.16.39-43) takes *pañcabhaṅgi* as model (*prakṛti*) and describes the others as its modifications (in fact, they are regarded as varieties of *paṇcabhaṅgi*):

श्रीविलासः स्वरादिः स्यात् श्रीरङ्गः पाटपूर्वकः ।
पञ्चाननः पदादिः स्यात् बिरुदादिस्तु मातलिः ।
तेन्नादिरुपाधिः प्रोक्तो गीतलक्षणवेदिभिः ।
एवं पञ्चप्रकारेण पञ्चभङ्गी प्रगीयते ॥

Umātilaka is not found in this passage; '*stu mātaliḥ*' may be construed with unwarranted strain and implausibility into '*stūmātilakaḥ*'. *Upādhi* is not found elsewhere. The last line suggests that the compositions *śrīvilāsa, śrīraṅga, pañcānana, mātali* and *upādhi* are sung as five aspects or modes of the same single composition, and are collectively known as *pañcabhaṅgi*. JS (p. 47) also takes *pañcabhaṅgi* as the model but describes the five *prabandhas* differently; these may be regarded as derived by systematic permutation for concluding and initial positions among sv pd pt bd and tn.

स्वराः बिरुदाः पदाः पाटास्तेन्ना परोदिताः ।
तेषां प्रस्तारविन्यासे प्रान्ते तेन्नादिके यदा ।
एकतालैकरागश्च पञ्चभङ्गिस्तदा भवेत् ।
एतेषामेव विन्यासात् प्रान्ते पाटादिको यदा ।
रागाभ्यां तालयुग्मेन तदा पञ्चाननो भवेत् ।
प्रस्तारेण स्वरादीनां यदि प्रान्ते पदादिकाः ।
रागैस्त्रिभिस्तालैः श्रीरङ्गः कथितस्तदा ।
प्रत्यङ्गपञ्चकेऽमुष्मिन् प्रस्तारे चरे सति ।
बिरुदादिर्यदा प्रान्ते तु तालसमन्वितः ।
रागपञ्चकसंयुक्तस्तालैः पञ्चभिरन्वितः ।
श्रीविलासस्तदा ज्ञेयः प्रबन्धो गीतवेदिभिः ॥

On the other hand, SR and following it, NN etc. take *śrīraṅga* as the model and describe the others viz. *śrīvilāsa* etc. relative to it. The differences in details among these authorities show that these compositions were in fluid, varied usage. SS (5.7.142cd-147ab, pp. 225, 226) also takes *pañcabhaṅgi* as *prakṛti* but describes *pañcānana* and *śrīraṅga* relative to it; however it does not depict *śrīvilāsa* and *umātilaka*.

The *lakṣaṇas* of all these five *prabandhas* are common and are summarised into a single formula by PS (4.37.38, p. 26) and JS 2d, six *aṅgas*—pd pt bd tl tn sv; an.

193a. śrīdaḥ: This *lakṣaṇa* of *umātilaka* is found only in NN.

193cd-196 6. *Tripadī*

194d. rati-manmatha: Ratigaṇa, also called *brahmagaṇa* is a variety of the prosodial prototype *atyuktā* and assumes four forms viz. SS IS SI II; *manmathagaṇa,* also known as *viṣṇugaṇa* is a variety of *madhyā chandas* and assumes eight forms viz. SSS ISS SIS IIS SSI ISI SII III (SR 4.64.65). These are bisyllabic and trisyllabic prosodial units respectively; the number of syllables is fixed but the moraic quantity/duration is variable, so that the poet has a wide choice. See comm. on NN 3.2.26cd.

195-196a. Manner of singing the *tripadī* is compiled by Paṇḍarīka Viṭṭhala from Kallinātha (pp. 313, 314):

तत्राद्यं पादद्वयमुद्ग्राहः । द्वितीयं पादद्वयं ध्रुवः । विप्रकीर्णेषु ''ओव्यादयश्च चत्वारो भवन्त्याभोग-वर्जिताः'' इति वक्ष्यमाणेन वचनेन चतुर्णामेवाभोगनिषेधात्, इतरेषां पुनः ''अनुक्ताभोगवस्तूनां पदैराभोग-कल्पना'' इति वक्ष्यमाणत्वादत्र पदैराभोगः कल्पनीयः । तेनायं त्रिधातुः । गणभाषानियमान्निर्युक्तः । अस्या द्विपदीप्रकृतित्वात् ''अनुक्तमन्यतो ग्राह्यम्'' इति न्यायेन तत्रोक्तः स्वरप्रयोगोऽपि प्रबन्धतासिद्धये ध्रुवानन्तरमध्या-हर्तव्यः। अन्यथा तालादिहीनत्वेन पदैकाङ्गतया तारावल्यादिप्रबन्धजात्ययोगादप्रबन्धतैव स्यात् । अतोऽयं पदस्वरबद्धत्वात् द्व्यङ्गः तारावलीजातिमान् ।

So, if sv also is omitted, only pd remains as *aṅga* and *tripadī* is no longer a musical composition (*prabandha*), nor of *tārāvalī* etc. *jātis*; hence sv should be used and *tāla* to accommodate it (only). So *tripadī* has two *aṅgas*—pd, sv, i.e. it is a *tārāvalī.* NN does not concur with this view (according to which the *aṅgas* should be three viz. pd sv tl, and not two), and holds that restricted use of *tāla* for sv alone does not elevate it to the status of a fullfledged *aṅga.*

196a. Tripadī is an ancient, classic metrical song in Kannaḍa, also known as *tividi, tivadī* and *trivadhi.* An epigraphic example is available as early as c. 700 A.D. Nāgavarma (*Chando'mbudhi,* 5.11) and Jayakīrti *(Chando'nuśāsanam,* 7.9) describe its two varieties viz. *citrā* and *vicitrā* of which *citrā* has survived today in wide popularity in poetic and epigraphic usage. The latter is also known as *citralatikā.* The *citrā* has four feet with two, four and three *gaṇas* respectively; among these, the sixth and tenth (second in the third foot and fourth foot respectively) are *rati gaṇas* while the rest are *manmatha gaṇas. Citralatikā* (or *vicitrā*) is different from this in only one respect; the eleventh *gaṇa* is not *manmatha*; it is a *bāṇa* (or *rudra*) *gaṇa* commencing on *guru* (Jayakīrti, op. cit. 7.10). That this was a music composition is evident from Jayakīrti who, in the very next two verses clearly states that, notwithstanding this rigid *aṁśagaṇa* (syllabic structure), its *mātrā* (moraic) frame (of sixtytwo *mātrās*) is elastic enough to expand or contract to accommodate various prosodic situations (ibid., 7.11); thus if it contains only *laghus,* its duration is only fortytwo *mātrās*; and he is aware (ibid., 7.12, 13) that a *sarvagaru tripadī* is not viable. Such elasticity is of the very essence in metrical (or nonmetrical) forms if they are to be feasible as music compositions also. According to these authorities, the composition rhymes on the second syllable in every foot. Its first two feet are sung along with part of the third: then this part is sung again, the third foot is completed and the fourth foot is finally sung.

AC (4.16. 276,282, pp. 30, 31) concurs with the above and offers on illustration. D.L. Narasimhachar (*'Mānasollāsadalli Chandassu'* in *'Pīṭhikegaḷu, Lekhanagaḷu'* p. 691) has carefully edited it into the following correct version:

मेदिनि वर्णिसल्कादियोळ् मीनागि
वेदवोत्तगेयनेत्ति तन्दित्तवन
पादंगळिगे महिमेयम् ॥

We learn from AC (4.7.32; 4.16.551) that the *tripadī* was sung as *onakevāḍu* (an occupational folksong sung while pounding corn) and as *aṅkamālā* (a song of irony containing a small number of *touché* taunt words directed at a rival defeated in battle or combat). For an excellent account of the origin, evolution and use of *tripadī* in classical and folk literature, see T.V. Venkatachala Sastri, *Kannaḍa-Chandaḥ-svarūpa*, pp. 384-425).

JS p. 51: as in NN; adds that the conclusion is on second foot after reverting to the first. JS and PS summarise thus: 2d, two *aṅgas*—pd tl (!sv?); n (4.27, p. 25)

197-199. 7. *Catuṣpadī*

197a. karnāṭa-bhāṣayā: Early authorities such as AC, JS and SR do not declare this *bhāṣā-niryukti* openly, for they must have been aware of the occurrence of *catuṣpadī* in other languages also.

But Kallinātha extends the Kannaḍa language to *catuṣpadī* from *dvipadī* and *ṣaṭpadī* on the strength of the rule: '*anuktam-anyato grāhyam*' (p. 315), because they also have Kannaḍa and lack *tāla*. Paṇḍarīka Viṭṭhala and Veṅkaṭamakhin (CDP 9. 298) have followed him.

It is known as *caupada* in Telugu and is a very popular metre, described by Kākunūri Appakavi (*Appakavīyamu*, 4.288), Vemulavāḍa Bhīmakavi (*Kavijanāśra-yamu*, 3.32) and a variety of folk song (*gilakala padyamu*). In Hindī also, it is a very popular metre called *caupāī*. It is defined in *Chandaḥprabhākar* (p. 49) thus:

सोरह क्रमन 'जतन' चौपाई, सुनहु नासु गति अब मनलाई ।
निकल परे समकल नहिं दीजै, दिये कहूँ तो लय अति छीजै ।
समसमसमसमसुखदाई विषमविषम सम समूह भाई ।
विषमविषमसम विषमविषमसम विषम दोय मिलिजानिय इकसम ।

It is a *mātrāsama vṛtta*, related to चउपइया (*Prākṛtapaiṅgala*, 1.97) and renowned under the name *jayakārī*. Jagannath Prasad 'Bhanu' (*Chandaḥprabhākar*, p.46) and Bikhāridas (*Chandārṇavapiṅgal*, p. 22) describe it as consisting of fifteen *mātrās* followed by a *guru* and *laghu* at the end in each foot. It is used by Chandbardāyi

(*Prithvīraj-rāso*), Sūrdās (*Sūrsāgar*), Nanddās (*Jñānamañjarī, Virahamañjarī*), Keśavadās (*Vīranarasiṁhadev carit*); it is employed as a *sama-mātrā vṛtta* of sixteen *mātrās* per quarter (sometimes relaxed to fifteen *mātrās* by these poets and Tulasidās, Jodhrāja, Jaṭmal, Gore-ul, Sūdan, Gulab, and in·*dohas* (for love-lyrics) by Katuban, Jayasi, Usmān, Noor Muhamad etc. (See *Hindī Sāhityakoś* Ed. Dhirendra Sharma, p. 290.)

197cd. nṛpa-daśapañca: *Catuṣpadī* is known to Kannaḍa as *caupadi(ge)*. Nāgavarma (*Chando'mbudhi,* 5.14) and Jayakīrti (*Chando'nuśāsanam,* 7.15) describe it as containing a *viśṇugaṇa* followed by a *rudragaṇa* (or *kāma* followed by *bāṇa gaṇa*) per quarter. Candrarāja (*Madanatilakam,* 8.34) agrees with this *lakṣaṇa* and gives two illustrations. However, *catuṣpadī* as a *prabandha* differs from this literary analogue, and has been experimented with extensively. Someśvara (AC 4.16.283, p. 31) gives a variable *pāda* of sixteen, twentyone or twentyfour *mātrās*; Jagadekamalla (JS p. 25) prescribes seven or eight *mātrās* per foot. SR, NN and others declare sixteen *mātrās* in even numbered feet and fifteen *mātrās* in odd numbered feet; this is corroborated in the *caupāyī* of Hindī as mentioned above. Numerous *caupadas* are available in Kannaḍa: *Rāvaṇa-digvijaya, Śaraṇalīlāmṛta, Cikadevarāya-caupada, Gaṅge-gauri-caupada, Vīrasaṅgayyana-caupada, Alamelurmaṅge-lālipada, Maisūru-doregaḷa caupada* etc.; these consist of eighteen *mātrās,* more or less, per quarter. It is sometimes argued that *catuṣpadī* is a modified form of *chandovasanta* and that it is derived by the fusion of two *dvipadīs.* The statement of Jagadekamalla (JS loc. cit.) that *tripadī* is derived from *dvipadī* may be recalled here. Someśvara (AC 4.16.284, p. 31) gives an illustration (which is not in Kannaḍa):

सुरगिरगिरहू आसूड इतलुतिर्द सुरकुजदुर्यलेरि मिक्क ।
सुविलासिनि पुरोलड्डुदाडि दरुहरि अयं कामाले गला ॥

198a. yamaka: See comm. NN 3.2.71a.

198a-199b. kramāt...catuṣpadī: these details are compiled by Paṇḍarīka Viṭṭahala and Veṅkaṭamakhin (CDP 9.295-302) from Kallinātha (p. 315).

199c. niryukta:, because of restriction on language and *mātrā* number.

199d. tārāvalīyakaḥ: cf. Kallinātha (p. 315): पदस्वरतेनकबद्धत्वात् त्र्यङ्गः । भावनीजातिमान्। *catuṣpadī* lacks *tāla* from *dvipadī lakaṣaṇa*; pt and bd are not prescribed. So it had only sv pd tn. It is not clear how it is classified as a *tārāvalī.* This has a variant reading: '*syādatra dīpanī*' from C. This is also plausible; for, there are two instances of corroboration of this from JS and PS: 3d, four *aṅgas*— tl tn pd sv; n , (4.53, p. 27). JS (p. 25) says that *catuṣpadī* has seven or eight *mātrās* per quarter and is composed in the metre named *catuṣpadī*; rhyming occurs in line-pairs or in all lines; all *pādas* are equal. A third source ascribes for it *dīpanī jāti* also: SS (5.7.79cd-81c): *catuṣpadī* consists of sv, tn, tl, sv-pd; but the text is somewhat ambiguous: '*svarāḥ satennakāsta-*

tra tālaḥ svarapadābhidhaḥ). It further prescribes a *yamaka* in each half, and conclusion on *tenaka.* BD (406, p. 144) also seems to prescribe *tāla, tenaka, svara* (and *pada*?) for the composition.

200-202. 8. *Ṣaṭpadī*

200c. kāmagaṇa: see comm. NN 3.2.26cd; 3.2.194d.

201b. bāṇagaṇa: see comm. NN 3.2.26cd.

201c-202. Manner of singing *ṣaṭpadī* is borrowed from Kallinātha (p. 316).

202b. jīvanāda: This is merely '*nādamuktikā*' in SR(4.274), but interpreted by Kallinātha as *jīvanāda* which he explains as the *sthāyi svara* of the *rāga*, but to be executed as *svara* sequence carried on vowels and not by uttering the names of *svara*-symbols (p. 316):

नादशब्देन स्थायिस्वरो विवक्ष्यते । तं सरिगादिवर्णोच्चाररहितं नादरूपमेवोच्चार्य न्यासं कुर्यादित्यर्थः ।

202b. Ṣaṭpadī is at once an ancient, classic metre and a music composition in Kannaḍa; it should be distinguished from the *ardhasama-catuṣpadī varṇavṛtta* named *ṣaṭpadā* (Kedārabhaṭṭa, *Vṛttaratnākara,* 4.12.1) which has twentynine syllables per quarter (17:12) and is structured with the *gaṇa* sequence तभरजरगग; रजरय. BD mentions it (c. fifth-seventh cent A.D., 386, p.142) but the description is lost in a lacuna. *Ṣaṭpadī* occurs in two forms—*aṁśagaṇa* and *mātrāgaṇa.* Its definition by Nāgavarma *(Chando'mbudhi,* 5.21), Jayakīrti *(Chando'nuṣāsanam,* 7.17) and others conform to its definition in the musical tradition such as by Someśvara (AC. 4.16.287-289); the latter adds other considerable information: it is composed in Kannaḍa in six feet among which 1=2=4=5, 3=6; each of the former feet consists of two *kāma* (=*viṣṇu*) *gaṇas* and each of the latter consists of the same and an additional *bāṇa* (=*rudra*) *gaṇa* at the end; it is not set to *tāla;* its lines rhyme (usually on the second syllable) and alliterate; it narrates a story (4.16.289, 552, 1125) and is used for this purpose. As mentioned above, *sūḍakrama* is according to him, the singing of long and classic *prabandhas* (*mahān*) such as *elā, ḍheṅkī,* followed by shorter, miscellaneous (*alpa*) *prabandhas.* The latter include *tripadī, ṣaṭpadī, dhavala, maṅgala, ovī, carcarī, caryā, rāhaḍī* and *dantī.* These were *laukika prabandhas,* i.e. their themes were mundane (AC 4.16.549, 550), to be sung in one's own language (mother-tongue, regional language; AC 4.16.557). This authority also offers an illustration, the text of which is ably reconstructed by D.L. Narasimhachar ('*Mānasollāsadalli Chandassu*', in *Pīṭhikegaḷu, Lekhanagaḷu,* pp. 692, 693) thus:

गडणदिन्दुरगन
पेडेवणिगळदीप्ति
गेडेगोण्डु तमगेत्तुवारतिया ।

सोडर्गळ पोले पाल्
गडलोळिर्दा विष्णु
कुडुतिक्के नमगिष्टसंसिद्धियम् ।

The form of *ṣaṭpadī* described by prosodists such as Nāgavarma and Jayakīrti as well as music authorities like Someśvara is archetypal. The *śivaśaraṇa* poets of Karnataka of the 11th-12th century A.D. expanded the *ṣaṭpadī* in scope and variety by systematic experimentation and came up with six forms, through a progressive increment of 2 *mātrās* in the first, second, fourth and fifth feet and adding half of this quantity again and a *guru* in the third and sixth feet. Thus the six varieties are *śara*-8 (4, 4), *kusuma* -10 (5, 5), *bhoga*-12 (3, 3, 3, 3) *bhāminī*-14 (3, 4, 3, 4), *parivardhinī*-16(4, 4, 4, 4) *vārdhaka*-20 (5, 5, 5, 5). The above illustration conforms to the *kusuma-ṣaṭpadī* format. (For a detailed discussion of the *ṣaṭpadī* —both *aṁśa gaṇa* and *mātrā gaṇa* varieties, see T.V. Venkatachala Sastri, *Kannaḍa Chandaḥ-svarūpa*, pp. 488-544.)

Śārṅgadeva is fully aware of the potential for evolution and proliferation of *tripadī* and *ṣaṭpadī* when he says (SR.4.274): भेदा वेद्यास्त्रिपद्यादेश्छन्दोलक्ष्मणि भूरयः at the conclusion of the *ṣaṭpadī prabandha.* P. Basavanna has offered a most comprehensive, latest proof of this statement in his *Śrī Śivakumaracaritam.* He has classified the *ṣaṭpadī* metre as *sama, asama, samasama, samāsama, asamasama, asamāsama, viṣama* and miscellaneous. His innovation lies in the concept of repeating prosodial units and verse feet to yield larger matrices for *ṣaṭpadī.* Such repetition consists in doubling, trebling, quadrupling etc. up to six times the original units e.g. thirtythree, thirtyfour, fortythree, fortyfour, thirtyfive, fiftythree, fortyfive, fiftyfour, fiftyfive of *mātrā* dispositions. The experimental range is from the smallest *ṣaṭpadī* of 6 *mātrās* per foot (*tāla*) to the largest consisting of forty *mātrās* per foot e.g. *mahāvārdhaka, mahāmaruvaka, mahāmallikā, mahāmandāra* and *mahoddaṇḍa.* His achievement consists in composing *lakṣaṇa-lakṣya* stanzas for all the varieties.

JS defines *ṣaṭpadī* as composed in Kannaḍa, in six feet consisting of two *gaṇas* in each of 1, 2, 4 and 5 and three in each of 3 and 6 so that there are altogether fourteen *gaṇas* in the stanza; it features many *yatis* and concludes on *nāda* (*svara* passage carried only on vowels); the seventh and fourteenth *gaṇas* are *bāṇa* while the rest are *kāma.* SS (5.7.178cd-181ab) concurs with all this, and says additionally that it has no *tāla* and the language is *deśya* (however, no examples of *ṣaṭpadī* are available in other *deśya* languages than Kannaḍa of his times; so, he probably means Kannaḍa by this expression). PS shows a lacuna for the *lakṣaṇa.*

203-205. 9. *Vastu*

204a. ebhiḥ: U consists of the five feet and *tenaka* at their end.

204d. dodhaka: see comm. NN 3.2.154a. Siṁhabhūpāla reads it as *dohaka.*

205b. tālayuk: SR is silent on *tāla* (4.275, 276); Kallinātha interprets this (p. 317) as the absence of *tālaniryukti*, not of *tāla*. Paṇḍarīka Viṭṭhala in turn interprets it positively. Veṅkaṭamakhin (CDP 9.148) is content with '*tālādi niyamābhāvāt*'.

205c. Ānandinī:,. because the *vastu* has all *aṅgas* except bd.

205d. niryukta: because of prescribed *mātrā* quantity and *dodhaka* metre; but *aniryukta* in *rāga, tāla, bhāṣā* etc. Veṅkaṭamakhin (loc. cit.) defines it as *aniryukta.*

205d. vastu: AC gives an illustration for *vastu* in Prākṛta (4.16.296, 297, p. 32):

जेच्छातिहणुसयलु निछिसे हु गम्भीरिं वजस्मापरसपलकालसश्नहिन विद्रुह ।
नामाविहसत्वम् ॥
पघुची णोच्चिया गणिजूइसोदाणचक्कुल निर्दलषुहयण किय आनन्दु ।
वृचुद्वोउक्षिउअ वहरउसलद्विपर गोविन्दु ॥

According to AC the *vastu* has five feet; 1, 3, 5 have each fifteen *mātrās* while 2, 4 have twelve *mātrās* each; at the end of fifteen *mātrās* is composed a *dodhaka*; it is sung in plays; according to Bharata's dictum, it arises from many *rasas*. JS and PS (4.55, p. 27) summarise it thus—3d, five *aṅgas*, pd pt sv tl tn; an.

Vastu is depicted in JS (p. 25) in five feet with fifteen *mātrās* in 1, 3, 5 and twelve *mātrās* in 2, 4: it has sv, tn, pt, pd and no tl (?). A is composed in other words; conclusion is no tn. *Dohaka* precedes A and follows D. SS (5.7.71d-84), gives the same details: it adds *dohalika* at the end (of each foot? of 5th foot?). First half (U) has pd while second half (D) has tn. This is followed by *dohalika*; A is composed in other words. Conclusion is on tn; tl is of one's own choice. BD (407, p.144) has an incomplete description: *vastu* has *tena*; it is a *deśī gīta*, sung in plays.

206-207ab. 10. *Vijaya*

206a. Vijaya is a *tālaniryuka-prabandha. Vijaya tāla* is (NN 1.193): विजये स्यु: पगपला: (ऽऽऽ।) which agrees with its description in SR (5.283).

206cd. pāṭaiḥ...kṛtaḥ: NN is not clear in stating the content of U or D; nor is SR (4.277). The translation of this passage is based on Kallinātha (p. 318). Veṅkaṭamakhin (CDP 9.149, 150) agrees with this. JS (p. 47) gives the contents as '*tenapāṭapadasvaraiḥ*'; if this also implies sequence, U consists of tn pt; D has pd sv.

207a. vijayo nāma: JS (loc. cit.) describes the composition as an eulogy of the victory (*vijaya*) of heroes and Siṁhabhūpāla (p. 318), of kings. So the name is apt. This is enhanced by the use the namesake *tāla.*

207a. pañcāṅga: All *aṅgas* except bd; hence *ānandinī* in *jāti.*

207b. niryuka because of *vijaya-tāla.*

207cd-208ab. 11. *Tripatha*

207c. Tripatha has three feet (JS p. 48; SR 4.278): the first has pt, the second, bd; both constitute U; the third foot has sv and is D.

208a. Pañcāṅga includes *tāla* by implication; JS (loc. cit.) explicitly mentions the application of a *tāla* of one's choice. All *aṅgas* except tn are present. So *tripatha* is an *ānandinī*. PS: 2d, four *aṅgas*—sv pd tn tl; n,(4.34, p. 26)

208cd-209. 12. *Caturmukha*

208d. varṇagaiḥ: As *'tri'* is significant in *tripatha*, *'catur'* is so in *caturmukha* because the *prabandha* has four feet: the first has *sthāyi varṇa* and (separate) sv (passages); the second is composed in *ārohī varṇa* and tn. The first two together constitute U; the last two, D.

209d. tripathavat: conclusion on U (SR 4.279), an, five *aṅgas* (sans bd)—and so an *ānandinī* (Kallinātha p. 319); these bear out the similarities with *tripatha*.

AC (4.16.35-38, p. 45; 4.16.396-398, p. 66): *Caturmukha* has four feet, the first two of which are sung like *svarāṅka*, the third with *tenakas* and the fourth with *gamakas*. The four parts (feet) are rendered with sv, pt, pd and tn respectively; no example of this is available.

SS (5.7.138-139ab): *Caturmukha* is composed of sv pt pd tn and of *sthāyī*, *ārohī*, *avarohī* and *sañcārī varṇas* respectively. A is in other words; conclusion is on U.

PS—

210-211ab. 13. *Siṁhalīla*

210c. siṁhalila-tāla (NN 1.189): ।ooo

210d. siṁhalīlake: This depiction of *siṁhalīla prabandha* conforms to that given in JS (p. 47), SR (4.279, 280). PS (4.30, p. 27; 4.33, p. 27); 2d, three *aṅgas*—pd tl **bd**, an/ 2d, five *aṅgas*—sv pt bd tn tl; an. Allocation of U etc. are compiled by Paṇḍarīka Viṭṭhala and Veṅkaṭamakhin (CDP 9.107-111) from Kallinātha (pp. 311, 312); it has all six *aṅgas;* so it is a *medinī* (SS 5.7.149cd-152a): composed of bd sv pt in *siṁhalīla tāla*.

211cd-212. 14. *Haṁsalīla*

211c. haṁsalīla tāla (NN 1.189, SR 5.267): 'विरामान्तं लघुद्वन्द्वं '।ĺ. But Kallinātha says (p. 320): "हंसलीलो यगणश्च लघुर्गुरुः" (।ऽऽ।ऽ) 'इति तस्य लक्षणं वक्ष्यते'. But this *lakṣaṇa* of *haṁsalila tāla* is not found in any available source—impressi typis or MS of SR.

212c. niryukta, because of *haṁsalīla tāla*.

212d. bhāvanī jāti because of three *aṅgas:* pd pt tl.

213-214. 15. *Daṇḍaka*

213a. Daṇḍakacchandas is a well known *varṇasama* metre of ancient origin. It is found in as many as thirty forms. Its prototype is defined by Piṅgalanāga (*Chandaḥśāstram*, 7.37) as consisting of two *na-gaṇas* followed by seven *ra-gaṇas* in each of four equal feet. This is named *caṇḍa*, *caṇḍavṛṣṭiprayāta*(*-prapāta*) and *suvarṇa*. In general, *any vṛtta* having more than twentysix syllables per foot is called *daṇḍaka*; the ones beyond *caṇḍa* are collectively called *pracita* by Piṅgala (ibid.,

7.35); others have grouped them into two classes, *daṇḍaka* and *mālāvṛtta*. Jayadeva (*Jayadevacchandas*, 7.34) regards *pracita* not as a collective name but as a specific instance wherein occur two *nagaṇas* followed by seven *ya-gaṇas* (instead of *ra-gaṇas* of *caṇḍa daṇḍaka*)

Daṇḍaka varieties may be grouped under three heads: variation in the initial six (two *na-gaṇa*) syllables, variation in the number of *ra-gaṇas* and substitutes for *ra-gaṇa*. If the initial six *laghus* are substituted with three, four, five or seven *laghus*, the *daṇḍaka* is respectively called *siṁha, abda, caṇḍa* and *vāta;* if the six *laghus* are retained at the beginning but the *ra-gaṇas* are increased from eight to fourteeen (by one, progressively), the following forms are obtained (n = *na-gaṇa*, r = *ra-gaṇa*; number of syllables is given after hyphen). (i) *caṇḍavṛṣṭiprayāta* 2n7r-27 (ii) *arṇava* 2n 8r-30 (iii) *arṇa* 2n 9r-33 (iv) *vyāla* 2n 10r-36 (v) *jīmūta* 2n 11r-39 (vi) *līlākara* 2n 12r-42 (vii) *uddāma* 2n 13r-45 viii *śaṅkha* 2n14r-48. These are described by most of the prominent prosodists such as Rāta, Māṇḍavya, Varāhamihira, Jayadeva, Jayakīrti, Kedārabhaṭṭa, Virahāṅka etc. Varāhamihira adds two more: *samudra* 2n 15r-51 and *bhujaṅga* 2n 16r-54. Nāgavarma (*Chando'mbudhi*, 3.23) mentions three viz. *racita, pracita* and *nacita*; the text is too opaque by corruption for decipherment. The third departure from the prototype is to substitute *ra-gaṇa* with *ya-, ta-, bha-* or other *gaṇas*. Jayakīrti *(Chado'nuśāsanam*, 6.32-37) is more detailed and informative in describing *daṇḍaka* among prosodists as is Jagadekamalla among musicologists (JS pp. 17-20). Both classify the *daṇḍaka* under *gaṇa-, mātrā-,, ubhaya-, vṛtta-* and *mālā* and characterise such forms as *mattamātaṅga, līlākara, siṁhavikrīḍā, anaṅgaśekhara, puṣpamañjari, kusumāstaraṇa, utsava, vilāsa, siṁhavikrānta, mṛgāṅka, bhujaṅgavilāsa, citramālā, citra.* JS adds that if one sings the *daṇḍaka prabandha* in song or dance in a *tāla* which is appropriate to the *yatis* and in words which accord with *śruti* (Veda), one is redeemed of all blemishes. Velankar holds (Velankar, H.D., *Kavidarpaṇa*, Introduction, pp. xii, xiii) that "the *daṇḍaka* was originally a *tālavṛtta* sung to the accompaniment of a time keeping instrument or of a regular rhythmic dance" as in the fifth Act of the *Mālatīmādhava* of Bhavabhūti. "It was sung in a *tāla* of eight or ten *mātrās* according as the particular *akṣara-gaṇa* contained four or five *mātrās* in it." This conjecture is plausible; but there is no musicological evidence to support the specificity of the *tāla* size.

Daṇḍaka may be composed in *padya(=vṛtta)* or *gadya*. H.D. Velankar (*Jayadāman*, pp. 147, 148) compiles the following thirtythree forms of *daṇḍaka* from various sources (abbreviations: *l*—*laghu*; g—*guru*; r—*ra-gaṇa*, n—*na-gaṇa*, t—*ta-gaṇa*, y—*ya-gaṇa*, b—*bha-gaṇa*, s—*sa-gaṇa*, z—any *gaṇa*, x—any number).

No.	Name	Composition	No.	Name	Composition
1.	*anaṅgaśekhara*	(*lg*) x	18.	*pracita*	6*l*, 7y
2.	*abda*	4*l*, z	19.	*bhujaṅga*	6*l*, 16r
3.	*arṇa*	6*l*, 8r	20.	*bhujaṅgavilāsa*	xb, *gg*
4.	*arṇava*	6*l*, 9r	21.	*mattamātaṅga*	xr
5.	*aśokapuṣpamañjarī*	(*gl*), x	22.	*mālatī*	ng, 11r
6.	*utkalikā*	6*l*, any *pañca-mātrā gaṇas*	23.	*meghamālā*	6*l* 3g, xy
7.	*uddāma*	6*l*, 13r	24.	*līlākara*	6*l*, 12r
8.	*kaṅkelli*	*ng*, 13r	25.	*līlāvilāsa*	ng, 14r
9.	*kāmabāṇa*	xt, *gg*	26.	*varṇaka*	6*l*, 7b
10.	*kusumāstaraṇa*	xs	27.	*vāta*	7*l*, z
11.	*keli*	ng, 12r	28.	*vyāla*	6*l*, 10r
12.	*caṇḍa*	5*l*, z	29.	*śaṅka*	6*l*, 14r
13.	*caṇḍakā(pā)la*	5*l*, xr	30.	*samudra*	6*l*, 15r
14.	*caṇḍavega*	6*l*, xy	31.	*siṁha*	3*l*, z
15.	*jīmūta*	6*l*, 11r	32.	*siṁhavikrīḍa*	5*l*, xy
16.	*dambholi*	*ng*, 9r	33.	*helāvali*	*ng*, 10r
17.	*pannaga*	*ng*, 8r			

Nāgavarma claims that the formula 2n+xr for *daṇḍaka* yields varieties upto x=333.

Most authorities in prosody or music are content to illustrate the *daṇḍaka* with the model of *caṇḍavṛṣṭiprayāta*. Some examples of this *daṇḍaka* form are: Bharatamuni, NŚ 15.153,154, p. 281 (MSS. ट, ठ, ड).

मुदितजनपदाकुला स्फीतसस्याकरा भूतधात्री भवन्तं समभ्यर्चति
द्विरदकरविलुप्तहिन्तालताली वनास्त्वां नमस्यन्ति विन्ध्यादयः पर्वताः ।
स्फटित(१)कलशशुक्तिनिर्गीर्णमुक्ताफलैरूर्मिहस्तैर्नमस्यन्ति वः सागराः
मुदितजलचराकुलाः सम्प्रकीर्णमलाः कीर्तयन्तीव कीर्तिं(२) महानिम्नगाः ॥

This is found in *Chandoviciti* (*Jānāśrayī*) with the variant readings (१) विमल (२) कीर्त-यिष्यन्ति वर्णं ।

Halāyudhabhaṭṭa, *Mṛtasañjīvanī* (comm. on Piṅgalanāga, *Chandaḥśāstram*, 7.37):

इह हि भवति दण्डकारण्यदेशे स्थितिः पुण्यभाजां मुनीनां मनोहारिणि
त्रिदशविजयवीर्यदृप्यद्दशग्रीवलक्ष्मी(१)विरामेण रामेण संसेविते ।

जनकयजनभूमिसम्भूतसीमन्तिनीसीम सीतापदस्पर्शपूताश्रमे(२)
भुवननमितपादपद्मा(३)भिधानाम्बिका तीर्थयात्रागतानेकसिद्धाकुले ॥

This is borrowed by Kallinātha (p. 321). Veṅkaṭamakhin (CDP 9.314) borrows in turn form the latter with minor variants: (१)लक्ष्म्या (२)पूताश्रये (३)पादपंपा

Nāgavarma, *Chando'mbudhi*, (3.22, p. 58: *lakṣya-lakṣaṇa-padya* in Kannaḍa):

अमरयुगदमुन्दे सन्दग्रिगळ् चण्डवृष्टिप्रयातक्केयेळप्पुदेण्टप्पुद
त्तमेनिसिदोडेयर्णमोंबत्तरिन्दर्णवं पत्तरिं व्याळजीमूतक ।
ग्रिमदे बरलदोन्दु लीलाकरं मत्ते तानग्रिगळ् (सुन्दरं, मुन्देरळ्)सन्दिरल् पुट्टुगुं (निश्चयं)
कमलवदने केडळ् प्रसिद्धङ्गळी तोरली दण्डकङ्गळ्गडा कन्तुकान्तोपमे ॥
[कमलवदने लोकप्रसिद्धमा(दाररिं मुन्ते नानाविधं दण्डकं पुट्टुगुं) ॥]

Someśvara (AC 4.16.250-253, pp. 27, 28) delineates *daṇḍaka* with the *caṇḍavṛṣṭi-prayāta* structure, numerous feet (note that this is a medial property of *daṇḍaka* between *padya* and *gadya*; but the illustration which follows has only four feet); it has *svara, tāla* and *pāṭa;* ṣv is interspersed in the words; according to some, single *tāla* is used; elsewhere two or three *tālas* are prescribed; after singing the name (of *prabandha*, patron, hero and composer), the song rests on U. He offers an illustration:

अजमजरमजस्त्रतेजस्विनं चिन्तयन्तीह यं तापसाः क्वापि पुण्यप्रदे
नियमितमनसः स्थिरीभूतभूतेन्द्रियाः क्षान्तिभाजः समीभूतभूकाञ्चना ।
रुचिरचितसुरायुधं विभ्रतं विभ्रमादर्शमम्बोधिजायाहृदा कौस्तुभं
हरिमद्यसमाश्रये (हरिमहरहमाश्रये) ज्यायसे श्रेयसे भूषणं भूर्भुवः
स्वस्त्रैलोक्यस्य ताम् (-स्त्रिलोकस्य तम्)॥

Gadyadaṇḍaka on the other hand, is not regulated by rules of *pāda* or *gaṇa*. It is enough if the same single *gaṇa* recurs continuously and constantly. It is described only by Jayakīrti (*Chando'nuśāsanam*, 6.34) among prosodists and by Jagadekamalla (JS pp. 12-20) among musicologists. Neither gives illustrations. From available examples it would seem that the initial *na-gaṇa* pair is absent and that the *prabandha* starts with pure prose (not *gadya prabandha*), and assumes the *daṇḍaka* form after some time. The repeating unit may be *ra-gaṇa* or *ta-gaṇa*.

Some illustrations of *gadya-daṇḍaka* may be given here: Bandhuvarma, *Harivaṁśābhyudaya*, (13.31pr. *ta-gaṇa*):

द्विव्यान्वयावासदोळ् पुट्टियुं किल्बिषस्थानियागिर्दु किंकुर्वाणंगैदु निचंमनोदुःखादिं सुय्दु हा कष्टदल्लीयन्दमेन्दन्ते मत्तं मनुष्याधरान्तस्थानदागळा ---

Śrīpādarāya: *Lakṣmīnṛsiṁhaprādurbhāvadaṇḍaka,* called *uddaṇḍadaṇḍaka* by the composer (*Śrīpādarājara-kṛtigaḷu,* pp. 229, 230):

जगत्स्वामि तानागले । त[स]भांगारशृङ्गारवल्ल्यंते कांगळ् समुद्यत्जटा केसरंगळ् विजृंभत् कराळास्पदं उग्रनासासमुच्छ्वासनिश्वासगळ् संचलद्व्यस्तव्याळक्षुरांतोग्र जिह्वाग्र लेलीहनं । गळ् भ्रमद् भ्रूल्पलंगळ् हनूरोषभीष्णंगळुं ऊर्ध्वकर्णंगळुं भूमिभृत् कंदराश्चर्यवव्यातघोरास्यनासापुटंगळ् अदीर्घोन्नतग्रीववुं दीर्घदंतोप्पुवो देहवं ---

Śaṅkaradeva, *Nijaliṅga-cikkayyana daṇḍaka* (*Prasanna Śaṅkaraliṅga ragaḷegaḷu,* Dharawada, 1976, pp. 51-356) shows *ta-gaṇa* in the main, occasionally substituted by *ra-gaṇa* and *ya-gaṇa.*

श्रीमन्महास्वर्णशैलाग्रलालित्यराजगृहव्याप्ति सन्दीप्तिलोलं सदानन्दसन्धानसन्मानशीलं प्रमोदप्रबोधा-विनोदानुकूलं त्रिलोकाधिपत्यासुरक्रियासारविद्याविशालं यथान्यायपालं परब्रह्मतत्त्वार्थ-संस्तोत्रपारम् --

BD mentions *daṇḍaka* (397d, p. 142), but its description is lost through a lacuna. **Someśvara** (AC loc. cit.) states that *daṇḍaka* is composed of tl pd sv. Haripāladeva **(SS 5.7.64, 65)** depicts it with pd sv, suitable tl-, *rāga;* decorated with numerous *yatis:* **Pārśvadeva** (PS 4.46, p. 27) summarises its *lakṣaṇa* thus: 3d, three *aṅgas* —pd tl **sv; n, Śārṅgadeva** is very crisp (SR 4.281): पदैः स्वैरैर्दण्डकेन छन्दसा दण्डको मतः । **Kallinātha (p. 321)** expands this to say that U is made of pd, D of sv, A of other words; **three** *dhātus, niryukta* because of *daṇḍaka* metre, *bhāvanī jāti* because of three *aṅgas* viz. sv pd tl. Paṇḍarīka Viṭṭhala and Veṅkaṭamakhin have followed this.

Many important authorities on music recognise that *daṇḍaka* had vastly proliferated: e.g. JS (p. 18);

नानविधा ज्ञेया दण्डकाः । SS (5.7.64): दण्डको गणवृत्तादिभेदेन बहुधा भवेत् । SR (4.281): तस्य भूरितरा भेदाश्छन्दोलक्ष्मणि भाषिताः । NN however, does not observe this.

215-216ab. 16. *Jhampaṭa*

215a. tripadīgāthā: see comm. NN 3.2.151a, 3.2.153a; *gāthā* is *āryā* metre composed in Prākṛta words. It has 3,5 or 6 feet (NN 3.2.153b). When it has only three feet it is called *jhampaṭa.* Kallinātha compiles its *lakṣaṇa*—'*jhampaṭam tripadaiḥ*' (p. 321). *Gāthā* is defined by Kedārabhaṭṭa (*Vṛttaratnākara,* 5.12):

विषमाक्षरपादं वा पादैरसमं दशधर्मवत् ।
यच्छन्दो नोक्तमत्र गाथेति तत्सूरिभिः प्रोक्तम् ॥

Piṅgalanāga (*Chandaḥśāstram,* 8.1) and Jayadeva (*Jayadevacchandas,* 7.36) concur with this, while Hemacandra, (*Chando'nuśāsanam,* 7.73) merely says '*gāthātrānūktam*'. The *gāthā* is a *viṣama-catuṣpadī,* in which the four feet have eight, ten, seven and nine syllables respectively; the number of these syllables may vary. The following is an illustration:

युधिष्ठिरो धर्ममयो महाद्रुमः ।
स्कन्धोऽर्जुनो भीमसेनोऽस्य शाखा ॥
माद्रीसुतौ पुष्पफले समृद्धे ।
मूलं कृष्णा ब्रह्मा ब्राह्मणाश्च ॥

Thus the *jhampaṭa* is a metre of three (mutually) unequal feet, composed in Prākṛta words.

215cd. yatra...padaiḥ: first two feet of *jhampaṭa* form its U; the last foot, is D. A is composed of words other than those of U and D.

216a. krīḍā tāla (NN 1.143): क्रीडा द्रुतौ विरामान्तौ । (००́)

216a. niryukta in metre, *tāla* and language.

216b. tārāvalī: because it has two *aṅgas*—pd, tl. NN. has derived details of *jhampaṭa prabandha* from Kallinātha (pp. 321, 322).

BD

AC (4.16.79, p. 49): *jhambaḍa*: omits two feet in *dohada-vṛtta*; the second is repeated in part.

JS (p. 51) mentions *jhampaṭa-chandas* and *krīḍā tāla*; three feet. The rest is lost.

SS (5.7.175d-176a): *sompaṭa*? *sompaṭa-tāla* and *sompaṭa* metre(?)

PS (4.27, p. 25): 2d, two *aṅgas*—pd tl, n.

216cd-217. 17. *Kanduka*

216d. Kanduka is explained by Kallinātha (p. 322) as a variety of *gāthā* like *jhampaṭa*: *'ayam api gāthābhedo draṣṭavyaḥ'*: NN omits this. This *prabandha* also has three feet; the first two, consisting of pd and pt respectively, constitute its U. The third foot, composed of pt is D. A consists of words not found in the first and third feet. SR NN or CDP do not mention the conclusion of the song. But Kallinātha declares that the conclusion of *kanduka, siṁhalīlā, haṁsalīla, daṇḍaka* and of *jhampaṭa* is on the respective U.

217c. Dīpanī jāti because it has four *aṅgas*—pd pt bd, tl.

AC (4.16.53, p. 47) *kantuka*; many kinds of (unequal) feet, pd, bd; tl, *rāga* of composer's choice.

JS (p. 48): *kanṭuka:* composed of pd pt bd.

PS (4. 33, p. 26): 2-d; four *aṅgas*—pt tl bd pd; an

218-221ab. 18. *Tribhaṅgī*

218c. Tribhaṅgī vṛtta is a *samacatuṣpadī varṇavṛtta* of twentyseven syllables to the quarter, with *yati* at 7, 7, 13 and a *gaṇa* disposition: नसभनतजतसय (Jayakīrti, *Chando'nuśāsanam*, 2.268)

218d. tribhaṅgi tāla (NN 1.195): ताले त्रिभङ्गिसंज्ञे तु लघुद्वन्दं गुरू तथा । (।।ऽऽ)

219b. tribhiḥ: including or excluding the *tribhaṅgi tāla.*

219c. brahmaviṣṇuśivastutyā: SR(4.284) merely says: '*yad-vā devatraya stutyā*'. Siṁhabhūpāla expands this into '*kaścit trayāṇām stutyā yuktaḥ*' (p. 323). Kallinātha is silent (p. 323).

220abc. svara-padāsaktaḥ: Allocation of the four *aṅgas* pd pt sv tl in the three *dhātus* UDA is not found elsewhere, including Kallinātha. This is a general or uniform distribution. In parallel treatises such allocation is specific to particular varieties of the *tribhaṅgi* or allowed to be arbitrary. So, even though most authorities describe the same five forms of *tribhaṅgi*, these latter differ slightly from each other. These may be epitomised here from early authorities.

BD (418, 419, p. 145) gives application of pd pt sv only generally, and merely states

वृत्तत्रयपदेन तालत्रयमिश्रेण त्रिभङ्गिरभिधीयते ।

AC (4.16.345-352, pp. 39, 40) distinguishes *tribhaṅgī* varieties by (a) three *vṛttas* (b) three feet, each composed of sv pt (c) three *tālas* (d) each of three feet composed in a different *vṛtta.* It offers two illustrations:

अमरराजशिखामणिरश्मिभी रञ्जिताङ्घ्रिसरोरुहयुग्मम् ।
वन्दे देवं त्रिभुवनगुरुं पावनं वासुदेवम् ॥
नीलनीररुहरोचकमूर्तिः कौस्तुभद्युतिविराजितवक्षाः ।
पाञ्चजन्यपरिभूषितपाणिः सचि(पात्वि)नां शुभबलाकय(लसितोत्पल)नाभः ।
सृजसि देव जगन्ति रजोन्वितस्तदनुपालयसि स्फुटसत्त्ववान् ।
अपि च संहरसे तमसावृतो जगति चित्रमिदं तव चेष्टितम् ।
नाभीसरोरुहजुषा चतुराननेन
संस्तूयमानपदपङ्कजपुष्कराक्ष ।
दुग्धाम्बुराशिभुजगाधिपभोगशायिन्
त्रायस्व मां दुरितनाशकृते नमस्ते ।

It is not known how his words भिन्नपादत्रयस्येयमुदाहृतिरीरिता may be conciled with this illustration. He gives an additional information: *tribhaṅgi* has no rule about meaning (i.e. theme) or *rasa.*

Jagadekamalla (JS p. 45) describes the following five kinds: i. composing sv pd pt in three suitable *rāgas* and in ii. three *tālas* iii. composing sv pd pt in *tribhaṅgi-tāla* or in three different *vṛttas* iv. composing all three feet in three *aṅgas* in a single *vṛtta* called *tribhaṅgi* v. composing in propitiation of three gods. It is suggested that in the first two varieties the sequence of *aṅgas* is sv-pd-pt and pt-pd-sv respectively in each of three feet, in the third, each foot is in a different *vṛtta;* in the fifth, each foot is devoted to praise or propitiation of one god.

Haripāladeva (SS. 5.7.125-128) gives slightly different *lakṣaṇa* for these five: i. sv-pt-pd (probably in this order) should be sung in each foot separately, thus repeating them three times in all three feet; ii. composed in three *rāgas,* three *tālas;* iii. composed in *abhaṅga* (*tribhaṅgī?*) *tāla;* iv. and v. are the same as above.

Somarājadeva (*Saṅgītaratnāvalī,* extr. *Bharatakośa,* p. 262) gives the same five varieties in the same way.

Pārśvadeva (PS. 4.54, p. 27): 3d, four *aṅgas*—pd pt sv tl.

Veṅkaṭamakhin (CDP 9.187-193) adds that (iii) is composed such that each of the three feet is devoted to one of the three *aṅgas* and to one of the three *tālas.*

It may be recalled that *tribhaṅgi vṛtta* has been described as a *catuṣpadī* (3.2.218 c). But the above descriptions relate to three feet only. This may be conciled by assuming that the fourth foot is A (which has words different from these in the other two; but whether the names of the *prabandha* etc. can be incorporated into the metrical structure of *tribhaṅgī* metre is ponderable). On the other hand Kallinātha says (it is not known on what authority) that *tribhaṅgi vṛtta* is a variety of *gāthā* (of three feet, p. 322). In this case, A is composed separately.

221a. aniryukta: with no restriction of *rāga, tāla, vṛtta* etc. e.g. (v)

221a. niryukta: with restriction of *rāga, tāla, vṛtta* etc. e.g. (ii), (iii)

221b. yathāsambhava: in any arbitrary order.

221cd-223ab. 19. *Haravilāsa*

222d. haravilāsa: There is unanimity in the *lakṣaṇa* of this *prabandha* among the authorities. It is not described in BD and AC. But Jagadekamalla (JS p. 46) and Jagannātha (? extr. *Bharatakośa,* p. 768) ascribe the following *lakṣaṇa* of *haravilāsa* to Mataṅga:

पदैः सबिरुदैः पाटैस्तेन्नकैर्यो विरच्यते ।
तथैवान्यपदाभोगः पाटन्याससमन्वितः ।
मतङ्गमुनिना प्रोक्तो नाम्ना हरविलासकः ॥

This, if genuine, is more likely to be a paraphrase or summary than an extract; BD does not reveal any specific distribution of *aṅgas* among *dhātus,* i.e. allocation of this or that particular *aṅga* or *aṅgas* to a particular *dhātu.* However, the possibility of the above passage or its purport in BD cannot be completely ruled out because of the large lacunae and corruption in the available text of BD.

SS (5.7.141,142) gives a somewhat different sequence of the *aṅgas:*

पदैश्च बिरुदैः स्तोभैः पाटैरपि विरच्यते ।

Veṅkaṭamakhin (CDP 9.155-158) agrees with previous authorities e.g. SR (4.2.58).

The conclusion of the song on *pāṭa,* ascribed to Mataṅga in the above passage, is not mentioned elsewhere.

PS (4.56, p.27): 3d, five *aṅgas*—sv bd tl tn pt; an.

223b. Ānandinī: because it is composed in all *aṅgas* except sv; *rāga* and *tāla* are to be assumed.

223cd-224. 20. *Sudarśana*

224b. sudarśana. Kallinātha is silent, but Paṇḍarīka Viṭṭhala and Veṅkaṭamakhin (CDP 9.179-181) adopt his method to interpret thus.

BD, AC, SS have not described this *prabandha*; its description in JS (p. 48) is the basis for later accounts.

224d. Dīpanī because it is composed in four *aṅgas* viz. pd bd tn tl.

PS (4.32, p.26: 2d), three *aṅgas*—bd tl pd; n.

225-226. 21. *Svarāṅka*

225. svaraiḥ... svaraiḥ: The structure first segment—sv-1tl, second segment—pd-2 tl, third segment—bd-3tl is agreeable to most authorities. In some instances pd is substituted by pt (e.g. SS 5.7.123a). Only Śārṅgadeva and later authorities give a different order: pd-sv-bd (SR 4.286).

226b. mālavaśriyā: Kallinātha adopts this reading for SR (p. 324) and is faithfully followed by Paṇḍarīka Viṭṭhala and Veṅkaṭamakhin (CDP 9.184). This reading is not supported elewhere; the former has conflated both versions.

226c. caturdhātuka: Here NN and CDP (9.185) have followed Kallinātha (p. 324); from the expression '*udgrāhāditrayam*' (SR 4.286b) follows the arrangement: U—first foot composed of pd in a single tl; M—second foot composed of sv in 2 tl; D—third foot composed of bd in 3 tl. According to others, the order is U—first foot, sv-1tl; M—second foot, pd-2tl; D—third foot, bd-3tl. With both schools A is fourth *dhātu*, composed of words other than those in the first (or second) foot. Thus the *prabandha* is *caturdhātuka.*

226d. Dīpanī: because it has four *aṅgas*: pd sv bd tl.

PS (4.50, p. 27): 3d, four *aṅgas*—pd sv bd tl. Thus Pārśvadeva does not recognise the occurrence of M in this *prabandha.*

BD does not describe *svarāṅka.*

AC (4.16.30-33, pp.44-45) mentions the three segments clearly:

स्वैरेको पदैरेको बिरुदैश्च तथा परः ।
एवं खण्डत्रयं कार्यं स्वराङ्के तालसंयुतम् ॥

It records (4.16.33, p.45) for the first time the admission of the Kannaḍa word *bayakāra* (composer) as a technical term into the perimeter of music theory. It further adds that this composition may have its own god or king as hero. An illustration is given:

अचिन्त्यो योगिभिश्चिन्त्यो निर्गुणोऽप्य(?स)गुणस्तथा जयति भगवान् भक्तवत्सलः ।
श्रीवत्सलाञ्छन गोविन्द रावणमहाशैलकुलिश ।
घातककंसासुरगजपञ्चानन बाणदावानल हिरण्यकशिपूरुफलकविदारणचक्र ॥

JS (p. 45) concurs with AC.

227-228ab. 22. *Śrīvardhana*

227. yatra-padātmakaḥ: Paṇḍarīka Viṭṭhala and Veṅkaṭamakahin (CDP 9.173-175) have followed Kallinātha (pp. 324, 325) in this distribution of *aṅgas* among *dhātus.*

228a. Śrīvardhana prabandha is not described by Mataṅga and Someśvara. But JS (p. 47) and SS (5.7.154, 155) give the same *lakṣaṇa* as in SR.

228b. Ānandinī: because of five *aṅgas,* pd pt sv bd tl.

228cd-229ab. 23. *Harṣavardhana*

228c. padaiśca birudaiḥ: This is U of *harṣavardhana.*

228d. svarapāṭakaiḥ: This is its D.

229a. udgrāhe nirvāṇaḥ: This *lakṣaṇa* is not found elsewhere.

229b. śeṣaḥ: aniryukta, tridhātuka, ānandinī jāti (not found in Kallināha).

229b. Harṣvardhana is not found in BD or AC. But Jagadekamalla (JS p. 48), Haripāladeva (SS 5.7.155, 156), Pārśvadeva (PS 4.33), Śārṅgadeva (SR 4.288), Veṅkaṭamakhin (CDP 9.176, 177) have described it in the same terms as in NN JS and SS add a *tālaniryukti* of *citra tāla*; this *tāla* is described in NN (1.192) thus:

चित्रे दो लौ द्रुतो दौ द्वौ द्रुतौ लघुः (०।।०।।००।)

229cd-231. 24. *Vadana*

229c. *Cha-pa-da* are *mātrā-gaṇas* defined by moraic quantity viz. *cha*—six *mātrās* (ऽऽऽ), ca—five *mātrās* (ऽऽ।), *da*—four *mātrās* (ऽऽ), *ta*—three *mātrās* (ऽ।) and *da*—two *mātrās* (ऽ), as described in SR (4.63). These were used largely to compose metrical structures in Prākṛta and Apabhraṁśa languages; they are discussed by Hemacandra (*Chando'nuśāsanam,* 1.3), Virahāṅka (*Vṛttajātisamuccaya,* 1.15, 16, 27-29), Svayambhū (*Svayambhūcchandas, inter alia*) with alternative symbols; two *mātrās*—*da, dāra*; three *mātrās*—*ta, tāra, tāṁśa*; four *mātrās*—*ca, cāra, cāṁśa*; five *mātrās*—*pa, pāra, pāṁśa*; six *mātrās*—*cha, chāra, chāṁśa.* Hemacandra employs *ṣa* in place of *cha.* It is interesting that Jagadekamalla also employs the same in describing *vadana* (JS p. 50).

229cd-230a. udgrāhe....padaiḥ: Both Paṇḍarīka Viṭṭhala and Veṅkaṭamakhin (CDP 9.198-205) have followed Kallinātha (pp. 325, 326) in the distribution of *aṅgas* among the *dhātus. Vadana* and its varieties are not found in BD, AC or SS. JS describes *vadana, upavadana* and *vastuvadana* (p. 50) thus:

वदनं वस्तुवदनं तथोपवदनं त्रिधा ।
मध्ये मध्ये स्वरैः पाटैस्तालैरपि विराजितः ।
पचयुगकलितं वदनः(?नं) स्याच्छगणयुग्मतदेर्मतमुपवदनं
वस्तुवदनकं चयुगलदतषषैः कार्पटिकानाम् (?)

PS (4.27, p. 25); 2d, two *aṅgas*—pd tl; n.

232-234. 25. *Caccarī*

232b. ***Carcarī chandas*** is a *varṇavṛtta-samacatuṣpadī* with eighteen syllables in each quarter, which is divided into three natural segments with two *yatis* at 8 and 5 syllables having the structure रसजजभर (*Prākṛtapaiṅgala*, 2.184). It is called *ujjvala* by Hemacandra (*Chando'nuśāsanam*, 2.313), *mallikottaramālikā* by Jayakīrti (*Chando'nuśāsanam*, 2.220), *vibudhapriyā* by Piṅgala (*Chandaḥśāstram*, 8.16) and *haranartana* by Kedārabhaṭṭa (*Vṛttaratnākara*, 3.94.14). But SR (4.290) remarks that *carcarī* has many feet of sixteen *mātras* each. NN is silent about this.

But Kallinātha says (p. 326) '*ṣoḍaśamātrātmakapādayuktam cacchariccandaḥ*'. It is not known on what authority he does so or if he infers this because Śārṅgadeva mentions a foot of sixteen *mātrās*. This is not necessarily *carcarī* metre, for SR gives *carcarī chandas* according to another school of thought; hence, this would be alternative to a sixteen *mātrā* foot and could well be the eighteen *mātrā* foot mentioned above. NN seems to reject or ignore the *carcarī* of sixteen *mātrā* foot, but to favour the *carcarī* metre. SR (4.290-292ab) gives altogether four versions of *carcarī* viz. i. *caccarī tāla*, many feet, each of which has sixteen *mātrās*, every pair of lines possesses a rhyme; Prākṛta words; *hindola rāga*; sung in the Spring Festival; ii. same, but *caccarī* metre instead of sixteen *mātrā* foot; iii. same, but *krīḍā tāla* instead of *caccarī tāla;* iv. same, but *ghattā* etc. *chandas* instead of sixteen foot *mātrā.* When *caccarī prabandha* is composed in a metre other than *caccarī,* its name is associated with the other metre e.g. *ghattā caccarī* NN omits the last three.

Ghattā is described in *Prākṛtapaiṅgalam* (extr. by Narahari Cakravarti, *Saṅgītasārasaṁgraha,* (6.22-24, p.133) as consisting of seven four-*mātrā* units in each of two feet (*dvipadī*) with three (*laghu?*) *yatis.*

इह सप्त चतुष्कलगणनिर्मितपदत्रिलघुविरामं भवति यदि ।
नागाधिपपिङ्गलभणितसुमङ्गलघत्तावृत्तमिदं वदति ॥
पिङ्गले- सा घत्तह कुलसारकित्तिअ पारणा अवाय पिङ्गल कहयि ।
एआरह वीसाम णन्दउ णाम पुण विसओ तेरह विरइ ॥

If, instead, the *ghattā* metre has caesurae at 11, 7, it is called *ghattānanda.*

232b. *caccarī tāla* (NN 1.144):

विरामान्तद्रुतद्वन्द्वान्यष्टौ लघवः स्मृतः । (००́। ००́। ००́। ००́। ००́। ००́। ००́। ००́।) If the definition of SR (5.266) is preferred viz. विरामान्तद्रुतद्वन्द्वायष्टौ लघु च the *tāla* is ००́००́००́००́००́००́००́००́।

Krīḍā tāla prescribed in (iii) above of SR is (NN 1.143): क्रीडा द्रुतौ विरामान्तौ –००́

233c-234a. atra...padaiḥ: Paṇḍarīka Viṭṭhala has borrowed information on distribution of *aṅgas* among *dhātus*, number of *dhātus* and *prabandha jāti* from Kallinātha (pp. 326, 327).

Car(c)carī is not found in BD and SS. CDP has suffered a lacuna for the *lakṣaṇa* of this *prabandha*. Jagadekamalla (JS p. 24) offers an elaborate description including *carcarī* metre, *carcarī tāla*, *krīḍā tāla*, *ghattā* metre (and some explanation of this metre in a text which is now snarled), frequent medial recurrence of '*dhātu*, *pada* and *prāsa*', words of Prākṛta languages, god-theme, performance in Spring Festival etc.

Someśvara (AC 4.16.301-303, p. 33) is evidently the source for SR in its treatment of the *carcarī* and contains all the details; it is interesting that the prescription '*rāge vasante*' occurs in the middle of the song(see below). This is called *deśī hindola* in AC (4.16.143, p.14); it is called *vasanta*, a *janya* of *hindola*, *pūrṇa*, also called *deśī hindola*; *hindola* is performed in the spring season, in the fourth watch of the day; it is dear to *Makaradhvaja*, i.e. *Manmatha* (SR 2.2.95cd-96). This seems to be the basis for '*kāmadevataḥ*' in NN for *carcarī* which is to be sung in the *hindola rāga* in *vasantotsava*.

AC offers the following illustration of *carcarī* in a Prākṛta language (4.16.302, p. 33):

मधुरिपुनायकु पहुतरसाहारकिसलयकिवउः
विचकिल परिमालाग्रोषुम्यौं ।
अलिकुलझङ्कारबहुकुसुमैः कोइल कउरउ करइ ।
मुहावउ तरणींह कुसुमसररक्राखारउ हालकैं ।
नरवैकचुपविनसितालिहिछं देगारि पुडिज्जइ ।
कुङ्कुमसलिले नणुरञ्जइ तरुणियणिम्मटुरुणजिज्जयि ।
पठहिदो लउवडि खेलिज्जइ । जुवति हं चरण हं दिउदुपेल्लज्जइ ।
चन्दणे अच्च इले वेणु किज्ज इमल्लि य मञ्जरि शिरे तुरुं विज्जइसि अधु विश्व ।
अवरुड विज्जइनो भाहलनवसरूप हरिज्जइकश्रूरमन्त्रिपुमसिसे विज्जइा रागे वसन्ते ।
पीउ गाइज्जइ हंसे तुलायिमुं । देसो विज्जइ । विरुलं तउवाणि नाणिज्जै ।

It may be noted that the *pāda* does not have sixteen *mātrās*, nor set to the *caccari* or *ghattā* metre.

Pārsvadeva (PS 4.27, p. 25) and JS summarise the *caccarī*: 2d, two *aṅgas*—pd, tl; n.

235-237ab. 26. *Caryā*

235ab. āryā...vinā: Paddhaḍī etc.metres are prescribed in parallel treatises. This metre is explained in comm. NN 3.2.237cd. SR (4.292) reads: पद्धडिप्रभृतिभिच्छन्दाः। Siṁhabhūpāla expands this (p. 327) to पद्धडीराहडी मुख्यानि छन्दांसि ।

236a. dvitīya: SR gives a larger option (4.293): द्वितीयादितालतः '*Ādi*' here means, according to Kallinātha (p. 327) any *tāla* which is equivalent in *mātrā* quantity to *dvitīya tāla.*

Dvitīya tāla is explained in NN (1.140) thus: द्वितीयो दद्वयं लश्च । (i.e. ००।). This is explicitly stated in the NN.

236d. udgrāhadhruvakau: U consists of the first two feet of the *paddhaḍī* (or *rāhaḍī*) metre; D is made of its third and fourth feet. A is composed of other words. Paṇḍarīka Viṭṭhala has not derived this *aṅga* distribution from Kallinātha, but has inferred it by using the latter's method. CDP has a lacuna for this *prabandha.*

237a. dvyaṅga: pd, tl; hence a *tārāvalī.*

235c. caryā: SR (4.293cd-294ab) describes the following four forms of *caryā*:

सा द्विधा छन्दसः पूर्त्या पूर्णाऽपूर्णा त्वपूर्तितः ।
समध्रुवा च विषमध्रुवेत्येषा पुनर्द्विधा ॥

Kallinātha expatiates on this (p. 327): i. *pūrnā*: full metre ii . *apūrṇā*: uncompleted metre iii. *samadhruvā*: D= U in length iv. *viṣamadhruvā*: D and U are unequal in length. According to Siṁhabhūpāla however, *samadhruvā* consists of repeating all four feet; *viṣamadhruvā* repeats only D.

The *caryā* is not found in BD and JS. CDP has a lacuna. AC (4.16.57-59, p. 47) characterises it as composed with a spiritual theme, rhyming in every two feet the second half is similar to the first. It offers an illustration:

संसारसोपूहदरैः कायहीनं चण्डिया ।
कोहलोहमोह बहुकेण तरिया ।
इन्दियपयणखरवेगेन हंसि ।
दुक्ति हलाहणिम नडिन पाचधि(सि?) ।

PS (4.27, p. 25) says that *carijā* has two *dhātus*, two *aṅgas* (pd tl) and is *niryukta.* SS (5.7.176-178, p. 230) gives its *lakṣaṇa* thus: its theme is spiritual; *yogins* sing it in many forms; it has terminal rhyming, uses *paddhaḍī* etc. metres and *dvitiya* etc. *tālas.*

Caryā means religious or spiritual conduct. Songs pertaining to such practices are known as *caryā gītis* and are more than a thousand years old. Some fifty *caryā gītis* composed by *vajrayāna* and *mahāyāna* Buddhist monks and others are known; their authors are *Lui, Kukkurī, Guṇḍarī, Cāṭilla, Bhusuku, Kānha, Kambala, Ḍombī, Kṛṣṇā-*

cārya, Vīṇā, Sarahā, Kaṅkaṇa, Śabara, Tāḍaka, Āryā, Viruvā and *Jayanandī*. Several *dohas* of *Saraha*(*pāda*) are also available.

The *caryā* is undoubtedly the archetype of *pada* and *kīrtan* in the music of North India (Oriyā, Bihāri, Beṅgāli, Hindī, Gujarāti) and of *pada, kṛti* or *kīrtana* in Karnataka music. I have discussed this in some detail in *Śrīpādārāya: A Literary and Musical Study* (ready for the press). These *caryāgītis* have some common features: they are composed in a mystic language, usually allegorical, called *saṁdha, saṁdhyā* or *iṅgitabhāṣā*, which is variously claimed to be the precurser of Beṅgāli, Oriya and Bihāri languages. Only three of these songs are in Sanskrit; the others are in the one or the other of Prākṛta *bhāṣās*. The songs are always in couplets, divisible into four quarters. The second of these couplets is always *dhruvapada*, and is not counted as a *caraṇa*. Here the two lines are sometimes unequal. *Dhruvapada* is repeated at the end of each stanza (*caraṇa*). The stanza line (*pāda*) is usually of sixteen *mātrās*, occasionally (slightly) more or less. The number of *caraṇas* is usually four (there are only three exceptions viz. with 5, 5, 6 stanzas). The *rāga* is invariably mentioned, but never the *tāla*. This was probably to enable the performer to choose a *tāla* or rhythm frame appropriate to the metre or rhythm frame of the words. Terminal rhyming occurs invariably, including *dhruvapada* and varies from stanza to stanza. The stanza lines in each couplet are of approximate equal length and vary from stanza to stanza. Composer's name is found always in the last stanza.

A *caryā* of *Vīṇāpāda*, consistng of an allegory on the musical instrument *vīṇā* is offered below; this is in Prākṛta; its Samskṛta *chāyā* is also given: (*Caryāgītikoṣa*, ed. P.C. Bagchi and Śānti Bhikṣu Śāstrī, pp. 58, 59)

राग पटमञ्जरी; वीणापादानाम्	छाया
सुज लाउ ससि लागोलि तान्ती ।	सूर्योऽलाबू शशिनि लग्नः तन्त्र्याम् ।
अनहा दांडी एकि किअत अवधूती ॥ १ ॥	अनाहतो दण्डिका एकीकृत्य अवधूत्या ॥ १ ॥
बाजइ अलो सहि हेरुअ वीणा ।	वाद्यते भोः सखि हेरुकवीणा ।
सुनतान्तिधनि विलसइ रुणा ॥ (ध्रुवपद)	शून्यतन्त्रीध्वनिः विलसति करुणम् ॥
आलिकालिबेणि सारिसुणिआ ।	आलिकालीं द्वे शारिके श्रुत्वा ।
गअवर समरस सान्धि गुणिआ ॥ २ ॥ (ध्रु)	गजवरसमरससन्धिं गणयित्वा गुणयित्वा वा ॥ २॥
जबे करहा करहकले चापिउ ।	यदा करहः करहकलेन पीडितः ।
बतिस तान्तिधनि सअल विआपिउ ॥ ३ ॥ ध्रु ॥	द्वात्रिंशत्तन्त्रीध्वनिभिः सकलं व्याप्तम् ॥ ३ ॥
नाचन्ति बाजिल गाअन्ति देवी ।	नृत्यति वज्रिलः गायन्ति देव्यः ।
बुद्धनाटक विसमा होइ ॥ ४ ॥ ध्रु ॥	बुद्धनाटकं विसमं भवति ॥ ४ ॥

From the general features of the *caryās* described above and the foregoing illustration, the resemblance of the *caryā* with the *pada* (both northern and southern analogues) becomes evident.

237cd-240ab. 27. *Paddhaḍī*

237c. chandaḥ: The requirement that *paddhaḍī prabandha* should be composed in the namesake metre is found implicitly in JS (p. 25): its foot has sixteen *mātrās* amongst which *jagaṇa* should be avoided in the odd numbered positions and the ninth syllable must be a *guru*; this is explicitly stated in SR (4.295). NN has lifted the *lakṣaṇa* of *paddhaḍī* metre from Kallinātha who quotes it from an unnamed source (p. 329); this verse is found in JS (p. 25) which reads '*navama guru*' vice '*caramaguru*' in the last quarter:

षोडशमात्राः पादे पादे यत्र भवन्ति निरस्तविवादे ।
पद्धडिका जगणेन विमुक्ता चरमगुरुः सा सद्भिरिहोक्ता ॥

CDP (9.170) contains a secondary extraction of this. Jayakīrti derives this metre from *raghaṭā* (*Chando'nuśāsanam*, 1.24). *Paddhati* may be a Sanskritisation of *paddhaḍi* which is primarily a Prākṛta metre, very popularly employed in Apabhraṁśa languages (e.g. Hemacandra, *Chando'nuśāsanam*, 3.73 regards this as a Sanskrit metre). It is a *catuṣpadī mātrā vṛtta*, each foot being formed of four four-*mātrā gaṇas*. Those in odd positions cannot be a *ja-gaṇa*; the last one must be *guru* or *ja-gaṇa* or *sarvalaghu*.

The *paddhaḍī* is also called *paddhaḍikā*, *paddaḍiā*, *pajjhaṭikā*, *pajjhaḍiā*, and *paddhaṭikā*. It is a Prākṛta metre. Svayambhū (*Svayambhūcchandaḥ*, 6.169 et seq) characterises it thus: *savra-sama catuṣpadī*: each foot has sixteen *mātrās*; terminal rhyming (*yamaka*) in the even feet. Eight such *yamakas* constitute a *kaḍavaka*. This is called *paddhaḍika dhruva*. In actual compositions, it is found that the end of the foot is *ja-gaṇa* or *sarvalaghu*. Nanditāḍhya's description (*Gāthālakṣaṇam*, st. 74, 75) agrees with this. Rājaśekhara (*Chandaḥśekhara*, 5.137) says that the *paddhaḍī pāda* is composed of four four-*mātrā gaṇas*. Hemacandra (*Chando'nuśāsanam*, 3.73, comm.) avers that each of the four quarters has four *ca-gaṇas* with terminal rhyming; *ja-gaṇa* is proscribed in odd places; there may be *jagaṇa* or *sarvalaghu* at end of the foot. *Kavidarpaṇa* gives a similar account except that the last *caturmātrā gaṇa* must have a *madhyaguru* (*ja-gaṇa*) or a *dvilaghu*. *Prākṛtapaiṅgala* also states (1.125) that each of the four equal feet has four four-*mātrā gaṇas*, but the fourth must be a *ja-gaṇa* only.

The following illustrations may be cited for *paddhaḍī*:

Paddhaḍī vṛtta: Hemacandra (Sanskrit)

छत्रायमाणधरणोरगेन्द्र पार्श्वजिनेन्द्र स्मर मृगमृगेन्द्र ।
दर्शय दीर्णदुरित तिमिरनिकरसत्पद्धतिमास्यजितरजनिकर ॥

Idem. (Apabhraṁśa)

उन्निद्दकमलदल दीहरच्छुकंचणकवाडदढवि अडवच्छु ।
सुरव इकरिन्द करसरलबाहु एक्कङ्गिण अरिबलु धरइ नाहु ॥

Kavidarpaṇam (Apabhraṁśa):

धन्नह उद्दामप्रणामरङ्गि बालत्थलि पडिसङ्कन्तचङ्गि ।
गुरुसमुद्रसूरि पयनक्खुकन्ति कप्पद्धडिआइ तुलं वहन्ति ॥

Note that the name of the *vṛtta* in the first and third examples occurs in paronomasia.

Paddhaḍī prabandha: AC (4.16.317, pp. 35, 36):

जनितकमलानन्द प्रणतसुरगोविन्द
दनुजकुलसंहार अद्य(घ)कमलनीहार
भक्तजनभयहरण सुरसङ्घनतचरण
पुण्यसञ्चयसदन सरसीरुहनिभवदन
नीलजलधरवर्ण मकरकुण्डलवर्ण
तरुणरविनिभचक्र दमिल(त?)कालियसर्प
कंसभुजबलनाश दक्ष ----

BD (404, p.144): *pāṭalī*(?) is composed of sv pt tl bd in any language.

AC (4.16.316-318, pp. 35-56): sv pt, at end of foot, tl bd, any language; for illustration see above.

JS (p. 25): bd sv pt tl, in any language; defines *paddhaḍī: 'ṣoḍaśamātrā... proktā'* (see above).

PS. (4.34, p. 26) 2d, four *aṅgas*—bd pt sv tl; n.

240cd-242ab. 28. *Rāhaḍī*

240d. saṅgrāmaracitastutiḥ. SR (4.296) reads the same. But the sense of *'saṅgrāmacaritam jayaḥ'* in AC (4.16.419, p. 36) seems more appropriate.

241a. bahubhiścaraṇaiḥ (SR 4.296c) is taken by Kallinātha to mean that some are made U and some D without regard to precedence or antecedence (p. 329). NN extends Kallinātha's prior method to arrive at this detail.

241b. Rāhaḍī may be a *niryukta prabandha* in namesake metre like *gāthā, āryā, kalahaṁsa, cakravāka, tripadī, caccarī* and *paddhaḍī;* cf. Siṁhabhūpāla (p. 327) *'paddhaḍī-rāhaḍīmukhyāni chandāṁsi'*; but no indication of this is available in music treatises. Jagadekamalla (JS p. 51) requires (*'rāhaṭi'*) to be composed in words of *paddhaṭī* etc. metres.

242b. Niryukta: because *vīra rasa* is prescribed. But Kallinātha says (p. 322): *tālādyaniyamād aniryuktaḥ'*. Since NN draws upon Kallinātha for this portion of the text, the reading could be emended to *'-ābhogo'niryukto'* to align with him; but *niryukta* is a better reading.

242a. dvyaṅgaḥ: pd tl; so a *tārāvalī prabandha.*

242b. guṇadhātukaḥ: U, D, A.

AC (4.16.74, p. 49): *Rāhaḍī* is composed in *vīra rasa* relating to victory in a battle.

JS (p. 51): composed in *pādas* of *paddhaṭi* etc., terminal rhyme.

PS (4.26, p. 25), 2d, two *aṅgas*—pd tl; an.

242cd-243. 29. *Vīraśrī*

242c. padaiḥ: in words of prose or verse (see below, AC, JS *et al*).

242cd. udgrāha-dhruva: The allocation of pd to U and bd to D is due to Kallinātha (p. 329). NN and CDP (9.303, 305) follow him.

243d. bhāvanī: because of pd bd tl; but tl is left implicit by other authorities also: AC, and JS permit the use of any *tāla.*

AC (4.16.369-370, p. 63): pd bd any *tāla,* prose or verse; addressed to god or king on any desired theme. An illustration is given:

अनेकदुर्धरदैत्यदानवराक्षसक्षयकारिणं सृष्टिस्थित्यन्तकरणैकनिरन्तरमचिन्त्यं स्मरभरविवश-राधाहृदयवल्लभ-बालगोपाल-धूलिक्रीडाविकूणितविकृतवदनदर्शित जनितहासकोष्णनयनोदकस्नान-मन्दोदरी प्रलापदीक्षादानदक्ष अनन्तकालस्वीकृतभीरुभैरववपुर्विरचितसकलसङ्गरशास्त्रकोविद-रुचिसञ्ज्ञात-सन्धानविजय-बहु बाहु शालीन-देदीप्यमान-सुदर्शजातकम्पावसाद-दैत्यदयितासम्मोह कारिन्-गरलदानप्रवृत्तपूतनास्तनपानव्याजकृष्टरुधिरवसामस्तिष्कपङ्ककलुषकृत-नन्दगोपगृहप्राङ्गणदसदैत्येन्द्र-स्तम्भास्फालनमात्राविर्भूतनरहरि वपुर्विलोकनोत्पन्न-रोमाञ्चकञ्चुकसाश्चर्यार्यजनप्रवर्तितबहुस्तोत्र जय जय नारायण ।

JS (p. 49): *nibaddha* (with *tāla*) or *anibaddha* (without *tāla*), pd, bd, one *tāla.* PS has lacuna.

244-245. 30. *Maṅgalācāra*

244ab. yastu...kṛtaḥ: Thus *maṅgalācāra* is of three kinds (cf. CDP 9.307).

AC (4.16.359, 360, p. 41, 62): alliteration: previous words should be repeated and then next words taken up.

JS (p. 50): should be composed like *catuṣpadī; svaras* should be sung now and then in the middle.

SS (5.7.171) agrees with JS.

PS (4.31, p. 25): 2d, three *aṅgas*—pd sv tl; n-an.

244c. niḥsāru tāla: (NN 1.189, 190) also called *haṁsalīla:*

हंसलीले विरामान्तं लघुद्वन्द्वमुदाहृतम् ।
इममेवोचिरे तालं केचिन्निःसारुसंज्ञया ॥ (।ı́)

SS prescribes *jhampā tāla* (।০০́।, 2.68 p. 95) instead of *niḥsāru*(3.2.171-172c, p. 229).

244c. śrīrāga: AC (loc. cit.), JS. (loc. cit.), SS (loc. cit.) and Somarājadeva (*Saṅgītaratnāvalī*, extr. *Bharatakośa*, p. 451) ascribe *kaiśikī rāga* instead of *śrī*. The last authority admits *boṭṭa rāga* also. For descriptions of these *rāgas*, see *śrī rāga*, Paṇḍarīka Viṭṭhala, *Sadrāga-candrodaya*, 2.23.25; 3.43, 44; idem, *Rāgamālā*, 179; idem. *Rāgamañjarī*, 2.68, 69, NN 3.1.201), *kaiśikī-rāga*, SR 2.170, 171; *boṭṭa-rāga*, SR.2.50-52)

244d. ardhānte svararājitaḥ: at the end of each half; i.e. *svaras* are composed at the end of U and at the end of D. This seems to be the meaning of JS and SS: '*madhye madhye svarāśritaḥ*'.

246-251. 31. *Dhavala*

246a. Dhavala is also an ancient Prākṛta metre of 19 syllables to the quarter structured as six *na-gaṇas* followed by a *guru* (*Prākṛtapaingala*, 2.192). *Dhavala* also means bull. This *prabandha* derives its name from the ancient panegyrics comparing the hero to a bull. Its residue is now available in three forms viz. *kīrti-dhavala, vijaya-dhavala* and *vikrama-dhavala*. Then it was extended to benediction and therefore to all auspicious occasions, and received a pan-Indian experimentation and application. Examples of the *dhavala* varieties are available in Sanskrit, Prākṛta, Kannaḍa, Telugu and Hindī; it developed largely as folksong or in what is today called '*sampradāya*' songs i.e. songs, rendered traditionally by womenfolk on auspicious occasions and religious rites etc. Svayambhū (*Svayambhūcchandas*, 7.32) implies its acceptance by the learned and the skilled, despite its lack of *śāstra* characterisation, crystalline prosodial structure and purity of *yamaka* because it has an elastic form which could suit all auspicious occasions.

246a. trividhaḥ: Dhavala appears to have flowed in two separate streams in music and poetry like the *elā*. The metre is recognised in Prākṛta prosody as early as the 7th-8th century A.D. Svayambhū, Rājaśekhara, *Kavidarpaṇam* etc. describe its varieties. But Someśvara, Haripāladeva etc. do not distinguish various forms of *dhavala*. Haripāla mentions differences in the number of the *pādas*, but does not treat them as separate forms. Jagadekamalla has inaugurated its diversification in terms of prosodial differences. He seems to be the source for Śārṅgadeva.

246c. caraṇaiḥ: Dhavala varieties are related to the number of *pādas* in both music and poetry. *Kīrtidhavala* has four *pādas*; *vijaya*, six; and *vikrama*, eight. Svayambhū, Rājaśekhara and Hemacandra distinguish them, giving however, different names. e.g. Hemacandra (*Chando'nuśāsanam*, 5.32-38): *śrīdhavala, yaśodhavala* (8), *kīrti* (6), *guṇa-*, *bhramara-*, *amara* and *maṅgala-*(4). Rājasekhara (*Chandaḥśekhara*, 22-28) describes *utsāha-dhavala, helā-dhavala* etc. corresponding to *utsāha-maṅgala* etc. *Kavidarpaṇam* describes *kīrtidhavala* in agreement with parallel depiction elsewhere. The *kīrtidhavala* of six feet known to *chandaḥśāstra* has become *kīrtidhavala* of four feet in *saṅgītaśāstra*.

247c. kīrtidhavala: S. (4.299, 300) has a more readily intelligible account:

विषमे तु छयुग्मं स्यात् तो वा दो वाऽधिकः समे । तदा स्यात् कीर्तिधवलः

This version is accepted here since NN has based itself here on SR. According to this, the first and third feet of *kīrtidhavala* each carry two *cha* (i.e. six-*mātrā*) *gaṇas* while the second and fourth each carry a larger quantity in terms of *ta* (i.e. three *mātrās-)* or *da* (two *mātrās-) gaṇas.* So even feet have twelve *mātrās* each and the odd feet, fourteen (4*ta+da,* 2*ta+4da*) or fifteen (5*ta*) *mātrās.* This structure is unanimously accepted in the musical stream.

Prākṛta prosody offers its own subvarieties for the *catuṣpadī dhavala* in terms of *cha, ca, ta, da gaṇas.* For example

Svayambhū (*Svayamabhūcchandas,* 4.17-19) 1-3: *cha ca ta* instead of 2 *cha* 2-4: *cha ca*

Rājaśekhara (*Chandaḥśekhara,* 22-28) 1-3: fourteen *mātrās;* 2-4: sixteen or seventeen *mātrās.*

Hemacandra (*Chando' nuśāsanam,* 5.32-38)
guṇa dhavala 1-3: *cha* 2 *ca;* 2-4: *cha* 2 *ca da* or *ta*
bhramara dhavala 1-3: *cha ca ta;* 2-4: *cha ca*
amara dhavala 1-3: *cha ca ta;* 2-4: *cha* 2*ca*
maṅgala dhavala 1-2 (not 1-3): *cha* 3*ca da;* 3-4 (not 2-4) 5*ca da*

247d. Vijaya dhavala is characterised in SR (4.300bcd) thus:

विजये त्वाद्यतुर्ययोः ।
दौ द्वौ षष्ठे द्वितीये च शेषौ द्वौ छेन पेन वा ॥

This *lakṣaṇa* is adopted in other music treatises also. NN has

षष्ठे द्वितीये छौ शेषौ द्वौ छेन सेन वा

in the majority of its collative sources: B replaces '*sena*' with '*pena*'. If the reading '*sena*' is adopted, there would be two *da-gaṇas* (in excess of two *cha-gaṇas)* in the *pādas* 1, 2, 4, 6 than in the *catuṣpadī* analogue, resulting in sixteen *mātrās.* All four *pādas* would then have the same moraic quantity uniformly, differing only in *gaṇa* disposition; the remaining *pādas* 3-5 also have sixteen *mātrās* (2 *cha* + *sa-gaṇa).* Such structure is unacceptable. So, rejecting '*sena*', the minority reading '*pena*' (which also accords with SR) is preferred. In this case, the *mātrā* quantities in the six *pādas* are 16-18(19)-17(18)-18(19)-17(18) and 18(19) respectively.

Treatises on Prosody delineate the *ṣaṭpadī-dhavala* thus:
Svayambhū (loc. cit.) 1-3: 3 *cha;* 2-5 : 2 *cha;* 4-6: 2 *cha ca/pa*
Rājaśekhara (loc. cit.) 1:14; 2:8; 3:16(17); 4:14; 5:8; 6: 16(17)
Hemacandra (loc. cit.) 1-4:2 *cha da;* 2:5: 4*ca;* 3-6: 2 *cha ca/pa*

Kavidarpaṇam (loc. cit.) 1-2-3: 2*cha da*/2 *ca* 2 *cha ca*; 4-5-6: same: 1-3: *antyaprāsa.*

249d. vikrama-dhavala: NN has literal correspondence with SR(4.301cd-302ab) on the *lakṣaṇa* of this *prabandha.* According to this, the eight *pādas* have the following *gaṇa/ mātrā* disposition:

1- 3ca da/fourteen (*mātrās*); 2-3*da*/six; 3-3*da*/six; 4-3*ca da*/fourteen; 5-3*ca da*/ fourteen; 6-4*da*/eight; -7-3*da*/8-4*da*/eight. There is accord on this *lakṣaṇa* in other treatises.

The *aṣṭapadī-dhavala* is delineated in treatises on Prosody as follows:

Svayambhū (loc. cit.) 1-3: 3.5 *ca*; 2-4: 3*ca* 5-7: 3*ca,* minus one *mātrā* 6-3 *ca;* 8-2.5 *ca.* In other words, 14-12-14-12-11-12-11 and 10 *mātrās* respectively.

Rājaśekhara (loc. cit.) 14-12-14-12-11-10-11 and 10 *mātrās* respectively.

Hemacandra (loc. cit.) *śrīdhavala* 1-3: 3 *ca* 2-4: 2ca (?)

yaśodhavala 1-3: 3*ca;* 2-4: 3*ca;* 5-7: 2*ca ta;* 6-8: 2*ca* 2*da* or 3*ca*; i.e 14-12-14-12-11- 12-11 and 12 *mātrās* respectively.

250b. vimala: *Dhavala prabandha* contains words such as *vimala, dhavala* etc.

250c. yadṛcchayā: as one pleases, without observing any rule of *prāsa, mātrā* or *yati.*

250d. lokaprasiddhitaḥ: This means that there were numerous other forms of *dhavala* with variable or elastic *lakṣaṇa.*

251abc. yatra...padaiḥ: for this distribution of *aṅgas* among *dhātus,* Paṇḍarīka Viṭṭhala draws upon Kallināṭha (pp. 331, 332). U: 1,2 in *kīrtidhavala;* 1, 2, 3, 4 in *vijayadhavala*; 1, 2, 3, 4 in *vikramadhavala.* D: remaining *pādas.* (A in other words containing names of *prabandha,* patron/hero, composer.)

251d. dvyaṅga: pd tl; so a *tārāvalī.*

251d. niryukta: because of rules of prosody.

251d. tridhātuka: UDA

AC (4.16.14-16, p. 43): contains *dhavala* etc. words; divided into *pādas*; words of benediction; any metre; an illustration is given in a Prākṛta language.

धवलु हिमालउ धवलु गङ्गा धवलु एरावणु धवलु ।
चन्द्र धवलु महेसरु । धवलु छत्रु ब्रम्हदेछपसने धवलु जसु ॥

JS (p. 50): source for SR: sung in any *tāla.*

SS (5.7.172d-173ab): composed in four, six or eight *pādas*; sung on auspicious occasions only like weddings; set to *ekatāla.*

PS (4.27, p. 25) 2d, two *aṅgas*—pd tl; n

Hemacandra (*Chando'nuśāsanam,* 5.39, 1) gives an illustration of *maṅgala-dhavala*:

तुह असिलट्ठिहि नरवइ मङ्गलकारणि वित्थारिअ निम्मलयर सत्थिअधोरणि ।
सङ्गररङ्गि विवाहमुहूसवि जयच्छिहिल दारिअमयगल कुम्भत्थलमोत्ति आगुच्छिहि ।

Numerous *dhavalas* are available in Kannaḍa for auspicious occasions such as *jātakarma, sīmanta, upanayana, vivāha* etc. as well as devoted to deities e.g. *maṅgalagaurī dhavala, gaṅge dhvala* and so on. Many *dhavalas* are available in Telugu too. All these may be comprehended in 'यदृच्छया वा धवलो गेयो लोकप्रसिद्धितः' (NN 3.2.250 cd). I have discussed an actual *dhavala* elsewhere (Sathyanarayana, R., *Dhavala: A Hoary Song of Karnataka*, Bihar Theatre).

252-254ab. 32. *Maṅgala*

252a. yatreṣu...pāde: An explicit *niryukti* that *maṅgala-prabandha* should be sung in *maṅgalacchandas* is seen in Jagadekamalla (JS p. 50):

मङ्गलं मङ्गलाख्येन छन्दसा तालसंयुतः ।
---पञ्च चकारगणाः प्रतिपादगताश्चेन् मङ्गलमाहुरिदं सुधियः खलु वृत्तम्

SR(4.304):

मङ्गलं --- गेयं मङ्गलच्छन्दसाऽथवा

and SS (5.7.174, 175). Kallinātha has quoted the above definition of *maṅgala* metre from an unnamed source. NN has described the metre without naming it. But Śrīkaṇṭha (*Rasakaumudī*, 3.96, 97) says implausibly that the *maṅgala-pāda* has five *bha-gaṇas.*

Like *dhavala, maṅgala* also has evolved in two streams—the literary and the musical; the two *prabandhas* are closely affined. For example, Svayambhū (*Svayambhūcchandas,* 4.20, 21) takes up *maṅgala* immediately after *dhavala* and declares that its feet 1-2 have *cha* 2*ca gaṇas,* 3-4: *5ca* or 4 *pa*; '*tan-maṅgalacchandaḥ jānīhi maṅgalārthe*', i.e. it should be performed on auspicious (*maṅgala*) occasions. Thus the name of the *prabandha* is appropriate thrice: *maṅgala* metre, *maṅgala-tāla* and *maṅgala* occasions. Further, Svayambhū says that the prosodial forms such as *utsāha, helā, vadana,* performed on auspicious occasions may be suffixed with *maṅgala* e.g. *utsāha-maṅgala, helāmaṅgala, vadanamaṅgala* (*dhavalamaṅgala, dohāmaṅgala*). Apabhraṁśa *vṛtta-jātis* employed in the panegyric to gods are called *pullaḍka;* if used on auspicious occasions such as wedding, the selfsame are called *maṅgala* (ibid., 7.32)

252c. śaṅkha cakrādi racitaiḥ: This *lakṣaṇa* is not found elsewhere.

253ab. śrīrāge... mālavaśriyā: *Maṅgala* is restricted in the use of *rāga* and *tāla* also as in metre. As mentioned above, JS (p. 50) prescribes *maṅgala tāla* for it (००।). SR (loc. cit.) and AC (loc. cit.) require it to be sung in *kaiśikī* or *boṭṭa-rāga.*

253c. pūrvāparayoḥ: U—first two *pādas*; D—last two *pādas.*

254. tridhātu: UDA

254a. dvyaṅga: pd tl; so a *tārāvalī*

AC (4.16.17-19, p. 43): composed with auspicious words and sentences; sung in *kaiśiki* or *boṭṭa rāga, antyaprāsa; tṛtīya tāla* (NN 1.151): ooo' An illustration is available:

दधिदूर्वाक्षतचूतपल्लवकनककलशमातुलुङ्गस्वस्तिकनन्द्यावर्त सितकुसुमचन्दनकुङ्कुमलाजादि मङ्गलद्रव्याणि विप्राः पुण्यतमा योषितः महर्षयः देवमातरः नवग्रहा लोकपालाश्च ब्रह्मविष्णुमहेश्वराः । एते प्रयच्छन्तु मम मङ्गलम् ।

JS (p. 50): composed in *maṅgala* metre (defined above), *maṅgala-tāla, vilamba-laya*; example?

निलययुवतिजनसंतोषकुर्वाणमशेषजन(श्रव-?)णोत्सवं (?) मङ्गलम्

SS (5.7.174cd-175c): composed in *maṅgala* metre, *vilambita-laya,* and sung on festive occasions (*utsava*).

PS (4.28, p. 25) 2d, two *aṅgas*—pd tl; n.

254cd-256. 33. *Ovī*

255a. Ovī is also called *uvī. Ovī* is a well known folksong of Maharashtra; this may be the *deśabhāṣā* mentioned in NN (254d) and elsewhere. AC (4.16.553, p. 81) asseverates that the womenfolk of Maharashtra sing it while pounding corn— '*ovī tu kaṇḍane*'. Thus it is a *prabandha* sung to the rhythm of the stamp or pound (=*onakevāḍu* in Kannaḍa). *Ōvī* is a Kannaḍa word also. Keśirāja (*Śabdamaṇidarpaṇam, Dhātuprakaraṇam,* 666) explains it as *ōvu-pālane* (to succour). A sonnet relating to elephants—*gajāṣṭaka*—was composed as '*ōvanige*' by *Saigoṭṭa Śivamāra* (*Epigraphia Carnatica* 7, *Nagara,* 35-37, 1077A.D). Ācaṇṇa (*Vardhamānapurāṇam,* 4.36) mentions *ōvanige.* Many other Kannaḍa poets mention *onakevāḍu* (pounding or stamping song) from early times e.g. Nemicandra (*Līlāvati,* 2.32-41), Suraṅgakavi (*Triṣaṣṭipurātanavilāsa,* 24.149-152), Somarāja (*Udbhaṭakāvyam,* 10.88,89), Bhīmakavi (*Basavapurāṇam, passim*), Siddhanañjeśa (*Gururāja-cāritram,* 13.100,101), Ṣaḍakṣari (*Vṛṣabhendra vijaya,* 36.2.51), Tirumalārya (*Karṇavṛttāntakathe,* 20.27). In all these instances, the *ovī* is composed in three segments (cf. *khaṇḍatrayam,* NN 3.2.254c).

This *ovī-lakṣaṇa* has literal correspondence with SR (4.304cd-306). Many *ovīs* are formed by rendering each of the three segments or all three together in different ways (in melody), by composing them in different metres, by incorporating rhyme (or according to others, alliteration) at the beginning, middle or end of the verse line etc.

256d. Ovī is not found applied to any particular *rasa.* AC (4.16.21, 22, p. 43) says that the song *uvī* has the word *uvī* at the end (of each foot), in any desired *tāla,* with abundant alliteration; the theme is in *vipralambha śṛṅgāra* of the separated beloved. It is composed in couplets. A short illustration is available:

गोत्रलिङ्गोलिनिह्मंवि अचलुवलितो मझपडिहे कन्नोसचलूला उविए

JS (p. 51): couplets; any desired *tāla;* provincial language; alliteration; the word '*ovi*' at end; many varieties because of repetitions; applied in *vipralambha-śṛṅgāra.*

SS (5.7.181cd-182): desired *tāla*; provincial language; terminal rhyme; contains the word '*ovi*'.

PS (4.29, p. 25): 2d, *aṅgas*— tl tn (!); n-an.

I recall a cradle song, lullaby, which my mother (a musician) used to sing in couplets in Telugu, at the end of each stanza of which (there were some four stanzas) the words *ovi-ōvī* were sung. Its theme was not *vipralambha śṛṅgāra* but *vātsalya* (*ōvu-pālane*); this may have been included in *'ovyo janamanoharāḥ'* (SR 4.306d).

257 34. *Lollī*

257. sānu... vicakṣaṇaiḥ: There is unanimity in music treatises in respect of Prākṛta language, alliteration and the word *'lolli'* at end. Someśvara (AC 4.16.83, p. 49; 427, p. 68) adds that it is composed in a couplet, at the end of which occurs the word *'lolli'*. NN gives three segments for *lolli.*

JS (p. 52): many stanzas, alliteration, '*lolli*' at end, Prākṛta language.

SS (5.7.183, 184a): couplets, alliteration, '*lolli*' at end, Prākṛta language.

PS (4.26, p. 25): 2d, two *aṅgas*—pd tl; an.

A song form called *lālī* occurs in Telugu and Kannaḍa. It is composed in couplets with initial and/or terminal rhyming, with the word '*lālī*' occurring at the end of each stanza. It has a good rhythmic frame but no discernible *tāla.* It is a lullaby. Several *lālis* are composed by the *haridāsas* of Karnataka in Kannaḍa; it is also a popular folksong.

258. 35. *Ḍhollarī*

258a. Dohaḍa-prabandha is assumed without explanation or description by SR (4.308) from which NN borrows this passage. JS describes *ḍhollarī* without reference to *dohaḍa.* Someśvara's description of *dohaḍa* (AC 4.16.75-78, p. 49) may be summarised here for the sake of completeness. It is composed in *lāṭa* language in four *pādas* such that 1-3 have fourteen *mātrās* and 2-4, twelve *mātrās* with *yamaka* at the end of each line. An illustration is found in AC:

गोविनयनहजोरस्वैजो कंसखयकालु ।
सो अम्हदुरिइवहर उकन्हभराडावालु ॥

The former half is sung with or without *tāla.* If in such *prabandhas* (of one or more couplets) the word *ḍhollarī* occurs at the end of each stanza, it assumes the name *ḍhollarī.*

AC (4.16.80-82, p. 49; 424-426, p. 68): if the word '*ḍhollarī*' occurs at the end of the *dohaḍa prabandha,* it is called *ḍhollarī*; each of three *pārasirā* (? a Persian word ? *pārasika*? *pānasī*?) has twentyseven *mātrās*; the second is repeated after the third;

the song concludes on the third *pāda*; it is composed in any desired *tāla* and *rāga*, in *lāṭa* language and is '*tauruṣkī prāsasaṁyutā*'.

JS (p. 51): *Ṭhollarī* is composed in couplets, with the words *ṭhollarī* at the end of the second foot, in *krampā (jhampā) tāla* and *gauḍa rāga*; in *lāṭa* language, *vipralambha* (*śṛṅgāra*) and *vīra rasa*, in many feet.

259. 36. *Dantī*

259. anuprāsa... nigadyate: AC (4.16.84, 85, p.49; 428, 429, p. 68): one foot (stanza?) is composed in *śṛṅgāra rasa*; the name of god occurs at the end(?) of another foot (stanza) the two are unrelated, and have alliteration; the word '*dantī*' occurs at the end.

JS. (p. 52): two unrelated feet, dominated by rhyming; numerous caesurae; the word.'*dantī*' occurs at end. There are other *prabandhas* such as *prahelikā* (riddles), (related to *dantī*?) but are not described in the work.

SS (5.7.200cd-201): two unrelated feet with dominant rhyming, strange (charming, variegated) caesurae; '*dantī*' occurs at end.

PS (4.26, p. 25): 2d, two *aṅgas*-pd tl; an.

The last four *prabandhas* viz. *ovī, lolī, ḍhollarī* and *dantī* are probably folksongs; they derive their names from the terminal word, and so are *niryukta*. The absence of A is specially mentioned for them lest the general rule अनुक्ताभोगवस्तूनां पदैराभोगकल्पना be inadvertently applied.

DESCRIPTIONS OF SĀLAGASŪḌA PRABANDHAS

262 cd-276ab. 1. *Dhruva*

The *lakṣaṇa* of *dhruva prabandha* coincides completely with that in SR (4.315-332) in respect of division of *dhātus*, sixteen varieties and their application in *rasa* and *tāla; komala* in SR has become *kamala* in NN. NN athetises the mention of invisible fruits accruing to the singing of these sixteen *dhruvas*.

AC does not describe the *sālagasūḍa prabandhas*. This is true of JS also. SS (5.7. 184-188 c) classifies *dhruva prabandha* into *uttama, madhyama* and *adhama*, on the basis of the number of *padas* (foot? stanza?). *Uttama prabandha* is composed in five *padas* in U, five in A, in sv, pt and attractive *deśī-rāgas*. The fifth *pada* in A carries bd. *Madhyama dhruva* is composed correspondingly in four *padas* each and the *adhama*, in three; any *tāla* may be used. This is indeed remarkable in view of the many varieties of the *prabandha* and the severe *niryukti* for their *tālas* in SR etc.

Śārṅgadhara describes a similar classification (*Sārṅgadharapaddhati*, 1965-2034, pp. 293-303) of the *dhruva*. He depicts the *sālagasūḍas* in much the same way as SR. but adds that they are governed by a twofold rule of *varṇa* (syllable) and of *pada* (foot) (1974). The *dhruva prabandha* is indispensable amongst all songs: music without *dhruvaka* is like knowledge without wisdom, contemplation without spirituality, chairty or gift without faith (1965). *Uttama dhruva* is composed of six feet, among which two segments set to the same *dhātu* constitute U; the third is in a higher pitch and contains *gamakālapti.* Next two segments form A; the third incorporates the composer's name. The song concludes on U. The *madhyama dhruva* has five feet, of which the first two are U; the third is auxiliary, sung twice. In both *uttama* and *madhyama dhruvas* the initial two parts of U also served as D by repetition, and the third, as *antara.* In both, one more line was added to the A, which was used for signatures of *prabandha,* patron and composer, and was sung in a higher key. The *kaniṣṭha* (*adhama*) *dhruvaka* had only four parts; U had two segments, the second being in a somewhat higher key. A also had two sections, the second containing the patron's name. The injunction of *pāda niyaṁa* (i.e. conformity to the prescribed number of sections or parts) and *varṇa niyama* (i.e. conformity to prescribed syllabic quantity) was relaxed into *pāda niyama* and/or *varṇa niyama.* Even so, if the *varṇa niyama* was followed in (the first) two sections, other segments were exempted from this rule. Sārṅgadhara bases the foregoing on the authority of *Rāgārṇava* (1977).

Pārśvadeva (PS 4.192, p. 38) gives the mode of singing *dhruva prabandha* thus:

आदौ पादौ समगणयुतौ धातुसाम्यौ ततस्तत्
तुल्यो वाऽङ्घ्रिस्त्वधिक इतरो धातुनान्येन युक्तः ।
स्यादुद्ग्राहेऽत्र पदसहितो गेय एव द्विवारं
त्वङ्घ्री गीत्वा सकृदपि पुनर्न्यस्यते चोद्ग्रहे सः ॥

265c. ṣoḍaśadhā: The number of syllables per foot of these sixteen *dhruvas* is: *jayanta* 11, *śekhara* 12, *utsāha* 13, *madhura* 14, *nirmala* 15, *kuntala* 16, *kamala* 17, *cāra* 18, *nandana* 19, *candraśekhara* 20, *kāmoda* 21, *vijaya* 22, *kandarpa* 23, *jayamaṅgala* 24, *tilaka* 25, *lalita* 26.

Pārśvadeva differs somewhat in the division of *dhātus,* mode of singing and varieties of *dhruva prabandha.* Instead of applying to *rasa* or *tāla,* he relates them to *gamaka* and occasion etc. Depending on the use of the different *gamakas* in the three registers, he describes eleven *dhruvas* viz. *śaśi, hāsa (bhāsa?), haṁsa, mādhava* (*vasanta*) *nīlotpala* (*kumuda*), *tāpasa, prajānātha* (*kamalabhava,*) *hari* (*kamalāpati*), *hara, narapati* and *śakra.* These are not found elsewhere (PS 4.193-198, p. 38).

268c. rāsa tāla: The forms of the *tālas* named for the sixteen *dhruvas* are collected from NN (1.138-195) and shown along with the *dhruvas.* These are the translator's additions and are not part of the original text.

275c. Vicārapratimaṇṭha is not known to NN, SR etc. Catura Dāmodara (*Saṅgītadarpaṇam,* p. 166) has compiled it from *matāntara*: विचारप्रतिमण्ठोऽसौ नगणो दौ विरामवान् । (IIIoó) Elsewhere, *pratimaṇṭha tāla* is prescribed for *lalita dhruva.*

276cd-283ab. 2. *Maṇṭha*

277b. vikalpena: *Antara* may or may not occur; *antara* is an expedient device functioning as bridge between D and A. It was used in *uttama dhruva* and *madhyama dhruva* (but not in *kaniṣṭha dhruva*). Its application transgressed the *sālagasūḍas* into *pañcatāleśvara, vadana* etc. also. This was used occasionally in *maṇṭha* and other *sālagasūḍa prabandhas.* Kallinātha says that this was popularly referred to as *upāntara* (p. 341). The *dhruva dhātu* of some *sālagasūḍas* e.g. *ekatāli* was also sometimes called *antara* (SR 4.358).

280-281ab. jena...sena: The *aṅgas* of these *tālas (laghu, guru)* correspond exactly to their prosodial analogues; see comm. NN 3.2.17, 26d.

296-299. 6. *Rāsa*

296c. caturvidho: Since none of them is prescribed in respect of specific *tālas,* they may be assumed to be sung in *rāsa tāla* itself.

298-299ab. kautuke...abhyudaye: Such application of *rāsakas* to different occasions is reminiscent of similar applications of the *dhruvas* by Pārśvadeva (PS 4.193-198, p. 38)

300-303. 7. *Ekatāli*

300b. trividhā: Particular *tālas* are not ascribed to these three *ekatālis.* So they may be assumed to be performed in *ekatālī-tāla* itself.

304b. dvyaṇga: pd tl

305. kecil-lakṣyaviśāradāḥ: Music treatises describe the *sūḍakrama* by and large in the same way as above. However, there existed a parallel tradition of grouping different *prabandhas* as *sūḍakrama.* Paṇḍarīka Viṭṭhala is probably implying the haridāsas of Karnataka, especially his senior contemporary, the saint singer Puranadaradāsa who is venerated as the Father of Karnataka music. For, while Śrīpādarāya (15th century A.D.) inaugurated the seven *tālas dhruva, maṭhya, rūpaka... eka* in musical practice, it is his disciple Vyāsarāya, and his disciples Purandaradāsa, Vādirāja and Kanakadāsa who consolidated and stabilised them in usage. However, these *tālas* were not created by them. They were known at least since the 12th cent. and are mentioned in Kannaḍa literary sources up to the 17th century Aggaḷa (1189 A.D. *Candraprabhapurāṇam,* 15.52, 72), Janna (1209 A.D. *Anantanāthapuāṇam,* 10.8 pr.), Somanātha, Pālkuriki (C.1300 A.D., *Paṇḍitārādhya-caritramu, Parvataprakaraṇamu,* pp. 446, 447, 449), Padmaṇāṅka (c. 1400 A.D., *Padmarāja-purāṇam,* 5.62), Candraśekhara (c. 1430 A.D. *Pampāsthāna-varṇanam,* 74, p. 27), Bāhubali (1539 A.D., *Nāgakumāracaritam,* 22.98), Govindavaidya (1648 A.D. *Kaṇṭhīrava-narasarāja-vijayam,* 8.61).

The *haridāsas* sang in effective changes in these, made them simple and comprehensive and established them exclusively in musical practice by conferring on them conceptual and empirical validity. I have discussed this at length elsewhere (*Sulādis* and *Ugābhogas of Karnataka Music,* pp. 45-62).

'*Sālagasūḍa*' is made of the adjectival term *sālaga* and the nominal term *sūḍa*. *Sālaga* is phonetic deterioration of *chāyālaga*, which means partaking of the shade (of the *śuddha*) i.e. being similar to the *śuddha* (in some respects); in this context, having some likeness with *śuddhasūḍa prabandhas*. This is discussed above: (comm. NN 3.2.106ff. '*śuddhasūḍa prabandhas*'). Next, *sūḍa* is not a Sanskrit word, but is a vernacular (Kannaḍa) term referring to a special group of songs (Kallinātha p. 213); Narahari Cakravarti goes to the length of describing it as a collective term for many *tālas* employed in a single composition (*Saṅgītasārasaṅgraha*, 1.209-211 pr. pp. 26, 28):

बहूनां तालानामेकत्र गुंफनं सूडम्

How ancient are the *sālagasūḍa prabandhas*? Siṁhabhūpāla (p.335) attributes to Bharatamuni the ascription of *chāyālagatva* to the *elā* etc. Śrīkaṇṭha (*Rasakaumudī*, 3.143) states that Mataṅga mentions the *sālagasūḍas*. Kṛṣṇadatta (cit. Nārāyaṇadeva/ Puruṣottama-miśra?, *Saṅgītasaraṇi*, extr. Bharatakośa, p. 737) traces the *sūḍamadhya prabandhas* to Dattila Muni. As mentioned above (comm. NN 3.2.106ff.) there is no evidence whatsoever to support these claims. Someśvara and Jagadekamalla do not describe *dhruva, maṇṭha* etc., though they do mention *sūḍakrama*. Pārśvadeva does not treat them as a special group of songs, but has interspersed other (*ālikrama*) compositions. Indeed, *sūḍakrama* appears to have been coined in analogy with *ālikrama*. Haripāladeva is the first known authority who has grouped together *dhruva, maṇṭha* etc. including the archetypes of the subsequent *rūpaka, jhampā* and *triviḍa tālas*. Aggaḷa offers, as shown above, an independent corroboration at about the same time. Thus the two parallel lines *dhruva, maṇṭha, pratimaṇṭha* etc. and *dhruva, maṭhya, rūpaka* etc. appear clearly in the 12th century A.D. The former appears to have enjoyed a 'classical' status and adopted in textual tradition while the latter, probably indigenous, remained largely empirical, taken up and promoted by Śrīpādarāya and *his* school of Haridāsas. The two seem to bear a mutual (evolutional) relationship somewhat like the *grāma rāgas: rāgas* or *bhāṣā rāga: antarabhāṣā* and *vibhāṣā rāgas*. There is a difference, however: the *elā* etc. '*śuddha*' *sūḍas* themselves appear in a bewildering variety and prolificity (a staggering total of 4044 against 184 *ālikrama prabandhas*); these were still growing and were firmly established in practice, coexisting with the *sālagasūḍas* (which totalled only 35!) for at least 500 years. The *sālagasūḍas* were themselves in the crucible of change in the 15th-16th century as revealed by Kallinātha in the South and Narahari Cakravarti in the North respectively—and of course by Narahari Tīrtha, Śrīpādarāya and others. Tulaja records in the early 18th century that the *sālagasūḍas*, now frankly called *sulādis*, were still in a flux of evolution. Even though their first mention is by Haripāladeva 11th century A.D.) and Aggaḷa (1189 A.D.), the first actual example of *sulādi* is found in Narahari Tīrtha (14th century A.D.). I have discussed the evolution of the *sālagasūḍas* into *sulādis* in some detail in two works: *Sulādis* and *Ugābhogas of* Karnataka Music (pp. 21-33) and *Śrīpādarāya: A Literary and Musical Study* (mentioned above). They gained the collective name *'sulādi'* in *Saṅgīta Śāstra* in the 17th century due to the sustained effort of Tānappācārya and of his worthy disciple's disciple Veṅkaṭamakhin (CDP 8.3, 4).

The *sālagasūḍa prabandhas* are required to be composed in their namesake or other well defined *tālas* and to be performed in a predetermined sequence. This is why they were *sūḍa-krama,* like *ālikrama.* Because *'ḍa'* readily degenerates phonetically to *'ḷa', sūḍa* became *sūḷa.* The group of *dhruva* etc. is collectively known as *sūḍādī* or *sūḷādi* since at least the 15th-16th century A.D. in Kannaḍa; e.g. Padmaṇāṅka (*Padmarājapurāṇam,* 5.62), Bāhubali (*Nāgakumāracaritam,* 22.98), Govindavaidya, *(Kaṇṭhīrava-narasarāja-vijayam,* 8.61), Purandaradāsa, the song *'vāsudevana nāmāvaḷiya klptiyanu'* extr. Beluru Keśavadāsa, (*Karnāṭaka-bhaktavijaya,* p. 205), Aṣṭāvadhāna Somanārya (*Svararāga-sudhārasa,* MS. copy, Sri Varalakshmi Academy, Mysore), Catura Dāmodara (*Saṅgītadarpaṇam,* 6, p. 154) and Veṅkaṭamakhin (CDP 2.111) etc.

305cd-306ab. dhruvo... kramāt: These were not originally a group of *tālas* bearing such names or *prabandhas* named after the *tālas.* By the 16th-17th century A.D. two more were added to these: in the South, *jhompaṭa* and *ragaṇa maṭhya* (Veṅkaṭamakhin, CDP 2.83-111); Catura Dāmodara calls *tripuṭa* as *tṛtīya* and *maṭhya* as *jagaṇamaṭhya;* in the North, Narahari Cakravarti *(Saṅgītasāra Saṅgraha,* 1.212) groups *dhruva, maṇṭha* as *jagaṇa maṭhya;* in the North, Narahari Cakravarti (*Saṅgītasārasaṅgraha,* 1.212) groups *dhruva, maṇṭha, pratimaṇṭha, niḥsāru, rāsa, prati, ekatālī, yati* and *jhumari* as *sālagasūḍa gītas* on the authority of *Saṅgītadāmodara* and *Pañcamasārasaṁhitā.* The *yati* mentioned here is obviously, the *jati* (*jate*) which occurs at the end of the *sulādis.* In due course, *jhompaṭa* inverted its *aṅgas,* was called *ādi tāla* (which should be distinguished from the namesake (*deśī tāla*) and was comprehended in *tripuṭa tāla.* So, the *sulādi tālas* were reduced again to seven. Kallinātha has shown (p. 338, comm. on SR 5.261, 262, pp. 139, 140) that confusion was rampant in the *deśī tālas* in his day because of different *tālas* with same names and same *tālas* with different names. The haridāsas brought logical and conceptual basis, unambiguity and fixity to the *tāla* system and derived from *virāmānta na-gaṇa/pratimaṇṭha, niḥsāru, yatilagna/laghuśekhara/jambunāla* (see Siṁhabhūpāla, comm. on SR 4.314-316, p. 343), *jhampā, dvitīya, aḍḍa/kuḍukka, ādi/rāsa tālas* respectively the *sulādi tālas* viz. *dhruva, maṭhya, rūpaka, jhampā, tripuṭa, aṭṭa* and *eka.* The *dhruva* and *jhampā tālas* which were used in *vīṇādaṇḍī* and *nāṭyadaṇḍī* also participated in this transformation.

This is briefly, how the *sālagasūḍa tālas* evolved in the South-chiefly in Karnataka. In North India they took a different course. They retained their names and structures and found application in discrete compositions dedicated to Viṣṇu. Narahari Cakravarti (ibid., 1.228 pr.) offers an illustration of such a *dhruva prabandha.* Similar illustrations are found in Krishnadas Badajena Mohapatra (*Gītaprakāśa*, 2, pp, 11-23) and Haladharamiśra (*Saṅgītakalpalatikā*, 1.20ff, pp. 3-10 and appendix, pp. 73-93). Besides these, Kumbhakarṇa creates a new form of *sūḍas* called *miśrasūḍa prabandhas* (*Saṅgītarāja*, 2.4.2.28 pr. b. 553): there are twentyeight of these somewhat fancifully and bombastically named: *daśavatāra-kirtidhavala, harivijaya-maṅgalācāra, mādhavotsava-kamalākara, sāmodadāmodara-bhramarapāda, madhuripu-ratnakaṇṭhikā, akleśavakuñjaratilaka, mugdha-madhusūdana haṁsa-krīḍa, harivallabhāśokapallava, snigdhamadhusūdana-rāsavalaya, harisamudaya-garuḍapadā, sākāṅkṣapuṇḍarīkākṣa-bhramararuta, dhanya-vaikuṇṭha kuṅkuma, hariśa-raṇa-kadalīpatra, hariramita-campakaśekhara, harirasa-manmathatilaka, nārāyaṇa-madanāvāsa, lakṣmīpati-ratnāvalī, amandamukunda makaranda, caturacaturbhuja-rāgarāji-candrodyota, harihāratālarāji-jaladhara vilasita, tālarāgārṇavamurāri-maṅgala-kusumalatā, sānandagovinda-rāgaśreṇī kusumāstaraṇa, madhuripu-modavidyādharalola, suratārambhacandrahāsa, kāma-tṛptikāmahāsa, pauruṣarasapremahāsa, kāmādbhutābhi-nava-mṛgāṅkalekhā* and *pitāmbaratālaśreṇi-muktāphala.* These are his adaptations of the *aṣṭapadis* of Jayadeva Sarasvati's *Gītagovinda* to music and are treated by him in his *Rasikapriyā* commentary on *Gītagovinda.*

It has been mentioned above that *yati, jhumarī, jhompaṭa* and *ra-gaṇa maṭhya* were suffixed to the *sālagasūḍa tālas.* of these, *jhompaṭa* was ००।; this was inverted to ।०० and became *āditāla* which even today enjoys a semi independent status in Karnataka music, *ra-gaṇa maṭhya* became diminished to half its quantity and became the modern *caturaśra maṭhya. Yati* and *jhumari* may be compiled here from Śubhaṁkara (*Saṅgītadāmodara*, 2, pp. 27, 28). *Yati prabandha* has four varieties: *līlā* consisting of thirteen syllables per *pāda*, is sung to *karuṇa rasa* in the *tāla*-ऽ, *āndolitā-yati*, fifteen syllables per *pāda* in *sṛṅgāra* and *vīra rasa*, in the *tāla* ।।́० ;*kaumudī*, seventeen syllables per *pāda*, is sung in *hāsya rasa* in *lalita tāla* (ऽ́।); *haṁsamālā yati*, nineteen syllables per *pāda*, is sung in *śānta rasa* in the *tālas* ००००ऽ. *Jhumari* has no varieties, and has no rules regarding number of syllables, *rasa* or *tāla.*

Narahari Cakravarti describes, besides *śuddhasūḍa* and *sālagasūḍa prabandhas*, fourteen *saṅkīrṇasūḍa prabandhas* viz. *caitra* (*caccarī?*), *maṅgala, nagaṇikā, carcā* (?*caryā*), *bhilā* (*dhavala?*), *ṭollarī, doha, ovi, hnevāka* (?) *kārika, tripadi* etc. and prescribes them to be sung in the month of Caitra.

The admissibility of the *sālagasūḍa* as *prabandha* is questioned by Narahari Cakravarti on the authority of Dāmodara *et al* and by Mahāpātra (see Comm. NN 3.2.11a, 12cd-13). *Saṅgītasaraṇi* (extr. *Bharatakośa*, p. 723) quotes some quaint views on *sālaga*(*sūḍa*) *prabandhas* from Kṛṣṇadatta:

शुद्धश्चेदङ्गरहित: सालग: । अङ्गै: स्वरपाटैस्तेनैर्विरहित: शुद्ध(:) सालगो भवति । वाक्यं तु सालगोऽपि भवति । तेन विना तादृशी रञ्जकता जायते । मातृकाप्रबन्धसूडप्रबन्धादिषु जात्या वैलक्षण्यविधानात्तु

सालगव्यवहार: । : सूडकल्पित: रञ्जको नवभिस्तालै: गीतवाद्ये च नर्तने । यद्यप्यन्येऽपि सूडकल्पिता मुक्तकाश्च सालगा: सन्ति । तथा सूडो नवतालात्मक: ।

He describes the *sūḍa prabandhas* somewhat differently (extr. ibid., p. 737):

ताला सञ्चारिका यत्र पाटादिरहिता यदि ।
आद्यन्तयो: पाटवे तु युतास्ताला यदृच्छया ।
सूडमध्यप्रबन्धोऽयं ख्यातो दत्तिलसम्मत: ।
ताला नवादिका यत्र बद्धा: पाटादिवर्जिता: ।
सूडप्रबन्ध: कथित एकरागनिवेशित: ॥

Paṇḍarīka Viṭṭhala's description of the *sālagasūḍa prabandhas* should be read together with his account of *sālagasūḍa vādyaprabandhas* (NN1.82-85) and *yati prabandha* (NN 1.86-91).

As indicated above, the *sālagasūḍas* were also *nṛtta prabandhas,* i.e. dance compositions. Catura Dāmodara has explained them (*Saṅgītadarpaṇam,* 7.220-234) under the name '*śuddhapaddhati*'. Veda depicts them thus (*Saṅgītamakaranda,* MS. copy in Sri Varalakshmi Academy, Mysore):

काता वाग्गेयकारैस्तु ये गीता: सूडतालत: ।
तेषां भावानुसारेण नृत्तं स्यात् सम्प्रदायत: ।
सूडादिगीतनृत्तं तत् कथितं पूर्वसूरिभि: ॥

Thus the *sulādi nṛtta* had a long line of traditional descent (*sampradāya*) known to the early authorities. They were characterised by *nṛtya* according to the *bhāva* of the words rather than to composed dance or grammar of dance. Here is an independent corroboration of Veṅkaṭamakhin's synonymising the *sālagasūḍa* songs as *gītas*; it may be remembered that Veda was a junior contemporary of Veṅkaṭamakhin and flourished at the same royal court of Tanjore a generation later. The accounts of the *sūḍādi nṛtta* by Catura Dāmodara and Veda are widely different.

DESCRIPTIONS OF PRASIDDHA PRABANDHAS

306bc. prasiddhāḥ: All these *prabandhas* did not originate only in the days of Paṇḍarīka Viṭṭhala; for example, *navaratna, raṇaraṅga, caturaṅga,* and *śarabhalīlā* are of quite ancient origin. *Vīraśṛṅgāra* may be regarded as a hybrid of the *pañcatāleśvara* varieties *vīrāvatāra* and *śṛṅgāra-tilaka. Daśāvatāra* is already composed by Jayadeva Sarasvati in his *Gītagovinda,* and is a very popular song-type with nearly every haridāsa, right from Śrīpādarāya. So, only *candraprakāśa, sūryaprakāśa, ṛtuprakāśa* and *śṛṅgārahāra* may regarded as new.

308d. atha lakṣaṇam: Some of these eleven *prabandhas* find mention or description at approximately the same period in other works; thus they are corroborated with the stamp of contemporaneity.

Among such sources may be mentioned Śrīkaṇṭha (*Rasakaumudī*, 3.124-129), Paṇḍitamaṇḍalī (*Saṅgītaśiromaṇi*, extr. *Bharatakośa*), Catura Dāmodara (*Saṅgītadarpaṇam*, 4.514-525), Narahari Cakravarti (*Saṅgītsārasaṅgraha*, 1.191, 192), and compilation by Sourindra Mohan Tagore in *Saṅgītasārasaṅgraha* (3.134-136). Further, Abul Fazl who, like Paṇḍarīka Viṭṭhala flourished in Akbar's court mentions these '*prasiddha*' *prabandhas* in his *Āyeen-i-Akbarī*. Of these, *Saṅgītaśiromaṇi* is extracted only for *raṇaraṅga*; Narahari Cakravarti offers only this short passage (loc. cit.) without describing the *prabandhas*:

नवरत्नाभिधः प्रोक्तस्तथा शरभलीलकः ।
कण्ठाभरणनामा चेत्यथ षड्विंशतिर्मताः ।
चन्द्रप्रकाशकाद्याश्च विधत्ते षट् तथा परे ।

Sourindra Mohan Tagore has compiled the *lakṣaṇas* of eight among the above viz. *vīraśṛṅgāra, caturaṅga, sarabhalīla, sūryaprakāśa, candraprakāśa, raṇa-raṅga, nandana,* and *navaratna* from *Saṅgītadarpaṇam* without acknowledgement, and has omitted *vīrāvatāra, ṛtuprakāśa, daśāvatāra* and *śṛṅgārahāra*. Therefore, only *Rasakaumudī* (9RK) and *Saṅgītadarpaṇam* (SD) remain as the only original sources for comparison. *Caturaṅga, raṇaraṅga, śarabhalīla* and *navaratna* may be compared with the *lakṣaṇas* given by the ancient authorities.

Most of these names are also numerograms and indicate the number of *rāgas*, *tālas* or segments occurring in the song; e.g. *ṛtu* =6, *sūrya* = 12, *rudra*= 11, *candra* = 16, *śarabha* = 8.

309ab-311ab. 1. *Candraprakāśa*

309b. candrabhūpayoḥ: RK and SD do not prescribe double entendre between moon and (patron) king.

310. rāgaiḥ... parigīyate: RK condenses this to 'रागैः षोडशभिर्युक्तः षडङ्गो'

311cd. nāma...kaveriha: included by SD but omitted by RK.

This is called *candraprakāśa* because the king is compared with the moon in paronomasia and it is set in sixteen segments like the sixteen digits of the moon. Such comparison is a time honoured poetic convention and is both defined and illustrated by Daṇḍin (*Kāvyādarśa*, 2.310, 311) in the context of explaining the *arthālaṁkāra* variety called *śleṣacakra:*

श्लिष्टमिष्टमनेकार्थमेकरूपान्वितं वचः ।
तदभिन्नपदं भिन्नपदप्रायमिति द्विधा ॥

If two or more meanings cling (*śliṣṭa*) to the same word, it is called *śleṣa*; it is of two kinds—*abhinnapada* and *bhinnapada*.

असावुदयमारूढः कान्तिमान् रक्तमण्डलः ।
राजा हरति लोकस्य हृदयं मृदुभिः करैः ॥

[Behold ! this *rājā* (moon/king) is on the ascent—*udāyārūḍha* (ascending the *udayācala*, the mount of moonrise/prosperous), *kāntiyukta* (tender/lustrous), *raktamaṇḍala* (red disc/has a bevy of affectionate ministers), and has plundered the hearts of the people with *mṛdu* (tender, not harsh) *kara* (rays/taxes). This is an instance of *abhinnapada śleṣa* or *abhaṅgaśleṣa* wherein the punning word does not have to be decomposed for the twofold meaning (e.g. as in *doṣākara* = *doṣā* + *kara*, *doṣa-ākara*).

311cd-312 2. *Sūryaprakāśa*

311cd. sūryaprakāśa: so called because *sūrya* signifies twelve; the *prabandha* has twelve segments; twelve *rāgas* and twelve *tālas* (one for each segment).

312b. caitramāsādi: RK and SD do not prescribe description of the twelve lunar months, but require panegyric to the Sun. So, one each of the twelve segments is devoted to the eulogy of one of the twelve *Ādityas.* (These twelve are somewhat differently named in different sources e.g. *Mahābhārata Ādiparvan*—65.14.16; *Śāntiparvan*, 208.15, 16 and *Anuśāsanaparvan*, 150.14.16; *Viṣṇupurāṇam*, 1.15.130, 131; *Bhāgavatapurāṇam*, 6.6.38, 6.18.1; 12.11.45; *Vācaspatyam*, 4.456 etc. The first mentioned source enumerates *Dhātṛ, Mitra, Aryaman, Śakra, Varuṇa, Aṁśa, Bhaga, Vivasvat Pūśan, Savitṛ, Tvaṣṭṛ* and *Viṣṇu.* Elsewhere, *Parjanya, Gabhastimat, Tvaṣṭṛ, Kratu, Yama, Hiraṇyaretas, Divākara, Citra* etc. are counted among the *dvādaśādityas*)

312d. śleṣaḥ: RK and SD do not speak of pun between king and the sun.

313-314. 3. *Navaratna*

'*Nava*' indicates nine in each of segments, *rāga, tāla* and *rasa*; i.e. each segment is composed in a separate *rāga, tāla* and *rasa.*

313a. aṅka: Nine digits 1, 2, 3…9 (zero is not regarded as a number here). *brahma*: nine *brahma mānasaputras* viz. *Bhṛgu, Pulastya, Pulaha, Kratu, Aṅgirasa, Marīci, Dakṣa, Atri* and *Vasiṣṭha* (*Viṣṇupurāṇa*, 1.7.5-8) are regarded as *Brahmā* himself. Elsewhere (e.g. *Bhāgavatapurāṇam*, 3.12; *Matsyapurāṇam*, 3.8; *Manusmṛti*, 1.35) *Nārada* is added to the list.

rasa: nine *rasas*: *śṛṅgāra, hāsya, karuṇa, raudra, vīra, bhayānaka, bībhatsa, adbhuta* and *śānta rasa;* nine *sthāyibhāvas: rati, utsāha, śoka, vismaya, hāsa, bhaya, jugupsā, krodha, śama.*

khaṇḍa: nine continents: *indradvīpa, kaśeru, tāmraparṇi, gabhastimān, nāgadvīpa, saumya, gāndharva, vāruṇa, sāgaradvīpa* (*Viṣṇupurāṇam*, 2.3.6,7) or *indrakhaṇḍa, śvetakhaṇḍa, tāmrakhaṇḍa, gabhastikhaṇḍa, nāgakhaṇḍa, saumyakhaṇḍa, gandharva khaṇḍa, cāraṇakhaṇḍa, bharatakhaṇḍa (Yājuṣaprayogapārijāta,* p. 104). *graha*: nine planets: *sūrya, candra, maṅgala, buddha, guru, śukra, śani, rāhu, ketu;* or *sama, anāgata, viṣama, atītā, anudyama, anūdana, sanāda, sābhinandana, sunāda* (*Saṅgīta-śabdārthacandrikā,* p. 233).

ratna: nine gems: *muktā, māṇikya, vaiḍūrya, gomeda, vajra, vidruma, padmarāga, marakata, nīla* (*Śabdakalpadruma,* 3.839).

rasa: nine essences: *pṛthivī, jala, oṣadhi, puruṣa, vāk, ṛk, āma, udgītha (Chāndogya-upaniṣat* 1.1.2) plus *ānanda* (*brahman*).

The foregoing is incorporated suitably in nine segments, each set to a different *rāga* and a different *tāla.* SD requires description of only nine gems (in pun with king?) in nine segments.

314a. sarvāṅgabaddha. The five *aṅgas* viz. pd pt bd sv and tn are employed in any arbitrary manner in the above nine segments; tl applies to the entire composition.

315-318. 4, *Vīraśṛṅgara*

315a. sakṛd... gātavyo: SD reads '*sakṛd-vāggeyakāreṇa*' implausibly (4.515a)

315b. vīraśṛṅgāra is not found in RK.

316ab. ādya... khaṇḍakāḥ: SD (4.516ab):आद्यखण्डं परित्यज्य गीयन्तेऽन्येषु मण्ठकाः ।

316cd. not found in SD.

317ab. tam... iti: cf. SD 516ab (extr. in comm. 3.2.316ab supra).

318cd. antya ... bhūṣitaḥ: This is A of the *prabandha.*

319-320ab. 5. *Rudraprakāśa*

319cd. purāṇa-rudrāṇām: *Mahābhārata: Ādiparvan,* 66.2, 3: *Mṛgavyādha, Sarpa, Nirṛti, Ajaikapāt, Ahirbudhnya, Pinākin, Dahana, Īśvara, Kapālin, Sthāṇu, Bhava; Anuśāsana; Ajaikapāt, Ahirbudhnya, Pinākin, Aparājita, Ṛta, Pitṛrūpa, Tryambaka, Vṛṣākapī, Śambhu, Havana, Īśvara; Viṣṇupurāṇam* (1.15.122,123): *Hara, Bahurūpa, Tryambaka, Aparājita, Vṛṣākapi, Śambhu, Kapardin, Raivata, Mṛgavyādha; Bṛhat-parāśara Smṛti* (2.190, 191): *Ajaikapāt, Ahirbudhnya, Virūpākṣa, Raivata, Hara, Bahurūpa, Tryambaka, Sāvitra, Jayanta, Pinākin, Aparājita; Bhāgavatapurāṇam: Manyu, Manu, Mahākāla, Mahat, Śiva, Ṛtadhvaja, Ugraretas, Bhava, Kāla, Vāmadeva, Dhṛtavrata.*

Each of the eleven segments describes one *Rudra* and is set to one different *rāga* and different *tāla.*

320cd-321ab. 6. *Raṇaraṅga*

Mataṅga, Śārṅgadeva, Narahari Cakravarti and Veṅkaṭamakhin do not describe *raṇaraṅga.* There is unanimity in the views of Someśvara (AC 4.16.361, p. 62), Jagadekamalla (JS p. 48). Haripāladeva (SS 5.7.162), Pārśvadeva (PS 4.30, p. 26), Paṇḍitamaṇḍali (*Saṅgītaśiromaṇi* extr. *Bharatakośa,* p. 522), Catura Dāmodara (SD 4.523): *raṇaraṅga* is composed in *vīra* and *raudra rasas* (appropriate to *raṇa*—battle field—in *raṅga tāla* (so that the name is apt), in pt, bd; in *sama, anāgata* and *atīta grahas* of *tāla*. So it is of three kinds. PS adds tn to the *aṅgas*. *Saṅgītaśiromaṇi* has:

अयं च द्विविधो भवेत् समातीतानागताख्यतालग्रहविभेदतः ।

Here '*dvividha*' should be corrected to '*trividha*'.
Raṅga tāla: (NN 1.175):

रङ्गश्चतुर्द्रुती गश्च (ooooऽ)

321cd-322. 7. *Daśāvatāra*

This *prabandha* is not described elsewhere.

322a. tadguṇam: one segment per *avatāra*; 2, 3, 4... segments per *avatāra*.

322b. vānchitakramaiḥ: Any of the five *aṅgas*, pd pt bd sv and tn may occur in any *avatāra*; tl applies to the whole composition, of course.

322c. Ābhoga is generally a separate segment containing the names of *prabandha*, patron/hero and composer; it is composed in words other than those of U, (M) or D. But by special decree here, there is no separate A but the tenth segment itself functions as A such that it describes the tenth *avatāra* and excludes all *aṅgas* other than pd.

323-324ab. 8. *Śarabhalīla*

323b. Śarabhalīla is an ancient *prabandha*; but it is not defined by Śārṅgadeva, Śrīkaṇṭha and Veṅkaṭamakhin. However, its development may be traced from Mataṅga to Paṇḍarīka Viṭṭhala. Thus according to Mataṅga (BD 415, p. 154), *śarabhalīla* has eight *pādas*, composed of sv, pt; set to eight *rāgas* and eight *tālas*. Someśvara (AC 4.16.336-338, p. 38) agrees with this *lakṣaṇa* and adds that each segment is composed in a separate *rāga* and separate *tāla*, and that sv and pt occur at the end of each segment. He gives a lovely illustration:

देव नीलोत्पलदलसमानकायकान्ते ।
विहितसकलभक्तलोकदुरितशान्ते ।
इच्छामात्रजनिताखिलजगज्जन्य ।
करकमलतलकल्पितपाञ्चजन्य ।
नाभिनलिनस्थपद्मासनस्तूयमान ।
पादस्पर्शपवित्रीकृतवैनतेययान ।
नाकिलोकनेत्रामृतायमानमूर्ते ।
तुभ्यं नमः प्रसादितधवलकीर्ते ।

This composition features alliteration and terminal rhyming in couplets. It is not known whether this is accidental, for no available authority mentions these features as characterising *śarabhalīla*. It may be noted that this composition has bd. Jagadekamalla (JS p. 48) delineates two forms of this *prabandha*: the first has eight *pādas* as above (each of which is set to a separate *rāga* and *tāla*) such that sv pt are performed in between the *pādas*, i.e. at the end of each *pāda*. He adds that the conclusion of the song is in two spans of the (final) *tāla;* the second variety is composed in namesake (i.e. *śarabhalīla*) metre and *tāla* only; the song concludes on sv, pt i.e. instead of sv and pt recurring at the end of each *pāda*, they occur only once, after the eighth *pāda*. Paṇḍarīka Viṭṭhala has given the first variety, but has incorporated partially the *lakṣaṇa* of the second: he includes *śarabhalīla* metre and omits *śarabhalīla tāla*. *Śarabhalīla tāla* is (NN 1.191ab): लौ द्वौ चतुर्द्रुती लौ द्वौ ताले शरभलीलके। (||oooo||). *Śarabhalīla* metre is defined by Jagadekamalla (JS p. 47) as '*iha hi śarabhalīla kaṅkajagaiḥ*' which is at one its *lakṣya* and *lakṣaṇa*.

Haripāladeva has the same *lakṣaṇa* of *śarabhalīla* (5.7.147-149) as given in AC and further adds that each *pāda* is composed in a separate metre. Pārśvadeva (PS 4.37, p. 26) mentions it is *niryukta*, *dvidhātuka*, composed in all six *aṅgas*; in other words, he adds bd, tn but omits A. Both Paṇḍarīka Viṭṭhala and Catura Dāmodara (SD 4.518) describe the *prabandha* with all six *aṅgas*. The former however, has a *misch* definition; for he prescribes the conclusion of the song on sv instead of on sv pt.

324a. Muktaka is a discrete, self-contained verse.

324cd-325ab. 9. *Caturaṅga*

Caturaṅga is not known to Śārṅgadeva, Haripāladeva, Śrīkaṇṭha and Veṅkaṭamakhin. However, like *śarabhalīla*, it also has a long and consistent history; the name is also a numerogram. It is composed of four *rāgas*, four *tālas*, four *aṅgas*, four segments and four languages. Mataṅga (BD 411, 412, p.145) mentions four *rāgas*, *tālas*, and languages only. Someśvara (AC 4.16.353-355, p.40) concurs with this definition but adds that it should be composed to make some sense in (four) languages such as Sanskrit. He also gives an illustration:

य: स्रष्टा चतुराननस्य विबुधस्त्राणैकबद्धस्थिति: ।
पदारविन्दरसलोकं दोदनीलप्यहे ।
जोगोची(पी)जगणे गाह(इ)जेबहुपरिरूपेनिर्हाम् ।
गोमयसैक: शेशनलेसु लधुशशजणभावंकसे ॥

Jagadekamalla (JS p. 45) justifies the name because of the use four *aṅgas* viz. pd pt sv tn and offers additional details: U has two segments as also D, thus making four *pādas*. Each of these is composed in a separate *rāga*, *tāla* and language. Pt should be sung after the first *pāda*, sv after the second, pd after the third and tn after the fourth. A should be composed with words in the second segment of D. The song is concluded on tn.

Pārśvadeva (PS 4.52, 57, p. 27) summarises it thus: 3d, four *aṅgas*—pd sv tl tn; an. Catura Dāmodara (SD 4.517) avers that *caturaṅga* consists of four segments and of six *aṅgas* omitting *rāga* (?). Paṇḍitamaṇḍalī (*Saṅgītaśiromaṇi*, extr. *Bharatakośa*, p. 197) declares that the name *caturaṅga* is well suited because it has four *aṅgas*, omitting bd tn. This contradicts JS who says that the song has tn, on which it concludes and contradicts Paṇḍarīka Viṭṭhala and Catura Dāmodara who attribute all six *aṅgas* to it; six *aṅgas* would mean the inclusion of tl and bd: each segment should be composed in a separate *tāla*. But where should bd be composed?

325cd-326. 10. *Ṛtuprakāśa*

325c. puṣpabāṇa: Manmatha is important because it is spring season; so *śṛṅgāra* is dominant.

326a. ṣaṭ: Ṛtu means season; there are six seasons. Therefore, *ṛtuprakāśa* has six segments, each of which carries a separate *rāga* (and *tāla*?); composed in all six *aṅgas*; each segment should be composed with words in praise of one season.

Ṛtuprakāśa is not found in RK and SD.

327-329ab. 11. *Śṛṅgārahāra*

329a. Śṛṅgārahāra is sung as follows: U is composed in sv; then *gamakālapti*; next D in words replete with *śṛṅgāra rasa*; this is followed by *antara*. (Note the use of *antara*; its use here is exceptional, as for example in *pañcatāleśvara* (NN 3.2.177-185.) Next comes A which contains composer's name, the word *śṛṅgārahāra*, *ālāpa* without *tāla* and pt with tl. Finally A, containing the name of the patron or hero is sung. The song concludes on U.

329b. lakṣyavedibhiḥ: Śṛṅgārahāra is not described in any other music treatise; hence the reference to practical exponents.

329cd-334. MERITS OF SONG

These are at once literary merits in poetry and musical merits in song. Rhetoricians in India have studied the merits and faults of both meaning (*artha*) and sound (*śabda*) in Sanskrit poetry in great detail from very early times. These are applied to melodised vedic prosodial strúctures—the *sāmans*—by Nārada in the *Nāradīyaśikṣā* (N) probably for tne first time. Ten of these are enumerated and described therein (1.3.1-11).

रक्तं पूर्णं अलङ्कृतं प्रसन्नं व्यक्तं विकृष्टं श्लक्ष्णं समं सुकुमारं मधुरमिति गुणाः ।

Śārṅgadeva has applied these, *mutatis mutandis* to secular music (SR 4.374-379).

Paṇḍarīka Viṭṭhala has borrowed from and abbreviated SR here. Therefore extracts from N and SR are given below to facilitate a comparative study.

331a. Vyakta N: व्यक्तं नाम पदपदार्थप्रकृतिविकारागमलोपकृत्तद्धितसमासधातुनिपातोपसर्गस्वरलिङ्ग वृत्तिवार्तिकविभक्त्यर्थवचनानां सम्यगुपपादने व्यक्तमित्युच्यते

SR: तत्र व्यक्तं स्फुटैः स्वरैः प्रकृतिप्रत्ययैश्चोक्तम्

331c. pūrṇa: N: पूर्णं नाम स्वरश्रुतिपूरणात् छन्दःपदाक्षरसंयोगात् पूर्णमित्युच्यते ।

SR: छन्दोरागस्वरैः पूर्णं पूर्णाङ्गगमकम् ।

331d. prasannam N: प्रसन्नं नाम अपगतगद्गदं निर्विशङ्कं प्रसन्नमित्युच्यते ।

SR: प्रसन्नं प्रकटार्थकम् ।

332a. sukumāram N: सुकुमारं नाम मृदुपदवर्णस्वरकुहरणयुक्तं सुकुमारमित्युच्यते

SR: सुकुमारं कण्ठभवम् ।

332b. alaṁkṛtam N: अलङ्कारं नाम उरसि शिरसि कण्ठयुक्तमित्यलङ्कृतम् ।

SR: त्रिस्थानोत्थमलङ्कृतम् ।

332c. samam N: समं नाम आवापनिर्वापप्रदेशप्रत्यन्तरस्थानानां समासः सममित्युच्यते ।
Bhaṭṭa Śobhākara's comm. *Vivaraṇa* on this passage:

स्वरस्य आपूरणं प्रक्षेपः आवापः निर्वापो न्यूनताकरणम् । तेषां आवापनिर्वापप्रदेशानां प्रत्यन्तरेषु व्यवहितेषु स्थानेषु समं समप्रक्षेपः न व्युत्क्रमेणेति समं गानं भवति ।

SR: समवर्णलयस्थानं सममित्यभिधीयते ।

333b. suraktam N: रक्तं नाम वेणुवीणास्वराणां एकीभावो रक्तमित्युच्यते ।

SR: सुरक्तं वल्लकीवंशकण्ठध्वन्येकतायुतम् ।

333d. ślakṣṇam N: श्लक्ष्णंनाम अद्रुतमविलम्बितमुच्चनीचप्लुतसमाहारं हेलतालोपनयनादिभिरुप-पादनादिभिः श्लक्ष्णमित्युच्यते ।

SR: नीचोच्चद्रुतमध्यादौ श्लक्ष्णत्वे श्लक्ष्णमित्युच्यते ।

334b. vikṛṣṭam N: विकृष्टं नाम उच्चैरुच्चारितं व्यक्तपदाक्षरमिति विकृष्टम् ।

SR: उच्चैरुच्चारणादुक्तं विकृष्टम् ।

334b. madhuram N: मधुरं नाम स्वभावोपनीतललितपदाक्षरगुणसमृद्धं मधुरमित्युच्यते ।

SR:मधुरं धुर्यलावण्यपूर्णं जनमनोहरम् ।

Pārśvadeva (PS cit. Siṁhabhūpāla, on SR 4.1, p. 209) relates different qualities of music with different temperaments and tastes.

i. *Ācāryas* (preceptors): high notes and low notes, neither fast nor slow, even in pd tl.
ii. *Paṇḍitas* (the learned): Correct syntactical construction, freedom from *sandhidoṣa* (faulty phonetic combination), clear articulation of notes (and vowels).
iii. *Paramours:* Charming syllabic content, coloured with the erotic sentiment, melodiousness.

iv. *Others* (Common folk): high notes, profuse *prayoga (gamakālapti? ālāpa?* experimentalism?)

v. *Śūras* (valorous): *ārabhaṭī vṛtti* (see comm. NN 3.2.114d), description of encounters of heroes, high and low notes, enthusiastic.

vi. *Virahi* (separated lovers): words intensifying or exciting love, full of erotic sentiment, of compassion (pity) and *kāku* (emotional inflexion of voice).

vii. *Viṭa* (sensuous *bon vivant,* keeper of prostitutes): reversed words or inverted meanings, enlarged with *svarabhaṅgi,* full of humour and jest.

viii. *Yogis:* profound and mystic meanings, theme of the ultimate, deprecating worldly pleasures, spiritual themes.

ix. *Women*: auspicious sentences, composed in *śuddha pañcama* (*rāga*), sung on festive, marriage etc. auspicious occasions.

x. *The Pious and Devoted:* prayer to gods, teaching its influence and effect, generating faith, attractive.

xi. *Argumentative, Contentious:* resists intelligibility, not defined in tl pt, profuse in *prayoga,* dry, uneven.

335-337. FAULTS OF SONG

NN has borrowed these three verses from SR (4.379-380). These ten faults pertain more to the *mātu* part of the song than to its *dhātu.* SR does not recognise this explicitly. But Paṇḍarīka Viṭṭhala states here unequivocally that the faults enumerated and described by rhetoricians for poetry in the context of *rasa* and *bhāva* apply equally to the *mātu* of song. However, music authorities are uniformly silent on the merits and faults of *dhātu.* An attempt is made below to apply these *doṣas* to the *dhātu,* shown in [ ]

Among the ten faults viz. *lokaduṣṭa śāstraduṣṭa śrutivirodhi kālavivcrodhi punarukta kalābāhya gatakrama apārthaka grāmya* and *sandigdha,* the early rhetoricians Daṇḍi, Bhāmaha etc. have counted *grāmyatā* and *sandigdha* among *padadoṣas, punarukta* and *apakrama* among *vākyadośas* and *apārtha* among *arthadoṣas.* Parallel definitions from Daṇḍi—D (*Kāvyādarśa*), Bhāmaha—B (*Kāvyālaṁkāra*) and Vidyānātha—V (*Pratāparudrīya,* based on the Telugu translation *Āndhra-Pratāparudrīyamu*) are given below for the ten faults to facilitate a comparative study.

1. Loka is totality of the behaviour of immobile and mobile beings (B 4.35); it is the activity or functioning of the aggregate of all inanimate and animate existence (D 3.162); *loka-duṣṭa* or *lokavirodhi* is being contrary to established norms of the world. This could be interpreted as being in conflict with provincial/ regional custom or with worldly knowledge; see V (p. 50). [Musical performance in conflict with established practice in *rāga, tāla* etc.]

2. śāstraduṣṭa: Faulty in or inconsistent with disciplines such as grammar, prosody, musicology etc.

3. Śrutivirodhi is called *āgamavirodhi* in *alaṁkāraśāstra*; *śruti* here means *Veda; śrutivirodha* is to be in discord with what is prescribed or required in *Veda* (D 3.177-184). B interprets this (B 1.47-49) as evoking disgust as soon as heard. He gives the following illustration, prohibiting the use of ambiguous words which also suggest disgusting meaning. He classifies verbal faults into four: *śrutiduṣṭa, arthaduṣṭa, kalpanāduṣṭa* and *śrutikaṣṭa*: *Arthaduṣṭa* is hard to understand, impausible imagery; *śrutikaṣṭa* is harsh to the ear:

विड्वर्चो विष्ठित क्लिन्नच्छिन्न वान्तप्रवृत्तयः ।
प्रचारधर्षितोद्गार विसर्गह्लादयन्तृताः ॥

[*viṭ*-merchant/excreta; *varcaḥ*—brightness/excreta; *viṣṭhita (vi-sthita)*—one who is exceeding/one who excretes; *klinna*—wet/soaked in blood; *chinna*—cut/murdered, hacked; *vānta*—emerged/vomit; *pravṛtti*—wish or interest in activity/excretion; *pracāra*—defeated/rape; *udgāra*-exclamation/vomit; *visarga*—escaped, liberty/excretion; *hrāda*—slight sound/to fart; *yantṛtā*—regulating/energy of coition.]

Vāmana (*Kāvyālaṁkārasūtravṛtti,* 2.6) has defined this as *śrutivirasam kaṣṭam* (rude, harsh to the ear) with an example: अचूचुरच्चण्डि कपोलयोस्ते कान्तिद्रवं द्राग्विशदः शशाङ्कः ।

[Singing/playing contrary to reference pitch (*śruti*) or contrary to the *śruti* quantity prescribed for a *svara.*]

4. Kālavirodhi is anachronism in time; *kāla* means night, day or seasons; D offers an exmaple (3.162, 167, 168): the lotus blooms at night: the swans are loquacious in the rainy season: peacocks are intoxicated in autumn etc. B says (4.30, 31) that *kāla* is of only six kinds because of the six seasons: *kālavirodhi* is description which is contrary to the season:

षण्णामृतूनां भेदेन कालः षोढेव भिद्यते । तद्विरोधकृदित्याहुः विपर्यासादिदम् । e.g. mango trees, laden with bloom, scent the air which carries rain drops of the rainy season. [singing/playing *rāgas* contrary to the time prescribed for their perfomance.]

5. Punarukti is also called *ekārtha*: This means the repetition of meaning using the same words again or with other words; it is of two kinds: *śabdapunaruktaka* (repetition of words and *arthapunaruktaka* (repetition of meaning), according to D (3.135-138) and B (4.12,16). If this is deliberately used to heighten an effect it becomes an *alaṁkāra* called *punarukta padābhāsa*, not a fault (V pp. 20, 21); *punarukta* may be a fault in both *pada* and *vākya.* [Singing/playing the same theme repeatedly.]

6. Kalā is defined as 'नृत्यगीतप्रभृतयः कामार्थसंश्रयाः' (D 3.162) and as कलासङ्कलना प्रज्ञा शिल्पान्यस्याश्च गोचरः । (B 4.32) i.e. music, dance etc. are instruments to attain *kāma* and *artha puruṣārthas* (D) and consciousness which concentrates, i.e. it conflates and collimates together various discrete elements and creates something original, new. *Kalābāhya* or *kalāvirodha* is being inconsistent with the spirit and practice of art (B 4. 33, 34)

> ऋषभात् पञ्चमस्तस्मात् सषड्जं धैवतं स्मृतम् ।
> अयं हि मध्यमग्रामो मध्यमोत्पीडितर्षभः ॥

In *madhyama-grāma pa* is not born of *ri*, nor *sa* from *pa* and *dha* generated by *sa*; nor are *ma-ri* mutually consonant. Hence this is *kalāvirodha*. [Performing three *drutas* for *ādi tāla* or *kalyāṇi rāga* with *śuddha madhyama*, or *ānandabhairavī rāga* with *śuddha sampūrṇa* scale, performing *tīntāl* with fifteen *mātrās* or a *ṭhumri* like a *tarāna*.]

7. Apakrama is a *vākyadoṣa*, a fault in which items appear in a wrong sequence or order. e.g. 'May *Śiva*, *Nārāyaṇa* and *Brahmā* who cause *sthiti* (sustenance), *nirmāṇa* (creation) and *saṁhāra* (destruction) of all the worlds protect you!' (D 3.144, 145). B concurs with this definition and illustrates with 'May *Śambhu* and *Viṣṇu* who are glorious and wear the crown and moon on their heads, lustrous with the complexion of the blueblack thunder cloud and snowwhite and hold in their hands the discus and trident...' (B 4.20, 21). This *doṣa* is called *kramabhraṣṭa* or *kramabhaṅga* and is of two kinds viz. *arthagata* and *śabdagata* (disorder in meaning and disorder in words respectively). [Performing the composition *varṇa* in Karnataka music in the sequence *ettugaḍe svaras-pallavi-ciṭṭasvaras-ettugaḍe caraṇa-anupallavi*; the *khyāl* in Hindustani music in the sequence *choṭa khyāl-baḍā khyāl,antara-āstāi* etc; the *jhampā tāla* in Karnataka music with *druta, laghu, anudruta.*]

8. Apārthaka is *arthadoṣa* and is defined by D(3.129) as an antilogical or inconsistent arrangement of the components so that the whole makes no sense. Any one—barring children, drunkards or the insane—speaking irrelevantly or disjointedly is committing *apārtha*. e.g. 'the gods drink the ocean; I am enervated with old age; these clouds are thundering; Indra is fond of the *Airāvata*'. According to B (4.3-8) *apārthaka* is lacking in collective sense. e.g. 'ten pomegranates, six puddings, seven chairs, two fish, one elephant.' V (p. 37) echoes this definition. [Singing snatches from *pallavi-svarajati-tillāna-varṇa-daru-sulādi-kṛti-ugābhoga-aṣṭapadi* in disjointed phrases of words, *rāgas* and *tālas.*]

9. Grāmya is being known only in the usage of the laeity; vulgar; according to V (p. 9). Vāmana (*Kāvyālaṁkārasūtravṛtti,* 2.7) defines it similarly: लोकमात्रप्रयुक्तं ग्राम्यम् and illustrates it with' 'कष्टं कथं रोदिति फूत्कृतेयम्' wherein '*phūtkṛteyam*' is vulgar usage.

D says (1.62-68), 'It is true that *mādhurya* is generated by *alaṁkāra* in poetry. But this is accomplished largely through the avoidance of vulgarity (*grāmyatā*). If there is a suggestion of obscenity in words, their combination and in the purport of a sentence, it is *grāmya.* [Singing *padam* or *jāvali* with indecent or obscene words or gestures.]

10. Sandigdha is a *padadoṣa.* It seems to have been occasionally referred to as '*sasaṁśaya*' by rhetoricians. It means ambiguity. D (3.139) defines it as *sasaṁśaya* wherein the very words which are meant to be decisive generate doubt. If two related propositions are described in exactly equal terms without adding a special or particular element or term in one of them, *saṁśaya* (doubt) is generated. A logical fallacy which generates *saṁśaya* is called *sasaṁśaya doṣa* according to B (4.17, 18) who offers this illustration:

> व्यालवन्तो दुरारोहा रत्नवन्तः फलान्विताः ।
> विषमा भूभृतस्तेभ्यो भयमाशु प्रमादिनाम् ।

(*Vyāla*—serpents/wicked people; *durāroha*—difficult to climb/ difficult to approach; *bhūdhara*—mountains/kings; *viṣama*—uneven/ruthless; *tebhyo*-serpents/ kings. Kings/mountains surrounded by wicked people/serpents and replete with gems and fruits or rewards but are difficult to approach/climb and are ruthless/ uneven. If one is not alert, there is immediate cause for fear/danger from them (kings/mountains). If the context is not known, it cannot be determined whether this refers to kings or to mountains. Hence the fault of *sandigdha* accrues. This may be cited as an illustration for *śleṣa* (paronomasia).

Vāmana defines *sandigdha* concisely: '*saṁśayakṛt sandigdham*' (*Kāvyālaṁkārasūtravṛtti,* 2.20) and explains: whenever a proposition is stated in only general or common terms and lacks specific terms, it generates doubt; it is then called *sandigdha.* He offers a beautiful illustration: स महात्मा भाग्यवशान्महापदमुपागतः । That great person attained to the great position due to good luck. It could also be स महात्माऽभाग्यवशान्महाऽऽपदमुपागतः । That great person became the target for great calamity because of ill luck. This ambiguity may be resolved only if the circumstances (or the context) are known. Vidyānātha defines (V p. 6) *sandigdha* as 'सन्दिग्धार्थप्रतीतिकृत्' and illustrates with

> विहाय च गृहान् तान् वै व्यत्यस्तवृत्तयः ।
> कदा भविष्यते वासः कटकेषु महीभृताम् ?

Here *mahībhṛt* means king or mountain; *kaṭaka* means the capital or foot of the mountain. So where is residence—the capital or the foot of the hill?

336c. padadoṣāḥ: Vāmana enumerates and describes (*Kāvyālaṁkārasūtravṛtti,* 2.4-10) five *padadoṣas* viz. *asādhu*, *kaṣṭa*, *grāmya*, *apratīta* and *anarthaka*; also, five *padārthas—anya, neya, gūḍhārtha, aślīla* and *kliṣṭa* (2.1.11-22). Vidyānātha (V p. 2-13) describes seventeen *padadoṣas*: *aprayukta, apuṣṭartha, asamartha, nirarthaka, neyārtha, cyutasaṁskāra, sandigdha, aprayojaka, kliṣṭa, gūḍhārtha, grāmya, anyārtha, apratīti, aślīla, paruṣa, avimṛṣṭavidheyāṁśa* and *viruddhamatikṛt.*

336. vākyadoṣāḥ: Vāmana elucidates three *vākyadoṣas (Kāvyālaṁkārasūtravṛtti,* 2.2.1-8): *bhinnavṛtta, yatibhraṣṭa, visandhi* and seven *vākyārthadoṣas*: *vyartha, ekārtha, sandigdha, ayukta, apakrama, lokaviruddha* and *vidyāviruddha* (ibid., 2.3.9-24) Vidyānatha lists and explains twentyfour *vākyadoṣas* (V pp. 13-37). *śabdahīna, kramabhraṣṭa, visandhi, punarukta, vyākīrṇa, vākyasaṅkīrṇa, apūrṇa, vākyagarbhita, bhinnaliṅga, bhinnavacana, nyūnopama, adhikopama, bhagnacchandas, yatibhraṣṭa, aśarīra, atireka, visargalupta, asthānasamāsa, vācyavarjita, samāptapunarātta, sambandhavarjita, patatprakarṣa, adhikapada* and *prakramabhaṅga.* He also defines (ibid., pp. 37-52) the following eighteen *arthadoṣas*: *apārtha, vyartha, ekārtha, sasaṁśaya, apakrama, bhinna, atimātra, paruṣa, virasa, hīnopama, adhikopama, asadṛśopama, aprasiddhopama, hetuśūnya, niralaṁkṛti, aślīla, viruddha* and *sahacaracyuta.*

336d. doṣāśca rasabhāvayoḥ: Some ancient rhetoricians allow the occurrence of a *rasa*—word signifying the respective *rasa.* But this is not acceptable: *rasa* such as *śṛṅgāra,* transient states (*vyabhicāribhāvas*) such as *nirveda* should not be mentioned by name as evoking the respective emotive state or concomitant; in other words, the *mātu* of a song should not contain words such as '*śṛṅgāra* is now generated; *hāsya* is here withdrawn or concealed, doubt has arisen, enthusiasm is evident' directly or in suggestion. *Rasa* should manifest only consequent upon *vibhāva* etc. It is a fault if, instead of inducing *rasa* through its concomitants, it is directly or indirectly invoked in words.

337cd-343. DESCRIPTION OF COMPOSER

Compare with SR (4.2-12). For explanation and commentary of the various terms see Sathyanarayana, R., Introduction, *Viśeṣa-kṛtimālā*; idem. Introduction, *Sirigannaḍadiñcara*; idem. New Creations in Karnataka Music in Journal of Indian Musicological Society, A special issue on 'Compositions in Indian Music' vol. 21,1 & 2, June -Dec. 1990, pp. 59-66.

श्लोकार्धानुक्रमणी

आ

इ

ई

उ

ऊ

ऋ

ए

ओ

क

ख

ग

ज

झ

ट

ड

ढ

त

ब

भ

म

य

र

श

ष

स

ह

आकरनामानुक्रमणी

विशेषपदानुक्रमणी *

अ (इ = इत्यादि, * = विकीर्ण:)

* Number before (:) refer to page number after (;) refer to *śloka*s and end in (;)

ध

न

प

य

र

ल

व

INDEX TO AUTHORS, COMPOSERS

Commentary on ch. 3.1 & 3.2

Names in italics are of Composers

D

E

F

G

H

I

J

INDEX TO WORKS

Commentary on ch. 3.1 & 3.2

R

S

INDEX TO TECHNICAL TERMS

Commentary on Ch. 3.1 & 3.2

A

C

D

H

I

J

L

U